Advances in Spatial Science

For further volumes:
http://www.springer.com/series/3302

Juan R. Cuadrado-Roura • Patricio Aroca
Editors

Regional Problems and Policies in Latin America

Springer

Editors
Juan R. Cuadrado-Roura
Economia Aplicada
Facultad de Ciencias Económicas
Alcalá de Henares
Madrid
Spain

Patricio Aroca
Business School
University Adolfo Ibañez
Viña del Mar
Chile

ISSN 1430-9602
ISBN 978-3-642-39673-1 ISBN 978-3-642-39674-8 (eBook)
DOI 10.1007/978-3-642-39674-8
Springer Heidelberg New York Dordrecht London

Library of Congress Control Number: 2013955908

Printed on acid-free paper

Springer is part of Springer Science+Business Media (www.springer.com)

Contents

Part II Analysis by Countries

Part III Horizontal and Comparative Analysis

List of Contributors

Alem, Mauro. Ph.D. in Economics from the University of Chicago (2003). Bachelor in Economics, Universidad de Buenos Aires (1996). He currently works as President of the Banco de Inversión y Comercio Exterior (BICE).

Aroca, Patricio. Professor at the Universidad Adolfo Ibáñez in Chile. He is also main researcher of the nucleus of the Millennium Scientific Initiative of the Chilean Ministry of Economics – "Regional Science and Public Policy" – and affiliated Associate Professor at the Regional Economics Applications Laboratory (REAL) of the University of Illinois, USA. He has consulted for World Bank, UNCTAD, IADB, CELADE-ECLAC-UN, and several national and regional governments. He is also member of the boards of the RSAI and the PRSCO and President of the RSAmericas (Regional Science Association of the Americas).

Asuad-Sanén, Normand. Professor of Regional and Urban Economics and Director of the Center of Studies for Regional and Urban Sustainable Development (CEDRUS), Faculty of Economics, National Autonomous University of Mexico (UNAM). Author of numerous books and articles on regional problems and policies.

Atienza-Ubeda, Miguel is Ph.D. in Economics from the Universidad Autonoma de Madrid (Spain) and M.Phil. in Development Studies from the Institute of Development Studies (IDS) at the University of Sussex. He is Professor in the Economics Department in the Business Faculty of the Universidad Catolica del Norte, Antofagasta (Chile). His specialization is in regional and urban economics. His main research areas are spatial location, productive clusters in developing countries, and small- and medium-enterprise economics.

Azzoni, Carlos Roberto. Professor of Economics, University of São Paulo, Brazil. His research interests include all regional issues related to economic growth, such as productivity differences, regional inequalities, the role of social programs on inequality, the impact of global warming on regions, and regional policy. He has published numerous books and articles in prestigious international journals on these topics.

Boisier, Sergio. Economist (University of Chile), M.A. in Regional Science (University of Pennsylvania), Ph.D. in Applied Economics (University of Alcala, Madrid, Spain), former Director of Policies and Regional Planning of the Latin American and Caribbean Institute for Economic and Social Planning (ILPES/ECLAC/UN). He is author of numerous books, articles, and reports on regional trends and policies.

Costa, Silvio M. de Azevedo holds a Ph.D. in Economics from the University of São Paulo. He works as economic advisor in the research department of the Brazilian Central Bank, where he develops studies on economic modeling, macroeconomic policy, and forecasting (silvio@usp.br).

Cuadrado-Roura, Juan R. Full Professor of Applied Economics and holds the Jean Monnet Chair, funded by the European Commission, University of Alcala, Madrid. Founder-Director of the Institute of Economic and Social Analysis. Former President of the ERSA and Director of the journal *Investigaciones Regionales*. He has published numerous articles, book chapters, and books, mainly on economic policy, European economy, regional growth and policies, productivity, and the analysis of service industries.

Cuervo, L. Mauricio. Economist, Licentiate from the University of Los Andes, Bogota, and Ph.D. in Urbanism from the University of Paris-Est. Former Associate Professor and researcher of CEDE, CIDER, and CINEP (Bogota) and visiting researcher at the IRD, the Institute of Americas (France), and the IDE (Japan). Actually Official of Economic Affairs at the ILPES, CEPAL, Chile. Main research fields: development theory and regional and urban development.

Cuervo B., Nicolás. Economist, Licentiate in Economics from the University of Los Andes, Bogota. Ph.D. student in Urbanism at the University of Paris-Est. He has been Associate Professor at the Universidad Autónoma de Manizales and consultant in urban management and residential policies in Colombia as well as in urban and regional economy.

Curbelo, José Luis. Vice President of Strategies of Development and Public Policies of the CAF Development Bank of Latin America and former General Director of Orkestra in the Basque Country, San Sebastian, Spain. Ph.D. in Economics, University of California at Berkeley. He is the author of 6 books and over 50 articles published in prestigious Spanish and overseas journals.

Del Pozo-Segura, Juan Manuel. Graduate in Economics from the Catholic University of Peru (2007). Assistant Professor of Economics in the Catholic University of Peru, Lima. He works on problems of economic development and territorial policies.

Elias, Victor J. Ph.D. in Economics from the University of Chicago (1969). Emeritus Professor of the University of Tucuman. Full Member of Argentine's National Academy of Economics. Author of *Sources of Growth: A Study of Seven Latin American Economies*, San Francisco, ICS Press (1992). Recent publication:

"Sources of Growth. Progress and Challenges" (2012), published in Progress in Economic Growth, Argentinian Economic Policy Association.

Elias, Julio Jorge works as Chief Economist of the Banco de Inversión y Comercio Exterior (BICE), Buenos Aires, and as Professor of Economics at the Universidad del CEMA. He is also Executive Director of the Center for Creativity Economics at the Universidad del CEMA. He received his Ph.D. in Economics from the University of Chicago in 2005.

Fernández-Núñez, Ma. Teresa. (Ph.D.) is Associate Professor of Applied Economics at the University of Extremadura (Spain). Her main research interests are external competitiveness and productive and commercial specialization. She has published different papers in several national and international journals.

Gallo-Rivera, María Teresa. Ph.D. in Economics, University of Alcala. Associate Professor of Economics and Business Management Department, and researcher at the Institute for Economic and Social Analysis (IAES), University of Alcala, Madrid, Spain. Main fields of interest: location, convergence, regional and household inequalities, regional policy, economics of institutions.

Galvis, Luis Armando. Ph.D., researcher at the Center for Regional Economic Studies (CEER), Banco de la Republica, Central Bank of Colombia. His research has been focused on urban and regional economic topics applied to the case of Colombia, for which he recently received the "P. Nijkamp RSAI Research Encouragement Award" (lgalviap@banrep.gov.co).

Garrido-Yserte, Rubén. Ph.D. in Economics, University of Alcala (2000). Master in European Economics from the Ortega and Gasset Institute, Madrid (1996). Associate Professor of Economics and Business Management Department, Director of the Area of Territorial and Urban Analysis of the Institute for Economic and Social Analysis (IAES), University of Alcala, Madrid, Spain.

Gonzales de Olarte, Efraín. Master in Economics from Université Catholique de Louvain, Belgium (1974). Ph.D. in Development Economics, Université Paris I Pantheon-Sorbonne (1976). Academic Vice President at Catholic University of Peru. Professor of Economics and Director of Master in Economics program at Catholic University of Peru, Lima. Senior Economist in the Peruvian Studies Institute and international consultant.

González-Catalán, Sergio. Agronomics Engineer; Master in Agrarian Economy, Pontificia Universidad Católica de Chile. Researcher at the Instituto Latinoamericano y del Caribe de Planificación Económica y Social (ILPES) of the United Nations Economic Commission for Latin America and the Caribbean (CEPAL), Santiago de Chile. His research focuses on regional development indicators and assessment of regional disparities in Latin America.

Haddad, Eduardo A. is Full Professor in the Department of Economics at the University of São Paulo, Brazil, where he teaches courses on regional and urban economics and general equilibrium modeling. He is the Director of Research at the

Institute of Economic Research Foundation (FIPE). He has acted as the President of the Brazilian Regional Science Association (2008–2010) and the first President of the Regional Science Association of the Americas (2008–2010).

Isaac-Egurrola, Jorge. Professor and member of the Research Program of the Faculty of Superior Studies (FES-Acatlán), UNAM. Economist at FES-Acatlán and specialized in political economy, spatial economics and High and Post-Graduate Education. Author and co-author of ten books and a large number of articles published in renowned academic journals.

Lima, Gilberto T. is a Professor in the Department of Economics at the University of São Paulo, Brazil. He holds a Ph.D. in Economics from the University of Notre Dame (USA) and his research interests and publications are mostly in macrodynamics of growth and development.

Luque, Carlos A. is a Professor in the Department of Economics at the University of São Paulo, Brazil. He holds a Ph.D. in Economics from the University of São Paulo (Brazil). He served as Assistant Secretary of the Secretariat of Economy and Planning of the State of São Paulo from 1995 to 2005. Currently, he is the CEO of the Institute of Economic Research Foundation (FIPE). His main areas of interest are economic growth, fiscal policy, and evaluation of public policies.

Mancino, Maria Antonella. Bachelor in Economics from the Universidad Nacional de Cuyo. Master in Economics from the Universidad del CEMA. Currently a Ph.D. student at the University of Western Ontario. Previous positions include Economist at the Banco de Inversion y Comercio Exterior (BICE) and External Economist at the Centre for the Implementation of Public Policies Promoting Equity and Growth (CIPPEC).

Márquez, Miguel A., Ph.D. (Economics), is Head of the Department of Economics at the University of Extremadura (Spain) and Scientific Secretary of the Spanish Association of Regional Science (AECR). He is Affiliate Research Professor at the REAL (University of Illinois, USA) and member of the European Union Regional Economics Applications Laboratory (EU-REAL). His major research work has covered a variety of topics on regional economics, particularly economic growth and economic models.

Máttar, Jorge. Mexican Economist. M.A., University of Cambridge, UK; from 2010, Director of the Instituto Latinoamericano y del Caribe de Planificación Económica y Social (ILPES, CEPAL). He coordinates and manages studies, assessments, and skilling courses on planification, public governance, evaluation of public policies, and economic and social prospective for Latin America and the Caribbean countries.

Meisel-Roca, Adolfo. Ph.D. (Economics). He works at the Banco de la República, the Colombian Central Bank (Director of the Regional Centre, Cartagena, Colombia). His research interests are in the fields of economic history of Colombia, anthropometric history, and regional economics. Currently, he is writing an economic history of the Colombian Caribbean Coast.

Mendoza, Miguel-Angel. Professor and tutor of Regional and Urban Economics at the Post-graduate Studies Division of the Faculty of Economics of the UNAM. Ph.D. in Economics from the UNAM, Facultad de Economía; M.Sc. in Economics from UACPyP-CCH of the Autonomous National University of Mexico (UNAM) and Licentiate in Economics from the Facultad de Economía, UNAM, Mexico.

Moncayo-Jimenez, Edgard. Economist (University of Rosario), M.Sc. in Public Administration (Harvard University), and Ph.D. (National University of Colombia). Director of the Institutional Program of Prospective and Strategy, Universidad Central, Bogotá; President of the Colombian section of RSAI and the Colombian Society of Geography. Research fields: economic growth, regional development, public policies. Formerly Director of the Colombian Institute of Foreign Trade, Member of the Junta of the Andean Pact, and Director of the ECLAC's Office in Bogota.

Ochoa-Moreno, Wilman-Santiago. M.Sc. in Urban and Regional Economics, Universidad Nacional Autónoma de México (UNAM). He is currently Professor of Economics and researcher at the Quantitative Methods Section of the Department of Economics, Universidad Técnica Particular de Loja (UTPL), Ecuador.

Ochoa-Jiménez, Diego Alejandro. M.Sc. in Applied Economics, Universidad Nacional Autónoma de México (UNAM). He is currently Professor of Economics and researcher at the Macroeconomics Section of the Department of Economics at the Universidad Técnica Particular de Loja (UTPL), Ecuador.

Penfold, Michael. Director of Public Policies and Competitiveness of the CAF, Development Bank of Latin America, and Associate Professor at IESA. He is the author of numerous books and articles, among them *Dragon in the Tropics: Hugo Chávez and the Political Economy of Revolution in Venezuela* (coauthored with Javier Corrales and published by Brookings Institution) awarded as the Best Book of 2011 in the Western Hemisphere by Foreign Affairs.

Quintana-Romero, Luis. Professor of Regional Economics and Econometrics and researcher of the Research Program of the Faculty of Superior Studies (FES), Acatlán, National Autonomous University of Mexico (UNAM). He has published numerous books and articles on regional economy, from a theoretical focus as well as empirical analysis and case studies.

Ramajo, Julián is Professor of Applied Economics at the University of Extremadura (Spain), Head of the Research Group in Applied Economic Analysis, and member of the European Union Regional Economics Applications Laboratory (EU-REAL). Main research interests: macro- and micro-econometric models and general equilibrium models in regional economics. He has published a large number of papers in major journals and has participated in many different research projects.

Ramón-Mendieta, Marlon Giovanni. M.Sc. in Urban and Regional Economics from the Universidad Nacional Autónoma de México (UNAM). He is currently a Professor of Economics and researcher at the Economic Theory Section of the Department of Economics, Universidad Técnica Particular de Loja (UTPL), Ecuador.

Riffo-Pérez, Luis. Economist. M.Sc. in Geographies of Globalization and Regional Development, University of Liverpool. Researcher of the ILPES (CEPAL), area of Local and Regional Development Management. Main fields of interest and research: socio-spatial disparities and economic and territorial development of Latin America and the Caribbean.

Rodríguez, Jorge. Researcher at the Latin American Demographic Center (CELADE) of the Population Division of ECLAC (Economic Commission for Latin America and the Caribbean). He holds a degree in Sociology and a graduate degree in Population and Development Programs Policies from CELADE and he is in the doctoral program in Economic and Social History in America of the Universidad de Santiago, Chile.

Rowe, Francisco. Queensland Centre for Population Research. Geography, Planning, and Environmental Management, Faculty of Science, University of Queensland, Brisbane, Australia.

Ruiz-Durán, Clemente. Professor of Economics, Faculty of Economy, UNAM, Mexico. His main research fields are regional and urban development, labor economics, software industries, clusters, information technology, and others. He has given lectures and conducted workshops in many universities in Latin America, the USA, and Europe.

Sakurai, Sergio N. is Assistant Professor in the Department of Economics at FEARP, University of São Paulo. He holds a Ph.D. in Economics from the University of São Paulo, and his main research areas are the economics of the public sector, public finance, and new political economy.

Salas, Carlos. Professor, CESIT (Center for Trade Union Studies and Labor Economics), Instituto de Economía, University of Campinas, Brazil. Ph.D. in Economics, UNAM, Mexico. Main research fields: labor economics and economic development and labor.

Santos, Anselmo. Ph.D. in Economics from the State University of Campinas (UNICAMP), Brazil. Professor at the Institute of Economics, researcher and Deputy Director of the Centre for Trade Union Studies and Labor Economics (CESIT), University of Campinas. Coordinator of the social economy and labor area of the graduate program in development. Research interests: labor market economics, labor and small businesses, informality.

Valdivia, Marcos. Researcher at the Regional Center for Multidisciplinary Research of the National University of Mexico (UNAM). Ph.D. in Economics for the New School for Social Research, New York. Main research fields: spatial economics, urban economics, computational modeling, migration and labor markets.

Vial, M. Camilo. Ph.D. (c) in Political Science, Universidad Complutense, Madrid. His research interests are decentralization, regional development, territorial policies, and poverty reduction, with special emphasis on Chile and South America.

Contributors

Mauro Alem Banco de Inversión y Comercio Exterior, Buenos Aires, Argentina

Patricio Aroca University Adolfo Ibañez, Viña del Mar, Chile

Normand Asuad-Senén Faculty of Economics, UNAM, México DF, Mexico

Miguel Atienza Universidad Católica del Norte, Antofagasta, Chile

Silvio M. de Azevedo Costa Research Department, Brazilian Central Bank, Brasilia, Brazil

Carlos R. Azzoni Faculty of Economics, University of Sao Paulo, Sao Paulo, Brazil

Sergio Boisier (Economics), CATS, Ases. Des° Territorial, Santiago de Chile, Chile

Juan R. Cuadrado-Roura Department of Applied Economics, University of Alcalá, Madrid, Spain

Luis Mauricio Cuervo ILPES, CEPAL, Santiago de Chile, Chile

Nicolás B. Cuervo Université de Paris Est, Paris, France

José Luis Curbelo Strategies of Development and Public Policies of CAF (Corporación Andina Financiera), Caracas, Venezuela

Julio Jorge Elías University of CEMA, Buenos Aires, Argentina

Victor J. Elías University of Tucumán, Tucumán, Argentina

Mª Teresa Fernández University of Extremadura, Badajoz, Spain

Maria Teresa Gallo Department of Economics and Business Management Department, University of Alcala, Madrid, Spain

Luis Armando Galvis Center for Regional Economic Studies, Banco de la República, Cartagena, Colombia

Rubén Garrido-Yserte Department of Economics and Business Management Department, University of Alcalá, Madrid, Spain

Sergio González ILPES (Latin America and Caribe Institute of Economic and Social Planning), CEPAL, Santiago de Chile, Chile

Eduardo Haddad Faculty of Economics, University of Sao Paulo, Sao Paulo, Brazil

Jorge Isaac-Egurrola Faculty of Superior Studies (FES) of Acatlán, UNAM, Acatlan, Mexico

Gilberto T. Lima Department of Economics, FEARP, University of Sao Paulo, Sao Paulo, Brazil

Carlos A. Luque Department of Economics, University of Sao Paulo, Sao Paulo, Brazil

Maria Antonella Mancino University of Western Ontario, London, Canada

Miguel Angel Marquez Department of Economics, University of Extremadura, Badajoz, Spain

Jorge Mattar ILPES (Latin America and Caribe Institute of Economic and Social Planification), CEPAL, Santiago de Chile, Chile

Adolfo Meisel Center for Regional Economic Studies, Banco de la República, Cartagena, Colombia

Miguel Angel Mendoza Post-Grado Division, Faculty of Economics, UNAM, Mexico DF, Mexico

Edgard Moncayo Research Associate Fellow (Non resident), United Nations University-Institute of Comparative Regional Studies (UNU-CRIS), Brugge, Belgium

Diego A. Ochoa-Jiménez Department of Economics, UTPL, Loja, Ecuador

Wilman-Santiago Ochoa-Moreno Department of Economics, UTPL, Loja, Ecuador

Efraín González de Olarte Catholic University of Peru, Lima, Peru

Michael Penfold Public Policies and Competitiveness of the CAF (Corporación Andina Financiera), Caracas, Venezuela

Juan Manuel del Pozo Catholic University of Perú, Lima, Peru

Luis Quintana-Romero Faculty of Superior Studies Acatlán (FESA), UNAM, Estado de México, México

Julián Ramajo University of Extremadura, Badajoz, Spain

Marlon G. Ramón-Mendieta Department of Economics, UTPL, Loja, Ecuador

Luis Riffo-Pérez Managing Regional and Local Development, ILPES – CEPAL, Santiago de Chile, Chile

Jorge Rodríguez CELADE, CEPAL, Santiago de Chile, Chile

Francisco Rowe Queensland Centre for Population Research, University of Queensland, Brisbane, Australia

Clemente Ruiz-Durán UNAM, Mexico DF, Mexico

Sergio N. Sakurai Department of Economics, FEARP, University of São Paulo, Sao Paulo, Brazil

Carlos Salas CESIT, Institute of Economics, University of Campinas, Campinas, Brazil

Anselmo Santos Institute of Economics, University of Campinas, Campinas, Brazil

Marcos Valdivia CRIM (Regional Center of Multidisciplinary Research), UNAM, Cuernavaca, Mexico

M. Camilo Vial Faculty of Political Sciences, Complutense University, Madrid, Spain

Part I
General Overview, Problems, Trends and Regional Policies in Latin America

Chapter 1
The Reason Why of This Book: An Introduction

Juan R. Cuadrado-Roura and Patricio Aroca

The quantity and quality of the research and publications on Latin American nations' territorial problems and policies have increased substantially over the past decade. However, the fact that the majority of the studies have been published in Spanish and Portuguese has limited their dissemination to the countries in which those languages are spoken. Today, there is a great deal of interest in Spanish- and Portuguese- speaking America for a variety of reasons. The region's increasing weight on a global scale is undeniable due to its population and the dynamism of some of its economies and to the interesting political changes that have taken place and continue to develop in these nations. As such, one should not be surprised by the interest that has developed in the problems, dominant trends, and policies of the countries of Latin America, which has increased both generally and in regard to the specific sphere of the regional, territorial and local.

For all of these reasons, we decided to publish an English language book about territorial issues and the regional policies that have been applied in Latin American countries over the past few decades. Nearly 3 years have passed since we began to develop an outline of the publication. During that period, Springer-Verlag agreed to handle the editing and marketing of the book, and we should note that it did so enthusiastically. This was without a doubt an important source of encouragement for us as editors and for all of the authors who prepared a set of original manuscripts for possible inclusion in the book. Springer-Verlag's support guaranteed that the book would be handled carefully and marketed on an international scale.

All of the manuscripts that were submitted during the first phase of the project were submitted to anonymous review, after which they were revised, edited and the

J.R. Cuadrado-Roura (✉)
Department of Applied Economics, University of Alcalá, Madrid, Spain
e-mail: jr.cuadrado@uah.es

P. Aroca
University Adolfo Ibañez, Viña del Mar, Chile
e-mail: parocanet@gmail.com

J.R. Cuadrado-Roura and P. Aroca (eds.), *Regional Problems and Policies in Latin America*, Advances in Spatial Science, DOI 10.1007/978-3-642-39674-8_1,

data used have been updated wherever possible. One of the conditions to which the authors agreed was that all of the texts be absolutely original.

The experience and earlier publications of the authors and teams that joined the project guaranteed the quality of their contributions. A second basic condition for the project was that all manuscripts contribute clear *added value* beyond that which was already known utilizing the most current data and information possible. An additional condition was placed on chapters that present a specific analysis of a series of countries. In addition to being original work, they were required to have a survey focus. The goal was to ensure that any reader would be able to come away from the text with a global vision of what had occurred in each country regarding the evolution of disparities and other regional problems and the policies applied. Each text also had to offer a selection of bibliographic references for those interested in expanding their understanding of the topic. Something similar was sought in the texts that provide more horizontal and comparative analyses of common issues and problems such as job markets, poverty, fiscal decentralization, and urban problems and the concentration of population and wealth.

The final result of this effort is this 24-chapter book which offers a very current and critical vision of regional problems in the countries of South America and Mexico. Of course, its contents are not exhaustive. It would be nearly impossible to address every single issue that merits attention. We do believe that this volume offers a broad vision of territorial matters in Latin America, the place that they occupy in the societies and economies of the region, the efforts that have been deployed to reduce interregional disparities in income and living conditions, and the challenges that must be faced now and in the coming years.

As the editors of this book, we are quite satisfied with the results, though we are aware that there are problems that we have not been able to address mainly due to a lack of available research. In any case, we trust that this publication will allow other studies to emerge that will complement, update, and expand upon its contents.

The texts that were selected have been organized into three parts. The first consists of more general analyses designed to provide an overview of the problems, dominant trends, and role of territorial policies in Latin America. The second is composed of texts that address a group of countries that is representative of the region but also reflects the differences that exist. The third presents studies that consider more horizontal issues, comparing the unique situations of several different countries. Below we mention some of the characteristics of the studies that make up these three sections.

1.1 General Overview: Problems, Trends and Territorial Policies in America Latina Along the Last Decades

The first part of the book includes seven chapters. As it has been pointed out the aim of this part is to offer a panoramic overview on the evolution of regional disparities in the Region, as a whole, and the most outstanding territorial trends. It also includes a first analysis of some regional programs and actions put into practice or recently planned.

The editors of this book, Profs. **Juan R. Cuadrado-Roura** and **Patricio Aroca**, are the authors of Chap. 2, which aims are clearly two. Firstly, to underline some arguments and characteristics of recent attitudes about regional problems in Latin America and the increasing interest of International Organizations about them. And, second, to propose the need for regional development policies in Latin America, taking advantage of the period of excellent performances in terms of macroeconomic growth that most economies of the Region are experiencing from the beginning of this century. A departing point supporting to this proposal is the fact that regional economic disparities are actually higher than in other continents. There are examples of Latin American countries where the richest region has an income per capita almost ten times the poorest. Even in cases not having so high differences, the dominant characteristic of such income disparities is that they have not changed significantly along the last decades.

As many authors point out, from politics and macroeconomics it would seem that Latin America is once again facing the dilemma of choosing between promoting more market and promoting more government in policy, particularly in regional policy. Increasing importance is given to the fact that inequalities are beginning to generate strong movements that are opposed to continuing with the concentration of power and wealth in some specific areas within each nation or certain groups within the population. From Central America to the Patagonia and from the Andean countries to Venezuela or Brazil, numerous political movements can be seen claiming for a better distribution of the income, both at personal and territorial level. Undoubtedly, as the authors establish in this chapter, there are sufficient elements and signs to suggest that interregional inequalities merit more attention than they have received over the past decades. But regional development policies cannot be confused with simple redistribution policies or measures taken to combat poverty and improve the wellbeing of low-income individuals or families. Structural changes and long term objectives to develop the backwardness regions cannot be identified to some social programs actually implemented by some Latin American governments. The development of more delayed areas requires profound changes that cannot be achieved through short term policies. They require policies having continuity and not being subject to changes derived from electoral processes or governmental changes. And they require also concentration of actions and policies and not dispersion over all regions of a country. Arguments justifying this type of regional policies and some specific requirements to get successful results are also pointed out in this chapter.

Chapter 3 provides an overview of some stylized facts of development models in Latin America and the dynamics of the socio-spatial inequalities in the past half century. **Jorge Máttar,** actual Director of the ILPES-CEPAL, and **Luis Riffo,** researcher of such Institute, are the authors of this text which is organized in two main parts plus some final reflections. The first part deals with an analysis of the prevailing development models in Latin American and the Caribbean throughout the last 50 years, paying particular attention to the observed changes in the role of the state and to the predominant ideological ideas. The second part offers a study of long-term trends of the regional economic disparities in some of the most representative countries of Latin America: Chile, Mexico, Brazil, Colombia and Peru, emphasizing the spatial concentration of GDP and population and the slow evolution of regional disparities in GDP per capita, which have even worsened in some cases. Finally, the chapter ends highlighting the increasing importance that territorial development policies seem to have recently, reviewing some particular cases of countries that have plans to implement new approaches and perspectives.

Some final remarks of the authors must be pointed out. The first is the radical change of approaches that can be observed between the decades of 1940–1970 and the 1980s onwards. The core of this important change is the degree of confidence on the role of the market and the state as instruments to promote development and the increasing internationalization of the economies. While, in the first stage the state was almost always the main agent to decide economic policies – including some regional policies experiences – in the second stage the market has been the main protagonist, mainly through privatization of public companies and public services, de-regulation processes, openness to FDI and supporting the role of private entrepreneurships and investments.

The second remark is on the evolution of regional disparities. The main trends observed is that while it is possible to observe interesting transformations in terms of population and the structure of production, as well as some evidence of convergence in GDP per capita, no substantive changes can be observed in the main core subsystems of each country and the strong interregional disparities. This last is calling for more active regional policies and to increase decentralization in terms of governance.

Territorial policy is the main topic of Chap. 4, which was written by renowned professor and expert **Sergio Boisier**. Boisier draws on a very important asset: his direct experience over the course of many years as a member of ILPES and consultant on the design and implementation of territorial policies in many South American and Caribbean nations. This chapter contains impressive ideas and conclusions that will no doubt be of interest to the reader. The text also has a very critical profile in regard to the handling of territorial policies, which are described in terms of benchmarks and in the context of the policy models that sustained them. The author describes the changes that have taken place in regional development policy in Latin America, situating all of this in the context of the nations' various governments and dominant ideological backgrounds. Two ideas are particularly noteworthy. The first is the general trend towards decentralization that has impacted the majority of the countries of Latin America. The second is that many of the changes observed have their roots in theories from those specific periods. As a result, there has been a clear lack of continuity in the actions implemented. Boisier argues that the failure of many policies has to do with both of these phenomena.

Professor **Juan R. Cuadrado-Roura**, from the University of Alcala, and the engineer and economist **Sergio González**, researcher at the ILPES–CEPAL, have been the authors of Chap. 5, which analyses the relationship between economic growth and regional disparities in Latin America. The first section of their paper underlines five stylized regional or territorial trends considered by the authors as the most relevant along the last decades in Latin America. That is: the high levels of product and population concentration; the high level of regional disparities within countries that barely have declined; the significant growth of some regions as producers of primary resources; the low progress in decentralization objectives; and the lack of effective regional development policies or the lack of continuity in several countries. Lately, the text analyses in-depth the spatial concentration of population and production as a characteristic of the majority of Latin American countries, as well as the very limited evolution, if not worse, of regional disparities compared to the most positive achievements of the national economies. The authors discuss and show the empirical results of the relationship between economic growth and regional disparities in eight Latin American countries, which should give support to the need of much more active and realistic regional development policies oriented not only to diminish the high territorial inequalities but to increase the economic and social cohesion. In this field the text suggests the three principles that international experiences show as the suitable starting point for a Regional Development Policy. They offer also some guidelines to be considered in terms of objectives, strategies and instruments of such policies, drawn from international experiences.

The problem of concentration and growth is also the central point of the contribution prepared by professors **Manuel Atienza** and **Patricio Aroca.** Their work is included as Chap. 6 of this book. It presents a rich analysis of the trend towards concentration and its effects. Specifically, the authors argue that concentration restricts the growth of many Latin American nations. In addition to reviewing theoretical ideas about the topic, Atienza and Aroca provide empirical analyses that demonstrate the evolution of spatial concentration over the past few decades in terms of both population and economics. Their goal is to show that that spatial concentration affects countries' growth based on the cases of nine very important countries in the region. Their work suggests that the polarized pattern of urbanization has become an obstacle to their growth. The authors identify two groups of countries for which it is recommended that the reduction of spatial concentration become a national policy objective, not only due to reasons of equity but to increase the growth potential of their economies. The first group includes almost all Southern countries: Argentina, Chile and Peru, followed by Uruguay and Paraguay. The second group is formed by most of the countries in Central America. The existing differences between these groups and countries requires particular case analysis, paying particular attention to evaluate the degree to which policies aimed at de-concentration of population and productive activity contribute to promoting their growth.

The last chapter of Part I have been prepared by **L.M. Cuervo,** an experienced researcher of the ILPES, and **N. Cuervo,** economist. Their work, which is presented as Chap. 7, complements the previous study and expands the analysis of the strong urban development that has taken place in Latin America (LA) over the past several decades, connecting it to the regional disparities that persist in the majority of the countries of the region. The analysis underscores urban primacy as a very dominant characteristic and provides an in-depth study of urban primacy and economic primacy, presenting a comparative empirical analysis based on seven countries. Special attention is paid to the cyclical nature of urban primacy over the past 60 years, showing that the ultimate phase of the diachronic function of primacy is saturation. Nevertheless, the authors remark that the decrease in primacy after saturation is much slower than its increase along its growth phase. Additionally, it shows the appearance of processes of stagnation or reversion of these trends; that is, a take-up of primacy growth again. As the chapter shows, these processes of revitalization of growth in Latin America primacy seem to be associated with the deep economic restructuring that large cities are experiencing across the continent. All this let the authors to analyze and propose the global effects produced by these changes. But, the authors underline some existing differences. Argentina, Peru and Brazil show a permanent relationship between changes in economic primacy and changes in disparities, whereas Bolivia, Colombia, Chile and Mexico show a significant but changeable direction of such relationship. An interesting epilogue closes this contribution proposing some final reflections about the public policy that seems convenient to apply and the need to confront seriously the urban concentration and their consequences in a good number of Latin American countries.

1.2 The Necessary Country Study Analysis

It is important to note that while the texts from Part I generally suggest that there are many characteristics that seem to be shared by all Latin American nations, it is also true that the there are differences among them. Part II presents seven chapters that provide analyses of regional development problems and policies in specific Latin American nations or groups of nations.

Professors **Luis Quintana and Norman Asuad** of FES-Acatlan and the UNAM School of Economics, respectively, are the authors of Chap. 8, which focuses on Mexico. The title of the chapter suggests the main points that the study addresses, all of which are quite closely linked: Growth, concentration, inequality and Regional Policy in Mexico. Three characteristics differentiate the focus adopted by the authors from other contributions already published on the Mexican case. First, they analyze the evolution of inequality in Mexico under the idea that the spatial unit of analysis is relevant. This leads the analysis to combine the traditional analysis by states with one by metropolitan areas, which they believe represent a regional disaggregation closest to what functional economic region should be. Second, they use new proposals to measure the inequality, not restricted to the traditional analysis of sigma and beta convergence. Third, the analysis seeks to contextualize inequality in the process of spatial concentration of economic activity in the country, showing at the same time how regional policies have helped to consolidate the current concentration pattern and the regional differences that arise in this process.

It is not our place to provide a detailed discussion here of how the authors delve into these three fronts, the empirical evidence that they present and the main conclusions that they reach. The reader can evaluate the quality of the analysis provided independently. He or she also can observe the very clear connections that exist between growth, economic and demographic concentration, and spatial inequalities in Mexico and the changing regional policy actions. The problems and challenges that the country faces from this territorial perspective require a clear strategy as well as continuity in the policies that are applied, the latter of which has always been absent given that policies are linked to government mandates that are limited to 6-year periods.

Colombia presents a set of unique characteristics in this regard as well as points in common with other Latin American countries. **Luis A. Galvis and Adolfo Meisel** of the Banco de la República de Colombia Center for Regional Studies (Cartagena) contributed Chap. 9 of this book. The main objective of this contribution is very clear: departing from some theoretical approaches on the origin and evolution of regional disparities they focus their attention on the Colombian case to show the facts associated to inequalities and regional imbalances. They also highlight the role of the central government through regional policies and the limited success that it has achieved. After a very robust and detailed analysis they conclude that regional economic disparities have been increasing in Colombia over the last decades and the lack of success of the policies implemented to reduce such disparities. Government transfers have actually benefited mainly the most prosperous regions, as there is a positive correlation between income per capita and transfers per capita by the central government. They conclude that a regressive policy has been practiced, which has not favored the poorer areas that are rural and mainly located in the periphery of the country.

As Professor **Carlos R. Azzoni**, from the Sao Paulo University, points out at the beginning of his contribution – Chap. 10 – "being a country with large territory, it is expected that regional disparities would be pronounced in Brazil". This is true, but it is necessary to analyze deeply the actual situation, the evolution along the last decades and the factors explaining the changes observed. General indicators are presented and analyzed in this text revealing the high degree of economic disparities in the country and its persistency. Figures cover a long period of seven decades end it is clear that concentration and regional inequalities of Brazil are high and relatively stable over time. As for spatial concentration of economic activities the main change is the growth in the north region, related to mining and logging, and in the mid-west region, related to agriculture and agribusiness. So, the main changes are related to resource-oriented activities, led by, or associated to, some governmental programs such as the establishment of a new state capital (Brasilia) in the Mid-west, the design and implementation of a free-import zone in the Amazon, the support given to technological improvement in agriculture making possible for the mid-west to become a great-basket for the world. Any case, it appears that income inequality decreased in the last decade, but this is associated with government social programs. But, it seems clear that there is a long way to diminish the concentration of economic activities. As Prof. Azzoni concludes "centripetal forces are still surpassing the centrifugal influences of de-agglomeration economies".

Argentina constitutes a rather singular case, but finally not so different from other LA countries. The text has been prepared by Professor **Victor J. Elias,** with **Mauro Alem, Julio J. Elias** and **M.A. Mancino** and it is an excellent contribution to a better knowledge of what has happen along the last four decades in Argentina, from a territorial point of view. The author's analysis, which has been included as Chap. 11, draw on several factors strongly related to economic development, on the basis of its initial and current value, including: education (human capital), financial sector development, urbanization, exports, productivity, tax burden, size of firms, among others, They also analyze the role of public policy on regional development of the country. As in other countries of the Continent, Argentina is characterized by a large concentration of population and economic activity in one region known as Pampeana, which includes Buenos Aires City and Buenos Aires Province, as well as Cordoba, Entre Rios, La Pampa and Santa Fe. Buenos Aires is, of course, the main concentration of population, economic activities and transportation infrastructures. Any case, as it is shown in the chapter, the main feature of regional development in Argentina is the remarkable diversity across regions and provinces in measured per capita income levels and in growth rates. The convergence in living standards between provinces has been very low along the four decades analyzed and there was little change in the income per capital raking of provinces. Only Catamarca's region has had an unprecedented growth performance due to the mining, but provinces of the Nordic region lag behind by any economic measure. Regional economic policies during the period have registered frequent changes and most of them were targeted to macroeconomic objectives as to increase exports, industrial production and, some, to innovation and education.

Patricio Aroca is the author of Chap. 12 on Inequalities and Regional Policies in Chile. Ten years ago Aroca and Hewings have yet shown that in the case of Chile, even when migration follows the market's signals, inertial concentrating forces around large cities, particularly around the Metropolitan Region, were stronger, leading to greater concentration rather than a reduction of inequalities of the country. The Aroca's contribution to this book not only confirms this result but it argues that Chile, starting from the basis that it is one of most inequitable nations in the world and that this situation has a strong territorial component. He argues that between 1990 and 2010, regional differences have grown, presenting a center-periphery type pattern. This is proved in the second section of the chapter where results from the analysis carried out by the author on the evolution of regional inequalities in Chile have increased over time and that their origins lie in government actions and the expansion of the market mechanisms for assigning resources to the production of goods and services. A particular remark can be picked up from the analysis carried out: the analysis of the country from a spatial shows the main profile of inequality in Chile, namely a high concentration of income and the benefits of growth around the Metropolitan Region despite the fact that the growth of production in other regions has been higher. In other words – the author says – this Region has a very strong capacity to appropriate the income generated by growth in the country. According to the statistical data, the Metropolitan Region shows the highest income of the country and the differences with the rest of regions has grown over the course of a decade. A second group is formed by the southern- and northernmost regions which produce primary goods (cooper, oil and salmon). The rest of regions, which are low-income, are located in the central part of the country to the north and south of the Metropolitan Region. The increase of inequality observed is not only due to the mechanisms of market, but to government actions, which fund designed to reduce regional inequalities has worked increasing the centralism of public spending, the allocation of grants for advanced human capital and the monetary policy of the Central Bank of Chile, mainly oriented to guaranty the prices stability.

Two more countries have been object of specific analysis: Peru and Ecuador, located as Chaps. 13 and 14 of the book, respectively. The Peru's analysis has been developed by an academic team constituted by professors **Maria-Teresa Gallo** and **Ruben Garrido** (University of Alcalá, Madrid) and **Efrain González** and **Juan M. delPozo** (Catholic University of Peru). These authors begin their analysis by showing that this country has experienced high levels of growth over the past few years which was motivated to a great extent by the exportation of primary resources. However, from a territorial perspective and even a sectoral one, this does not seem to have been capable of modifying the old tendency towards divergence among the regions of the country. Overcoming the limitations of the model of 'imbalanced economic growth', or non-inclusive growth as the authors prefer ton ame it, constitute one of the main challenges of the Peruvian economy. This growth continues to coexist with high levels of inequality and socioeconomic territorial disparities, and thus has not resulted in generalized welfare for broad sections of society and for more diverse territories. As factors explaining this process, the author point out: first, the primary material exports model, largely based in mining, which does not contribute to generate changes for the regions to be capable of endogenously activating regional demand and reducing their rates of rural poverty; second, the dynamism of imports, favored by the revaluation of the 'nuevo sol', does not generate the necessary incentives for investment in productive sectors; and third, the limited distributive capacity of the state, together with restrictions on undertaking and effective decentralization and to improve the efficiency of public expenditure. Final comments from the analysis carried out underline three final points: (1) the advances to close the gap among regions is very limited; (2) the strong and increasing spatial concentration of economic activity, accompanied by greater levels of inequality, configures a type of perverse dynamic of growth, with a strong divergent center (Lima) which scarcely integrates the remaining regions; and (3) that the fruits of decentralization are still scarce as it is not contributing to change territorial economic concentration or divergence among regions. All this is claiming for greater efforts to be implemented with a long-term view and assured continuity in actions.

The analysis of Ecuador has been developed by a group of young academics of the Private Technical University of Loja, **Marlon Ramón**, **Santiago Ochoa** and **Diego Ochoa.** Chapter 14 shows that the case of Ecuador is quite similar to those of other Andean nations. Over the past few years, Ecuador has managed to grow at fairly high rates. This was due to a significant extent to the exportation of primary products, as is the case in Peru and other neighboring countries. The authors utilize conventional convergence analyses to show that this growth has been accompanied by a moderate decrease in regional differences in terms of per capita product. This reduction is linked to migratory movements, which have resulted in high population and productive activity concentration in Quito and even to a greater extent in the area of Guayaquil. In fact, Ecuador is a highly polarized nation with areas or regions that present notable differences as a result of their physical/geographic characteristics. The analysis shows that the forces of growth are very dependent on elements outside of the country and that exhaustion may have begun, which suggests that there is also an incipient process of regional divergence. The estimates of beta convergence and the Moran index allow us to arrive at a more complete vision of that which is taking place in the country as a whole and to highlight the fact that what occurs in a given region is very much connected to the dynamics and productivity of neighboring regions. From the perspective of regional policy, several observations can be made: (1) notable changes have been introduced in regard to territorial division in Ecuador; (2) there is a limited presence of regional development policies as such with a predominance of sectoral policies that have benefited the most dynamic nuclei, especially Guayaquil; and (3) the current focus is on social equality policies which are more oriented towards the individual or families than an effort to decrease territorial disparities.

1.3 Horizontal and Comparative Analysis

The case studies in Part II of the book and the more general trends that are analyzed in Part I clearly do not exhaust the field of possibilities of analysis that a collection like this one should address. As such, a third of the space, or perhaps a bit more than that, was set aside from the outset to include a set of contributions focused on providing more specific analyses of relevant topics such as migration and population, education and human capital, poverty, progress and difficulties linked to greater decentralization, exports, and the regional policies implemented by some countries. The idea was for these chapters to provide information regarding several countries from the region in order to underscore the points of contact and differences in each specific case. It has not been possible to meet that objective in every case, but the great majority of the contributions selected for this book do so.

Part III has ten chapters. The first one, number 15 of the book, has been prepared by Professor **Patricio Aroca** and the researcher of the Population and Development of CELADE- ECLAC Population Division – **Jorge Rodríguez.** The central point is the analysis of demographic trends and internal migrations in several Latin-Americans countries, shows a strong tend to concentrate population around more developed areas.

Even though, the market signals as regional wage differentials, unemployment differentials and growth at regional level, tend to move people in the expected direction and one might be predict a reduction of territorial differences because the market job in reallocating workers, what the authors find is that a large share of the movement is associate to the size of the population at the destination region, which is also the main region of its country. This conclusion rises in the descriptive analysis of the data as well as in the model that allows controlling for several other characteristics.

The main implication of this results endure the conclusion of several other chapters of this volume, that concentration in Latin-America has a strong inertia that will need serious regional policy to revert.

Professors **Miguel A. Mendoza and Jorge Isaac** of the Schools of Economics at UNAM and FES-UNAM (Acatlan), along with researcher **Marcos Valdivia** of UNAM's Regional Center for Multidisciplinary Research, offer a study on Education, Innovation and Economic Growth in Latin America, which is Chap. 16 of this book. We have become familiar with these topics through earlier research but these authors revisit them and offer a truly interesting analysis. The main purpose has been to analyze how economic growth in the LA countries is affected by the linkages between population in school (net enrollment rate) and population with different educational skills enrolled in the job market. In particular, their study focus in whether skilled workers are engaged in the production processes through practices of imitation or innovation of technologies and how this affects growth performance. Figures used come from the Socio-Economic Database for Latin America and the Caribbean, the World Bank and the data set of Educational Attainment of Barro & Lee. The authors examined the challenges facing education in LA on the basis of UN's Millenium Development Goals, concluding that: (1) most countries in LA can achieve the goal of universal primary level education by 2015; and (2) that the workforce with primary level schooling yrs. is relatively homologous among LA countries. The situation is very different when analyzing the enrollment rates and the years of schooling for secondary and tertiary education. Great disparities exist between countries in this case; Argentina and Chile emerge as leaders and Peru, Panama and Chile came top in tertiary and higher education. Actually, the differences in the proportions of the population with complete secondary and tertiary education, accumulated over the past 60 years. do not seem easy to reduce in the short term. And, on the other hand, the links between levels of education and the capacity of innovate or imitate technological processes are very clear, according to the analysis carried out using five economic growth models.

At least in some aspects, the previous contribution is complemented by the paper included as Chap. 17, which adopts a much more regional approach. It has been produced by **Francisco Rowe**, from the University of Queensland, and its title is: 'The Geography and Determinants of Human Capital in Eight Latin American and Caribbean (LAC) Countries'. Using a unique dataset comprising 5,978 city-level regions from eight LAC countries, the paper investigates the evolution of the national stock and spatial distribution of human capital and explores the factors that influence a region's share of human capital. The analysis shows that the national stock of human capital has increased in all eight countries over the past last five decades to 2010, but it has remained smaller than in advanced economies, such as Japan, Australia and the US. On the other hand, the results accomplished reveal that human capital in LAC countries is concentrated in regions which include areas of main cities and their close surrounds. The findings also suggest that a unique combination of factors collectively play a role in explaining regional differentials in human capital accumulation. Of these, the provision of public amenities is shown to be the most prevalent factor influencing human capital differential in each of LA countries. In contrast, the share of regional foreign-born workforce as a measure of regional diversity only helps to explain regional differences in human capital in the case of Brazil. This original contribution opens a door to new researches on this interesting aspect of regional disparities inside the LAC countries.

The issue of poverty in Latin American nations and its connection to living conditions and particularly wages is without a doubt one of the overarching questions that could not be omitted from this book. Chapter 18 was prepared by Professors **Carlos Salas and Anselmo Santos** of the Universidade Estadual de Campinas in Brazil utilizing data from that country and Mexico. Their analysis show not only the crucial importance of this topic, but the differences which exist comparing both countries. In Brazil, due to a major policy change, incomes have been raising more than in Mexico, jobs were created in the last decade and poverty felt throughout the whole country. Job creation increased also the number of salaried workers protected by the labor and progress to a more egalitarian society has taken place. This let not ignore that there is a group of hardcore poverty areas in Brazil and that standard policies are not enough to rise the living standards of millions of people, due to their isolation, their low levels of education and the impact of poverty ridded generations. The Mexican case shows some specific characteristics and differences compared to Brazil. The greater integration of this country into the US (and Canada) economic area have not lead to a convergence process, whereby the less developed regions started growing faster to catch up the rest of the country, thereby diminishing poverty levels in a more clear and permanent way. Unfortunately, the impact of the actual crisis, starting in 2008, and the slow rate of creation of qualified jobs have had an impact on the general well-being of Mexican workers. Micro economic units (those having less than six workers, including self-employed workers) represent more than 80 per 100 of the Mexican enterprises; they create more jobs than the rest of the economy but their working and payment conditions are bad, which surely explain the surge in poverty levels. It is clear that more education is needed, but the type of jobs being created does not need qualified personal. The chapter includes tables supporting the results attained.

Two different papers included in the book as Chaps. 19 and 20 have focused the problem of decentralization in LA. The contribution of Professor **Clemente Ruiz Duran**, from the UNAM, offers a rich approach to the topic both from a theoretical point of view but also considering the consequences of the dominant 'centralization' being practiced in a great number of LA countries. On the other hand, the contribution written by **M. Camilo Vial,** Ph.D. candidate in Political Science, pays a much more specific attention to the fiscal decentralization through a comparative analysis of Bolivia, Chile, Colombia, Ecuador and Peru. Both are, without any doubt, two excellent papers, plenty of ideas to extend the debate on centralization versus decentralization, strongly supported by theoretical approaches and empirical analysis. It is difficult to summarize the chapter written by Professor **C. Ruiz Duran** (Chap. 19), from the UNAM, Mexico. His departing point is the Latin America debt crisis and their consequences to analyze later the strengthening local governance comparing the cases of Argentina, Mexico and Brazil structures and the tax distribution among different levels of government, the transfers systems in each of these countries showing a bargaining political process. Other aspects analyzed are expenditures and the trap of megacities, a topic strongly related with the urban and concentration trends studied in Part I of this book. Finally, the chapter try to answer a crucial question: How much decentralization has fostered development? His conclusion is that decentralization agenda has helped to strengthened territorial development in LA, but it has to be recognized that the lack of planning has diminished positive effects. Any case, he underlines the need of studies case by case because there are important differences by countries and the trends to centralize are still dominating.

The contribution by **M. C. Vial** (Chap. 20) offers a panoramic view on the political and fiscal decentralization in the Andean countries (Bolivia, Chile, Colombia, Ecuador and Peru). The aim of the first part of the chapter is focused to describe the decentralization processes held in these countries from the 1980s to now. This overview is complemented by a revision of the evolution of political-administrative division. Differences existing between the countries studied can be simplified considering two territorial units with their own governments that stand out because of their responsibilities, resources and territorial authority: the local governments (municipalities) and the intermediate ones governing the respective provinces, departments or regions according to the different names used). Finally, the author analyzes the processes of fiscal decentralization in each of the countries studied, differentiating transfers from self-generated incomes. The main conclusion is that three decades after the process began, there is no doubt that LA now presents a more decentralized face, which is linked to the advances to a democratic participation. But it is also true that some major decentralizing reforms are limited to formal aspects that do not manage to generate practice or fail to meet the high expectations created, which once again generates incentives for the center to take on greater leadership. Or, perhaps, this has been really due to the lack of real decisions to decentralize.

Chapter 21 offers an specific analysis on the procedures and effects of government transfers, taking Brazil as a reference case. This contribution, prepared by **E. Haddad, C.A. Luque, G.T. Lima, S.N. Sakurai and S.M. Costa**, from de University of Sao Paulo, complements some aspects studied in the two previous chapters. In fact, the Brazilian case is a very interesting example of how work the government transfers to attain social goals and the reduction of personal (and indirectly regional) disparities. Redistributive policies carried out by the central government in Brazil through interregional government transfers is a relevant feature of the Brazilian federal fiscal system. Regional shares of the central government revenues in the poorer regions have been recurrently smaller than the shares of central government expenditures in those regions. Appeal to core-periphery outcomes could be made, as Sao Paulo, the wealthiest state, concentrated in 2005 over 40 % of total Federal tax revenue, receiving less than 35 % of Federal expenditures. These figures suggest an effective process of redistribution of public funds from the core of the economy to the peripheral areas. The chapter analyses the role interregional transfers play in the redistribution of activities in the country, using an interregional input–output approach. Counterfactual simulations allow the authors to estimate some costs and benefits for the core and the periphery due to such fiscal mechanisms. The final conclusion is that the results are positive in the sense that the Northeast and North regions have increased their share in national GDP, as their shares in total value added effect exceed their respective shares in GDP. Thus, interregional government transfers seem to have had a favorable impact. But, the analysis carried out has also shown that interregional linkages within the Brazilian economy operate favoring the more developed regions, as there are relevant leakages from lagging regions to more developed regions. So, as the authors conclude, "the persistence of regional dualism in Brazil is nonetheless reinforced by the structure of productive interdependence of the economy, as our results have demonstrated".

The aim of Chap. 22, which author is Prof. **Edgard Moncayo,** has been to analyze the role of regional policies in the Andean countries and their evolution. To understand both is absolutely necessary, as the author underlines from the very beginning, to contextualize the political evolution of such countries, that is, Venezuela, Colombia, Ecuador, Peru and Chile.

From the perspective of major structural trends, Andean regional policies have evolved in a pattern quite similar to most LA countries. These, in turn, have followed the model of the dominant international trends. Such synchronicity can be explained by the fact that regional policies – just like all other public policies – evolve *paripassu* to the role assigned to the State in the processes of development. Regarding their public policies, two clearly distinct periods can be highlighted in the LA context: (a) the post-War period until the late 1980s, and (b) the period dating from that time until the present. In the case of three Andean countries – Bolivia, Ecuador, and Venezuela – it is relevant to distinguish yet another stage, characterized by "post-" or "anti-" neoliberal policies of governments that aim at establishing a new kind of socialism in their respective States.

The analysis carried out by the author concludes with some specific remarks. The first is the continuous presence of a centralism-federalism debate which caused several civil wars and conflicts in the nineteenth century and during the twentieth century. Such conflicts – and contradictions – remain unsolved today in the twenty-first century. The second underlines that during the second half of the twentieth century, Andean regional policies followed a path that is closely associated to the evolution of the role assigned to the State in development processes, and that is very similar to the cycles of the welfare state and regional policy in the developed countries. The third is that the ascendant stage of regional policy in the Andean countries was supported by the greater State interventionism and 'developmentalism' (Bolivia, Peru and Venezuela in particular) leaded towards a substitution of imports policies and the export of natural resources. Fourth, the international crisis of the 1970s, the impact of imbalances in the world economy in the 1980s, and the adoption of the neoliberal model in the 1990s determined the dismantling of previous statist policies – as in most of the other Latin American countries – and thus the decline of active public policies, including regional policies.

Finally, disenchantment with the results of structural reforms of the economy inspired by the neoliberal paradigm (the Washington Agreements) and the exhaustion of the political parties that promoted them led to a wave – unprecedented in Latin America – of governments on the left side of the political spectrum. From the point of view of regional policies it must be admitted that they aren't the most important in the political programs of the leftist governments of Venezuela, Bolivia and Ecuador, much more interested in personal redistribution policies through subsidies and actions oriented to facilitate lodging, healthcare and education without a clear territorial component.

The exports patterns in Latin America contrasts clearly to the one in the European Union. While the differences among the European countries export baskets are decreasing over time, the pattern among the Latin American countries shows a rise on specialization (less diversification). This pattern among the countries is also found within two Latin American countries (Chile and Colombia), showing regions more specialized than their country. This is a first remark set up by professors **Miguel A. Marquez, Ma. Teresa Fernandez and Julian Ramajo,** from the University of Extremadura (Chap. 23). There are two important implications of this pattern. Firstly, shocks abroad that impact demand for export will have different impact within the country according the specialization of the regions. While a negative shock might affects significantly to some regions, it might not affect at all other ones. The chapter includes empirical analysis showing both alternatives and their consequences.

From a regional policy point of view, a government that is aware of these potential impacts should have a policy that compensates those affected regions in order to reduce negative impacts. A model to estimate the potential impact for a country is estimated and the information for regional policy design is generated.

Finally, Chap. 24 includes the analysis of an important aspect of the recent development of Latin American countries: the presence of Foreign Direct Investments and their allocation by countries and sectors. It has been produced by **Michael Penfold and Jose Luis Curbelo,** both linked at CAF, Development Bank of Latin America. The chapter has three main sections. In the first one, the behavior of foreign investment in Latin America is characterized on the basis of various indicators. The second analyses the relevance that Asian investments have been acquiring, with a special focus on China, as well as the investment of the 'multilatins' as a mechanism of intra-regional integration. In this same section some incipient elements relating to FDI are dealt with, such as the location of Research and Development Centers by multinational companies and the emergence of a venture capital industry which has begun to channel investment resources towards local sectors and companies with innovative potential. Finally, the chapter concludes with the identification of new challenges which the Latin American countries are going to have to deal with in order to increase FDI and, above all, to positively impact in the different economies of the region. These final reflections constitute what the authors have named as 'the new agenda' of FDI in Latin America. It must be underlined that one of the characteristics of the most recent trends is the increasing presence of what the authors call 'multilatin' companies, which show not only an increasing activity but a much more sectoral diversification. In particular, investments in food and beverages, engineering and construction, steel and metallurgy, transport, petroleum and mining stand out. Furthermore, as they also remark, this is a process in which there is a growing participation of medium sized companies that attempt to emulate the internationalization patterns of large Latin American companies, through which they tend to be integrated as suppliers.

1.4 Some Final Remarks

As we stated at the beginning of this introduction, it is clear that we have not addressed every aspect and problem related to the issues that form the focus on these studies. However, the 23 chapters that comprise this book along with this introduction offer numerous elements that can be used to understand the problems and trends that can be observed from a territorial perspective in Latin American and Caribbean nations. These studies also elucidate the types of policies that have been implemented in order to address or reduce the severity of those problems. We have, of course, tried to provide rigorous and objective treatments of the issues. Though they respected basic formatting guidelines and accepted comments and suggestions based on early drafts, the authors prepared their texts with complete freedom.

The final result of the work of the authors and editors is this volume, which we are confident will be well-received and widely circulated as it clearly fills a void that existed in English-language literature on regional problems and policies.

We wish to emphasize two final points.

The first is that, as the reader will note and as we have tried to underscore in this introduction, although Latin American countries have a great deal in common in regard to territorial problems that allow one to identify dominant trends that have emerged over the past six or seven decades, the studies in this book also highlight differences between them.

The second point is that those differences among the countries of the sub-continent make it impossible to apply clichés to the interpretation of what has happened in each of them. This is not only valid in regard to the problems that the countries are facing, but also in terms of the policies (or lack thereof) applied in order to address them. In many cases, these policies present scant results and have been linked to instability and a lack of continuity derived from frequent political changes. In this sense, the much more stable situation of growth that many countries in the region are experiencing leads us to hope that regional development policies can be implemented that decrease territorial inequality and achieve a greater level of economic and social cohesion and thus increase political stability based on clear advances in terms of social equality in the areas of economics and quality of life.

Finally, as the coordinators and editors of this volume, we would like to thank Springer-Verlag for the support that it has provided for the publication since its inception and all of the authors whose names are listed in this book for their generous collaboration and willingness to bring this project to fruition.

Madrid and Santiago de Chile, December 2012.

Acknowledgments We acknowledge particularly the support of the Project NS 100046 of the Millennium Science Initiative of the Chilean Ministry of Economics, Public Works and Tourism and the Chilean FONDECYT Grant No 1111061

Chapter 2
Facing the Need for Regional Policies in Latin America

Juan R. Cuadrado-Roura and Patricio Aroca

2.1 Introduction

From the perspective of results in terms of growth as a whole, Latin America and particularly some countries of the continent are experiencing an economic stage that could be described as fairly pleasant. There are, of course, differences among countries, but several of them have reported GDP growth rates of over 4 % in real terms since 2000. The impact of the international economic-financial crisis had its worst manifestation in 2009, when Brazil, Chile, Venezuela and especially Mexico reported real negative rates in the variation in their GDP. However, in 2010, all of them returned to very positive rates of expansion (7.44 % in Brazil; 5.2 % in Chile; 5.39 % in Mexico; 4.13 % in Bolivia and over 8 % in Peru and Uruguay). This put the average real growth in the region for 2010 at around 4.1 %, which was estimated to have increased two more decimals in 2011 and would only decrease to slightly below 4 % in 2012.[1] As some reliable reports have suggested, Latin America and the Caribbean (LAC) confirmed its economic power in 2012 because the region was capable of resisting international economic instabilities and maintains expectations of growth of 3.5–4 % for the next 2 years.[2]

[1] Data extracted from World Bank reports, *Anuario Estadístico de América Latina y Caribe 2012*, and statistics and forecasts through 2012 published by ECLAC (CEPAL). When this text was written, reliable data on 2012 results were not available.

[2] See *Perspectivas económicas de America Latina 2012* (OECD-CEPAL 2011) and the more recent report by the International Monetary Fund.

J.R. Cuadrado-Roura (✉)
Department of Applied Economics, University of Alcalá, Madrid, Spain
e-mail: jr.cuadrado@uah.es

P. Aroca
University Adolfo Ibañez, Viña del Mar, Chile
e-mail: parocanet@gmail.com

J.R. Cuadrado-Roura and P. Aroca (eds.), *Regional Problems and Policies in Latin America*, Advances in Spatial Science, DOI 10.1007/978-3-642-39674-8_2,

One of the factors that explain these results has undoubtedly been the exporting sector, in which the two most important clients – the United States and Europe – were recently joined by a third that has become a source of stimulus: China, the recipient of many of the exports of mining products without any prior processing. However, one must keep in mind that the national accounting data also reflect a notable and nearly constant increase in internal consumption, domestic investments, and flows of entries of external investments, though this latter is more limited than it was in the past. In several countries on the continent all of this has been accompanied by the application of macroeconomic policies designed to maintain stability. In fact, the policies applied during the years of strong growth (2003–2008) frequently allowed the margin for other social policies to be generated and broadened. For example, some Latin American nations used monetary policy and particularly fiscal policy (OECD-CEPAL 2011) in a counter-cyclical manner during the worse period of the international financial crisis of 2008–2009, which helped them to avoid a deep recession and soften the negative effects of the crisis on the most vulnerable sectors of society.

The data provided and consolidation of adequate macroeconomic policies should not hide the fact that some countries present behavior and results that are far from the average for the region. This is the case in several Central American nations, for example. Furthermore, there continue to be risks for the future derived from the strong dependence on some exports to the evolution of China and other emerging nations, the low levels of productivity in some economic sectors and inflationist movements that gain steam from the increase in the prices of primary materials and energy and from social spending policies.

It would not make sense to continue to expand upon the issues mentioned above in this text, though they undoubtedly merit more extensive comments and some fine-tuning. There are, however, three problems or questions that merit special attention, one of which will be taken as the foundation for the thesis that is set forth in this chapter.

The positive data in terms of growth, exports and social improvements do not impede the existence of significant problems now and looking to the future. The need to maintain the stability of macroeconomic balances may be the first of them, as the goal of closing gaps in infrastructure, education and innovation is maintained, which would allow most Latin American economies to continue to grow more and better in the long term. But there are two others that are directly related to income distribution and the well being of the citizens who also are and should be a cause for concern. The first is the unequal distribution of income at the individual or household scale given that the differences that exist in this area in Latin America and Caribe (LAC) are well-known. Some countries in the region are even among those that have the greatest level of inequality in the world. The second, different but strongly related to the first, is the significant economic disparities that exist in Latin America from the territorial perspective, that is, among the states, provinces or regions of each country. This is not something new, as it is a problem that began decades ago and has barely improved over the past few years. In some cases, it has been exacerbated as a result of clear processes of concentration of production in metropolitan areas or specific sectors of the country, as several chapters in this book demonstrate. In Argentina, the highest per capita GDP in 2010 (Santa Cruz province) was 7.85 times that of the poorest province in the country (Formosa).[3] In Brazil, the per capita GDP of the Federal District is 7.35 times higher than that of the state of Alagoas. In Mexico, the richest state's per capita GDP is 9.3 times that of the poorest state (Campeche and Guerrero, respectively). In Peru, that figure is 7.8 and in Colombia it is four. The differences are just as high or higher in other LAC countries.

These strong interregional economic disparities in terms of production per inhabitant also frame very important differences connected to the productive structures of states, provinces or regions and very limited or null perspectives for improvement for the most delayed territories if one does not measure the implementation of specific regional development programs to promote their transformation. This also should affect regions that are temporarily in a phase of high growth rates and the expansion of employment based on the exportation of natural resources, because the continuity of that activity may be limited due to changes in international markets or the economies of the countries that are their main clients.

This chapter starts from the need to promote new regional development policies, capitalizing on the positive economic situation that many countries in the region enjoy. In the case of LAC, implementing regional policies is not a whim or an 'accessory' policy. The realities that the content of several chapters of this book reflect lead us to state that the territorial issue and the development of the most delayed regions should occupy a very high-profile position on government agendas. The reflections presented in the pages that follow are designed to justify the need for such policies and underscore some of the characteristics that should accompany those that are implemented as well as those that are ongoing, of which there are undoubtedly few at this point in time.

2.2 Regional Policy in Latin America: Preliminary Observations

2.2.1 A Brief Description of the Recent Historical Context

The recent economic history of Latin America (LA) has been marked by a set of policies generated in order to address the varied problems that have emerged not only as individual countries but as a set of nations that shares histories, from their Independence processes to their languages, culture, some characteristics of their productive systems, and certain policy proposals and economic strategies.

[3] It is important to keep in mind that Santa Cruz is responsible for exceptional energy production that increases the average per capita production.

The 1950s and 1960s were marked by an economic policy proposal built by the group of LA countries and formalized by the Economic Commission for Latin America (ECLAC) in which the development of a continent that was closed off to commerce with developed countries was proposed. There was active promotion of import substitution for domestic products and the specialization of the countries in different manufactured goods.

The main justification for this approach lay in the fact that evolution in terms of exchanges mainly benefited developed nations, which exported manufactured goods, unlike LA nations, which exported basic agricultural, mineral and energy products. At the same time, the model proposed defended the need for the government to play a very active role in the production of goods and services in both the manufacturing and agricultural sectors. In the latter case, agrarian reforms were implemented based on the fact that a significant portion of the land was purchased with speculative intentions.

This set of changes with a strong emphasis on the role to be played by the government was complemented by political reforms dominated by a liberal governing class that sought greater equality and affected the economic interests of large multinational corporations that had investments in those countries and local wealthy groups. This lead to a significant decrease in both local and foreign investment and governments used inorganic emission to finance the growing demand of its operations. This led to growing inflation in numerous countries on the continent towards the end of the 1960s and throughout most of the 1970s.

The 1960s saw serious attempts to implement regional policies, as several chapters in this book point out, rampant inflation and the stalling of production generated characteristics that were described as 'stagflation.'[4] The solution to this was the focus of most of the economic policies of the following decade, and the approach taken was the application of stabilization programs.

The stabilization plans applied in Latin America in order to manage the imbalances were accompanied by military dictatorships and characterized by a strong contraction of government demand in order to decrease budgetary deficits and try to reduce the continuous increase in the level of prices that was seen in most Latin American nations.

The majority of these adjustment programs enjoyed the support and conditioning of the International Monetary Fund (IMF), whose set of recommended measures for countries, which they were required to implement in order to have loans approved by that agency, had positive consequences for control of inflation but not economic growth with one exception. However, at the same time the reduction of the size of the government through privatizations and particularly through spending reductions oriented towards the poorest sectors of society caused a significant increase in

---

[4] The content of this expression – stagflation – was also applied to several European nations, neither the causes, the levels that inflation reached, nor the limited growth and scant job creation are comparable to the situation of various Latin American nations, as in the cases of Peru, Ecuador, and Brazil.

inequalities of income at the individual level. A second and equally or more important element was the increase in territorial inequalities within each country, as many studies have shown for years and as is very clearly reflected in several chapters of this book. Existing interregional differences were not decreased and in many cases, they worsened or remained unchanged.

Despite the fact that these territorial inequalities are recognized in the political discourses of various governing coalitions, the economic policies that were given priority after the stabilization are those that promote growth and, with much less importance, those focused on reducing poverty. In fact the poverty levels increased dramatically during the adjustment period that took place throughout nearly the whole of the 1980s and that have allowed it to be described as "the lost decade of Latin America."

The following decade – the 1990s – began to show signs of economic and social recovery in the region. The military dictatorships gave way to returns to democracy and, as part of this process, decentralization policies were implemented in order to ensure the transition towards a full republican government. However, though these policies were the subject of proposals and were implemented in some countries, as Burki et al. (1999) note, progress in that direction was only made in a few cases. Otherwise, there is no clear link between the limited decentralization efforts and the reduction in territorial economic inequalities.

2.2.2 *The Intellectual Contribution*

There is a long history of intellectual contributions to understanding the effect of location, interaction and spatial heterogeneity in economies and the generation of territorial inequalities. However, it was likely Nobel Prize-winning economist Paul Krugman who helped focus the consideration of space in the center of the discussion or at least in the mainstream of traditional economics in the 1990s. This gave way to a new area of Economics as a science that took shape and continued to grow stronger based on then-new contributions known as the "New Economic Geography" (NEG). One of the main conclusions that this analytical current proposed starting from a look inside of the countries was that concentration or increased density promotes growth (Fujita et al. 1999). This complements and supports one of the main recommendations of economic policy that were present in the 1990s through the early twenty-first century: grow and then distribute.

This idea, which has existed for some time in traditional regional economics (Capello 2007), was presented in a much more formalized context and thus adapted more and in a better fashion to the current mode of doing economics, with microeconomic foundations and a piece that had been absent of a greater puzzle that sustained the design of regional policies (Baldwin et al. 2003). At those time, mainly following these approaches, the majority of Latin American nations not only smiled upon processes that favored concentration but also promoted them, generating a significant increase in the already concentrated distribution of economic activity and population in space.

The extension of a theoretical body of NEG has begun only recently in which, motivated by the fact that some countries present behaviors similar to those suggested many years ago by Williamson (1965), more attention has been paid to the thesis that the excesses of concentration negatively affect growth. In fact, various contributions show that under certain conditions, excessive concentration around a region of a country may negatively affect the entire growth process (see Cerina and Mureddu 2010) and may produce new increases in socio-economic disparities among the regions within countries.

2.2.3 The Interest of International Organizations

The territorial inequality that exists in Latin America undoubtedly has deep roots. It began to show signs of reaching concerning levels some time ago, levels that could affect economic efficiency as well as the stability of the region. The emergence of the Zapatista movement in Chiapas, in southern Mexico, to the north, and more recent protests in Punta Arenas, Chile, on the southern end of the continent, were based mainly on the resentments produced by territorial inequalities, as Armstrong and Taylor (2003) have observed. It is likely that this has moved international organizations to increasingly pay attention to the growth of territorial inequalities.

In its flagship report from 2009, *Reshaping Economic Geography*, the World Bank began the study of the countries in the world with an intra-country gaze. This work, which was strongly influenced by the ideas of NEG, proposes adopting policies that generate concentration or increase density in order to continue to grow. The companion book for Latin America and the Caribbean that was published by the same entity extends and expands this idea for Latin American nations (World Bank, 2009).

Also in 2009, ECLAC (CEPAL) published the book *Economía y Territorio en América Latina y el Caribe*: *Desigualdades y Políticas* in which regions within countries on the continent are classified as winners and losers. However, the analysis is again focused on growth of the GDP and ignores how it is distributed in the territory and how that affects the wellbeing of different areas of countries, which present fairly strong internal disassociations. This is particularly true for regions or areas that focus on the exploitation of natural resources, an activity that is highly intensive in use of capital and strongly oriented towards exports. The noteworthy aspect of the ECLAC analysis is how aligned it is with the position adopted by the World Bank given that the two institutions have traditionally promoted clearly contradictory visions of development in Latin America.

That same year, the OECD published volume focused on the study of Chile and its regions (OECD 2009a) following the formal invitation extended to that nation to become a member state of the organization. The OECD's perspective is different than the one described above for the World Bank and ECLAC. The main conclusion of the OECD report is that Chile needs to make better use of its regional assets and reduce concentration around the Santiago metro area given that this would allow the country to achieve greater economic growth and a reduction in territorial inequalities. Other OECD publications (2009b, 2010) have more generally presented this same idea, though with a fairly formal and even more ascetic approach.

In 2010, the Corporation for Andean Economic Development (Corporación Andina de Fomento, CAF) focused its annual report on economics and development on the topic (CAF 2010). The publication was entitled: *Desarrollo Local: hacia un nuevo protagonismo de las ciudades y regiones(Local Development. Towards a new protagonism of cities and regions)*. In it, the CAF argues that there are territorial and city-region cases that have been very successful with their goal of promoting the productivity of their firms and industries and improving inhabitants' quality of life. The report shows and concludes that regional policy and regional development are key for explaining the cases of successful cities and regions of its member states that were considered for the study. As was the case with the OECD report (2009a), the influence of NEG on the CAF study is minor and, as is noted in the text, the goal is to "contribuir al entendimiento de los patrones de desarrollo local y regional, asícomo aidentificar opciones de políticas públicasque con una fuerte participación de los gobiernos e instituciones sub-nacionales, tanto en el diseñocomo en la ejecución, permitan compatibilizar el crecimiento económico con un desarrollo balanceado de los territorios al interior de laseconomías" (*to contribute to the understanding of the patterns of local and regional development and identify public policy options that with strong participation by sub-national governments and institutions in their design and execution, allow economic growth to be made compatible with balanced development of the territories within the economies*).

2.2.4 The Challenges for Politicians and Regional Policy

It would seem that LA is once again facing the dilemma of choosing between promoting more market and promoting more government in policy, particularly in the case of regional policy. Increasing importance is being given to the fact that inequalities are beginning to generate strong movements that are opposed to continuing with the concentration of power and wealth in certain territories within each nation or certain groups within the population.

Over the past few years, we have moved from the privatizing current of the 1980s and 1990s to nationalization processes, which have been implemented in several nations. Also, there are a growing number of localized movements on the periphery of the countries that are fighting to achieve more and greater opportunities for their inhabitants. In this context, there is no doubt that regional policy has an important role to develop and that the current circumstances also constitute a great opportunity because several countries are experiencing a clear overall economic improvement of their economies. Whether said policies are designed, implemented and successful in their results depends a great deal of the related assessments. Understanding the processes of concentration and the creation of greater opportunities on the margins of the territories is thus a key aspect, as is discovering the right institutions for the culture and levels of development of the different areas of LA. All of this constitutes a fundamental task that will allow policymakers to be provided with the tools they need to design the new regional development policies that Latin America currently needs. The issue clearly merits more careful study, which is what we propose to do in the following sections.

2.3 On the Advisability of and Justification for Implementing Regional Policies

The need for Latin American nations to implement 'regional policies' finds clear support in everything that has been presented in the introduction and preceding section. It is very especially clear when one considers the persistence of territorial disparities over the past few decades and in the majority of the region's nations.

As we have already indicated, and as some of the texts included in this book have underscored, the implementation of this kind of policy has a notable history in the region, mainly through the 1980s. Currently, however, the agendas of Latin American governments rarely include policies of this kind despite the fact that they have recognized the need for them formally and in many government programs. Over the past 10 years, administrative decentralization programs and territorial development policies have been approved, but many of them continue to be stuck in a very primary phase or are under review.

The processes of economic concentration and strong interregional disparities that exist in Latin America are clearly manifest in many chapters of this book. The authors highlight the need to design and implement regional development policies and do so *precisely now*, when the evolution of the economies is very positive in terms of economic growth. South Korea may represent an interesting reference in this regard. Its officials understood a little over a decade ago that the strong growth that the economy was experiencing could not continue to be concentrated in and around the capitol and that there was a need to take advantage of the economic abundance to achieve more territorially balanced development (Sang-Chuel Choe 2012). In fact, from the beginning of this century, South Korea has re-centered the focus of its problems on *local and territorial development* rather than on national problems, on *quality of life* rather the economic problems, and on *local and regional government* rather than problems of administrative centralization.

When this type of approach is shared, the objective that we present here is to try to clarify what we are talking about when we talk about regional policies, the motivations that justify it and the types of fronts or lines of action that seem to be most important based on the international experience that has been accumulated.

The ideas and suggestions presented below require more space than we can provide for them here.[5] However, we must present them – albeit in a summary format – during such a crucial phase in Latin America's history in which issues of politico-administrative decentralization and the need to correct disparities between states, provinces and/or regions is the focus of demands that merit a clear response.

2.3.1 Regional Policy, Social Equality Policies or Regional Development Policies?

The role of the market in the economies and the one that officials should play when it comes time to correcting the market's 'faults' has been one of the liveliest topics of debate that has taken place among economists and, of course, at the political level. The *critical* literature on the effective functioning of the markets is fairly extensive. In many studies, the list of problems that the market fails to address or does not resolve properly[6] has allowed authors to defend *the need* for officials to intervene in order to resolve these problems or at least to alleviate their consequences. However, there is another set of studies whose critiques of the market have evolved towards much more radical positions. They demonstrate that the capitalist system based on the free market does not function adequately and fails to address real needs and social objectives. The conclusion to which the latter approach leads one is the need to 'substitute' the system, albeit radically, through the annulment of private property and creation of a system of planning and centralized decisions or a combination of central planning and market. By contrast, the option initially presented leads to a mixed system of market economy[7] in which government interventions is legitimated though in a level that is comparatively uneven by country and according to their respective constitutions.

If we situate ourselves in the context of mixed economies, which is what we find in nearly every Latin American economy currently and, of course, the system in place in the majority of the most developed nations, the issue of *disparities of income and wellbeing among the various regions in a country*[8] is introduced or forms part of the concern over the improvement in *income distribution* among

[5] See for ex.: Cuadrado-Roura, 2010, 2012.

[6] These 'lacks' include at least the following: the existence of non-competitive markets; the failure to consider external effects; the deficient or non-existent assessment of public goods; the existence of increasing production of scale; the lack of consideration for income distribution; the failure to resolve imbalances and growth of the economy; the existence of preferential and undesired needs; the lack of solidarity that the market promotes in social conduct; the flawed allocation in relation to the 'moral risk'; and the ineffectiveness of the market when urgent problems develop.

[7] This is also sometimes called the '*social* market economy.'

[8] Or of a set of countries if one is considering nations linked to an economic integration process, like the European Union, or connected through an agreement that is more limited to the commercial realm, as MERCOSUR essentially continues to be, or like NAFTA.

citizens, an aspect that market mechanisms clearly do not address. However, it is important to note that one must not confuse inequality in terms of personal income (inequality in the *level of wellbeing* or in regard to the level of *per capita income*) with inequalities in the *spatial distribution of production* and the population, though both types of inequality are or can be linked.

In theory, one would have to present the possibility that the social inequalities that a country suffers in terms of per capita income would be reproduced equally in all of its regions, states or provinces. This would mean that, in practice, disparities between regions, provinces or states would not exist and that the objective of economic policy to be considered in this area could consist only of ensuring that socio-economic inequalities among individuals would be progressively reduced (Polèse and Shearmur 2005; Polèse and Rubiera 2009).

However, this type of situation is unthinkable in reality because in all nations both types of inequality or disparity exist simultaneously and require different treatments. In effect, though they are related, these are actually two different issues. On the one hand, there is a problem of personal distribution of income and, on the other, disparities in the levels of development that can exist among provinces, states or regions within a country. The latter also have to do with the former, mainly in terms of average levels, but personal inequalities in income can and tend to occur in more dynamic and developed regions as well as more delayed ones. In fact, the struggle against regional disparities does not in and of itself ensure the achievement of greater social equality.

As simple as it seems, the above reasoning allows one to reach a clarifying conclusion: introducing income redistribution policies through the tax system and spending and subsidy or government aid policies is not the same as implementing territorial or regional rebalancing policies or vice versa, though they may influence each other. In some Latin American countries, regional policies as such are not being implemented at this time, but the governments are introducing social and income and quality of life policies for the poorest citizens through subsidies, aid and personal transfers like those are included in anti-poverty programs. However, confusing these types of policies would be and clearly is an error, particularly when we introduce the concept of *regional development policies*.

The question that must be asked is thus, what do we call regional policies and/or regional development policies?

The answer is simple, at least on the surface. Both are policies that take as their point of reference *the territory* and, as such, the whole of the population that utilizes it, the economic activity developed in it, its economic structure and the endowment of social and wellbeing-related infrastructures. However, it is possible to identify two major types of socio-economic policies in regional matters: regional policies (RP) and regional development policies (RDP).[9]

[9] The possible confusion may increase when the concept of 'territorial organization policies' is included. These policies have a different meaning than the other two, though they can be incorporated as part of them. 'Organizing' a territory is not the same as economically balancing

The former essentially seek to reduce regional disparities or inequalities in terms of per capita income and employment (Armstrong and Taylor 2003). In order to achieve this, actions are developed that generally try to refocus the spatial distribution of economic activities throughout the entire countries as sources of new income and employment. For example, business location incentives may be offered or specific public investments may be made. In the context of such policies, transfers may be made to the regions in order to even out the availability and access to basic social services such as education and healthcare, thus reducing disparities that may exist between poorer regions and more dynamic and better endowed ones.

Regional development policies (RDP) are aimed at the 'development' of some regions that are more delayed than others or have suffered some sort of setback due to the exhaustion of their main resources or as a result of a crisis in specific productive sector, be it agriculture, manufacturing or services. From this perspective, the concept of 'development' looks to achieve in the medium and especially long term economic, social and qualitative objectives[10] that truly imply a profound change in favor of one or several delayed regions and their inhabitants. The action is thus *more selective* from the territorial perspective given that it focuses on *developing* a specific number of regions, states or provinces and the goals that are sought cannot be compared to those of *redistribution* policies, nor do they only seek regional economic growth. They are clearly different from regional parties, whose nature is frequently more 'aid-oriented' than the promotion of 'development.' This is particularly the case because RDPs must always incorporate a *long term vision* aimed at resolving the economic and social problems that delay or under development of a specific territory or territories within a country pose, transforming their structures from the outset.

From a conceptual perspective, the difference between the two policies is fairly clear, though it is not as much in practice given that they can and tend to become entwined. There is often a move to promote the 'development' of delayed or less favored regions as part of an anti-inequality policy. An important differential characteristic is that regional *development* policies (RDP) always require the participation of the region and the various agents present in it, while regional policies tend to be more horizontal – they cover or tend to cover an entire nation, though there are some differences – and vertical at the same time: the protagonist is the State, that is, the central government.

---

the regions of a country or a group of countries. Territorial organization looks to do something that is much more closely linked with a respectful treatment of space, evaluating the consequences – mainly physical, of respect for nature, etc. – that may come from any public action (transportation networks and new infrastructure) and urban problems and systems, rural areas, natural spaces that must be protected, etc.

[10] The differentiation between simple economic growth and 'development' is the subject of a broad body of literature that we do not need to list here. See Furtado (1968); Thirlwall (1972, 1999) and Eatwell et al. (1987).

2.3.2 *Economic and Non-Economic Arguments That Justify the Implementation of Regional Development Policies*

There is broad agreement with the idea that regional policies in general and *regional development policies* in particular can be justified and have been justified *not only* due to *economic* reasons but also because of *political and social* reasons based on principles of *equity*. This has led economists who believe that the market is a mechanism that guarantees greater efficiency in the allocation of resources to criticize the implementation of any type of regional policy, just as they do with practically all policies that involve government intervention in economic processes derived from the free market.[11] The reason that they give is that the application of such policies is not justified from the perspective of efficiency or improved allocation of resources in the short or especially the long term.

However, it seems clear that there are *economic arguments*, and not only extra-economic ones that justify the application of regional rebalancing policies in favor of the most delayed regions of any nation.

2.3.2.1 Economic Arguments

These arguments revolve around two clearly related issues: (i) whether interregional disparities in terms of income and employment exist and their causes and (ii) whether the mechanisms of the market will tend to correct disparities or if they will tend to remain and even increase. It is important to note the following regarding these matters, however briefly:

(i) The empirical evidence shows that *economic imbalances exist at the territorial level* in all types of economies both in those considered more developed and those that are emerging or developing. From this point of view Latin American nations are not only an exception but, as was noted in the introduction to this chapter and as many of the texts included in this book show, the territorial disparities of Latin American countries are – almost without exception – higher than in other areas of the world and with strong resistances against decreasing over time.

    The reasons for the existence and development of territorial inequalities in Latin America can be attributed, as in other cases, to various causes. There are clear differences in available resources; the geographic location of the regions, in some cases very far removed from the more dynamic centers of the country; the play of certain favorable or unfavorable effects of attraction for different regions, such as the 'capital effect,' which generally favors the city named as the capital of the country; the attraction that large urban nodes exercise, which

[11] By contrast, deregulation policies, privatizations, etc., that is, elements that are favorable to the free movement of the market and competition, are accepted.

means that they constitute to grow; certain policy decisions made in the past such as transportation networks, the priority nature of a port, etc.; the differences in terms of the entrepreneurial spirit or 'social capital'; the climate, etc. But over the past few decades, industrial relocation processes and the crises suffered by specific productive activities also have played a role. In some cases, these activities are very concentrated due to technological changes, the development of substitute products or simply the exhaustion of the natural resources that constituted their initial basis. As a result, regardless of the causes, it is the existence of elevated interregional differences, in terms of production, average per capita income and employment.

(ii) The immediate question to be asked is whether the territorial disparities that existed within each country would tend to *increase* or *decrease over time* thanks to economic evolution if authorities do not intervene or specific development programs are not implemented (Cuadrado-Roura 2012).

Economists have offered fairly different responses. This should not come as a surprise given that Economics is a social science and, as such, the theories and arguments implicitly or explicitly take up 'values' and value judgments[12] that, along with some, suppositions, condition the recommendations of said theories or models and their results, as eminent economists such as Myrdal (1953), Blaug (1962), David (1988), Higgins (1951) and Schlefer (2012) have noted. This is also what happens in the interpretation of economic disparities at the territorial level and their possible evolution. Those who base their claims on and defend the principles of the *neoclassical model* argue that the existence of said territorial disparities should not be a reason for special concern. The system of exchange of the market, if it acts freely, handles or adjusts the prices and quantities in a certain time period (Borts and Stein 1964; Harris and Trainor 1997; Hulten and Schwab 1984; Barro and Sala-i-Martin 1992, 1995) such that, in the long term, interregional convergence in terms of income, employment and productivity will be assured. According to this approach, which is associated with neoliberal policies, the free play of the market is always better than any type of regional policy given that the latter involves introducing restrictions or impediments to the free circulation of goods, services and factors of production that push the market when it is allowed to operate with the necessary freedom. Convergence – in terms of per capita income, productivity, etc. – will be the result of successive adjustments through the functioning of the market if the distortions that affect its operative capacity are reduced or removed.

This approach comes, as is known, from a set of previous suppositions such as the existence of perfect information, constant performance of scale and the

[12] Some could qualify them as 'preferences' or 'value judgments' of those who build any theory. Regarding the 'Hume rule' on the need to establish a border between what 'science' can contribute and preferences around specific 'values' have been – as G. Myrdal demonstrated in his doctoral thesis – a common note for all economists (Myrdal 1953).

complete divisibility of all of the factors, which lead, through the key factor, – *free trade* and *free mobility* – to a world of perfect competition.

However, many other authors have been openly critical in regard to the real operation of market mechanisms in economies and their ability to resolve the existing disparities in the regional environment and elsewhere. These include the arguments developed years ago by Myrdal (1957), Hirschman (1958), Friedmann (1963), and Kaldor (1970), among others. There are also more recent theoretical developments including some of the conclusions of the modern 'new' theories of growth.

The accumulative model of economic development states, for example, that "el libre juego de las fuerzas en el mercado tiende normalmente a aumentar, en lugar de disminuir, lasdesigualdades entre las regions" ('*the free play of market forces normally tends to increase rather than decrease inequalities among regions*') (Myrdal 1957). Once some regions have out-performed others thanks to an initial advantage (Clark 1966), there tend to be new increases in activity and growth in expanding regions due to their own advantages and the dynamic that the markets develop. As a result, the convergence among countries and long-term convergence of regions in a specific country is not something that one can take as a given (Kaldor 1970; Dixon and Thirwall 1975; Thirwall 1980). And though effects of concentration and dispersion stand in opposition to one another, there is a need for policies to promote the development of delayed regions and promote the "effects of dispersion" through investments in social capital and/or the use of specific development and stimulus funds in order to create businesses and attract new domestic or direct foreign investments.

The contributions of modern international commerce theory and theories on super national integration processes also support the idea that it is very unlikely that commercial and economic integration processes among countries will reduce regional disparities. In fact, these tend to increase. Those integrating processes reinforce the advantages of "central" regions or nuclei for the location of new businesses and increase competition in the markets, not infrequently to the detriment of more marginal or rural regions. All of this has a negative impact on less efficient producers or those that have a lower capacity to react as seen, for example, in the cases of NAFTA and the European Union.

Based on the ideas and approaches presented above, regional policies have found support in a set of important economic arguments:

- Efficiency is not fully guaranteed by the market and its mechanisms of adjustment.
- The market is blind to the redistribution of wealth and it alone does not contribute to decreasing disparities in terms of income and wealth.
- The lack of adaptation and delay of some regions implies improper use or underutilization and the abandonment of their resources and infrastructures, which will always hurt the country as a whole.

- The movements of the population (migration from less developed areas to capital cities and more dynamic areas) present economic, social and cultural costs that the market does not assess.
- In addition, the accumulation of the population from rural areas in large urban centers creates high costs related to problems of infrastructure, sanitation equipment and education apart from negative externalities such as congestion that tend not to be considered.
- Finally, numerous analyses have shown that the development of a delayed territory benefits the entire country given that it promotes better use of the resources available in that area and avoids the abandonment of facilities and equipment.

Several recent studies, specifically Chaps. 5 and 6 of this book, offer empirical evidence showing that the *income disparities* among regions and *production and income concentration* processes in Latin America hamper the overall growth of the countries analyzed.[13]

2.3.2.2 Ethical-Political and Historical Arguments

In addition to the economic arguments there are *extra-economic reasons and arguments* that have provided clear support for the need to introduce RDP or at least RP. Thus the principles of *equity and solidarity* support the need to move towards greater equality in the living conditions of all citizens and in favor of the distribution of global benefits provided by economic growth. In this sense, the existence of significant economic and quality of life differences among the regions of a country is not socially acceptable or advisable because it will eventually produce instability. Nor is it acceptable from a collective perspective for a large number of citizens and their families to be forced to leave their places of origin and roots in order to be able to find a job and sufficient income to live, which generally produces negative impacts for the individual and their family.

The need to implement regional policies also has found support in some *political arguments* which underscore the need to balance a country's social and economic situation and suggest that it is generally difficult to maintain the social and political stability and cohesion of a State when there are territorial conflicts or significant inequalities among its various regions or areas. Several Latin American countries (Bolivia, Brazil, Colombia, etc.) provide solid examples of this. On the other hand, it is easy to 'believe in' the advantages and benefits of a process of supranational integration (such as that of the EU, for example[14]) or the benefits derived from the

---

[13] See Chap. 5, Cuadrado and González: "Growth and Regional Disparities in Latin America" and Chap. 6: Atienza and Aroca, "Concentration and Growth in Latin American Countries."

[14] In the case of the EU, the main argument in favor of a shared regional policy is linked to the concept of social and territorial 'cohesion,' which was introduced for the first time in the Maastricht Treaty of 1992. This document states (Art. 130 a) that "Con el fin de promover un

intensification of free trade through various global agreements (such as NAFTA and MERCOSUR) when some of the countries or regions affected by that integration feel that the advantages of it do not benefit them at all.

Finally, the arguments that are not strictly economic in nature that justify the implementation of regional policies also have included *historical reasons* or some punctual facts of the past that allow one to suggest that some of the decisions that have been taken have led to territorial inequalities that must be corrected or "compensated." These include the location of the capital of a country, the design of the highway or railway network, or the existence of international borders that decisively influence behavior in border regions.

2.4 The Objectives of an RDP: Long Term Vision, Concentration, and Continuity

The main problem that justifies the implementation of regional policies is, as we have just noted, the existence of disparities among the regions, states or provinces of a country and the need to ensure that they do not increase or to reduce them. But given that it is not a matter of generating subsidies or turning more delayed regions into 'aided' ones, the idea is to create the basis for *promoting a development process* in those areas. The problem cannot be limited to the economic sphere. The goal is not only to foster growth in the regional production level (GDP) or, where possible, to put that number somewhere over the national average, which could guarantee a process of convergence. Nor is it true that the differences in territorial per capita income lead exclusively to a line of convergence. On the one hand, the GDP and per capita income are indicators that leave aside many non-economic elements that should be considered. On the other, one must refer to what other authors have called *the tyranny of the averages*, which is a result of the use of very simple indicators such as per capita GDP that inadequately reflect the real economic and social differences. RP in general and RDP in particular are currently posited as a basic objective for the achievement of a *greater social and economic cohesion*. This does not only mean reducing economic territorial gaps within a nation, but something more. 'Economic cohesion' implies reducing differences in terms of economic variables, GDP, per capita GDP, productivity and employment, which should lead to greater collective wellbeing. And, on the other hand, 'social cohesion' means that one must move towards other fronts that

desarrollo armonioso del conjunto de la Comunidad, ésta desarrollará y proseguirá su acción encaminada a reforzar su cohesión económica y social. En particular, la Comunidad tendrá por objetivo reducir las disparidades entre las diversas regiones y el retraso de las regiones menos desarrolladas, incluidas las zonas rurales" ('*In order to promote harmonious development of the entire Community, it will develop and pursue action aimed at reinforcing economic and social cohesion. Specifically, the Community will seek to reduce disparities among its various regions and the delay of less developed regions including rural areas*').

imply the reduction of territorial differences in terms of the quality of life of all citizens. This means health, education, access to transportation and communications as well as the wellbeing of needier groups and the lack of differences based on gender, race and/or culture.

This goal of achieving increasing 'social and economic cohesion' at the territorial level is what should represent the basic goal of RDP. This would eliminate the search for possible short-term results, always so highly valued by politicians, given that it forces a country to introduce *long term goals*. The essential condition for this is that the policies and actions that are designed must have *continuity* over time. This condition has not exactly been the dominant characteristic of the policies designed in Latin America. When they have existed, political changes have frequently led to the abandonment of programs and policies before the results were visible and the design of new actions that also were not implemented properly or for long periods of time.

In the context of the OECD and in the EU the most positive regional development experiences present two main conditions or principles. On the one hand, there is the *principle of concentration*, which means that RDP are presented for regions with problems and not as policies for the distribution of incentives, subsidies and investments throughout the entire territory of the country or 'sprinkler' policies, as some call policies that try to address all regions in one way or another. On the other hand, it has been found that successful policies are designed and applied with *long term* objectives and actions because both structural changes and the development of new activities or improvement of social conditions and quality of life require time and continuity. RDP can never be short term policies.

Several years ago, the OECD (2009a, b) identified the factors that would seem to be most relevant for regional growth. In a more recent report (OECD 2012), the entity has reaffirmed and developed this idea at the general level and based on the lessons learned from the analysis of 23 cases of regions in OECD member states, including four regions in Mexico (Chiapas, Durango, the State of Mexico and Jalisco). Those factors are listed below in no particular order:

- *Infrastructure*. They have a positive impact on regional growth when other key factors such as human capital and innovation are also present.
- *Human Capital*. The absence or limited presence of people of working age with only primary school education and the presence of individuals with tertiary education has a positive impact on regional growth.
- *Job Market*. The activation of the labor force[15] can play a very positive role in regional development.
- *Innovation*. In the long term – 10 years or more-, this factor can and tends to have an important impact on regions' growth.

---

[15] This concept includes both unemployment and labor participation rates. Policies related to labor activation seek to improve skills and abilities, looking to better match supply and demand and other aspects of the labor market rather than simply focusing on the reform of labor markets in terms of salaries.

- *Productivity*. This is a key factor (measured in GDP by employee) whose improvement is decisive and depends on various factors including efficiency in the use of factors and the organizational aspects of companies, their size and their competitiveness within the country and abroad.
- *Clustering and connectivity*. Clustering also has an effect that is generally positive on regional growth. It stands in contrast to the dispersion of actions.

2.5 Policy Design: Centralization Versus Direct Participation of Regions

There is a final question that must be pointed out. It addresses who should take responsibility for designing and implementing RDP. Offering an answer is not merely a technical issue – though it is also this-, but implies matters directly related to power and distribution. The matter of whether government officials are seen as being linked to such policies or whether responsibility for the development of any state, region or province should be shared and cooperative between the central government and regional officials and social agents definitely does have an impact.

Three options can be presented in regard to who can play a leading role in the design and implementation of any RDP, though there can be formulas with a less Cartesian profile.

The first basic option is the top-down RDP. This corresponds – with some slight variants – to cases in which these policies have been or are clearly centralized. Territorial problems and aspirations are considered, but the central power – the government and its administration – handles the design and to a significant extent the execution of development programs. In other words, here RDPs are designed in the 'center' and managed from the 'center,' though there may be 'delegations' responsible for the monitoring and execution of the programs with limited levels of autonomy. This type of approach was the most common one during the 1950s and 1960s in Latin America as well as Europe, and it continues to be present in the approaches that have emerged much more recently.

The second option corresponds to cases in which the government is much decentralized, as it occurs with countries that have very well developed a decentralized confederal or federal systems. In this case, the RDP can come 'from' and 'by' the state or province – if it is called that – to which the policy refers. This could be described as a 'down – down' policy and it requires, as a premise, significant decentralization of power in terms of both strictly political-administrative aspects and the finance system that has been adopted in the country for its states, which must ensure the high level of territorial autonomy.

Finally, it is important to refer to a *mixed* RDP in which priority is placed on cooperation between central and regional officials with broad autonomy of the latter in the design and execution phases of the regional program. This could be described as a '*top+down*' distribution of responsibilities during the design phase given that the elaboration of the program and its policies is handled jointly by the central government and that of the state or region that would benefit. The process continues with the execution of actions that would mainly be handled by the region or state (down) and a final assessment of the execution and results obtained that would again involve cooperation between the center and the state/region (*down+top*).

From various points of view, one can state that in order to be effective, RDPs require *very significant participation of the involved regions* in regard to the existence of a government or authority in that region and the incorporation of various agents – business people, social representatives, civil organizations, etc. – in the planning and final assessment phases. The most adequate political-administrative setup is thus the third option. The executor agency also should have a regional profile, though the national officials also should be present. The essential aspect of the model is that it is decentralized, though based on cooperation between the central and regional administrations and representatives of the same. With various nuances, this final option has been used for years to implement the European Union's Regional Policy for Cohesion – and others – under the principle of partnering, that is, participation and cooperation between the European Commission, the governments and the regions.

The aspect considered in this section is undoubtedly a very important one. It is clearly an issue that is directly related to governance and the structure that is adopted. A *very centralist* approach can be successful when the country is small and the administration is very centralized without any or almost any power being transferred to regional and local administrations in the territories for which the RDP is designed. The best experiences, however, – as the OECD has stated and as can be deduced from the EU experiences-correspond to a *decentralized* approach similar to the one described above as the third general option. This approach is based on the principles of self-reliance and cooperation, which are absolutely essential to the achievement of successful results.

There is one additional condition: RDPs must have a duration and implementation that is not subject to possible political changes at the national or regional levels. This is frequently simply the result of elections (national, regional, municipal) and their calendars. There is no doubt that political changes introduce – or can introduce – levels of instability that are contrary to one of the characteristics that must accompany RDPs so that they can be effective: their *continuity* and the *long term as a horizon*.

2.6 Final Remarks

The issues presented in this chapter cannot be fully explored in a text whose length must be limited. There is no denying that many of them require significant development and careful consideration. However, we can outline some important points that represent the messages that we have wanted to communicate. They can be summarized as follows:

- A significant number of LAC countries have experienced a fairly pleasant economic phase over the past few years in function of the growth rates reported for their economies, the level of stability that they have achieved, their improved position on an international scale, and the positive results that all of this has provided for the people and their wellbeing.
- Territorial socio-economic disparities in LAC countries are very concerning for two reasons: (1) their magnitude; and (2) the fact that they have continued for several decades without variation (and where there were variations, they have not been always positive).
- There are sufficient elements and signs to suggest that interregional inequalities merit more attention than they have received over the past few decades. The need to correct them or ameliorate their real effects is included in political and government agendas but there are very limited current examples of regional policy.
- The most recent theoretical arguments and reports issued by many organizations los (OECD, ECLAC, CAF, World Bank) contribute more than enough arguments for LAC countries to consider the need to promote policies focused on the development of the most delayed regions in their respective countries. These arguments are entwined with others that are already known but forgotten that were very much present in the past.
- RDPs cannot be confused with simple redistribution policies or more horizontal measures taken to reduce poverty and improve the wellbeing of low-income individuals or families.
- RDPs cannot only be justified on the basis of equity or political arguments but are equally justified from the economic results and better and more efficient use of each country's resources. In fact, the empirical evidence demonstrates that excessive concentration even threatens growth.
- Some principles must be taken into account and respected when designing and implementing new regional development policies. One very important principle is accepting that this policy is and always must be a long term one. The development of more delayed areas requires profound changes that cannot be achieved through short term policies.
- This requires that the policies designed have the continuity that they require and that they must not be subject to changes that may be produced as a result of electoral processes or governmental changes. However, this continuity does not exclude the revision of the objectives and the efficiency of the measures so that they may be refined. This also requires the existence of a medium term (ongoing) assessment system as well as evaluation at the end of the program (ex post).
- Another condition that the available experiences support is the concentration of actions regarding dispersion. Regional development policies must be selective in regard to the regions at which it is directed and not address all regions or states.
- Finally, a necessary institutional question is that of regions/state/provinces that are the object of the RDP participating very directly in the assessment and design of the actions to be developed as well as their execution. This implies transferring power to the territories – decentralization – and the implementation of

principles of cooperation and partnering between the central government, the regions, and social agents.

References

Armstrong H, Taylor J (2003) Regional economics and policy, 3rd edn. Blackwell, Oxford, particularly chapter 8

Baldwin R, Forslid R, Martin P, Ottaviano G, Robert-Nicoud F (2003) Economic geography and public policy. Princeton University Press, New Jersey

Barro R, Sala-i-Martin X (1992) Convergence. J Polit Econ 100:223–251

Barro R, Sala-i-Martin X (1995) Economic growth. McGraw-Hill, Boston

Blaug M (1962) Economic theory in retrospect. Cambridge University Press, Cambridge, Trad. al español del FCE con el título: *Teoría Económica en retrospectiva,* México, 1985

Borts GH, Stein JL (1964) Economic growth in a free market. Columbia University Press, New York

Burki SJ, Perry GE, Dillinger WR (1999) Beyond the center: decentralizing the state. World Bank, Washington DC

CAF (2010) Desarrollo local: hacia un Nuevo protagonismo de las ciudades y regiones. Publicaciones CAF, Caracas

Capello R (2007) Regional economics. Rutledge, London

Cerina F, Mureddu F (2010) Is agglomeration really good for growth? Global efficiency, interregional equity and uneven growth. Working Paper, CRENoS

Clark C (1966) Industrial location and economic potential. Lloyds Bank Rev 82:1–17

Cuadrado-Roura JR (2010) Regional policy, economic growth and convergence. Springer, Heidelberg

Cuadrado-Roura JR (2012) Regional policy: what (it seems) we have learned from some European experiences. In: Cooke P, Parrilli MD, Curbelo JL (eds) Innovation, global change and territorial resilience. E. Elgar, Cheltenham, chapter 14th

David WL (1988) Political economy of economic policy. The quest for human betterment. Praeger, New York/London

Dixon RJ, Thirwall AP (1975) A model of regional growth rate differentials along Kaldorian lines. Oxf Econ Pap 27:201–214

Eatwell J, Milgate M, Newman P (1987) Economic development. McMillan, London

Friedmann JRP (1963) Regional economic policy for developing areas. Pap Proc Reg Sci Assoc 11:41–61

Fujita M, Krugman P, Venables AJ (1999) Spatial economics. MIT Press, Boston

Furtado C (1968) Teoría y política del desarrollo económico. Siglo XXI, México/Madrid

Harris RID, Trainor M (1997) Productivity growth in the UK regions, 1968–91. Oxf Bull Econ Stat 59:485–510

Higgins B (1951) What do economist know? Melbourne University Press, Victoria

Hirschman AO (1958) The strategy of economic development. Yale University Press, New Haven

Hulten CR, Schwab RM (1984) Regional productivity growth in US manufacturing, 1951–1978. Am Econ Rev 74:152–162

Kaldor N (1970) The case for regional policies. Scott J Political Econ 18:337–348

Myrdal G (1953) The political element in the development of economic theory. Routledge and Kegan Paul, London

Myrdal G (1957) Economic theory and under-developed regions. Duckworth/Harper, London

OECD (2009a) Territorial review: Chile. OECD Publishing, Paris

OECD (2009b) How regions grow: trends and analysis. OECD Publishing, Paris

OECD (2010) Regional development policies in OECD countries. OECD Publishing, Paris

OECD (2012) Promoting growth in all regions. OECD Publishing, Paris
OECD-CEPAL (2011) Perspectivas económicas de América Latina, 2012. Publicaciones de CEPAL, Paris/Santiago
Polèse M, Rubiera F (2009) Economía Urbana y regional. Civitas-Thomson Reuters Ltd, Madrid
Polèse M, Shearmur R (2005) Économie Urbaine et régionale, 2nd edn. Economica, Paris
Sang-Chuel C (2012) Introduction: reshaping regional policy in Korea. In: Richardson HW, Chand-Hee CB, Sang-Chuel C (eds) Reshaping regional policy. E. Elgar, Cheltelham, chapter 1
Schlefer J (2012) The assumptions economist make. Belknap Press of Harvard University Press, Cambridge/London
Thirlwall AP (1999) Growth and development, 6th edn. Macmillan, London, First edition of 1972
Thirwall AP (1980) Regional problems are balance of payment problems. Reg Stud 14:419–426
Williamson JG (1965) Regional inequality and the process of national development a description of the patterns. Econ Dev Cult Chang 13:3–45
World Bank (2009) Reshaping economic geography in Latin America and the Caribbean. Companion Volume to the 2009 World Development Report, Washington, DC, World Bank

Chapter 3
Territorial Development in Latin America: A Long Term Perspective

Jorge Máttar and Luis Riffo

3.1 Introduction

It is a well-known fact that Latin America is the world region with the greatest inequalities in the various dimensions associated to development; economic (income), production, employment, social and territorial. Inequality, in its various forms, reinforces each other, and in the absence of public policy intervention, it is unlikely that these gaps that have characterized the region for decades will be reduced (ECLAC, *Time for Equality. Opening paths, closing gaps* 2010). This insight may explain why the development agendas of many countries of the region are aimed at reducing such disparities. Furthermore, these disparities could be a barrier to long-term growth of national economies. High levels of income inequality usually go hand-in-hand with stark differences in terms of organization and socio-spatial disparities. The current configuration of continental socio-spatial disparities was consolidated when industrialization processes began to develop around the early 1940s which as a result, led to accelerating urbanization and a growing rural–urban gap in terms of living conditions. At the same time, it also accelerates the economic and demographic concentration in a few parts of the country.

From the mid-1970s the region experiments a gradual change in its style of development, in which emphases are placed on increased openness and economic deregulation, privatization and divestiture of public enterprises and a deepening of the external integration as part of an overall strategy that attempts to assign a leading role to the market, to the detriment of state intervention. As in other

J. Máttar (✉)
ILPES (Latin America and Caribe Institute of Economic and Social Planification), CEPAL, Santiago de Chile, Chile
e-mail: Jorge.Mattar@cepal.org

L. Riffo
Researcher, Managing Regional and Local Development, ILPES – CEPAL, Santiago de Chile, Chile
e-mail: luis.Riffo@cepal.org

J.R. Cuadrado-Roura and P. Aroca (eds.), *Regional Problems and Policies in Latin America*, Advances in Spatial Science, DOI 10.1007/978-3-642-39674-8_3,

dimensions, the strategy lacked accompanying polices for the reduction of inequality gaps, and socio-spatial inequalities did not change substantially, accounting for strong inertia dictating territorial concentration processes. Reducing inequality therefore, seems to require an explicit public policy for that purpose. It is a long journey in which the market could and should be a positive contributor to this strategy.

This paper aims to provide an overview of some stylized facts of development models in Latin America and the dynamics of socio-spatial inequalities in the past half century and is organized as follows. The first part deals with an analysis of the prevailing development models in Latin America in the last 50 years, especially considering the observed changes in the role of the state and forms of international integration. In the second part, an analysis of long-term trends of territorial disparities is made for a group of Latin American countries, with emphasis on the spatial concentration of the gross domestic product (GDP) and population and disparities in GDP per capita. We will analyze the cases of Chile, Mexico, Brazil, Colombia and Peru, which have longer series of sub-national GDP. Finally, we highlight the growing importance that territorial development policies have acquired recently, reviewing some particular cases of countries that are implementing new approaches or perspectives.

3.1.1 Styles of Development in Latin America and the Caribbean Countries

The discussion on the problems of development in Latin America and the Caribbean over the past three decades has been very intense and insightful. Departing from theories and concepts of industrialized countries about the developed world itself and developing regions, the region has been able to articulate an own vision of development, based on the different realities that most industrialized countries today experienced more than a century ago, including their patterns of socio-spatial organization. The remainder of this section provides a brief tour of the development stages of Latin America, starting in the 1950s, when the promotion of development plans begin to consolidate from the state apparatus and a variety of sectoral policies are implemented, and to a lesser extent, territorial development.

Prior to the 1950s, the relatively developed Latin American economies had advanced in their process of import substitution of manufactured goods of low technological complexity (mainly consumer goods, such as processed foods, clothing, shoes, etc.). A more challenging period followed, which extended to the replacement of durable consumer goods (appliances, electronics, cars), whose output was very dynamic in the subsequent decades, elicited by changes in the structure of demand of the highest income groups. Progress in this process was important due to the multiplier effects on the manufacturing of parts and components of certain capital goods and related services. The type of complex and sophisticated products that high-income groups demanded of industrial processes required more capital intensive and imported technologies designed to operate larger scales (in terms of larger markets). This, given the low import capacity, "forced the Latin American industrial development towards greater openness on admission and participation of foreign capital." (see ECLAC/ILPES, "Regional development and economic development in Latin America", Training program, DCPC document – B/19, 1976, pp. 4–5).

In the 1950s and 1960s, the development plans expanded their scope and sophistication. Governments created capabilities to develop and expand their technical foundation; generally, focusing on sectors (manufacturing, as an engine of growth and leader of import substitution, and agriculture, for its procurement of food and export surplus) and priority projects (mainly infrastructure and the development of production clusters in certain regions). The development plans did not have a broad and long-term view of development, but government action was considered essential to address the many social economic problems to be solved. They begin to lay the groundwork for sub-regional planning (in the sense of regions within countries). Furthermore, the concept and dialogue of territorial development and its relationship to national development begins to take shape. Geography matters and there is concern for development with harmony, through territorial convergence, which is reflected in national planning initiatives for regional development.

At the beginning of the 1960s, the tensions that the development process showed in the region during the previous decade endured or worsened in most countries. In fact, the outlook of accelerating the process of import substitution in a protected environment strengthened, but it lacked powerful instruments in order to strengthening the industrial process, which, later in the context of competition with the international economy, could give a new qualitative leap in its development. Thus, a limited development persisted, dependent and vulnerable on international integration.

In territorial terms, on the one hand, disparities between town and country, and urban-rural increased, and on the other, the processes of urban marginality intensified, due to increasing migration to the large Latin American cities. During the 1960s and 1970s socio-spatial structure is subject to large subsystems or diversified metropolitan areas, resulting in a high dependence condition for the rest of the territories. In the domain of ideas, support for approaches that attributed to increased state responsibilities had strengthened in solving development problems. Responding to the requirements of various sectors, several governments were creating organizations and institutions with the capacity to develop national and regional development plans with prescriptions based on increasingly rigorous studies, clearly defined options and precise policy proposals. These studies were intended to guide and modify the development of all the major economic and social sectors of the country and intended to guide decisions on the allocation of public resources and the use of instruments to influence private decisions.

A milestone in the 1960s was the institutionalization of development as a central objective of public policy, achieved with the creation of the Charter of Punta del Este, adopted by the member countries of the Organization of American States, except Cuba, in August, 1961. In this letter, a commitment was established

(Alliance for Progress) to undertake an effort to develop economic cooperation, previously unprecedented, in which the United States, international financial organizations and the governments of Latin America would participate. The Charter committed signatory governments to ambitious targets for economic growth, income distribution, production modernization, social welfare, price stability and regional integration. Essentially that is the same agenda of today.

In the 1970s the import substitution scheme and the political consensus on industrialization as the path to development paradigms, were left behind, as was the idea of planning as a development tool. Meanwhile, the international economic system would begin a process of financial internationalization; from the withdrawal of the fixed exchange rate system of Bretton Woods in 1971, and the development of foreign exchange markets and Eurodollars after 1973. The governments of the region were engaged in the search for development models to respond to new realities and challenges posed by the tensions created by the aspirations of different social groups. Inequality, in its various dimensions, and beyond its clear ethical repercussions, was shown as an obstacle to development, but public policies did little or nothing to attack. The influence and even the institutional functions, of systems planning and development strategies endured significant changes.

At this time, signs of tiredness (or, from another point of view, requests to move to the next stage) of the development scheme of the two previous decades started to appear. It was recognized and recommended (by ECLAC, among others) that a transition was necessary from a specialization model in commodities//infant industries//import substitution//protection, to one based on a more open development, with an external integration based on competitiveness of manufactured or semi-manufactured products, taking advantage of the relative abundance of labor, increasingly well educated, qualified and trained; and gradually leaving behind specialization in production//exports of raw materials, commodities or semi-finished products.

From the mid-1970s, countries' foreign trade expanded rapidly. As did imports – and even faster – capital inflows to the region, above all in the form of foreign loans, which accelerated the growth of the foreign debt, tripling between 1978 and 1982. In 1982 the volume reached more than three times the value of exports to Latin America annually. As the international interest rate exceeded double digits since 1979, the payment of interest on debt, especially since 1981, gravitated very heavily towards the current account of the balance of payments, exceeding 30 % of the value of exports.

In 1982, three developments were added to stress the deteriorating international payments position of the countries in the region: exports declined, the terms of trade fell due to the deterioration of the central economies, and international interest rates rose again. In August of that year, Mexico was forced to suspend debt service and a rough interruption of commercial bank loans to all countries in the region was produced. Without those loans, no country was able to maintain the debt service on the originally agreed terms, except for Colombia. The balance between net capital inflows and debt service became negative. Financial transactions caused a considerable drain on resources that swept the exchange reserves of the region and forced countries to sharply reduce their domestic spending. There were severe contractions of public spending, depreciation, investment contraction with a powerful impact on economic activity, income and consumption per capita, unemployment and inflation. The result was the worst crisis since the Great Depression of the 1930s; the economy lost competitiveness and poverty and social inequalities sharply increased. What followed was the "lost decade" for development of the region. The external sector crisis was followed by renegotiation attempts of the foreign debt, repeated in each country for the rest of the decade. These became the determinants of economic and social policies of the governments of the region. The GDP per capita stagnated 10 years, inflation overflowed in many countries, government deficits exploded and the voluntary debt international markets of remain virtually closed for Latin American countries.

The objectives of economic and social development were subordinated to financial constraints that the external debt service imposed. In this sense, the adjustment plans that each government presented to re-balance their external accounts were constituted with the basic definition framing public policy. Mid to long-term considerations yielded to short-term problems. The incipient search of territorial development in harmony with national development was abandoned when growth and development ceded priority to economic survival.

In the late 1980s, a "pillar" of development starts to gain global importance – Latin America is no exception – that while having existed from the time of Malthus's writings of the late eighteenth century about population and economic growth, it had failed notoriety, to the extent that prior to the 1990s little was known about the threats to the sustainability of development in the long term, especially in an environmental context. It must be recognized, however, that since the United Nations Conference on the Human Environment in 1972, the subject starts to become relevant and raises awareness on the dangers of environmental degradation and its impact on the welfare of the population.

The term sustainable development was popularized with the presentation in 1987 of the Brundtl and Report (Our Common Future). Its use became especially popular after 1992, when it spread to the Earth Summit in Rio de Janeiro, Brazil, in which it was defined as "development which meets the needs of the present, without compromising the ability of future generations to meet their own needs." Today it is inconceivable to talk about development without considering sustainability as a critical component. Knowledge and ideas have evolved and the discussion on differentiated strategies for sustainable growth in the North and South is not over, issues which were discussed at the Rio+20 Summit in June 2012 in Brazil.

The 1980s left the idea of a failed "model" import substitution as a legacy. It was argued from the mainstream that the region had not been able to substitute imports efficiently, not having achieved a high international competitiveness and thus kept the fragility and vulnerability of the external sector, and whose most vivid expression was the manufacturing sector, unable to generate their own currencies for self-sustaining development. External constraints persisted to growth: increases in exports were accompanied by increases of equal or greater magnitude in imports, which ultimately put a ceiling on output growth, as inferred by Thirlwall's model (1982).

In this context, the foundations were laid in virtually all countries of the region to change "model", based on the market and private sector acting as the support and leader of the development process. It was introduced like that, and a new period was conceived, which was immediately characterized by a wave of structural transformations, emphasizing privatization and divestiture of public enterprises, spreading the participation of the private sector, opening the external sector, both regarding goods-services and the capital account, and deregulation of markets, including in many cases urban land markets. In the 1990s structural reform programs were executed, inspired by the Washington Consensus (1989), which systematically reduced activity and influenced public policy and planning – and the role of the state – in development. In this decade the market was assigned the role of leader in the development process, with a key ally – the private sector – that did not responded accordingly. The governance effort was concentrated on restoring the macro "balance" (key prices: consumer, interest rate, exchange rate, wages). As in the "lost decade," on the 1990s the effort of the region turned to short-term objectives, first to overcome and survive the crisis, and then to balance the economy. The reforms of the 1990s – that, in principle, were expected to succeed in the structural change in favor of a more active role of the market and private sector development – , were not successful as many hoped for.

The privatization of enterprises or institutions that were previously from the State, the divestiture and deregulation of activities was due to policy approaches that directly contradicted the views that prevailed in Latin America in previous decades, in which the state had a fundamental role in the development process. A new economic model and national development started to take place where the market was principal in resource allocation and income distribution; private initiative was called to be the engine of growth and the state reduced its intervention to a subsidiary and secondary role. That is, the pendulum was inclined to the other end, when what was needed was to balance the market with the state.

Unlike what happened in the countries of Southeast Asia, which adopted strategies of industrialization with strong public support decades ago, the Latin American States stopped acting as the authority which should have ensured, through appropriate policies, resource allocation and progressive improvements in income distribution. In the new market approach, the state was limited to providing legal and regulatory frameworks that the market requires to function. The state was replaced as a corrective mechanism of the allocation of resources by the marketplace.

Under the new paradigm, the state's orientation of economic and social development was unnecessary. Policy instruments were removed, and policies on productive sector development were minimized, including agricultural and industrial policies that had been important in the past. Social policies were focused on reducing poverty, which had soared in the previous decade, supported by a sustained increase in social spending, reversing the deterioration experienced in the previous decade. Public investment is maintained, meanwhile, at very low levels, around 4 % of GDP, due to the divestiture of public enterprises.

Private sector intervention, with appropriate market signals (liberalization, privatization, neutrality, ad-hoc instruments), should result in increased competitiveness. It sought to reinsert the Latin American economies in the global scene, on the basis of a model based on exports of dynamic products in world trade. In a context of economic expansion and global trade, an elevated dynamism of Latin American exports was expected which would lead to global economic growth ("export led growth"). Ten years later, however, it could be said that there was growth in exports, but low output growth, i.e., "export led, but no growth."

With regard to the field of territorial development, even though one might think that the new strategy could boost several lagging regions, rich in natural resources for export, and therefore would mitigate the unbalanced regional development, the available evidence indicates that, in general, the main winners that remained were the major metropolitan areas while less developed regions failed to take off, with what remained was a heavily unbalanced socio-spatial structure.

On the public institutional space, the reforms proposed by the Washington Consensus were limited to promoting the modernization of public finance, the effectiveness of fiscal and tax instruments and the ability of information systems to facilitate financial decisions, and developments were scarce. Public investment in infrastructure recorded a decline. The expansion of the role of markets was conducted in the absence or inadequacy of regulatory frameworks that promoted competition and protected the interests of consumers.

In the last decade, many of the countries in the region showed a satisfactory economic performance, which was associated with a downward trend of poverty and inequality. Economic growth – highest in South America – was encouraged by the external sector, and in South America was supported by demand from China, prompting high growth in agricultural and mining exports, mainly through the increase in international prices and, to a lesser extent, by increases in physical volume. Such is the demand for this type of goods, that South America has been deepening its specialization in production and export of raw materials. In some countries, this dynamism is expressed in subtle processes of territorial convergence, measured in terms of GDP per capita, where certain less developed regions have managed to slightly increase their relative position, which has not implied a significant structural change.

This situation resulted in favorable trade balances that allowed stabilizing the external sector, diminishing in this period the structural constraint of the balance of payments that dragged them for decades. The good performance of the region was confirmed both in the period of growth of the world economy, and during the financial crisis that began in late 2008. Although the region was hit by the worldwide recession, it learned how to overcome financial instability and the fall in demand with disciplined macroeconomic management, which in some countries even allowed implementing countercyclical measures to avoid a greater impact. Despite the dominant "neoliberal" stage of the past 20 years, it is clear that the state has been able to "remain at the scene", with a new role in the conduct of public policy in the countries of the region, which has been instrumental in regional performance in the last 20 years: the percentage of people living in poverty fell from over 48 % in 1990 to just over 30 % in 2011, while employment increased in quantity and improved in quality. Inflation has stabilized in single digits in most countries (average 6.6 % in 2011), public debt is better in quality and low in quantity (below 35 % of GDP) and international reserves have reached record levels, about $765,000 million dollars in 2012 (ECLAC 2012).

Improved governance has been fundamental in the progress aforementioned. It is worth noting the modernization of budgetary planning processes and performance management, the fiscal consolidation status, the greater transparency of fiscal exercise, the efficiency of expenditure and accountability, improved budget execution, and the decrease of the public debt ratio, in some cases accompanied by fiscal surpluses (ECLAC//ILPES, *Panorama de la gestión pública* 2011; and ECLAC// ILPES, *Haciaunanuevaarquitectura del Estado para el desarrollo*, SerieEspaciosIberoamericanos 2011).

In terms of territorial development, in several countries we see major progress particularly in the areas of infrastructure, poverty reduction and access to basic social services. Likewise, there are interesting local democratization processes which form an important part of a new concept of territorial autonomy and social participation.

On the side of the future development policy agenda, the current effort is aimed at attaining a high, sustained and inclusive growth: the region continues with a very uneven – yet improved – income distribution and wide inequalities in other dimensions, such as the territorial one. Nor was there a substantial improvement in reducing the heterogeneity of production, which was associated with widening internal and external productivity gaps, reflecting in turn, the technological distance against global competitors. On the contrary, in many cases, the dynamic primary products exports emerged as the new specialization of countries in the region in the international economic context, giving importance to the former and current ECLAC ideas of unequal international linkages between the Center and the Periphery.

Thus, the crisis has highlighted the region's ability to confront it; the existence of vulnerabilities of the growth plan followed in past years, the importance of planning the development to be better prepared to face these crises, and therefore, this reveals an opportunity to continue the discussion regarding development, not simply development, but inclusive and sustainable development.

The elusive path towards development with equality continues to manifest itself strongly in most countries. While recognizing the resilience of Latin American macroeconomics, we still notice weaknesses of the manufacturing base (the "meso" economy), and the risks of an external integration scheme that is accented with the continued rise of raw materials, especially for South America. Central America and the Caribbean are not taking advantage of this boom and therefore, do not run the same risks; however, Central America and Mexico face declining or stagnant terms of trade and vulnerability to the low dynamics of the United States economy. The Caribbean remains with high debt ratios and structural weaknesses, as these economies depend on the external sector, whether in the provision of inputs and finished products, or through international tourist arrivals.

The question remains of how to move towards higher stages of development, where (in fact an intrinsic part of the process) development gaps are closed simultaneously, such as income inequality, employment, productivity and territorial gaps. The region still exhibits unequal growth, exclusive and concentrated, with expressions of territorial divergence within most countries. Development is a long-term issue that requires an enormous effort for a long time (in fact, it never finishes), led by state policies that are beyond the reach of government administrations. State policies should look at long-term horizons. Hence countries might be increasing their attention on building visions of the future, in which the reduction of inequality is a widespread aspiration. This is a remarkable phenomenon in Latin America and the Caribbean, because it means a real and concrete role for development. Envisioning a desired scenario is a way of committing to a development path, which in the Latin American experience, has been truncated by the difficulty of articulating the social and political actors around long-term goals.

Planning is a powerful tool capable of articulating interests of different actors (the state, society, external environment, national and subnational actors) public policy (the state, plans and programs, national and subnational), with a long-term (sustainable) vision, political economy towards less unequal societies.

As part of what could be described as a good performance against the crisis, the economic and social actors recover elements of public policies left behind by the prominence of the Washington Consensus and seem to regain the interest of public policy makers. In that debate, the need resurfaces for medium and long term policies, with economic policies not only for nominal stability (inflation, interest rate, exchange rate), but also with a greater role for real stability (output and employment to rise and with less volatility, interest rates and exchange rates to promote growth and reduce poverty).

Likewise, there is renewed interest in promoting territorial development policies, which should be complemented by regional and local initiatives, starting with the search for efficient and participatory coordination mechanisms.

In this brief summary we have shown that over the past five decades Latin America and the Caribbean has experienced significant sociopolitical and economic changes associated with different proposals for development strategies. Within them, the state has played consistent roles with the interpretations that have emerged in recent decades, more active and structured during the developmental stage; more subordinate and absent during the neoliberal stage; and more regulated in the most recent stage. Despite these strong transformations, what has survived without significant changes is a socio-spatial organization that is strongly unbalanced and expressed as high territorial concentration and high disparities in economic and social development. This does not mean that there was no absolute progress during these decades, which are relatively evident, but the differences between the territories show a strong inertia, without observing emerging regions that balance the importance of large metropolitan areas, along with their areas of influence. This path will be analyzed in the following section from the available evidence.

3.1.2 Long-Term Regional Economic Dynamics in Latin America

As was discussed in the previous section, in the early 1970s, the main features of the spatial economic structure of Latin America that emerged in the context of import substitution industrialization processes had consolidated, which was essentially characterized by a strong geographic concentration of production and population in a few places in the territory and generated profound socio-spatial disparities in living standards. This concentration process resulted in the formation of a limited set of core subsystems of accumulation within each country, which comprised its most dynamic parts, coexisting with peripheral subsystems which are linked from various channels, mainly investment, migration and trade (CEPAL 1968; ILPES 1978; Rofman 1974).

From the mid-1970s and especially during the 1980s, the continent experimented with substantive changes in their styles of development, towards further deregulation of their economies and increasing openness. This new style will have as the background; the external debt crisis, the balance of payments and structural adjustment processes undertaken by several countries from the indications of the International Monetary Fund and the World Bank. For some Latin American authors, this new context seemed suitable to drive decentralized spatial processes which would reverse three decades of unbalanced regional development (Boisier 1993). Others remained skeptical as to the new scenario and argued that the prevailing capitalist rationality would prevent substantive changes to the spatial structure in Latin America (De Mattos 1986).

In this context, the purpose of this section is to analyze long-term trends of territorial inequalities in Latin America, starting in the 1970s, and identify the major transformations in the last four decades. The focus of the analysis will center on the changes in the relative shares in GDP (or value added) and in the population, along with changes in the relative differences in GDP per capita.

On this last indicator we should clarify certain points. Firstly, this is not a measure of welfare, and although it does measure wealth generated from the production processes, it is not an indicator of disposable income of the population of the different territories. In this sense, it does not allow conclusions about the distribution of income, which can be very high in spite of a higher GDP per capita. Secondly, measurements of sub-national GDP for Latin America and the Caribbean have made substantial improvements in the last two decades, whereas the measurements available for previous decades are subject to a number of limitations of basic statistics and estimation methods, which may include some bias for interpretation.

One last important note regarding the methodology refers to the type of political administrative division available for each country, which should be considered for this analysis. In the case of Mexico City in Mexico, and Bogota in Colombia, its administrative limits are substantially lower than their actual spatial dimension, usually referred to as large metropolitan area, while in the case of Lima in Peru,

Sao Paulo in Brazil and Santiago in Chile the reverse follows, its administrative limits include more than the major metropolitan area, to include the entire Department, the state or the region. One option for a comparable analysis would be to consider the major stratum for the first three countries, which is left for the reader's consideration.

3.1.2.1 Chile

In 1970 36.7 % of the population was located in the Metropolitan Region of Santiago (RMS), home of the nation's capital, 13.9 % in the Bio-Bio region and 10.9 % in the region of Valparaiso. Together the three regions accounted for 62.5 % of the total and formed the main industrial centers of the country. In terms of contribution to production, the focus on the three clusters was even higher, reaching 72 % of the total, where the RMS only realized 47 % of total GDP. These strong concentration levels coexisted with high levels of disparities in GDP per capita (GDP pc), which ranged from the Araucanía Region with GDP pc representing less than 40 % of the national GDP pc average and the Magallanes region with GDP pc that exceeded 164 % of the average.

The analysis of the major socio-spatial trends from the 1970s allows us identify four broad areas. First, there is a significant increase in the relative weight of The North (Tarapacá, Antofagasta and Atacama), highly specialized in the mining sector, both in terms of population and GDP, and a clear improvement in the relative levels of GDP pc. In second place, the RMS increases its relative weight in both population and GDP and there is a slight reduction in the level of GDP pc, even if it still exceeds the national average. Thirdly, there is a clear decline in the share of total GDP of the regions of Valparaiso and Bio-Bio, and less clear in terms of population as well as a reduction in their relative levels of GDP pc. In fourth place, a relatively small improvement occurs in several regions that were under the relative levels of GDP pc, and with low contribution to GDP and total population, although still maintaining strong differences with the national average, as in La Araucanía, Coquimbo, Maule and Los Lagos. Finally, in the context of the new parameters of the deregulated and externally open model, regions such as Magallanes, which had a free trade zone status, see a quick decline in their positive differentials of GDP pc in the period.

As a primary result of increases in GDP pc of the northern regions, as well as a strong reduction from that of Magallanes, a convergent trend is recorded throughout the period, expressed as a decrease in the standard deviation of GDP pc from 58.2 to 42 (Table 3.1).

3.1.2.2 Brazil

In 1970 Brazil was structured around two major socio-spatial subsystems: the Mid-South, with Sao Paulo as the main pole and the Northeast, with Bahia as the

Table 3.1 Chile: GDP, population, and GDP per capita (percentages and indices) 1970–2010

	GDP (percentages)			Population (percentages)			PIBpc VApc (Chile = 100)		
Regions	1970	1992	2010	1970	1992	2010	1970	1992	2010
Chile	100.0	100.0	100.0	100.0	100.0	100.0	100	100	100
Tarapaca	2.4	2.9	3.8	2.0	2.6	2.9	122	113	131
Antofagasta	4.6	5.9	6.8	2.8	3.1	3.4	167	187	203
Atacama	1.8	1.8	2.3	1.7	1.7	1.6	105	107	139
Coquimbo	2.0	2.3	2.7	3.8	3.8	4.2	52	61	63
Valparaiso	12.4	9.5	8.9	10.9	10.2	10.3	114	92	87
RMS	47.1	47.5	49.1	36.7	39.5	40.3	128	121	122
O'Higgins	4.0	4.1	4.0	5.3	5.2	5.2	76	78	77
Maule	3.5	3.9	3.7	6.8	6.2	5.9	52	63	63
BioBio	12.5	11.6	9.4	13.9	12.9	11.9	90	90	79
Araucania	2.4	2.7	2.7	6.6	5.8	5.7	37	46	47
Los Lagos	4.3	4.5	4.8	8.1	7.1	7.1	52	64	67
Aysen	0.6	0.6	0.6	0.5	0.6	0.6	111	92	101
Magallanes	2.4	2.3	1.3	0.9	1.0	0.9	264	216	141
Standard deviation							58.2	47.7	42.0

Source: Authors estimations based on National Statistics Institute and Central Bank of Chile

largest state, where both differ strongly in their development conditions. While the former subsystem consisted of 53 % of the population and 80 % of the country's total GDP, the latter subsystem accounted for 28 % of the population and 10 % of total GDP. Sao Paulo, by itself, accounted for almost 40 % of total GDP, even though its weight in the population was significantly lower, at around 20 %. Following behind Sao Paulo were Rio de Janeiro and Minas Gerais.

In terms of GDP pc, the differences were also very noticeable. While Sao Paulo doubled the national average and Rio de Janeiro exceeded it by 75 %, at the other end, the GDP pc of Bahia and Pernambuco were 60 % below average and 50 % below average, respectively. A special case is the Federal District, home to the country's capital, that although in 1970 represented only 3.1 % of GDP and 0.6 % of the population, it had a much higher GDP pc national average, on the order of four times and a half. This can be explained by its particular condition as seat of government, which is characterized by a high share in total employment of public officials (above 50 % of the total), which receive an income above the average.

On the other hand, while the Central South had a production structure with a high degree of industrialization and a diversified agricultural economy, the Northeast kept a very intensive production structure of export commodities.

In the last 40 years, Brazil has experienced a very important series of economic and social transformations, particularly during the 2000s, although large gaps remain in their levels of socio-spatial development.

In the first place, it has expanded strongly pushing the agricultural frontier, the so-called Midwest region, comprising the states of Mato Grosso, Mato Grosso do Sul, Goiás and the Federal District. Secondly, the North has had an important dynamism sustained in large part by the dynamics of the city of Manaus, State of

Table 3.2 Brazil: GDP, population and GDP percapita (percentages and indices) 1970–2009

	GDP (percentages)			Population (percentages)			GDPpc (Brasil = 100)		
States	1970	1991	2009	1970	1993	2009	1970	1993	2009
Brasil	100.0	100.0	100.0	100.0	100.0	100.0	100	100	100
Acre	0.2	0.2	0.2	0.2	0.3	0.4	81	71	63
Alagoas	0.6	0.8	0.7	1.7	1.7	1.6	33	47	42
Amapá	0.1	0.2	0.2	0.1	0.2	0.4	112	84	70
Amazonas	0.3	0.7	1.5	1.0	1.4	1.8	26	48	82
Bahia	3.1	4.3	4.3	8.0	8.1	7.4	39	53	59
Ceará	1.5	2.1	2.1	4.7	4.3	4.4	31	48	47
Distrito Federal	3.2	3.9	4.2	0.6	1.1	1.3	558	354	309
Espírito Santo	1.2	1.8	1.9	1.7	1.8	1.8	69	100	105
Goiás	1.8	2.7	3.2	3.4	3.4	3.9	53	79	83
Maranhão	1.1	1.3	1.3	3.3	3.4	3.3	34	37	39
Mato Grosso	2.4	2.0	3.0	1.7	2.6	2.9	141	75	103
Minas Gerais	7.8	9.4	9.0	12.3	10.7	10.3	64	88	88
Pará	1.0	1.8	1.9	2.3	3.4	4.0	44	53	47
Paraíba	0.8	0.9	0.9	2.6	2.2	2.0	32	42	47
Paraná	4.4	5.5	6.0	7.4	5.7	5.5	59	95	109
Pernambuco	2.9	2.5	2.4	5.5	4.8	4.6	52	52	52
Piauí	0.4	0.6	0.6	1.8	1.8	1.6	25	31	37
Rio de Janeiro	16.8	12.7	10.8	9.6	8.7	8.4	174	146	129
Rio Grande do Norte	0.5	0.9	0.9	1.7	1.6	1.7	31	53	53
Rio Grande do Sul	8.3	7.0	6.8	7.1	6.2	5.6	116	113	120
Rondônia	0.1	0.5	0.6	0.1	0.8	0.8	80	62	79
Roraima	0.1	0.1	0.2	0.0	0.1	0.2	116	101	78
Santa Catarina	2.8	3.8	4.1	3.1	3.1	3.3	91	123	124
São Paulo	38.5	33.9	32.6	19.0	21.5	21.7	202	158	151
Sergipe	0.3	0.6	0.6	1.0	1.0	1.1	27	61	59
Standard Deviation							106.2	63.5	54.8

Source: Authors estimations based on Brazilian Institute of Geography and Statistics (IBGE) and Institute of Applied Economic Research (IPEA)

Amazonas, home to a major industrial complex supported by regional incentive policies. Finally, as a result of active industrial and social policies, we see a greater dynamism of GDP pc of the most lagging regions like the Northeast, with respect to the most prosperous regions of the country (South and Center South), which has resulted in a significant convergence process, as shown by the sharp reduction in the standard deviation of the index of GDP pc (Table 3.2).

3.1.2.3 Mexico

In 1970 the main socio-spatial subsystem was located in the center of the country around the metropolitan area of Mexico, covering all parts of the Federal District and State of Mexico and Hidalgo. The sum of the three territorial entities accounted for 25 % of the total population and 34 % of total GDP. Far behind were the states of Jalisco, with 7.7 % of GDP and 6.8 % of the population, Veracruz, with 7.0 % of GDP and 7.9 % of the population and ultimately New Leon, with 6.1 % of GDP and 3.5 % of the population.

Major gaps were observed between the Southwest, Guerrero, Chiapas and Oaxaca and northern and central Mexico. Indeed, in the first three states, GDP pc was lower between 60 % and 40 % to the national average, while in Nuevo Leon and Mexico City GDP pc was above 70 % of the average. Other areas of high GDP pc, such as Campeche and Tabasco to the southeast, were important hydrocarbon production centers, which do not necessarily mean better living conditions for the population.

In the period under study, one can see three types of processes. Firstly, we are witnessing a process of spatial de-concentration around the metropolitan area of Mexico and to the northern axis, mainly to the State of Mexico, Querétaro, Guanajuato and Aguascalientes. Secondly, it strengthens the relative GDP of several northern states like Nuevo Leon, Coahuila and Chihuahua, derived in large part to the expansion of assembly plants for exports (*maquiladoras* in Spanish), also increasing their levels of GDP pc. Thirdly, the most lagging states of Mexico, Guerrero, Chiapas and Oaxaca, large gaps remain with respect to the national average, with GDP pc around 50 % of the national average.

The cases of greatest relative increase in GDP pc were produced in Aguascalientes, Queretaro, Quintana Roo, Campeche, Zacatecas, Chihuahua, San Luis Potosi and Mexico City. At the other end, the main relative decreases were recorded in Mexico, Baja California, Veracruz and Chiapas.

The high fluctuations in GDP pc of some oil states such as Campeche, have influenced the volatility of the convergence indicator which increases significantly between early 1970s and early 1990s, and then subsequently declined sharply in 2009, it is necessary to explore in more detail future dynamics of territorial disparities estimates without considering any oil activity (Table 3.3).

3.1.2.4 Peru

In Peru's case, the concentration levels were very high compared to the average for Latin America in 1970. Indeed, the region of greatest weight relative to the early 1970s was Lima, with 28 % of the population and 55 % of the GDP. Far behind was Cajamarca, with 6.8 % of the population and 2.3 % of the GDP, and Piura, with 6.3 % of the population and 5.4 % of the GDP.

Lima, Madre de Dios and Tacna and recorded the highest relative levels of GDP pc, while in five departments, Cuzco, Ayacucho, Amazonas, Cajamarca and Apurimac, GDP pc did not exceed 40 % of the national average.

After a long period of political, economic and social instability, Peru has shown, in the first decade of the century, a strong dynamism which has repositioned the country in the Latin American context. An important part of this rise is related to the development of the mining sector, which has fueled the growth of various

Table 3.3 Mexico: GDP, population and GP per capita (percentages and indices) 1970–2009

	GDP (percentages)			Population (percentages)			GDP pc (México = 100)		
States	1970	1993	2009	1970	1993	2009	1970	1993	2009
México	100.0	100.0	100.0	100.0	100.0	100.0	100	100	100
Aguascalientes	0.5	0.8	1.2	0.7	0.9	1.0	69	91	112
Baja California	2.5	2.6	2.9	1.8	2.2	2.8	141	120	106
Baja California Sur	0.3	0.5	0.7	0.3	0.4	0.5	129	120	135
Campeche	1.8	4.8	3.5	0.5	0.7	0.7	347	712	483
Coahuila de Zaragoza	2.7	2.8	3.0	2.3	2.4	2.4	115	114	126
Colima	0.5	0.6	0.5	0.5	0.5	0.6	92	107	99
Chiapas	1.8	2.0	1.9	3.2	4.0	4.2	56	50	45
Chihuahua	2.6	2.9	3.3	3.3	3.0	3.1	78	96	104
Distrito Federal	24.5	20.8	18.1	14.2	9.7	8.4	172	214	214
Durango	1.4	1.3	1.3	1.9	1.6	1.5	73	80	87
Guanajuato	3.7	3.6	4.0	4.7	4.9	4.7	78	74	84
Guerrero	1.8	1.9	1.6	3.3	3.2	3.0	54	59	52
Hidalgo	1.4	1.6	1.5	2.5	2.3	2.3	58	68	65
Jalisco	7.7	7.0	6.6	6.8	6.5	6.5	113	107	102
México	7.7	9.0	9.4	8.1	12.5	13.6	95	72	70
Michoacán de Ocampo	2.8	2.5	2.5	4.8	4.3	3.8	58	59	65
Morelos	1.0	1.3	1.2	1.3	1.5	1.6	76	86	78
Nayarit	1.0	0.7	0.6	1.1	1.0	0.9	85	73	70
Nuevo León	6.1	6.5	7.6	3.5	3.9	4.1	173	169	187
Oaxaca	1.6	1.8	1.6	4.2	3.7	3.4	40	49	46
Puebla	3.2	3.1	3.4	5.2	5.1	5.2	62	61	66
Querétaro de Arteaga	0.8	1.3	1.9	1.0	1.3	1.5	76	99	120
Quintana Roo	0.2	1.2	1.5	0.2	0.7	1.1	94	174	137
San Luis Potosí	1.6	1.8	1.8	2.7	2.4	2.3	61	73	79
Sinaloa	2.5	2.3	2.1	2.6	2.7	2.5	96	87	83
Sonora	2.8	2.3	2.5	2.3	2.3	2.3	124	101	108
Tabasco	2.4	2.7	2.8	1.6	1.9	1.9	154	141	146
Tamaulipas	3.5	3.0	3.3	3.0	2.8	2.9	116	107	114
Tlaxcala	0.4	0.5	0.5	0.9	1.0	1.0	50	57	53
Veracruz – Llave	7.0	4.9	4.8	7.9	7.5	6.9	89	65	70
Yucatán	1.1	1.3	1.5	1.6	1.7	1.8	72	75	84
Zacatecas	0.9	0.7	0.8	2.0	1.5	1.3	46	48	64
Standard Deviation							56.7	114.1	77.5

Source: Authors estimations based on National Institute of Statistics and Geography (INEGI)

departments. Moreover, a significant expansion of agricultural exports was recorded.

Nevertheless, apart from a few marginal exceptions, the socio-spatial structure has not experienced fundamental changes, even reinforcing the relative demographic weight of Lima, which in 2007 amounted to 34 % of the population, that is, a growth of six percentage points with respect to 1972, and maintaining a high contribution to total GDP of 52 %. Some departments such as Arequipa, La

Table 3.4 Peru: GDP, population and GP per capita (percentages and indices) 1970–2007

	GDP (percentages)			Population (percentages)			GDP pc (Perú = 100)		
Departments	1972	1993	2007	1972	1993	2007	1972	1993	2007
Perú	100.0	100.0	100.0	100.0	100.0	100.0	100	100	100
Amazonas	0.5	0.8	0.6	1.4	1.5	1.4	38	55	47
Ancash	4.2	3.5	3.8	5.4	4.3	3.9	79	81	97
Apurimac	0.7	0.6	0.5	2.3	1.7	1.5	32	33	31
Arequipa	4.0	5.1	5.8	3.9	4.2	4.2	103	123	139
Ayacucho	1.3	0.9	1.0	3.4	2.2	2.2	38	41	44
Cajamarca	2.3	2.4	2.7	6.8	5.7	5.1	33	41	53
Cusco	2.1	2.5	2.6	5.3	4.7	4.3	39	53	62
Huancavelica	1.1	1.1	0.9	2.4	1.7	1.7	44	63	51
Huánuco	1.2	1.3	1.0	3.1	3.0	2.8	40	42	36
Ica	2.7	2.7	2.8	2.6	2.6	2.6	101	105	106
Junín	3.3	3.7	3.3	5.1	4.7	4.5	65	79	74
La Libertad	3.9	4.2	4.9	5.8	5.8	5.9	67	73	83
Lambayeque	2.2	2.8	2.7	3.8	4.2	4.1	58	68	66
Lima	55.6	50.7	52.0	28.0	31.9	34.0	199	159	153
Loreto	1.6	3.8	3.1	3.7	4.5	4.8	44	83	63
Madre de Dios	0.4	0.4	0.4	0.2	0.3	0.4	226	139	99
Moquegua	0.5	1.4	1.4	0.6	0.6	0.6	83	231	243
Pasco	1.1	1.3	1.2	1.3	1.0	1.0	88	130	119
Piura	5.4	5.1	4.1	6.3	6.3	6.1	85	80	68
Puno	2.6	2.5	2.2	5.7	4.9	4.6	45	51	47
San Martín	0.7	1.1	1.3	1.7	2.5	2.7	42	45	47
Tacna	2.2	1.7	1.4	0.7	1.0	1.1	311	170	134
Tumbes	0.4	0.6	0.5	0.6	0.7	0.7	75	79	63
Standard Deviation							68.1	48.8	47.8

Source: Authors estimations based on National Institute of Statistics and Informatics (INEI)

Libertad, Loreto or Moquegua achieve slight increases in their relative contributions to total GDP, about one percentage point, mostly derived from a higher mining production.

Regarding the GDP pc some significant changes were seen. On the one hand there are relatively strong reductions in cases of Tacna and Madre de Dios; while on the other hand, Pasco, Moquegua, Arequipa, Cuzco and Loreto experience a relative increase. The latter department has been positively impacted by the increasing flow of tourists.

When considering the general trends in convergence//divergence we observe a clear reduction of territorial disparities in the first period from 1972 to 1993, however, when looking at the period from 1993 to 2007, there is a stagnation regarding the gaps measured by the standard deviation (Table 3.4).

3.1.2.5 Colombia

In the case of Colombia, Bogota had almost a third of the country's total GDP in 1975, but only 14 % of the total population. The existence of two departments with a demographic weight slightly less than Bogota, corresponding to Antioquia and Valle del Cauca, helped to create a socio-spatial structure slightly less concentrated than in other Latin American countries. These three departments formed the most developed part of the country.

In terms of GDP pc, Bogota largely exceeded the rest of the territory with a level 135 % above national average. Other departments with high GDP pc were Meta, which exceeded the national average by 68 % and the new departments, which had an intensive productive base in mining.

The strong territorial gaps in Colombia is particularly exemplified by the case of Chocó, which had in 1975 a GDP pc of only 25 % of the national average, but also with the Departments of Huila, Córdoba and Magdalena, with a GDP pc lower than 50 % of the average.

The analysis of the evolution of recent decades shows a strong demographic expansion of Bogota, whose population rose from 12.7 % to 16.1 % of the total population, with a relative reduction in its contribution to total GDP, from 30 % in 1975 to 26.3 % in 2009. Departments that slightly increase its share in total GDP are Meta, Santander and the new departments.

In terms of GDP pc, we can observe a higher growth relative to various departments located in the lowest levels in 1975, such as Huila, Chocó, Quindío, Córdoba and Magdalena, which is indicative of a process of convergence. It also shows significant increase in the Department of Santander.

In the case of Bogotá, it decreases its level relative to the average, even though it still exceeds it by 62 %.

In terms of the overall dynamics of disparities, we notice a reduction between 1975 and 2005, while the estimates for the second period recorded a slight increase in the standard deviation index of GDP pc (Table 3.5).

3.1.2.6 Some Remarks from the Cases Studied

From the previous discussion, we can draw some conclusions about the long-term regional economic dynamics of Latin America, which can be complemented by more recent analysis prepared by ILPES (ILPES 2010, 2012).

First, it can be seen that with regard to the structure of relative weights of subnational GDP and population, the cases of Chile and Peru show the greater stability of the primacy of core subsystems. One the other hand, significant declines are noticeable in some regions that were traditionally relevant in the early 1970s yet have been losing their relative weights in recent decades, as in the case of Rio de Janeiro in Brazil, Valparaiso and Bio Bio in Chile and Veracruz in Mexico. In contrast, parts of Argentina, Brazil, Peru and Chile with few resources have

Table 3.5 Colombia: GDP, population and GP per capita (percentages and indices) 1970–2009

	GDP (percentages)			Population (percentages)			GDP pc (Perú = 100)		
Departments	1972	1993	2007	1972	1993	2007	1972	1993	2007
Perú	100.0	100.0	100.0	100.0	100.0	100.0	100	100	100
Amazonas	0.5	0.8	0.6	1.4	1.5	1.4	38	55	47
Ancash	4.2	3.5	3.8	5.4	4.3	3.9	79	81	97
Apurimac	0.7	0.6	0.5	2.3	1.7	1.5	32	33	31
Arequipa	4.0	5.1	5.8	3.9	4.2	4.2	103	123	139
Ayacucho	1.3	0.9	1.0	3.4	2.2	2.2	38	41	44
Cajamarca	2.3	2.4	2.7	6.8	5.7	5.1	33	41	53
Cusco	2.1	2.5	2.6	5.3	4.7	4.3	39	53	62
Huancavelica	1.1	1.1	0.9	2.4	1.7	1.7	44	63	51
Huánuco	1.2	1.3	1.0	3.1	3.0	2.8	40	42	36
Ica	2.7	2.7	2.8	2.6	2.6	2.6	101	105	106
Junín	3.3	3.7	3.3	5.1	4.7	4.5	65	79	74
La Libertad	3.9	4.2	4.9	5.8	5.8	5.9	67	73	83
Lambayeque	2.2	2.8	2.7	3.8	4.2	4.1	58	68	66
Lima	55.6	50.7	52.0	28.0	31.9	34.0	199	159	153
Loreto	1.6	3.8	3.1	3.7	4.5	4.8	44	83	63
Madre de Dios	0.4	0.4	0.4	0.2	0.3	0.4	226	139	99
Moquegua	0.5	1.4	1.4	0.6	0.6	0.6	83	231	243
Pasco	1.1	1.3	1.2	1.3	1.0	1.0	88	130	119
Piura	5.4	5.1	4.1	6.3	6.3	6.1	85	80	68
Puno	2.6	2.5	2.2	5.7	4.9	4.6	45	51	47
San Martín	0.7	1.1	1.3	1.7	2.5	2.7	42	45	47
Tacna	2.2	1.7	1.4	0.7	1.0	1.1	311	170	134
Tumbes	0.4	0.6	0.5	0.6	0.7	0.7	75	79	63
Standard Deviation							68.1	48.8	47.8

Source: Authors estimations based on National Administrative Department of Statistics (DANE)

experienced slight increases derived from the boost of some activities, primarily mining or agriculture, while in the case of Mexico, there were increases in the north derived from assembly plants for exports. Finally, there are also central territories that have lost weight in population or GDP, due to a greater increase in their immediate areas of proximity or influence, as in the case of Mexico City with respect to the State of Mexico.

And second, when analyzing trends in GDP per capita, we notice strong deviations, either positive or negative, which as a hypothesis could be explained by two types of phenomena. (a) the development, expansion or decline, for extractive activities (primarily mining) strongly impacting on levels of GDP per capita, because they are usually located in states with low population levels as they are resource and capital intensive. (b) the relative decline of more industrialized or diversified areas that have failed to insert themselves dynamically into the current globalization processes but on the contrary, have experienced deterioration processes of their production structures.

3.1.3 Recent Experiences of Regional Development Policies

Several Latin American countries have recently promoted new territorial development agendas, which have been included into the national policy strategies and objectives designed to reduce the strong internal imbalances. These new policies include: processes of decentralization, territorial competitiveness agendas, cluster promotion, infrastructure development, and cross-border integration, among others.

This new interest in the territorial dimension of development could be supported by a set of objective factors that have emerged in the last decade and that require a more explicit territorial approach of public policy. Firstly, it is clear that in spite of showing a positive social and economic performance in many countries, this has not enabled to overcome the relatively high distances between advanced and lagging regions. Secondly, in contrast to the rise of the integration of countries into the global economy, the need for public policies to promote regional competitiveness has come to light, understood in a broad sense, the set of dimensions of the territorial environment where companies operate. Thirdly, the growing environmental risks generated either by climate change, strong urban expansion, or by the growing number of natural resource-intensive activities have triggered concern about national approaches to territorial development. Finally, and derived from growing democratizing desires, concerns for issues of decentralization and social participation have emerged, which has been expressed in various cases of new institutions.

Given this framework of reemergence of the territorial dimension, a few examples have been selected: Ecuador, Argentina, Peru and Brazil, which express the diversity of approaches to the problem of uneven regional development. The common element in all four experiences is its explicit objective to modify or change the current pattern of socio-spatial organization, interpreted as highly unbalanced, for which different actions are proposed in the economic, infrastructure, decentralization and coordination among others.

In the case of **Ecuador**, the new territorial agenda is embedded in the 2009–2013 National Plan for Good Living, under the name of National Spatial Strategy SENPLADES (2009). Within its organizational outline it aims to create seven planning areas, their main emphases being: (a) Polycentricity, (b) Rurality and food sovereignty, (c) Infrastructure, connectivity and energy, (d) Sustainability, (e) Diversity and cultural heritage, (f) External Insertion and regional integration, and (g) Decentralization and participation.

The graph of the strategy presented in the following map, which shows in order of appearance: (1) Ecological valuation; (2) Rural Good Living, (3) Infrastructure corridor, (4) local support hub, (5) Regional link hub, (6) National structuring hub and (7) International articulation hub (Map 3.1).

In the case of **Peru**, the territorial agenda is embedded in the Bicentennial Plan: Towards 2021. Relevant to this discussion is the strategic axis number 5; regional development and infrastructure CEPLAN (2011). The main emphases of the strategy are: (a) Decentralization and transfer of capabilities, (b) Reconfiguration

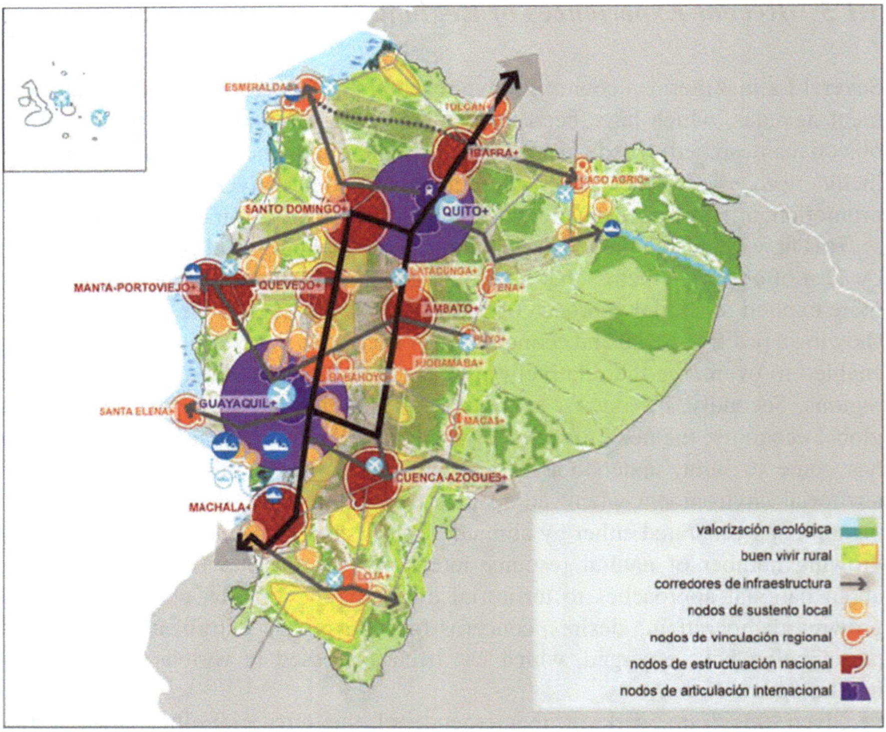

Map 3.1 Graphics expression of the Brazilian National Territorial Strategy (Source: National Territorial Strategy, National Secretary of Planning and Development (SENPLADES))

of political administrative division, (c) economic corridors, (d) Partnerships and clusters, (e) Public-private partnerships and investment promotion, and (f) Development infrastructure.

One important dimension is the development of economic corridors, identified from special studies conducted by the Presidency of the Council of Ministers, which is shown on the maps below. On the left side its shows Cities classification: Metropolis, Major City, Intermediate City and Minor City. On the right side its shows Corridors: Coastal, North, East, Center and South (Map 3.2).

In the case of **Argentina**, the most recent territorial agenda is in the National Development Policy and Land Management, which is embodied in the National Spatial Strategy Plan. Argentina 2016 (PET). The main emphases are:

- Participate on the territorial composition of the country and each of its regions MINPLAN (2008).
- Improve the level of development of national urban networks, provincial and local.
- Increase and rationalize the provision of infrastructure and services in each province.

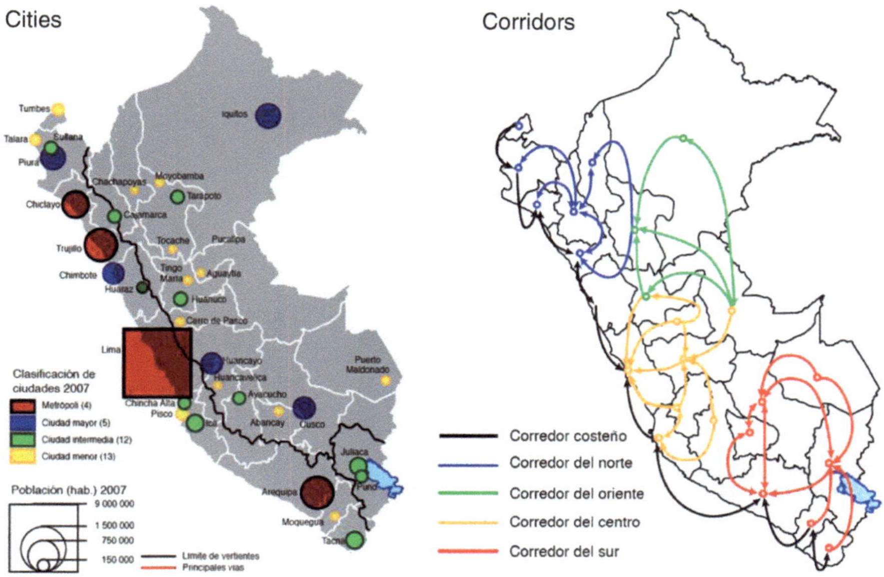

Map 3.2 Classification of cities and economic corridors in Peru (Source: National Center for Strategic Planning (CEPLAN))

- Work on the most lagging and less dynamic areas.
- Stimulate and maintain the order territorial and make the management capacity in government more dynamic.

The graphic expression of the desired spatial development model is shown below. Its identify three categories of Territorial Dynamic and Organization: To qualify; to potentiate and to develop. Also it identified: Connective tissue, structuring network, structuring hub, city to potentiate and city bigger or equal to 30,000 inhabitants (Map 3.3).

Finally, in the case of **Brazil**, the new Regional Development Policy was institutionalized in 2007, and is conducted by the Ministry of National Integration (MI 2007). It has as a general goal to reduce regional inequalities and enable development potential of regions. The specific objectives are:

(a) Provide regions the necessary conditions – infrastructure, credit, technology, etc. – to take advantage of economic-productive opportunities for its development.
(b) Promoting integration of social productivity in the population, human resources training and improving the quality of life in all regions.
(c) Strengthening regional socio-productive organizations, with the expansion of social participation and encouraging construction practices of plans and sub-regional development programs.

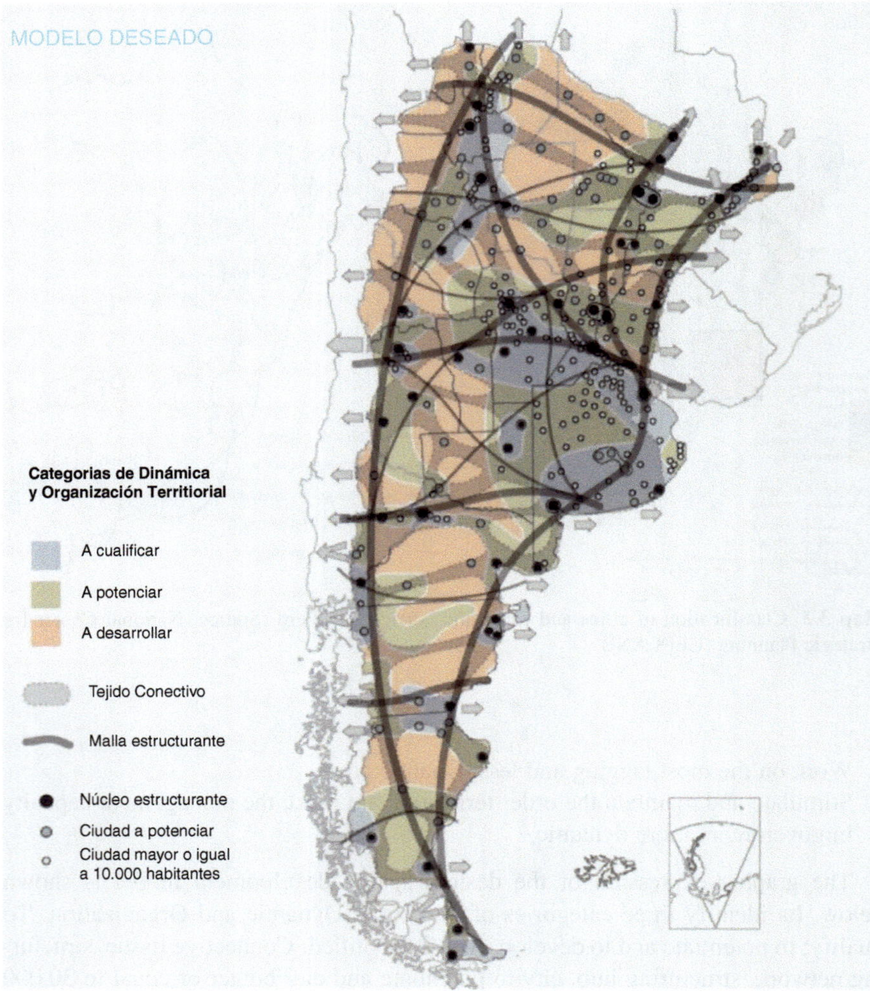

Map 3.3 Argentina's desired territorial model (Source: Territorial Strategic Plan 2016, Ministry of Federal Planning, Public Investment and Services)

(d) Encourage the sub regional exploration potential arising from the magnificent cultural and socioeconomic diversity of the country.

For the National Regional Development Policy it was build a typology of territories, shown below, which identify four categories of territories: (a) Low income (b) Stagnant (c) Dynamic and (d) High income (Map 3.4).

These examples do not exhaust the range of initiatives being carried out in other countries in the region, as recorded in most efforts to confront subnational imbalances.

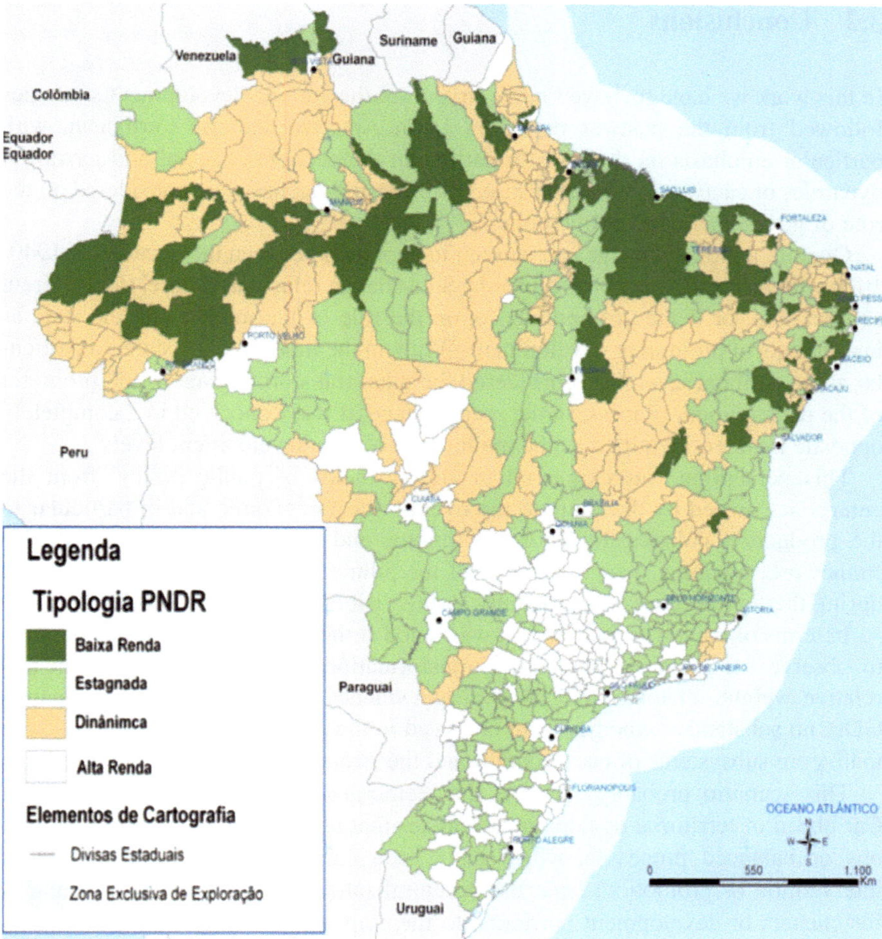

Map 3.4 Brazil. Typology of the National Regional Development Policy (Source: Ministry of Integration, Brazil)

In conclusion, we can say that in Latin America and the Caribbean there exist a new context of territorial development policies, framed in new approaches that exploit the state's role as an active agent in the development process, and which give the territorial element greater importance in strategic thinking and foresight.

3.2 Conclusions

In this work we have reviewed in the first place the various development strategies followed from the postwar period in Latin America and the Caribbean, with particular emphasis on the transformations in the economic, social and territorial dynamics of each period. In each case, different approaches were considered on the role of government and public policy.

Overall, a radical change can be seen in approach between the decades of 1940-1970 with respect to the 1980s onwards. Said change refers, at its core, to a different appreciation, or degree of confidence, on the role of the market and the state as instruments of promoting development. While in the first stage the state, in particular at the national level, was considered the main transforming agent and promoter of the development process; in the second stage, it was conceived in a completely opposite manner, identified as the main cause of low development levels.

This perception was expressed in various fields of public policy, from the enterprises owned by the state, to the overall macroeconomic and in particular to the production policies, to labor institutions, and to territorial policies. In this framework, planning, which was one of the pillars of the strategies implemented during the first decades was gradually losing visibility in many countries.

In terms of the territorial trends it was noted at the outset that while it is possible to observe a number of interesting transformations in terms of population and relative weights of total GDP, as well as evidence of convergence in per capita GDP, no substantive changes were observed in the situation of the primacy of the main core subsystems of each country and the strong interregional disparities.

This scenario probably supports the reemergence in Latin America and the Caribbean of territorial development policies that seek to generate more harmonious or balanced processes, which have been considered for various areas of intervention or promotion, from the decentralization of power, through demands for clusters or development corridors, to the emphasis on more traditional heavy investment in infrastructure observed in recent years in several countries. A relatively new element is forward planning processes that delineate seeking future scenarios in relation to models of socio-spatial organization.

In short, Latin America and the Caribbean has shown in these last five decades transforming processes of different ideological persuasions, seeking to direct development towards new horizons, accumulating a wealth of successes and failures that must be considered in the formulation of current development strategies.

Methodological Annex

The information that was considered was based on estimates of GDP and population for the first level of the political and administrative division of each country (e.g., region, province, department, etc.), due to this level having greater availability of official information.

First we selected those years for which there was a Census Population and GDP estimates. This was possible mainly by the early 1970s and early 1990s. For the most recent year we considered population estimates or projections for Chile, Mexico, Colombia and Brazil, the 2007 census for Peru, and the ECLAC-Argentina estimate for 2005.

For the purpose of having constant prices we performed a single splice using varying rates between series with different base years for the cases of Mexico, Chile, Colombia, Peru and Brazil.

Sources for GDP original series.

Mexico: 1970–1988, INEGHI Estimate, 1993–2009, Regional Accounts of Mexico, INEGHI.

Chile: 1970–2001, MIDEPLAN, regionalized GDP Estimate 1960–2001, 2003–2010, Central Bank of Chile.

Colombia: 1975, ILPES, 1993 and 2009, Regional Accounts, DANE.

Peru. Departmental Accounts, INEI.

Brazil: 1970–2009. IPEA.

References

Boisier S (1993) Las transformaciones en el pensamiento regionalista Latinoamericano, Serie Investigación, documento 93/07. ILPES, Santiago

CEPAL (1968) Estudio económico de América latina 1968. CEPAL, Santiago

ECLAC (1976) Desarrollo Regional y Desarrollo Económico de América Latina

ECLAC (2010) La hora de la igualdad. Brechas por cerrar, caminos por abrir. CEPAL, Santiago

CEPLAN (2011) Plan bicentenario, El Perú hacia el 2021. CEPLAN, Lima

De Mattos C (1986) Paradigmas, modelos y estrategias en la práctica latinoamericana de planificación regional, Pensamiento Iberoamericano Nº10, CEPAL/ICI.

ECLAC (2012) Structural change for equality. An integrated approach to development. ECLAC, Santiago

ILPES (1978) Desarrollo regional y desarrollo económico en América Latina. Documento CPRD-B/19, Santiago

ILPES (2010) Economía y territorio en América latina y el Caribe: desigualdades y políticas. ILPES, Santiago

ILPES (2011) Panorama de la Gestión Pública en América Latina en la Hora de la Igualdad.

ILPES (2012) Panorama del desarrollo económico territorial de América latina. ILPES, Santiago

Ministerio Integración de Nacional (2007) Política nacional de desenvolvimento regional. MI, Brasilia

MINPLAN (2008) Plan estratégico territorial. Argentina del bicentenario. MINPLAN, Buenos Aires

Rofman A (1974) Dependencia, estructura de poder y formación regional en América latina. Siglo XXI, México
SENPLADES (2009) Plan nacional para el buen vivir 2009–2013. SENPLADES, Quito
Thirwall AP, Hussain MN (1982) The balance of payments constraint, capital flows and growth rate differences between developing countries. Oxford Economic Papers, Oxford

Chapter 4
The Origins, Development and Current State of Territorial Policies in Latin America in the Twentieth and Twenty-First Centuries

Sergio Boisier

4.1 Introduction

This chapter is organized as follows: The introduction identifies the purpose of the document and redefines the concept of *territorial policy*. Next, a theoretical approach is described that includes a discussion of the nature of *territorial issues*, a fundamental aspect of policy interventions in the territory. The historical overview traces the origins of policy interventions in Latin America on the basis of two foundational experiences: the Tennessee Valley Authority, which was established by Roosevelt in the 1930s, and the *Cassa per ilMezzogiorno*, a development agency created in southern Italy in 1950. In each case, I present the most important Latin American replicas of those experiences. The section on paradigmatic territorial policies provides a detailed examination of the evolution of these instruments. Next, the discussion of the objectives of territorial interventions and their results reviews the goals that were set and the outcomes. My hypothesis regarding a more than evident failure explains the reasons why success was not achieved. The section on key events from the twenty-first century addresses new interventionist trends in Brazil and Chile and the World Bank's 2009 report on the global economy as a significant milestone from this century. Finally, the conclusions describe the overarching weaknesses of the approaches and interventions that have been developed thus far.

This article provides a general and transversal framework for reading the Latin American experience with the formulation and application of first, second and third generation territorial policies over a period of almost half a century. I look at the origins of these policies, which represent an essential point of reference if *path dependence* adopted as a hypothesis, as well as the theoretical referents, objectives and results, examining the causes of what could be called *a more than evident*

S. Boisier (✉)
CATS, Ases. Des° Territorial, Santiago, Chile
e-mail: sboisier@vtr.net

J.R. Cuadrado-Roura and P. Aroca (eds.), *Regional Problems and Policies in Latin America*, Advances in Spatial Science, DOI 10.1007/978-3-642-39674-8_4,

failure. In the current century, we have witnessed the emergence of new approaches and practices that promise improved results. In this article, special attention is paid to the new role of civil society in the construction of regions.

It should be noted from the outset that the contemporary concept of *territorial policy* refers to a *set of policies or to a global policy goal* that includes four *mega-policies*: (a) territorial organization; (b) decentralization; (c) the *promotion* of territorial economic growth; and (d) the *promotion* of societal development in the various territories.[1] Each of these mega-policies includes diverse sets of *meso-policies* (e.g. territorial organization policy includes infrastructure localization policies, land use policies, etc.) and each one of these is ultimately expressed as a vector of specific instruments. This is an interpretation that is far more complex than the simple idea of a *territorial policy,* which refers exclusively to interventions concerning certain territorial sections which are called *regions* based on various criteria.

4.2 Theoretical Approach

From a functionalist perspective, as Talcott Parsons might say, all socio-economic systems seek to achieve three over-arching and immanent, irrevocable, and long-term objectives: (1) to systematically increase the capacity to produce goods and services; (2) to obtain a certain social stability that makes the process of savings and investment viable, a condition that is necessary in order to achieve the first objective; and (3) to maintain territorial sovereignty, a basic condition of the permanence of a national government.

In classical literature on planning, the clash between objectives and their obstacles is defined as a problem, and thus an issue that contributes to defining the field of intervention.

According to this reasoning, over the course of a country's evolution, a process that is framed within the logic of capitalism in the case of Latin America, several types of problems begin to emerge at different levels and with varying degrees of importance. At some point, a special class of problems will develop within this group: those defined by aggregate (national) objectives and impediments of an evident territorial nature. This in turn generates a set of problems that we refer to as *territorial issues* (formerly known as *regional issues*).

The objective of "systematically increasing production capacity" (the achievement of a sustained high rate of growth of the GDP) begins to be impeded by an excessive level of **territorial concentration of the means of production** due to the emergence of the phenomena of external diseconomies and agglomeration that surpass the increasing positive yields of concentration. The "problem of hyper-

[1] The fact that the word *development* is underlined is not coincidental: it denotes the change of the role of the government in neoliberalism.

territorial concentration of production and population" thus begins to take shape, and the effort to address it will take the form of a policy that seeks to reverse the situation by means of both positive measures (varied stimuli to peripheral localization) and negative ones (differentiated taxes, restrictions on industrial building at the *core*, etc.).

The goal of maintaining a social system free of recurrent extreme tensions in order to facilitate the process of saving and investment is threatened when the pattern of distribution of the results of the growth process is questioned. This is particularly true in relation to the unequal distribution of income, which shows, in all cases, a strong, *highly visible territorial component*, which in turn generates "the problem of territorial disparities in income, well-being and opportunities," with their attendant social and political tensions. These may lead to the formation of frankly challenging political movements and center/periphery conflict in addition to causing migratory patterns that introduce true vicious circles in sub-national territories. Proposals for transfer policies, social endowments and distributive and redistributive policies will emerge in response to this.

The objective of maintaining the territorial integrity of the nation/government is threatened by excessive economic and demographic concentration accompanied by perceptibly higher income levels in the "center" of the system. This creates a political situation associated with a highly *unequal distribution of power* (in its variety of guises). Combined with Latin America's Bourbon tradition in the shaping of the government, it results in the "problem of centralism" that is so evident in the sub-continent. According to Claudio Veliz (1982), this also feeds off of a true *centralist culture*. The government's response will take the form of policies of deconcentration and/or administrative, political and territorial decentralization.

These problems, taken together or in individually, tend to appear at the intermediate stages of growth, and are inherent to them. This multivariate dynamic is typical of the evolution of all systems of social relations of production, in this case capitalism. Processes that are clearly positive during initial periods, such as concentration or centralism, become negative after a turning point and require the implementation of various forms of social self-intervention.

In Latin American countries that presented "early industrial evolution," such as Mexico, Argentina and Brazil, the government's response began to form half-way through the twentieth century.

4.3 Historical Overview

The above observations help to elucidate the rationality of territorial policies, but rarely does rationality alone support them.

At the global level, the first relatively explicit attempt by a national government to intervene in addressing the issue that is now described as a "regional problem" was the TVA (Tennessee Valley Authority). The project, which was undertaken in the United States in the early 1930s, was the work of Roosevelt's government. The

TVA was enormously successful and influential, and its theoretical foundations were based on Keynesian economic policy. The establishment of the TVA was a typical Keynesian response to the crisis of 1929. As such, it was an intervention that, by nearly mathematical derivation, became the icon of regional developmentism (*desarrollismo*). After World War II, it would be followed by the creation of the *Cassa per il Mezzogiorno* in Italy, a clearly ideological state intervention (aiming to avoid the Communist Party's taking of Presidential power) and again, it became an icon of regional policy but for different purposes.

Scholars agree that Mexico has been the cradle of territorial policy development in Latin America since the establishment of the Papaloapan River Basin Commission in 1947. The body was created to manage approximately 47,000 km^2 of basin area. Its main objectives were linked to flood control, though several other objectives were eventually assigned to it. In fact, its authority included investment in hydraulic resources for controlling floods, irrigation, hydro-electric power and drinking water as well as the establishment of all sorts of communication systems for all matters of industrial and agricultural development, urbanization and colonization (Barkin and King 1970, p. 100).

Commissions would later be formed to intervene in the Grijalva and Usumacinta (120,000 km^2) basins as well as Tepalcatepec (17,000 km^2), Balsas (100,000 km^2), Fuerte (29,000 km^2) and Lerma-Chapala-Santiago (126,700 km^2). Such entities would eventually cover over 20 % of the country's territory.

In Brazil, the National Department of Works Against Drought (DNOCS) created the Commission for the Development of the São Francisco River Valley (known as CODEVASF for its acronym in Portuguese) in 1948. It later formed the Commission for the Development of the Rio Doce River Valley Basin. In both cases, the strategy is very similar to the one that had been tested in Mexico.

Brazil also created the Office for Northeastern Development, or "SUDENE," in 1959. This is probably the most emblematic body in the area of territorial policy in Latin America (de Oliveira 1977). The name of Celso Furtado and his *Northeast Operation* had been linked to the creation of SUDENE. Next steps were the Offices for Amazon Development (SUDAM) and the Manaus Duty Free Zone (SUFRAMA). The decades that followed would bring similar agencies for the macro-regions of west-central, south-central and southern Brazil.

That same year, Argentina created the Federal Investment Council (CFI) through a constitutional agreement between the provinces, the municipal government of the City of Buenos Aires, the National Territory of Tierra del Fuego, Antarctica and the South Atlantic Islands. This is another agency that was considered an icon of regional development practice. Perhaps one of the most important features of CFI was the *exclusion* of the national government from the constitutional pact, which reaffirmed federalism and regionalism.

Another historic milestone which also became an icon in this field was the establishment of the Venezuelan Corporation of Guayana (CVG) in 1960. The entity was framed by the sort of philosophy of development and planning that was brought to the government of Venezuela in 1958 by President Rómulo

Betancourt. The development of the Guayana, project hinged on the foundation of a new city Santo Tomé of Guayana and on the development of hydro-electric power and iron and steel mining. John Friedmann wrote a classic text on the Venezuelan experience (Friedmann 1966).

The final stages of the first half of the twentieth century saw the creation of Colombia's Cauca Valley Development Corporation, first as an electricity producing company and later as a development agency. The La Sabana Autonomous Corporation was created soon after, followed by several departmental corporations that were more closely linked to issues of territorial organization.

By the 1960s, regional policies changed in their form and footing following the emergence of *national* regionalization plans that were more in line with the functionalist rationale described above. The policies would take on a more systemic character, opening up the field to two variants: (a) *intra-regional policies* and (b) *inter-regional policies.* A number of countries adopted this method, including Argentina, Bolivia, Brazil, Colombia, Chile, Mexico, Peru, and Venezuela.

Austrian economist Walter Stöhr took stock of regional development programs in Latin America in the late 1960s. He gathered information on no fewer than 75 programs in total and organized them into the following five categories:

Policies for the decentralization of decision-making
Policies for depressed areas
Policies for the colonization of new areas of natural resources
Policies for the development of border areas
Policies for metropolitan areas and new poles of development.

The same author assesses the degree of implementation and success of these policies, and here his judgment is generally more negative. It would seem that most were more semantic than real (Stöhr 1972).

Later on, in the 1970s, an even more drastic change would develop in the field of regional policies. This issue will be examined in greater detail below.

4.4 The Paradigmatic Models of Territorial Policies

The influence of the institutional model of the TVA remained on the front lines for about a decade. By the mid-1950s, the "hydraulic" paradigm model would give way to another model, a European one that was founded more on political lines than economic ones. As we have already noted, the post-war period raised the possibility that the Communist Party could take control of Italy by means of accession to the presidency. Fear of this was one of the causes of the passage of the Constitution of 1947, which divided Italy into 22 regions. The strategy was to form territorial and political spaces in which the Christian Democrats could find refuge and strength and build resistance. The Communist Party never won the presidency, though it did gain control of several regions and cities that would later become the stars of Italian development (industrial districts). As part of the same political construction and under the Marshall Plan, the U.S. pushed for the creation of a funding and projects implementation agency that would channel investment resources to the impoverished southern area of the Italian peninsula, where it was thought that communism would find a favorable environment.

The result was the emblematic Italian experience (*Cassa per il Mezzogiorno*). Between 1950 and 1980, the agency would receive the enormous sum of $36 billion (nominal) earmarked for investments in infrastructure and industrial equipment for the south. *La Cassa* had considerable success in increasing per capita income in that region, but income in the north increased much more rapidly during the same period, exposing the duality of disparities in absolute and relative terms.

SUDENE would become the main replica of *La Cassa* in Latin America. Like its parent model, this institution owes its creation to political developments. It represents the Brazilian government's response to the social and political unrest caused by poverty that had developed in the northeastern region of the country. The situation had already created a powerful and menacing movement, *Las Ligas Camponesas,* which were led by Francisco Juliao (Juliao would later be co-opted by the system and become a federal deputy). Through Furtado, Kubistchek's government created a device whose main purpose was to make visible the transfer of capital from the center-south to the northeastern region, creating companies, entrepreneurs and employment. Francisco de Oliveira said -using clear Marxist language – that SUDENE made viable the expansion of Brazilian oligopolistic capitalist accumulation with a nationalist air while creating a local oligarchy similar to the one that was already in place, mainly in São Paulo. The tax exemptions created through Article 34/18 would be the main instrument for raising capital.

The "invisible hand" of the United States soon became visible: Hollis Chenery, one of the architects of the *La Cassa* model, and Stephan Robock, a prominent economist, would serve as advisors to the Superintendency and contribute decisively to its organization and the definition of its strategy. Later, according to Oliveira, "the action of the USAID in the northeast specifically aimed to undermine the authority of SUDENE by offering direct aid to state governments that were capable of politically opposing populist political forces, which were in turn labeled as 'radicals'" (Oliveira, op. cit, p. 122).

The 1960s began, in a sense, with the Punta del Este Conference of 1961, which saw the creation of the Alliance for Progress. This was at that time that the U.S. used its power to veto the use of planning, transforming it into a legitimate instrument of progressive interventionism endowed with a supposed *fundamentum in re*. On the other hand, it was a decade marked by utopias, ideological visions (today the term is *metanarratives*) and a clash of ideologies, at least in Latin America. This confrontation involved various schools of thought and interpretation of development: dependency theory in its Marxist versions (Frank, dos Santos, Marini, Quijano) and non-Marxist ones (Cardozo, Faletto, Sunkel), and social modernization theory, which was mainly espoused by Gino Germani.

According to this latter position, the lack of development of Latin American countries was mainly due to a set of structural barriers that prevented these countries from following the path of progress already trodden by the industrialized nations (there was an implicit assumption that a single path to development existed). The list of barriers included –rightly so, it seems – the educational system and land ownership. Educational and agricultural reforms were put on the agenda.

Another barrier, and one that is of particular interest in this field, was the low degree of internal integration of Latin American economies. The concept of low "internal integration" referred to *physical* integration, which was clearly very deficient; *economic* integration as the lack of a national market; and *socio-political* integration. These processes had not been completed during the construction of the nation-state, which led to a lack of a national framework of values and the precarious position of the government in its own territory. Colombia may be the best example of these shortcomings.

Although not included in the assessment of the lack of Latin American development made in the framework of modernization theory, one could easily take from it a recommendation that would be central to the design of territorial policies beginning in the 1960s: the advisability of modifying the political and administrative structure of national territories in order to create a sort of a new geographic policy that was more in line with contemporaneity. This would allow for the elimination of the old internal territorial boundaries of the Conquest and of a new political geography the Hispano-Portuguese colony which had ceased to reflect the contemporary organization of the territory. It was thought that this intervention would contribute strongly to improving internal integration conditions. *Regionalization* of a national scale comes onto the scene at this point. This process involved the definition of a comprehensive and exclusive division of the national territory which would serve as a basic framework for the implementation of national regional or inter-regional policies and intra-regional policies or simply regional policies. We must note that this proposal comes at a key time for the cognitive framework known as *regional science* developed mainly by Walter Isard in the United States (University of Pennsylvania), an elegant neoclassical synthesis of the contributions of European geographers and economists starting with von Thünen.

As often happens within the Latin American intellectual arena -particularly in the field of economic thought-, in most countries, an "all or nothing bet" in favor of regionalization comes to the fore. (Magical properties are attributed to certain economic models, and there is hardly any country of a significant size that will not make an attempt at regionalization, including Panama, which has only 57,000 km^2, and the Dominican Republic and Honduras, which are even smaller.) In some cases, such as Argentina, the respective proposal was based on the application of the gravitational models of social physics that were so widely disseminated by Isard. In other cases, such as Chile, the proposal combined ecological, geographic, and economic criteria. In all cases, the move constituted a political and social "experiment" imposed by the government but did not respond to any social demands and was markedly economist in character. In almost all cases, regionalization created regions *ex nihilo*.

In a sense, regional planning entered a golden decade in the early 1960s. This period also saw the advent of very significant political change in countries like Colombia, Chile, Panama, Peru and Venezuela, where government control was transferred to single parties, party coalitions or military factions. In general, these entities shared their adhesion to Social Democratic or Christian Democratic political positions and could be described as progressive and modernizing governments (although the conciliation of these terms with a dictatorial practice would be difficult to carry out). There is also a link in generic terms to the ideas of social modernization. As such, there is a certain tendency towards regionalization. In the case of Chile, Frei was always a fervent supporter of the regions as entities that helped to balance out the excessive weight of the capital. Once regions were defined, specific policies for the whole and the components of the system relied heavily on Paul Rosenstein-Rodan's central idea of *a great destabilizer and multiplying boost* and François Perroux's concept of *poles of development,* an industrial destabilizer.

The 1970s bore witness to the enthronement of de facto military and right-wing governments, which destroyed the idea of planning. In some cases, such as Chile, formal regional planning would continue until 1978. This effort was supported by the military, which took charge of CONARA (the National Commission on Administrative Reform) until economists belonging to the group known as the Chicago Boys (in reference to their *almamater)* took full control of ODEPLAN (the National Planning Office). A thorough examination of the experience of the military government is found in Boisier (1982).

From this point on, Chile's national regional development policy would take other directions. In general, it disappears from government discourse and is replaced by a kind of *non-strategy* that transfers responsibility for regional development to the regions by removing the government's role on this area. A kind of subliminal message was sent from the center to the peripheries, often without a clear target audience: *From now on, responsibility for development is in your hands; take note of the external opening of the economy and pull yourselves up by your bootlaces, and understand that the State is limited in its ability to ensure the permissiveness in the exploitation or over-exploitation of both natural resources and also manpower. Try your best!* Prominent Brazilian SUDENE economist Tania Bacelar de Araujo has been a harsh critic of this self-marginalized position of the government, and has denounced this *laissez faire* policy for leaving less competitive regions adrift.

Regionalization began to unravel throughout the region with the exception of Chile. Over the years, however, a kind of regionalist reorganization emerged in several nations. In Argentina, the constitutional reform of 1994 opened the door for *adjoining* provinces to form regions (as occurred with the formation of the Patagonia Region, which is composed of five provinces and a regional capital, Santa Rosa de la Pampa, and the Central Region). The five macro-regions of planning disappeared in Brazil. In Colombia, Article 306 of the Constitution of 1991 made the establishment of regions mandatory. This was achieved through the association of adjoining departments (RAP regions, Administration and Planning). The five CORPES (Regional Council of Economic and Social Planning) regions that were created in 1985 disappeared. In Bolivia, *departmentos* were reinforced. In Peru, the sophisticated regional institutional architecture created by Alan Garcia in his first term of office was erased at a single stroke. Meanwhile, the Constitution of 1993 allowed for the formation of regions based on voluntary association of neighboring departments. This occurred in Argentina in 1994.

Ray Bromley (1990) made a significant contribution to this field through his article "Development, Underdevelopment, and National Spatial Organization," in which he provides the perspective of a British geographer with an extensive knowledge of Latin America.

Roberto Camagni, a leading Italian specialist, has prepared a sequence of the most common regional intervention concepts (see list below). It should be noted that Latin America is following the same conceptual path but with a significant time lag.

KEY CONCEPTS IN LONG-TERM REGIONAL POLICIES

1950-1960	**Infrastructure as a condition for growth**
1960-1970	**Attracting inward investment, development poles, exportation bases**
1970-1980	**Endogenous development: Small and Medium Size Enterprisess, local competences**
1980-1990	**Innovation, technology difussion, innovative methods**
1990-2000	**Knowledge, intangible factors, collective learning**
2000-2010	**Relational capital , interconnection, local culture, electronic labor**

Poland's Katarzyna Dembicz (2005, pp. 149–164) provided a lucid examination of the contributions of ECLAC in regard to the concepts of region and regional development in Latin America.

4.5 The Objectives and Results of Territorial Interventions

As we have seen, the multiple programs that were created in order to promote growth and development in the territory were based on various paradigms. Overall, they proposed a limited and more or less standardized set of goals.

The first of these is an *instrumental* objective: the implantation of a new political/administrative division of the territory, *regionalization,* which is clearly an instrumental objective or measure that, in the minds of many, became the ultimate goal.

A second common goal was limiting the expansion of large cities or the largest city in each case. The purpose of the *control of-metropolization* was to reduce both the volume of internal migration and the already visible social costs associated with sprawl and the exponential growth of the main center of each country.

Third, great importance was given to a vague notion of equality expressed as the need to reduce *territorial disparities* in per capita product, income or well-being. As we have noted, this objective was not removed from considerations of national political and institutional stability.

The fourth goal was that of the *decentralization of decision-making* in the public and private spheres, though this was presented in a rather vague manner. Even basic or theoretical knowledge of Latin American centralism was very limited.

Last, *regional development* appeared as an objective as the end or teleological result of the four preceding goals. It was presented as a process with two scales. The first was *national or inter-regional,* with a systemic conceptual background, and the second was *regional,* which refers to each one of the regions and addressed the impossibility of equal relative growth.

An assessment of the level of achievement of these objectives in the long term shows of the limited nature of the results.

By the late twentieth century, Chile was the only Latin American nation that presented the constitutional and political consolidation of regionalization. The Constitution of 1980 and subsequent reforms stated that "Chile is a unitary state. Its territory is divided into regions. Its administration will be functional and territorially decentralized, or deconcentrated where appropriate, in accordance with the law." (Article3) Peru (1996), Nicaragua (1996), and the Dominican Republic (1996) appear together with Chile in an undated UNDP report on the subject, but it was noted that in 1993 the Peruvian constitutional reform eliminated the regions and the political and administrative structures established during Alan Garcia's first government. Noted politician and Peruvian specialist Manuel Dammert (1999) maintains a position that is completely contrary to the one presented in the UNDP report, though it is true that in 1998 Congress approved a *Framework Law for Decentralization* in an effort to "departmentalize" regionalization. But in any case, it seems more accurate to note that in the year of the UNDP report's publication, only Chile, Nicaragua and the Dominican Republic could present *de jure* regional structures, and if one takes into account the size of these countries, it would not be unreasonable to point to Chile as the only relevant case in function of its geographic size.

Secondly, the purpose of setting limits on metropolization and urban primacy failed outright. It is well known that Latin America is characterized by a high rate of urbanization (84 % in South America and 72 % in Central America). This process is developing quickly in the region, which presented a rate of urbanization of 1.6 % annually between 2005 and 2010 (Population Division, Department of Economic and Social Affairs, United Nations 2011). As has been observed elsewhere, even the inability to contain metropolitan growth has led to the introduction of new words such as *megalopolis and megalopolization.* The figures show that the percentage of the population that lives in large urban areas has surpassed 47 % in Mexico, 48 % in Brazil, 42 % in Argentina, 42 % in Peru, 39 % in Chile, 34 % in Venezuela, and so on (see www.unpopulation.org). In some cases, the population figures for the largest cities exceed 20 million inhabitants.

The hopes for a shift in the economic model, in the spread of post-Fordism and in decentralization have not become a reality.

Third, the reduction of territorial disparities in per capita product and income, another objective noted above, was an issue that merited the attention of empirical analysts from early on. This was the case with Gilbert and Goodman (1976) for Brazil and the northeast; Leon for Colombia, Panama and Venezuela; Martin (1984) for those same countries based on Leon; and Boisier and Grillo (1969) for Chile. Currently, the issue has been taken up with the vision of convergence/divergence analyses. Luis M. Cuervo (2003) prepared an excellent review of the "state of the art" for ILPES to which we refer the reader with an appetite for numbers. The most general conclusion is that there is no clear pattern of convergence in Latin America; rather, convergence containment patterns appear. The ILPES study written by Ivan Silva (2003) offers an even more complete overview of the disparities, territorial competitiveness, and local and regional development in the sub-continent and is recommended reading. A more recent and complete study on Chile that includes mathematics which are only for the initiated was published by Robert Duncan and Rodrigo Fuentes of the University of Wisconsin and the Central Bank of Chile, respectively (2006, pp. 82–112). The document presents two points of view and a comprehensive bibliography featuring many Chilean publications on the topic.

Empirical evidence provided by Duncan and Fuentes tends to support the hypothesis of convergence in per capita GDP both in terms of *beta* convergence (convergence in levels) and *sigma* convergence (convergence in the dispersion).

However, this result is accompanied by slow rates of convergence of slightly less than 1 %, implying that the time needed to halve the gap between "rich" and "poor" regions is between 81 and 96 years! It is difficult to appreciate the practical utility of studies of this nature.

One of the most important empirical studies on territorial disparities in Latin America was prepared by Emmanuel Skoufias and Gladys Lopez-Acevedo for IBRD/World Bank (2009, p. 9). It states that:

> *The eight Latin American countries examined in the study show significant differences in poverty rates in and within regions. For example, some countries such as Brazil and Peru have large differences in poverty rates both within and between regions, while other countries such as Ecuador, Guatemala and Nicaragua have higher differences in rates of poverty between urban and rural areas than within regions in general.*
>
> *Each country has a clearly determined "leader" region and one or two straggling regions. People living in straggling regions experience even higher levels of poverty, as measured by poverty rates, levels of well-being, and consumption rates. In an extreme case, some regions of Brazil have poverty rates slightly above 10 percent, while others are above 50 percent. Mexico and Peru also show large differences in poverty rates in the regions. In all of the Latin American countries analyzed, poverty rates are higher in rural areas than in urban ones, with very high rates in straggling regions, such as the Northeast of Brazil, the South Pacific states of Mexico, the Andes mountains in Peru, and the Pacific region of Colombia.*

Fourth, the objective of decentralizing public and private decision-making systems has demonstrated an erratic temporal trajectory as a result of serious limitations in the culture, the tradition of government organization, the sub-culture of public administration, and Latin American's individualist mentality. The latter was inherited from the model of rule by rural landowners in which the peasant (later to become the urban worker) cultivated a model of dependence with respect to the land owner and later the government. The distinction between federal and unitary countries is naturally mandatory in this area. Ivan Finot (2001) prepared a careful study for ILPES in which he reviews the "state of the art" in this field which we recommend for all readers. Ultimately, however, we must recognize that progress in decentralization – where there is progress – seems to respond to changes connected to globalization and neo-liberalism rather than to the strength of the statements.

The final objective encourages regional development processes in the region's countries. It has always failed from the standpoint of evaluation due to the vague, inexplicit nature of the objective itself. However, if we use a criterion that is very simple but not without rationality, namely, describing *regional development* as processes that generate or promote cities (as a "device" for a region, to use Mumford's terms) that become competitive centers in the process of capitalist accumulation of one (or a few) traditional and historical accumulation centers, one could tentatively state that there has been a process leading to a condition which could be classified as "regional development."

If this criterion is used to take a new look at the map of Latin America, we see that situations like the one described are seen in Monterrey and Guadalajara in Mexico; Medellín, Barranquilla and Cali in Colombia; Guayaquil in Ecuador; Arequipa in Peru; Concepción in Chile; Mendoza, Rosario, and Cordoba in Argentina; Santa Cruz in Bolivia; and São Paulo in Brazil. However, a more detailed analysis would reveal that the thrust of development in most of these cities/regions began in the nineteenth century, before there was talk of regional policy, though there could have been implicitly.

Based on a more contemporary understanding of development, the following cases should be highlighted: Neuquén in Argentina; Ceará, Santa Catarina and Paraná in Brazil; and San Pedro Zula in Honduras along with cases arising from the action of the "developmentist government" such as Córdoba in Argentina and Concepción in Chile. In any case, the results, once again, are quite precarious. Something has not worked out as planned.

4.6 Hypothesis of a More Than Evident Failure

Disappointment caused by the poor performance of regional policies has led to extensive discussions of its possible causes. These discussions were not without ideological approaches, at least in the beginning.

First, we must mention – and only a mention is sufficient – radicalized sectors' thesis of the impossibility of relatively harmonious regional development in the context of the capitalist system at least until the late 1970s. This thesis would not have held up under even the most basic theoretical examination and was not at all validated by empirical evidence.

Next, a hypothesis was presented concerning coherence between the *styles of development* and *regional policies.* This discussion was held at an important seminar in Bogota in 1979 during which participants concluded that most regional policies had been conceived as highly functional in terms of the style that had begun to gain ground, a style heavily biased towards economic growth. This went against the suppositions that had been made. Some of the papers presented at that seminar (including those of Hilhorts, Uribe-Echevarría/Helmsing, Boisier, Haddad, Pineda, Stöhr, and others) helped highlight coherence and opened up new avenues for reflection in view of the empirical results.[2] In recent years, regional policies strongly associated with international competitiveness have been perfectly consistent with external liberalization and globalization, at least in discourse, even though this has meant that the less favored regions have been neglected.

Certainly, the political and economic policy "discontinuities" that prevailed in Latin America from the mid-1970s were also noted as possible causes of the results.

A first look at the search for an operational causality – that is, explanations that clearly give rise to new forms of intervention, and not a self-contained explanations – must point to the following: if the processes of growth and development in the territory are understood as *complex evolutionary processes,* as real systemic emergencies associated with evolutionary complexity, then it must be admitted that causality *is also complex* by explaining successes or explaining failures, as Rubén Utría states in a book on the development of nations (Utria 2002).

This leads us to argue that a whole range of causal factors comes into play, from the kind of international integration that a country presents, with the entire system of domination/dependency that is usually involved, to the national economic policy (macro and sectoral) to the culture and behavior of specific stakeholders and agents. However, here a selective analysis that intends to point to two *radical* causes (in the sense of being at the root of the matter) are given priority and have been exposed on numerous occasions and still have not, to this day, been rejected. It is important to keep in mind that lessening the complexity of an operation is fraught with danger, given that, as per Cartesian dualism, this reduction in complexity dilutes the very question being considered and eventually makes it disappear.

Beginning with a strict differentiation between the concepts of *growth* and *development,* that were framed initially in a synonymy (since at least the time of the Atlantic Charter signed by Churchill and Roosevelt in 1941), it became increasingly clear that the most significant specific difference between them was relegating the concept of growth (as a process and government) to material achievements (certainly important in and of themselves) while the concept of development is linked to immaterial, intangible, subjective, and value-related achievements

---

[2] See *Experiencias de planificación regional en América Latina: Una teoría en busca de una práctica, 1981. Compiled by S. Boisier, F. Cepeda, J. Hilhorst, S. Riffka, Uribe Echevarría, ILPES, SIAP, Santiago de Chile*

strongly influenced by the thinking of Seers, Sen, Goulet, Furtado, Hirchmann and others.

A precise definition of development was not available (and is one available now?). This has led to a lack of understanding of its structure and its dynamics. Even worse, development on the sub-national scale had a great deal of scale reductionism, which led to a failure to recognize the qualitative changes between scales. The lack of a definite *corpus* makes interventions mere bets; the desired results may be achieved, but surely these will result from chance, from good luck.

Even on firmer theoretical ground concerning growth, current theorizing about *endogenous growth* at the sub-national level has been adopted a bit lightly, ignoring issues such as the considerable degree of systemic openness of sub-national societies and their also systemic insertion in areas of high command –the country and the world-, levels at which major initiatives are undertaken. (For example, this may include the specification of the framework of the economic policy, the specification of a "country project," or long-term national project, regulations of various forms, investments, etc. etc.).It neglects the fundamental fact that the growth process (and also development) is the result of an *enormous decision-making structure* that involves a multiplicity of "agents." When the elemental question of where most of these agents are found is asked, the answer is unequivocal: *outside of the territory (region, province, neighborhood,* etc.*) in question.* As a result, economic growth in the territory should be considered highly *exogenous* regardless of whether knowledge and technical progress adheres to a strictly economic rationality.

From a strictly theoretical point of view, it has been argued (Boisier 2003) that both growth and regional development are *systemic emergences.* In the case of growth, such emergence arises from the intense interaction *of the system with its own environment* (with the decision-makers in charge of capital accumulation, technical progress, human capital, external demand, the formulation and implementation of economic policies, and design of the "country project" if it exists). In the case development, due to the strong interaction *between the subsystems of the system* (axiological, accumulation, organizational, procedural, decision-making, and subliminal subsystems whose interaction (synapses) depend on the complexity of evolution). This reasoning supports the *exogenous* growth thesis as well as the *endogenous* development theory.

Theory and practice in the area of interventions designed to encourage development have been steeped in positivism (with all of the limiting assumptions of this paradigm) and analytic Cartesian thought, ahistoricism, and action programs such as "disjointed instrumentalism" *á la Lindblom.* They are impregnated with a belief that development results from the *sum* of projects and programs, rather than the result, metaphorically speaking, from the *multiplication* of cognitive social synergy.

The key to designing successful territorial interventions, which necessarily assume their consonance with contemporaneity, probably lies in considering that processes of social change in the territory (growth + development) require *decentralized* interventions in order to maximize the endogeneity of the of processes (we already know that it will be relatively low in the case of growth and high in the case of development). The requirement is broad decentralization in institutional terms, i.e., in the public and private spheres, and simultaneously political and territorial in nature (governments with the autonomy to govern, endowed with resources and legitimate authority, having been elected by the people). Without understanding decentralization as such, it would be difficult for the indispensable public/private associativity to emerge, and it has been increasingly recognized as a necessary condition for generating the social energy required to trigger and sustain the process of change.

4.7 Key Events of the Twenty-First Century

4.7.1 Globalization and Geography: Tension Between Change and Conservation

Globalization, that Buñuelian *obscure object of desire* which we all want to capture,[3] is a game in which everyone (individuals, organizations, territories) is required to participate in order to survive or avoid death, where possible. By decoding the concept of globalization, we find a systemic process that is not determined, as some naively believe, by a perverse conspiracy of world leaders located in different areas and parts of the world. Rather, far from Manichaeist simplism, globalization is nothing more, for better or for worse, than *the current techno-cognitive phase in the development of the capitalist system*. This system began in the Netherlands back in the seventeenth century as commercial proto-capitalism. A century later, it would give way to industrial capitalism in England and then morph into financial capitalism in the twentieth century mainly in the United States and most recently into techno-cognitive capitalism, as can be seen in several locations around the world.

This phase, which cannot even be considered as a final phase or the end of history, shows the interaction between two underlying processes that are the main cause of what appears as *globalization's world economic landscape*. The key elements of the landscape are the intense external opening of economies, gradual replacement of material elements by information as the currency of international trade, and mobility of capital, people and knowledge,[4] including the transformation of the structure of the distribution of political power at both supra-national and sub-national levels, allowing for decentralization. The two underlying processes referred to are: (i) the exponential systematic reduction of the life cycle of

[3] This does not mean that it is a matter of greater free mobility. On the contrary, knowledge is increasingly privatized, to say nothing of capital.

[4] This metaphor should be understood as referring to the cognitive and innovative nucleus of globalization.

manufactured products, and (ii) the exponential systematic increase of the added cost of research, innovation and marketing.

Given that the capitalist system is a social system, it does not escape the tight categorical imperative inscribed in the genetic code of all biological and social systems: its permanent reproduction. As Althusser[5] once said, "Therefore, the final status of production is the reproduction of the conditions of production." In order for this to occur, the system must recover the resources spent on the research, development and marketing involved in the transition process from "n" product generation to "n+1" generation, in modern parlance, as quickly as possible. As a result, the system does not tolerate borders, customs, tariffs, para-tariff ruses, or other mechanisms that hinder the formation of *a single trade area* that will go hand in hand with *multiple spaces of production.*[6] One can now understand the search for more and more bi- or multi-lateral free trade agreements.

4.7.2 Three Events That Change History

The years 2005, 2007 and 2009 brought new milestones in the field of territorial policy in Latin America.

The first event occurred in Chile. In August 2005, the Constitution of Chile was modified in order to remove Article 49, which had established the existence of 13 regions in Chile. This text rigidly divided the country into regions and made it impossible to create new ones. The modification was orchestrated by civil society in the province of Valdivia, part of the Lakes District in the south of the country. For 30 years, the entity had demanded the right dismantle the current regional structure in order to establish a full, legitimate region. In October of that year, the President signed the bill to create the Rivers Region, which was enacted by Law 20.174 on March 16, 2007. All of this occurred in the country that is most tightly bound to the political model of a unitary, centralist, and presidential government in Latin America. The regional government was installed and began to execute an unprecedented process of development strategy for the region with broad citizen participation and methodological support from the highest level.

Finally, Law 20390 was passed on October 16, 2009, establishing the direct election of Regional Councilors. On October 12, 2011, the President sent a message (133–159) to Congress containing the bill to amend Law 19175 (the Statutory Law of Government and Regional Administration). It is currently being discussed in Congress and may allow for the direct election of Regional councilors by October

[5] Althusser L. *Ideology and ideological state apparatus, Freud and Lacan*, 1969, http://www.sociologia.de

[6] Certainly, the logic of the system does not always match the logic of its individual actors. This explains behavior and ambivalence in the discourse and in the practice of free trade by the more industrialized countries. However, there can be no doubt as to who will impose their logic. This temporal contradiction had already been noted by Gramsci.

of this year. The country would then move from territorial decentralization of the regions to a form of decentralization that is also political.

The second of these events occurred in Brazil. In this case, the date February 21, 2007 becomes a symbol of another revolution in Latin America. On that day, President Ignacio "Lula"[1] da Silva signed the Presidential Decree 6047 *re-establishing the federal government's obligation to design and implement a National Territory Policy,* an issue that had disappeared from the national political agenda at the beginning of the twenty-first century. This Decree grants political and legal recognition to the new meso-regions formed as a result of civil society initiatives (initially in southern Brazil). These entities are composed of regions of adjoining territories belonging to different states. For example, the first of these is the MERCOSUR Northern Border Meso-Region, which includes the states of Rio Grande do Sul, Paraná and Santa Catarina, adjoining territorial sections. A real regional revolution!

According to Decree 6047, the National Policy for Regional Development defines regional development strategies in the following territorial scales:

(a) Macro-regional scale, for which the Superintendents of the North, Northeast and Central-West were recreated and identified as priorities
(b) Sub-regional or meso-regional scale, which is based on the definition of the *differentiated meso-regions* (currently 13 differentiated meso-regions and nine sub-regions)
(c) The semi-arid area, border area and Integrated Development Regions (RIDEs) are defined as priorities.

The greatest contribution to the issue of territorial development in Latin America found in the Decree is most likely the definition of the *Differentiated Meso-regions.* It states that: "... Differentiated Meso-Region is understood to mean the continuous sub-national space, smaller than existing or proposed macro-regions, with a common identity, which includes areas of one or more federal states, defined for purposes of identifying potential strengths and vulnerabilities that will guide the formulation of socio-economic, cultural, political, institutional and environmental objectives."

Not all the contents of Decree 6047 are worthy of praise. Its greatest weakness may be the lack of *completeness and uniqueness* that all *national* regionalization *must respect* in the interests of consistency of national territorial development policy. This is also a necessary condition for the mathematical modeling of some aspects of this policy.[2] It might seem at first glance that Brazil presents a high degree of decentralization given that it is has a federal government. However, history does not support this thesis at all.

As Celso Furtado (1999) argues, "We must recognize that centralism was instrumental in the formation phase of nationality and, to some extent, in the construction of an economic system that is integrated enough to allow for the absorption of modern technology. In a country with low income levels, regional fragmentation of the domestic market was a serious obstacle to the formation of an industrial system." He adds, "You cannot ignore the fact that the historical mission of centralism is spent."

A group of case studies that offer a wide range of analyses is found in the book *Políticas de desenvolvimento regional: desafíos e perspectivas á luz das experiências da União Europea e do Brasil* edited by Clelio Campolina Dinitz (2007). The study by Bandeira, Araujo, Becker, Haddad, and Galvao is particularly important in this field. A recent and significant contribution to studies of Brazil is the book *Governança territorial e desenvolvimento* (Dallabrida 2012).

Rui de Britto Alvares Affonso (1999) discusses the recurrent tension between centralization and decentralization *(decentralization by demand and decentralization by supply)* in Brazilian history. *At the end of his study he states*, "The remaining problem is the absence of an integrating perspective that is broad enough to restructure the foundations of the federative pacts in a context in which conflicts between spheres of government and the regions are expanding. The problem is compounded by the profound changes underway in the Brazilian economy, society, and in its international insertion."

One of the objectives of a national territorial development policy in a country like Brazil is to complete the construction of the nation in a global context that questions the importance of national governments, as Bertha Becker, the outstanding Brazilian geographer, writes. In that sense, Decree 6047 is a step ahead of the trend that was anticipated in the Constitutions of Colombia (1991), Peru (1993) and Argentina (1994).

All of these countries are pushing for a new form of regionalization through the formation of *associative regions,* between adjacent sub-national territories. They are introducing a strong democratic content by basing their efforts on the initiatives of the communities. The Colombian process, which is expressed in Articles 306 and 307 of the Constitution of 1991, is stopped. That is not the case in Argentina, where the Patagonian Region and Central Region have already been formed. The situation of Peru is similar. It has seen the formation of the La Libertad region in the north of the country. It is clear that what lies ahead is a gradual expansion of these examples, which the current economic crisis will favor given the need to expand the range of anti-crisis measures, not only from national governments, but also at regional level. Clearly, a country the size of Brazil, with its federal policy-making, can live with the problem of coordinating large and disparate systems.

The third event occurred in Washington. It concerns a report on the world economy that was published by the World Bank in 2009.

The World Bank publication, *World Development Report 2009:* was quite surprising. The first sentence of the Preface signed by Robert B. the World Bank President, reads as follows: "Production is concentrated in large cities, advanced provinces and wealthy nations." It may be said that the Bank has abandoned its belief in territorial floating economy, a belief so entrenched in many international organizations, even those that were icons of developmentist thinking decades ago. Many now highlight the importance of "the three Ds" (density, distance, and division) in development and promote *balanced growth and inclusive development.*

This "three Ds" approach provides a novel view that is not without interest and merit. For the World Bank, *density* is the most important dimension at the sub-national or local level, and indeed it is! Certain sizes and scales are essential for generating economies of scale and external economies, and proximity is a key factor in associativity in that it is a facilitator of trust (social capital). *Distance* from density is the most important dimension at the national geographical scale. The distance between prosperous areas and those which are lagging behind is crucial in efforts to disseminate progress. In this case, the reduction of the cost of overcoming the friction of this distance is an important tool, as is favoring labor mobility. According to the World Bank, *division* is the most important dimension from an international point of view. The concept of "division" is used here to denote the divisions associated with the impermeability of borders and differences in currency and regulations that hinder international trade. The race to sign bi- or multilateral free trade agreements is proof of this.

Of course, the World Bank has spoken *urbi et orbi* from its Washingtonian cathedral and the world must behave according to this new behavioral norm. We must pay attention to the territory. Welcome to the territory!

From another angle, the World Bank paper that I have cited has an impressively limited bibliography. Paul Krugman is not cited anywhere, not even in a footnote, despite the fact that he was the clear inspiration for the change in perspective. The same is true for Perroux, Boudeville, Rosenstein-Rodan, Myrdal, Hirschmann, Friedmann, Furtado and many other creators of thought on territorial development. ECLAC (Economic Commission for Latin America), which houses, *malgré tout,* ILPES (the Latin American and Caribbean Economic and Social Planning Institute), the clear Latin American institutional center which shares the approach that has now been (re)created by the World Bank, does not merit a reference either.

4.8 Conclusions: A Theory in Search of a Practice, or a Practice in Search of a Theory?

This is not a play on words but a fundamental question regarding the task at hand. In fact, the aforementioned seminar held in Bogota in 1979 was entitled *National Strategies of Regional Development.* The book that was produced as a result of the event was called *Experiences of Regional Planning in Latin America: A Theory in Search of a Practice.* Both titles reflect what seemed to be a vision of consensus: there is more theory than successful practices. Over time, this judgment has been called into question.

Three factors stand out as shortcomings: the lack of a *government policy* regarding territorial matters, the lack of scientific knowledge of the field in question, and the attachment to productive structures based on comparative advantages. There are several other issues to which I cannot refer given the limited space available to me in this format.

References

Althussser L (1969) Ideología y aparatos ideológicos del Estado, Freud y Lacan, http://www.sociologia.de

Barkin D, King T (1970) Desarrollo económico regional. Siglo XXI Editores, Mexico

Boisier S (1982) La vocación regionalista del Gobierno Militar. Revista EURE #72, Universidad Católica de Chile, Santiago de Chile

Boisier S (1986) La articulación Estado-Región: clave del desarrollo regional. Pensamiento Iberoamericano # 10, (Desarrollo Regional. Nuevos Desafíos), ICI/CEPAL, Madrid

Boisier S (2003) El desarrollo en su lugar, Serie GEOLIBROS. Instituto de Geografía, P. Universidad Católica de Chile, Santiago de Chile

Boisier S, Grillo C (1969) Sobre la comparación internacional de las disparidades regionales, Mimeographed document. ODEPLAN, Santiago de Chile

Boisier S, Cepeda F, Hilhorst J, Riffka S, Uribe-Echevarría F (Comps.) (1981) Experiencias de planificación regional en América Latina. Una teoría en busca de una práctica, ILPES/SIAP, Santiago de Chile

Bromley R (1990) Development, Underdevelopment, and National Spatial Organization, http://sites.maxwell.syr.edu/clag1990/bromley6.pdf

Camagni R (2000) Rationale, principles and issues for development policies in an era of globalization and localization: spatial perspectives. Politecnico de Milano, Milan

Campolina DC (ed) (2007) Regional development policy: Challenges and perspectives from the European Union and Brazilian experience. MNI, Brasilia

Cuervo LM (2003) Evolución reciente de las disparidades económicas territoriales en América Latina: estado del arte, recomendaciones de política y perspectivas de investigación, Serie Gestión Pública # 41, ILPES, Santiago de Chile

Dallabrida RV (coord.) (2012) Governanza territorial e desenvolvimento. UNC, Universidad de Contestado, S.C.

Dammert M (1999) Desborde territorial descentralista, edición propia, Lima, Peru

de Oliveira F (1977) Elegia para umare(li)giao. Editora Paz e Terra, Sao Paulo

Dembicz K (2005) La región y el desarrollo regional en los conceptos socioeconómicos de la CEPAL, Actas Latinoamericanas de Varsovia, Tomo 28, CESLA, University of Warsaw

Duncan R, Fuentes R (2006) Regional convergence in Chile: new tests, old results. Cuadernos de Economía, vol 43, Facultad de Ciencias Económicas, Pontificia Universidad Católica de Chile, Santiago de Chile

Finot I (2001) Descentralización en América Latina: cómo hacer viable el desarrollo local. Serie Gestión Pública # 38, ILPES, Santiago de Chile

Furtado C (1999) A nova dependencia. Paz e Terra, Sao Paulo

Friedmann J (1966) Regional development policy. A case study of Venezuela. MIT Press, Cambridge

Galvão Filgueira CA (2004) Política de Desenvolvimento Regional e Innovação. Garamond Universitaria, Rio de Janeiro

Germani G (1981) Sociology of modernization. Transaction Books, Rutgers, TSU, New Brunswick

Gilbert A, Goodman D (1976) Desigualdades regionales de ingreso y desarrollo económico: un enfoque critic, Revista EURE Vol. V, # 13, CIDU-IPU, Universidad Católica de Chile, Santiago de Chile

Higgins B, Savoie DJ (1995) Regional development, theories and their application. Transaction Publishers, New Brunswick/London

León A Dimensión territorial de las disparidades sociales. El caso de Colombia, Doc. CPRD-B/30, Programa de Capacitación, ILPES, Santiago de Chile (similar studies were published for Venezuela and Panama with the acronyms CPRD- B/29 and CPRD-B/28), undated document

Martín J (1984) Disparidades regionales y pobreza, Doc. CPRD-B/31, Programa de Capacitación, ILPES, Santiago de Chile

Rui de Brito Alvares A (1999) *Descentralizacao e Reforma do Estado: a Federacao Braileira na* Encruzilhada. Economia e Sociedade # 14, Campinas
Scott A (2009) Book review. J Econ Geogr 9:583–586, U.S.A
Silva I (2003) Disparidades, competitividad territorial y desarrollo local y regional en América Latina, Serie Gestión Pública # 33, ILPES, Santiago de Chile
Skoufias E, Lopez-Acevedo G (2009) Determinantes de las Desigualdades Regionales de Bienestar al Interior de los Países de América Latina, BIRF/BM, Washington, DC
Stöhr W (1972) Regional development. Experiences and prospects in Latin America. Mouton, Geneva
UNDP, Cooperación política para la descentralización del Estado, Santiago de Chile (undateddocument)
United Nations, DESA (2012) Urban population, development and the environment, New York
Utria R (2002) El desarrollo de las Naciones Hacia un nuevo paradigma. Sociedad Colombiana de Economistas, Bogotá
Véliz C (1982) La tradición centralista de América Latina. Editorial Ariel, Barcelona

Chapter 5
Growth and Regional Disparities in Latin America Concentration Processes and Regional Policy Challenges

Juan R. Cuadrado-Roura and Sergio Gonzalez-Catalán

5.1 Introduction

The focus of this chapter is centered on the process of product concentration and the evolution of regional disparities in Latin America and its relationship to countries' economic growth. For this purpose, a group of eight countries have been taken into account: Argentina, Bolivia, Brazil, Colombia, Chile, Mexico, Panama and Peru. To carry out the empirical analysis these countries offer the advantage of having uniform regional and national data that enables the comparison between them. Nevertheless, figures from Ecuador will also be considered to study some specific aspects, as regional disparities of income per capita, the concentration of population and the increasing exports of raw materials to other American, European and Asian economies.

Using regional GDP data, the analysis clearly establishes high levels of regional disparities and economic concentration in Latin America and that the countries' progress in both matters has been both limited and uneven. Although in various 'regions'[1] there has been positive economic growth, these advances have not been able to reduce the gaps that exist between them. In fact, many of those regions still remain stagnated and regional disparities trends have been stable in the countries throughout the last decades. This confirms the idea that high level regional inequalities persist in access to the wealth of its citizens, which at the same time

[1] Here we take as 'regions' the political administrative divisions named according to the different countries: states, provinces and regions.

J.R. Cuadrado-Roura (✉)
Department of Applied Economics, University of Alcalá, Madrid, Spain
e-mail: jr.cuadrado@uah.es

S. Gonzalez-Catalán
ILPES (Latin America and Caribe Institute of Economic and Social Planning), CEPAL, Santiago de Chile, Chile
e-mail: Sergio.Gonzalez@cepal.org

J.R. Cuadrado-Roura and P. Aroca (eds.), *Regional Problems and Policies in Latin America*, Advances in Spatial Science, DOI 10.1007/978-3-642-39674-8_5,

encourages also considering what effect those differences have on the activity and the overall economic performance of each country.

Regions with low levels of productivity could be, and in fact, have been, sources of low economic growth, that results in decrease of aggregated national growth. On the other hand, the high economic activity that other regions/provinces/departments have recently shown in Chile, Peru, Bolivia, Ecuador or Colombia is mainly due to the primary sector, which is receiving high external demand for goods, and results in high contributions to national GDP and an improvement in their relative economic ranking position within the country.

This shift, which national data conceal, raises questions about the long-term sustainability of this growth and for the destination of the funds obtained through exports, which are largely allocated to social policies and subsidies rather than to a genuine development policy. This kind of reallocation of resources does not contribute to structural changes in these regions or to reduction of interregional differences.

The empirical evidence obtained through several studies suggests that the level of regional inequalities, measured as differences in GDP per capita between regions, could provide medium and long-term obstacles to national GDP growth, including an increase in the gap between real and potential GDP. This justifies the need for systematic and long term strategies. In this matter, the role of a regional development policy is essential. Such policy should focus on both reducing regional income per capita disparities and on ensuring an inclusive economic growth that reduces social inequalities.

From these ideas and in accordance with the objectives stated at the beginning, the contents of the chapter are organized as follows. Section 5.2 provides some considerations regarding stylized facts and trends in recent decades in Latin America from the regional point of view. This presentation is a starting point for our analysis, which will focus primarily on the concentration of wealth and the evolution of interregional disparities that have occurred. These two are not, however, the only issues related to recent trends in Latin America. But we considered that it was necessary to describe those dominant tendencies as a framework for the analysis that is developed here.

Section 5.3 focuses on the territorially unbalanced economic growth that characterizes Latin America. References are taken from well calibrated data from eight countries that allow us to observe the relations between territorial inequalities, measured through a Gini territorial index, and economic growth, measured by changes in country GDP per capita. Section 5.4 explores in detail the relationship between economic growth and regional inequalities through a regression analysis that provides very significant results.

Finally, considering the results, Sect. 5.5 seeks to justify the need for regional policies aimed to the correction of regional disparities in Latin America, and the encouraging and developing of sustainable and long term growth policy. It was not imperative to close the chapter with reflections contained in Sect. 5.5,since any economic policy decision(including regional policy)involves introducing preferences and value judgments that cannot be derived from a scientific analysis.

However, in this section a few suggestions are made using experience and good practices from other countries. The chapter closes with brief endnotes that summarize the most important research results.

5.2 Regional Stylized Features and Trends in Latin America for the Last 35–40 Years

The evolution of Latin America economies at a regional scale allows the extraction of facts and dominating trends that have characterized them in the last decades. However, it's important to remember that there are important differences between countries, which respond not only to different scales but to different historic as well as cultural, political and economic outlines that have drawn the development of the Latin American and the Caribbean countries. Recall, for example, that Panama is a country whose extension is 27.5 times smaller than Colombia, with whom it shares a border, and represents only 0.9 % of the territory and 1.6 % of the population of Brazil. Uruguay is also equivalent to only 6.3 % of the Brazilian territory and an 8.7 % of Argentina.

However, establishing the existence of clear differences between Latin American countries – in terms of territory and population, history and culture – the study of their regional economy allows to pick out some facts and trends that can be qualified as 'stylized' and which are common to most of the Latin America countries. In our opinion, the most relevant on what has happened over the last four decades are the following[2]:

- High levels of product and population concentration in most countries.
- High regional economic disparities within countries that barely have declined in recent decades.
- Significant growth in some regions in recent years due to the exploitation and export of primary resources.
- Low progress in decentralization objectives.
- Lack of effective regional development policy or lack of continuity in several countries, replaced in recent years by social and income redistribution policy.

The characteristics of these dominant trends are discussed and illustrated below in a very synthetic way.[3]

---

[2] The origin of many of them is located in distant historical periods, but it has been since the 1950s. and 1960s. when these facts and trends are reinforced.

[3] Some of them could be clearly differentiated – for example, the concentration of production and population – and even incorporate some more, but we present the most remarkable from an economic and regional perspective.

5.2.1 Regional Product and Population Concentration

The trend towards spatial concentration of production and population is undoubtedly one of the dominant features in most of the countries in Latin America, although there are some differences between them. The capital of each state and its metropolitan area generally occupy a dominant position in this matter. This is something that also happens in many countries in the world, but not to the extent that has occurred in the Latin American region.

Some facts should be noted, in this regard.[4] In Brazil, the states located in the South Central region, including Sao Paulo as the dominant pole, represented 80 % of the country's production and 53 % of the population in 1970. Sao Paulo alone contributed around 38 % of GDP of the country with only 19 % of the population. Figures for 2009 indicate that this concentration has declined, but is still very significant: the macro south-central region of the country accounts for about 70 % of the country's GDP and the population has increased to nearly 60 %.

In Peru, the concentration levels were and still are very high. In 1970, Lima contributed to more than 55 % of GDP and 28 % of the national population. In 2007, the relative weight of the population of Lima was 34 % and the contribution to total country production was situated above 52 %, only three points below the level of the last 40 years.

In Chile, the Santiago metropolitan region represented 47.1 % of GDP and 36.7 % of the population in 1970 and four decades later both figures have risen to 49.1 % and 40.3 %, respectively. Something similar has happened in Argentina, where the metropolitan area of Buenos Aires is dominant both in population and its contribution to the national product. In 1970, the city and province of Buenos Aires accounted for 62.6 % and 50.3 % of the production and population respectively. Both percentages have declined (55.5 % of GDP and almost 46 % of the population in 2005), but the area is still very dominant in relation to the rest of the country.

Some countries show a comparatively lower concentration to the ones mentioned above, although the numbers are still maintained at very high levels. In Mexico, its metropolitan area (Mexico City and Mexico and Hidalgo states) currently represents just over 29 % of GDP (with a relative decline of four points from 1970) and 24.3 % of the population, a percentage level practically unchanged after four decades, although the area's total population has increased by more than ten million inhabitants. In the Mexican case, however, two facts should be noted. First, there has been some effect of productive activities spread from metropolitan cities cited above to other cities located in the State of Mexico (for example Toluca) and to other near states, like Queretaro and Guanajuato, besides Puebla and Aguascalientes. On the other hand, some northern states like Nuevo Leon, Chihuahua and Coahuila, have strengthened their weight due to industrial dynamism and to industrial exports (the 'maquila' industries).

In Colombia, the concentration in the capital area, Bogota, was and remains high (almost 30 % of production in 1975 and 26.3 % in 2009), but the weight of Antioquia and Valle del Cauca, which was already high in terms of production in

[4] See chapter written by J. Máttar and L. Riffo included in this book (Chap. 3)

the 1970s., has risen to almost 14 % and over 10 %, respectively, in late 2009. Several Colombian departments weighing less (Meta and Santander) have become increasingly important in the period, but at the same time, a number of other departments do not reach 1 % of total GDP or only slightly exceed it, although in terms of population, that weight is duplicated.

The analysis of recent trends in Latin America in terms of product spatial concentration shows at least two types of configurations: 'primatial' and 'multi-pole'. In Argentina, Chile and Peru a primatial structure is observed, which is characterized by a single region – the metropolitan area of the state capital – that concentrates economic activity. The multi-pole structure can be seen in Bolivia, Brazil, Colombia and Mexico, where economic activity is concentrated in more than one region. None of these countries have shown a strong tendency to decrease the concentration of population or product in the 1990–2010period (ECLAC 2009).

The same stagnation can be seen when monitoring trends of the geographic concentration index for GDP[5] from nine countries in Latin America (Fig. 5.1). Stable trends are observed in most countries, in other words, no strong increases or decreases in product concentration levels. The figure shows that the largest concentration index values correspond to Brazil, Peru, Colombia and Chile. Intermediate values are observed in Panama, Argentina and Mexico, while the lowest are Ecuador and Bolivia. The value of the index for the average of the OECD countries in 2005 was 0.43. Regarding the countries shown in Fig. 5.1, only Ecuador and Bolivia have product concentration levels below the OECD average.

Moreover, the strong concentration of production and population centres in some Latin American countries, that can even qualify as hyper-concentration in the case of Peru, Brazil, Argentina, Bolivia and Mexico, should be related to the central role that the nation's capital and its metropolitan area play. This is explained by centralization policies,[6] always enhancing the role of the state capital and the concentration of power.

5.2.2 High Regional Economic Disparities Within Countries That Barely Have Declined in Recent Decades

From the regional point of view, this is definitely a very dominant feature in virtually every country in Latin America. Extreme differences between regions within the same country vary between 4 and 5 times until ten or even 12 times between the richest region and the poorest in the country (CEPAL, 2010). The data that reflect regional disparities are indisputable. In Argentina, the relationship between GDP p.c. in Buenos Aires (metropolitan area) and the provinces of

[5] This index is the sum of the differences between surface and GDP ratio for country regions. The index takes values from 0 when the surface and GDP all have the same regional ratio and tends to 1 when the differences between product and area ratios of each region are higher.

[6] See chapters by S. Boisier and L.M. Cuervo and N. Cuervo in this book.

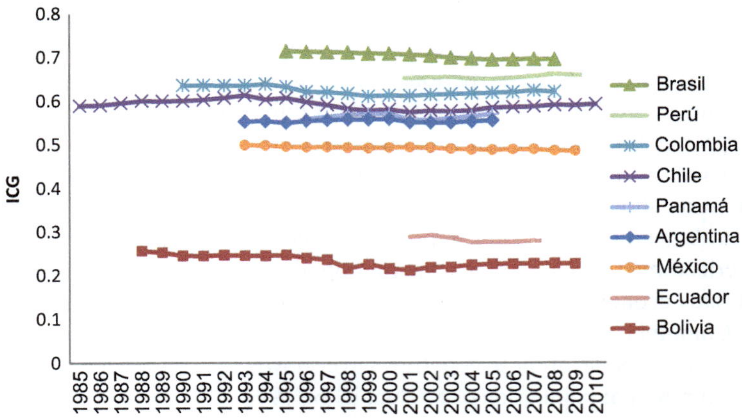

Fig. 5.1 Geographic concentration index for GDP for countries in Latin America 1985–2010 (Source: Cepal/ECLAC (2012), based on official country data)

Formosa and Santiago del Estero, shows a difference of almost 7.4 times, which was lower four decades ago. In Brazil, the difference between the state with highest GDP p.c. and the lowest state (Piauí) is 8.4 times, having decreased compared to 1970 due to the relative decline of Distrito Federal and Sao Paulo. In Peru, the difference between the region with highest GDP p. c and the lowest is 8.1 times, Lima has a GDP pc which is five times higher than the poorest region, although the capital has concentrated population coming from the poorest regions, which has resulted in a lower GDP p.c. growth. Finally, in Mexico, Campeche GDP p.c. is equivalent to almost 11 times than the one of Chiapas.

When considering all regions from each country, the trend observed in regional disparities is practically stable. Obviously this hides movements related to progress in some areas and setbacks in others. Only a few of the Latin American countries in our study recorded a slight tendency to interregional convergence. Figure 5.2 shows the results obtained when estimating the Gini coefficient of regional inequalities during the period 1995–2009 for nine countries.[7] Higher values correspond to countries where regional disparities are greater, in which Panama, Colombia,

[7] The Gini coefficient expresses regional differences in GDP per capita and varies in a range between 0 (low disparity) and 1 (high disparity). Regions are defined as the first subnational administrative scale.

Gini coefficient of regional inequalities: $\frac{2}{N-1} * \sum_{i=1}^{N-1}(F_i - Q_i) \quad F_i = \frac{i}{N} \quad Q = \frac{\sum_{j=1}^{i} y_i}{\sum_{j=1}^{N} y_j}$

$y_{i:}$ GDP per capita for region i N: number of regions

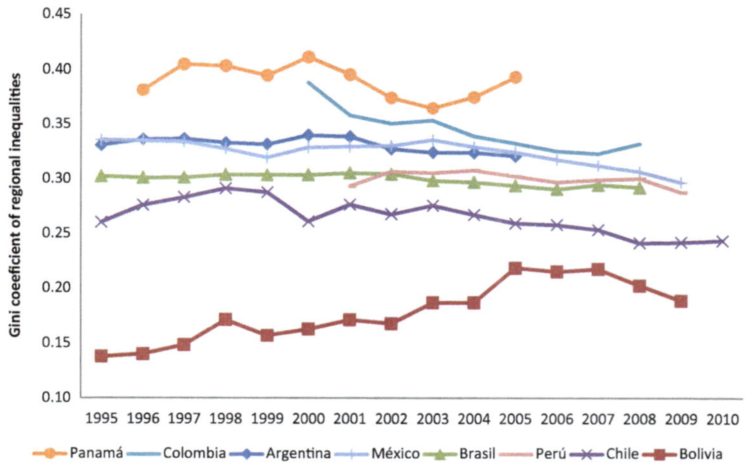

Fig. 5.2 Gini coefficient of regional inequalities during the period 1995–2009 (Source: Cepal (2012), based on official country data)

Argentina and Mexico are included. Brazil and Peru recorded slightly lower levels of regional disparity and the lowest levels correspond to Chile and Bolivia.

More important is to observe the evolution of disparities over time, allowing us to observe either a convergent or a divergent trend. What our estimation shows (Fig. 5.2) is, as anticipated, a significant indicator of stability, with a very slight converging trend since 2003 in Chile, Colombia and Mexico. Bolivia, which recorded almost divergence from 1995 to 2007, seems to be undergoing a process of convergence in recent years. Nevertheless, we must take into account, that the exploitation of primary resources is driving to the expansion of some very specific regions, which undoubtedly influences the slight trend showed by our analysis.

5.2.3 Significant Growth in Some Regions in Recent Years Due to the Exploitation and Export of Primary Resources

This is also a feature that characterizes the evolution of many Latin American countries in the past and in recent years. The exploitation of primary resources, whether mineral, energy related or agricultural, has always played an important role in the development of a good number of countries in the region. Historically, Chile, Mexico, Colombia, Peru and others lived in the past because of strong economic expansion stages based mainly on the exploitation of mineral resources. Strong

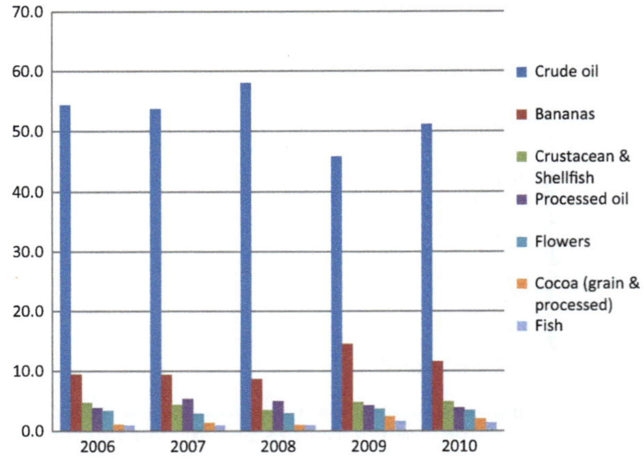

Fig. 5.3 Ecuador – primary products exported 2006–2010 (in % of total exports) (Source: Figures from the World Bank data base and the Statistic Services of each country)

external demand was usually the driving factor, but not infrequently these very positive trajectories were dashed by the fall – sometimes dramatic – of such external demand due to the evolution of the international situation, the relative prices or the appearance of substitutes.[8]

Since the beginning of this century, and even somewhat earlier, several Latin American countries have been experiencing, again, an extremely positive step in terms of the exploitation of some commodities, which are subject to strong external demand and enjoying high prices in the markets, like copper, gas, oil, zinc, gold, soybeans, cocoa, flowers and fish. The exploitation of these resources – in many cases with great intensity – is allowing the provinces or departments to have high rates of GDP growth, which in turn contributes to strong growth rates of country GDP.

The following figures (Figs. 5.3, 5.4, and 5.5) show the case of three countries – Ecuador, Bolivia and Peru – where primary exports have expanded strongly. The regions obtained logically significant growth of GDP, although the real impact the growth has on them is doubtful, from a regional development point of view and regarding modification of their productive structures in the medium/long term. In fact, we must question the long-term sustainability of growth through primary exports. Also we must consider the effect that the exploitation of some mining and energy products generate on the environment.

Examples of 'successful' regional growth due to natural resource exploitation are Atacama and Antofagasta in Chile, Santa Cruz, Chubut and Tierra del Fuego in Argentina, Arequipa, Loreto and Libertad in Peru, some regions of northeastern

[8] A paradigmatic example is the exploitation of nitrates in Chile, Peru and Bolivia in the nineteenth century and its rapid decline after 1920 as a result of the occurrence of chemical nitrates and fertilizers

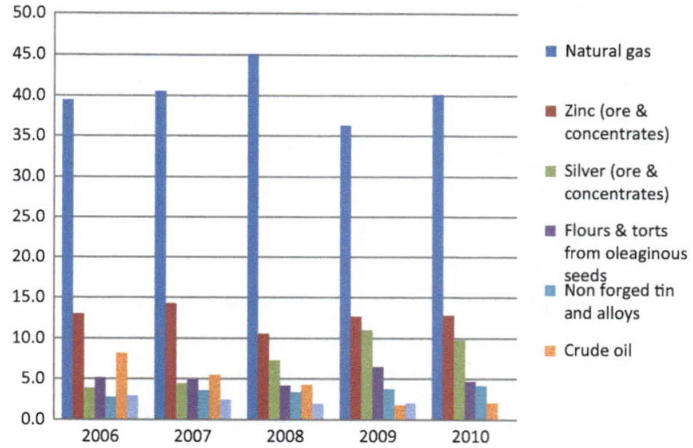

Fig. 5.4 Bolivia – primary product exported 2006–2010 (in % of total exports) (Source: Figures from the World Bank data base and the Statistic Services of each country)

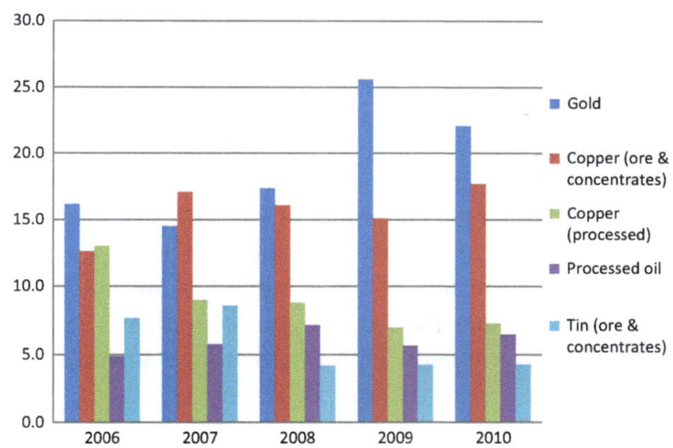

Fig. 5.5 Peru – primary products exported 2006–2010 (in % of total exports) (Source: Figures from the World Bank data base and the Statistic Services of each country)

Brazil, through agricultural production and export mining, and the department of Tarija in Bolivia, due to gas exploitation. Some authors have called this kind of success the 'curse' of natural resource abundance, because instead of helping them in the generation of economic development, it condemns them in some way to a final situation of stagnation and social conflict (Auty 1993; Gavin and Hausmann 1998; Sachs and Warner 1995, 2001).

5.2.4 Limited Progress on Political and Administrative Decentralization

Some Latin American countries are defined constitutionally as federal states, as it is the cases of Mexico and Brazil. Others have made political and even legislative commitments to move towards decentralization, like Chile and, more recently,

Bolivia, Ecuador and other states of the region. However, a very common feature in Latin American countries is the preference for a highly centralized political organization. From the regional point of view, this means that the basic decisions that could be placed on what is understood as a regional policy – infrastructure development, industry promotion, granting benefits to the location, etc. – are taken almost exclusively at the central level. Furthermore, its implementation is instructed by the central government of the country, using established channels; governors, delegates from government or ministries, and even delegates clearly defined as an organization of regional action. Sergio Boisier has clearly described this feature in Latin America, which can be seen in most of the regional policy experiences carried out in the region.

In recent years, the concern about citizen involvement in the development process of different regions, departments or provinces has rather clearly expanded in several countries. In fact, some new initiatives have been approved that might be important on modifying the centralizing trend we have outlined. In 2005, Chile adopted an amendment to the Constitution that proclaims the country's decentralization objective, while approving the creation of new regions. In Brazil, in2007, President Lula signed a presidential decree mandating design a national regional policy. Other countries have taken steps in the 'decentralization' direction or recognition of the regions role in the overall development of the country, like Bolivia, which has incorporated the regional autonomy principle in its new constitution, although the commitment has hardly developed. Ecuador has also officially endorsed a process aimed at decentralization.

So far, the results of these initiatives are not too obvious. It may be early to speculate whether the tendency to 'centralism' and the maintenance of power by national governments will finally move towards an effective decentralization process.

5.2.5 *Regional Development Policies Occupy a Very Secondary Position and Are Subordinated to Sectoral and Macroeconomic Policy*

During the period identified with import substitution policy[9] many countries launched regional development policies largely inspired by the ones that had been designed in some European countries, such as France or Italy. Two well-known and studied examples are Venezuela and Brazil, but other countries – Colombia, Peru, Argentina and Chile, among others – also developed initiatives to promote the industrialization of particularly lagged sectors. For this purpose instruments related to public enterprises and the granting of incentives to attract investment allocation in some particularly underdeveloped regions were used.

[9] See the chapter written by J. Máttar y L. Riffo on this volume (Chap. 3).

The shift that took place in most Latin American countries since the mid-1980s., related to neoliberal policies, privatization, foreign investment and trade liberalization, settled in the Washington Consensus in the early 1990s, and determined the disappearance of conventional regional policies. Actually, these had already disappeared from the agendas of Latin American governments, concerned about overcoming the crisis that led to the highly interventionist policies of the past, as well as macroeconomic imbalances (inflation, trade deficit, debt) that they had to face.

The clearest consequence is that, with specific exceptions, few regional development plans that favor backward provinces or departments were designed and approved. It can also be argued that land use planning, in the French manner, has not been very present, although in the previous decades it had its place, even if sometimes it was much more of a policy formulation rather than a true framework to be reflected on sectoral, infrastructure development and education and health policy.

In the last decade, public policy has been oriented towards social policy, where the income redistribution has played a major role. Venezuela, Bolivia, Ecuador and Brazil are good examples. In the first three cases, the abundant resources obtained through primary exports have provided funding for the implementation of such policy, which can be better identified with an income redistribution policy and not with a regional development policy. These are accompanied by education policy and support to higher education (Ecuador), subsidy for primary goods, social housing schemes and public health policy. Although some of these actions have been positive for very poor regions, it is clear that their objectives cannot be identified with what should be a regional development policy in favor of the most backward regions, based on medium/long term approaches to modify production structures, diversify production and promote growth and the creation of long-term sustainable jobs.

Undoubtedly, social policies often have more immediate results than policies that promote structural changes in undeveloped areas or conversion issues, so they have greater political appeal. Brazil may be the country that has made the greater effort to combine social and regional development policies. In other cases – Mexico, Argentina, Chile and others – regional development policies have been – for years – practically absent from the government objectives. This does not prevent the government from designing very ambitious if not utopic regional plans, as the 'Plan Puebla-Panama' (later re-named 'Project Mesoamerica') in 2001, conceived in Mexico and intended for the further the development for South and southeast Mexico and for strengthening cooperation and coordination with Central American countries. This important plan has been languishing due to the lack of financial resources and the postponement of regional integration priorities and objective.

5.3 Spatial Concentration of Wealth, Regional Disparities and Territorial Performance

Knowing the trends and traits in Latin America regarding spatial concentration of wealth and population and territorial disparities, it is important to establish what kind of relationship exists between these factors and how they affect the economic and social performance of the territories and countries. There is broad debate concerning urban concentration levels of wealth and population and its relationship to the economic and social performance. The question about the relationship between variables associated with regional concentration of wealth/population and economic/social performance is less clear and hasn't been studied with such depth.

Wheaton and Shishido (1981) suggest the existence of a U-shaped relationship between the degree of decentralization, measured as the inverse value of urban primacy index, and level of development, measured by the value of country GDP p.c. In their view, an increase in the levels of GDP p.c. initially will be accompanied by greater centralization up to a certain level and then as GDP p.c. grows an increased level of decentralization will occur.

Henderson (2000) states that urban concentration levels are a key factor in country growth and that the relationship between growth and urban concentration is not linear, but also with a U-shaped in which the growth rate increases as the degree of urban concentration increases in the country and decreases after reaching certain level of urban concentration. Henderson also argues that there is an optimal degree of urban concentration which maximizes a country's growth and that this optimal level varies according to the level of country development. Under this logic, there will be high growth losses in non-optimal levels of urban concentration. He also establishes a curvilinear between regional disparities and levels of urban primacy. In the case of Chile, for example, while the concentration of population and the product have increased between 1990 and 2007, territorial disparities levels decreased slightly (Cuervo and González 2010).

Nevertheless, the relationship between growth and regional disparities was approached initially by Jeffrey Williamson (1965). In his well-known article on the evolution of differences in state per capita income in the U.S. he demonstrated that as state economic growth begins inequality increases and then decreases in the presence of high levels of development. There is evidence, as shown above, that Latin America and the Caribbean have very high levels of inequality, which is also expressed in territorial disparities. However, De Mattos (1986) suggests that in Latin America the theoretical approaches about concentration levels and disparities are not met, due to the presence of structural rigidity.

Yet the debate persists about the need for no government intervention in order to take advantage of economies of agglomeration and to allow economic development processes with geographically unbalanced growth, but ensuring at the same time, inclusive development (World Bank 2009). But in Latin America territories with low population density (hab./km^2) have managed to maintain high levels of growth

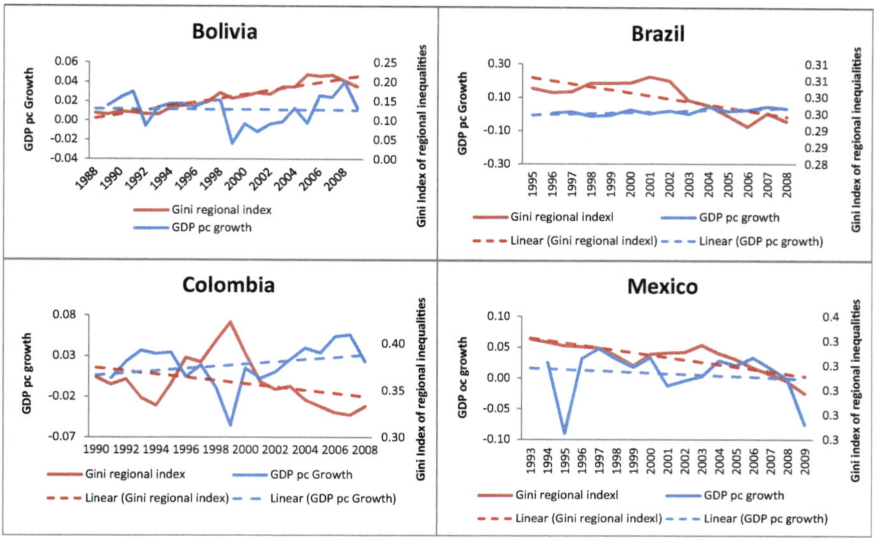

Fig. 5.6 Country GDP p.c. growth (Expressed as a percentage of regionalized GDP annual growth (sum of all regional GDP). It does not include extra-regional GDP) and regional inequality Gini index (*% y Coefficient*)

during the period 1990–2007, so it seems that economies of agglomeration are not a requirement to achieve a sustained growth process and economic development (Panorama of Territorial development; CEPAL 2010).

While high levels of regional disparities result in an unequal access to welfare between territories, what is the effect of these inequalities on economic performance? To answer this question, Figs. 5.6 and 5.7 show the evolution of growth and an regional inequality Gini coefficient in eight Latin American countries. In dotted lines trends in both indicators are presented. Overall, in the sample of countries, the existence of a negative relationship between regional inequalities and growth of GDP pc is seen. Although it is not initially possible to demonstrate that the level of regional disparities determines the level of country growth, or vice versa, this data suggests that there is a relationship between the economic growth of countries and the levels of territorial inequalities.

Research that deals with the relationship between national growth and regional disparities is rare and has not yet established a clear relationship between the two variables. Productivity gaps between regions can contribute to the discussion on this relationship. Gatto (2007) notes that in Argentina, the post-crisis macroeconomic conditions from 2001 to 2002 enabled strong economic growth and exports for several provinces, but that this was conditioned by their productive profile. In some provinces entrepreneurial, human, technological, and financial skills were deficient, leading to unequal production rates.

Gatto also states that the lag in some regions of Argentina is mainly due to de-accumulation of public and private investment that occurs in regions that lack

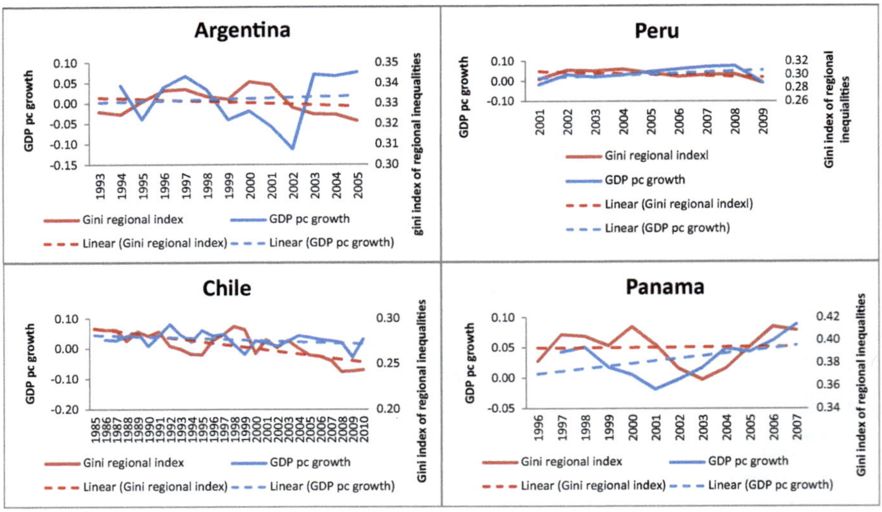

Fig. 5.7 Country GDP p.c. growth and regional inequality Gini index(*% y Coefficient*) (Source: authors based on country official data)

productive, social and human capital. He also concludes that the territory, defined as a space of socioeconomic and cultural relationships, has an influence on aggravating, containment or improving socio-economic inequalities and can become a specific objective for socio-economic policy in order to improve and transform the lives of large population groups that otherwise can't be achieved with a general (national) or sector policy instrument.

Regions with low productivity can be a source of lower growth, affecting national aggregate growth. This may be exacerbated in the presence of high levels of productivity gaps between regions. Gaps in productivity between regions reduce potential growth, thus domestic growth will be lower. Another effect on national growth can be caused by the pattern of investments in the presence of high levels of regional productivity gaps, as these will be aimed at the most productive regions, which already have capital and labor availability, in order to maximize returns, but at the expense of the loss of growth potential of regions with lower productivity.

Other effects can be explained by neo-classical economic theory and refer to the existence of saturation points produced by negative externalities from the agglomeration processes (increase in rent prices, land prices, pollution, increased time of travel and other difficulties in transportation). Investment in dense rare as will lead to a diminishing of marginal product, so that in larger and denser territories, production and population will present a saturation process that will result in lower growth levels, which have a negative effect on national aggregate output.

Although a clear link between regional disparities and growth has not been established, Barro (2008) has studied the impact of income inequality on national economic growth using panel data for several countries between 1960 and 2000. The results conclude that there is a negative relationship between the levels of income Gini coefficient and levels of economic growth of the countries. He also states that the impact of income inequality on growth is stronger in poor countries. Barro concludes that the relationship between the initial level of GDP pc and growth is given by the Kuznets curve. Inequalities increase at low levels of GDP pc and then decrease once high levels are reached. Based on this model, and using information on per capita GDP from 9 Latin American countries (Argentina, Bolivia, Brazil, Chile, Colombia, Ecuador, Mexico, Panama and Peru), results of empirical research to determine the relationship between regional disparities and national growth are shown below.

5.4 Regional Inequalities and Growth: Empirical Evidence

To determine whether there is a causal link between regional disparities and national growth a regression analysis is performed. The dependent variable is annual country per capita GDP growth and the independent variable is the level of regional inequalities in the previous period. This analysis will capture the effect that regional disparity levels have on national growth.

Based on the model of Barro (2008) we use national GDP pc growth and the Gini coefficient of regional disparities lagged in one period. The analysis uses data from1995 to 2008 due to uniformity and availability of data for the countries. Subperiods 1995–2000 and 2000–2008 are also analyzed; in these periods is where stable and convergent trends are observed in several countries.

The model is expressed in Eq. 5.1 below:

$$\text{GDPpc growth}_{i,t} = \alpha + \beta_i X_{i,t} + \lambda \text{ regional Gini coefficient}_{i,t-1} + \mu_i$$

where

GDPpc growth$_{i,t}$ = Annual GDP per capita growth from country i in year *t (percentage)*
Xi,t = Binary variable for country i
Regional Gini coefficient$_{i,t-1}$ = Gini coefficient of regional inequalities for country i in year *t-1 (coefficient)*
μ_i = error

The estimation is made using a fixed effects model using Ordinary Least Squares.[10]

The results of the fixed effects model for the nine countries that have been taken as reference show the existence of a negative relationship between national GDP pc growth and regional inequality level lagged in a year (Table 5.1). For the

[10] Panel data from nine countries is used in the analysis (Argentina, Bolivia, Brazil, Colombia, Chile, Mexico, Panama, Ecuador, Peru) for the 1988–2010 period. The data corresponds to an unbalanced panel, due to lack of information for all the years in the period.

Table 5.1 Results for the fixed effects model for national growth and regional disparities

Period	Coefficient	Standard error	t-statistic	P value	Significance (5%)	R-2
1995–2008	−0.349335	0.140509	−2.486212	0.0148	SI	0.278670
1995–2000	−1.152043	0.228128	−5.049992	0.0000	SI	0.585126
2000–2008	−0.341945	0.162250	−2.107523	0.0393	SI	0.310420

Source: Authors elaboration using countries official data and (CEPAL 2012). The period 1995−2000 period does not include information for Colombia, Peru y Ecuador

1995–2008 period we can observe a negative coefficient (−0.349335) associated to the Gini coefficient of regional inequalities lagged in a year, with a 5 % of significance. The negativity of the coefficient indicates that a higher level of regional disparity has an adverse effect on GDP per capita growth for the following year, in other words, the high level of regional disparities will result in lower country growth.

For 1995–2000 and 2000–2008, statistically significant coefficients with negative values are also obtained. However, the magnitude of the coefficient and R2 value are higher in 1995–2000, indicating that regional disparities had a stronger effect on the level of aggregate growth in this period and that the model is explaining a greater proportion of the variability of growth.

These results allow us to establish that in these Latin American countries the level of regional disparities between 1995 and 2008 has had a negative impact on national economic growth. Therefore, a reduction of regional disparities would be important not only to ensure greater population welfare, but also to allow higher levels of economic growth.

5.5 The Need for Regional Development Policy and the Lessons from International Experience

Economists and policy-makers know that national economies, as well as world economy, are developed unevenly from the spatial perspective. Economic activity and population tend to concentrate and this involves a self-feeding process in which concentration stimulates growth through the productive potential due to the proximity between enterprises and individuals. Agglomeration economies reflect the economy of scale's cumulative effect; greater labor market supply, forward and backward link ages of production units, networks effects, spill-over and other internal and external economies that firms may be able to exploit when activity is geographically concentrated (OECD 2012).

Evidently, economic forces alone do not explain regional imbalances or the spatial concentration process. The territories show differences in resource endowments and offer certain advantages and disadvantages in order to achieve a development process. The soil, climate, geographical position and endowments may be considered too simple explanations of regional disparities (Higgins and Savoie 1995), but no one denies that they play an important role. Human and cultural factors, which could be considered 'mobile' compared to natural resources or geographical conditions, are also closely linked to the territory. In any case, there are numerous examples showing that the lack of natural resources cannot be an impediment to economic development if the answer to the 'challenge' – in the sense of Toynbee – determines the development of entrepreneurial, organizational and specialization senses, or the application of disciplined principles of conduct and assessment.

Whatever the reasons for unbalanced regional development and concentration, what is clear is that both – regional disparities and concentration- are very present in Latin America, as shown in the three previous sections. This suggests the need to implement regional development policies to reduce the differences between the most dynamic and the stagnated regions and to balance the concentration process.

The question is, in any case, very clear: Why governments should worry about improving performance of the less developed regions, instead of focusing only on a few key regions as engines of growth?

This is certainly an important question, posed also by the OECD (2012). The answer is not an easy one. In fact, economics offers several arguments to disagree with government intervention, as has been shown for years by the supporters of the 'school of divergence' (from Myrdal and Hirschman to Thirlwall and other contemporary authors), supporting only the need for the authorities to correct territorial imbalances produced by market mechanisms, arguing that the free mobility of capital and labor eventually will lead to convergence in the long term (as argued also by the neoclassical approach of the 1960s., and still do today).

Underdeveloped regions – as emphasized by (OECD 2012) – are often seen as a negative factor or as national performance obstacle rather than strengths or advantages to be potentially exploited. OECD further notes that "in the past, most policies aimed at supporting such regions sought to "prop them up" through fiscal transfers and subsidies, an approach that yielded very poor results. However, a new OECD report: Promoting Growth in All Regions (2012), provides fresh analysis that shows how relatively backward regions can in fact be potentially important sources of growth, but that a very different approach is needed to tap that potential" (p. 1).

A striking result from research by OECD (2009b , 2011) is based on analysis of the member countries and regional case studies, and states that the less developed regions make a vital contribution to national growth. In fact, during 1995–2007, such regions accounted for 43 % of aggregate OECD growth. It also notes that the predominantly rural regions have, on average, enjoyed faster growth than urban or intermediate regions. Concentration of economic activity and population is neither necessary nor sufficient for success.

Although OECD countries are quite different from those in Latin America (Chile and Mexico are OECD members and Brazil is in the process), these results should be taken into account. Likewise, results reported in the preceding sections of this chapter suggest that it would be very positive, both for country and regions, to implement policies that correct regional disparities and the high concentration that characterizes most Latin American countries.

If economic potential of poorly developed regions (provinces, states, departments) is put into value they can contribute significantly to national growth, and at the same time will improve the economic welfare and stability of its people. Internal migration processes have costs that are not valued by the market and high concentration of population and production in certain areas also carries important social costs. Finally, developing a territory can bring benefits to the whole economy, not only because of its direct contribution to growth but also because of the use of otherwise abandoned facilities and resources. The efficient allocation of resources is not guaranteed by the market and its adjustment mechanisms, but they do determine the under–utilization marginalized regions.

Besides economic arguments there are ethical arguments (equal living conditions and equal distribution of benefits to the population) and political arguments (the existence of large economic and welfare differences among regions is not socially or politically acceptable and has the risk of generating political and social instability), which also justifies the need to carry out regional development policies (RDP).

As outlined in Sect. 5.2, the majority of Latin American countries haven't applied clear nor effective RDP for years. In some of them, the place of these policies has been occupied by social welfare focalized on individuals and families, not the region. In others, there are regional programs, but with ineffective implementation, either because of lack of resources or by the political changes in governments, that do not undertake long-term projects. Interesting initiatives in Latin America are the "National Regional Strategy" in Ecuador, the strategic territorial "Bicentennial Plan: Towards 2021" in Peru, the "National development and land use policy" in Argentina and the "Regional Development Policy" in Brazil. In urban areas specific policies have been developed, some successful, though very disassociated from the regional and national levels (Rojas et al. 2008).

It would be inappropriate to try to develop here how the RDP should be formulated, mainly because of the fact that such policies must always conform to the conditions of each country and its regions, as well as objectives to be achieved.

However, it does seem possible to learn some lessons from both the past experience with in Latin America, as from the European Union and some member countries of the OECD. The analysis and review of many of them can point out some principles that should prevail, and some conclusions about "what we have learned" (Cuadrado-Roura 2010, 2012).

There are **three principles** that experience shows that should be taken into account as a starting point for a Regional Development Policy:

- **Concentration**. Interventions or actions of the RDP should focus on specific geographical areas in order to achieve maximum effectiveness. It makes no sense to pretend RDP that benefits all regions. The RDP should be selective and directed essentially to try to boost the less developed regions. There is no sense in a "sprinkler type" policy which profits all regions.[11] To narrow the scope or

[11] For example, the EU has rectified its regional policy towards increasing shares and benefits for prioritized regions according to a criterion: that GDP pc. is below 75 % of the Community average. The margin for grant aid to the remaining regions has been reduced, linking them with the general objectives of the Community.

areas that may be 'eligible' to benefit from RDPsetting a threshold is useful; for example, a benefit directed only to regions whose GDP pc is below 50 or 55 % of the national average. (Obviously, this principle does not apply to 'land use planning', which by its very nature must include the entire country and even coordinate with other neighboring countries).

- **Medium/long term programs**. The RDP should be programmed for periods exceeding the duration of governments (national and regional); the lack of continuity will result in failure. All RDP should always have long time horizon, because structural change, development of new activities or empowering others require time and continuity. Thus, the RDP should be a state policy, not a government policy. The duration of a regional program should be 5–6 years with the possibility of continuing for a second period of similar duration.
- **Co-participation**. Although the central government takes significant responsibility for the design, realization and conducting a RDP, it is necessary to involve regional authorities and representative social partners. Both the diagnosis and the priorities should be set together through a consensual process and such co-operation must also be present along the implementation of programs and activities.

In addition to these principles, some RDP have established '**additionality**',[12] so that the actions that the central government or the local authorities had already planned on the basis of regular budget resources are not taken as a part of the RDP. This principle also applies for large public companies investments. Thus, this principle implies that there will be an 'additional' financial, political and economic effort.

On a more concrete level, the experiences of RDP also allow drawing some guidelines for the objectives, strategy and regional policy instruments (Cuadrado-Roura 2012). Objectives and strategies should be consistent with the current situation, characterized by the internationalization of the economies (which implies that RDP results must be competitive and sustainable in the long term).

The main guidelines are:

- A RDP is not a redistribution policy. Its objectives are to remove obstacles and enable development of lagging regions and to promote long-term structural changes in the production scheme. It cannot be a social welfare policy, nor guided only by ethics and equality.
- The 'regions' (departments, provinces, states) are always 'open economies', which means there is no room for isolated projects or for promoting activities only on a local or regional level. New activities must be competitive nationally and internationally.
- Making a region 'competitive' means that a positive effect is added to the competitiveness of a company installed in the territory. To achieve that status action in three areas is required: financial capital, human capital and public capital.

---

[12] For example: in the European Union.

- Regarding the instruments the RDP has moved from a public support and incentives system (credit, tax, etc.) to a more 'horizontal' scheme, aimed at the production structure of regions and the increasing companies efficiency and competitiveness, by improving basic infrastructure, providing innovation facilities for the development of new technologies, business services, supporting exports, among other initiatives.
- Public companies can play an important role in the development of stagnated regions, but always under the condition that they operate with a high level of efficiency. There is much experience regarding the perverse effect of public companies with no prospect of long-term sustainability.
- Modern RDP emphasize two key factors for development: human capital and 'entrepreneur' support.
- Experience shows that some institutions and regional development instruments (Development Agencies, Institutes for small and medium company support, technology parks, business networks, etc.) work effectively when social actors – employers, trade unions, chambers of commerce – participate and engage in their activity. To do this, the public authority must give the leading role to other actors.
- The RDP must consider real possibilities of development in each region. This means that it is pointless to imitate or copy instruments or schemes that may have been successful in other regions (e.g. high technology areas) and underestimate the potential of the available natural resources, agricultural products and livestock or certain handcrafts by increasing their added value.
- The efficiency and effectiveness of any PDR is always a long-term project and its main enemies are improvisation and changes in guidelines or strategy.
- The RDP should have evaluation mechanisms. *Ex ante* to assess its coherence, *on going* to assess their development and midterm results, and *ex post* at the end of the period (5–6 years). The evaluation should be objective and technical, carried out by an outside party and with measurable objectives.

5.6 Final Remarks

The purpose of this chapter has been to link regional disparities and product/population concentration in Latin America with its influence on the overall economic country performance.

To meet this purpose the starting point was to highlight some stylized facts that characterize the behavior of regional economy in recent decades. Among them, the tenacious process of economic and demographic concentration that has occurred from the territorial point of view, the fact that regional inequalities are much higher than anywhere else in the last decades. Other features can be identified; centralized decision–making, high economic performance of some regions thanks to the exploitation and export of natural resources and the almost total lack, in recent years, of regional development policies.

Sections 5.3 and 5.4 are the core of the chapter. In them, the reality of interregional disparities and the concentration of production are analyzed using a sample of nine countries in Latin America. Using econometric techniques we reached the thesis, also supported by several authors, that regional disparities apparently have a negative effect on aggregate growth of the country. The results suggest that regional disparities are a burden to national economic development. Recent studies of the OECD (2012) reinforce the validity of this thesis and state that in advanced countries, the least developed regions contribute about 43 % to aggregate growth in the OECD, and predominantly rural regions have presented a faster average growth than intermediate, urban and developed regions.

This invites us to reflect on the need for a regional development policy (RDP) of a highly selective character and medium to long term target for countries in Latin America. This is clearly supported by economic arguments, as well by other ones related to the achievement of equality within countries. Political reasons and social cohesion are also very relevant. Section 5.5 presents some principles and possible aspects to consider in terms of objectives, strategies and instruments of RDP, drawn from international experiences. We pointed out, however, that any policy must adjust to country specifications and, especially, to regional characteristics, problems and potentials.

References

Auty RM (1993) Sustaining development in mineral economies: the resource curse thesis. Routledge, London

Barro R (2008) Inequality and growth revisited. Working papers on regional economic integration, n. 11. Office of Regional Economic Integration. Asian Development Bank

Cepal (2009) Economía y territorio en América Latina y el Caribe: desigualdades y políticas. Libros de la Cepal, Santiago, p 206, n. 99

Cepal (2010) La hora de la igualdad: brechas por cerrar, caminos por abrir. Documento del Trigésimo tercer período de Sesiones de la CEPAL. Santiago. 289 pp

Cepal (2010b) Panorama del desarrollo territorial en América Latina y el Caribe. Documento de proyecto, Santiago, p 165

Cepal (2012) Cambio estructural para la Igualdad: una versión integrada del desarrollo. Documento del Trigésimo cuarto período de Sesiones de la CEPAL, Santiago, p 330

Cuadrado-Roura JR (ed) (2010) Regional policy, economic growth and convergence. Springer, Berlin

Cuadrado-Roura JR (2012) Regional policies. What (it seems) we have learned from the European experiences. In: Cook P, Parrilli D, Curbelo JL (eds) Innovation, global change and territorial resilience. E. Elgar, Cheltenham, ch. 14

Cuervo L, González S (2010) Concentración espacial y disparidades económicas territoriales en Chile. Revista Chilena de Estudios Regionales 2(1):25–37, Temuco

De Mattos C (1986) Paradigmas, Modelos y Estrategias en la Práctica Latinoamericana de planificación regional. Pensamiento Iberoamericano Nº10, CEPAL/ICI, Madrid, España

Gatto F (2007) Crecimiento económico y desigualdades territoriales: algunos limites estructurales para lograr una mayor equidad. Documento de proyecto de la CEPAL. Crisis, Recuperación y Nuevos dilemas: la economía Argentina 2002–2007. Oficina de la Cepal en Buenos Aires

Gavin M, Hausman R (1998) Nature, development and distribution in Latin America: evidence on the role of geography, climate and natural resources. Working Paper No. 378, Washington, DC: I-A Devt. Bank

Henderson V (2000) How urban concentration affects economic growth. Policy Research Working Paper no. 2326. The World Bank, Development Research Group, Washington, D.C. United States

Higgins B, Savoie DJ (1995) Regional development theories and their application. Transaction Publishers, New Brunswick

OECD (2009a) Territorial reviews: Chile. OECD, Paris

OECD (2009b) How regions grow: trends and analysis. OECD, Paris

OECD (2011) Regional outlook: building resilient regions for stronger economies. OECD, Paris

OECD (2012) Promoting growth in all regions. OECD, Paris, March

Rojas E, Cuadrado-Roura JR, Fdez-Güell JM (2008) Governing the metropolis. Principles and cases. D. Rockefeller Center, Harvard University and IADB

Sachs JD, Warner A (1995) Natural resource abundance and economic growth. National Bureau of Economic Research Working Paper No. 5398, National Bureau of Economic Research, Cambridge

Sachs JD, Warner AM (2001) The curse of natural resources. Eur Econ Review 45(4–6):827–838, Elsevier, http://ideas.repec.org/a/eee/eecrev/v45y2001i4-6p827-838.html

Wheaton W, Shishido H (1981) Urban concentration, agglomeration economies, and the level of economic development. Econ Dev Cult Chang 30(1):17–30, University of Chicago Press, Chicago

Williamson J (1965) Regional inequality and the process of national development: a description of patterns. Econ Dev Cult Chang 13(2):1–84, University of Chicago Press

World Bank (2009) World development report: reshaping economic geography. Washington, DC

Chapter 6
Concentration and Growth in Latin American Countries

Miguel Atienza and Patricio Aroca

6.1 Introduction

Despite urbanization and recent development, many Latin American countries, such as Chile, Peru, Uruguay and Argentina, still maintain very high levels of urban primacy (United Nations 2012). Most studies about the region have analyzed economic and social problems derived from the existence of urban giants but have not considered in which ways urban primacy is currently affecting national growth. In this respect, Brülhart and Sbergami (2009) show, using a sample of 105 countries and controlling for 18 variables used in various convergence studies worldwide, that when a country achieves a GDP per capita level of $10,000 an increase in the level of urban concentration, negatively affects the national growth rate. Consequently, it is plausible that in some Latin American countries spatial concentration not only has become an equity problem but also a constraint for national efficiency whose reduction should be taken into account in development strategies.

The aim of this chapter is to analyze to what extent, relative excess of spatial concentration of economic activity and population has become a constraint for growth in Latin American countries in order to know whether or not spatially focused policies oriented towards the reduction of concentration are necessary. For this purpose, the chapter, first, describes theoretical approaches that have analyzed the evolution of spatial concentration as countries develop and how spatial concentration affects aggregate economic growth. Afterwards, the second section of the chapter analyzes the characteristics of Latin American urbanization and the evolution of spatial concentration in the last decades and presents, based in previous

M. Atienza (✉)
Universidad Católica del Norte, Antofagasta, Chile
e-mail: miatien@ucn.cl

P. Aroca
University Adolfo Ibañez, Viña del Mar, Chile
e-mail: patricio.aroca@uai.cl

J.R. Cuadrado-Roura and P. Aroca (eds.), *Regional Problems and Policies in Latin America*, Advances in Spatial Science, DOI 10.1007/978-3-642-39674-8_6,

empirical studies, which are the countries where concentration is affecting national efficiency. Finally, conclusions are drawn.

6.2 Economic Geography and Growth

6.2.1 Economic Development and Spatial Concentration

Experts are increasingly recognizing the strong relationship that exists between nations' development and their economic geography (World Bank 2009). It is well known that the process of development is spatially unbalanced (Hirschman 1958; Myrdal 1957). Early stages of development are characterized by the strong spatial concentration of economic activity. Industrialization favors the transition from a rural to an urban society and emerged an internal geography concentrated in one or two cities. This spatial pattern is beneficial to the economy as a whole, as it allows companies located in a single place to benefit from increasing returns of scale arising from proximity that firms would not have been able to obtain if they were dispersed due to the reduced size of the economy and high trade costs resulting from a lack of infrastructure. During this period, the agglomeration of the population is intimately linked to the structural change derived from urbanization, and public policies have a limited impact on spatial concentration (Davis and Henderson 2003).

As the economy develops, circumstances that are favorable for spatial dispersion appear. On the one hand, companies located in regions with a higher level of concentration face pure external diseconomies of agglomeration and a relative increase in the cost of land, commuting and salaries. On the other hand, economic growth favors increases in local markets demand and allows the internal trade costs to fall thanks to regional investment in infrastructure. In addition, the growth of the industry and related activities lead to greater productive diversification and favor the appearance of economies of scale in peripheral regions. As countries further develop, deconcentration begins to be efficient for the economy and it is plausible to expect the beginning of a process of regional dispersion of industry.

The Williamson hypothesis (1965) takes up these ideas and proposes that the relationship between economic geography (concentration) and economic development follows a quadratic distribution in the shape of an inverted "U."[1] The Williamson hypothesis has been theoretically formalized by some of the models of New Economic Geography, in which development is equated to diminishing trade costs and the resulting integration of domestic markets (Fujita et al. 1999; Puga 1999; Puga and Venables 1996; Van Marrewijk 2005). The empirical

[1] In his study, Williamson (1965) refers to the evolution of per capita income inequality among different regions. His argument was later used to address inequality in the location of activities and population, particularly by Urban Economics and New Economic Geography.

evidence on the relationship proposed by Williamson has been proved in various cross-country and panel data studies (Ades and Glaeser 1995; Alonso 1980; Barrios and Strobl 2009; Bertinelli and Strobl 2007; Brülhart and Sbergami 2009; El-Shakhs 1972; Gaviria and Stein 2000; Henderson 1999, 2003; Junius 1999; Wheaton and Shishido 1981).[2]

The hypothesis of the inverted "U" also has been corroborated in the case of specific countries, though the number of studies is reduced due to the long periods of time required to estimate the evolution of urban systems. El-Shakhs (1972) found that Williamson's hypothesis held in the case of the United Kingdom and Alperovich (1992) in Israel. Parr (1985) utilizes the Zipf coefficient to analyze the level of asymmetry of the urban systems of 12 countries and obtains mixed results. In more developed countries, a pattern similar to Williamson's is found, but that is not observed as the level of development of the nations decreases. Along these same lines, Vallone and Atienza (2012) analyze the evolution of the Zipf coefficient in Chile between 1885 and 2002 and show that the trend towards an increase in spatial concentration has not yet been reverted in that country. By contrast, Combes et al. (2011) analyze the case of France between 1860 and 2000 and find evidence of a bell-shaped process of spatial concentration in manufacturing and services over time.

This empirical regularity is not found systematically but it is known that the process of spatial agglomeration that accompanies development in its initial stages tends to occur very quickly, while the dispersion of activity and population tends to be slow and to come at different speeds depending on the geographic, historical, economic and political conditions of each nation (Henderson 1999). The persistence of the concentration in one or two cities despite the increase in per capita income has been a usual characteristic, particularly in countries with intermediate development where urbanization has already finished. In this sense, it could be said that it is a characteristic that extends to the great majority of Latin American nations, which currently present some of the highest primacy index in the world (United Nations 2012).

The persistence of spatial concentration depends on diverse factors such as the size of the country, the level of urbanization, the level of trade openness, the size reached by the industrial sector and whether or not the main concentration is found in the nation's capital. However, one characteristic that differentiates the persistence of the concentration from urbanization is that the former is a phenomenon that is directly and significantly influenced by the institutional framework and public policy. Ades and Glaeser (1995) find that political factors such as dictatorships, political instability and centralized government explain urban concentration. Junius (1999) highlights the influence of historical patterns of location, related to the institutions of the colonial period, on current rates of primacy. Along the same lines, Kim and Law (2012) compare differences between historical decentralized forms of government in the United States and Canada, and centralist Latin American

[2] This relationship has not been verified in some studies, such as Rosen and Resnick (1980), Richardson and Schwartz (1988), Mutlu (1989) and Lemelin and Polèse (1995).

nations, and find that this is one of the factors that explains the greater concentration that exists today in Latin America. Moomaw and Alwosabi (2004) point out the importance of rent-seeking opportunities that occur in large concentrations for explaining primacy, particularly if the agglomeration occurs in the country's capital city.

As Hirschman (1958) has noted, public policies play a key role in the transition from a polarized economic geography to a more balanced one. It has been empirically verified that the institutional framework and specific policies can favor the excess of concentration, generating the phenomenon known as "favoritism." This term refers to the existence of economic and political incentives for ensuring that resources are mainly directed at large concentrations of people (Ades and Glaeser 1995; Davis and Henderson 2003). Other policies such as investment in interregional infrastructure throughout a nation in order to integrate its markets, greater fiscal decentralization and increased levels of democracy facilitate the deconcentration of activity from central regions to peripheral ones (Davis and Henderson 2003). Furthermore, actions of this nature not only contribute to greater spatial equity but also can have a positive impact on the growth of middle income countries.

The existence of profound regional imbalances and urban systems dominated by large metropolises that are maintained despite national development posits key questions in two areas. On the one hand, the problem of equity in the spatial distribution of resources emerges, and could become a focus of social tension in the long-term if it is not resolved (Stöhr and Tödtling 1977). On the other hand, the problem regarding the way in which the excessive concentration affects the country's efficiency and growth is posited (Henderson 1999, 2003). In this chapter, we will focus on later point.

6.2.2 *Spatial Concentration and Growth*

The Williamson's hypothesis implicitly establishes a close link between development measured as per capital GDP, concentration, efficiency and equity. During the early stages of development, the trade-off between efficiency and spatial equity dominates (World Bank 2009; Brülhart and Sbergami 2009). This can mean that policies focused on improving the regional distribution of factors can become prejudicial to growth. As the country develops, this effect gradually weakens and the nation can reach a situation in which high spatial concentration does not only present problems of equity but also negatively affects growth (Davis and Henderson 2003). In this section, we will analyze the theoretical approaches that have addressed this relationship and the empirical studies that have tried to verify it.

6.2.2.1 Theoretical Approaches

Two main approaches have been used to address spatial concentration and growth from a theoretical perspective. One involves the system of cities model that originated in Henderson's study (1974) and the other is composed of the models of New Economic Geography that are developed based on Krugman's work (1991). Attempts to reconcile these two lines of research have been incomplete and their complexity has made their empirical contrasting partial and limited (Combes et al. 2005). Specifically, the theories reach opposite conclusions in most cases for the analysis of the relationship between spatial concentration and national growth.

The main objective of the system of cities theory is to explain how differences in size and productive specialization emerge in a set of cities within a single nation. With different levels of complexity regarding the original arguments (Abdel Rahman and Anas 2004), this theory is posited based on general equilibrium models in which the production of goods has increasing returns of scale that comes from the existence of some type of economy of agglomeration, such as economies of location in Henderson (1974), or the accumulation of qualified human capital. At the same time, the concentration of production and workers in a city causes diseconomies of scale that normally are modeled as increases in the price of land and the cost of urban commuting. Due to the opposed impact of these two forces, cities cannot grow indefinitely and reach an optimal size based on the difference between the diseconomies and economies of agglomeration. As a result, cities cannot produce all of the goods and tend to specialize in some activity. The number of cities emerges in an endogenous manner by introducing a set of city developers into the model. These developers can enter the land market and promote the creation of new cities according to the Henry George's theorem. In this way, the economy is composed of a system of cities that present efficient sizes related to the agglomeration economies that correspond to their productive specialization.

Based on this theory and in combination with a model of endogenous growth, Henderson (2003) finds that empirically there is an optimum level of primacy depending on the size of the economy, measured as urban population, and its level of development, measured as per capital GDP. However, when the market of land developers has coordination problems or there are situations of favoritism that create excess of concentration in some cities in the system, the result is a situation of inefficiency in the economy as a whole. This situation has a negative impact on national growth. From a static perspective, the loss of efficiency caused by excess concentration has its origins in both resources wasted by diseconomies of agglomeration caused by the existence of cities that exceed their optimal size and economies of scale that are not used in cities that are too small. Both effects cause lower income levels, potentially cause less saving and lower accumulation of capital and, as a result, lead to a lower rate of growth (Henderson 2005, 2010). From a dynamic perspective, these losses emerge from the deviation of resources that could be used for investment and innovation in productive activities in the periphery towards large agglomerations in order to maintain the quality of life in congested local spaces (Duranton and Puga 2001; Henderson 2003).

One of the main problems of the system of cities models is that they do not incorporate transportation costs, which is a key element in the models of New Economic Geography for explaining the organization of space. These models initially were presented in order to explain the processes of agglomeration in an economy with two regions and two sectors, agriculture and industry (Krugman 1991). Industry possesses internal returns of scale and its demand is adjusted to a function with constant elasticity of substitution in a context of monopolistic competition. The preference for diversity on the part of consumers makes each industrial company specialize in a product. These assumptions coupled with the existence of positive transport costs and the mobility of industrial workers generate an explosive mechanism of agglomeration that is activated as transport costs decrease, favoring the concentration of the industry in a single region. This sector benefits from the productive advantages that emerge as a result of pecuniary economies of agglomeration that are derived from a greater market potential. As a result, that region is capable of offering higher real wages and attracting more workers. According to Krugman's model, when the transport costs are low enough, the stable equilibrium is the complete concentration of industry in a single region, which determined a core-periphery pattern. Later studies based on the same frame of reference (Helpman 1998; Puga 1999; Van Marrewijk 2005) incorporate new centrifugal forces such as the price of land or diseconomies of agglomeration. These studies were capable of reproducing an inverted "U" pattern similar to the one proposed by Williamson's hypothesis. As transportation costs decreased, a process of industrial concentration was produced. This was later reverted and the stable equilibrium returned to symmetry among regions. However, these models had the limit of not being dynamic and being unable to incorporate the relationship between the structure of the economic geography and growth.

More recent models (Baldwin and Martin 2004; Baldwin et al. 2004) introduce endogenous growth à la Romer (1990) in the context of the core-periphery models of the New Economic Geography. This allows them to incorporate the dynamism that they were lacking and to analytically estimate how spatial organization affects economic growth. These models give special importance to the mobility of qualified human capital and capital and are capable of including technological agglomeration economies and innovation through the incorporation of a research and development sector. The main result of the models of the New Economic Geography that incorporate endogenous growth is favorable to the idea of the existence of a trade-off between spatial equity and efficiency (Martin and Ottaviano 2001; Baldwin and Forslid 2000; Fujita and Thisse 2003). When transportation costs are sufficiently low, the concentration of activity (industrial and innovative) in a single region is a stable equilibrium that favors greater national growth due to the endogenous creation of knowledge and innovations produced in the core. The result is that the growth of the real income of the periphery is, in the long term, equal to that of the core. The gap between core and periphery increases, but the inhabitants of the latter are "better off" than if the activity were deconcentrated. All regions win, but some win more than others. From the policy perspective, the models of the New Economic Geography that incorporate endogenous growth, in contrast to the system of cities models, consider that while there is room for spatial compensation policies oriented towards development in peripheral regions such as the construction of infrastructure, these measures will reduce the rate of growth of the economy as a whole. From this perspective, policies that help reduce the costs of innovation would be more profitable than spatial policies.

As we will see below, the predictions of the models of the New Economic Geography that incorporate endogenous growth have not found support in empirical studies and lack robustness because their results heavily depend on the form of the Cobb-Douglas function utilized (Cerina and Mureddu 2011). In this same vein, Dupont (2007) states that the link between concentration and growth depends on the assumptions made about the mobility of capital and the diffusion of knowledge. Recently, Cerina and Mureddu (2010) have made some modifications to this type of model which allow them to reach results that are closer to those forecasted by the system of cities theory and that reconcile the approach of the New Economic Geography with empirical research. These authors add a third sector – services – to core-periphery models. This sector produces non-tradable goods and benefits from the knowledge externalities that exist in manufacturing sector thanks to research and development. The existence of localized knowledge spillovers between sectors implies incorporating an "anti-growth" effect in the periphery, where the rate of growth is reduced due to the loss of manufacturing activity, but also in the core. This reduction of growth due to industrial concentration is produced when: (1) the spatial range of the spillover effects within the research and development sector; (2) the force of the technological externalities towards the services sector; and (3) the expenditure on non-tradable goods (services) are sufficiently high. In this case, which adjusts to a situation of relatively advanced development, the losses of growth that occur in the periphery due to the reduction of manufacturing are not compensated by the lower costs of innovation in the core region. As a result, in this model, the trade-off between growth and spatial concentration does not occur in the case of economies that have reached high levels of development, where, consequently, the policies oriented towards reducing regional inequalities could positively affect growth.

6.2.2.2 Empirical Studies

The empirical studies that analyze the relationship between spatial concentration and national economic growth tend to confirm the implicit idea of the "Williamson hypothesis." For relatively low levels of per capita income, there is a trade-off between concentration and growth. However, after a certain income threshold, concentration can become an obstacle to economic efficiency. Several studies (Henderson 1999, 2003; Sbergami 2002; Bertinelli and Strobl 2007; Barrios and Strobl 2009; Brülhart and Sbergami 2009; Pholo Bala 2009; Gardiner et al. 2010) have recently verified that the excess of primacy in one or two cities within the urban system significantly reduces productivity and national growth. It is important to keep in mind that the empirical studies that have been conducted thus far have not verified the models proposed by the system of cities theory and the New Economic Geography. They are based on growth models using cross-country and panel data analyses. One of the reasons that these theories remain without strict empirical verification has to do with the difficulty of measurement of economies and diseconomies of agglomeration that are at the basis of their explanations. The absence of studies on the specific experience of countries is also noteworthy. This may be due to difficulties with unraveling the determinants of long-term growth.

Henderson (2003) presents what could be considered one of the most complete and technically solid studies written thus far on the relationship between concentration and national growth. He utilizes data on the period between 1965 and 1995 in 5-year intervals for a sample of 69–81 countries depending on the variables utilized. In order to analyze the direction of the causality, Henderson takes the first differences of all of the variables that eliminate permanent effects by country that could be correlated to growth and the primacy rate. He then uses the Generalized Method of Moments estimation technique, utilizing the primacy rate from 10 years earlier as an instrumental variable. The main results of the study suggest that the process of urbanization does not in and of itself promote growth. Urbanization is rather a by-product of the structural shift from a primary economy to an industrial one, a process that takes place as a country develops. However, he does not rule out the possibility that there may be an optimal level of urbanization that could favor growth. In contrast, he does find that growth is strongly impacted by the level of spatial concentration. Economic growth increases and then decreases in relation to urban primacy. There is also an optimal level of urban concentration that maximizes growth. Deviations with respect to that optimal level due to excess or defect of primacy have a significant impact on growth. An increase in urban primacy over a standard deviation from the mean would reduce the rate of growth of the GDP by approximately 1.5 % per year.

Another noteworthy study is that of Brülhart and Sbergami (2009), who conducted extensive research on the determinants of growth, selecting 18 of 80 variables that were robust in a significant number of studies in an effort to explain regional growth in different countries. To this group of variables they added the concentration of the population measured through an index of primacy (*Urban750*) calculated as a percentage of the population that lives in cities with over 750,000 inhabitants. One of the main results of this study is presented in Fig. 6.1, which shows that the sign of the relationship between concentration and growth depends on the level of the country's per capital product. Concentration positively affects growth for low levels of per capital product. However, once it passes a certain level, that relationship changes its sign or is not significant. More specifically, the authors use a database of 105 countries and show that the threshold of the per capita product in which this relationship changes its sign is US$10,048 estimated based on purchasing power parity from 2006.[3] In other words, for countries with a per capita product of over US$10,000, it is recommended that they reduce concentration in order to achieve greater growth.

[3] Earlier studies like the one conducted by Wheaton and Shishido (1981) identified a slightly lower per capita product threshold of US$8,384.

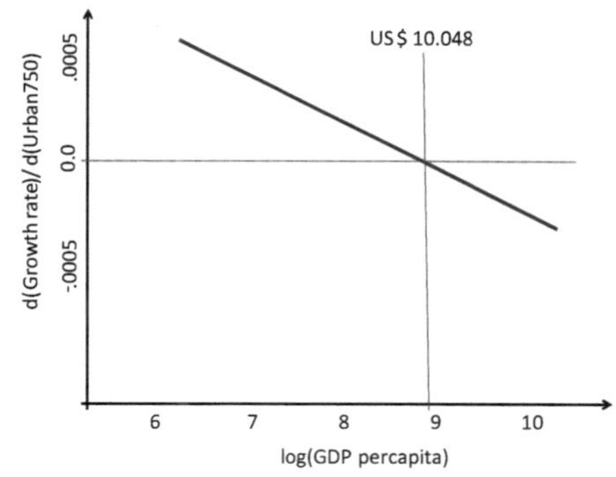

Fig. 6.1 Effect of urban concentration on growth (Source: Authors based on Brülhart and Sbergami 2009)

Bertinelli and Strobl (2007) and Pholo Bala (2009) do not analyze the relationship between spatial concentration and growth using structural models. Instead, these authors utilize semi-parametric techniques, which allow them not to impose a functional form on the relationship between growth and concentration and to estimate the degree to which the growth rate varies for each level of the variable utilized to measure urban concentration. This approach also allows them to analyze the differences that exist between groups of countries. Bertinelli and Stobl (2007) analyze a data panel of 70 countries that covers the period between 1960 and 1990 and estimate the form of the relationship between the growth of the product and primacy, comparing developed and underdeveloped nations according to criteria established by the World Bank. The main result shows that in the case of developed nations, this relationship tends to be positive while in developing nations it is closer to an inverted "U." There is a level of primacy that the authors situate at 35 % of the urban population after which the spatial concentration has a negative effect on growth. Pholo Bala (2009), for his part, conducts an analysis that is similar to the one described above, though he controls for the potential endogeneity of the results, uses different concentration measurements to estimate the robustness of the results, and calculates the significance of the differences between groups of countries. The results show significant differences by continent. In Europe, the relationship between concentration and growth is a positive one, which coincides with the results reported by Bertinelli and Strobl (2007). Asia and Latin America are located in what the author describes as a "concentration trap" in which the relationship is basically negative, especially in the case of Latin America. Finally, Africa presents an inverted "U" shape. The author also shows that the differences between the continents are significant among developed and underdeveloped nations but not among underdeveloped ones.

Both studies highlight the need to examine the relationship between concentration and growth keeping in mind the differences in the urbanization and growth processes that the different groups of countries have followed. Specifically, they state that developed countries may have reached a growth trajectory that is different from that of underdeveloped nations, which could affect the relationship between concentration and growth. Different patterns of urbanization and concentration could have an impact on this relationship. In developed nations, urbanization led to a progressive improvement in the qualification of human capital, industrialization, the development of a formal economy and to economic growth. It does not seem that this process has followed the same path in continents such as Latin America and Africa. There, urbanization can mean concentration without growth characterized by cities with large informal economies, poverty and a mixture of rural and urban activities (Fai and Opal 2000; Yuki 2007). In the rest of the chapter, we will focus on the processes of urbanization and spatial concentration of activity in Latin America.

6.3 Spatial Concentration and Growth in Latin America

In contrast to European countries, Latin America completed its urbanization in less than a century at a speed that is unprecedented elsewhere in the world. At the same time, the urbanization of this region was characterized by high levels of spatial concentration and primacy that persist in most countries despite the levels of growth and per capita income that its nations have achieved over the past two decades. These characteristics make Latin America a particularly interesting case study for evaluating the relationship between spatial concentration and growth. In this section, we will address the process of urbanization and spatial concentration in Latin America in order to understand its unique characteristics. We will then analyze how the current economic geography of its countries could become an obstacle to growth. It is important to note that not all of the countries on the continent have followed similar paths. As a result, one of the tasks to be completed -which we will only partially address in this section- is the specific analysis of each nation.

6.3.1 Urbanization and Spatial Concentration in Latin America

At this time, Latin America presents the second greatest level of urbanization in the world and is just three percentage points behind North America. In 2010, nearly 80 % of the region's population lived in cities and the urban population is expected to reach nearly 87 % by the year 2050 (United Nations 2012). These statistics were difficult to anticipate at the beginning of the twentieth century. In 1925, when censuses began to be generalized throughout the sub-continent, the urban population was barely 25 %, significantly lower than that of North America, Oceania and Europe, where the urbanization process was already at an advanced level (Cerrutti and Bertoncello 2003). Over the past 60 years, between 1950 and 2010, the percentage of the urban population in Latin America has doubled (Fig. 6.2),

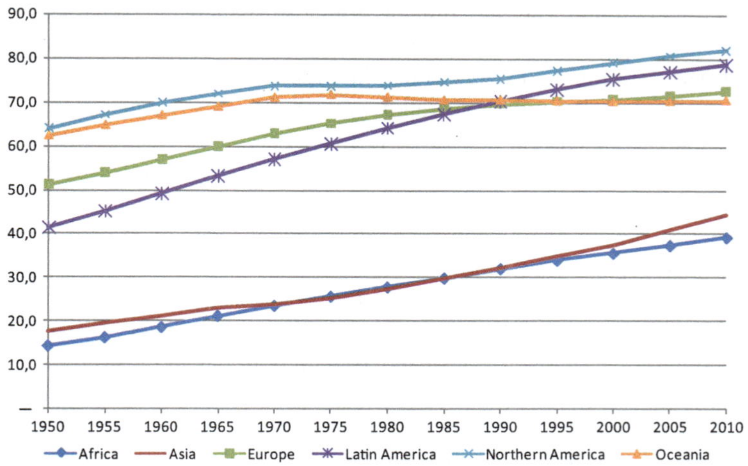

Fig. 6.2 Percentage of urban population by continent, 1950–2010 (Source: Created by the authors based on United Nations data from 2012)

growing at an annual rate of 3.2 %, which is twice the rate of North America and triple that of Europe. The speed of Latin American urbanization,[4] which occurred in just one century, is unprecedented (Kemper 2002) and shows patterns that are significantly different from those observed in the case of more developed nations, in which urbanization was a process that took several centuries and led to a more balanced economic geography.

Between the years prior to Independence and the first half of the nineteenth century, the urban growth of Latin American nations was weak. Paradoxically, the region was characterized by a process of urbanization that was faster in peripheral cities as part of an effort to make use of the exploitation of natural resources, plantation and export economies and in order to avoid conflicts and crime in border areas (Morse 1974). It was at the beginning of the second half of the nineteenth century, once national unification was ensured and political systems were centralized (with investments in railroads, ports, telegraph services and other infrastructure), when the position of main cities was reinforced as places of political clientelism and financial intermediation, and early industrialization. During the second half of the nineteenth century, all of the capitals grew more quickly than the rest of the nation, though the process of concentration was not accelerated and

[4] It is important to recall the diversity that existed among Latin American nations in its urbanization process. Table 6.1 in the Appendix describes the evolution of urbanization in larger countries.

there were exceptions. The situation of primacy,[5] which later characterized the economic geography of Latin America, was not initially the dominant pattern, though it was the most widespread once in 1920. At that point, Argentina, Cuba, Mexico, Chile and Peru demonstrated greater primacy in contrast to Brazil, Colombia and Venezuela (Morse 1974; Kemper 2002).

The creation of asymmetrical systems of cities, in many cases dominated by a single city, which begins between the second half of the nineteenth century and the first three decades of the twentieth century, gives way to a path-dependence trajectory that persists until today in most countries. The origin of this spatial pattern is not based on the industrialization of these nations, as the models of New Economic Geography predicted, because the development of manufacturing was limited until the 1930s. It is instead based on political and institutional factors. The dominant hypothesis about this situation point out the economic dependence of Latin American countries compared to more developed nations, which favored the concentration of political and economic power in the main cities. This situation attracted the political and commercial elite to the major cities, mainly the capitals, along with owners of land and other natural resources, creating a "metropolis-hinterland" pattern (Morse 1962) and fundamentally centralist states (Kim and Law 2012). In contrast to the European case in which there were complex systems of cities organized into small centers formed over the course of centuries, the rural and peripheral areas of Latin America presented large extensions with scant population density without transportation and communication infrastructure. In those spaces, material development was very precarious due to the economic model of the plantation and enclave. This model of internal colonization provided scant benefits to the peripheral areas where production took place. These benefits were concentrated abroad and in national urban centers, which favored the concentration of migrants from the impoverished periphery and, particularly during this period, from foreign countries (Rodgers et al. 2011).

The pattern of highly concentrated urbanization was consolidated and accelerated significantly between the 1930s and 1970s. Between 1925 and 1975, the urban population increased from 25 % to 61.2 % (Cerrutti and Bertoncello 2003). In countries like Argentina, Chile, Uruguay and Venezuela, the process of urbanization was nearly complete, with over three out of every four inhabitants living in cities. While many of the previous political and institutional conditions remained in place, most authors have assumed that one of the main reasons for the accelerated and concentrated urbanization that took place during this period is related to the adoption of Import Substitution Industrialization (ISI) strategies in most of the countries of the continent (Kemper 2002; Portes 2005; Rodgers et al. 2011). The growth of industrial activity in the main cities produced large

[5] Measured as the ratio between the population of the first and second cities of the system. It is assumed that there is primacy when that ratio is greater than two. This convention is related to the expected value if a system of cities meets Zipf's law according to which the size of the principal city is double that of the second, triple that of the third, and so on.

flows of internal migration from rural areas, giving way to a rapid increase in primacy rates that ended up exacerbating the preexisting pattern. Also, the cities' inability to accommodate the large influx of migrants led to socially segregated and polarized areas with high levels of informal labor (Portes 1989). The characteristics of this process have led some authors (Polèse 2005) to question the relationship between the high level of urbanization achieved by the countries of the Southern Cone (Chile, Argentina and Uruguay) and its long-term growth.

Beginning in the 1980s, the urbanization rate exceeded 60 % in nearly every Latin American country. As a result, the growth of the urban population progressively decreased. Despite the abandonment of ISI policies and the adoption of neoliberal macro-economic stabilization policies, trade openness and privatization, there was no substantive change in the high rates of primacy in most countries, though in some of them increasing growth of secondary urban centers was observed (Portes 1989, 2005). In any case, on this point, it is important to keep in mind the diversity of experiences of these countries. Some have maintained high concentration levels and others seem to have initiated a process that would reverse this trend. Figures 6.3 and 6.4 present the evolution of primacy rates of nine Latin American countries that have at least two cities with over 750,000 inhabitants. In Fig. 6.3, primacy (primacy 1) is calculated as the percentage of the urban population that lives in the main city, while in Fig. 6.4 primacy (primacy ½) is calculated as the ratio between the population of the first and second cities of the system.

The rate of growth of the participation of the main city in the urban population tends to decrease or level out in the majority of countries beginning in the 1980s with the exception of Chile, which grows slightly, and Colombia. This case is special given that the internal violence associated with paramilitaries and guerrillas caused massive waves of migration of displaced persons towards the capital city of Bogotá. These results confirm that which was observed by Ades and Glaeser (1995) regarding the positive relationship between violence and political instability and primacy. By contrast, the most significant reductions in primacy took place in Bolivia and particularly in Venezuela where, since the 1970s, it has been reduced nearly to half. Though in these two cases an urban system dominated by two cities – La Paz and Santa Cruz in Bolivia and Caracas and Maracaibo in Venezuela- has been formed.

Among the countries analyzed, which correspond to the largest nations of the continent, Bolivia, Colombia, Ecuador and Mexico had a primacy rate of around 25 % of the urban population and three countries stood out for having primacy rates of over 35 %. In 2010, Chile and Peru had the highest rates but seemed to have stabilized, while Argentina presented a marked downward trend (Fig. 6.3). In smaller Latin American nations that have not been included in the figure such as Costa Rica, El Salvador, Nicaragua, Paraguay and Uruguay, the primacy rates are over 30 % and up to even 40 % (United Nations 2012). This is due to factors such as small size, which contributes to concentration, and the fact that the process of urbanization is more delayed in nearly all of these countries with the exception of Uruguay.

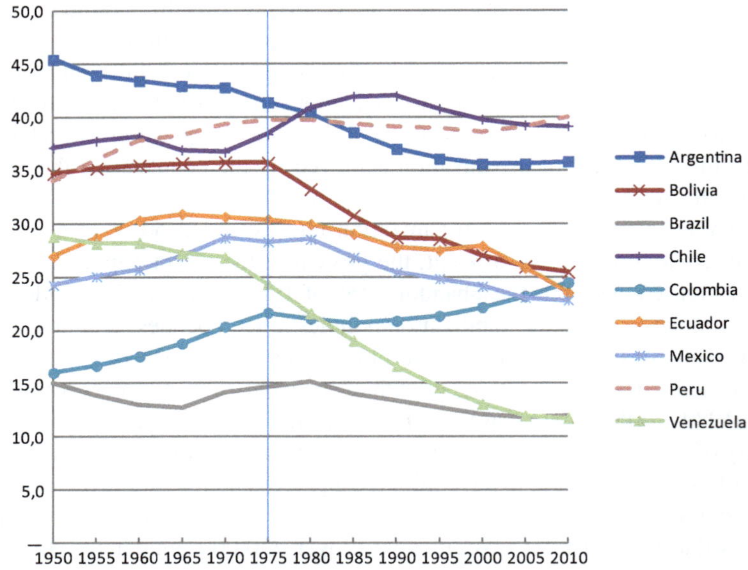

Fig. 6.3 Primacy rate 1, 1950–2010 (Source: Authors based on United Nations data from 2012)

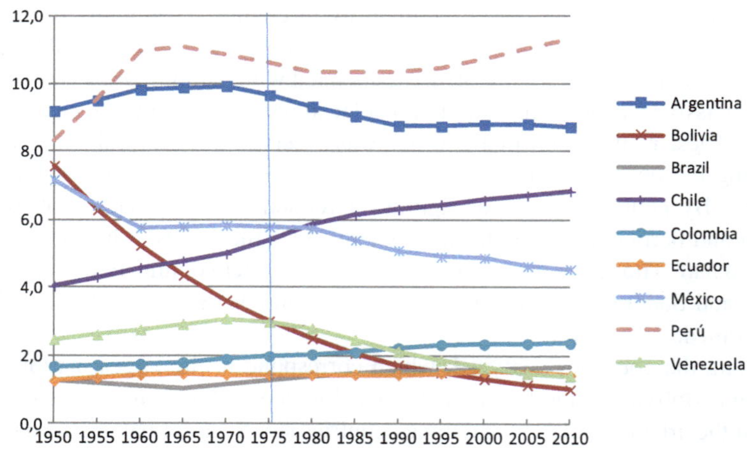

Fig. 6.4 Half primacy rate, 1950–2010 (Source: Authors based on United Nations data from 2012)

The ½ primacy rate indicates the degree to which the country is moving towards an unpolarized urban system and develops at least two large urban concentrations. When spatial concentration is measured in this way, only four of the countries analyzed would not be in a situation of primacy (index of less than two): Bolivia,

Venezuela, Ecuador and Brazil (Fig. 6.4). In this group, the marked downward trend of Bolivia caused by the accelerated growth of the city of Santa Cruz stands out, as does that of Venezuela, due to the growth of Maracaibo. Among the countries with primacy, one observes a high dispersion of values and trends. Argentina and Mexico, for their part, present a clear downward trend, particularly since the late 1970s, which indicates the development of a less asymmetrical urban system. However, their main cities continue to be significantly larger than the second city in the system, nearly nine times in the case of Argentina and over four times in Mexico. On the other hand, Colombia, Chile and Peru have reinforced the position of their main city in the system. Note the strong growth of primacy in Chile, where the city of Santiago has gone from being four times the size of Valparaíso in 1950 to nearly seven times its size in 2010. Peru follows a variable trend that could be related to migratory flows to Lima caused by the terrorism of "Sendero luminoso", and shows the largest primacy among the countries analyzed (Fig. 6.4).

6.3.2 *Spatial Concentration and Growth in Latin America*

The results of the previous section show that while Latin America is one of the sub-continents with the highest rate of urbanization in the world, it presents an economic geography that is characterized by high primacy that has been maintained despite the growth experienced over the past two decades. In fact, of the countries analyzed, only Venezuela and Bolivia present a clear tendency to reduce primacy according to the two indicators utilized, though both of these countries have moved to a city system dominated by two cities. Several of the Latin American countries analyzed have achieved or are close to reaching the level of 10,000 dollars after which, according to Brulhart and Sbergami (2009), it would be recommendable to reduce the primacy rate because it could have negative effects on national growth. In this section, we will analyze the position that Latin American nations occupy in the international context in terms of primacy and per capita GDP, and we will review empirical studies that have analyzed the relationship between primacy and growth in order to more precisely identify where in the sub-continent concentration could be acting as an obstacle to growth.

Figure 6.5 presents the per capita GDP on the abscissa axis and percentage of the total urban population that lives in the main city on the ordinate axis (primacy 1). The per capita GDP has been divided arbitrarily into intervals of US$5,000 for which the average primacy 1 rate has been calculated in order to observe which Latin American countries are situated significantly above the average in their group. The average level of primacy 1 for each per capital GDP interval is presented as a dotted horizontal line within each interval. The countries with a per capita GDP of less than US$5,000 are mainly African nations. On average, these countries present the highest levels of primacy, 34 %. Among the Latin American nations in this group, Paraguay stands out because of its high concentration (over 50 %), as

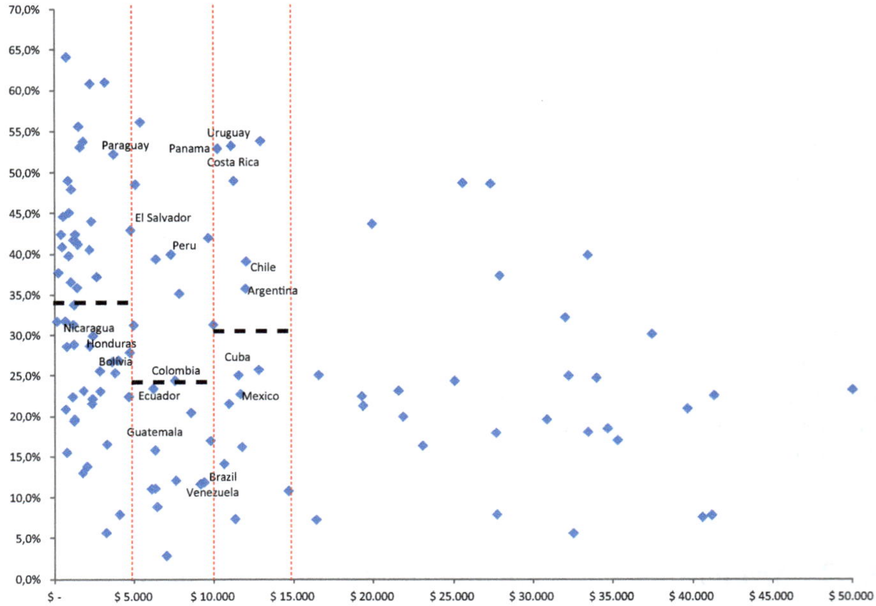

Fig. 6.5 Primacy 1 rate and per capita GDP, 2010 (Source: Authors based on United Nations data from 2012)

does El Salvador (over 40 %). The group with per capita GDP of between US$5,000 and US$10,000, whose average primacy is 24 %, includes Peru, which has high primacy of just over 40 %. In this group, the majority of Latin American nations (Brazil, Venezuela, Guatemala, Ecuador and Colombia) are close to or below the average primacy rate. The opposite is found in the group with per capita GDP of between US$10,000 and US$15,000, in which the average primacy is around 30 % and most Latin American countries (Argentina, Chile, Costa Rica, Panama and Uruguay) present clearly higher levels of primacy. Only Cuba and Mexico are below the average. As a whole, nearly 50 % of the Latin American countries considered in Fig. 6.5 have a level of primacy that is significantly higher than the average of their per capita product range.

The position of the Latin American nations in the international context leads one to suspect that primacy has managed to become an obstacle to their growth in a significant number of cases. The review of existing empirical studies confirms it. Table 6.1 shows the results of various studies that identify the Latin American nations in which spatial concentration could have a negative impact on economic growth. These estimates consider various indicators of primacy and analytical techniques and, in general, the results tend to coincide. In the first place, three countries in the Southern Cone that are present in all of the studies – Argentina, Chile and Peru – are highlighted. In that same area, Uruguay and Paraguay also appear, though with less frequency. The majority of the countries in Central America are found along with this group from the southern part of the continent,

Table 6.1 Latin American countries with excess of concentration

Paper	Primacy index	Latin American countries with excess of concentration	Estimation method
Henderson (2000)	Primacy 1	*Argentina*, *Chile*, Uruguay, Paraguay, *Peru*, Panama, Costa Rica, El Salvador, Nicaragua, Guatemala	Panel data
Henderson (2003)	Primacy 1	*Argentina*, *Chile*, Mexico, *Peru*	Panel data
Bertinelli and Strobl (2007)	Primacy 1	*Argentina*, *Chile*, Uruguay, Paraguay, *Peru*, Costa Rica, El Salvador, Nicaragua, Guatemala, Honduras	Semi-parametric estimation
Brulhart and Sbergami (2009)	Primacy 1 and primacy > 750,000	*Argentina*, *Chile*, *Peru*, Uruguay, Venezuela	Panel data
Pholo Bala (2009)	Primacy 1 and density > 750,000	*Argentina*, *Chile*, Dominican Republic, Guatemala, Nicaragua, *Peru*, El Salvador	Semi-parametric estimation

Source: Authors

particularly Nicaragua, Guatemala and El Salvador.[6] In principle, these countries would form two groups with different characteristics. On the one hand, the countries of the Southern Cone tend to be medium in size with very advanced urbanization processes, higher incomes and primacy rates that have tended to stall. On the other, the Central American nations are small and many have not yet completed their urbanization process. They have lower incomes and higher rates of primacy in the cases of Costa Rica, Panama and El Salvador. It is likely that the study of the relationship between concentration and growth will require different approaches for each group.

6.4 Conclusions

Over the past 10 years, a great deal of attention has been paid to the study of the relationship between spatial concentration and growth. While the predictions of the main theoretical lines of research are not in agreement, empirical studies have tended to confirm that, based on a specific threshold of development; concentration does become an obstacle to growth. The most recent studies also have highlighted the need to differentiate between groups of countries due to the fact that the relationship between concentration and growth could be affected by their different patterns of urbanization and growth trajectories. An exploration of the process of

[6] The differences, regarding the data, presented in Fig. 6.5, where Guatemala and Nicaragua, which show relatively low levels of primacy, may be due to the time periods analyzed by the studies gathered in Table 6.1, which frequently refer to the period between 1960 and 1995.

urbanization in Latin America reveals that it has had very specific characteristics. These include velocity – it has taken just one century for the continent to become urbanized – and high levels of primacy. It is also noteworthy that trajectories of primacy have tended to be more diverse since the 1980s, once maximum levels of spatial concentration were reached.

The levels of per capita income reached by a significant number of the countries of the sub-continent suggest that the polarized pattern of urbanization has become an obstacle to their growth. This is confirmed by nearly all of the empirical studies available for a significant number of countries. Two groups are identified for which it is recommended that the reduction of spatial concentration become a national policy objective not only due to reasons of equity but also in order to increase the growth potential of their economies. The first group includes nearly all of the countries in the Southern Cone, notably Argentina, Chile and Peru followed by Uruguay and Paraguay. The second group is formed by most of the countries in Central America. Given the differences that exist between the two groups and the different trajectories observed between countries with similar incomes, there is a need to analyze the experience of each country in Latin America and evaluate the degree to which policies aimed at deconcentration of productive activity as well as the population contribution to promoting their growth.

Appendix

Table A-1 Urbanization rates in Latin American countries. 1950–2010 (%)

	1950	1960	1970	1980	1990	2000	2010
Costa Rica	33.5	34.3	38.8	43.1	50.7	59.0	64.2
El Salvador	36.5	38.3	39.4	44.1	49.2	58.9	64.3
Guatemala	25.1	31.1	35.5	37.4	41.1	45.1	49.3
Honduras	17.6	22.7	28.9	34.9	40.5	45.5	51.6
Mexico	42.7	50.8	59.0	66.3	71.4	74.7	77.8
Nicaragua	35.2	39.6	47.0	49.9	52.3	54.7	57.3
Argentina	65.3	73.6	78.9	82.9	87.0	90.1	92.3
Bolivia	33.8	36.8	39.8	45.5	55.6	61.8	66.4
Brazil	36.2	46.1	55.9	65.5	73.9	81.2	84.3
Chile	58.4	67.8	75.2	81.2	83.3	85.9	88.9
Colombia	32.7	45.0	54.8	62.1	68.3	72.1	75.0
Ecuador	28.3	33.9	39.3	47.0	55.1	60.3	66.9
Paraguay	34.6	35.6	37.1	41.7	48.7	55.3	61.4
Peru	41.0	46.8	57.4	64.6	68.9	73.0	76.9
Uruguay	77.9	80.2	82.4	85.4	89.0	91.3	92.5
Venezuela	47.3	61.6	71.9	79.2	84.3	89.9	93.3

Source: Authors based on United Nation 2012

References

Abdel Rahman H, Anas A (2004) Theories of systems of cities. In: Henderson JV, Thisse JF (eds) Handbook of regional and urban economics, Vol 4, Chapter, 52. Elsevier, Amsterdam/Boston pp 2293–2339

Ades A, Glaeser E (1995) Trade and circuses: explaining urban giants. Q J Econ 110:195–227

Alonso W (1980) Five bell shapes in development. Pap Reg Sci Assoc 45:5–16

Alperovich G (1992) Economic development and population concentration. Econ Dev Cult Chang 41(1):63–74

Baldwin R, Forslid R (2000) The core-periphery model and endogenous growth. Economica 67:307–324

Baldwin R, Martin P (2004) Agglomeration and regional growth. In: Henderson JV, Thisse JF (eds) Handbook of regional and urban economics, Vol 4, Chapter, 60. Elsevier, Amsterdam pp 2671–2711

Baldwin R, Forslid R, Martin P, Ottaviano G, Robert-Nicoud F (2004) Economic geography and public policy. Princeton University Press, Princeton

Barrios S, Strobl E (2009) The dynamics of regional inequalities. Reg Sci Urban Econ 39:575–591

Bertinelli L, Strobl E (2007) Urbanisation, urban concentration and economic development. Urban Stud 44(13):2499–2510

Brülhart M, Sbergami F (2009) Agglomeration and growth: cross-country evidence. J Urban Econ 65:48–63

Cerina F, Mureddu F (2010) Is agglomeration really good for growth? Global efficiency and interregional equity. Working paper CRENoS 200913, Centre for North South Economic Research, University of Cagliari and Sassari

Cerina F, Mureddu F (2011) Agglomeration and growth with endogenous expenditure shares. J Reg Sci 52(2):324–360

Cerrutti M, Bertoncello R (2003) Urbanization and internal migration patterns in Latin America. Paper prepared for conference on African migration in comparative perspective, Johannesburg, pp 4–7, June

Combes PP, Duranton G, Overman H (2005) Agglomeration and the adjustment of the spatial economy. Pap Reg Sci 84(3):311–349

Combes P, Lafourcade P, Thisse JF, Toutain JC (2011) The rise and fall of spatial inequalities in France: a long-run perspective. Explor Econ Hist 48(2):243–271

Davis JC, Henderson JV (2003) Evidence on the political economy of the urbanization process. J Urban Econ 53:98–125

Dupont V (2007) Do geographical agglomeration, growth and equity conflict? Pap Reg Sci 86 (2):193–213

Duranton G, Puga D (2001) Nursery cities: urban diversity, process innovation, and the life cycle of products. Am Econ Rev 91(5):1454–1477

El-Shakhs S (1972) Development, primacy, and systems of cities. J Dev Areas 7:11–36

Fay M, Opal C (2000) Urbanization without growth. A not-so-uncommon phenomenon. Policy research working paper 2412, Banco Mundial

Fujita M, Thisse JF (2003) Does geographical agglomeration foster economic growth? And who gains and loses from it? Jpn Econ Rev 52(4):121–145

Fujita M, Krugman P, Venables A (1999) The spatial economy. Cities, regions and international trade. MIT Press, Cambridge

Gardiner B, Martin R, Tyler P (2010) Does spatial agglomeration increase national growth? Some evidence from Europe. J Econ Geogr 1–28. doi:10.1093/jeg/lbq047

Gaviria A, Stein E (2000) The evolution of urban concentration around the world: a panel approach. Working paper 414, Inter-American Development Bank

Helpman E (1998) The size of regions. In: Pines D, Sadka E, Zilcha I (eds) Topics in public economics. Cambridge University Press, Cambridge, pp 33–54

Henderson JV (1974) The sizes and types of cities. Am Econ Rev 64:640–656

Henderson JV (1999) The effect of urban concentration on economic growth. NBER, Working paper 7503
Henderson JV (2003) The urbanization process and economic growth: the so-what question. J Econ Growth 8:47–71
Henderson JV (2005) Urbanization and growth. In: Aghion P, Durlauf S (eds) Handbook of economic growth, Vol 1B, Chapter 24. Elsevier, Amsterdam, pp 1543–1591
Henderson JV (2010) Cities and development. J Reg Sci 50(1):515–540
Hirschman A (1958) The strategy of economic development. Yale University Press, New Haven
Junius K (1999) Primacy and economic development: bell shaped or parallel growth of cities? J Econ Dev 24:1–22
Kemper R (2002) Urbanization in Latin America. In: Ember M, Ember CR (eds) Encyclopedia of urban cultures, vol 1. Grolier Publishing, Danbury, pp 88–100
Kim S, Law M (2012) History, institutions and cities: a view from the Americas. J Reg Sci 52 (1):10–39
Krugman P (1991) Increasing returns and economic geography. J Polit Econ 99:484–499
Lemelin A, Polèse M (1995) What about the bell-shaped relationship between primacy and development? Int Reg Sci Rev 18(3):313–330
Martin P, Ottaviano G (2001) Growth and agglomeration. Int Econ Rev 42(4):947–968
Moomaw M, Alwosabi A (2004) An empirical analysis of competing explanations of urban primacy evidence from Asia and the Americas. Ann Reg Sci 38:149–171
Morse R (1962) Some characteristics of Latin American urban history. Am Hist Rev 67 (2):317–338
Morse R (1974) Trends and patterns of Latin American urbanization, 1750–1920. Comp Stud Soc Hist 16(4):416–447
Mutlu S (1989) Urban concentration and primacy revisited: an analysis and some policy conclusions. Econ Dev Cult Chang 37(3):611–639
Myrdal G (1957) Economic theory and under-developed regions. Duckworth, London
Parr J (1985) A note on the size distribution of cities over time. J Urban Econ 18(2):199–212
Pholo Bala A (2009) Urban concentration and economic growth: checking for specific regional effects. CORE Discussion Paper 2009/38
Polèse M (2005) Cities and national economic growth: a reappraisal. Urban Stud 42(8):1429–1451
Portes A (1989) Latin American urbanization during the years of the crisis. Lat Am Res Rev 24 (3):7–44
Portes A, Roberts B (2005) The free-market city: Latin American urbanization in the years of the neoliberal experiment. Stud Comp Int Dev 40(1):43–82
Puga D (1999) The rise and fall of regional inequalities. Eur Econ Rev 43(2):303–334
Puga D, Venables A (1996) The spread of industry: spatial agglomeration in economic development. J Japan Int Econ 10(4):440–464
Richardson H, Schwartz G (1988) Economic development, population, and primacy. Reg Stud 22:467–475
Rodgers D, Beall J, Kanbur R (2011) Latina American urban development into the 21st century. UNU WIDER Working paper 2011/05
Romer P (1990) Endogenous technological change. J Polit Econ 98:71–102
Rosen K, Resnick M (1980) The size distribution of cities: an examination of the Pareto Law and primacy. J Urban Econ 8:165–186
Sbergami F (2002) Agglomeration and economic growth: some puzzles. HEI Working paper No: 02, Institut Universitaire de Hautes Etudes Internationales
Stöhr W, Tödtling F (1977) Spatial equity-some anti-theses to current regional development doctrine. Pap Reg Sci 38(1):33–53
United Nations (2012) World urbanization prospects. The 2011 revision. Department of Economic and Social Affairs, Population Division, New York

Vallone A, Atienza M (2012) Concentration, development and evolution of the urban system in Chile between 1885 and 2002. Working paper WP2012-03 Departamento de Economía, Universidad Católica del Norte

Van Marrewijk CH (2005) General geographical economics model with congestion. Tinbergen Institute Discussion Paper no 05-100/2

Wheaton W, Shishido H (1981) Urban concentration, agglomeration economies, and the level of economic development. Econ Dev Cult Chang 30:17–30

Williamson J (1965) Regional inequality and the process of national development. Econ Dev Cult Chang 13(4):1–84

World Bank (2009) World development report 2009. Reshaping economic geography. World Bank, Washington, DC

Yuki K (2007) Urbanization, informal sector, and development. J Dev Econ 84:76–103

Chapter 7
Urban Primacy and Regional Economic Disparities in Latin America

Luis Mauricio Cuervo G. and Nicolás Cuervo B.

7.1 Introduction

The purpose of this paper is to attempt to understand the relationships between urban primacy and regional economic disparities in Latin America. It tackles, therefore, the investigation of the interactions between two different dimensions of regional development. On one hand, the spatial, that of urban primacy understood as a special kind of regional configuration. On the other hand, the socio-economic, that is to say, disparities understood as a determined distribution of opportunities for growth and wellbeing between regional territories in a determined national space.

Regions are heterogeneous and disparate spaces. Heterogeneous in the sense of being made up of areas of very diverse qualities and structures in terms of their economy, or their social, cultural aspects, their landscape, habitat or type of settlement. Inequalities exist in the levels of access to services, employment opportunities and wealth creation. In contemporary societies, the city possesses a peerless power to have an effect on both dimensions; that is to say, the organization of space and the distribution of opportunities for wealth creation and wellbeing for members of society.

The city's power to have an effect outside its boundaries is explained, mainly, by the fact that it is part of an urban system whose operation is politically determined by the presence and actions of the nation state. In economic terms, the constitution

L.M. Cuervo G. (✉)
ILPES, CEPAL, Santiago de Chile, Chile
e-mail: Mauricio.Cuervo@cepal.org

N. Cuervo B.
Université de Paris Est, Paris, France
e-mail: nicolas.cuervo@gmail.com

J.R. Cuadrado-Roura and P. Aroca (eds.), *Regional Problems and Policies in Latin America*, Advances in Spatial Science, DOI 10.1007/978-3-642-39674-8_7,

and the dynamics of the urban network respond, in the main, to the process of emergence, integration and the evolution of the internal market.[1]

Under these conditions, the nation state[2] and the domestic market provide political and economic significance for the relationship between urban primacy and regional disparities. Indeed, the relationships between cities and between regions are highly conditioned by this legal-political entity (Nation State – National Territory) – where specific ideas of prosperity and solidarity between individuals, social groups and also regions take place. Moreover, national state regulations and operations also take care of the promotion of each of these two ideas, and the management of their interrelationships. Finally, but of no lesser importance, because of regulations governing customs, finances, the freedom and restraint of the economy, and also the physical infrastructure which results, are a fundamental to the domestic market and of the conditions in which they relate to the outside world.

The paper begins with a deliberation on the theory, with the aim being to identify and organize what it adds to the comprehension of these relationships. Even though special importance is granted to economic theory, other disciplinary contributions are also considered, especially those of a geographic and historical base. Then, the available regional economic information for Latin America will be organized to form the most panoramic comparative view possible, centered on events over the past two decades.

7.2 Urban Primacy Economic Policies and Regional Disparities

There is no integrated theoretical corpus that accounts for the basic interrelationships between urban primacy and regional disparities. Therefore, this section will establish the theoretical fundamentals of this relationship, beginning with a review of most relevant and pertinent approaches. For argumentative ease, disparities are considered as the dependent variable, and primacy as the explanatory variable.

To begin with the dependent variable, the economic explanations for the behavior of regional disparities will be reviewed. Continuing then with the independent variable, where economic theory concerning city size will be examined, along with the main empirical research available, in an attempt to explain urban primacy in general terms, and in Latin America specifically. The section is concluded with a text considering, by means of a hypothesis, the main relationships between urban primacy and region disparities.

---

[1] Without implying that the global is not fundamental

[2] Under very special conditions, such as with the European Union, these relationships take on the sense of a multinational space.

7.2.1 Economic Explanation for Regional Inequalities

In this part, a brief description of what theory and empirical research offer us in the discovery and explanation of the evolution of regional economic disparities.[3]

In terms of the description of the phenomenon being explained, there are two commonly used alternatives employed for the theory and empirical research. The first, derived from neoclassical theory of growth, is based on the calculation of a convergence coefficient. This coefficient calculates statistical relationship between the level of per capita wealth of a region in the initial year [$Log(y_{i,t-1})$] and its growth rate during a reference period [$\text{Log}(y_{it}/y_{i,t-1})$]. In accordance with the theory's underlying assumptions, it is expected that the poorest regions grow at higher rates ($\beta > 0$) and that, over time, they will tend to close the gap in wealth between regions (and also between countries). This is known as convergence and it is usually calculated by the use of the Eq. 7.1:

$$\text{Log}\left(y_{it}/y_{i,t-1}\right) = a - \left(1 - e^{-b}\right).Log\left(y_{i,t-1}\right) + u_{it}(1) \tag{7.1}$$

The second family of descriptions is centered on the calculation of different indicators of inequality. The most elemental of which are standard deviation and others such as the GINI or Theil coefficient. Within this family, Williamson (1981), in his studies of regional economy has used a particularly pertinent index, the Weighted Variation Coefficient (V_w), as defined by the Eq. 7.2:

$$V_W = \frac{\sqrt{\sum_i (y_i - \bar{y})^2 \frac{f_i}{n}}}{\bar{y}}, \tag{7.2}$$

Where:

y_i: per capita income of the i-th region
$\check{Y}$: national per capita income
f_i: population of the i-th region
n: national population

Even though the first type of indicators became widely accepted during the 1990s and during parts of this century, for several reasons the use of the second type, and especially V_w, are advisable. Among the most significant limitations of the β convergence indicator are the following: In substantial terms, it has drawn the debate towards a discussion of little consequence, in as much as whether to prove or

[3] For the effects of this paper, regional economic disparities are understood as the inequality of access to opportunities for wealth creation and well-being between subnational unities within the same country. In the area of empirical research, GDP and per capita earnings are the most commonly used indicators to measure these inequalities.

reject convergence hypothesis. As will be seen, regional systems pass through alternating periods of convergence and divergence, and as so, efforts should be centered on identifying the factors that explain the trends at each moment and the ruptures that induce movement from one phase to another. In place of this, the debate over convergence hypothesis has been taken to levels of ever more sophisticated measurement and has become remote from the identification of explanatory factors of one or another behavior. In operative terms, the β convergence coefficient manifests difficulties of varying magnitudes that transforms it into an unreliable measurement: the result can vary from one extreme to another quite opposite one, depending upon the initial year and final year chosen; by admitting or taking out of some of the component regions in question, a considerable impact on the value and significance of the statistics results; every region is treated as a component of comparative importance irrespective of the percentage of population that lives there; finally, it doesn't allow for the tracking of year by year figures, but only for defined periods. The variations resulting from any of these reasons mentioned, makes it very difficult to distinguish whether they are the result of the calculation methods used, or, on the contrary, of the phenomenon observed.

In accordance with the arguments above, CVP (Eq. 7.2) will be taken as a reference point for the empirical exercises developed throughout this article. The long-term historical study undertaken by Williamson (1981) concerning regional disparities in the USA is particularly inspiring. This historical undertaking, however, will not be considered as a prediction as to what is likely to happen in lesser developed countries. It will be used instead, as an opportunity to identify significant features of the historical evolution of this phenomenon and of its explanatory factors.

With the long-term experiences for the USA, Williamson (1981) and Barro and Sala-i-Martin (1995) together indicate convergence as the predominant trend. However, the former's research reveals the cyclicality of the process, with its changing speeds, its regional diversity (North–south) and the changing composition of base determinants. *In agreement with the above, the particular interest of this research is the identification and characterization of cycles of regional economic disparities for Latin America*. From this characterization, the convergence, stagnation and divergence phases should appear, which should allow for the identification of their determinants and explanations. In addition, given that our research takes into account a sample of countries of varying sizes and characteristics, *identifying the differences and similarities in the countries' cycles will be of particular interest, as well as the levels around which these cycles oscillate*.

The direction and the speed of these trends are explained by Williamson (1981) in relation to productivity and salary gaps between sectors and regions (rural–urban). The free movement of capital and work explains the lack of constancy of these gaps. Only during a specific period, from 1900 to 1930, have the relative prices of some strategic goods, cotton in this case, been used as an additional explanation for the development of productivity and salary gaps. In his previous research, Williamson (1965) explains the economic mechanisms that are the basis for these convergence and halting of these processes: "That spatial inequality, depressed areas, and backward regions appear to persists may simply suggest to some that internal factor flows (tending to reduce internal inequality) do not occur with sufficient speed and quantity to offset the dynamic indigenous conditions which cause relatively faster resource augmentation and technological change in the rich developing regions (tending to increase inequality). In fact, one could reasonably appeal to the high degree of sectionalism, fragmentation and general national disintegration in the youthful stage of national development to predict increasing regional inequality during those early decades" (Williamson 1965, p. 5).

One aspect that is more explicit than implicit, but of paramount importance, is that these explanations start with a representation of the radial focus of the processes of development. Innovation, prosperity, and growth appear in specific nodes (focuses), from which their dynamism spreads. Economic theory of disparities center their attention on the conditions in which this process of spread is produced or impeded, leaving aside the emergence of innovative focuses as a factor.

Although by different routes and by different arguments, Williamson's reasoning is complemented by the work of Barro and Sala-i-Martin (1995). The model of growth proposed here predicts *convergence between economies with very similar structural characteristics and parameters*. This is what has been known as conditional convergence (Cuervo 2003, p. 12): "In order to answer these questions, a group of closed economies (regional or isolated economies) are considered that are structurally similar, in the sense that they have the same values for the *s*,[4] *n*[5] y δ[6] parameters, and they also have the same production function *f*(•). Therefore, the economies have the same *y** y *k** values as are found in a state of stagnation. Imagine that the only difference between these economies is the initial level of capital per capita, *k(0)*. These differences in the initial levels could reflect past disruptions, such as wars or temporary conflicts in the production functions. The model therefore implies that less advanced economies – with lower *k(0)* and *y(0)* values – have higher levels of growth than *k*. The *y* level of growth will be typically higher in less advanced economies (Barro y Sala-i-Martin 1995, p. 26). "Therefore, the model does not always predict convergence in all circumstances; a poor country can grow at a lower rate than a rich country. (...) Countries with a lower level starting point *y(0)*, are probably there because they are in a state of stagnation, *k**, probably owing to their low levels of investment or due to bad, persistent government policies that effectively lower the production function" (Barro y Sala-i-Martin 1995, pp. 29–30).

Williamson's work and arguments make evident the importance of *free spatial mobility* as conditions for convergence. In agreement with the neoclassical theory of growth, more than just this freedom, it is also important to have regional socioeconomic homogeneity. In effect, the underlying assumption of convergence

---

[4] Savings rate

[5] Rate of demographic growth

[6] Depreciation rate

is the existence of the same stagnant state between areas that are being compared, that is to say, in terms of technological, labor, and financial similarities, manifest in the existence of "the same values for s, n and δ parameters, and also having the same level of production function $f(\bullet)$" (Barro y Sala-i-Martin 1995, p. 26). Accordingly, *physical and institutional integration of the economic space* will form the base for the freedom of movement of factors, while *socio-regional cohesion* will be fundamental for homogeneity.

7.2.2 Economic Explanations for Urban Primacy

Urban primacy is understood as the percentage of national population living in the countries' largest city. The concept of economic primacy will also be considered, and is understood to be the relative economic weight of the largest city with respect to its country. This constitutes a particular aspect of more general phenomena such as urbanization[7] and urban concentration.[8] To focus attention on this particular feature of contemporary regional organization in Latin American countries is justified by the singular importance of this phenomenon for the subcontinent (see Fig. 7.1).

The analysis of this incorporates various theoretical contributions: the economic history of the city, the economic theory of urban size and also the theory of primacy, as already mentioned.

Paul Bairoch's research (1985) on urban economic history provides evidence of the *external constraints* for urban growth. The city depends on the region, on its capacity for the production of *surplus food commodities*, for water and energy supplies – vital for sustaining an urban population dedicated to non-agricultural activity. Under these conditions, the maximum size of the city depends upon the magnitude of these surpluses and upon the form of provision of these elements. Bairoch (1985) calculates and shows that to sustain a million inhabitants in Imperial Rome depended upon the capacity to provide sufficient food provisions the sourcing of which was dependent upon the entire Mediterranean bay. Under the agricultural production conditions of the time, in terms of transportation and conservation methods for food-stock, it proved difficult for Rome to increase its size beyond this historical level, and for there to have developed other cities of a similar size. This dependency relationship still exists today, though, in today's world we resolve some of these problems by means of global networks of food-stock provision and energy supply.

Alonso's (1971) and Richardson's research (1977) may be considered pioneering in their inquiry of the explanations for urban growth. Using theory of the firm, a city's growth is explained as the result of the coming together of opposite

[7] Extent of the city as a general form of human settlement

[8] Trend of fastest growth witnessed in largest cities

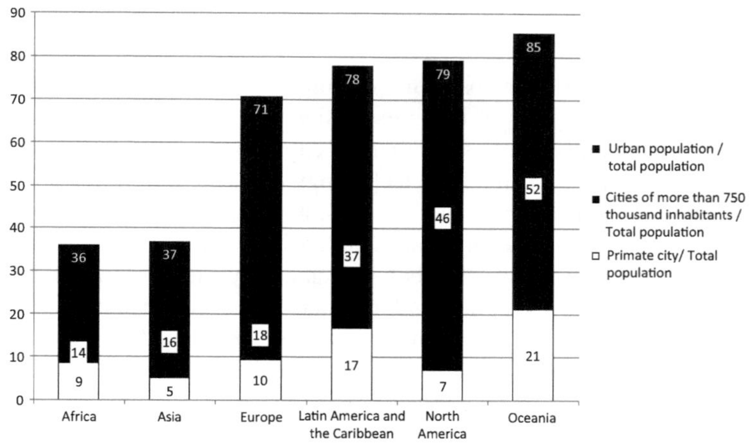

Fig. 7.1 Weight of urban population (distinct groupings) nationally by world continents (Source: Own calculations based on United Nations–*World Urban Prospects*: *The 2009 Revision*)

forces – the costs and benefits of urbanization – that model rhythms of growth, saturation and decline. The theory predicts a cyclical expansion dynamic for the city: an accelerated expansion phase, ever slowing, followed by a point of saturation, and then a final phase of decline. Given the microeconomic inspiration for this theory, it can be assumed that the definitive parameters of cycle's thresholds (that is to say, its beginning and its end) are the extension of fixed urban capital[9] and of technological changes.

Research into urban history and geographical history provide empirical support to the prediction of cyclical urban growth and it places it, moreover, in its chronological dimension. As already mentioned, Bairoch's research (1985) illustrates the long cycles of expansion, saturation and decadence in the cities of Rome and London, where epochs are measured in centuries, rather than decades or years. Research by Yazaki (1968) illustrates, on the other hand, the transition of Edo, from the imperial capital of medieval Japan, to Tokyo, the country's industrial center, taking almost a century and including a pronounced decline in the population (from one million to 500,000) and then returning to growth (from 500,000 to one million). Research undertaken by Sassen (1991) on New York, as well as studies carried out on Bogotá (Cuervo 1995) reveal the existence of shorter cycles and phases of transition, calculated in decades (around 50 years). In accordance with historical observation, *the cycle of urban expansion is part of a process of long waves* (*over various centuries*), *medium* (*over various decades*) *and short* (*over years*), *determined by very different changes in magnitude and intensity*. In the interests of this

[9] As known, it is assumed that this type of capital can be extended continuously and infinitely until a certain threshold, from which the only possible expansion is by means of a discontinuous leap.

paper, the center of attention is in identifying the determiners of medium and short waves.

Research by Hall (1998) helps with the comprehension of the factors that place limits on the medium cycles of urban expansion and explain the transitions from one to the next. Its reflection stresses that the city as an economic challenge is the result of not only physical capital and technology, but also from forms of organization, ideology and ethical and moral agreements that, together, constitute virtual capital that operates alongside physical capital, being the city's spirit and its engine. Cities and countries, says Hall, react before change opportunities in many different ways and are obliged to invent new and ingenious *methods to combines public and private funds* and build new urban infrastructures; new *regulation systems* must appear and other cease to exist; all of which involve the creation and preservation of moral order, a process of social construction, and a sense of shared social order as well (Hall 1998, p. 617; italics are ours).

To comprehend medium and short cycles of urban growth requires, therefore, the understanding of the city as an aggregate product, composed of and determined by the behavior of at least three great types of capital (a) physical capital supporting the general workings of the city, of collective consumption, subject to their own life cycles[10] (gestation, expansion and obsolescence); (b) immaterial capital, principally relationships, providing meaning, cohesion and integration of individual, corporative and social human behavior; (c) sectorial capital, with its own dynamics and cycles of expansion and obsolescence.

The historic research into Latin American urban primacy undertaken by Cuervo (2004), reaffirms the predictions of economic theory in respect to its cyclical evolution, indicating its magnitudes, and identifying some of its most important socioeconomic determining factors. It takes as its reference, the proposal of the existence of a *diachronic function of urban primacy*, with at least four historical phases proven for Latin America and also for Europe. Before industrialization, urban primacy never achieved such levels as now. (i) The phase before industrialization was accompanied by negative growth in levels of urban primacy; however, in Latin America, Southern Cone countries did not experience this decline. (ii) The moment at which industrialization takes off, signals the beginning of a long phase of growth in urban primacy. (iii) Growth in primacy continues until saturation is reached, and this is the turning point for primacy. (iv) Finally, the expectation is that the declining phase with eventually come to an end at some point. Taking this function as a reference, and by comparing Europe and Latin America, the differences seen in the latter are derived from the presence of various particularities: the lack of phase (i) for various countries and a higher intensity and duration of phase (ii). Under these conditions, if, at the beginning of the period,

[10] In accordance with Hall (1998, p. 616): an innovative push, giving rise to a Kondratieff expansion, produces new forms of transportation and communication, which in turn alters the accessibility patterns and the popular perception thereof; as a result, urban space is revalued, resulting in great changes to urban form and structure.

levels of primacy in Europe and Latin America are comparable, by the end of the period, the latter has more than double the level of the former.

How is this peculiarity in Latin America explained? Empirical research from geographic and economic standpoints identifies some factors that appear to be of little significance. Various empirical studies establish an inverse relationship between primacy and the size of the nation (Mehta 1964; Linsky 1965; De Cola 1984; Henderson 2000). Even though the size of Latin American countries would predict lower levels of primacy than is the case for Europe, this is not the case. Other factors that appear to be more significant are geographic traits derived from political and economic processes. Some possess a clear and direct impact, as in the positive relationship found by Henderson (2000) as to whether the primate city is at the same time a maritime port and/or political capital of the country. Finally, there are other ambivalent impacts, positive in some cases, and negative in others, as occurs with the level of physical integration in national territory. For some, favoring primacy, while for others, the impeding it: for Henderson (2000), urban primacy in a country is an inverse function of the density of its road network infrastructure.

More forceful explanations seem to come from industrialization modalities, the configuration of the internal market, and the characteristics of the urban labor markets. The Latin American peripheral industrialization mode, present between 1930 and 1970, weakened the spatial de-concentrative forces and heightened some of the concentrative ones. Latin American industry came about in the presence of large gap between the optimum size and the real size of production. These means that from just one city or one company (or from a very reduced number of companies) the national market demand is satisfied. Therefore, a highly monopolist or oligopolistic industrial structure is formed. In contrast, dispersing forces are weaker. This weakness is expressed principally through the absence of an industrial base and production branch of means of production that normally tends to develop close to sources of primary materials or energy provision (generally outside of large cities). This industrial base only started to appear at the end of the 1960s and early 1970s.

On the other hand, levels of urban salaries do not encourage geographic dispersion of industry. Non-salary incomes and the self-sufficiency activities in goods and services make up important complements to salary incomes. This combination of income types (salary and non-salary) helps to keep urban salaries surprisingly low, in spite of the growing costs of urbanization and city life.[11] This over-priced cost of urbanization is financed by the non-salary part of working income, and, by this means, has no effect in encouraging industry to relocate to areas outside of the big cities. Finally, the orientation and priorities of public investment reinforce industry's location in the big cities, as urban infrastructure is maintained at a superior level in comparison to the countries' other cities or regions.

[11] Economic incentives for the dispersion of industry are lessened, as expressed in theories by Richardson.

7.2.3 Possible Relationships Between Urban Primacy and Regional Disparities

Economic theories of size and urban primacy establish the role that the biggest city undertakes as a generator of, and focus for, demographic and economic growth, prosperity and innovation. They allow for the comprehension of the external conditions (food-stock and environmental surplus) for city growth (Bairoch 1985), the internal opposing conditions (agglomeration economies and diseconomies) that regulate the cycle, and the underlying fundamentals (urban technologies, organizational structures, moral order, obsolescence of collective physical and sectorial capital installed) around which the transition from one medium term cycle to another is produced.

For various reasons, which are numbered below, this primate city cycle is neither parallel to the cycle of disparities, nor does it condition it:

- Firstly, empirical evidence suggests that the cycle of primacy possesses a great inertia and that its direction does not coincide with cycles of disparities: the examination of this coincidence or discrepancy is one of the proposals to be followed up by means of the research undertaken here and is expressed below.
- Secondly, there is no coincidence, nor clear correspondence, between urban expansion and the increase in prosperity and standards of living in the big cities. Depending on the balance between agglomeration economies and diseconomies, the growth of the city and an increase in well-being and standard of living coincide at the early stage; after which, their direction diverges until a saturation point is reached where they again synchronize and both witness a decline.
- Thirdly, this impact is conditioned by national regional characteristics, which are outlined below. First, the properties of the urban network, specifically, if this network is headed by only one city, or by many. Second, the impact of primacy on the integration and homogeneity of national space, that is to say if this is accompanied by a process of segmentation, or by the integration of national economic space.

7.3 Recent Evolution of Regional Economic Disparities in Latin America

This part characterizes the disparities, from which questions will be stated and discussed. Figure 7.2 shows the evolutions of Weighted Variation Coefficient (V_w) for the seven countries included in this analysis and for a period of time of around two decades (1990–2010) that are to be analyzed here. By observation of these, conclusions will be drawn related to the absolute values of V_w and their trends.

In terms of levels, Fig. 7.2 prompts the distinction of three groups of countries: (a) of the highest value, Argentina; (b) the most numerous grouping, of four

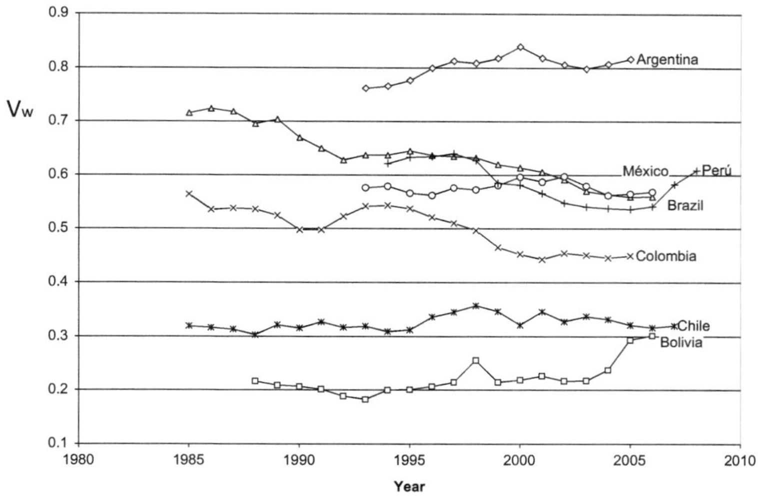

Fig. 7.2 Latin America, seven countries 1985–2007. Weighted regional disparities (V_w) (Source: Cuervo and González 2010)

countries with intermediate values (Mexico, Brazil, Peru and Colombia); (c) finally, two countries, Chile and Bolivia, form the group with the lowest values. These groups are clearly staggered since the intermediates oscillate between values of almost two times those of the lowest group, and the highest show values almost 1.4 times those of the intermediates.

Concerning trends, various groupings are also identified: Mexico and Chile with oscillations around a stable value; Brazil (since 1985), Colombia (since 1993) and Peru (since 1998) with decreasing trends; and Argentina and Bolivia (both since 1993) with growing ones.[12] For all countries, except Brazil, the 1990s were a period of change in trends, though not in the same sense for all. These trends, moreover, do not appear to alter with the advent of the twenty-first century.

The fact that for political and social reasons V_w is considered priority as an index for disparity, doesn't mean that the evolution and behavior of VC should be ignored[13] as illustrated in Fig. 7.3, that demonstrate very different observations than those seen in Fig. 7.2. In accordance with this, the classification by level goes from three countries to only two: Brazil and Peru, those countries with a high regional disparity, and the five remaining countries have an intermediate level.

[12] Classifications of countries previously made in publications, CEPAL (2009) and Cuervo and González (2010), based on Variation Coefficient (VC): standard deviation of GDP per capita for region divided by the average) Sigma (standard deviation) classifies Chile as a country with medium levels of disparities and Colombia as a country with low levels. On the other hand, the 1990s are often spoken of as an era of growing inequality, upending a variety of trends (stagnation, decline and increase) as here found.

[13] Defined as Standard Deviation divided by the average.

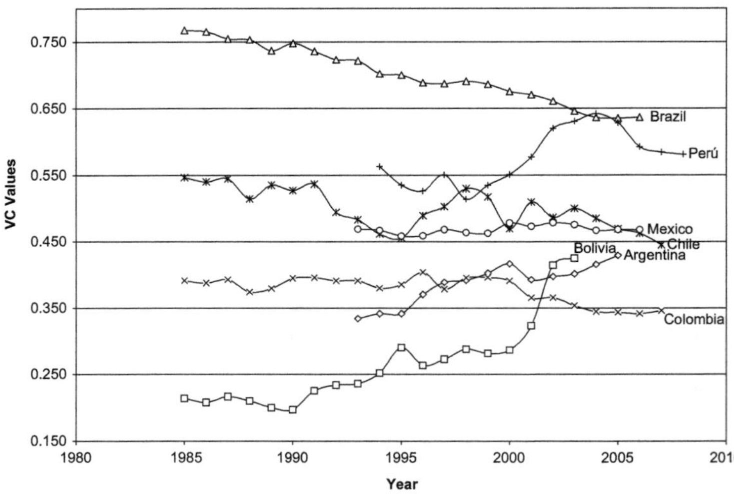

Fig. 7.3 Latin America 1985–2007. Evolution of variation coefficients (VC) for seven countries (Source: Cuervo and González 2010)

Argentina lowers abruptly from a country with very high levels of socio-regional disparities (V_w) to a country of moderate levels of regional disparity. Observations related to trends are very similar to those seen in Fig. 7.1, with the exception of Chile, which shows a moderate decreasing trend in V_w.

7.4 Characterization of Recent Evolution of Urban Primacy in Latin America and Its Relationship with Disparities

In a similar manner to the way in which regional disparities were characterized, urban primacy should also be characterized in each country in accordance with its absolute level, and also by its change trends.

Figure 7.4 represents data available for the selected countries between 1950 and 2010. Taking these levels as points of reference, of the seven countries studied, three clearly differentiated groups are configured:

- Chile, Argentina and Peru, with very high levels of primacy, between 30 % and 35 % of the national population residing in the primate city.
- An intermediate group, made up of Colombia, Mexico and Brazil, with values of around 17 %.
- And finally, Bolivia, with very low values, of around 10 %.

In terms of making sense of temporary evolution or trends, Fig. 7.4 shows the classification of countries into two large groups. The first, most numerous group,

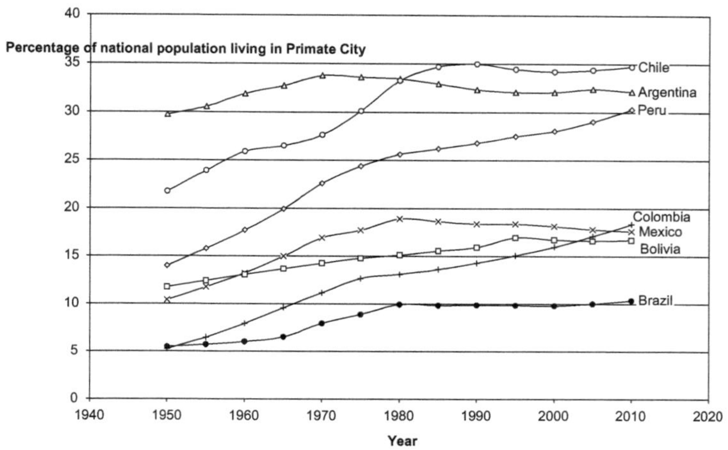

Fig. 7.4 Evolution of urban primacy in Latin America, 1950–2010. Selected countries (Source: Own calculations based on United Nation's–*World Urban Prospects*: *The 2009 Revision*)

being made up of five countries, have a decreasing or stable trend: Argentina (since 1970), Chile, Mexico and Brazil (since 1980), and Bolivia (since 1995). The second group, made up of only two countries, Peru and Colombia, show an increasing trend.

From the information provided by Fig. 7.4, various conclusions of singular importance can be drawn. The cyclical behavior of primacy, forecast by the theory and by statistical research, is validated by these results: confirmation that the primacy saturation phase has been reached in five of the seven cases. Additional, complementary observations may also be made. The figure shows, firstly, the slow process of primacy reversion: after reaching a saturation point, the downward side is always less steep than the upward growth in primacy. *The trend in primacy reversion, therefore, is significantly slower than during its increasing phase*. Secondly, observations can be made concerning some countries such as Chile, Argentina and Brazil, where the decreasing trend in primacy is halted, and, although slowly, follows a growth path: in Chile, since 2000, in Brazil, since 2005, and in Argentina since 2000, although this falls back after 2005.

The data here presented and interpreted allows for the testing of one of the central questions asked in this paper, by exploring the statistical relationship between urban primacy and regional disparities. Figure 7.5 reveals the relationship for the most recently available data concerning levels of urban primacy and regional disparities.

As seen, there is no significant statistical relationship between urban primacy and regional disparities. Two groups of countries are identified with very similar levels of urban primacy, but with very different values of disparities: Mexico, Colombia and Bolivia with primacy rates of around 17 %, but with V_w levels between 0.3 in the case of Bolivia and up to 0.6 in the case of Mexico; Chile, Peru and Argentina have primacy rates of between 30 % and 35 % and V_w values of between 0.3 in Chile's case, and up to 0.8 in Argentina's.

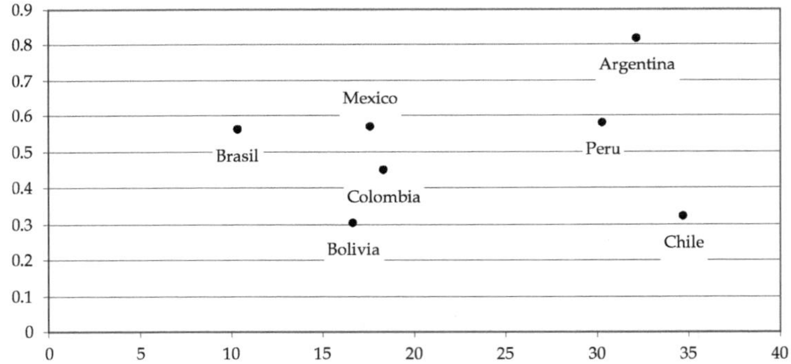

Fig. 7.5 Simple relationships between levels of urban primacy (2010) and V_w (2005–2007) (Source: Own calculations based on United Nations–*World Urban Prospects*: *The 2009 Revision* and Regional Records by country)

As posed from the beginning of this paper, urban primacy and regional disparities are related to two very different orders or empirical dimensions: firstly, with reference to demographic processes and the spatial distribution of the population, while the second is related to the economic activity conditions and wealth creation in the region. There is no reason to rule out a close and direct relationship between the two; even though there is no reason to think that this relationship, if it is produced, has to be invariable and lasting. The theory suggests, as witnessed above, that cyclical behavior trajectories in both cases have factors and explanations that in some cases coincide, and in others, do not. What this statistical study shows is that, at this precise and exact period (the last 20 years of Latin American history) this coincidence has not resulted.

As a consequence to this first result, a second essay was made necessary, using a different definition of primacy, a direct economic one. The proposal and results for which are given in the next section.

7.5 Characterization of Recent Evolution in Economic Primacy in Latin America and Its Relationship with Disparity

Economic primacy is defined as the percentage of GDP (Gross Domestic Product) resulting from the Intermediate Administrative Division (IAD)[14]) where primate city is located. As seen in Figs. 7.6 and 7.7, the countries with a high economic primacy, over 40 %, are Argentina, Chile and Peru, while those with intermediate

[14] Category using censual language, corresponding to intermediate regional entities, such as Provinces, States, Regions or Departments.

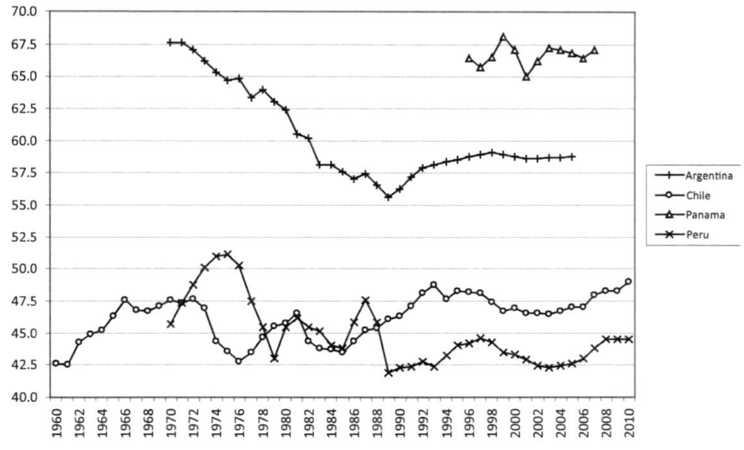

Fig. 7.6 Levels and evolution of economic primacy in Latin America, 1960–2010, countries with high primacy level (Source: Own calculations based on National Accounts data by country)

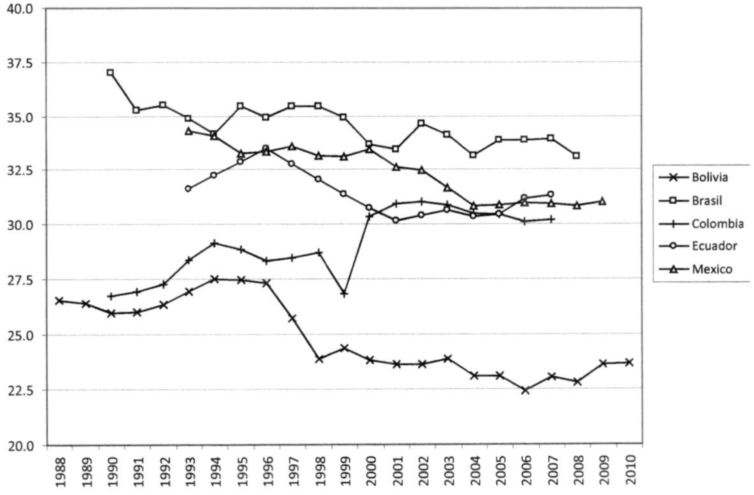

Fig. 7.7 Levels and evolution of economic primacy in Latin America, 1988–2010. Countries with intermediate primacy levels (Source: Own calculations based on National Accounts data by country)

values are Bolivia, Brazil, Colombia and Mexico. Distinguishing them by trend, the first group of three countries:

- Brazil, Mexico and Bolivia show a persistent decline in the medium term, that, however, is slowed at the beginning of the 1990s.
- A second group (Argentina and Peru), with initial early declines, again over a long period, and with a trend reversal after 1990.
- Finally, Chile and Colombia, with prolonged rising trends from the middle of the 1970s, and with a final slowing down phase after 1992 in Chile's case, and after 2000 in Colombia's.

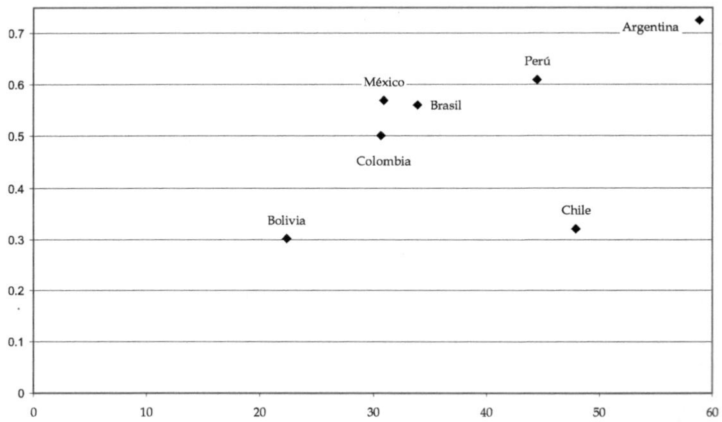

Fig. 7.8 Simple relationship between levels of economic primacy and V_w (2005–2007) (Source: Own calculations based on: Cuervo and González 2010 and National Accounts data by country)

For six of the seven countries studied, the beginning of the 1990s represented a break from previous trends: Brazil, Mexico and Bolivia with a slowing down in the rhythm of falling economic primacy; Argentina and Peru, with falling trend reversals, and Chile with a slowing down of previous growth. Colombia is the only country that seems not to have felt the impact in its incremental trend since the early 1990s. In Colombia's case, the impact of the arrival of the 1990s is more uniform, thus, five cases deal with the mitigation of the decrease or in reverting to increase; only in Chile's case is an inverse impact seen.

From the results above, a similar procedure was carried out to that of urban primacy. Fig. 7.8 explored the simple statistical relationship between economic primacy and regional disparities, with a very different result from that achieved from urban primacy. In this case, with Chile as the only exception, levels of economic primacy are directly associated with regional disparities (V_w).

Econometric studies of the relationships between economic development and urban primacy have not considered[15] the existence of a possible discrepancy in the behavior and the evolution of the two expressions of primacy here examined: demographic and economic. The additional conclusions show evidence that a correspondence, or symmetry, between levels of economic primacy and demographics is non-existent. In accordance with what was found, from now on, economic primacy will be taken as the central observation.

Next, the dynamic relationships between economic primacy and regional disparities will be examined. A graphic illustration, by means of Figs. 7.9 and 7.10, will be given as the source for these relationships. Figure 7.9 groups four

[15] Absence probably explained by the difficulties of obtaining specialized economic information. Thus, generally speaking urban primacy has been assumed to be proxy for economic primacy.

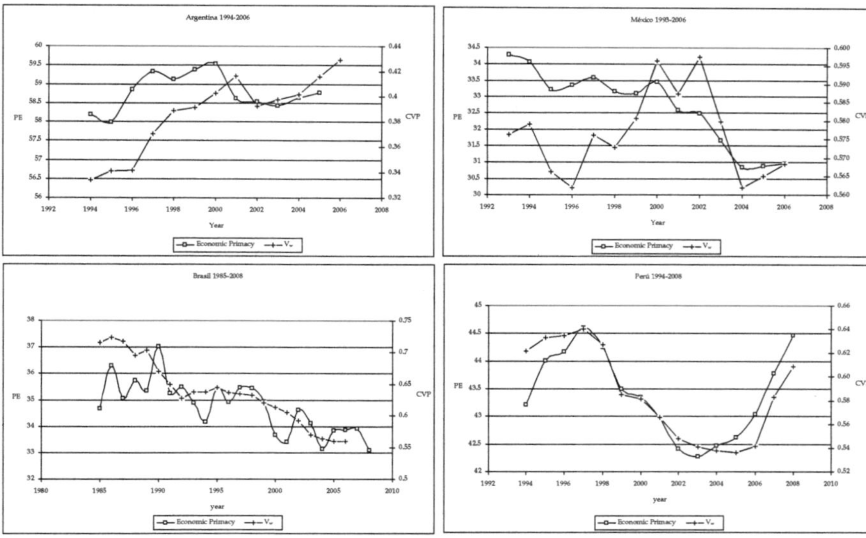

Fig. 7.9 Dynamic relationships between economic primacy and regional disparities. Countries with a strong and direct association (Source: Own calculations based on: Cuervo and Gonzalez 2010 and National Accounts data by county)

countries which show a close and direct association between economic primacy and regional disparities (V_W): Argentina, Brazil, Mexico and Peru:

- In Argentina, two sub-periods are identified: from 1994 to 2001, with a concomitant growth in economic primacy and in regional disparities; from 2002 to 2006, with stagnation in both variables and a slight upturn in both at the end.
- In Brazil, data over a longer period is available, which shows, during the period observed, a systematic fall in disparities accompanied by an oscillating but sustained decline in economic primacy.
- In Peru, an almost parallel movement in both variables is seen: an increase from 1993 to 1997, and a decline from 1997 to 2003, with another increase from 2003 to 2007.
- In Mexico, two periods are identified, from 1993 to 1996 where movement in the two variables do not coincide, and, from 1997 onwards, where a direct relationship is seen, an increase between 1998 and 2000, and a decrease from then until 2004, and then upturn between 2004 and 2006.

Figure 7.10 includes three countries in which more complicated relationships are identified that seem to involve break-down processes or structural change.

- In Colombia, from 1976 to 1993, both economic primacy and regional disparities are increasing. However, after this date, this relationship disappears since a profound decrease in regional disparities is accompanied by stagnation, and even a slight decline, in economic primacy.

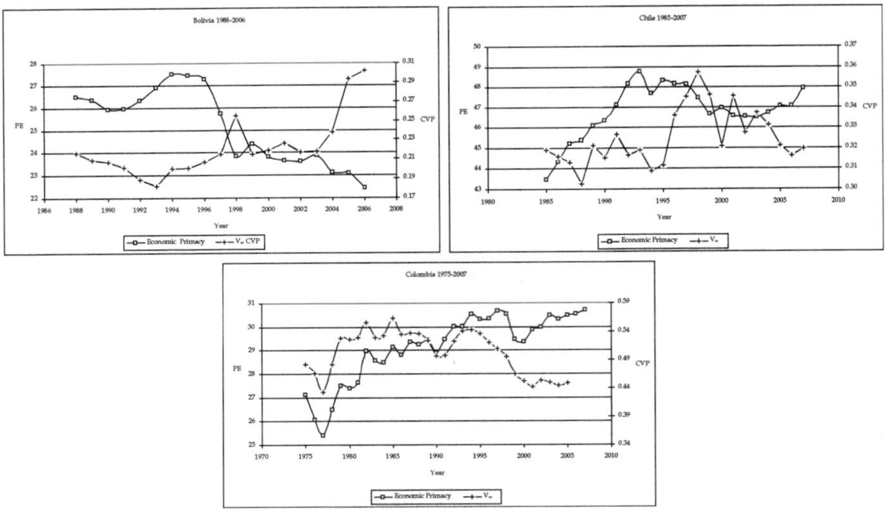

Fig. 7.10 Dynamic relationships between economic primacy and regional disparities. Countries with a strong and direct association (Source: Own calculations based on: Cuervo and Gonzalez 2010 and National Accounts data by county)

- In Chile, from 1985 to 1994, an independence or absence of a simple relationship between the two variables is seen, as the increase in economic primacy is accompanied by stagnation in regional disparities. After which, an inverse relationship appears: from 1994 to 2004, where a slight decrease in economic primacy is accompanied by an increasing growth trend in regional disparities; while from 2004 to 2007, an increase in economic primacy is accompanied by a decrease in regional disparities.
- In Bolivia, from 1988 to 1993 there is a parallel decrease in economic primacy and disparity; from 1993 to 2001 however, this relationship changes and movements in opposite directions appear, a decline in economic primacy and an increase in disparities; finally, after a brief pause between 2002 and 2006, this inverse relationship continues, but now, disparities fall while urban primacy increases.

Moreover, it's worth making a distinction between a group of three countries for which data exists over a longer period than for the others. This is the case for Brazil, Colombia and Chile. Additional information can be learnt by focusing on this group. In the case of Brazil, for example, the difference between a more volatile behavioral rhythm and oscillation of economic primacy and disparities is evident. However, owing to the length of time for these observations, it is shown that these oscillations occur with a longer, more marked trend in disparities. There is, it seems, a process of structural change with a great inertia that is a feature of the Brazilian evolution. In the cases of Chile and Colombia, the presence of break-ups and deep changes are seen, with radical transformations in the types of relationships between the two variables in question. It is of great importance to consider this moment of change in order to identify its conditions and explanations.

In the countries with shorter timelines, these two forms of behavior are also reproduced. However, the conclusions drawn are less sure as it's not possible to know whether these oscillations are the same as in Brazil's case, along a large and inert trend, or if they foreshadow the existence of structural break-ups, or if, finally, they concern marked behavioral dynamics of volatility. The outstanding task for future research is to form statistical series over a longer period of time that would clear up any of these questions.

The countries with very high levels of economic primacy (Peru and Argentina) show a very close relationship between both variables, with the only exception being Chile. In the countries with an intermediate level of economic primacy (Brazil, Mexico and Colombia), more complex relationships are seen, from intense to slight, direct to inverse, or even with independence between the two variables; only during some periods is the relationship as close as that seen in the first group. Finally, Bolivia, the country with the lowest level of economic primacy, shows very uneven dynamics for the two variables in question.

7.6 Urban Cycle and Regional Disparities

In this section, the relationship between urban primacy and regional disparities will be examined focusing on the role undertaken by big cities as a center for innovation. This role, as was concluded in the previous section, is changing in its intensity as in its meaning and direction.

The empirical evidence that has been examined up to now has shown that the early 1990s represented, for an important number of countries, a change in the previous trends of economic primacy. In the trend analysis, a first group of three countries was shown to have a persistent medium term decrease that, however, *is slowed* by the early years of the 1990s: Brazil, Mexico and Bolivia; a second group, with early initial growth and with prolonged periods of decreases, but with a *trend reversal* after 1990: Argentina and Peru. A third group consisting of two countries, Chile and Colombia, escapes this relationship, with growing and prolonged trends, from the middle of the 1970s, with a final phase of slowing down, after 1992 in Chile's case and as late as 2000 in Colombia's.

Between 1990 and 2010, the Latin American primate city experienced a deep transformation in its economic structure. This urban economic restructuring would be a reflection of the process of renovation experienced by primate cities, together with, and affected by, the changes in trends as already mentioned. The sectorial participation of the primate city against the national total for three strategic groupings is used as an indicator of this change: industry; commerce, restaurants and hotels; and financial activities.

Figures 7.11, 7.12, and 7.13 show the participation of the sectorial production generated by the primate city against the national total. The years 1990, 2000 and 2010 are compared. For each year, moreover, the percentage of each sector measured against GDP is taken as reference. In spite of the differences in structure and levels of sectorial primacy for each country, the sense of the evolution is quite uniform for this collection of countries:

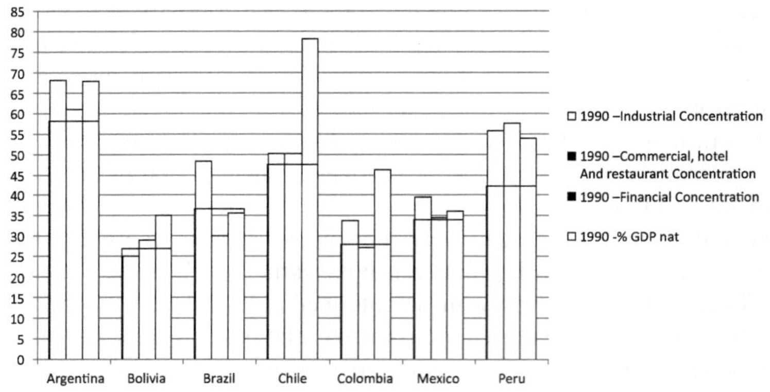

Fig. 7.11 1990 – Primate metropolis participation in economic sectors against national total (Source: National Accounts data from each country. Calculations were made for this research)

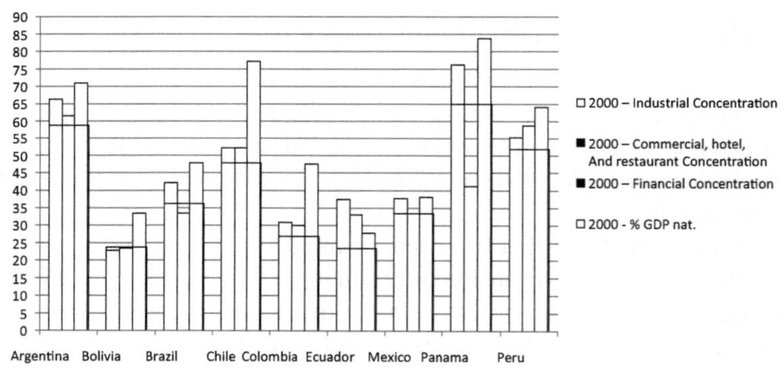

Fig. 7.12 2000 – Primate metropolis participation in economic sectors against national total (Source: National Accounts data from each country. Calculations were made for this research)

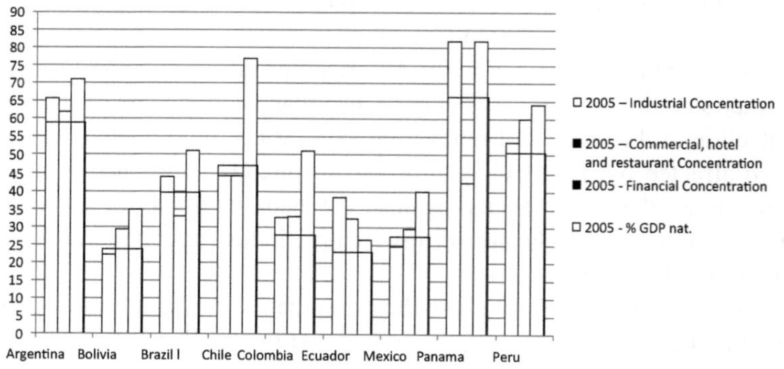

Fig. 7.13 2005 – Primate metropolis participation in economic sectors against national total (Source: National Accounts data from each country. Calculations were made for this research)

- Firstly, albeit with differences in intensity, there is a considerable decline in the weight that industry has in the primate city in relation to the national total. The extremes are Mexico with a decline of almost half from its initial level, and Colombia with a stable participation.
- Secondly, a considerable increase in the primate city's financial activity is seen for each country. The highest increase is presented by Lima-Callao in Peru[16] and the lowest by Santiago de Chile. However, in the latter case, its participation was even more significant in 1990, at almost 80 %.
- The evolution of the relative weight of commercial, hotel and restaurant activity is, however, more disparate. Peru, Colombia, Brazil and Argentina show growth in this field. Chile and Mexico show a decrease, while Bolivia is stagnated.

These figures suggest that the revitalization of the primate metropolis is associated with a major structural change connected with the consolidation of the city as a financial center, and with the relative weakening of its role as an industrial pole. However, it might be prudent to underline that, even with this weakening; the industrial weight of the Latin American primate city is still significant (Table 7.1).

7.7 Conclusions

The revised economic theory of regional disparities identifies the factors that determine and explain the direction of its evolution. Work undertaken, and arguments developed, by Williamson (1965, 1981) underline the importance of *free spatial mobility* of factors as a condition for convergence. On the other hand, in accordance with neoclassical theory of growth, in addition to this freedom, a condition of *regional socioeconomic homogeneity* is also required. In effect, the basic assumption of convergence is the existence of the same stationary state between entities that are compared, which means similar technologies, labor, finance, manifested in the existence of "the same values for s, n y δ parameters and also the same for production function $f(\bullet)$" (Barro y Sala-i-Martin 1995, p. 26). Consequently, the *physical and institutional integration of the economic space* will form the base for the free movement of factors, while *socio-regional cohesion* will be fundamental for homogeneity.

Even though no explicit observations were carried out of these determiners, nor of their influence on the explanation of the recent evolution of regional disparities, it is possible to put forward some interpretive hypotheses. Recent experiences for the seven Latin American countries studied, suggests that the fundamental factors in operation and existence are very varied. In accordance with the trends observed, countries can be grouped into three categories:

[16] Available data for Peru only indicates services in general, not financial services.

Table 7.1 Latin American Urban Primacy and Regional Economic Disparities. Main Indicators circa 1990 - circa 2010

Country	V_w Level	VC Level	V_w Trend	VC Trend
Argentina	High	Medium	↑ accelerated between 1993 and 2000 ↑ slower (2001–2005)	↑(since 1993)
Bolivia	Low	Medium	↓(1988–1993) ↑(1993–2006)	↑(since 1990)
Brazil	Medium	High	↓ accelerated (1985–1992) — (1992–1998) ↓ slower (1998–2006)	↓(since 1985)
Colombia	Medium	Medium	↑(1975–1985) ↓(1985–1991) ↓(1993–2005)	↓(since 1998)
Chile	Low	Medium	↓(1985–1988) ↑(1988–1998) ↓(1998–2007)	↓(since 1985)
México	Medium	Medium	↓(1993–1996) ↑(1996–2002) ↓(20032–2006)	—
Perú	Medium	High	↑(1994–1997) ↓(1997–2005) ↑(2005–2008)	↑(since 1998)

Key Notes:
Source: Own material, based on Cuervo and González 2010
Taking these characteristics as reference, it's possible to propose the following questions to be considered:
- What is the impact or effect of primacy on socio-regional disparities in each country?
- How does primacy contribute to the explanation of each country's inclusion at the determined level of V_w (High, Medium, Low)
- What role does the primacy dynamic play in the explanation of witnessed changes in trends for each country during the period of time studied?
↑: Increasing trend;
↓: Decreasing trend;
—: Stable

– Two groups, each made up of an extreme case and of opposite directions: Brazil, with a long trend of decreasing V_w values, and Argentina with the opposite trend. Both countries seem to be under the influence of long-term socio-spatial processes and relative inertia. Brazil, with a process of growth spreading from its most dynamic pole, Sao Paulo, towards the entire south of the country; Argentina, with its long period of primacy in terms of the vast Buenos Aires, in absence of regional poles (potential and eventual receivers) to spread this dynamism towards, which might include the most developed, central provinces of Santa Fe, Cordoba and Mendoza.
– The remaining group, the other five countries, with changeable relationships, very probably determined by the experienced transformations caused in the regional economic structure for each country. The identification of these relationships and relevant factors make up part of the fundamental task for future research.

Theories on size and urban primacy establish the role of the biggest city as a central generator for growth in terms of demographics, the economy, prosperity and innovation. They identify the external conditions (food-stock and environmental surplus) for city growth (Bairoch 1985), and the opposing internal forces (economies and diseconomies of agglomeration) which regulate the cycle. Likewise, among these fundamental factors (urban technologies, forms of organization, moral order, obsolescence of installed physical and sectorial collective capital) from which the transition from one medium term urban cycle to another is produced. The theory//theories forecast a dynamic cyclical expansion of the city, with an accelerated initial expansion phase, followed by a point of saturation and then a final phase of decline. In accordance with developed historical observations made in different regions of the world, *the urban expansion cycle would be part of a process with long wave (over several centuries), medium waves (over various decades), and short waves (in years), determined by very differing changes in magnitude and intensity.*

The historic study of Latin American urban primacy undertaken by Cuervo (2004) reaffirms the predictions made by economic theory with respect to its cyclical evolution, specifying its magnitudes and identifying some of its most important socio-economic determiners. It proposes and measures the existence of a diachronic function of urban primacy, with at least four historical phases proven in Latin America as well as in Europe: a phase beginning before industrialization with decreasing levels of primacy, a long phase of growth in primacy beginning with the process of industrialization, a moment of saturation and then a final phase of decline. In the case of Latin America, the phase for growth in primacy is longer and more intense, and this forms the base for the generation of the high levels of primacy witnessed on this subcontinent.

The empirical evidence developed and presented in this paper contributes to the development of knowledge of the theme in many ways and for various reasons. On one hand, the evolution of Latin American urban primacy over the last 60 years reaffirms the cyclical character of urban primacy, and shows evidence of the ultimate phase of the diachronic function of primacy: saturation. It specifies, moreover, that the decrease in primacy after saturation is much slower than its increase during its growth phase. Additionally, it shows the appearance of processes of stagnation or reversion of these trends, that is to say, a take-up of primacy growth again. These processes of revitalization of growth in Latin American primacy seem to be associated with, as shown in the last part of this paper, the deep economic restructuring that large cities are experiencing across the continent. This restructuring lessens, without destroying, the role of industry as a generator for regional disparities and boosts the role of financial activity. The collection of cities studied has experienced a similar transformation, with varying degrees of intensity and scale.

As forecasted at the end of the theoretical review in this paper, the primate city cycle is not parallel to, nor completely conditions cycles of disparities. The first contribution to this comes from establishing the inexistence of a significant statistical relationship between levels of urban primacy in the seven countries studied and levels of disparities (measured by means of V_w). The revised statistical evidence does not allow us to rule out of the possibility that this relationship was valid at other times in history. To verify this would require the use of long-term data, which was not available at the time of writing of this paper.

The examination of the relationship between economic primacy and regional disparities produced very different results: Firstly, a significant and direct statistical association between the former and the latter. Secondly, very close dynamic relationships between changes in economic primacy and changes in disparities. Though close and lasting, this association occurs in a various guises: from a direct and permanent relationship in the case of some countries like Argentina, Peru and Brazil; from a significant but changeable direction in the remaining countries: Bolivia, Colombia, Chile and Mexico. The explanation for these differences between countries, and the variations over time, are themes to be explored for future research.

7.8 In Epilogue Form: Reflections on Public Policy

Though the purpose of this research is not to formulate regional or urban economic policy recommendations, by its very nature, it provides an opportune moment to make some reflections on the theme. In as much as these reflections are not the direct result of presented arguments, we prefer to present them in the form of an epilogue.[17] Thinking about public policy means centering attention on institutional, political and even ethical processes; areas that have not been closely related to the exercise in hand. Objective knowledge of the casual relationships between variables, factors and dimensions is only one of the varied ingredients necessary for creating satisfactorily prepared economic policy. Therefore, in spite of recognition of the limitations of the presented reflections in the following lines, we consider it appropriate to make them, more to open up the debate, than to finalize it.

These reflections take their starting point from two findings. The first: from research (Cuervo and Williner 2009) and from direct contact with Latin American national realities,[18] where there is a notable lack of concern about urban concentration and the size of the biggest cities as a phenomenon related with regional policy objectives.[19] An interesting theme in itself, for its undeniable environmental, social,

[17] The definition of ″epilogue″ according to the Spanish Royal Academy es: "the last part of a piece of work, detached in some way from earlier parts, representing an action or referring to events that are a consequence of the main action or are in some way related to it.

[18] There is a renaissance in the theme of spatial decentralization//de-concentration of economic activity in public policy and regional regulatory plans in countries such as Venezuela, Ecuador and Trinidad and Tobago.

[19] Gained interest at the end of the 1970s when some countries in the region implemented measures to dis-incentivize growth in the biggest cities and promote growth in the intermediate cities and in new poles, as this was called in that era.

political and institutional impacts; but not for its possible impact on regional economic disparities. The second: from the 1970s (a time when this area for concern existed) until today, advances made in theoretical and empirical research are noteworthy. Starting with that research, it would be possible, and also necessary, to reformulate quite drastically, the fundamentals there established. Some of these advances have been taken up again in this paper, and others have been raised in previous publications (CEPAL 2009). We have taken up some of the most significant public policy suggestions deriving from these.

The most important reference for the 1970s was early work carried out by Williamson (1965). From this work, many considerable advances have been made in the knowledge of the relationships between economic development and urban primacy. There was the acceptance of the idea that urban primacy is neither positive nor negative in itself, but that its economic significance depends upon the development phase of a particular country; additionally, it was established that states of excessive concentration or de-concentration, with long-term growth possibility implications, can result at any moment of the process (Henderson 2000). The relationships between urban primacy and development are situated thus, in the context of a multifaceted and multidimensional argument that suggest and oblige placing the county in the specific context that corresponds to it, without pigeonholing it with supposedly universally valid affirmations. Research inspired by neoclassical models of growth, undertaken during the 1990s, made evident the extremely slow process of regional convergence before, and its halting thereafter. It identified and quantified the importance of qualitative research, already documenting these phenomena, but little studied at a statistical level; such was the case for regional fragmentation of national space (Cuervo 2003). This fragmentation is the reason for the presence of losing and winning regional clubs, the expression of socioeconomic and infrastructural heterogeneity of Latin American national space.

Along with progress made in theory, consideration for the institutional learning undertaken in the region is also indispensible. The most notable of which concerns decentralization policies applied in Latin America. Though very different in context – in terms of institutions, continuity and also in the tools applied – they have shown that decentralization is a necessary condition, but not in itself sufficient, in achieving a decrease in levels of regional disparities. Moreover, experiences in local development and in regional competitiveness pertaining to the 1990s, but still valid today, show a similar conclusion: regional involvement is a necessary condition, but not sufficient in itself, to weaken or lessen regional economic disparities.

As stated above, some countries begin to bring concerns about excessive concentrations of activity and economic power in their biggest cities into the sphere of public policy, and put in place programs which attempt to mitigate the effects of this concentration. The scattered and incomplete data that exists suggest that the design of these new generation of spatial economic de-concentration policies haven't absorbed the previously mentioned theoretical knowledge, or knowledge gleaned from research or institutions. In the majority of cases, these policies are concerned with the formulation of plans, which a lack clear articulation and with imprecise instruments of execution and financing, and with no intersectional coordination space. Additionally, instead of making the most of the policy and institutional strengthening that some subnational and local governments have enjoyed thanks to decentralization, policies put forward by national governments are formed by consultation neither with, nor in coalition with, regional levels below. Finally, there is a lack of effort: (a) from academia to carry out research for the purposes of making historical and institutional memoirs and creating reflections and arguments that help us avoid making the same mistakes as in the past; (b) from multilateral organizations to aid with the identification and interchange of relevant experiences that accelerate the processes of improvement in the quality of public management in areas as specific as this.

References

Alonso W (1971) The economics of urban size. Pap Reg Sci Assoc XXVI:67–83

Bairoch P (1985) De Jéricho à México. Villes et économie dans l'histoire. Gallimard, Paris

Barro RJ, Sala-i-Martin X (1995) Economic growth. MacGraw-Hill, New York

CEPAL (2009) Economía y territorio en América Latina y el Caribe. Desigualdades y políticas. Cepal Naciones Unidas, Santiago de Chile, p 206

Cuervo LM (1995) Génesis histórica y constitución de Bogotá como ciudad moderna. Bogotá, Corporación SOS Viva la Ciudadanía, Mimeo, Mayo, 134 p

Cuervo LM (2003) Evolución reciente de las disparidades económicas territoriales en América Latina: estado del arte, recomendaciones de política y perspectivas de investigación, Serie Gestión Pública No.41. ILPES, CEPAL, Naciones Unidas, Santiago de Chile, p 110

Cuervo LM (2004) Desarrollo económico y primacía urbana en América Latina. Una visión histórico comparativa, 2004. In: Ana Clara Torres Ribeiro (ed) El rostro urbano de América Latina. CLACSO, Agencia Sueca de Desarrollo Internacional (ASDI), Buenos Aires, pp 77–114, 384 p

Cuervo LM, González S (2010) Disparidades económicas territoriales en América Latina: 20 años de trayectoria (1990–2010). Mimeo/ILPES, CEPAL, Naciones Unidas, Santiago de Chile, p 186

Cuervo LM, Williner A (2009) Políticas e instituciones para el desarrollo económico local, 2009, pp 57–83. Revista *LIDER*, Vol 13, Año 11. In: Alberto Abalerón (ed) Desigualdades Socio-Espaciales en América Latina, 20 p, Chile

De Cola L (1984) Statistical determinants of the population of a nation's largest city. Econ Dev Cult Chang Chic 33(1):71–98

Hall P (1998) Cities in civilization. Culture, innovation and urban order. Phoenix-Giant, London, p 1169

Henderson V (2000) How urban concentration affects economic growth, Policy research working paper 2326, The World Bank, 42 p

Linsky AS (1965) Some generalizations concerning primate cities. Ann Assoc Am Geogr (LUGAR) 55:506–513

Mehta SK (1964) Some demographic and economic correlates of primate cities: a case for revaluation. Demography 1(1):136–147, Washington

Richardson HW (1977) The theory of city size. In: Richardson HW (ed) The Economics of urban size. Saxon House/Lexington Books, Lexington, pp 11–20, 243

Sassen S (1991) The global city. New York, London, Tokyo. Princeton University Press, Princeton, 397

Williamson JG (1965) Regional inequality and the process of national development. Economic development and cultural change 13, July, pp 3–45

Williamson JG (1981) Inequality and regional development: the view of America. In: Bairoch P, Lévy-Leboyer M (eds) Disparities in economic development since the industrial revolution. MacMillan, London, pp 373–391

Takeo Yazaki (1968) Social change and the city in Japan. From earliest times through the industrial revolution. Japan Publications, Tokyo

Part II
Analysis by Countries

Chapter 8
Growth, Concentration, Inequality and Regional Policy in Mexico

Luis Quintana-Romero and Norman Asuad-Sanén

8.1 Introduction

During the period from 1970 to 2010 the Mexican economy grew at an average rate of 3.3 %, a disappointing long run performance. To a large extent, this situation is due to the end of the import substitution industrialization period, during the late 1970s, and the subsequent transition to a new model based on exports, during the 1980s.

Slow growth of the Mexican economy has been associated with an increase in regional disparities (Appendini et al. 1972 Hernández 1984; Garza 1997; Unikel et al. 1976; Ruiz 1997; Ramirez 1986; Juan-Ramón and Rivera-Batiz 1996; Messmacher 2000; García-Verdú 2002). Since the late 1990s, numerous studies of the convergence hypothesis in Mexico have found greater regional inequality (Navarrete 1995; Esquivel 1999; Esquivel and Messmacher 2002; Gamboa and Messmacher 2002). These studies agree on the existence of a process of convergence in the early years of Mexican industrialization and one of stagnation in the years following its demise. That is particularly true after 1985 when a unilateral liberalization process started, that was later completed with the signing of the North American Free Trade Agreement (NAFTA) in 1994 (Hanson 1998, 2001; Sanchez and Rodriguez 2002; Esquivel and Messmacher 2002; Aguayo 2004; Rodriguez-Orregia 2005; Chiquiar 2005; Serra et al. 2006; González Rivas 2007; Calderon and Tykhonenko 2007; Cermeño and Garrido 2009).

This work was carried out with the support of the Special University Chair "José Vasconcelos" FES-Acatlán and the DGAPA PAPIIT IN308911 "Economic regionalization program" in FE-UNAM. The authors want to thank to Cristina Vázquez Ruiz and Jaime Prudencio Vázquez for his valuable work of research documents, sources and for mapping.

L. Quintana-Romero (✉) • N. Asuad-Sanén
National Autonomous University of Mexico, FES-Acatlán and FE-UNAM, Mexico
e-mail: luquinta@apolo.acatlan.unam.mx; nasuad@economia.unam.mx

J.R. Cuadrado-Roura and P. Aroca (eds.), *Regional Problems and Policies in Latin America*, Advances in Spatial Science, DOI 10.1007/978-3-642-39674-8_8,

In addition to the studies conducted, the use of new spatial analysis techniques (spatial econometrics, kernels and conditional densities) has provided additional elements to evaluate regional inequality Anselin (1988). Asuad et al. (2007a, b), using spatial growth models, have shown that inequality is a process that has a regional feedback. Meanwhile Aroca et al. (2005) note that the envisioned consolidation in the northern region of the country, derived from NAFTA, has indeed occurred. For them the regional divergence is explained by the development of a convergence club at the country's central region. Sastre and Rey (2008) show that the divergence is associated with a deepening of regional polarization.

In relation to the existing evidences of regional inequality in Mexico, this paper starts from a different perspective, one which we believe can provide new evidence on what happens to the country's regions. First, we analyze the evolution of inequality in Mexico under the idea that the spatial unit of analysis is relevant. That is why we combine the traditional analysis by state with one by metropolitan areas, which we believe represent a regional disaggregation closest to what a functional economic region should be. Second, it makes use of new proposals to measure inequality that are not restricted to the traditional analysis of sigma and beta convergence. Third, the analysis seeks to contextualize inequality in the process of spatial concentration of economic activity in the country, and shows how regional policies have helped to consolidate the current concentration pattern and the regional differences that arise in this process. We think these three elements allow us to present a better analysis of the regional inequality process, and also raise new research issues on regional analysis.

For these purposes, the text is divided into three parts. The first presents some stylized facts about concentration and regional growth in Mexico. The second part we present several inequality indicators at the state and at the metropolitan area level. Finally in the third part we examine the central elements of a regional policy that has helped to consolidate the current structure of inequality.

8.2 Patterns of Regional and Urban Development

Mexican regional development maintains essentially the same economic characteristics and population concentration that existed in traditional regions, during de 1970s. Although there have been changes at the intra-regional level, derived from economic liberalization and the outward orientation of the economy, they have not been strong enough to solve the structural problems of regional and urban development.[1]

[1] The data used in this section are author's calculations based on the Economic Census of 1989, 1994, 1999, 2004 and 2009, and the Population Censuses of 1970, 1980, 1990, 2000 and 2010. The inter-census population data were estimated using the method of interpolation.

To analyze the basic features of growth in Mexico, we use a regional delimitation combining physical, economic, social and spatial criteria. The results are three major areas (Central, North and South) composed of nine regions.[2] National regional development pattern is characterized by high economic and population concentration in a few regions and urban areas, due to differences in the formation of market areas, the agglomeration of fixed capital in the global and sectorial productivity of their economies.

8.2.1 Central Zone and Its Regions

From 1970 until 2008, the Central zone accounted for about 50 % of the national gross product production. It also provided more than half of the jobs in the country (57 %) and concentrates up to 55 % of the total population according to 2008 data. It is worth noting that the aggregate share of the area in production, employment and population, remained practically constant during the period 1970–2008.

Moreover, the central zone contributes most of the production of services and manufacturing activity. The zone accounted for 73 % and 64 % respectively, of the national total in 2008. It is in the central region where employment is concentrated in the central zone, as it accounts for 37 % of manufacturing employment and 43 % of the services jobs of the Central zone enter. However, Central zone's productivity and per capita output are the smallest among the country's zones.

Inside the Central zone there have been significant structural changes, while the North Central region and the Central West have been more involved in manufacturing, and the central region has increased its relative share of services. In fact, the Central zone is characterized by a change in its production structure moving from manufacturing to services, both in terms of production's value, and in terms the structure of jobs created.

Alongside with economic concentration processes, Central zone is also distinguished by its high urban population, hosting cities with over 15,000 inhabitants. In 2008, the Center had more than half of the total population of the cities of that size. For example, the metropolitan area of Mexico City had about 20 million people, while the next most important city in the Zone is Puebla, which is Mexico's fourth largest city.

[2] The North zone comprise three regions and its respective federative states; Northwest (Baja California, Baja California Sur, Sonora, Sinaloa), North (Chihuahua, Durango, Coahuila), Northeast (Nuevo León and Tamaulipas). The Central zone is form for the next regions; Central (Distrito Federal, Estado de México, Puebla, Hidalgo, Morelos, Querétaro, Tlaxcala), Central west (Jalisco, Michoacán, Nayarit and Colima), North Central (Guanajuato, Aguascalientes, San Luis Potosí and Zacatecas). Finally, the South zone comprise the next regions; Southeast (Guerrero, Oaxaca and Chiapas), Southwest (Tabasco and Veracruz), and Yucatan peninsula (Yucatán, Campeche and Quintana Roo).

8.2.2 Northern Zone and Its Regions

The Northern zone was second in importance in terms of the share of production and employment generation, corresponding to 23 % and 27 %, respectively, of the national total in 2008. This Zone accounts for 22 % of the total population of the country and its relative importance has remained virtually unchanged from 1970 to 2008.

The Zone held the second place in its share of manufacturing (23 %) and services (16 %) in 2008. Inside this Zone, the Northeast region stands out as it contributes with a little more than half of manufacturing activity and half of the services in the Zone.

In the case of employment, it ranks in second place in terms of the Zone's manufacturing and service jobs, but it also has a high share in the creation of jobs in the primary sector, contributing with 40 % to the national total.

Within the Zone, there are significant regional differences in the manufacturing and service sectors performance, as the Northeast region noted for its even greater participation in production and productivity levels, even in the national figures. The high industrial productivity of the northeast region has led to an increased participation at national level between 1970 and 2008, although the Zone to which it belongs has lost relative weight in the country's totals.

The Zone accounts for 28 % of the population of the major cities of the country and 20 % of the total urban population. It also includes within its boundaries, the third largest city in the country, Monterrey with 3.9 million inhabitants in 2008.

8.2.3 Southern Zone and Its Regions

The Southern zone area ranks third in importance for its contribution to production and employment generation, with 27 % and 16 %, respectively, in 2008. However, much of that weight is due to the oil extraction southeastern sector and to the Yucatan peninsula. The area has a primary productive structure, contributing with 94 % of the sector's national total. It concentrates only 10 % of the population of the major cities, Merida being the most important city inside this zone relevant.

8.3 Regional Inequality and Spatial Effects on Regional Performance

The evolution of regional economic inequality in Mexico must be examined in accordance with the different ways in which it expresses itself in the country's regions. We begin with the analysis at the administrative region level (i.e., at the state and municipal level). State level is relevant because the allocation of federal public spending. While the municipal level is the locus of economic concentration upon which economic activity takes place. It is within these levels that the economic links are generated inside a region. Our analysis of inequality includes the administrative regions of the country, that is, states and their municipalities, as well as representative regions of economic concentration, in this case Metropolitan areas. Inequality measurements, at these different levels of spatial aggregation, are complementary and enrich the discussion of the evolving regional growth and its nationwide disparities.

We begin our analysis with a review of the evolution of GDP per capita (GDPPC) dispersion levels, over the 32 states in which the country is divided administratively. In this analysis we introduce two novel aspects in relation to the vast literature that has been published since the 1990s on regional inequality in Mexico: the use of a wide range of indicators of inequality and use of population weights to account for size differences in the spatial units.[3]

Following Ezcuarra and Rodriguez-Pose (2010), the degree of inequality among the states during the period 1970–2010, is analyzed by means of the coefficient of variation (c), the standard deviation of the logarithms (v), the Gini index (G), generalized entropy indexes (GE) and the Atkinson index (A).

Figure 8.1 includes the results for the different inequality indicators, that has been unable to overcome inequality levels that prevailed in the 1970s. According to the indicator used, inequality levels are currently in the range from −4 to 7 percentage points relative to 1970.

During this time span there are five stages of regional inequality reductions. They are shaded in the graph at its lowest point, corresponding to the periods of 1970–1978, 1980–1987, 1993–1995, 2000–2004 and 2008–2009. In the first two periods the reduction of inequality reached its historical peak, in 1970–1978 is reduced from 5 to 15 percentage points, while from 1980 to 1987 is reduced from 8 to 26 percentage points. In studies related with convergence or divergence of regional growth in Mexico, the coefficient of variation has been used as a key indicator of inequality. What can be seen in our results is that this indicator undervalues the dimensions of the problem. Most of the alternative measures of inequality have higher values than those derived from the values of the coefficient of variation. Therefore, is possible to argue that the sigma convergence process was much deeper in the 1970–1987 phase, than previous studies have argued. In that period, the Mexican economy still registered high growth dynamics. In spite of the oil prices collapse in 1986, when the oil revenues diminished to half its previous level, the economy grew at a rate of over 5 %.

The final three periods in which the regional dispersion is reduced, correspond to a stage of slower growth that begins with the process of structural reform in the mid-1980s, which promotes the country's trade liberalization and privatization of companies previously owned by the Mexican state. Since 1987, the year in which

[3] Annex describes broader the indicators of inequality, and the way in which were calculated.

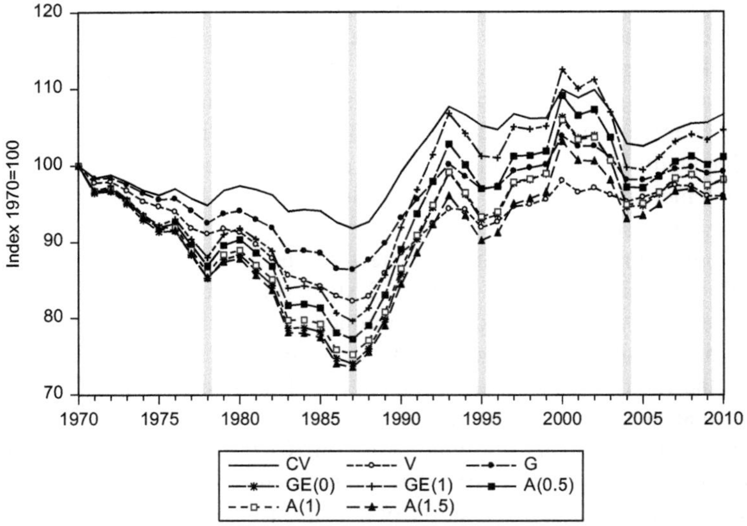

Fig. 8.1 Regional inequality in the Mexican States (GDP per capita, 1970 = 100) (Source: Authors' calculations based on Mendoza (2011))

the reduction of regional inequality is highest, there is a notorious economic slowdown of the country: between 1987 and 2010 the average annual growth rate drops to 3 %.

Since the 1990s, the processes of regional inequality reduction have two main characteristics. Its duration tends to be shorter, i.e., they are less sustainable than the processes that occurred in the 1970s and 1980s. Also their depth is less than what was achieved years ago. Clearly regional inequality is associated with the weakening in the pace of economic growth. Slower rates of growth are a consequence of a very orthodox conception regarding economic policies, which has prioritized the stability of macroeconomic indicators at the expense of growth.

The processes of reducing and increasing inequality that we have described, are related to a growing polarization. The graph below shows the results of generalized polarization indicator of Esteban et al. The first thing to observe is that the long-term regional inequality we have highlighted before, also corresponds to an increase in long-term polarization. This increase goes from 5 to 22 percentage points from 1970 to 2010, depending on the weights assigned to the sensitivity parameter used. The greatest polarization growths occurs after the process of trade liberalization in the mid-1980s (Fig. 8.2).

Between 1970 and 2010, we can find times when regional polarization is slightly reduced. This happens from 1970 to 1975, from 1979 to 1985, from 2000 to 2001 and from 2003 to 2010. There is no full correspondence in decreasing inequality and reductions of polarization. In fact, even after 1985 one observes increased polarization processes that correspond to processes of lower regional inequality.

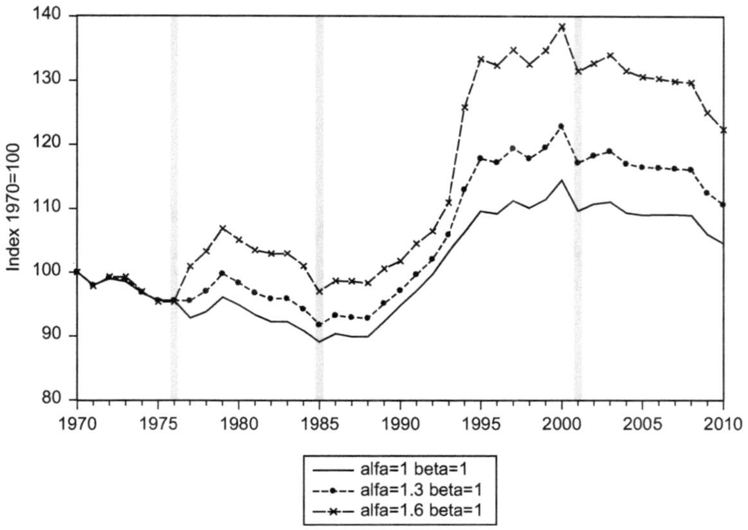

Fig. 8.2 Regional polarisation: two groups of Mexican States (1970 = 100) (Source: Authors' calculations based on Mendoza (2011))

As has been stated in the first section of this chapter, the spatial economic concentration is the dominant aspect in the growth processes of the country's regions. The main concentrations are located in metropolitan areas, so it is worth examining the behavior of inequality at that level of aggregation. In Mexico GDP data are not disaggregated by municipalities, so it is not possible to have this information directly for metropolitan areas. Therefore, in this paper we use Mendoza's estimates of (2011) for municipal GDP in the period 1989–2010.

Figure 8.3 shows the estimates of inequality in Mexican metropolitan areas. Regardless of the form in which it is measured, data indicates a process of greater inequality over the last 20 years. Inequality among states, as we have already observed above, also shows an increasing pattern in those years. When inequality is measured by metropolitan areas, its values are higher than those estimated considering only states. Overall, the data suggest that inequality among metropolitan areas has grown between 12 and 24 percentage points, a higher figure than the 4 percentage points, estimated using state level data.

In the long run the combination of greater divergence and greater polarization can be characterized if we look at the entire distribution of the data (Quah 1993, 1996a, b, 1997; Magrini 2009). Panel (a) of Fig. 8.4 shows the conditional distribution function (Hyndman 1996; Hyndman et al. 1996) of the states' per capita GDP in 1970 and 2010. The persistence of the distribution along the main diagonal, highlights the absence of regional convergence. At the same time, there can be seen a movement in the probability mass of high levels of income in 1970 to higher levels in 2010. The latter indicates greater regional polarization and the existence of

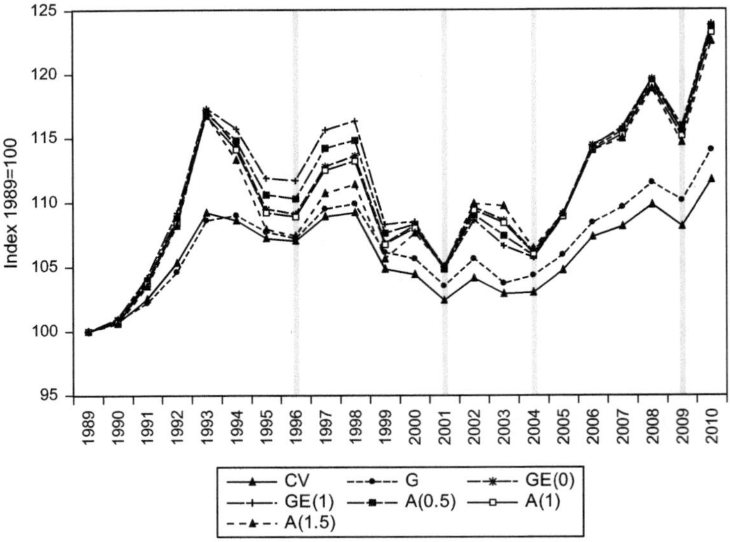

Fig. 8.3 Regional polarisation: two groups of metropolitan areas (1970 = 100) (Source: Authors' calculations based on Mendoza (2011))

a group of states that have been relatively more enriched, which is located between the DF and a group of central states such as Aguascalientes, San Luis Potosi and Queretaro. Panel (b) of the same graph shows the distribution for metropolitan areas. There we also find persistence, but there is greater mobility at higher income levels. Metropolitan areas that tend to improve their position more strongly are those of Coatzacoalcos, Aguascalientes, Chihuahua, Toluca and Morelia.

The problem of regional inequality lies not on its existence, but on its extent and in the fact that it leads to vicious cycles of growth, in which the rich regions become more rich and the poor ones, poorer. This has been possible to the extent that regional policy has proved unable to reverse this problem, as discussed below.

8.4 Change and Evolution of Regional Policy

8.4.1 Origins, Orientation and Regional Policy Change Until 1970

Since its origins, regional policy was oriented to diminish regional inequalities in the country.[4] This goal is included in the 1917 Constitution text, where is stated that national development will be based on the domestic market. In its first phase

[4] This section was developed based in Asuad (1995)

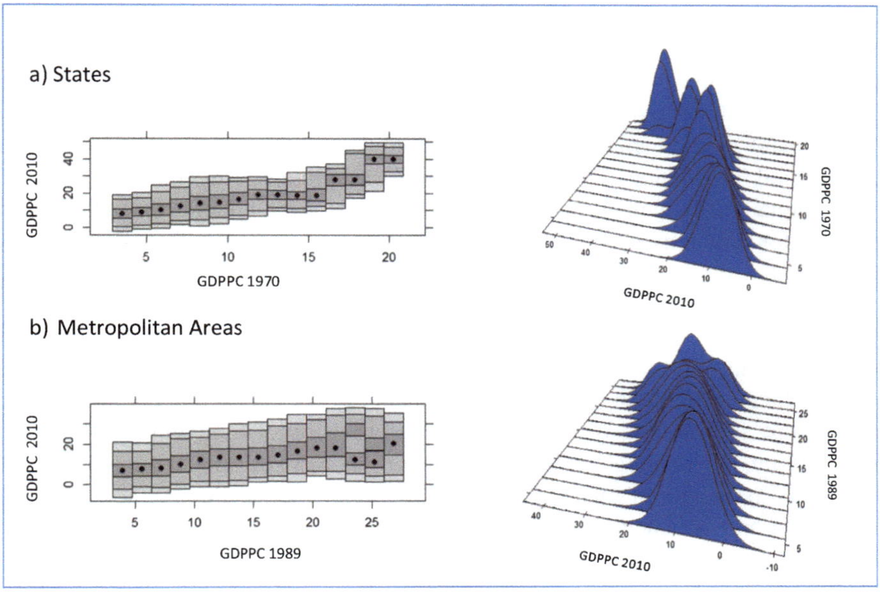

Fig. 8.4 Stacked conditional density plots and high density regions boxplots of per capita GDP (Source: Authors' calculations based on routine (Hyndman 1996; Hyndman et al. 1996))

(1915–1940), the main feature of regional policy was the creation of basic institutions for domestic market infrastructure development. These institutions include the creation of the Bank of Mexico and other public funding agencies, and the creation of government owned strategic industries such as electricity production and distribution, Railroads and Oil industries.

The main instrument to promote human settlements in the country was the 1915 land reform law, upon which 153 major agricultural settlements were established, some with significant impacts on the subsequent urbanization process.

The growth of a railroad network strengthened economic regions formed during the period before the 1910 Revolution. The country concentrated most of mining and metallurgy in the Central zone and railroads moved cargo from production sites to the ports. The economic regions that flourished during this period were the following:

1. Central Region based in Mexico City maintained its role as the main regional center of the country.
2. The Western Central Region based in the city of Guadalajara. It was consolidated as the second most important regional center, extending to the Bajio region, which today form the North Central region.
3. The Northeast Region based in the city of Monterrey as the third regional center.

Inside these regions, major market areas developed, mainly in the central and north regions. Mexico City stands out for its huge economic size and a population of 1.8 million people, representing 26 % of the urban population, while Guadalajara and Monterrey had more than 200,000 inhabitants.

From 1940 to 1970, based on import substitution, a major industrialization drive was promoted. This process resulted in the transition from a rural to an urban nation. During those years the population nearly tripled, from 20.2 to 60.0 million people, with about two-thirds of the population living in cities.

Regional policy focused on the expansion of industry and the development of agricultural production. Domestic industry was protected by means of import restrictions and helped through fiscal exemptions, credit facilities and massive support for productive infrastructure. This support for the manufacturing industry consolidated the major regional centers of the country, which still prevail, and which are articulated mainly around Mexico City, Guadalajara, Monterrey and Puebla (see Fig. 8.1). Industrial development was complemented by support for agriculture, through the expansion of irrigation districts, especially in the Northwest, which resulted in agricultural productivity increases the productivity of agriculture, increases that made possible the provision of food and raw materials required by the manufacturing development. In fact the model is adopted the traditional paradigm of regional policy of the Tennessee Valley Authority, which was based on watersheds (Barkin and King 1993) (Fig. 8.5).

8.4.2 Impulse, Reorientation and Change of Regional Policy 1970–1988

8.4.2.1 The Model of Shared Development and Institutionalization of Regional Policy During 1970–1976

In the late 1960s Mexican economy began reducing its growth rate and in 1968 went through a major political crisis because of the repression of the student's movement. Thus, to deal with social discontent, government policy in the early 1970s focused on income redistribution, job creation and the expansion of production capacity. Therefore, regional policy was aimed at combating centralism, reducing regional disparities, given attention to marginalized areas and creating integrated regional development areas. This stage is known as the shared development model, and coincides with the a reduction of regional inequality already alluded to in the previous section.

The main regional policy actions were aimed at creating growth poles, regional development regions and programs that promoted comprehensive regional development, details of which can be reviewed in Box 8.1.[5]

[5] Regional policy was analyzed from the Presidential reports and National Plans of Development of each Government (Presidencia de la República, Informes Presidenciales and Presidencia de la República Planes de desarrollo de los sexenios 1970–1976; 1976–1982; 1982–1988; 1988–1994; 1994–2000; 2000–2006; 2006–2012).

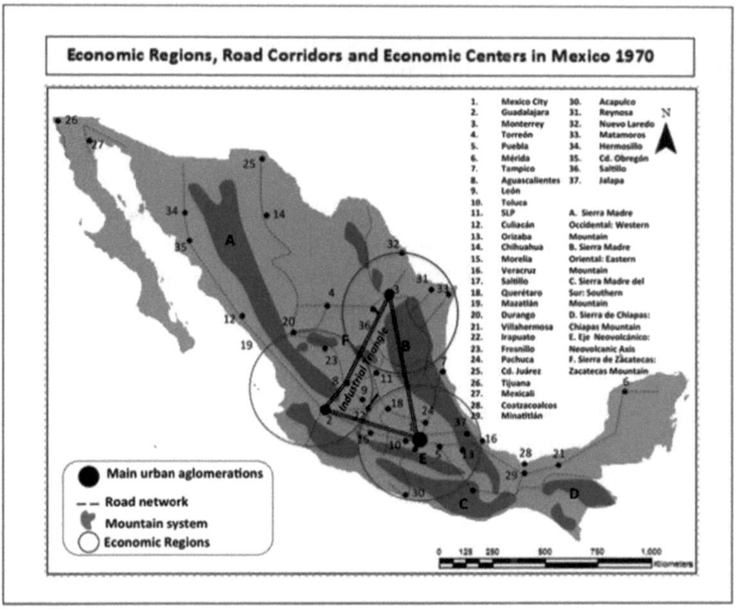

Fig. 8.5 Economic regions in Mexico 1970 (Source: Authors' elaboration)

The implementation of shared development policy was based upon expansive public spending, which led to monetary issues, inflation, debt, a decline in private investment, capital flight and devaluation of the exchange rate, which led to a reorientation both of economic policy and the development model between 1976 and 1982.

Box 8.1: Regional Policy 1970–1976

Rural Development Programs

1. National Commission for Arid Zones, (CONAZA 1971); Research, loans and subsidies.
2. Policies and programs for the development of indigenous groups of central Mexico, (1970), by providing communications infrastructure, agricultural inputs and education.
3. Public investment program for rural development (PIDER 1973), to boost its development.
4. National Plan of new population centers Ejidal (1971) to redistribute population to smaller centers.

(continued)

Box 8.1: Regional Policy 1970–1976 (continued)
Development Programs and Industrial Decentralization

1. Program for parks and industrial cities (1970).
2. Maquiladora Industry Extension Program (1972) to other parts of the country, except three main clusters.
3. Financial incentive scheme for small and medium industries (1972), outside the major industrial clusters.
4. Tax incentives for industrial decentralization outside the traditional industrial centers, (Decrees 1971 and 1972).

Creating Centers of Industrial and Tourism Growth

1. Iron and Steel complex Lazaro Cardenas Las Truchas (1971)
2. Resort in Ixtapa, Zihuatanejo, Guerrero
3. Resort in Cancun, Quintana Roo.

Creating Regions for Integral Development

1. Commission for the Integral Development of the Isthmus of Tehuantepec (1972).
2. Commission for Economic Development of the Peninsula of Baja California (1974).

Management and Coordination for Regional Development

1. National Regional Development Commission (1975), in order to develop plans for development for regions spanning more than two states with participation of private and public sector.
2. Committee for promoting socioeconomic development in states (Coprodes 1971–1975). Coordinate federal programs and implement their own programs.
3. General Direction for regional development (1974), to support and provide technical assistance to the Coprodes.
4. Administrative Decentralization of Mexico City government owned companies (1970).

8.4.2.2 The Model of Development Based on Oil and Regional Policy 1976–1982

The government officials that took office in the year 1976 made an agreement with the International Monetary Fund in order to carry out a plan of adjustment of the economy. However, the discovery of new oil fields, the increase in international oil prices and credit availability at the international money market, led to a new economic policy aimed to stimulate oil production and, eventually, its exports. In this period the policy has three main areas: (1) Direct stimulus for regional and territorial production by means of oil production and the creation of industrial ports and regional programs; (2) Creation and promotion of city regions, along with a decentralization of federal government expenditure and the creation of new federalism coupled with the creation of state institutions for the management and coordination of regional development, and (3) Regularization of human settlements and comprehensive urban planning (see Box 8.2). A remarkable aspect of this period is the creation of a system of tax coordination in 1980, under which a system of federal participation is created. This system is one of the main mechanisms for channeling federal resources to states and municipalities, as well as to promote fiscal coordination among federal, state and municipal authorities, as to become a resource balancing mechanism between states and municipalities.

The states, under the approved coordination agreement with federal authorities, were to receive 13 % of total federal tax revenues. Moreover, the agreement established the requirement that states in turn should transfer to municipalities at least 20 % of the federal proceeds received.

Regulation and planning of human settlements, was promoted through the creation of the Ministry of Human Settlements and Public Works, (SAHOP), in order to formulate policies for of human settlements through urban planning and some aspects of regional planning, and to promote and manage the planning activity and the principles of coordination with states and municipalities.

By early 1980, a fall in oil prices along with a higher credit cost and to high public debt levels, contracted based on the oil production potential, contributed to the collapse of this development model, as the country fell into a severe economic crisis in 1982.

Box 8.2: Regional Policy 1976–1982

Oil extraction, Construction of Refineries and Petrochemical Plant

1. Were completed and put into operation seven plants of the Refinery "Miguel Hidalgo" in Tula, Hidalgo, with combined capacity of extracting 150,000 barrels per day.
2. Exploitation of wells Cantarel and Maloob1, the largest in the country based on the oil region of Chiapas, Tabasco and Campeche, which provided 79 % of the country's total output.
3. Construction and operation of the refinery "Hector R. Lara Sosa" in Cadereyta, Nuevo Leon with a capacity of 100,000 barrels per day.
4. Construction and operation of the refinery "Antonio Dovali Jaime" in Salina Cruz, Oaxaca, with a capacity of 165,000 barrels per day.
5. Construction and operation of the Petrochemical Complex "La Cangrejera" with capacity to process 113,000 barrels of crude and liquids in Coatzacoalcos, Veracruz.
6. Construction and operation of the combined plant No. 2,135,000 barrels per day refinery in Cadereyta.

(continued)

Box 8.2: Regional Policy 1976–1982 (continued)
Creating Industrial Ports and Regional Development Programs

1. Industrial ports of Altamira, Tamaulipas; Coatzacoalcos, Veracruz; Lazaro Cardenas, Michoacan; Salina Cruz, Oaxaca.
2. Tax incentives for industrial location in the industrial port.
3. National program for the development of border areas and free trade areas (1977).
4. Coordination of National Plan for backward areas and marginalized groups, COPLAMAR (1977), replaced CONAZA's purpose of providing minimum welfare to zones and core areas of high deprivation.
5. It continued with the public investment program for rural development (PIDER 1973).
6. Mexican Food System, SAM (1980), which aimed to achieve self-sufficiency in basic foodstuffs, which was intended to be accomplished by coordinating the resources sector and the development of own programs.

Federal Public Expenditure Decentralization and Fiscal Federalism

1. Creation of the National System of Fiscal Coordination and Fiscal Federalism

Management and Coordination of Regional and Urban Development

1. It was established the Single Convention on Coordination (CUC) between the federal government and the states.
2. Creating committees for planning state development (COPLADES) in 1981.
3. Creation of the Directorate General of regional programming in 1977 to set standards for other regional planning agencies.
4. Program for territorial decentralization of the federal public administration, (PRODETAP), in 1978.

Managing the Urban Development

1. Creation of the Ministry of Human Settlements and Public Works, (SAHOP), in order to plan human settlements and some functions of regional planning and the principles of coordination with states and municipalities.
2. Development of the National Plan for Urban Development (PNDU 1978) in order to rationalize the distribution of economic activities and population.
3. National Urban Development Commission (1977).
4. Urban Development Plan for the Federal District in 1980, in order to induce urban growth deliberately.

8.4.3 Structural Adjustment, Orientation of New National Development Model and Regional Policy 1982–1994

The 1982 crisis forced a strong macroeconomic adjustment to improve public finances, pay interest on debt, reduce inflation and improve the balance of payments and the exchange rate. The reduction of public spending, privatization of public enterprises and trade liberalization of the economy are at the heart of economic policy during the 1982–1994 period.

In line with these national policies, regional policy was focused on three areas of action:

1. Stressing planning, programming and regional coordination through the development of an Industrial Plan, state plans, regional development programs and the creation of regional planning institutions;
2. Enforcing the regulations of federal public expenditure decentralization and fiscal federalism and expanding the fiscal powers of the municipalities, and
3. Promotion of sustainable urban planning by creating institutions. The main activities of the regional policy of this period are shown in Box 8.3.

It is worth noting that the new industrial plan (PRONAFICE) sought regional de-concentration, encouraging industrial development in new areas and regions. For those purposes it defined the following areas: Areas of high priority, areas of state priorities and/ or rest of the country, controlled growth areas and areas of consolidation. It also indicated as priorities for the first phase of diversification, the automotive, electronics, petrochemical and Maquiladora activities.

The strategy of industrial decentralization, as in previous administrations policies on economic growth centers, was aimed to the development of intermediate urban-industrial growth centers.

To supplement the general industrial plan, plans were developed by state and priority regions, highlighting the need for planned growth of the Mexico City Metropolitan Area (MCMA) as the most important national problem to ensure balanced regional development and the central region of the country in order to guide a planned decentralization of economic activity and population concentration.

Planning activities were regionally supplemented by promoting decentralization of public expenditure and fiscal federalism. This was done primarily through federal contributions and the support of municipalities by increasing their fiscal powers.

Meanwhile, population policy was also associated with decentralization policies, since it had the purpose of relocation, retention of population and redirection of internal migration. The basic thrust was to control the growth of the MCMA, the consolidation of Guadalajara, Monterrey and Puebla. Fifty nine middle size cities were selected as alternative locations to the large population centers of Mexico City, Guadalajara and Monterrey.

However, regional policy never left the paper as the developing plans and programs, were not carried out. Paradoxically decentralization of Mexico City, was only enacted as a result of the 1985 earthquakes and for environmental concerns.

In this context, the new government for the period 1988–1994, considered as exhausted the economic development model of industrialization based on import substitution and on the social policy of the Mexican Revolution.

The new model of development was sketched in the National Development Plan 1989–1994, using two basic strategies:

(1) Face financial and economic crisis in the country, and restore growth and social spending, as well as renegotiate public debt payment schedules, and (2) To promote the new development model based on an outward orientation of the national economy, which essentially meant the signing of the North America Free Trade Agreement in (1992) with the United States and Canada and its entry into operation 1994. In this context, regional policy focused on two main areas: (1) Social policy primarily through the creation of institutions and social development programs and through expenditure decentralization and fiscal federalism and regional institutions for the development of social development programs, and (2) Urban planning aimed at strengthening territorial decentralization, improved city services and municipal strengthening and the development of population centers (see Box 8.4).

Despite the achievements in reviving growth, and reducing debt, the Mexican economy at the end of this administration had strong pressures on the current account, which actually showed signs of trade imbalance and overvaluation of the peso, making uncertain the viability of the country's economy. This was reaffirmed with the political crisis of the ruling party, PRI, with the indigenous uprising in Chiapas and the ensuing devaluation in the first days of the new government.

Box 8.3: Regional Policy 1982–1988

Regional, Planning, Programming and Coordination

1. Development of Industrial and Foreign Trade Plan (PRONAFICE) from 1983 to 1988, with regional priorities and industrial decentralization strategy.
2. Preparation of 31 state plans, one for each state, where erroneously regarded each as regions.
3. Preparation of development Programs for priority regions: Sea of Cortes, Southeast Region, metropolitan area of Mexico City and Central Region, Arid Areas, Northern Border, Yucatan henequen zone and Zone of the Oaxaca Mixteca, and Coatzacoalcos Basin.

(continued)

Box 8.3: Regional Policy 1982–1988 (continued)

4. Creation of the National System for Democratic Planning, including for the first time an integrated manner for the global, sartorial and institutional levels to consult the public linked to state entities from the COPLADES. The entities acted as instances of coordination between the federal government and the states of the country.

Federal Public Expenditure and Fiscal Federalism Decentralization

1. Support fiscal federalism, number 25 budget branch appearance, in 1983 as a federal investment program operated by state governments, where resource transfers were made through the expenditure of federal executive agencies.
2. Large fiscal powers to municipalities through changes in Article 115 of the Constitution.

Sustainable Urban Development

1. Creation of the Ministry of Urban Development and Ecology, which replaced the SAHOP.
2. Mexico City Metropolitan Area (MCMA) Program and the Central Region, in order to guide a planned sustainable decentralization of economic activity and population.

Box 8.4: Regional Policy 1988–1994

Social Policy

1. Development of National Solidarity Program (PRONASOL), in order to provide the minimum population welfare in food, health, education and infrastructure services. In addition to supporting the primary activities production, especially for social sectors in poverty and marginalization and run micro-regional programs.
2. Creation of the Ministry of Social Development (SEDESOL) in 1992, replacing the SEDUE, to perform the functions of urban planning, territorial management, environmental control, coordination and implementation of micro – regional and social programs.

(continued)

Box 8.4: Regional Policy 1988–1994 (continued)

Federal Public Expenditure Decentralization and Fiscal Federalism

1. Creating Conventions for Social Development (CSD) of the Federation and the states to transfer fiscal resources directly to states and municipalities.
2. Federal Expenditure decentralization to States and Municipalities through fiscal federalism to allocate 20 % of tax revenue for the participation of States and Municipalities.
3. Transfer of fiscal resources to States and Municipalities untied according to the formula of federal participation, including equity criterion for attention to the poorer.

Urban Development

1. Preparation of the National Urban Development Plan for 1990–1994 was aimed to strengthen territorial decentralization, improving urban services and municipal strengthening and development of population centers.
2. One-hundred medium size cities Program, aimed to improve the distribution and quality of services in a concentrated form.

8.4.4 NAFTA, Post-NAFTA and Regional Policies 1995–2012

In the period 1995–2000, government seeks to continue and consolidate the new export oriented development. Therefore, in the National Development Plan for the period 1995–2000 very similar objectives to those of the previous period are set and continued with the privatization of public enterprises.

Similarly the regional policy adopted in the previous period was reinforced, along two main axes: social policy and urban planning and land use in cities. The main actions carried out are shown in Box 8.5.

During the period 2000–2006, a candidate proposed by the opposition right-wing National Action Party (PAN) was President. However, the new government followed the same precepts of neoliberal order that had been applied to the country since the mid-1980s.

Its proposals for regional planning, sought to promote the development of the south- southeast meso-region. The new government launched an initiative known as Plan Puebla-Panama, which until the date still has not materialized. In particular regional policy in this period is reduced to social policy, as the main tool is Oportunidades. This program aims to support 250 μ –regions of extreme poverty. The main regional policy actions of this government are shown in Box 8.6:

For the period 2006–2012 the second PAN government reduces the scope of regional policy to a series of actions and programs of the federal government with an aggregate and sectorial focus. It gives impetus to traditional programs to fight poverty, which were already implemented in the previous administration: Opportunities, temporary employment, 70 and over, Daily agricultural Workers, Social Milk Supply, kindergartens, health programs and access to medical attention, tec. The main actions are shown in Box 8.7.

The overall balance of the regional policy conducted since the mid-1980s and especially since the period of government of Salinas de Gortari (1988–1994) is one of a transition from an active policy supported by regional advocacy tools to passive policy supported by social policy instruments.

Box 8.5: Regional Policy 1995–2000

Social Policy

1. Development of 'Progresa' Program to combat poverty through integrated care: education, health, nutrition and training to work, promoting employment and housing and basic services like water, sewage, electricity, roads and roads to communities. Replaces Solidarity program.
2. Programs to combat poverty by population group targeted and micro-regions: 94 the number of priority areas, including 1,595 municipalities in which 32.7 million people live, just over a third of the national population. Program 39 regions in precarious conditions for immediate attention, comprising 989 municipalities in 22 states with a population of 16.8 million inhabitants.
3. Alliance Program for the country, temporary employment program for 129,000 jobs to benefit 705,000 families.
4. PROCAMPO mechanism for transferring resources to compensate domestic producers because subsidies received by their foreign competitors. Replacement of the guaranteed price scheme for grains and oilseeds. Support to about 1.1 million farmers on 3.2 million hectares.
5. Sustainable rural development programs (PRODERS) integrated planning model to drive sustainable development of 30 regions, located in 18 states, covering an area of 19.6 million hectares, distributed in 312 municipalities in which six million people reside.

Federal Public Expenditure Decentralization and Fiscal Federalism

1. Delegation to local and state congresses direct oversight of federal grants to states and municipalities, which corresponded to the federal resource transfers, conditioned to federal regulation and supervision by special agreements (1997).

(continued)

Box 8.5: Regional Policy 1995–2000 (continued)

2. The budgetary resources of the branch 26 which are for the states that previously drove regional development was redirected to combat extreme poverty through integrated social development in micro regions and were the most focused.
3. Institutionalization of social spending by state and municipal budget item branch 33, oriented to basic education, health services and municipal infrastructure.
4. It was promoted the creation and operation of the Municipal Development Councils – CDM – and Planning Committees for Municipal Development – COPLADEM – in the whole municipalities of the country.
5. The budget share formula was modified, including poverty criterion of the entity, so that both the criteria of number of inhabitants, 45 % of federal tax revenues (RFF) and 45 % of state revenue collection capacity and 10 % according to poverty rates. According to these rates, transfers corresponding to greater poverty entities were $230.00 per capita and the lowest $32.50 per capita. Thus 35 % of the resources allocated to the six states with the highest poverty.

Urban Development

1. The National Urban Development Program from 1995 to 2000 includes actions in 205 cities of the country: the four main metropolitan areas, 85 cities considered priority in states and 100 cities program which is the main Federal Government investment vehicle to promote urban development.
2. Development of State Plans for Urban Development.
3. Project for National Land Management (1996) which aims to achieve effective coordination between sectorial policies seeking to promote sustainable patterns of population distribution and economic activities in the country.
4. It was made studies titled Mexico 2020: a territorial approach to development, urban watershed, and Mexico 2020: a territorial approach to development, regional dimension, with the purpose of exploring the urban and regional development of the country in the long term.
5. Program for Planning Metropolitan Area of Mexico City (POZMVM), within the Metropolitan Commission on Human Settlements (COMETAH) between governments of Mexico City, State of Mexico and SEDESOL.

Box 8.6: Regional Policy 2000–2006

Strategic Planning, Regional Development and New Ways of Government Relationship

1. Create the Office of the President for Strategic Planning and Regional Development (OPEDR)
2. Adoption of a regional planning model based on the principle of voluntary association of states. This new bases were established and coordination schemes between the federation and the states and municipalities in the region to modernize public administration and possible social participation of inhabitants.
3. Five Meso-regions were created for intergovernmental coordination in the formulation of comprehensive sustainable development (PIDS). The general policy was: The freedom of each region and federal entity to control their own destiny in harmony with the rest of the country. Coordination regions are: (I) Northeast (Tamaulipas, Nuevo Leon, Coahuila, Chihuahua, and Durango) (II) Northwest (Baja California, Baja California Sur, Sonora, Sinaloa, Chihuahua, Durango) (III) Center (Mexico City, Queretaro, Hidalgo, Tlaxcala, Puebla, Morelos, Mexico) (IV) West Center (Jalisco, Michoacan, Colima, Aguascalientes, Nayarit, Zacatecas, San Luis Potosi, Guanajuato, Querétaro) (V) South – South East (Campeche, Yucatan, Chiapas, Oaxaca, Quintana Roo, Tabasco, Guerrero, Veracruz, Puebla)
4. Establishment and operation of five regional Trusts to carry out regional development plans and projects of regional impact. (FIDERCO: West Central Region), FIDCENTRO: Central Region; FIDENORESTE: Northeast Region; FIDESUR: South Region Southeast. The trust of the Northwest region did not succeed as a unifying body and catalyst of efforts.
5. Project Puebla-Panama Plan Initiative, which should boost regional development and Southeast region integration to the country and the Central American countries to Panama. It aims to provide basic transport infrastructure and production to integrate the region and promote regional development.
6. Creating Regional Coordination OPEDR dependent for Puebla – Panama Plan and the Northern Border.
7. Norms for Budget Regionalization issued by the Secretary of Finance and Public Credit.

(continued)

Box 8.6: Regional Policy 2000–2006 (continued)

8. March to the South Program: Providing federal resources of 493.7 million pesos for the implementation of 392 projects in the less developed regions of the country.
9. Strengthening Regional Road Infrastructure: South Southeast Region was the most favored. Were constructed/upgraded 7,965.7 km highway links, roads and feeder roads.
10. Nautical Ladder Plan for Gulf of California (2001–2006) to establish the Baja California port infrastructure.
11. Development programs of the Northern Border, to boost trade, employment and prevent environmental problems.
12. Development programs of the Southern Border.
13. Great Vision project to integrate central region of highland corridor to link the center with the Gulf Axis.

Social Policy

1. Creation of the National Human Development Program "Opportunities", which replaces the Progresa program.
2. Boosting regional micro SEDESOL programs, 250 μ regions of extreme poverty.
3. The resources were deployed from branch 33 of the federal budget that relates to the contributions from the federal government.
4. Supporting states accounted for about 21 % of federal revenues shareable and is comprised untied resources.
5. 3 × 1 Program for Migrants. For every peso that migrants bring to the realization of social impact projects that favor the development of their home communities, municipalities, states and the federal government provide, overall, three pesos.

Programs to Increase Regional Competitiveness

1. Micro region Program aims to promote the comprehensive and sustainable development projects through strategic – educational infrastructure, procurement, health, culture and recreation; basic social infrastructure, agricultural and service, and projects that increase the productivity of the beneficiaries. Their antecedents in the National Priority Regions Care developed in period 1994–2000 and the Care Strategy 250 μ regions, "With you, hands to work."
2. PROCAMPO direct support to field related to historical land use, resource-poor farmers, poor farmers, and the program introduced a grant scheme of support per hectare.

(continued)

Box 8.6: Regional Policy 2000–2006 (continued)

3. "Alliance With you" program incorporates over 100 programs to increase agricultural productivity and capitalization between producers.
4. Marketing Support Program for supporting transition from selling to CONASUPO towards market-based scheme.
5. Support Competitiveness of Productive Branches Fund (FACRP) seeks to strengthen production systems and production lines consumption, with greater sensitivity to international market conditions.
6. FIRCO operates the Shared Risk Fund for the Promotion of Agro Business (FOMAGRO).

Urban Development

1. Territory Management Policy and Urban and Regional Action:
   (a) Habitat Program establishes an institutional model to regulate, promote, manage and promote the development of the National Urban System. This aims to improve basic infrastructure, equip marginalized urban areas, and provide social services and community development actions. This was organized into six territorial aspects of performance: Border Cities, Cities Oil Producer, Tourist Cities, Metropolitan Areas, Overall Slope, and Historical Centers.
   (b) Program Soil: Land Reserve to integrate land suitable for development as a support tool for urban expansion to meet the requirements for housing and urban development.
   (c) Preventing and responding to impacts from natural disasters in urban and rural areas, through control works and prevention. Relocation of human settlements located in high risk areas, regulation and control of land use, limiting permitted uses in risk areas and warning and organization of society, to meet contingencies.
2. Creating of five Regional Planning Programs that will address the priorities of the Meso-regions with a criterion of territorial management policy.

Box 8.7: Regional Policy 2006–2012

Social Policy

1. Continue with actions to combat poverty and marginalization through 70 programs and more; Temporary Employment (PET) Social Milk

(continued)

Box 8.7: Regional Policy 2006–2012 (continued)

Supply; Daycare for Working Mothers Support, and Care for Farm Workers, among others.

Implementation

1. Continue with Human Development Program Oportunidades: main element in combating poverty through strategies and actions sectors to education, health, food. As for coordination with other social programs that promote employment, income and household savings in extreme poverty. In 2012, sum 5.8 million families served.
2. It drives the Planning Strategy and Land Management with Identity Development in 155 μ-regions, for 23 states that have indigenous population.
3. Programs to improve coverage and access to medical services, such as Universal Immunization Program, Dental Health Week and National Health Weeks.
4. Implementation of Popular Health Insurance, formerly known as "Health for All Program" in order to preserve the health of families and encourage affiliates timely health care.
5. 3 × 1 Program for Migrants. For every peso that migrants bring to the realization of social impact projects that favor the development of their home communities, municipalities, states and the federal government provide, overall, three pesos.
6. Programs of the National Business Support for Solidarity Enterprises (FONAES) whose focus towards boosting production projects, strengthening business and trade skills of the population: 100 × 100 strategy, rural municipalities, and predominantly indigenous municipalities.

Regional Development Programs: Infrastructure

1. National Infrastructure Fund, authorized since its inception in 2008 until June 2012, support for studies and projects for 103,816 million pesos for the implementation of various infrastructure projects in the country, estimated to detonate an investment 230,386,000 pesos.
2. Rural electrification programs and neighborhoods, construction and upgrading of roads and rural roads.

Funding

1. BANOBRAS funding from infrastructure to regions by 148,073 million pesos representing 67 % of its resources.

(continued)

Box 8.7: Regional Policy 2006–2012 (continued)

2. Financing provided by NAFIN: From January 2007 to June 2012, NAFIN provided financing to the private sector by 2,382.8 billion pesos with the following regional destination: Central – Country, 44.6 % Northeast, 23.5 %; Centre – West, 16.8 %; South – South East 7.6 %, and North West 7.5 %.
3. Financing issued by Rural Financial: working on financing lines for high environmental projects and to develop financing schemes for forest communities and ejidos.
4. Program "L@ Red de la Gente" ("The net of people") offers a wide range of financial products and services in regions where there is no presence of commercial banks.

Tourism

1. Strengthening tourism sector via Conventions Coordinating on resource reallocation to 1,090.9 million pesos allocated to 230 projects aimed at developing infrastructure and services; urban image, tourist facilities, improvement, rehabilitation or creation of tourist sites; support systems and tourist information materials, as well as the Program for Competitiveness and Tourism Training.
2. Strengthening tourism policy with the operation of the National Agreement on Tourism, based on coordination between governors, legislators, employers, trade unions and academics to the implementation of the 101 specific actions grouped into ten strategic favorably impacting domestic tourism and international, foreign exchange earnings, employment generation and improved quality of life of the population engaged in this activity.
3. FONATUR invested in tourism development studies, tourism infrastructure and conducted several support programs for tourism development: Maya World, Mexico gastronomic routes, Magic Towns.

Boost SMEs

1. It continues with the policy for the development of small and medium enterprises (SMEs), through mechanisms for specific attention to the size and production potential, among them funding for the creation of new businesses, training and reduction procedures for its establishment and operation.
2. Expanding the capacity of social enterprises and promotion of productive people in poverty, by National Fund for Business Support (FONAES). Programs to Promote SME Financing: Young Entrepreneurs, National

(continued)

Box 8.7: Regional Policy 2006–2012 (continued)

Business Incubation, Entrepreneurs Financing with Commercial Banking, Capital Seed SMEs.

3. National Microenterprise Program for the entrepreneur ensure its permanence in the market, growth and competitiveness.
4. Productive Projects Program of the Secretary of Economy in coordination with state governments and business organizations, the present administration has channeled a total of 3,592.9 million, in support of 11,510 MSMEs, contributing to the generation of employment sources 6,461.
5. Supplier Development Program, integrator enterprises Program and Parks of SMEs Program.

Urban Development

1. Through 14 offices, promotes cross-agency strategy called Integrated Sustainable Urban Developments (DUIS)
2. Habitat Program. It applies in cities of at least 15,000 inhabitants. Within these, focuses its activities in poor urban areas with high concentration of households in poverty.
3. Program recovery of public spaces: social action and implementation of physical works to regain community meeting places, everyday social interaction and recreation, located in urban areas with characteristics of insecurity and marginalization.
4. Program savings and housing allowance, your HOME: provides support for the acquisition or construction of a basic housing unit in urban, semi-urban and rural areas.

8.5 Conclusions

In the long term, the economic and social development of the regions in Mexico shows the existence of structural patterns based on processes of economic concentration and their impacts on social development. These patterns are expressed at the regional and territorial level, as they result in a spatial distribution of economic activity and population, in cities-regions that do not match the country's administrative political units. Regional and urban development in the country, exhibits the location, distribution and growth consequences of a cumulative causal process that has its roots in history and geography, one of economic activity in space whose natural tendency is towards concentration and generation of regional disparities.

Public policies have failed to reverse the processes of regional inequality that have emerged in the country, which has shown the inability of social policy and urban development to reduce disparities, largely due to an 'assistentialist' conception of the urban development process. The regional policy management is critical for achieving adequate results. However, it is designed nationally in the aggregate and sectorial, bonded to the political administrative units without reconciling their impact on specific regions and territories.

Economic growth in the activities and dynamic regions does not overflow spontaneously and naturally, so their natural tendency, lacking a deliberate policy, is to form enclaves or convergence clubs that do not allow pushing or pulling other regions towards economic and social development.

The strategy of the outward oriented development model has been successful for certain economic sectors. However it has led to an increased income polarization and to deeper regional disparities. The regional and urban policy has very limited scope since it has its focus on the use of fiscal transfers and welfare programs.

The regional and urban development problems show inertial and structural components. Thus problems cannot be solved just with the coordination of the Federal Government without a deliberately defined strategy. Such changes cannot be reversed in a 6-year period, as they require long term transformations. Since regional and urban policies have been changing every 6 years, as the Federal government changes, there is no continuity, no permanent direction, nor have those policies had the human resources and the needed information for their implementation. This calls for a rethinking of regional policy that takes into account the essential role of sub-national economies and their development for the advance of the country as a whole. Economic regionalization and development of the country based on subnational economies should be the basis of coordination between state and local entities, for the definition and implementation of economic policy and national development. Its implementation requires building upon functional economic regionalization, detailing the differences of subnational economic performance and proposing social managed policies to make regional equality a concrete reality.

Annex: Inequality Indicators

The next indicators are based on Ezcuarra and Rodriguez-Pose (2010):

The coefficient of variation (c), and the standard deviation of the logarithms (v), which are in the expressions (8.1) y (8.2):

$$c = \frac{\sqrt{\sum_{i=1}^{n} p_i (x_i - \mu)^2}}{\mu} \tag{8.1}$$

$$v = \sqrt{\sum_{i=1}^{n} p_i (\ln x_i - \widetilde{\mu})^2} \tag{8.2}$$

Where:

$$\mu = \sum\nolimits_{i=1}^{n} p_i$$

$$\widetilde{\mu} = \sum\nolimits_{i=1}^{n} p_i \ln x_i$$

p_i = population share of region i in a given year.
x_i = per capita GDP of region i.

The Gini index (G) can be written as:

$$G = \frac{\sum_{i=1}^{n}\sum_{i=1}^{n} p_i p_j \left|x_i - x_j\right|}{\mu} \tag{8.3}$$

The generalised entropy class of measures (GE) can be written as:

$$GE(\theta) = \begin{cases} \sum_{i=1}^{n} p_i \ln\left(\frac{\mu}{x_i}\right); \theta = 0 \\ \sum_{i=1}^{n} pi\left(\frac{xi}{\mu}\right)\ln\left(\frac{xi}{\mu}\right); \theta = 1 \end{cases} \tag{8.4}$$

The Atkinson's family of indices, A(ε), can be written as:

$$A(\varepsilon) = \begin{cases} 1 - \left[\sum_{i=1}^{n} p_i \left(\frac{x_i}{\mu}\right)^{1-\varepsilon}\right]^{\frac{1}{1-\varepsilon}} ; \varepsilon \neq 1 \\ 1 - \prod_{i=1}^{n} \left(\frac{x_i}{\mu}\right)^{p_i} ; \varepsilon = 1 \end{cases} \tag{8.5}$$

The Esteban and Ray's measures of polarization are in the following expressions:

$$P^{ER}(f, \propto, \rho) = \sum\nolimits_{j=1}^{m} \sum\nolimits_{k=1}^{m} p_j^{1+\alpha} pk|\mu j - \mu k| \tag{8.6}$$

$$P^{EGR}(f, \propto, \rho^*, \beta) = P^{ER}(f, \propto, \rho^*) - \beta[G(f) - G(\rho^*)] \tag{8.7}$$

where:

$\propto \in [1,1.6]$ parameter that reflects the degree of sensitivity to polarisation
$\beta \geq 0$ is a weighting parameter for the error term in expression (8.7)

Finally, the modified conditional density estimator proposed by Hyndman et al. (1996) takes the following form:

$$\hat{f}\left(y|x\right) = \sum_{j=1}^{n} w_j(x)\frac{1}{b}K\left(\left\|y - Y_j\right\|\frac{y}{b}\right) \tag{8.8}$$

Where:

$\hat{f}(y|x)$ is the natural kernel estimator of the conditional density $Y|X = x$

K is the kernel function

$\|.\|$ is a metrical distance

b controls the smoothness of each conditional density in the **y** direction

w_j can be estimated from:

$$w_j(x) = K\left(\frac{\|x - X_j\|}{a}\right) / \sum_{i=1}^{n} K\left(\frac{\|x - X_i\|}{a}\right) \tag{8.9}$$

where a controls the smoothness of each conditional density in the x direction

All the indicators were calculated with DASP (*Distributive Analysis Stata Package)* in STATA.12 (Araar and Jean-Yves 2007), and using the Hyndman's hdrcde package for R.

References

Aguayo E (2004) Divergencia regional en México, 1990-2000. Ensayos XXIII(2):29–42

Anselin L (1988) Spatial econometrics. Kluwer, Dordrecht

Appendini K, Murayama D, Domínguez R (1972) Desarrollo Desigual en México, 1900 y 1960. Demogr Econ 1(6):1–39

Araar Abdelkrim, Jean-Yves Duclos (2007) DASP: distributive analysis stata package, PEP, World Bank, UNDP and Université Laval

Aroca P, Bosch M, Maloney WF (2005) Spatial dimensions of trade liberalization and economic convergence: Mexico 1985–2002, The World Bank Economic Review, December

Asuad N (2007) Aspectos básicos que debe atender una política de desarrollo regional y urbano en México en el corto, mediano y largo plazo. Investig Econ LX(231):71–107

Asuad N (1995) Comprehensive polarized regional development. International Institute of Social Studies, Erasmus University Rotterdam, The Hague

Asuad N, Quintana L, Ramírez R (2007a) Convergencia espacial y concentración regional agrícola en México 1970–2003, Problemas del Desarrollo. Revista Latino americana de Economía, vol 38, núm 149, Abril-Junio

Asuad N, Quintana L, Ramírez R (2007b) Desarrollo y políticas regionales en México: retos y perspectivas 2006–2020. In: Políticas de desarrollo regional, agenda para el desarrollo, vol 13, coordinado por José Luis Calva Editores: H. Cámara de Diputados, LX Legislatura y UNAM, Editorial Miguel Ángel Porrúa, pp 231–263

Barkin and King (1993) Desarrollo Económico regional, enfoque por cuencas hidrológicas de México, Siglo XXI, México

Calderon VC, Tykhonenko A (2007) Convergencia regional e inversión extranjera en México en el contexto del TLCAN, 1994–2002. Investig Econ 66(259):9–41

Cermeño R, Garrido D (2009) Convergencia de las entidades federativas de México, 1940–2004: un enfoque de series de tiempo. Documento de trabajo, núm. 448, División de Economía, CIDE

Chiquiar D (2005) Why Mexico's regional income convergence broke down. J Dev Econ 77:257–275

Esquivel G (1999) Convergencia Regional en México, 1940–1995. El Trimestre Econ 66:725–761

Esquivel G, Mesmacher M (2002) Sources of regional (non) convergence in Mexico. Working paper, Colegio de México, México

Ezcuarra R, Rodriguez-Pose A (2010) Measuring the regional divide. In: Capello and Nijkamp, Handbook of regional growth and development theories, Edward-Elgar Publishing, pp 329–353

Gamboa, Messmacher M (2002) Desigualdad regional y gasto público en México, BID

García-Verdú R (2002) Income dynamics across States in Mexico: 1940–2000. Documento de trabajo, Banco de México

Garza G (1997) Tendencias de las desigualdades urbanas y regionales en México, 1970–1996. Estud Demogr Urbanos 15(3):493–501

González Rivas M (2007) The effects of trade openness on regional inequality in Mexico. Ann Reg Sci 41(3):545–561

Hanson GH (1998) North American economic integration and industry location. Oxf Rev Econ Policy 14(2):30–44, Oxford University Press

Hanson GH (2001) U.S.-Mexico integration and regional economies: evidence from border-city Pairs. J Urban Econ 50(2):259–287

Hernández LE (1984) La desigualdad regional en México, en Cordera Campos R, Tello C (coords), La desigualdad en México, Siglo XXI, México

Hyndman RJ (1996) Computing and graphing highest density regions. Am Stat 50:120–126

Hyndman D, Bashtannyk M, Gary KG (1996) Estimating and visualizing conditional densities. J Comput Graph Stat 5(4):315–336

Juan-Ramón VH, Rivera-Batiz LA (1996) Regional growth in Mexico: 1970–93. IMF Working paper núm. 96–92

Magrini S (2009) Why should we analyse convergence using the distribution dynamics approach? Scienze regionali – Italian. J Reg Sci 8:5–34

Mendoza MÁ (2011) Metodología de interpolación estructural-espacial para la generación de una serie continúa del PIB y población por entidad federativa y municipio: 1970-2010, Documento de trabajo, Facultad de Economía, UNAM

Messmacher M (2000) Desigualdad Regional en México. El Efecto del TLCAN y Otras Reformas Estructurales. Documento de Investigación, 2000–4, Banco de México

Navarrete J (1995) Convergencia: un estudio para los estados de la república mexicana. Documento de trabajo 42, División de Economía, CIDE

Presidencia de la República, Informes Presidenciales de varios años, México

Presidencia de la República, Planes Nacionales de Desarrollo de los sexenios 1970–1976; 1976–1982; 1982–1988; 1988–1994; 1994–2000; 2000–2006; 2006–2012, México

Quah D (1993) Empirical cross-section dynamics in economic growth. Eur Econ Rev 37 (2–3):426–434

Quah DT (1996a) Regional convergence clusters across Europe. Eur Econ Rev 40(3–5):951–958

Quah DT (1996b) Empirics for economic growth and convergence. Eur Econ Rev 40:1353–1375

Quah DT (1997) Empirics for growth and distribution: stratification, polarization and convergence clubs. J Econ Growth 2:27–59

Ramírez MD (1986) Las desigualdades interregionales en México de 1970 a 1980. Estud Demogr Urbanos 1(33):353–355

Rodríguez-Orregia E (2005) Regional disparities and determinants of growth in Mexico. Ann Reg Sci 39:207–220

Ruíz CC (1997) Desigualdades Regionales en México 1900 a 1993. Estud Demogr Urbanos 11 (3):553–557

Sánchez-Reaza J, Rodríguez-Pose A (2002) The impact of trade liberalization on regional disparities in México. Growth Chang 33:72–90

Sastré Gutiérrez ML, Rey SJ (2008) Polarización espacial y dinámicas de la desigualdad interregional en México. Problemas del Desarrollo. Revista Latino americana de Economía, vol 39, núm. 155

Serra M, Pazmino M, Lindow G, Sutton B, Ramirez G (2006) Regional convergence in Latin America. IMF working paper núm 06/125

Unikel L, Chiapeto C, Garza G (1976) El desarrollo urbano de México. Diagnóstico e implicaciones futuras, El Colegio de México, México

Chapter 9
Regional Inequalities and Regional Policies in Colombia: The Experience of the Last Two Decades

Luis Armando Galvis and Adolfo Meisel

Colombia has one of the worst income distributions in the world. This finding is a matter of concern since abundant empirical evidence at the international level shows a negative relationship between economic growth and inequality (Deininger and Squire 1996; Alesina and Rodrick 1994; Bertola 1993; Engermann and Sokoloff 2002). In Colombia large differences in the distribution of income have become worrisome. For the last three decades inequality has increased and the most impoverished areas, such as the Caribbean and Pacific coasts, continue to lag behind. What is observed in the Colombian context is an increasing territorial polarization. Moreover, several key economic policies seem to have worsened the situation of economic imbalances in this respect.

Regional income convergence matters because it is related to inequalities in income distribution and to economic welfare. Having an unequal income distribution is an issue that should warrant special attention, more so when polarization trends are evident. This is the case of Colombia in recent decades. In this country, inequalities have been persistent during the last two decades and with them the economic growth and welfare of the population may have been negatively affected. Furthermore, the most impoverished areas, such as the Caribbean and Pacific coasts, have not received special policy support from the central government. Besides this situation, the capital city has reached an unprecedented importance in the national economy. For all these reasons, Colombia is an interesting case to study from a local perspective to delve into the specificities of the Colombian regions and the economic policies needed for the reduction of the disparities.

This paper seeks to review the economic growth and the evolution of inequalities during the last two decades in Colombia (1990–2010). Employing the last two censuses (1993 and 2005) we evaluate the spatial distribution of poverty and its persistence over time.

L.A. Galvis (✉) • A. Meisel
Centro de Estudios Económicos Regionales -CEER-, Banco de la República, Cartagena, Colombia
e-mail: lgalviap@banrep.gov.co; ameisero@banrep.gov.co

J.R. Cuadrado-Roura and P. Aroca (eds.), *Regional Problems and Policies in Latin America*, Advances in Spatial Science, DOI 10.1007/978-3-642-39674-8_9,

The main regional policy that the Colombian government has implemented in the last decades, fiscal decentralization, is discussed. This policy has not resulted in a reduction of regional economic disparities. On the contrary, it seems that the majority of the resources transferred from the central government have ended up helping the most prosperous regions.

The first section presents a review of the theoretical issues that help understand the evolution of regional disparities and economic growth. In the second section we focus on the Colombian case with respect to the factors associated to inequalities and regional imbalances. We highlight the role of the central government in terms of the regional policies and the limited success that has achieved in this matter. It is stressed that previous National Development Plans have focused on sectorial strategies rather than regional ones. The third section presents the spatial aspects related to poverty and inequalities. The fourth section reviews the way resources from the central government have been allocated among administrative units. The fifth section presents an analysis of the convergence hypothesis during the last two decades. Finally, the seventh section offers some concluding remarks.

9.1 Theoretical Perspectives on Economic Growth and Regional Imbalances

Economists have long recognized that knowledge spillovers are one of the main sources of economic growth (Marshall 1920). According to this framework growth in some sectors or geographic areas is explained by the externalities they receive from knowledge created in other sectors (Romer 1986; Lucas 1988). When sectors grow because of knowledge that they did not create, but rather that they "borrowed" from other sectors of the economy it is said that the knowledge spills over. Inspired by these ideas, there has been much work in the empirical literature on the determinants of the growth in cities (Glaeser et al. 1992, 1995; Ades and Glaeser 1995; Black and Henderson 1999). These theoretical frameworks have highlighted knowledge spillovers as important elements of economic growth, especially in urban environments where, as opposed to the rural areas, ideas may flow quickly due to the intensity of interactions between people. The literature on agglomeration economies pioneered by Marshall (1920) provided an explanation for why firms are located in urban areas: the search for positive externalities in the form of knowledge spillovers from other firms. In this sense Marshall mentions that:

> When an industry has thus chosen a locality for itself, it is likely to stay there long: so great are the advantages which people following the same skilled trade get from near neighborhood to one another. The mysteries of the trade become no mysteries; but are as it were in the air. (Marshall 1920, p. 225).

Jacobs (1969) has been recognized for having started the discussion of why cities provide an environment that facilitates the interchange of ideas and thus, knowledge spillovers and externalities. More specifically, the recent literature studying the determinants of innovative outputs refers to the effects of industrial specialization as Marshall externalities and industrial diversity as Jacobs externalities (Paci and Usai 1999; Ejermo 2005).

In the same framework of Jacobs' (1969), Glaeser et al. (1992) put stress on the sources of technological spillovers and their effect on city growth. This new growth theory is relevant for the study of factors which make cities prosper, and is particularly important to understand the growth of the main Colombian cities, especially Bogota, which has become an enormous economy in comparison with the rest of the urban areas.

Studies based on the new economic geography, with its emphasis on scale economies, have influenced the recent literature on the determinants of economic growth (Krugman 1991). In particular, Krugman has shown that the interaction between economies of scale and externalities can lead to the agglomeration of economic activity (Krugman 1999). This agglomeration in turn strengthens urban concentration as this phenomenon may act in a virtuous cycle.

Other theoretical proposals which enrich the growing body of literature on the determinants of city growth have been made by Vernon Henderson, Andrei Shleifer, and Edward L. Glaeser (1992, 1995). The study by Ades and Glaeser (1995) explores why some cities grow and become excessively large by pointing to two elements, namely trade and circuses. In the case of urban growth in Colombia, these elements can be understood as opportunities and amenities. People migrate to the main cities in search of job opportunities, education and improved welfare conditions. Ades and Glaeser's (1995) study shows some of the pulling forces that lead to such concentrations such as the population of Buenos Aires, with 35 % of Argentina's total. Along the same lines, 10 % of the Japanese population lives in Tokyo, 25 % of the population in Mexico is concentrated in Mexico City, among other examples.

The study by Ades and Glaeser (1995) also highlights some prominent themes. The biggest cities tend to be the country's capital. The authors also stress the importance of the links to natural resources. The higher the share of labor force outside agriculture, the more labor not tied to natural resources, and hence, more people will choose to live in the main urban areas.

From a policy perspective, Krugman and Livas (1996) argue that protectionism will foster urban concentration due to the fact that higher import taxes negatively affect imports and therefore local industries (and thus workers) will locate in big cities in order to supply national markets. In this respect, Colombia has been no exception. For instance, the import-substitution-industrialization (ISI) policies during the 1950s mainly benefited the central areas of the country, especially those that had accumulated physical capital with the coffee export profits, i.e. the so called coffee belt (Antioquia, Caldas, Risaralda and Quindío). This was not the case for regions such as the Caribbean Coast that did not benefit from ISI policies and, on the contrary, due to the geographical advantage of its localization near the coast, would have benefited from an export led growth policy. The latter was not part of the core coffee producing areas located around Antioquia, Caldas, Quindío, Risaralda, and the northern part of Valle del Cauca.

The growth of the central government has also been an important source of imbalances in regional growth in Colombia. During the first half of the twentieth century government expenditures reached an average of 5 % of the Colombian GDP; by the decade of the 1990s it had surpassed 20 % (Junguito and Rincón 2004). This tremendous growth has mainly benefited Bogota, as this city employs the vast majority of public officials, and attracts the majority of the firms that engage in contracts with the public sector, especially with the central government (Bonet 2003).

Political factors also contribute to territorial economic imbalances. For instance, factors related to democracy and civil rights have various effects on population concentration. It has been argued that governments protect civil rights for people living in the main urban concentrations, as they are the ones that determine the results of elections (Ades and Glaeser 1995). This becomes a pulling factor towards the cities for people in the hinterland.

Following previous theoretical propositions, in the Colombian literature there have been studies linking regional development and the convergence hypothesis. For instance, Cárdenas (2005) argued that although between 1970 and 2002 economic growth permitted a small reduction in regional income disparities, since the ratio between the per capita GDP of Bogota and that one of Chocó declined, this was not reflected in the quality of life for people with lower incomes.

In 2006, CEGA (Center for Livestock and Agricultural Studies) published the series for income, consumption, and savings for Bogota and the states that existed before the Constitution of 1991. This allowed the analysis of the income of those states. Up to that moment, research was carried out using state GDP, which distorted the information for the mining regions, among other problems. Bonet and Meisel (2006) tested the convergence hypothesis using the dataset produced by CEGA. Their findings point to a polarization process between Bogotá and the rest of the country. Using stochastic kernel functions the authors show a highly persistent pattern of disparities, as the ranking, in terms of the per capita income, remains unaltered during the three decades analyzed.

Gaviria and Gelves (2009) also provide evidence of the highly persistent patterns of income inequalities. The authors also use kernel functions to represent these patterns, but using a long run view covering various population censuses starting from the beginning of the twentieth century.

Galvis and Meisel (2010a) discuss two dimensions of economic disparities, time and space. The authors show that poverty is clustered in space and that this clustering remains through time, which constitutes evidence of the highly persistent pattern of disparities in the country and the existence of spatial poverty traps in Colombia. As the economic literature has pointed out, these poverty traps are characterized by low-income equilibriums (Azariadis 2006). From a policy perspective it is necessary to think about the presence of an external authority that provides a "big push" to the impoverished areas to help them get out of the poverty trap (Rosenstein-Rodan 1943; Sachs 2005).

9.2 Factors Associated to Growth and Disparities in Colombia

In countries like Colombia, the spectacular population growth of Bogota, is a matter of concern.[1] In fact, Colombia is going through a process of urban polarization in which economic disparities between the main cities have been increasing (Galvis and Meisel 2001). In this context, Colombia seems to be an example of what Krugman and Livas (Krugman and Livas 1996) said about the consequences of trade policies followed by developing countries to promote import substitution industrialization: the growth of a huge metropolis (which very often is also the capital).

This phenomenon is known as urban primacy, and it appears when the principal city is oversized in relation to the rest of the cities. The latter begin to depend economically on the main city, since the most important economic opportunities are concentrated there. The same can be said about investment and infrastructure which strengthens the capacity to undertake projects and establish new companies, and the investment in social and cultural capital coming from private resources, as well as the resources from the central government. Thus, middle sized cities turn into net ejectors of population onto the principal city, which has the largest market and, therefore, the greatest capacity to obtain economies of scale. Facilities and urban infrastructure such as better schools or subsidies also play the role of "welfare magnets" which attract people. This phenomenon has also been observed for international migrants to the US, who are attracted by welfare programs (Borjas 1999).

The abrupt topography seems to have played an important role on the spatial distribution of population in Colombia. This factor made land communication relatively deficient between intermediate cities and Bogota and that was one of the reasons why urban primacy was not observed earlier (Gouëset 1988). A similar case occurs in Peru, where the geography seems to provide physical barriers that make it more difficult for people to migrate. Furthermore, high transportation costs as well as ethnic fragmentation are also found to represent impediments for poor households to relocate in more prosperous areas (De Vreyer et al. 2009).

The localization patterns of the population in Colombia were characterized by the presence of several relatively balanced growth poles. This was explained in the past by the country's topography. When the Andes mountain range enters Colombia through the south-west region it breaks up into three mountain ranges from which the Central Region emerges, with Bogota as the principal urban center; the Pacific Region, with Cali as the principal urban center; the coffee zone, with Medellin; and the Caribbean Coast, with Barranquilla, as the principal city of the region (See Fig. 9.1).

[1] This section is based on the paper by Galvis and Meisel (2009). Parts of it are reproduced here with permission from the editor of the journal Foreign Affairs- Latinoamérica.

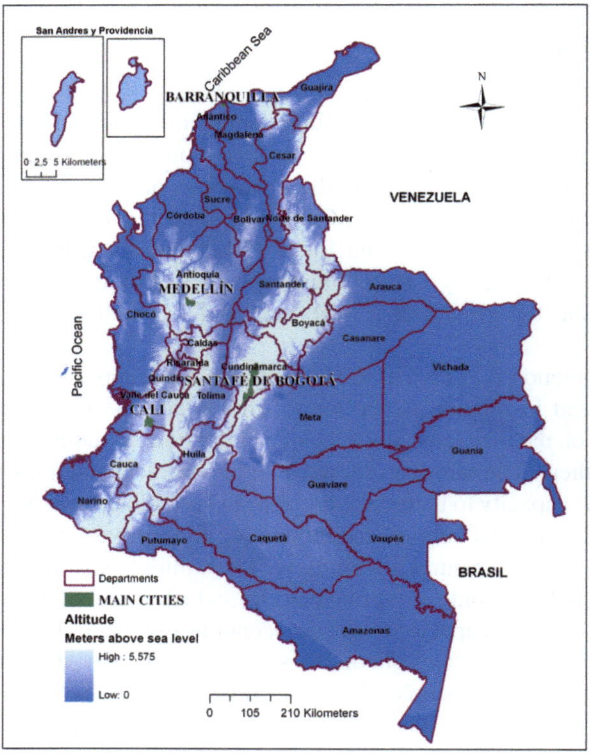

Fig. 9.1 Colombia: states and main cities (Source: Prepared by the authors based on the map database of the Agustín Codazzi Geographical Institute (IGAC))

9.2.1 *Path Dependence*

At the beginning of the twentieth century Bogota was the only city with more than 50,000 inhabitants, and the other municipalities were small and heavily dependent on agriculture, i.e., on immobile natural resources. With the industrialization of the mid-twentieth century, major cities were consolidated as an urban network, with each one becoming a nodal point in their respective regions. However, due to the stagnation experienced by Barranquilla since the 1950s (Posada and Meisel 1993), the main urban network was consolidated around the triangle Bogota-Medellin-Cali. A couple of decades later Bogota began to consolidate itself as the main urban area in a scheme of urban primacy. For example, in the 1973 Census, its population exceeded the sum of the following three main cities. By 2010 the population of Bogota represented 16.2 % of the country's total.

The importance of Barranquilla in the national context rested on that the fact that, despite being distant from other cities, it was connected to the Magdalena River, the primary mean of transporting merchandise and people from the Caribbean Coast to the interior of the country. However, following the opening of the

Panama Canal in 1914, it was easier to reach the interior cities through the Pacific Ocean. This, together with the large investments in roads and railways that occurred at the beginning of the century, allowed the central region to become well connected with the Pacific Coast.[2] As a result, the comparative advantage held by Barranquilla as a seaport connecting the center of the country with the rest of the world disappeared, and this role was taken by the port of Buenaventura.

As a result of the redefinition of road infrastructure and the growing importance of coffee in the national economy, the coffee belt became a center of development which concentrated a large portion of the country's population. In addition to the above, the country entered a period of import substitution policy. This policy favored some parts of the country, especially the industrial cities of the interior, and generated a process of concentration of wealth in those areas. The latter was the result of low import taxes on industrial raw materials, even with negative rates in real terms, which for other regions such as the Caribbean coast, was not as beneficial as it was for the regions where the industry was located.

The growing importance of the capital is more notable if one examines the participation of Bogota in the national GDP. While in 1960 Bogota contributed with 14 % of the GDP, this percentage increased to 22.6 % in 1995. It is estimated that in 2010 this percentage rose to 26 %.[3]

Further explanations for the regional imbalances in the economic growth of Colombia were studied by Galvis and Meisel (2001). The authors employ a series of variables to explain the economic growth of Colombian cities. The study concludes that the results obtained for urban income are consistent with the research of Paul Krugman and Edward Glaeser on regional economics, who emphasized the role of scale economies and knowledge spillovers to understand the growth of cities, rather than with the research of Jeffrey Sachs, which gives special importance to the role of physical geography. On the whole, the variables that stimulate economic growth also constitute pulling factors for population growth and Bogota has the best, or near the best conditions in terms of those "luring" factors.

Geographic variables may explain localization of people in the country from a historical perspective. Bogota is located along the Andean mountains and presents an average temperature of 65°, soil in the surroundings is fertile, and the main endowments in terms of infrastructure are located around it. For the latter situation there is also a historical explanation that goes back to the conquest period as the majority of indigenous population was concentrated around the Andean mountains (Zambrano 1997). Later the income generated by coffee growers was used for investments in communications and infrastructure along the Andean ranges. Thus, there is a sort of path-dependence through which the importance of geography in the more agrarian stages of development manifests itself in more recent periods and helps in the understanding of the localization of people in the territory.

---

[2] The infrastructure was built mainly with the resources obtained as an indemnity from the loss of Panama and with other resources coming from credits from US investors (Ramírez 1999).

[3] Calculations based on National Department of Statistics, DANE.

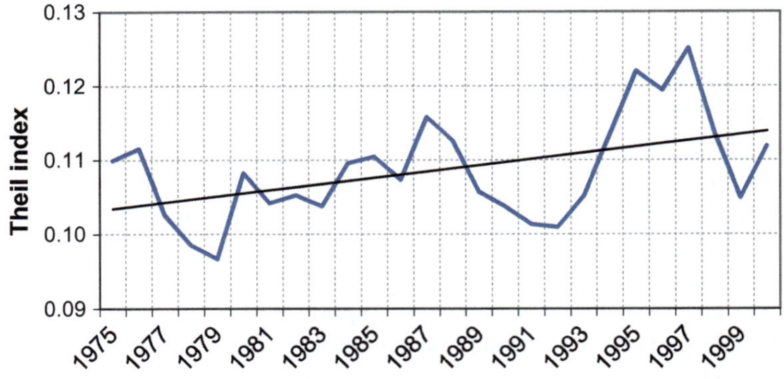

Fig. 9.2 Theil index of per capita income of the states, 1975–2000 (Source: Authors' estimates based on CEGA)

9.2.2 Income Concentration

The growing importance of Bogota in the national economy has been accompanied by an equal increase in regional disparities that is evident until the end of the decade of 1990. This can be seen in the concentration of income per capita in the states measured by the Theil index of concentration. This index is presented in Fig. 9.2, and evidences the polarization of income.[4] It can be observed that disparities in per capita income in Colombia have increased. This has resulted in a series of spatial imbalances in the distribution of wealth in the country, and regions such as the Pacific and Caribbean coasts have lagged behind. These two regions contribute with about 50 % of the population with unmet basic needs (UBN[5]), in spite of contributing with only 30 % of the national population.

The contrast in poverty levels between Bogota and the coastal regions is evident. For instance, according to the census results of 2005 the percentage of people with UBN in the Pacific Coast was 47.9 %, and 45.4 % on the Caribbean coast, while in Bogota that percentage was 9.16 %.[6] Moreover, the UBN index of the states along the so called "golden triangle" reached 15 % in 2005. This pattern provides evidence to posit that in Colombia the phenomenon of poverty has a spatial counterpart: the core of the country accumulates wealth while in the periphery the opposite occurs.

[4] Calculations were made until 2000, the latest date for which data is published for per capita income by CEGA.

[5] The UBN index is the percentage of households with deficiencies in at least one of the following characteristics: (1) quality of housing (2) public utilities (3) crowding (4) school attendance (5) dependency ratio.

[6] The Pacific coast is the sum of the departments of Chocó, Nariño and Cauca, together with the municipality of Buenaventura.

In conclusion, the phenomenon of poverty and inequality is present and persistent. Unfortunately, recent national government policies have not had any component aimed at reducing regional imbalances. With the exception of the national development plan of 2010–2014, no explicit policy related to reducing regional economic disparities has been formulated. Moreover, it had already been noted by experts in fiscal policy, that in Colombia the system of allocation of resources from the Government Transfers (GT) and the revenues derived from the exploitation of non-renewable natural resource royalties (NRR) have no explicit mechanisms to compensate for existing regional imbalances (Alesina et al. 2000, p. 14).

9.2.3 Regional Labor Market Segmentation

From a neoclassical perspective, labor market integration can be achieved through labor mobility. Under this view, if supply and demand are not in equilibrium the market will induce changes in prices of the commodity, in other words, wages will adjust to correct these disequilibria.

In a country like Colombia it would be expected that the adjustments occur via quantities i.e. through labor mobility as there is little chance for wages to fluctuate according to the market conditions, due to certain rigidities in the labor market (Echeverry and Santamaría 2005). Labor mobility constitutes, then, a very important element for understanding the dynamics of population and the adjustments of the labor market. What determines that mobility? Various factors are counted as determinants with wages being the one that exhibits an important weight. If labor were perfectly mobile we should observe an integrated national labor market and the equalization of wages across regions.

If we consider a representative market for any product, we could think of the integration in this market as the parity in the prices across regions. The same relationship may hold for the labor market if it is integrated. Why would there be differences in wages across regions? This question can be addressed in the framework of compensating wage differentials across labor markets in which these differentials reflect some desirable and non-desirable attributes associated with a given place of work or occupation. Those characteristics may generate some wage differentials as a form of compensation for the lack of amenities in certain jobs.

First, it is important to mention as background previous work, such as that of Galvis (2002) who used a gravity-type model to explain the interregional migration in Colombia. The author follows the framework employed by Aroca and Hewings (2002) to show that both the distance and the relative position of origin and destiny are important for migration flows. The study concluded that interregional mobility is of considerable importance and that economic conditions of destination and origin regions exert a significant influence on the migration flows. It was shown

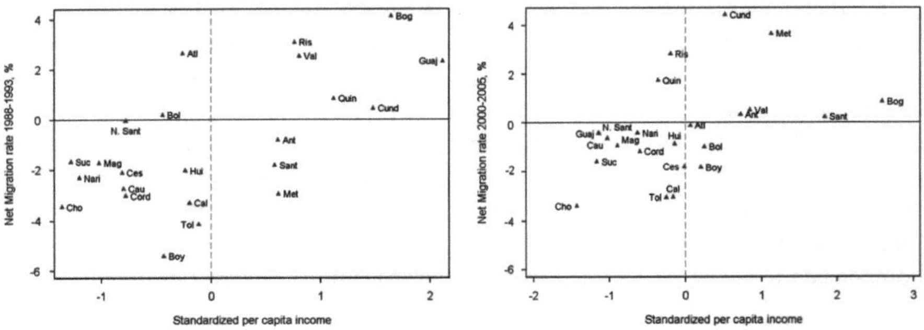

Fig. 9.3 Net migration rate and per capita average income 1988–1993 and 2000–2005 (Note: *Vertical dashed line* indicates the average per capita income. Net migration rates calculated with respect to the population in 1993 and 2005. Source: Authors' calculations)

that, for relatively similar time periods, the net interregional migration rate in Colombia was of comparable magnitude to that experienced by countries such as Spain, Ireland, Japan, and the United States.

The question that follows is if the labor market is integrated, given that there is a significant amount of labor mobility. In this regard, previous studies like Nupia (1997) investigated integration in the labor market of the four main metropolitan areas and Jaramillo et al. (2001) used urban and rural wages for unskilled workers to study the same issue. According to the results integration of the labor market of unskilled workers holds for the areas around the core of the country.

Considering both unskilled and skilled workers Galvis (2011) show that, for instance, Bogota presents the highest magnitudes of wages followed by Cali and Medellin, and show a similar behavior. On the other hand, urban areas that behave very differently with respect to the rest of cities are Barranquilla and Pasto. The particularities that are observed in those two cities which may explain that difference are related to the fact that they are located in the periphery of the country. Because of that reason, the possibility of movements of labor from or to these markets is even more limited.

What makes the results of the imbalances more profound is the fact that the regions that present higher per capita income are the ones which have positive net migration rates (see Fig. 9.3). What is expected is that those departments with higher per capita income or per capita income above average (right of the dotted line in Fig. 9.3) attract immigrants. In Romero (2010) it is shown that in Colombia, internal migration has contributed to human capital concentration in the largest and wealthiest cities, as more qualified people migrate to the main cities. This supports the hypothesis that the population with more economic resources is the one who can afford mobility across regions. For poorer people it seems that the costs of migration would prevent them from moving to areas in which there are greater opportunities to achieve higher living standards.

9.3 Spatial Analysis of Poverty

This section discusses spatial autocorrelation indexes in order to assess whether poverty in Colombia is randomly distributed across its territory. The spatial autocorrelation analysis considers that all phenomena are interrelated in space, but those which are closer are more correlated than distant ones. The foundation of this statement derives from the first law of geography, or Tobler's Law (1970). In this way, for spatial econometric analysis it is of relevance to evaluate statistically the existence of similar values in a variable, occurring in near spaces. Pearson's correlation coefficient does not account for similarities in close spaces between the variables that are geo-referenced, i.e., that have a reference to where the phenomenon occurs in space. In this case the Moran's I is used. This index parts from the definition of correlation coefficient, but adds the location of the observations in the space by including an array of spatial weights, W_{ij}, as follows:

$$I = \frac{N}{S_0} \frac{\sum_i \sum_j W_{ij} Z_j Z_j}{\sum_i Z_{\overline{i}}^{2}}$$

where $Z_i = X - \overline{X}$,, i.e. X is in terms of deviations from its mean and $S_0 = \sum_i \sum_j W_{ij}$. The term $W_{ij}Z_i$ is known as the spatial lag of Z. W_{ij} matrix allows us to identify the "neighbors" of the observations in Z. Based on the "first law of geography" the definition of the neighbors is achieved by building W_{ij} as a binary array whose cells are equal to one if observations i and j are neighbors and zero otherwise. Different criteria are used to restrict the neighbors such as contiguity criteria, distance weights, or the K-nearest neighbors.

For the calculation of Moran's I the covariance of Z with its spatial lag divided by the variance of Z is used. This can be obtained from the regression of the variable WZ with Z (Anselin 1996). Thus, if the sign of Moran's I is positive, it is said that there is a positive spatial autocorrelation in the Z variable, i.e., similar values occur in nearby locations.

Global Moran's I is useful to detect a general pattern of clustering. However, when it comes to local analysis the Moran's I index can be used to explore clusters. In this case the analysis is done by means of the Local Indicators of Spatial Association, LISA, which allows for the detection of patterns of spatial autocorrelation in small areas of the region of study (Anselin 1995). For this analysis if Z is set to be a variable resulting from the demeaned X variable, $Z_i = X_i - \overline{X}$, the LISA indicators, I_i, can be built in the following fashion:

$$I_i = \frac{Z_i}{m_2} \sum_j w_{ij} Z_j$$

Where: $m_2 = \sum_i Z_i^2$, which is equal to the variance of the Z variable.

The objective of this analysis is to find matching high values of a variable in a spatial location *i* as well as in neighboring observations *j*. This case corresponds to the High-High clusters. Low values in *I* surrounded also by low values, would correspond to the Low-Low. High-Low and Low-High combinations are also feasible and they would correspond with cases of local outliers. These cases are also of interest as they may indicate a phenomenon of resiliency in the sense that a poor area remains poor without experiencing spillovers to foster wealth coming from the prosperous places in the surroundings.

The inference, the same way as for the Moran's I, is performed by Monte Carlo simulations building a distribution of I_i, to serve as a reference to determine if clusters are statistically significant.

9.3.1 Spatial Poverty Traps

Regional economic disparities in Colombia have persisted over time (Bonet and Meisel 1999). This, however, is not a unique characteristic of Colombia, as it has been documented in the literature on economic development in other countries (Sawhill 1988; Morrill and Wohlenberg 1971; Levernier et al. 2000; Blanden and Gibbons 2006). Among the explanations for the persistence of economic disadvantage of some regions there is one that is related to "poverty traps", where the disadvantage maybe the result of conditions that lead to a vicious circle and a perverse equilibrium (Azariadis 2006). For instance, in the case of individuals low-income parents are not able to provide high-quality education for their children, who will in turn, have few opportunities to reach high income levels, thus maintaining the vicious circle. To bring these people to a sustained growth path, it is required that external forces provide some minimum level of wealth or human capital to exit the vicious circle.

Often the conditions that give rise to objective conditions of poverty are confined to specific geographical areas, where neighborhood effects are magnified (Durlauff 2006; Sampson et al. 2002). In these spaces the adverse consequences of poverty reinforce each other and thus there will be persistence of the unfavorable conditions. For example, poor local economies may have low quality of education that remains static for years, which implies a reproduction of poverty across generations (Bénabou 1996; Durlauff 1996). On the other hand, high income regions can invest in education, in order to provide better opportunities for their inhabitants. This process would imply not only persistence of disparities, but also the polarization of regional economic growth.

In this regard, fiscal decentralization processes may contribute to an increase in regional disparities, as documented in the case of developing countries (Rodríguez-Pose and Ezcurra 2010). This result may be related to differences in the ability of local authorities to lobby for resources from the central government, financial constraints, and differences in the quality of institutions that affect the efficiency with which regions use their resources.

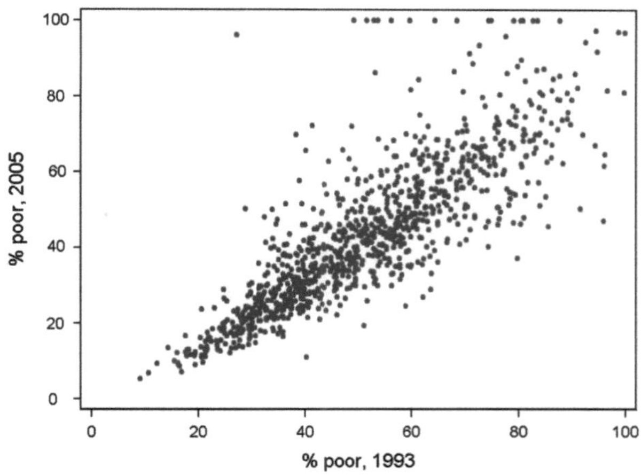

Fig. 9.4 Persistence of poverty among municipalities, 1993–2005 (Source: Authors' estimates based on DANE)

In Colombia, in the early 1990s decentralization policies, which were strengthened after the 1991 Constitution, promoted a system in which sub national units, such as municipalities and states, obtained resources from the national budget through transfers of the central government. One of the objectives of the fiscal decentralization was to reduce regional economic disparities. This objective, however, has not been achieved. Rather, the evidence shows that after the early 1990s there has been an increase in regional economic disparities.

Following Sampson and Morenoff (2006) study of durable inequality the persistence in poverty may be analyzed by means of a plot displaying poverty rates[7] based on in the last two Census, i.e., 1993 and 2005, as displayed in Fig. 9.4. There is a correlation of 0.87, between poverty rates in the municipalities in 1993 and 2005. This means that municipalities with high poverty rates in 1993 remain in poverty in 2005. The same correlation calculated between 1985 and 1993 yields a magnitude of 0.80, which is lower than the 0.87 found for 1993–2005 period, in spite of being calculated for a shorter period.[8] This means that the persistence of poverty rates increased after the decade of 1990.

To analyze the change in poverty rather than in its levels, it is important to see how the change in poverty is related to the initial conditions, and trying to understand whether the municipalities that increased their level of poverty between 1993 and 2005 "were those that were already very poor or those that were in the transition toward becoming poor" (Sampson and Morenoff 2006, p. 182). For that matter, Fig. 9.5 plots the poverty levels in 1993 against the "gains" in poverty from 1993 to 2005. In the figure we display the municipalities split into two categories:

[7] Poverty rates are measured as the percentage of population with unmet basic needs, UBN, (NBI for its Spanish acronym).

[8] Both correlation coefficients are statistically significant even at 1 %, using Bonferroni-adjusted significance levels.

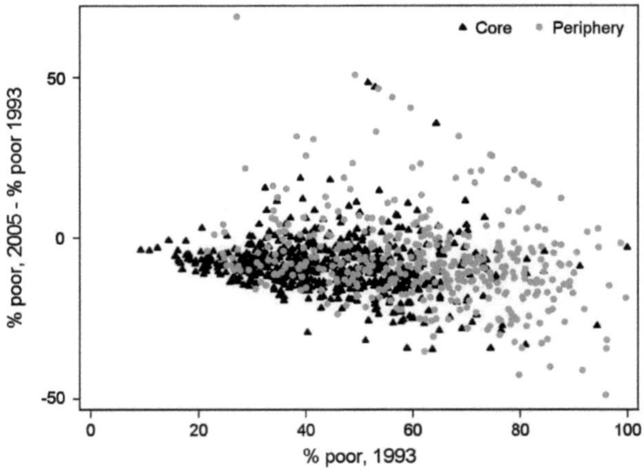

Fig. 9.5 Initial conditions and change in poverty levels, 1993–2005 (Source: Authors' estimates based on DANE)

the core municipalities and the peripheral ones, according to the c classification by Galvis and Meisel (2010b).

Figure 9.5 shows that most of the municipalities in the core present low poverty rates as opposed to the peripheral ones which are concentrated beyond the 50 % threshold. Furthermore, the municipalities with mayor decreases in poverty rates were the peripheral ones. This suggests that the poverty patterns and their dynamics have a spatial counterpart, which can be tested by estimating the equation relating poverty rates in 1993,UBN_{1993},to those in 2005, UBN_{2005}, in the following fashion:

$$UBN_{2005} = \beta_0 + \beta_1 UBN_{1993} + \varepsilon$$

In this case the residual change scores, denoted by ε, reflect the variation in poverty rates that are unaccounted for in the initial conditions. If only path dependence matters, the residual change would not have a spatial pattern, as the current level of poverty rates would be explained mainly by past poverty rates. To test for spatial dependence in the change scores, we use Moran's I test for regression residuals (Cliff and Ord 1981) as displayed in Table 9.1.

According to the results, the Moran's I is positive and statistically significant, which means that there is positive spatial autocorrelation in the residual change scores. This, in turn, provides evidence to suggest that the residual change scores are spatially clustered and, thus, the factors that explain current poverty levels, beyond past poverty rates, have a spatial dependence. To put this results into context we can refer to Durlauf (2006), who proposes that "poverty traps are nothing more than socioeconomic environments in which persistency in economic status is arbitrarily long" (p. 143). Spatial poverty traps, thus, may be defined as socioeconomic environments circumscribed in a given space that imply persistence in economic status. This may be precisely the explanation behind the results portrayed in Table 9.1. In other words, to understand the paths of poverty change in the municipalities of Colombia, it is necessary to make reference to spatial

Table 9.1 Regression of persistency in poverty rates

Dependent variable: UBN2005	Coefficients
UBN1993	0.8895***
	(0.0175)
Constant	−2.5655***
	(0.9814)
N	1,064
Adj. R-squared	0.71
Moran's I for regression residuals	0.1368***
Expected value	−0.0014
Std. Error	0.0176
Moran's I statistic standard deviate	**7.8535*****

Note: $^{***}p < 0.001$. Standard Errors in parentheses
Source: Authors' estimates

poverty traps as one of the main factors explaining the trajectories towards improving or reinforcing poverty and regional inequality.

9.3.2 Government Transfers and Decentralization Policies

The central government funds subnational units through participation in the national budget, also known as government transfers, GT. Besides the latter, royalties derived from the exploitation of non-renewable natural resources (NRR) are also transferred to territorial units. These funds originating from NRR were initially used by municipalities to finance basic needs programs.

It was expected that with the decentralization of fiscal resources, there would be an impulse to the strengthening of human capital and a reduction of inequalities in available incomes of local government. Nonetheless, it has been noted that in Colombia the clusters of municipalities where there are large amounts of per capita GT and NRR, do not coincide with clusters of poverty. Figure 9.6 shows an estimate of spatial clusters of poverty and transfers (GT plus NRR).

Clusters were identified based on local indicators of spatial association, LISA. The dark shaded areas correspond to municipalities with high values that are surrounded by municipalities with similar values, called high-high clusters. Consequently the low-low clusters, correspond to municipalities with low levels in the measured variable as well as its neighbors.

From this analysis we would expect that the high-high clusters in terms of UBN, correspond with areas of higher per capita transfers or high-high clusters. This is not the case and in fact, Panel A in Fig. 9.6 shows that a large fraction of municipalities with high levels of UBN, are surrounded by municipalities in the same condition without a level of national government transfers corresponding to the situation of poverty (they are located in clusters of low amounts of transfers, represented by gray areas). This happens in the southern part of the departments of the Caribbean

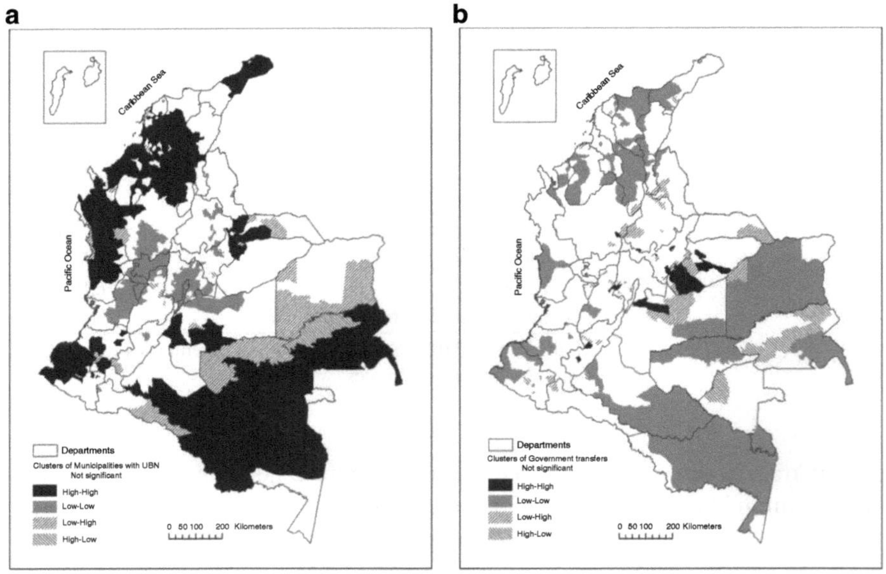

Fig. 9.6 Poverty clusters and transfers from the National Government. (**a**) Clusters of municipalities with UBN, 2005. (**b**) Clusters based on transfers (GT + NRR, 1996–1999) (Source: Prepared by the authors based on the National Administrative Department of Statistics (DANE), the National Planning Department (DNP) and the map database of the Agustín Codazzi Geographical Institute (IGAC))

Coast, and in some towns on the Pacific Coast, and in several municipalities in the eastern part of the country. Similar results were found for the UBN index for 1993, especially in the Caribbean Coast.

9.3.3 Trade Policy and Economic Geography

Trade liberalization can have an effect on the concentration of economic activity and thereby influence regional disparities. The effects of such policies depend on the relative accessibility to the domestic and the external markets, and how the regions are integrated via the transportation network. For instance, after NAFTA, manufacturing wages in the Mexico-US border increased relative to the existing ones in Mexico City. Specifically a 10 % increase in distance from the US border implied a decrease in the relative wage of 1.9 % (Hanson 1996). Relocation of manufacturing towards the border region was also documented after Mexico joined the NAFTA (Hanson 2004).

Regarding trade policy, it was expected that greater trade liberalization in Colombia in the early 1990s would help reduce regional disparities. The mechanism through which it would act to improve the living conditions in the coastal

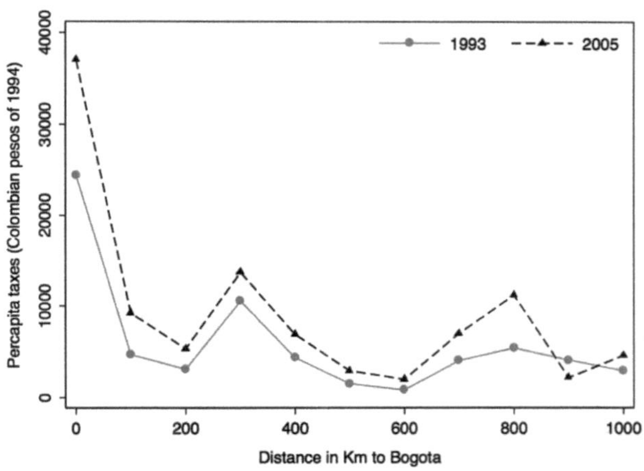

Fig. 9.7 Relationship between per capita taxes in retail and manufacturing and distance to Bogota (Note: Per capita taxes correspond to those collected from manufacturing and retail industries. Source: Prepared by the authors based on the National Planning Department (DNP))

economies relied on the location on shipping areas. This would, in turn, create jobs and wealth in those areas, among the most economically depressed in Colombia. However, the opposite has occurred and it seems that the effects of trade liberalization account for an increase in the size of the economy in the core of the country, specifically in Bogota (Fernández 1998). As a consequence of this, the highest concentration of companies in the capital and other areas with relatively high wealth may have increased regional disparities. This seems to be the case portrayed in Fig. 9.7, where we show a negative relation between the distance, in kilometers, to Bogota and the per capita taxes collected from manufacturing and retail. What is more interesting is that this negative relation strengthened from 1993 to 2005. The latter result shows that, more than a decade after trade liberalization, more income is generated in neighboring areas of Bogota than in cities near the seaports.

This last result could be expected, according to the approach of the so-called New Economic Geography, NEG. According to Paul Krugman, one would expect that in an economy with high transportation costs such as the Colombian, the concentration of economic activity would be localized in the center and not in the periphery.

The result expected from trade liberalization was that the Colombian economy would resemble an economy such as the US, which is more open to trade and, as a stylized fact, shows a great proportion of populous and wealthy cities and counties around the borders and in the seaports. In Colombia, however this has not occurred as it is shown in Fig. 9.8. This figure portrays the share of population in 1993 and 2005 living near the coastlines at different buffers of distance. It is shown in Panel A that the closer one gets to the coastline, the higher the share of population with UBN (i.e. under poverty conditions). On the other hand, in Panel B it is observed that as one approaches the coastline the share of population decreases. What is more surprising is that the average poverty rates near the coastline have increased from 1993 to 2005, even though the share of population has remained practically unchanged around those areas.

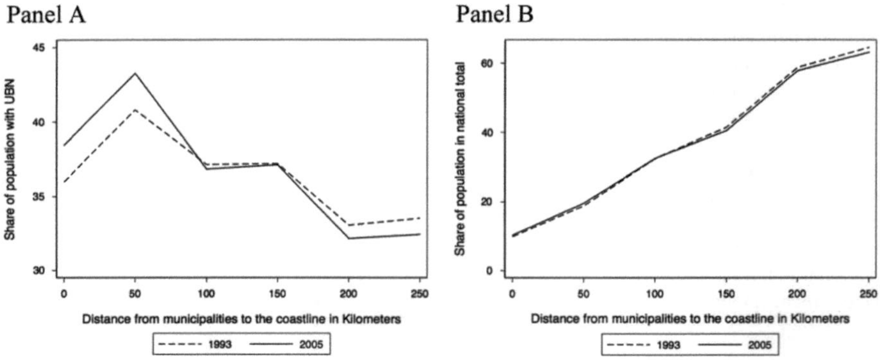

Fig. 9.8 Relation between distance to the coastline and the share of total population and population with UBN, 1993–2005 (Source: Prepared by the authors based on the National Administrative Department of Statistics (DANE))

9.4 Regressive Economic Policies

It would seem that the policies of the Colombian National Government follow a spatially regressive structure in which more transfers are allocated to more prosperous regions. This is evident when considering the relationship of departmental per capita GDP, as a measure of income, and the total transfers per poor people. This relation is presented in Fig. 9.9, showing that there is a positive association between the two. This result indicates a clearly regressive regional policy of fiscal transfers because the municipalities that have greater per capita wealth are receiving a greater portion of the resources transferred from the central government.

The latter results seem to justify the proposal of a regional policy that takes into account the elements of fairness. A recent report of the United Nations Development Program (UNDP 2007) estimates the Gini coefficient, and notes that in the global ranking of inequalities in income distribution Colombia (with a Gini coefficient of 0.586) is only exceeded by Haiti (0.592), Bolivia (0.601), Botswana (0.605), Central African Republic (0.613), Sierra Leone (0.629), Lesotho (0.632) and Namibia (0.743).

Economic and social policies should seek to reduce the gaps in income distribution which, as discussed above, have a strong regional component. That is, it requires a commitment from the National Government to be written into future development plans, taking into account these inequalities and identifying their causes in order to propose strategies to reduce them. In Colombia, perhaps because it was believed that the market would achieve a balance in regional income distribution, clear policies have not been formulated in this regard, with the exception of the latest National Development Plan 2010–2014. So far, the market has not eliminated regional economic disparities. For instance, in relation to the labor market, it is observed income differentials between regions do not tend to reduce over time. One explanation would be that this is the result of the most

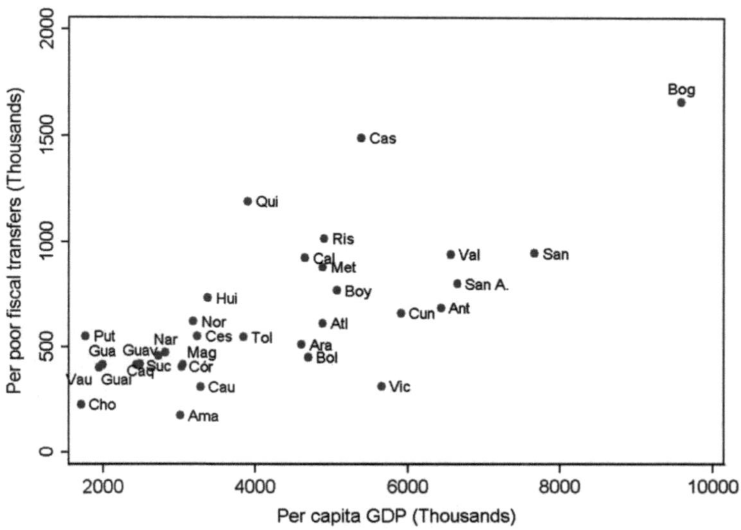

Fig. 9.9 Relation between total per poor transfers and the GDP per capita of the states (Average 2005–2007) (Note: Per capita fiscal revenues include Government Transfers, GT, plus non-renewable Natural Resources Royalties, NNR, sent to the states and municipalities. Source: Prepared by the authors based on the National Planning Department (DNP) and DANE, the National Administrative Department of Statistics)

qualified population groups moving to places where the income level is higher. This phenomenon has led to a larger gap in income generation among the territories of the country: those who are migrating are the most qualified people, and they migrate to areas with better income opportunities. This labor migration is causing that the most deprived areas lose human capital.

This migratory phenomenon in Colombia has been characterized by a concentration in Bogota, Cundinamarca, Valle, Antioquia and Atlántico. These territorial entities attracted over 50 % of the migration that occurred between 1988 and 1993 (Galvis 2002), according to the 1993 census and between the years 2000 and 2005, according to the 2005 census. Note that these are precisely the states where wealth is mostly concentrated.

9.5 Convergence Analysis

It has been argued that the reduction in disparities is supposed to help the country to achieve higher growth rates, as the reduction in inequalities is complementary to a more balanced growth (Lustig et al. 2002). Furthermore, the empirical literature has documented the existence of a negative relationship between inequality and growth (Deininger and Squire 1996; Alesina and Rodrik 1994; Bertola 1993; Engermann and Sokoloff 2002).

Inequalities between countries are found as a result of barriers to mobility. For instance, between countries it is less likely that factors move to places with higher returns until their relative supply becomes more balanced and income equalizes. On the other hand, within a country income disparities may arise as well but it is expected that these inequalities disappear faster than between countries, due to the higher mobility of labor and capital, which will lead to economic convergence. The latter may be studied by analyzing beta (conditional or non-conditional) or sigma convergence. Non conditional beta convergence exists when there is a negative relationship between the growth rates and the initial income. In this sense, the poorest regions, due to the higher returns to capital, will grow faster than the prosperous ones, experiencing a "catching up process" (Abramovitz 1986). Conditional beta convergence, on its part, occurs when this negative relation is found even if one controls for different attributes of the regions. On the other hand, sigma convergence refers to the reduction of disparities in income, measured though Theil's entropy index, the variation coefficient, Gini coefficient, among others.

Previous studies in Colombia have analyzed economic growth and convergence, suggesting evidence both in favor and against the convergence hypothesis. These research lines began with the pioneering study of Cárdenas et al. (1993), which found evidence in favor of the convergence hypothesis over the 1950–1989 period. On the contrary, various recent studies unanimously rejected the idea that income is converging towards one equilibrium level. Each study used different sets of data or estimation methods which rejected the convergence hypothesis (Rocha and Vivas 1998; Bonet and Meisel 1999; Galvis and Meisel 2001; Bonet and Meisel 2006).

Recent evidence on the analysis of disparities still shows no clear pattern of convergence. For instance, González-Quintero (2011) analyzes the period 1975–2005 and finds evidence of conditional beta convergence in income, at a speed of 1.5 % per annum. However, and bearing in mind that beta convergence is a necessary but not sufficient condition for the sigma convergence, when analyzing the dynamics of the distribution using Markov chains, González-Quintero finds that the distribution is characterized by a persistent pattern and a polarization of income. His results show, for instance that for the different classes in which the income is categorized, in most of the cases the probability of a spatial unit to remain in the same category is more than 90 %. The latter is an indicator of the great persistence shown by the distribution of regional income in the country. Moreover, for those categories where the probability of remaining in the same position is below 90 %, it is more likely that the spatial units move to a position where they will be worse off than before, which for the lower income classes will imply the occurrence of a polarization pattern. The latter results contrast with the ones obtained by González-Ramírez (2011) for the period 1994–2009. From his study, González-Ramírez concludes that Colombia has been a successful case of convergence as he finds evidence of absolute beta convergence and sigma convergence. However, as we have discussed, the persistent patterns of polarization of regional income distribution found by González-Quintero (2011) do not seem to coincide with this conclusion.

Table 9.2 Regressions for per capita GDP absolute convergence, 1990–2010

	(a)	(b)	(c)
	1990–2000	2000–2010	1990–2010
α	0.036*	0.065***	0.045***
	(0.015)	(0.013)	(0.008)
β	0.019	0.025*	0.021**
	(0.011)	(0.01)	(0.007)
N	33	33	33
Speed of convergence	1.74	2.26	1.74
Half-life (years)	36	27	33

Note: $^{*}p < 0.05$, $^{**}p < 0.01$, $^{***}p < 0.001$
Source: Calculations of the authors

9.5.1 *Beta Convergence*

The analysis of beta convergence is done following the approach proposed by Barro and Sala-I-Martin (1991):

$$\frac{1}{T}Log\left(\frac{y_{it}}{y_{i,\ t-T}}\right)=a-\left[\text{Log}\left(y_{i,\ t-T}\right)\right]\left(1-e^{-\beta T}\right)\left(\frac{1}{T}\right),$$

Where y_{it} and $y_{i,t\ -T}$ are the per capita income at time t and at the beginning of the period analyzed, respectively.

Estimation of the convergence equation indicates we can reject the hypothesis that there is no absolute convergence for the period 2000–2010, but not for 1990–2000. The speed of convergence, λ, is calculated using $\lambda = Ln(1 + \beta * T)/\text{T}$. For the first period λ reaches a magnitude of 2.52 %, and for second period λ is about 2.32 % per annum. For the combined periods λ is 1.93 % per annum. With those results, the time that it takes to reduce the initial spread by half, i.e. the half-life, is near three decades (Table 9.2).

As it has been stated, beta convergence is a necessary but not a sufficient condition for the reduction of disparities among regions or spatial units (Barro and Sala-I-Martin 1992). For this reason, complementary to the results found for beta convergence, we need to analyze the dynamics of the reduction of disparities by means of sigma convergence, which is of greater interest as it provides evidence of whether per capita income is becoming more equitable across spatial units (Quah 1993; Friedman 1992).

9.5.2 *Sigma Convergence*

Regarding sigma convergence we found that the coefficient of variation shows that up to 1999 inequalities increased. Later on, there was a decrease in the coefficient (Fig. 9.10). This result is confirmed by the weighted coefficient of variation

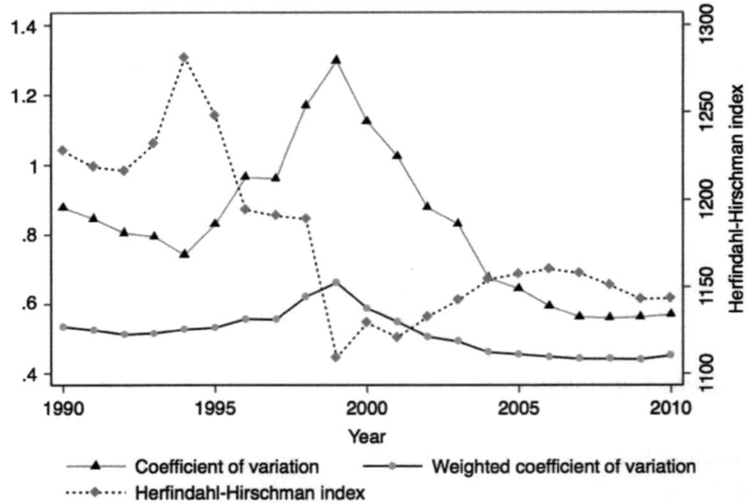

Fig. 9.10 Sigma convergence (Source: calculations of the authors)

(weighted by population share). It is observed that both coefficients show a first period of increase in inequalities followed by a period of improvement.

The spatial concentration of income is measured by the Herfindahl-Hirschman index. This index shows a different pattern since the concentration increases until 1994, from which it follows a period of decrease in spatial concentration until 1999. The spatial de-concentration trend breaks up from the year 2000 onwards. These results coincide with the ones presented by González-Arbeláez (2006) during the period 1990–2004.

It is worth mentioning that most of the previous evidence shown for this index in Colombia reports values near 1,000 or above (Bonet and Meisel 1999; Galvis and Meisel 2001; González-Arbeláez 2006). Moreover, if the Herfindahl-Hirschman coefficient were calculated for a full equidistribution for the 33 states the value obtained would be 303.03, a magnitude very close to the value of 325.7 presented by González-Ramírez.

Up to this point the evidence is non-conclusive regarding regional income concentration. Another common method to evaluate sigma convergence is to analyze the standard deviation of the logarithm of per capita income, v,:

$$v=\sqrt{\frac{1}{n}\sum\nolimits_{i=1}^{n}\left[Log\left(\frac{y_i}{y^*}\right)\right]^2},Log(y^*)=\frac{1}{n}\sum\nolimits_{i=1}^{n}Logy_i$$

As it is shown in the Fig. 9.11, this index shows a similar pattern as the one displayed by the variation coefficient.[9]

[9] This is not always the case, as documented by Dalgaard and Vastrup (2001).

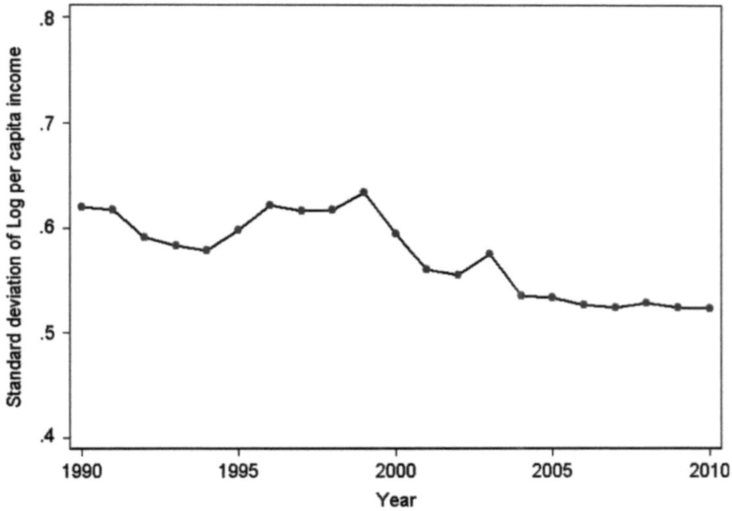

Fig. 9.11 Standard deviation of log per capita income (Source: Calculations of the authors)

Even though the coefficient exhibits a decreasing trend, is this enough evidence to conclude that disparities are decreasing? Note that the upward or downward trend exhibited by the coefficient may be an artifact of the scale. In fact, in order to verify whether there has been effectively a reduction in disparities we follow the work by Carree and Klomp (1997), who test the null hypothesis that variance of the initial year σ_{1^2}, is equal to the variance in the ending year, σ_T^2, i.e. the null hypothesis of no sigma convergence Ho: $\sigma_1{}^2=\sigma_T^2=\sigma^2$.We use the T_2 statistics proposed by Carree and Klomp (1997) that follows a $\chi^2(1)$ distribution.[10] The results show that the test for comparison of variances between 1990 and 2000, 2000–2010, and 1990–2010, do not allow us to reject the null hypothesis, as all values of the T_2 are below the threshold of $\chi^2(1) = 3.84$. This means that the variances are equal to each other for the three comparison periods, which in turn implies that disparities have not changed between the years 1990 and 2010 Table 9.3.

In sum, it is not plausible to conclude that Colombia is a successful story of convergence as the evidence is mixed. In fact, it is more plausible to suggest that there are convergence clubs for which the inequalities within groups decrease, and the inequalities between them increase. If that is the case, what may be happening is that the convergence clubs tend to separate from each other, showing a trend towards polarization.

[10] The T2-statistic is expressed as $T_2=(N-2.5)*ln\left[1+\frac{1}{4}\frac{\left(\sigma_1^2-\sigma_T^2\right)^2}{\sigma_1^2\sigma_T^2-\sigma_{1T}^2}\right]$, where σ_{1T} is the covariance between per capita income at time 1 and time T.

Table 9.3 Tests for equality of income variance, 1990–2010

Variable	N	Mean	Std. Dev.	Covariance	T_2
Log(per capita income 1990)	33	15.36	0.62		
Log(per capita income 2000)	33	15.45	0.59		
Combined				0.3174	0.20
Log(per capita income 2000)	33	15.45	0.59		
Log(per capita income 2010)	33	15.73	0.52		
Combined				0.2742	2.23
Log(per capita income 1990)	33	15.36	0.62		
Log(per capita income 2010)	33	15.73	0.52		
Combined				0.2532	2.22

Note: Calculations based on log of per capita income (Constant pesos of 2005). T_2 follows a χ^2 distribution with one degree of freedom which implies a critical value of $\chi^2(1) = 3.84$
Source: Calculations of the authors

9.6 Concluding Remarks

This document has pointed out critical issues regarding regional inequalities in Colombia. It has been shown that regional economic disparities have been increasing over the last decades. Moreover, the regional policies that the government has implemented in order to help in this matter do not seem to be successful in achieving this objective. On the contrary, government transfers have benefited mainly the most prosperous regions, as there is a positive correlation between per capita income and per capita transfers from the central government. From another perspective if the regions with the high poverty levels are compared to the places where the main government transfers are allocated, it is found that lagging regions are not the ones receiving the highest flows of resources from the central government. This is clearly a regressive policy that has not favored the impoverished areas which are mainly rural and located in the periphery of the country.

References

Abramovitz M (1986) Catching up, forging ahead, and falling behind. J Econ Hist 46(2):385–406
Ades A, Glaeser EL (1995) Trade and circuses: explaining urban giants. Q J Econ 110(1): 1953–227
Alesina A, Rodrik D (1994) Distributive politics and economic growth. Quart J Econ 109:465–490
Alesina A, Carrasquilla A, Echavarría JJ (2000) Decentralization in Colombia. Working papers series. Fedesarrollo, Bogotá
Anselin L (1995) Local indicators of spatial association. Geogr Anal 27(2):93–115
Anselin L (1996) The Moran Scatterplot as an ESDA tool to assess local instability in spatial association. In: Fischer MM, Scholten HJ, Unwin DJ (eds) Spatial analytical perspectives on GIS. Taylor & Francis, London
Aroca P, Hewings GJD (2002) Migration and regional labor market adjustment: Chile 1977–1982 and 1987–1992. Ann Reg Sci 36(2):197–218

Azariadis C (2006) The theory of poverty traps: what have we learned? In: Bowles S, Durlauf S, Hoff K (eds) Poverty traps. Princeton University Press, New York
Barro RJ, Sala-i-Martin X (1991) Convergence across states and regions, Brookings papers on economic activity, economic studies program. Brook Inst 22(1):107–182
Barro RJ, Sala-i-Martin XX (1992) Convergence. J Polit Econ 100:223–251
Bénabou R (1996) Inequality and growth. In: Bernanke BS, Rotemberg JJ (eds) NBER macroeconomics annual 1996, vol 11. MIT Press, Cambridge, pp 11–92
Bertola G (1993) Macroeconomics of distribution and growth. Economics Working Papers eco98/39, European University Institute
Black D, Henderson V (1999) A theory of urban growth. J Polit Econ 107(2):252–284
Blanden J, Gibbons S (2006) The persistence of poverty across generations. A view from two British cohorts. The Policy Press, Bristol
Bonet J (2003) Colombian regions: competitive or complementary? Revista de Economía del Rosario 6(1):53–70
Bonet J, Meisel A (1999) La convergencia regional en Colombia: una visión de largo plazo 1926–1995. Coyuntura Económica 29(1):69–106
Bonet J, Meisel A (2006) Polarización del ingreso per cápita departamental en Colombia, 1975–2000. Documentos de Trabajo sobre Economía Regional, Banco de la República-Cartagena
Borjas G (1999) Economic research on the determinants of immigration. Lessons for the European Union. World Bank Technical Paper, No.438, Washington, DC
Cárdenas M (2005) Crecimiento económico en Colombia: 1970–2005. Coyuntura Económica XXXV(2):49–59
Carree M, Klomp L (1997) Testing the convergence hypothesis: a comment. Rev Econ Stat 79 (4):683–686
Cliff AD, Ord JK (1981) Spatial processes: models and applications. Pion, London
CEGA (2006) Ingreso, consumo y ahorro en los departamentos de Colombia, 1975–2000. Sistema Simplificado de Cuentas Departamentales, vol 2, Bogotá
Dalgaard C-J, Vastrup J (2001) On the measurement of σ-convergence. Econ Lett 70(2):283–287
De Vreyer P, Herrera J, Mesplé-Somps S (2009) Consumption growth and spatial poverty traps: an analysis of the effect of social services and community infrastructures on living standards in Rural Peru. In: Klasen S, Nowak-Lehmann F (eds) Poverty, inequality, and policy in Latin America. MIT Press, Cambridge
Deininger K, Squire L (1996) A new data set measuring income inequality. World Bank Econ Review 10(September):565–591
Durlauff S (1996) A theory of persistent income inequality. J Econmic Growth 1:75–93
Durlauff S (2006) Groups, social influences, and inequality. In: Bowles S, Durlauff S, Hoff K (eds) Poverty traps. New York: Princeton University Press.
Engerman S, Sokoloff K (2002) Factor endowments, inequality, and paths of development among new world economies. NBER Working Paper No. 9259, Cambridge
Echeverry JC, Santamaría M (2005) The political economy of labor reform in Colombia. In: World Bank (eds) World development report 2005
Ejermo O (2005) Technological diversity and Jacobs' externality hypothesis revisited. Growth Chang 36(2):167–195, Wiley
Fernández C (1998) Agglomeration and trade: the case of Colombia. Ensayos Sobre Política Económica 33(June):85–123
Friedman M (1992) Do old Fallacies ever die? J Econ Lit 30:2129–2132
Galvis L (2002) Determinantes de la migración interdepartamental en Colombia, 1988–1993. Rev Econ del Rosario 5(1):93–118
Galvis L (2011) Real wages in Colombia: a conditional convergence analysis: 1984–2009. Rev Soc Econ 21(2):17–42
Galvis L, Meisel A (2001) El crecimiento económico de las ciudades colombianas y sus determinantes, 1973–1998. In: Meisel A (ed) Regiones, ciudades y crecimiento económico en Colombia. Banco de la República, Bogotá

Galvis L, Meisel A (2009) Tendencias de la Polarización Territorial y de las Inequidades en Colombia. Foreign Affairs Latinoamérica 9:21–32

Galvis L, Meisel A (2010a) Persistencia de las desigualdades regionales en Colombia: Un análisis espacial. Documentos de Trabajo Sobre Economía Regional, Banco de la República, #120

Galvis L, Meisel A (2010b) Fondo de Compensación Regional: Igualdad de oportunidades para la periferia colombiana. Documentos de Trabajo Sobre Economía Regional, Banco de la República, #122

Gaviria A, Gelves D (2009) A social history of the XXth century. Evidence from Colombian Municipalities. Paper presented at the first conference of the regional science of the Americas, Cartagena, February, pp 12–13

Glaeser EL, Kallal HD, Scheinkman JA, Shleifer A (1992) Growth in cities. J Polit Econ 100 (6):1126–1152

Glaeser EL, Scheinkman J, Shleifer A (1995) Economic growth in a cross-section of cities. National Bureau of Economic Research, Cambridge

González-Arbeláez A (2006) Convergencia regional y conflicto armado interno en Colombia, 1980–2004. Unpublished thesis, Universidad Javeriana

González-Quintero N (2011) ¿Otra vez? Una sencilla visión de la convergencia económica en los departamentos de Colombia: 1975–2005. Archivos de Economía, Departamento Nacional de Planeación, # 384

González-Ramírez J (2011) Convergencia económica regional en colombia: Un análisis para el periodo reciente de descentralización fiscal 1994–2009. Unpublished master's thesis, Universidad de los Andes

Gouëset V (1988) Bogotá: Nacimiento de una Metrópoli. Tercer Mundo Editores, Bogotá

Hanson GH (1996) Localization economies, vertical organization and trade. Am Econ Rev 86(5): 1266–1278

Hanson GH (2004) What has happened to wages in Mexico since NAFTA? In: Estevadeordal A, Rodrik D, Taylor A, Velasco A (eds) Integrating the Americas: FTAA and beyond. Harvard University Press, Cambridge

Jacobs J (1969) The economy of cities. Vintage, New York

Jaramillo CF, Nupia C, Romero C (2001) Integración del mercado laboral colombiano: 1945–1998. In: Adolfo M (ed) Regiones, ciudades y crecimiento económico en Colombia. Alfacolor, Bogotá

Junguito R, Rincón H (2004) La política fiscal en el siglo XX en Colombia. Borradores de Economía, Banco de la República, #318

Krugman P (1991) Increasing returns and economic geography. J Polit Econ 99(3):483–499

Krugman P (1999) The role of geography in development. Int Reg Sci Review, 22(2):142–161

Krugman P, Livas R (1996) Trade policy and the third world Metropolis. J Dev Econ 49(1): 137–150

Levernier W, Patridge M, Rickman D (2000) The causes of regional variations in U.S. poverty: a cross-county analysis. J Reg Sci 40(3):473–497

Lucas R Jr (1988) On the mechanics of economic development. J Monet Econ 22(1):3–42

Marshall A (1920) Principles of economics. Macmillan, London

Morrill R, Wohlenberg E (1971) The geography of poverty in the United States. McGraw-Hill, New York

Nupia O (1997) Integración espacial en los mercados laborales: evidencia para las regiones colombianas. Desarrollo y Sociedad 40:83–131

Paci R, Usai S (1999) Externalities, knowledge spillovers and the spatial distribution of innovation. Geo J 49(4):381–390

Posada Carbó E, Meisel A (1993) ¿Por qué se disipó el dinamismo industrial de Barranquilla? Y otros ensayos de historia económica de la Costa Caribe. Ediciones Gobernación del Atlántico

Quah D (1993) Galton's Fallacy and the convergence hypothesis. Scand J Econ 95:427–443

Ramírez MT (1999) The impact of transportation infrastructure on the Colombian economy. Borradores de Economía, Banco de la República, #174

Rocha R, Vivas A (1998) Crecimiento Regional en Colombia: "Persiste la Desigualdad". Revista de Economía del Rosario 1:67–108

Rodriguez-Pose A, Ezcurra R (2010) Does decentralization matter for regional disparities? A cross-country analysis. J Econ Geogr 10(5):619–644

Romer PM (1986) Increasing returns and long-run growth. J Polit Econ 94(5):1002–1037

Romero J (2010) El éxito económico de los costeños en Bogotá: migración interna y capital humano. Documentos de TrabajoSobre Economía Regional (129)

Rosenstein-Rodan P (1943) Problems of industrialization of Eastern and South-Eastern Europe. Econ J 53:202–211

Sachs J (2005) The end of poverty: economic possibilities for our time. The Penguin Press, New York

Sampson R, Morenoff J, Gannon-Rowley T (2002) Assessing neighborhood effect: social processes and new directions in research. Annu Review Sociol 28:443–478

Sampson RJ, Morenoff JD (2006) Durable inequality. In: Bowles S, Durlauf SN, Hoff K (eds) Poverty traps. Princeton University Press, Princeton, pp 176–203

Sawhill I (1988) Poverty in the U.S.: why is it so persistent? J Econ Lit 26(3):1073–1119

Tobler WR (1970) A computer movie simulating urban growth in the Detroit Region. Econ Geogr 46:234–240

United Nations Development Program – UNDP (2007) Human development report 2007/2008. New York

Zambrano Pantoja F (1997) Valoración y diagnóstico del territorio. Análisis Regional y Empleo. Un Enfoque Multidisciplinario. Ministerio de Trabajo y Seguridad Social – Universidad Nacional de Colombia, Bogotá

Chapter 10
Concentration and Inequality Across Brazilian Regions

Carlos Roberto Azzoni

10.1 Introduction

Being a country with a large territory, it is expected that regional disparities would be pronounced in Brazil. There is a wide range of natural conditions, since the distance between its north and south extremes reaches 2,700 miles. Weather and natural conditions are varied, since 6 % of the area and 5.3 % of the population are located in the northern hemisphere, close to the equator line, while 7 % of the area and 14.5 % of the population are situated in the temperate zone, with occasional episodes of snow in the high mountains. The majority of population is located in the coast, while 20 % is located in in-land states. Different biomes, with at least ten different types of vegetation, a variety of soil types, and different landscapes compose the natural basis of the country.[1] The largest part of the population and production is located in the southeast region, which accounts for only 11 % of the area and 43 % of the population.

As one would expect, regional inequalities are important and persistent (Azzoni 2001; Baer 2001). As Table 10.1 indicates, the poor northeast region, encompassing nine states, 28 % of the population, and 18 % of the country's total area, accounted for 18 % of the national GDP in 1939; in 2009 that share had dropped to 13.5 %. On the other hand, the southeast region represented 63 % of the national GDP in 1939 and 56.3 % in 2009.

In general, it can be said that few changes have occurred in the relative positions of the two most populated regions, the poor Northeast and the rich Southeast. It is true that their combined share in population has dropped from 79.5 % in 1940 to 69 % in 2010 and their combined share in national GDP has also dropped. But the Southeast remained the richest and the Northeast remained the poorest. The most

[1] http://www.ibge.gov.br/home/geociencias/cartogramas/ctb.html).

C.R. Azzoni (✉)
University of Sao Paulo, Sao Paulo, Brazil
e-mail: cazzoni@usp.br

J.R. Cuadrado-Roura and P. Aroca (eds.), *Regional Problems and Policies in Latin America*, Advances in Spatial Science, DOI 10.1007/978-3-642-39674-8_10,

Table 10.1 Indicators of regional concentration

		Share in population		Share in national GDP				
	Share in area	1940	2010	1939	2009	2009		
				Total		Agric.	Mining	Manuf.
North	45.3	3.9	8.3	2.7	5.0	7.5	11.6	4.2
Northeast	18.3	35.0	27.8	16.9	13.5	18.5	9.1	9.6
Piauí St.	2.9	2.0	1.6	0.9	0.6	1.1	–	0.3
Southeast	10.9	44.5	42.1	63.0	56.3	28.7	75.0	60.6
S. Paulo St.	2.9	17.4	21.6	31.3	33.5	11.5	2.3	43.0
South	6.8	13.9	14.4	15.3	16.5	26.3	2.0	21.1
Mid-West	18.9	2.7	7.4	2.1	9.6	19.0	2.4	4.6

relevant changes in regional shares are related to the rise of the north and mid-west regions. In the first case, natural resources played an important role, for the region is rich in minerals and timber, whose extraction started during the period; in 2009 it hosted 11.6 % of the national mining production. Also, a free import zone was established in the city of Manaus, which boosted the growth of that area, especially in the 1970s and 1980s, when import tariffs in the country were still very high. The north region moved from a share of 2.7 % in the national GDP in 1939 to 5.0 % in 2009, almost doubling its economic importance. The mid-western region benefited from the transfer of the national capital to the newly built city of Brasilia in 1961, which nowadays is a metropolitan area with over 2.5 million inhabitants. Another decisive factor was the technological development in agriculture promoted by government-funded agricultural research, which made the region the most important producer of grains, cotton, and ranching products in the country. The share of that region in the national GDP moved from 2.1 % in 1940 to 9.6 % in 2009.

Another way of looking at the process over time is to observe the changes in the center of gravity, defined as the average latitude and longitude of the state capital cities, weighted by the shares of the respective states in national GDP. As a simplification, it is assumed that the state's GDP takes place in the capital city of the state. This assumption is a good approximation for the majority of the states, since the areas around the capital cities tend to host most of the economic activity, especially in manufacturing and in the tertiary sector. The value obtained for a specific year, expressed in degrees of latitude and longitude, reflects both the geographical disposition of the capital cities and the state shares in national GDP, and it is not useful as an economic indicator. However, since the coordinates of the capital cities do not change over time, any movement in the gravity center is determined by changes in the economic importance of the states. Therefore, observing how the center of gravity moves over time indicates the economic forces pushing/pulling it, basically, the changing shares in the economic importance of the states in the national context.

Figure 10.1 exhibits the evolution of the center of gravity of the Brazilian economy over the period 1939 and 2009, covering a period of seven decades. Those were years presenting many important economic changes that could have

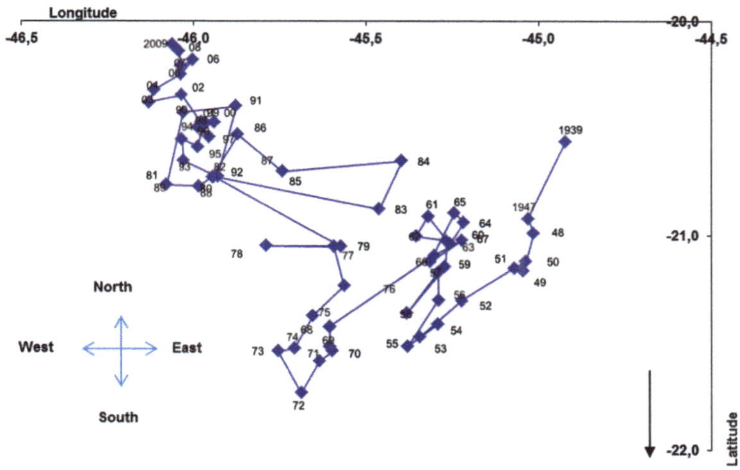

Fig. 10.1 Center of gravity of the Brazilian economy

led to modifications in the regional concentration in the country (Baer 2001). The World War II years were positive for the economy, since Brazil supplied raw materials for the allies. The following years were also positive, but the country burned all the international currency accumulated during the war, leading to a slow grow period in the early 1950s. National planning institutions were established in the second half of the 1950s and a concern about regional concentration was included in the planning toolkit. This period was followed by troubled times, with high inflation, political instability and, eventually, recession in the early 1960s. A military coup occurred in 1964 and important institutional modifications were implemented, leading to a boom period known as "the Brazilian miracle", which died off in 1973, along with the first international oil crisis. The mid 1970s were years of moderate growth and increasing inflation. This situation moved to the 1980s, which are known as the "lost decade", due to its low growth. The early 1990s continued in the low growth situation up to 1994, when inflation stabilization was finally achieved. Since the mid-1990s the country has grown steadily, although at a moderate pace. An important aspect is the opening-up of the economy from 1990 on, which took at least half a decade to mature and produce important results. The first decade of the twenty-first century presented much better years, with higher rates of GDP growth.

In spite of all those ups and downs, regional concentration remained almost the same. The poor northeast region, for which regional development instruments were developed and implemented, given its relevant share in population, possibly at a very high cost (Carvalho et al. 2006), lost participation, as presented before. It is clear that the booming years of the early 1950s and early 1970s brought the center of gravity to the strongest economies in the country, located in the southeast

Table 10.2 Indicators of regional inequality

	Per Capita GDP respective to the national average	
	1939	2009
North	0.75	0.63
Northeast	0.48	0.48
Piauí St.	*0.43*	0.33
Southeast	1.41	1.31
S. Paulo St.	*1.8*	1.55
South	1.11	1.14
Mid-West	0.7	1.32[a]

[a]The capital city, Brasília, established in 1961 in the region, presents the highest per capita income level in the country, 2.98 times the national average

region.[2] Years of economic difficulties tended to move it towards the northeast. After the mid-1980s, however, the center clearly moved towards the northwest. This can be explained by the development of high-performance agriculture in the mid-west, driven by government policies towards technological development in the sector, the establishment of the nation's capital in the core of the mid-west, the implementation of a free import zone in Manaus, in the core of the Amazon, the exploitation of mining activities in the state of Pará, in the North (bauxite, iron ore), as well as logging in that area.

Another way to look at the regional disparities is through the inequality in regional per capita income. Table 10.2 presents the relationship of the per capita income level in the regions in relation to the national average. The northeast region was never able to achieve a per capita income level higher than half the national average, in spite of massive out-migration movements, especially in the 1960s and 1970s. The per capita income level of the rich southeast region was 1.4 times the national average in 1939 (which includes that of the region) and dropped slightly to 1.31 times in 2009. The north region, in per capita terms, moved from 75 % of the national per capita income average in 1939 to 63 % in 2009, a movement that was caused by high population growth in the period, which more than doubled the regional share (from 3.9 % to 8.3 %). That is, the impressive increase in the regional share in GDP was out shadowed by the even more intensive growth in population. As for the mid-west, another gainer in terms of GDP, its per capita income level was 70 % of the national average in 1940 and moved to 32 % over the average in 2009. At present, Brasília shows the largest per capita income level of any large city in Brazil, almost three times the national average. As compared to the north region, the mid-west was able to gain both population and GDP, but the later was more intensive than the former, leading to an upgrade on the regional per capita income.

The above numbers are eloquent in showing both the impressive disparity levels and how little they have changed over seven decades. Recent changes, however, are calling the attention of researchers, since, for the first time over a sequence of years,

[2] Azzoni (1997) concluded that booming years tended to increased concentration, which was decreased subsequently.

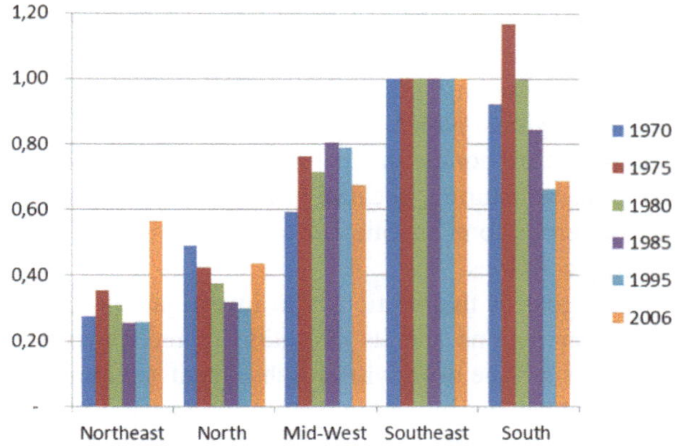

Fig. 10.2 Total factor productivity in Brazilian agriculture, 1970–2006 (Source: Vicente (2006, 2011))

inequality levels are decreasing. And this is not only for regional inequality, but also for personal income inequality, with the Gini coefficient dropping from 0.60 in 1997 to 0.51 in 2009, a movement that was accompanied by a decrease in the shares of poor and indigent people[3] (Barros et al. 2006; Ferreira et al. 2006; Hoffmann 2006; Soares 2006a, b; Neri 2010). As for regional inequality, as pointed out in Silveira-Neto and Azzoni (2011a, b), the numbers are also striking, since trends started to change in the late 1990s. The spatial Gini (across 27 states) and the standard deviation of the logarithm of per capita income, indicating sigma convergence, presented important decreasing trends. Employment in manufacturing shows similar behavior.

These new trends might raise some optimism about the future of regional concentration and regional inequality in the country. This paper sets to investigate some factors that could reinforce those trends, such as the recent levels and the evolution of productivity in the regions. It is well-established that human capital is a key aspect in regional development, and we will present some indicators in this area also. The paper has two sections besides this introduction and the concluding section. In Sect. 10.2 we present indicators of productivity across states, and in Sect. 10.3 we present higher education indicators. We set aside government influences, especially through interregional transfers, since we have a specific chapter to deal with them (Chapter 21st in this book).

10.2 Regional Productivity in Agriculture

Competitiveness differentials and their development over time are associated with regional disparities, especially with the regional concentration of production. By being more competitive, some regions tend to receive more investment and may

[3] http://www.ipea.gov.br/082/08201002.jsp?ttCD_CHAVE=3128

generate economies of agglomeration, which reinforce the initial level of competitiveness. Given their level of production and their importance for the competitiveness of the country, generally these regions are able to influence national policies and the regional allocation of public investment. These factors can consolidate or stimulate their competitive environment. This logic applies in general, but specially so in manufacturing, because of its greater potential geographical mobility and its sensitiveness to economies of agglomeration. But it also applies to primary and tertiary activities.

The goal of this section is to investigate productivity levels of agriculture in Brazilian regions and its evolution in recent years. Manufacturing and tertiary activities will be dealt with in subsequent sections.

Brazil has become an important food producer in the world in the last decades, thanks to government-led massive investments in research and technology. The evolution of total factor productivity for the country as a whole between 1970 and 2006 is impressive, as shown by Gasques et al. (2010). But this evolution was not homogeneous across regions, as the regional productivity differentials in agriculture calculated by Vicente (2006), presented in Fig. 10.2, indicate. Regional levels are expressed in relation to the southeast region, the one with the highest productivity level. The first thing that comes to sight are the low levels in the northeast and north regions. Not only that, but also these regions became progressively less competitive in the period, with an important inversion in 2006. The south region had comparable levels of productivity as the southeast up to 1980, but lost competiveness in the following periods. The uprising region is the mid-west, although in 1995 it was still 20 % below the southeastern level, and lost competitiveness in 2006.

The latest agricultural census was performed in 2006, from which two studies provide similar results. Vicente (2011) measures levels of total factor productivity and technical, allocative and economic efficiency in agricultural crop production at the state level, using a nonparametric frontier model (DEA). Imori (2011) uses stochastic production frontiers and inefficiency effects models at the municipal level. As the results in Table 10.3 indicate, the southeast region held its first place as the most productive in the country in 2006, followed more closely by the mid-west and south regions. Figure 10.3 reinforces this conclusion, at a finer geographical disaggregation.

In conclusion, the analysis of competitiveness in agriculture reveals that the southeast region holds the first position in the national ranking. The neighboring south and mid-west regions present the second best levels. Even considering that the southeast is basically the manufacturing core of the country, it is still responsible for 28.7 % of the national agricultural production (Table 10.1). It is followed by the south region, which held the second place until 1995. In more recent years, the downwards trend in this region, coupled with the upwards trend in the mid-west, made the latter to approach the former as the second most important region in agriculture in Brazil. This result is compatible with the changes in regional concentration presented in the introduction of this paper.

Table 10.3 Indicators of Competitiveness for Brazilian States, 2006

Region	State	Share in production	TFP	Efficiency Technical	Allocative	Economic
Northeast	Alagoas	1.16	86.17	1.00	0.51	0.51
	Bahia	8.00	94.31	1.00	0.53	0.53
	Ceará	1.52	54.39	0.85	0.56	0.47
	Paraíba	0.89	87.26	1.00	0.65	0.65
	Pernambuco	1.83	83.74	1.00	0.49	0.49
	Piauí	0.63	33.23	0.43	0.58	0.25
	Rio Grande do Norte	0.41	61.74	0.81	0.56	0.45
	Sergipe	0.48	71.27	0.87	0.52	0.45
	Maranhão	1.29	43.71	0.69	0.52	0.36
	Region	**16.21**	**80.50**	**0.93**	**0.54**	**0.50**
North	Acre	0.17	69.97	1.00	0.54	0.54
	Amapá	0.02	53.40	0.92	0.49	0.45
	Amazonas	0.37	40.32	1.00	0.35	0.35
	Pará	1.00	39.37	0.63	0.54	0.33
	Roraima	0.10	80.08	1.00	0.90	0.90
	Rondônia	0.74	88.15	1.00	0.70	0.70
	Tocantins	0.59	75.91	1.00	0.51	0.51
	Region	**2.99**	**61.97**	**0.88**	**0.56**	**0.49**
Mid-West	Distrito Federal	0.16	97.98	0.98	0.63	0.62
	Goiás	5.54	108.03	1.00	0.88	0.88
	Mato Grosso	9.42	88.02	1.00	0.62	0.62
	Mato Grosso do Sul	2.97	97.32	1.00	0.62	0.62
	Region	**18.09**	**95.76**	**1.00**	**0.70**	**0.70**
Southeast	Minas Gerais	11.20	112.28	1.00	0.76	0.76
	Espírito Santo	1.60	86.18	1.00	0.49	0.49
	Rio de Janeiro	0.44	97.77	0.97	0.55	0.53
	São Paulo	21.46	162.65	1.00	1.00	1.00
	Region	**34.70**	**142.04**	**1.00**	**0.89**	**0.89**
South	Paraná	12.25	97.73	0.84	0.78	0.65
	Santa Catarina	4.14	111.43	1.00	0.78	0.78
	Rio Grande do Sul	11.62	92.26	1.00	0.75	0.75
	Region	**28.01**	**97.49**	**0.93**	**0.77**	**0.71**
Brazil		**171.99**	**100.00**	**0.91**	**0.61**	**0.55**

Source: Vicente (2011)

10.3 Manufacturing

Manufacturing is an interesting sector to analyze because it is the most potentially mobile in space, as compared to resource-oriented activities, such as agriculture and mining, and to the tertiary activities. While accounting for 22 % of GDP, Brazilian manufacturing accounts for almost 70 % of exports and one-third of total R&D investment. It also employs 26 % of Brazilian workforce and buys 40 % of its inputs from other sectors of the economy (CNI 2010).

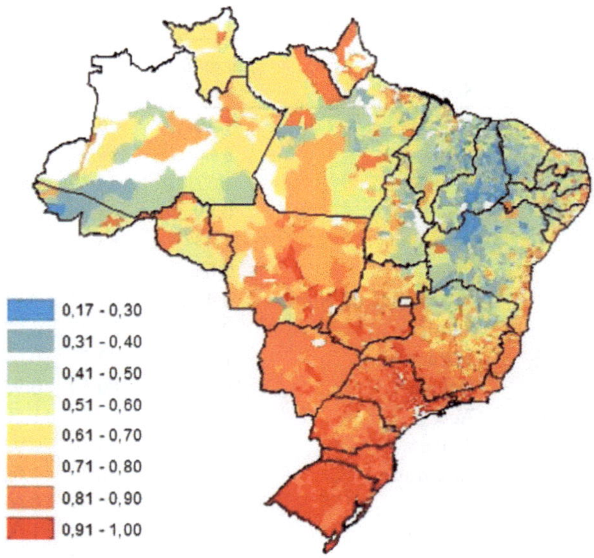

Fig. 10.3 Technical efficiency at the municipal level, 2009 (Source: Imori (2011))

Azzoni and Ferreira (1998) have computed indicators of relative profitability for the period 1970–1995. They are based on a comparison of efficiency wages, which consider both productivity and wage levels at the regional level. Their results are presented in Fig. 10.4. Due to data limitations, only five regional units are presented, with three states (São Paulo, Minas Gerais and Rio de Janeiro, all in the southeast region) and two regions (Northeast and South). The numbers indicate that the northeast region lost competitiveness over time, reaching 80 % of the national profitability level in 1995. The state of Rio de Janeiro also lost competitiveness. The south region was able to remain around the national average, but lost positions in more recent years. The most important state in manufacturing in the country, São Paulo, was able to remain above the national average all the time. Since the national average includes all states, it is right to say that the distance between São Paulo state and the remaining states is larger than in relation to the national average. Finally, Minas Gerais state presented an outstanding performance, due to the establishment of an important automobile plant (Fiat) in the mid-1970s, and its relevant metal-mechanic sector, which is related to the iron ore mines present in that state.

Schettini and Azzoni (2011) have computed efficiency indicators for states and regions. Figure 10.5 shows how concentrated the manufacturing production was in the country in 2006. Using data by the 137 meso regions from yearly manufacturing surveys, the authors were able to estimate stochastic frontiers, which allowed for the calculation of efficiency indicators. The focus was on the first years of the twenty-first century, given that important economic changes occurred in the country, associated with the opening up of the economy and the stabilization of prices from the mid-1990s on.

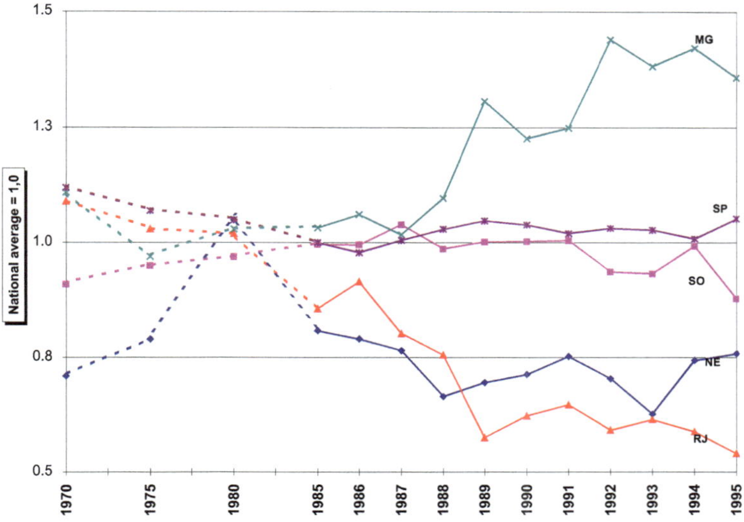

Fig. 10.4 Manufacturing profitability indicators for some Brazilian regions (Source: Azzoni and Ferreira (1998))

Their results in terms of levels are shown in the maps of Fig. 10.6. The numbers refer to the average of the period 2000–2006. Taken Sao Paulo Metropolitan area, the most important manufacturing center in the country, as a benchmark, only one region presents higher productivity. It is the "Extremo Oeste Baiano" meso region, a recent expansion area of grain production, hosting processing plants from the big international players in that activity. There are some few areas with the same level of productivity as São Paulo metropolitan area, basically in the mid-west and north regions, related to agribusiness, mining extraction and logging. Other than those, productivity is concentrated in the traditional manufacturing area of the country.

Another topic refers to the changes in productivity in this century. Figure 10.7 shows the rate of growth of productivity in the period 2000–2006. The national average growth was 3.9 % per year, but it ranged from −6.4 % to 7.6 %. As the figure shows, all states with negative productivity growth belong to the north and northeast regions. On the other extreme, the largest growth rates were from the north region (Amazonas) and the mid-west (Mato Grosso).

In Fig. 10.8 the possible existence of convergence across states is considered. The horizontal axis portrays the share of each state in national manufacturing; the vertical axis shows the rate of growth in productivity in the period. States with low participation in national production would have to present higher productivity growth to improve their situation over time. That is, the line relating these variables should be decreasing in order to indicate reduction of inequality. As it can be seen, that is not the case. Even if we did not formally test for the existence of divergence, it is clear from the picture that convergence in productivity is out of perspective.

Fig. 10.5 Manufacturing value added by km^2, 2006

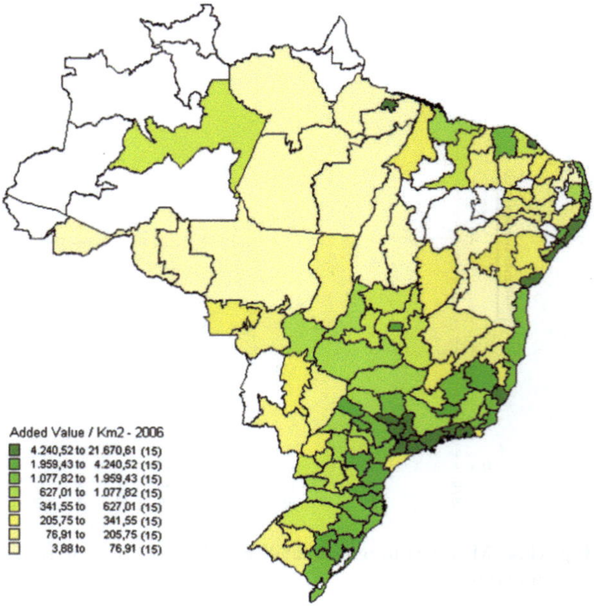

10.4 Tertiary Activities

Although typically tertiary activities are not considered in regional analyses and regional policies, it is important to consider their role in regional disparities. First of all, their quantitative role is too big to ignore: in Brazil, their share in GDP was 53 % in 1950 and 67 % in 2011. That is, more than two-thirds of GDP come from this sector; and its importance is increasing, as it happens everywhere in the world. Secondly, these are urban activities by nature, which adds another aspect to regional disparities: changes in the distribution of cities. The effects can be seen in Fig. 10.9, which portrays the changing shares of some important capital cities in their respective state's population. It seems clear that the capital cities in the most important areas of the country, in economic terms, have lost importance, due to an in-state decentralization process provided by the strength of their economic fabric (Panel a, in Fig. 10.9). At the same time, capital cities of peripheral states gained importance, possibly indicating a growing role in the economic system of the state (Panel b).

Considering these activities, Azzoni and Andrade (2005) analyzed the role of tertiary activities in regional inequality in Brazil in the period 1970–2001. They computed competitiveness indicators based on the limited information available. The authors concluded that the most important centers of Brazilian economy were either below average in terms of competitiveness or loosing competitiveness over time in commerce activities, but the same did not hold for services in general,

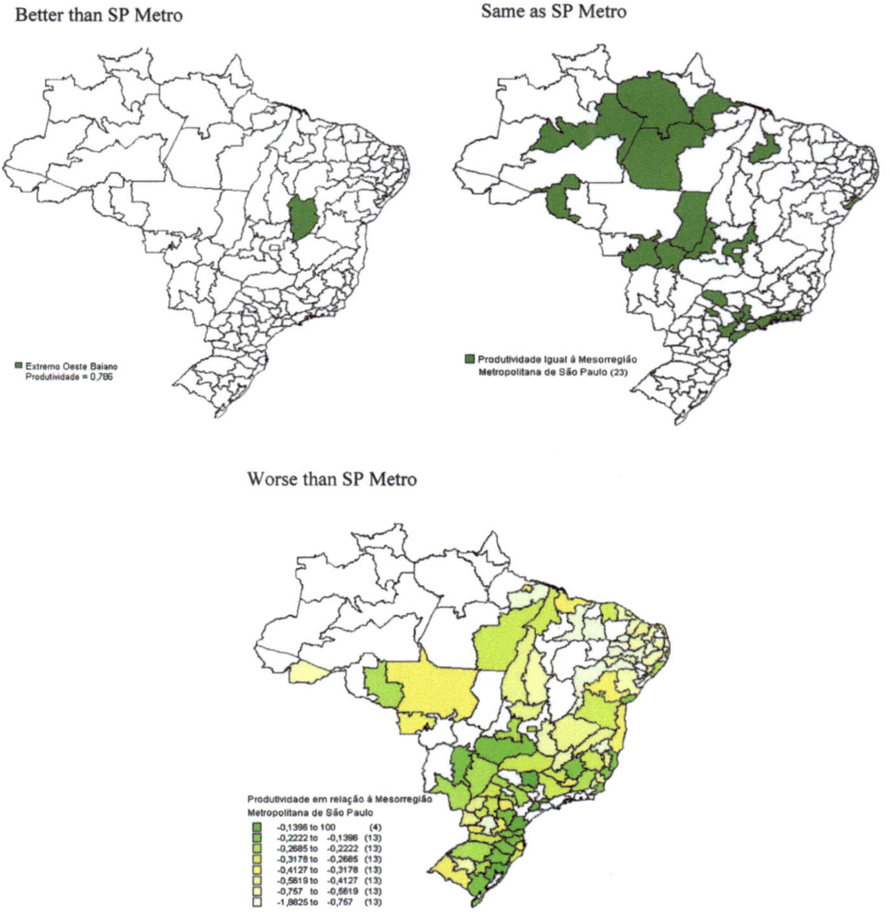

Fig. 10.6 Efficiency levels in comparison to São Paulo Metropolitan region, 2000–2006

as their results reproduced in Table 10.4 indicate. In this direction, Table 10.5 offers information on some sub-sectors within services. The results indicate that hotels and restaurants and real state presented a similar behavior as commerce, except for revenue/establishment, for which rich areas show increasing competitiveness. For transportation, São Paulo state presented improvements in revenue/worker and in revenue/establishment, as did the southeast region in this latter case. The really interesting modifications occurred in services to firms and miscellaneous, in which the rich areas moved from below to above average in revenue/wages, and increased their advantage in the other two indicators, with one exception only in the southeast region. These are more sophisticated sectors, for services to firms are related to outsourcing, consulting, etc., and miscellaneous tends to include new innovative activities not included in the previous classifications. Computing activities were only present in the surveys after the 1980 census, with only data for the late 1990s

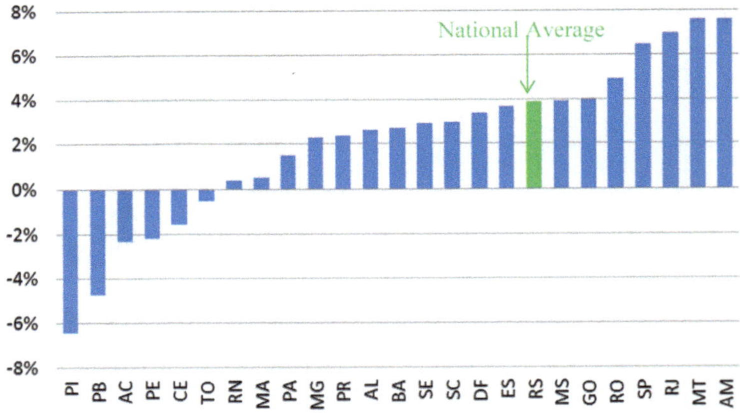

Fig. 10.7 Productivity growth across states, 2000–2006

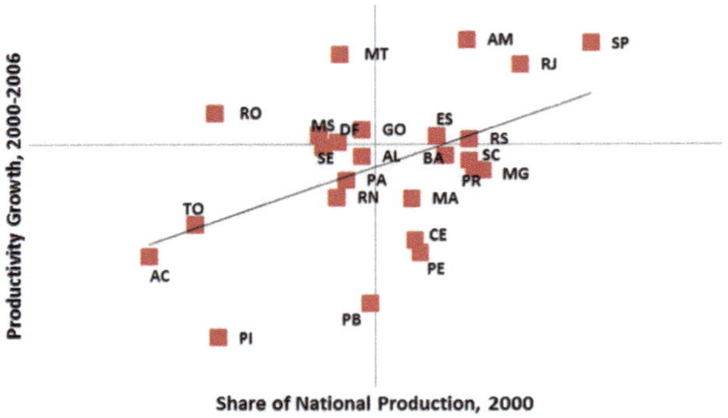

Fig. 10.8 Evolution of productivity across states, 2000–2006

available. The results indicate high competitiveness in all indicators for the richer areas, especially for the state of São Paulo. In the case of the mid-west region, results are biased by the presence of the federal government in Brasília, concentrating all data processing for federal activities in Brazil. It seems clear, thus, that in the most sophisticated sub-sectors within services, the rich regions are not only above average, but have increased their competitiveness over time.

Tertiary activities were disaggregated into 24 sub-sectors, and a spatial concentration index based on Devereux et. al. (2004) was calculated for each year. Results displayed in Fig. 10.10 indicate that, in general, sectors highly concentrated presented lower growth rates, with some exceptions, such as publicity, marketing and decoration. Over time, only six sectors increased spatial concentration as measured by employment: miscellaneous; security; communication; commercial representation, storage and agriculture; household services and travel agencies. The

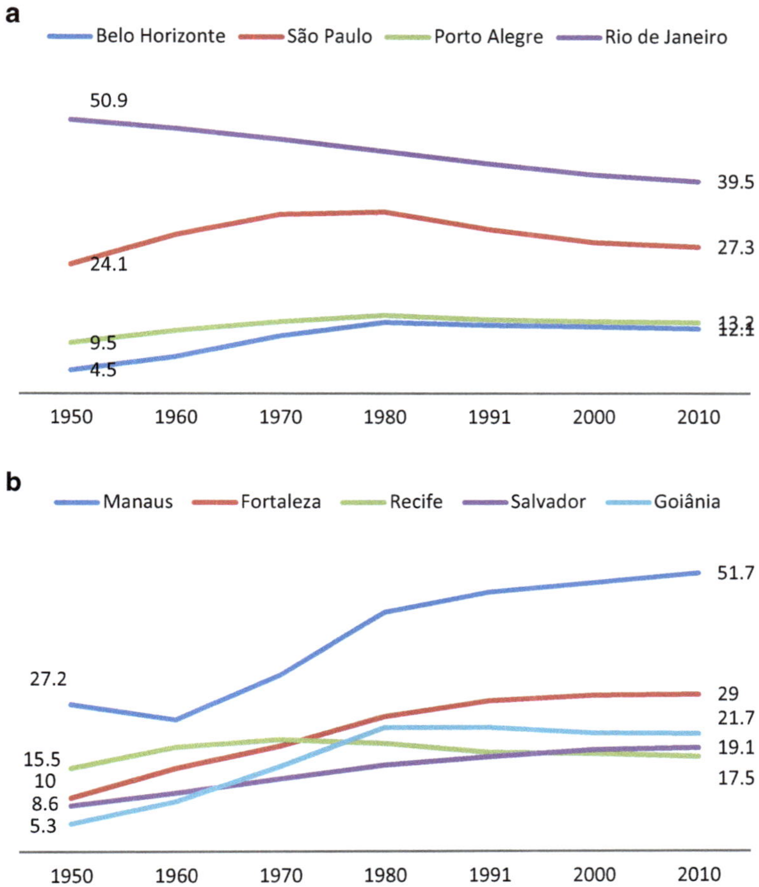

Fig. 10.9 Shares of capital cities in state's population (%) (**a**) Core states (**b**) Non-core states (Source: IBGE, Demographic Census, various years)

sectors for which increased concentration was the highest were household services and commercial representation, storage and agriculture. No statistically significant relationship between the two variables was found, that is, employment growth and end-of-period concentration do not seem to be associated.

The analysis of tertiary activities indicates that the rich areas are losing competitiveness in commerce and in traditional services, but are becoming more competitive in the modern sub-sectors within the tertiary, such as in services to firms, computing, etc. The analysis of growth and concentration revealed a great variety across sub-sectors, indicating that it is important to develop detailed analysis to come to relevant conclusions. As for spatial concentration, the majority of sub-sectors presented decreasing concentration in the period, although six sub-sectors presented increasing concentration. An income convergence analysis was performed, indicating that only a sub-set of sectors presented convergence. By

Table 10.4 Competitiveness indicator

	Commerce					
	Wholesale		Retail		Services	
	Late 1970s	Late 1990s	Late 1970s	Late 1990s	Late 1970s	Late 1990s
Revenue/wage bill						
North	1.03	1.36	1.20	1.27	1.04	1.09
Northeast	1.13	1.27	1.39	1.16	1.19	0.94
Southeast	0.99	0.89	0.92	0.93	0.97	1.01
South	1.01	1.09	0.99	1.05	0.92	0.98
Center-West	0.85	1.37	1.15	1.19	1.24	0.98
São Pauo State	0.95	0.83	0.94	0.88	0.86	1.02
Revenue/worker						
North	0.70	1.30	0.67	1.31	0.75	0.96
Northeast	0.65	0.89	0.57	0.88	0.57	0.68
Southeast	1.16	1.03	1.21	1.03	1.18	1.13
South	0.89	0.94	1.13	0.99	0.73	0.83
Center-West	0.74	1.09	0.99	1.01	1.10	0.83
São Pauo State	1.16	1.06	1.36	1.14	1.15	1.27
Revenue/establishment						
North	0.55	1.56	0.53	2.24	0.75	1.80
Northeast	0.36	0.96	0.38	0.78	0.39	0.92
Southeast	1.44	1.07	1.56	1.06	1.37	1.17
South	0.96	0.80	1.35	0.93	0.71	0.59
Center-West	0.75	1.31	1.00	1.18	1.12	0.93
São Pauo State	1.44	1.12	1.84	1.10	1.38	1.27
Brazil	1.00	1.00	1.00	1.00	1.00	1.00

Source: Azzoni and Andrade (2005)

correlating convergence with concentration and concentration changes, none, or very weak, association was found. The authors concluded that that there was no association between the increasing share of tertiary activities in GDP and spatial income inequality in the country in the period.

10.5 Conclusions

We have presented indicators of regional disparities for Brazil over the last seven decades. It was made clear that concentration and inequality are high and relatively stable over time. As for concentration, the important phenomena in terms of changing the long last distribution of activities are the growth in the north region, related to mining and logging, and in the mid-west region, related to agriculture and agribusiness. Therefore, the main changes are related to resource-oriented activities, led by, or associated to, governmental programs such as the establishment of a new capital city in the mid-west, the design and implementation of a free-import zone in the Amazon, the intense allocation of resources for technological

Table 10.5 Competitiveness indicators for services sub-sectors

	Hotels and restaurants		Real state		Transportation		Services to firms		Miscellaneous		Computing
	Late 1970s	Late 1990s	Late 1970s	Late 1990s	Late 1970s	Late 1990s	Late 1970s	Late 1990s	Late 1970s	Late 1990s	Late 1990s
Revenue/wage bill											
North	1.16	0.91	0.85	1.06	0.80	1.34	1.11	0.94	2.26	0.78	0.65
Northeast	1.49	0.99	1.01	0.96	0.93	0.98	1.64	0.95	1.48	0.84	0.70
Southeast	0.93	1.02	1.01	1.02	0.99	0.98	0.84	1.03	0.94	1.09	1.04
South	0.97	0.92	1.11	0.98	0.82	1.02	1.54	0.96	0.89	0.84	0.97
Center-West	1.16	1.04	0.83	1.07	1.34	1.19	1.34	0.83	1.27	0.85	1.06
São Pauo State	0.92	0.94	0.99	0.84	0.83	0.96	0.93	1.08	0.84	1.21	1.18
Revenue/worker											
North	0.93	0.88	0.31	0.82	0.75	1.18	1.07	0.72	0.97	0.73	0.71
Northeast	0.61	0.83	0.86	0.70	0.69	0.75	0.67	0.63	0.63	0.63	0.44
Southeast	1.21	1.11	1.08	1.09	1.11	1.08	1.07	1.14	1.18	1.25	1.20
South	0.86	0.82	0.89	0.94	0.59	0.90	1.11	0.86	0.96	0.66	0.69
Center-West	0.84	0.96	0.87	0.89	1.26	0.90	1.02	0.73	0.87	0.68	1.04
São Pauo State	1.31	1.15	1.10	0.95	0.97	1.18	1.18	1.31	1.21	1.65	1.51
Revenue/establishment											
North	1.16	1.76	1.06	1.07	1.05	2.24	1.11	1.38	1.01	0.87	3.86
Northeast	1.49	1.20	1.32	0.76	0.57	1.09	0.55	0.88	0.51	0.80	0.75
Southeast	0.93	1.06	1.00	1.15	1.26	1.29	1.20	1.16	1.27	1.32	1.05
South	0.97	0.68	0.85	0.75	0.42	0.50	0.97	0.60	1.02	0.50	0.56
Center-West	1.16	1.21	1.17	0.91	1.40	0.80	0.97	0.73	0.85	0.76	11.39
São Pauo State	0.92	1.02	0.94	1.05	1.12	1.27	1.24	1.29	1.33	1.78	1.14
Brazil	1.00	1.00	1.00	1.00	1.00	1.00	1.00	1.00	1.00	1.00	1.00

Source: Azzoni and Andrade (2005)

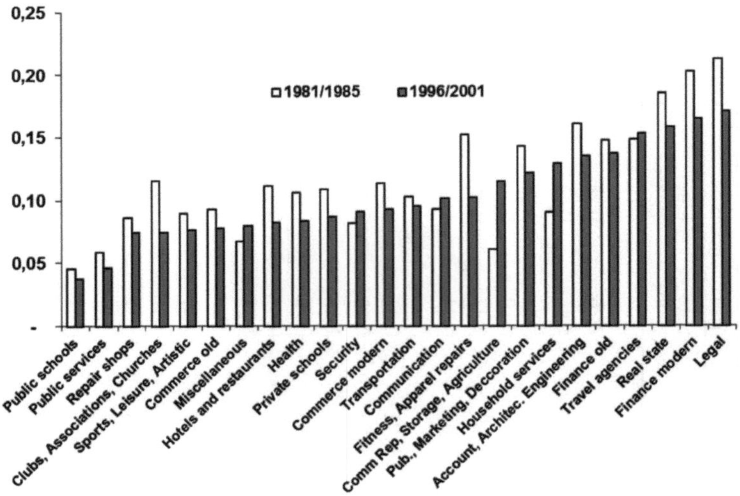

Fig. 10.10 Evolution of sectoral spatial concentration

improvement in agriculture – which made possible for the mid-west to become a bread-basket for the world.

However, even in agriculture the inequality in productivity levels are practically the same as it was in 1970, with the southeast region still leading in terms of competitiveness. As for the urban activities, with the exception of agribusiness activities in the mid-west, the situation in terms of competitiveness is also similar as it was in the past. No signs of regional convergence in productivity levels in manufacturing were found. On the contrary, indicators suggest that the industrial core of the country became even more competitive in the beginning of the twenty-first century. As for the tertiary activities, there are signs of de-concentration in the more traditional ones, such as commerce or basic services, whereas the more sophisticated services typically present a more concentrated pattern, both in levels and in growth.

Studies show that regional income inequality decreased in the last decade, but this is associated with government social programs, such as the appreciation of the minimum wage and the implementation of cash transfers to poor families, typically located in the poorer regions (Silveira-Neto and Azzoni 2011a, b). From the indicators presented in this chapter, it seems that there is a long way to go before the highly concentrated distribution of activities in the country could present significant changes. Even with all the changes that took place in the economy of the world and of the country over the last two decades, it seems that the centripetal forces are still surpassing the centrifugal influences of disagglomeration economies.

Acknowledgement I thank Prof. Eduardo Haddad, Department of Economics at the University of Sao Paulo, for his insightful comments.

References

Azzoni CR (1997) Concentração regional e dispersão das rendas per capita estaduais: análise a partir de séries históricas estaduais de PIB, 1939–1995. Estudos Econômicos. Instituto de Pesquisas Econômicas. v.27

Azzoni CR (2001) Economic growth and regional income inequality in Brazil. Ann Reg Sci 35:133–152

Azzoni CR, Andrade AS (2005) The tertiary sector and regional inequality in Brazil. Rég Dev 21:155–172

Azzoni CR, Ferreira DA (1998) Competitividade regional y reconcentración industrial: el futuro de las desigualdades regionales en Brasil. EURE (Santiago) XXIV(73):81–111, Santiago, Chile

Baer W (2001) The Brazilian economy: growth and development, 5th edn. Praeger Publishers, Westport, Connecticut and London

Barros R, Carvalho M, Franco S, Mendonça R (2006) Uma análise das principais causas da queda recente na desigualdade de renda brasileira. Econômica 8:117–147

Carvalho A, Lall SV, Timmins C (2006) Regional subsidies and industrial prospects of lagging regions. World Bank Policy Research working paper 3843, February 2006

Confederação Nacional da Indústria (CNI) (2010) A indústria e o Brasil: uma agenda para crescer mais e melhor. CNI, Brasília

Devereux M, Griffith R, Simpson H (2004) The geographic distribution of production activity in the U.K. Reg Sci Urban Econ 34:533–564

Ferreira F, Leite P, Litchieeld J, Ulyssea G (2006) Ascensão e queda da desigualdade de renda no Brasil, Econômica. Rio de Janeiro 8(1):147–171

Gasques JG, Bastos ET, Bachi MPR, Valdes C (2010) Produtividade total dos fatores e transformação da agricultura brasileira: análise de dados dos censos agropecuários. In XLVIII Congresso Brasileiro de Economia, Administração e Sociologia Rural. SOBER, Campo Grande

Hoffmann R (2006) Transferências de renda e a redução da desigualdade no Brasil e cinco regiões entre 1997 e 2004. Econômica 8(1):55–81

Imori D (2011) Eficiência produtiva da agropecuária familiar e patronal nas regiões brasileiras. MS thesis, Department of Economics, Universidade de São Paulo, Paris

Neri M (2010) The decade of falling income inequality and formal employment generation in Brazil, In OECD, Tackling inequalities in Brazil, China, India and South Africa: the role of labour market and social policies. OECD Publishing, Paris. pp 57–107

Schettini DD, Azzoni CR (2011) Diferenciais Regionais de Competitividade Industrial do Brasil no século 21, Prêmio CNI de Economia, 2°. Lugar, 2011

Silveira-Neto RM, Azzoni CR (2011a) Non-spatial government policies and regional income inequality in Brazil. Reg Stud 45:453–461

Silveira-Neto RM, Azzoni CR (2011b) Social policy as regional policy: Market and nonmarket factors determining regional inequality. J Reg Sci 52(3):433–450

Soares S (2006a) Distribuição de renda no Brasil de 1976 a 2004 com ênfase no período entre 2001 e 2004, vol 1166, Textos para discussão. IPEA, Brasília

Soares S (2006b) Análise de bem-estar e Decomposição por fatores da queda na desigualdade entre 1995 e 2004. Econômica 8(1):83–115

Vicente JR (2006) Comparação de produtividade agrícola entre as unidades da federação, 1970–1995. Agricultura em São Paulo 53(2):69–83

Vicente JR (2011) Produtividade total de fatores e eficiência no setor de lavouras da agricultura brasileira. Rev Econ Agronegócio 9(3):303–324

Chapter 11
Argentina's Regional Performance: 1970–2010

Victor J. Elias, Mauro Alem, Julio J. Elias, and Maria Antonella Mancino

11.1 Introduction

The aim of this chapter is to characterize and explain the evolution of provincial and regional GDP per capita in Argentina in the period 1970–2010 and the difference on its levels across provinces and regions. We draw on several factors related to economic development, on the basis of its initial and current value, including: education, financial sector development, urbanization, exports, inputs, productivity, tax burden, size of firms, among others. We also analyze the role of public policy on regional development.

Argentina, like most Latin American countries, is characterized by a large concentration of population and economic activity in one region known as Pampeana,[1] mainly in Buenos Aires. This feature of the economy is more

[1] The regions of Argentina are defined as follows: PAMPEANA includes Buenos Aires, Buenos Aires City (CABA), Córdoba, Entre Ríos, La Pampa and Santa Fé; PATAGONIA includes Chubut, Neuguén, Río Negro, Santa Cruz and Tierra del Fuego; NOA includes Catamarca, Jujuy, La Rioja, Salta, Santiago del Estero and Tucumán; CUYO includes Mendoza, San Juan and San Luis; NEA includes Chaco, Corrientes, Formosa and Misiones.

V.J. Elias (✉)
University of Tucumán, Tucumán, Argentina
e-mail: ieatuc@yahoo.com.ar

M. Alem
Banco de Inversión y Comercio Exterior, Buenos Aires, Argentina
e-mail: malem@bice.com.ar

J.J. Elias
Banco de Inversión y Comercio Exterior, Buenos Aires, Argentina

University of CEMA, Buenos Aires, Argentina
e-mail: JElias@bice.com.ar

M.A. Mancino
University of Western Ontario, London, Canada
e-mail: mmanci3@uwo.ca

J.R. Cuadrado-Roura and P. Aroca (eds.), *Regional Problems and Policies in Latin America*, Advances in Spatial Science, DOI 10.1007/978-3-642-39674-8_11,

pronounced at the beginning of the past century, on the first centennial of the country, in which great territorial expansion in Buenos Aires, an important migration inflows from Europe and the expansion of transportation, accompanying the development of agriculture in the region, contributed to an even stronger concentration around Buenos Aires and its port.

Although at the beginning of the settlement some regions had a variety of activities, they were characterized then by regional products such as sugar cane and snuff in the Northwest (NOA), the vine in Cuyo, and yerba mate and cotton in the Northeast (NEA). The economy of the Patagonia region was defined mainly over the second century around the petroleum industry. Only late in the second century, these regions were able to diversify their activities as they were more likely to participate in foreign trade.

Over the last century, regional economies of Argentina grew unevenly and uncoordinated. The convergence in living standards between regions was very low. The convergence rate recorded over the period was less than half the level observed in the more affluent countries. However, the main features of levels and rates of growth of incomes of regional economies vary across period. According to the available data, it looks that the large differences between provinces and regions were given before 1970. After 1970, the data shows a certain catch up for some regions.

This chapter is organized as follows. Section 11.2 presents a short discussion on different views on the process of regional development. Section 11.3 describe briefly the framework used to organized the data and think on the causes of regional development in Argentina. Section 11.4 presents the main patterns of economic growth by region and province in Argentina and in Sect. 11.5 we explore correlates of development. Section 11.6 discuss the main public policies implemented in the regions during the period. Section 11.7 summarizes and concludes.

11.2 Some Views on Regional Development: Human Capital and Cities

Human Capital accumulation and technological progress, accompanied by investment, are the main factors involved in development processes. Robert Lucas Jr. of the University of Chicago stress the role of human capital as an engine of growth by saying "the central idea. . .is that a successful transformation from an economy of traditional agriculture to a modern, growing economy depends crucially on an increase in the rate of accumulation of human capital".

Lucas (1988) suggests that cities may enhance growth by facilitating the accumulation of human capital, by generating ideas. Glaeser (2011) estate the connection between human capital and cities as follows: "The success of cities depends on the demand for physical connection. . .Newer cities have grown because technological change has increased the returns to the knowledge that is best produced by people in close proximity in each other. Cities thrive when they have many small firms and skilled citizens."

On thinking in regional development, the statesman and seventh President of Argentina Domingo Faustino Sarmiento wrote in 1845 that "The evil that afflicts Argentina is its extension: the desert is all around,. . ., the loneliness, the wilderness without a single human habitation, are generally unquestioned boundaries between the provinces."[2] Even though Argentina has an extensive system of rivers, "the greatest favor that Providence has in store for a country, the Argentine gaucho disdains it".[3]

Sarmiento was convinced that the key for regional development were the cities: "But progress is stifled because there can be no progress without the permanent possession of the ground, without the city, which promotes man's industrial capacity and allows him to extend his acquisitions."[4]

In the period 1875–1915, just after the end of Sarmiento's term in office in 1874, Argentina grew at an annual rate greater than 5 % with little increase in productivity. This is explained in part by the increase in land input, mainly in Buenos Aires (Acemoglu 2008; Krugman 1991; Marshall 1961; Schultz 1968).

11.3 Economic Framework

There are many approaches to studying the process of regional development (Acemoglu 2008). Different theories emphasize different factors as the engines of economic growth and development. In this chapter we follow the Neoclassical Solow model of economic growth extended with human capital input to think about regional development and organize the data (Solow 1956). In order to account for the main features of regional development in Argentina, we go beyond the determinants of inputs and its importance for economic growth by looking at the role of cities, migration, public policies and other factors.

Even though the Solow model cannot account for endogenous growth processes, the model is a useful framework to organize the data. The model emphasizes physical capital accumulation and technological change in the process of economic growth. This framework allows to quantify the contribution and effects of various factors, such as policy changes, on growth. In its crude version, the workhorse of the model is the Neoclassical production function $Y_{i,t} = A_{i,t}\ F(L_{i,t}, K_{it})$ for the output of the i economic unit in a given period t, where A stands for technology, or

[2] "el mal que aqueja a la República Argentina es la extensión: el desierto rodea por todas partes, se le insinúa en las entrañas; la soledad, el despoblado sin una habitación humana, son por lo general los límites incuestionables entre unas y otras provincias."

[3] "el favor más grande que la Providencia le depara a un pueblo, el gaucho argentino lo desdeña"

[4] "Pero el progreso está sofocado, porque no puede haber progreso sin la posesión permanente del suelo, sin la ciudad, que es la desenvuelve la capacidad industrial del hombre y le permite extender sus adquisiciones."

any factor that augment labor and capital productivity, L for labor and K for capital utilization.

Following the model, to account for economic growth and differences in income across economic units we look at different measures of labor (population) and its quality (education) and technological progress. We do not have good measures of capital at the regional level, so we do a poorer job in characterizing the patterns of this input.

It is important to notice that the basic Solow model predicts convergence in the growth on the standards of living of different economic units to a common rate and, under certain conditions, on its level, both outcomes that do not adjust exactly to the facts that we observe for the province and regions of Argentina. However, there are other factors that help to explain the patterns that we observe in the data.

In what follows we provide a detailed analysis of what happened in the Argentinean provinces in the last 40 years. It is important to notice that the analysis of the evolution of certain province or region cannot be easily isolated from what happens at the country level (Elias 1992; Hoselitz 1953; Solow 1956).

11.4 Economic Performance of Provinces and Regions: 1970–2010

We can characterize the main features of regional development in Argentina through tables and graphs. In Table 11.1 we present characteristics and trends of different variables for the provinces of Argentina for the period 1970–2010. Part of the analysis is concentrated in provinces rather than regions. When convenient, we group the observations in regions. In Table 11.2 we present the data at the regional level. Table 11.5 presents the shares of each province in GDP, public and private employment and profits.

The first thing that the observer can notice is the remarkable diversity across regions and provinces in measured per capita income levels. In 2010, the income per capita of NEA region was less than half of the average for the country. While the income per capita of the Patagonia region almost double it.

In order to look at these differences and its evolution, Figs. 11.1 and 11.2 provides an estimate of the income and the log of income distribution, respectively, across provinces in the years 1970, 1985, and 2010. Both figures show that today there is greater inequality among provinces, coincident with an increase in the average per capita income. Figure 11.1 shows that in 1970 most provinces had an income per capita below $4,000 (in US$ of 1995), the mode of the distribution is $3,000. From 1970 to 2010, the figure shows that there is a spreading out of the distribution of income across provinces. Part of this is due to the increase in average income from $5,210 in 1970 to $8,707 in 2010 (both values expressed in US$ of 1995).

Table 11.1 Provinces indicators

Indicator/province	BA	CABA	CDB	EnR	LaP	SFE	SHU	NQN	Rne	SCR	TDF	CAT
Average annual GDP growth rate (1970–2010)%	2.2	2.4	2.9	2.6	2.5	2.2	3.4	6.3	2.3	4.5	5.4	7.4
Average annual GDP per capita growth rate (1970–2010)%	0.7	2.4	1.7	1.5	1.0	1.2	0.9	3.0	0.1	1.5	–0.4	5.4
Average annual wage growth rate (1985–2010)%	2.2	1.2	1.8	2.5	1.6	1.4	3.1	1.3		2.1		1.9
Average annual land price growth rate (1977–2007)%	4.5	–	4.8	4.5	6.5	4.3	4.9	4.9	4.9	4.9	–	3.3
GDP per capita 1970, 1995 constant prices	4.843	9.137	3.961	2.817	6.145	5.088	8.999	5.999	5.976	11.404	19.893	2.435
GDP per capita 1985, 1995 constant prices	5.020	13.042	4.894		8.117	6.150	12.676	11.687		14.344	33.988	3.506
GDP per capita 2010, 1995 constant prices	6.424	23.887	7.886	5.159	9.071	8.173	12.909	19.634	6.126	20.810	17.264	20.133
GDP pc 2010 relative to BA 1884	2.5	9.3	3.1	2.0	3.5	3.2	5.0	7.7	2.4	8.1	6.7	7.9
Population 2010 (1,000)	15.625	2.890	3.309	1.236	319	3.195	509	551	639	274	127	368
Average years of education of the workforce (2011)	9.1	11.5	9.8	9.2	8.9	9.4	9.0	9.3	9.1	9.7	9.7	9.8
Infant mortality per 1,000 live births (2008)	12.4	7.7	12.1	13.5	14.9	11.5	10.4	7.4	11.7	10.6	6.8	15.3
Weekly hours of work (2009)	39.6	41.2	41.0	41.8	38.9	39.4	42.6	43.0	38.3	43.4	44.2	39.8
Activity rate (2010)	45.3	55.0	45.0	46.9	43.8	42.7	40.2	42.5	44.4	49.5	47.1	40.0
CONICET researchers per 1,000,000 inhabitants (2010)	112.0	768.0	198.0	15.0	59.0	156.0	187.0	51.0	398.0	38.0	183.0	17.0
Provincial exports as% GDP (2007)	22.8	0.5	38.6	24.8	10.5	62.8	39.9	14.0	13.4	34.2	40.1	111.7
Percentage of population not covered by banking services (2005)	3.1	0.0	13.5	16.4	7.4	11.5	6.1	8.2	19.3	1.6	1.6	28.5
Provincial public expenditure as% PBG (2005)	11.4	5.4	13.3	24.0	24.2	12.0	18.1	19.4	23.1	22.4	25.0	16.4

(continued)

Table 11.1 (continued)

Indicator/province	BA	CABA	CDB	EnR	LaP	SFE	SHU	NQN	Rne	SCR	TDF	CAT
Companies per capita ('1,000) (2009)	12.6	45.9	18.4	15.3	22.6	17.5	18.2	16.6	17.5	15.6	19.5	8.8
Number of cities that cover 80% of the population (2010)	33.0		10.0	9.0	10.0	8.0	4.0	4.0	3.0	2.0	2.0	7.0
ATM per 100,000 inhabitants (1998)	9.6	44.9	9.0	7.6	5.2	6.5	9.4	7.4	8.6	6.1	14.4	2.3
Provincial exports as% GDP (1994)	6.3	0.5	7.7	3.8	5.6	13.0	13.0	13.9	5.8	21.3	18.6	2.2
Total public employees per capita (1983)	0.061	0.024	0.088	0.127	0.215	0.094	0.180	0.209	0.170	0.367	0.399	0.289
Population in households with NBI as% population (1980)	19.9	7.4	19.4	27.9	18.8	20.0	29.8	33.9	32.8	22.7	25.6	37.6
Share of agriculture in GDP (1980)	11.0	–	19.0	23.6	42.8	19.3	3.4	3.6	17.0	8.8	3.4	16.4
Provincial public spending by km2 (2005)	2.150		1.118	1.036	219	1.522	167	310	262	150	292	228
Crimes per 10,000 population (1980)	39.7	87.8	125.1	67.5	194.0	127.0	65.1	112.4	108.4	96.3	105.6	124.9
Illiteracy rate (1980)	3.8	1.4	5.2	7.7	6.2	5.8	7.7	9.7	9.5	3.8	2.3	8.1
% of people aged 13 to 17 who attended secondary (1980)	53.0	78.1	54.7	40.8	44.4	51.3	42.7	36.8	37.6	49.2	51.5	38.8
% of urban population (1980)	93.2	100.0	80.7	68.8	64.9	82.0	81.4	76.1	71.8	86.8	95.1	57.5
Average years of education of workforce (2001)	9.2	12.1	9.6	8.7	8.7	9.4	8.9	9.0	8.6	9.5	10.1	9.2
Activity rate (1980)	35.9		38.8	35.6		36.0	36.3	39.4		39.8		35.9
% Industrial employment (1996)	34.5	19.4	27.3	22.1	14.9	31.6	18.1	11.7	11.3	7.5	28.4	34.5
Average wage (1995 pesos)	711.3	1152.3	623.5	519.3	823.4	716.4	943.3	873.6		1029.3		711.3
Average TFP growth rate (1980–90)	0.0	0.0	4.4	46.8	0.0	10.4	8.8	–43.1	0.0	26.2	0.0	–6.5
Firm size 1996	8.1	10.0	6.7	6.1	4.2	7.2	7.4	8.1	7.3	9.5	9.3	9.2
Firm size 2009	9.5	11.9	7.7	6.8	5.1	8.4	10.2	9.9	8.8	12.8	11.0	9.5

Indicator/province	JUJ	LaR	SAL	SDE	TUC	MDZ	SaJ	SaL	CHA	COR	FOR	MIS	Correl
Average annual GDP growth rate (1970–2010)%	2.5	1.9	2.7	3.1	1.7	3.1	1.7	3.0	2.5	2.1	2.8	3.1	0.69
Average annual GDP per capita growth rate (1970–2010)%	0.5	–0.3	0.5	1.6	0.1	1.6	0.3	0.9	1.0	0.7	0.7	0.8	1.00
Average annual wage growth rate (1985–2010)%	1.4	1.4	1.9	1.4		1.8	1.7	1.8	1.3	1.6	0.5	1.2	0.07
Average annual land price growth rate (1977–2007)%	4.2	4.9	3.5	3.6	4.7	4.9	4.9	4.3	4.1	5.6	5.2	6.9	–0.32
GDP per capita 1970, 1995 constant prices	3.631	3.459	3.370	2.135	3.678	4.698	3.139	3.974	2.578	2.890	2.710	2.091	–0.16
GDP per capita 1985, 1995 constant prices	4.010	6.178	4.359	2.545	4.593	5.024	3.366	6.425	2.353	3.915	2.848		–0.15
GDP per capita 2010, 1995 constant prices	4.361	3.018	4.111	4.039	3.788	9.035	3.475	5.599	3.769	3.844	3.571	2.885	0.61
GDP pc 2010 relative to BA 1884	1.7	1.2	1.6	1.6	1.5	3.5	1.4	2.2	1.5	1.5	1.4	1.1	0.61
Population 2010 (1,000)	673	334	1.214	874	1.448	1.739	681	432	1.055	993	530	1.102	–0.03
Average years of education of the workforce (2011)	10.0	9.4	9.9	8.8	9.1	9.8	9.2	9.0	9.1	9.7	9.0	9.5	0.30
Infant mortality per 1,000 live births (2008)	14.0	15.0	14.4	10.4	13.8	10.8	14.4	13.1	18.0	17.1	19.2	13.9	–0.14
Weekly hours of work (2009)	38.9	40.5	42.1	42.0	41.9	43.0	42.3	41.5	44.5	41.9	41.3	43.5	–0.05
Activity rate (2010)	41.2	39.6	45.0	37.2	44.6	43.6	40.6	38.7	33.0	38.4	32.4	40.8	0.09
CONICET researchers per 1,000,000 inhabitants (2010)	34.0	22.0	39.0	9.0	138.0	114.0	69.0	178.0	20.0	50.0	7.0	17.0	0.04
Provincial exports as % GDP (2007)	19.4	9.5	29.1	21.7	17.9	20.8	29.5	13.3	12.0	5.5	3.6	11.2	0.58

Table 11.1 (continued)

Indicator/province	JUJ	LaR	SAL	SDE	TUC	MDZ	SaJ	SaL	CHA	COR	FOR	MIS	Correl
Percentage of population not covered by banking services (2005)	24.1	18.7	22.4	36.6	28.5	23.3	26.7	11.3	24.7	21.5	31.6	33.9	0.00
Provincial public expenditure as% PBG (2005)	32.9	52.2	23.1	37.3	28.9	13.4	30.5	21.6	37.5	29.6	55.9	28.6	–0.43
Companies per capita (‘1,000) (2009)	7.3	7.9	8.2	6.4	9.5	14.3	11.0	12.1	8.7	8.6	5.3	8.4	0.19
Number of cities that cover 80% of the population (2010)	5.0	5.0	6.0	11.0	8.0	8.0	8.0	3.0	11.0	11.0	4.0	10.0	0.01
ATM per 100,000 inhabitants (1998)	2.4	3.0	4.1	1.1	5.9	7.9	6.4	12.1	2.0	2.9	3.1	4.0	0.13
Provincial exports as% GDP (1994)	4.4	3.4	6.1	4.4	5.0	6.6	1.7	2.5	9.3	3.4	3.8	3.6	–0.07
Total public employees per capita (1983)	0.177	0.307	0.144	0.158	0.123	0.110	0.176	0.238	0.148	0.168	0.223	0.131	–0.05
Population in households with NBI as% Population (1980)	45.1	31.6	42.4	45.8	36.6	20.4	26.0	27.7	44.8	40.6	46.8	39.2	–0.10
Share of agriculture in GDP (1980)	22.3	15.3	15.8	18.8	14.8	12.4	16.1	29.4	24.5	20.2	16.3	18.4	–0.04
Provincial public spending by km^2 (2005)	581	221	280	323	2.743	875	521	280	461	655	384	1.268	–0.16
Crimes per 10,000 population (1980)	153.9	86.1	96.4	165.6	104.0	104.7	114.2	42.7	144.1	58.5	106.5	45.4	0.15
Illiteracy rate (1980)	11.6	6.4	11.1	12.6	8.4	7.3	7.1	7.7	16.5	14.8	12.3	11.9	–0.06
% of people aged 13 to 17 who attended secondary (1980)	41.0	41.7	41.0	28.6	43.8	46.3	47.6	44.3	28.7	30.4	28.1	27.8	0.09
% of urban population (1980)	73.6	61.7	71.8	51.9	70.9	68.9	72.0	70.0	60.9	64.4	55.7	50.4	–0.08
Average years of education of workforce (2001)	8.6	9.3	8.7	7.8	8.9	9.0	9.0	9.1	7.5	8.1	7.9	7.6	0.19

Activity rate (1980)	35.6	34.8	33.2	34.6	36.8	39.2	34.1	37.4	36.2	32.6	34.4	36.0	0.03
% Industrial employment (1996)	29.6	44.4	16.3	15.5	26.2	26.5	28.2	53.3	17.2	18.1	11.5	30.9	–0.17
Average wage (1995 pesos)	504.8	555.2	509.0	494.6		613.5	524.5	579.1	543.8	534.1	685.4	583.2	0.20
Average TFP growth rate (1980–90)	3.6	95.6	10.8	–21.5	–15.3	–14.5	10.4	149.0	13.6	31.9	35.1	–9.4	–0.28
Firm size 1996	10.6	8.8	9.3	6.8	10.7	8.3	7.9	10.1	5.6	6.6	6.6	7.7	0.01
Firm size 2009	10.6	10.5	10.6	8.0	11.4	9.3	10.0	10.2	6.9	7.8	7.9	9.4	–0.05

Note: The GDP per capita for 1970 and 2010 was extrapolated using the GDP per capita for years 1953, 1985, 1995, and 2005 and the average annual GDP per capita growth rate. The GDP per capita for each province was obtained from the book "La Economía de Tucuman". The population data and the number of cities was extracted from the censuses conducted in 1970, 1980, 1990, 2001, and 2010. The average years of education of the workforce, weekly hours of work and the share of people who attended secondary school were calculated using the National household survey (EPH, INDEC). The data regarding mortality was obtained from the Interior Ministry Database for Provinces. The share of agriculture on GDP, activity rate, illiteracy rate, public expenditure and exports data were derived from the CIAP database for provinces and Porto (2004). The number of CONICET researchers was drawn from the CONICET webpage (http://www.conicet.gov.ar). The data regarding banking services was extracted from Anastasi et al. (2006) and Banco Central de la Republica Argentina (BCRA). The companies data came from the Ministry of Labour, Employment and Wages. Observatorio de Empleo y Dinamica Empresarial Cerro and Meloni (2000). Productivity was calculated based on GDP, capital stock (UNLP) and employment data (CIAP Database). The firms' data came from the Ministry of Labour, Employment and Wages. Observatorio de Empleo y Dinamica Empresarial. The data was deflated using INDEC price index. The last column "Correl" shows the correlation between the variable and the annual average GDP per capita growth between 1970 and 2010

Table 11.2 Regional indicators

Variables	Regions					Country
	Pampeana	Patagonia	NOA	CUYO	NEA	
Population (1,000)						
1970	16,926	705	2,382	1,541	1,808	23,362,286
1980	19,778	1,033	3,012	1,877	2,248	27,947,446
1990	22,404	1,452	3,654	2,219	2,799	32,527,095
2001	24,128	1,738	4,458	2,568	3,368	36,260,130
2010	26,574	2,100	4,911	2,852	3,680	40,117,096
Population (ratio 2010–1970)	1.6	3.0	2.1	1.9	2.0	
Non native population % population						
1970	7.50	21.35	3.57	3.93	9.28	9.33
2001	3.54	9.13	1.61	2.01	2.67	4.21
2010	3.98	7.64	1.50	1.98	2.34	4.50
% Urban population						
1970	88.09	77.01	61.76	68.36	50.94	
1980	81.52	80.93	64.58	70.31	57.84	82.99
1990	86.59	88.49	73.91	79.75	68.26	87.42
2001	89.78	91.13	78.53	84.13	76.81	89.44
2010	93.46	87.05	86.07	90.49	85.11	91.56
Density (excluding CABA)						
1970	13.7	1.0	8.3	4.4	7.5	
1980	16.3	1.5	10.6	5.3	9.6	
1990	18.7	2.3	12.6	6.3	12.2	
2001	20.6	3.0	15.0	7.4	14.9	
2010	22.5	3.7	16.4	8.3	16.5	
GDP per capita relative to Buenos Aires in 1884						
1884	0.8	nd	0.6	0.6	0.5	

1953	1.6	2.7	0.9	1.2	0.9	
1985	2.9	7.1	1.6	1.9	1.2	
1995	3.4	4.6	1.5	2.3	1.4	
2007	3.8	5.4	2.8	2.8	1.5	
Intern migration rate						
2001	−0.13	1.41	0.45	1.05	−1.04	
GDP per capita, 1995 pesos						
1953	4,212	6,906	2,296	3,187	2,390	4,823
1985	7,445	18,174	4,199	4,938	3,039	6,698
1995	8,589	11,688	3,825	5,897	3,498	7,697
2005	10,248	15,531	5,338	6,675	3,541	8,505
GDP per capita (ratio 2005–1985)	1.4	1.0	1.3	1.3	1.2	1.3
GDP (ratio 2005–1985)	1.7	1.8	1.9	1.8	1.6	1.6
GDP (ratio 2010–1970)	2.7	6.4	5.1	2.9	2.9	2.6
Illiteracy rate						
1980	5.02	6.60	9.70	7.37	13.88	6.81
2001	2.06	2.48	4.08	3.04	6.66	2.59
2010	1.52	1.71	2.76	2.04	4.49	1.92
Average years of education of workforce between 25 and 65 years old						
1996	8.1	8.6	8.8	8.6	8.0	
2001	9.6	9.2	8.7	9.0	7.8	
2011	9.7	9.3	9.5	9.3	9.3	
Share of people aged between 13 and 17 that attended secondary school						
1980	53.70	43.54	39.17	46.10	28.73	
2001	70.85	70.01	61.75	64.79	53.47	

(continued)

Table 11.2 (continued)

Variables	Regions					Country
	Pampeana	Patagonia	NOA	CUYO	NEA	
2011	89.91	89.76	84.29	89.52	88.45	
Educational quality	1.9	1.8	1.6	1.8	1.7	
Share of students attending private schools						
1996	28.3	12.6	13.1	14.0	10.4	24.7
2010	32.1	17.0	16.6	18.7	13.6	28.3
Health: average weight of children at birth in kg (2006)	3.3	3.4	3.3	3.3	3.3	
Percentage of live births of low birth weight (<2,500 g,) (known weight)						
2003	8.0	7.5	7.3	8.1	8.1	8.0
2010	7.1	6.5	6.9	7.2	7.3	7.5
Infant mortality per 1,000 newborn						
1980	28.6	31.4	44.7	33.0	47.2	33.2
1990	23.0	21.8	31.4	25.1	33.1	25.6
2000	14.4	14.3	19.9	17.0	24.4	16.6
2008	12.0	9.4	13.8	12.8	17.1	12.5
Weekly hours of work						
1985	40.4	44.1	40.0	41.2	41.1	
1996	50.9	44.2	46.6	47.4	46.7	
2001	41.5	42.6	41.0	41.9	40.9	
2009	40.8	42.3	40.9	42.3	42.8	
Employment rate						
1984	35.7	36.4	32.0	32.2	33.3	36.2
1993	36.4	36.5	32.1	35.2	32.3	37.1
2003	36.9	36.8	32.8	33.6	31.1	36.2

Activity rate						
1974	39.0	38.1	38.4	38.4	38.4	40.1
1980	36.6	38.5	34.6	36.9	34.8	38.5
1990	38.7	39.7	35.4	37.1	34.0	39.0
2000	43.0	40.6	37.4	39.4	34.1	42.7
2010	46.5	44.7	41.3	41.0	36.2	46.0
Industry employment as % of total employment						
1996	24.98	15.39	26.63	36.03	19.41	26.58
2002	20.14	12.54	23.94	29.62	16.32	21.64
2010	19.88	13.09	18.98	24.87	14.11	20.28
Provincial public employment per capita ('1,000)						
1983	27.5	59.2	54.9	42.7	45.3	27.2
1990	34.6	75.4	66.6	42.8	56.7	34.5
2000	39.1	71.1	52.0	43.8	47.1	37.4
2009	27.1	88.8	66.5	29.6	42.8	39.4
Total public employment per capita						
1983	0.068	0.210	0.164	0.141	0.160	0.095
1990	0.063	0.164	0.141	0.115	0.135	0.086
2000	0.049	0.115	0.083	0.074	0.082	0.061
Average wages in accordance with household survey EPH (pesos as of 1995)						
1985	758	949	519	572	587	677
1995	676	920	504	503	477	616
2005	481	775	368	454	357	487
2011	1,011	1,587	830	942	808	1,036
Mobility rate						
1997–2002	21.5	20.6	21.7	19.2	20.9	21

(continued)

Table 11.2 (continued)

Variables	Regions					Country
	Pampeana	Patagonia	NOA	CUYO	NEA	
Population in households with NBI as % of population						
1980	18.89	28.97	39.85	24.70	42.83	27.72
1991	12.97	19.97	28.99	17.07	31.09	19.93
2001	11.16	14.12	22.69	13.48	25.78	17.66
Institutional quality (2005/2010)	1.9	1.6	1.4	1.6	1.4	
CONICET researchers per 1,000,000 inhabitants (2010)	218.0	171.0	43.0	99.0	24.0	2879.0
People devoted to research per 1,000 inhabitants						
2001	4.69	0.40	0.55	0.94	0.29	37.44
2008	7.06	0.57	0.85	1.59	0.48	57.02
R&T expenditures per researcher, constant pesos 2008						
2001	66,077	56,116	126,999	60,257	62,724	69,941
2008	95,774	93,009	197,069	89,902	104,756	99,654
Share of agriculture on GDP (1985)						
1980	23.14	7.23	17.25	19.30	19.85	12.71
1985	22.00	7.60	15.50	21.30	21.70	15.27
1995	18.44	7.80	11.54	7.06	17.00	10.70
2001	20.39	7.76	11.53	7.16	17.04	9.14
Exports % PBG						
1994	6.16	14.54	4.23	3.58	5.03	5.93
2007	26.65	28.33	34.88	21.21	8.07	20.45
Land price, weighted by production weight (u$s per hectare)						
1977	1,323	714	1,488	1,083	1,227	

1987	984	435	980	741	914	
1997	2,393	1,034	2,517	1,900	2,434	
2007	5,587	3,035	4,770	4,142	5,852	
Total factor productivity relative to Bs As 1884						
1980	1.03	2.83	1.13	1.11	0.96	
1990	1.57	3.49	1.25	1.78	1.17	
Percentage of population not covered by banking services						
1998	9.68	9.42	31.52	22.53	32.45	13.40
2005	8.65	7.36	26.47	20.43	27.93	12.00
Banking agencies per 100,000 inhabitants						
1998	34.37	23.44	9.32	19.60	9.20	23.20
2005	41.55	38.18	15.12	20.93	13.25	28.50
Banking branches per 100,000 inhabitants						
1998	15.58	12.54	5.58	9.90	6.10	11.10
2005	14.92	12.34	5.13	7.83	5.23	10.20
ATM per 100,000 inhabitants						
1998	13.80	9.18	3.13	8.80	3.00	10.60
2005	22.12	24.24	9.58	12.90	7.90	17.20
Delinquency						
1991	20.28	21.50	26.04	4.63	27.50	19.42
2000	20.14	25.77	31.35	26.32	24.74	16.89
2011	3.34	4.50	5.94	6.08	6.15	3.45
Public expenditure % GDP						
1970	7.18	11.89	13.47	10.52	12.51	7.99
1980	11.55	14.08	21.82	17.95	22.02	9.25
1990	10.47	15.37	28.69	13.76	30.97	8.84

(continued)

Table 11.2 (continued)

Variables	Regions					Country
	Pampeana	Patagonia	NOA	CUYO	NEA	
2000	15.26	20.33	32.68	22.27	32.69	10.92
2005	15.06	21.61	31.79	21.80	37.89	
Public expenditure per km2 (2005 pesos) – excluding CABA						
1970	1,209	236	729	559	692	689
1980	2,345	645	1,767	1,183	1,773	1,466
1990	20,030	8,625	18,344	9,401	18,331	14,737
2000	30,952	10,259	21,620	14,782	24,207	20,926
2005	34,022	18,282	30,766	15,983	30,041	25,041
Provincial tax pressure (% PBG)						
1990	6.57	3.12	3.51	3.95	3.98	
2005	4.55	3.54	3.41	4.15	3.21	
Provincial Debt % GDP						
1996	3.18	7.22	16.26	9.36	19.06	7.64
2004	13.82	17.75	33.53	19.48	67.16	20.29
Paved roads per capita (km)						
1990	38.46	49.79	36.92	47.12	20.09	19.37
2005	39.53	53.06	38.58	59.56	20.81	20.13
Pave roads per km^2 (km)						
1990	360.23	89.96	245.38	257.64	225.02	226.61
2005	405.39	143.55	299.13	387.49	305.63	276.50
Logistics costs as a% of FOB value of exported goods						
2006	12.40	–	16.00	11.60	11.60	
Number of companies per capita ('1,000)						
1996	18.9	16.4	7.0	11.5	7.9	10.5
2009	22.1	17.5	8.0	12.5	7.8	15.4

Average size of firms						
1996	7.0	8.3	9.2	8.7	6.6	7.9
2009	8.3	10.5	10.1	9.8	8.0	9.5
FDI per caoita, 2004 pesos						
1990	0.02	0.01	0.01	0.01	0.00	0.01
2000	0.58	1.57	0.19	0.70	0.06	0.46
Crimes per 10,000 inhabitants						
1980	106.9	97.6	121.8	87.2	88.6	81.6
1997	289.8	267.7	266.5	295.2	192.5	230.0
Not registered employment (%)						
1990	26.9	17.4	23.1	23.0	25.1	
2000	35.4	24.0	41.3	39.5	41.3	
Collection of income tax per capita (2009 constant pesos)						
2009	2603.5	656.0	257.3	607.0	212.9	
Farms						
1960	306.641	28.305	28.305	14.153	94.351	471.756
1988	189.292	21.313	72.183	53.184	85.249	421.221
2008	110.392	15.469	58.513	35.525	56.682	276.581

Note: The GDP per capita for 1970 and 2010 was extrapolated using the GDP per capita for years 1953, 1985, 1995 and 2005 and the average annual GDP per capita growth rate. The GDP per capita for each province was obtained from the book "La Economía de Tucuman" Elias (1992). The population data and the number of cities was extracted from the censuses conducted in 1970, 1980, 1990, 2001, and 2010 and the Ministry of Education. The intern migration rate, average years of education of the workforce, weekly hours of work and the share of people who attended secondary school were calculated using the household survey (EPH, INDEC). The data regarding mortality was obtained from the Interior Ministry Database for Provinces and the Ministry of Education. The share of agriculture on GDP, activity rate, illiteracy rate, public expenditure and exports data were derived from the CIAP database for provinces and Porto (2004). The number of CONICET researchers was drawn from the CONICET webpage (http://www.conicet.gov.ar). The data regarding banking services was extracted from Anastasi et al. (2006) and BCRA. The companies data came from the Ministry of Labour, Employment and Social Security. Crime data was taken from Cerro and Meloni (2000). The data was deflated using INDEC price index. The mobility rate was extracted from Paz (2003). The data regarding R&D was obtained Anuario FONTAR from the Ministry of Science, Technology and Innovation. The land Price was calculated using the land value Compañia Argentina de Tierras (CADETIERRAS), corn, soya, cattle and wheat production data (Ministry of Agriculture, Fisheries and Forestry). Productivity was calculated based on GDP, capital stock (UNLP) and employment data (CIAP Database). National public employees for each province were calculated using the number of national public employees Zeller and Rivkin (2005) and the relative share of each province in the total national transfers (Porto 2005). Logistics costs were obtained from the Banco Mundial (2006). The number of farms was extracted from the National Agricultural Census from 1960, 1988, and 2008 (IERAL and Fundaicion Meditarranea (2010); Barro and Lee (2010); INDEC, Censo Nacional de Población, Hogares y Viviendas 1970, 1980, 1990, 2001, 2010; INDEC, Encuesta Permanente de Hogares (1970–2011); Universidad de Buenos Aires; Consejo Nacional de Investigaciones Científicas y Técnicas (CONICET))

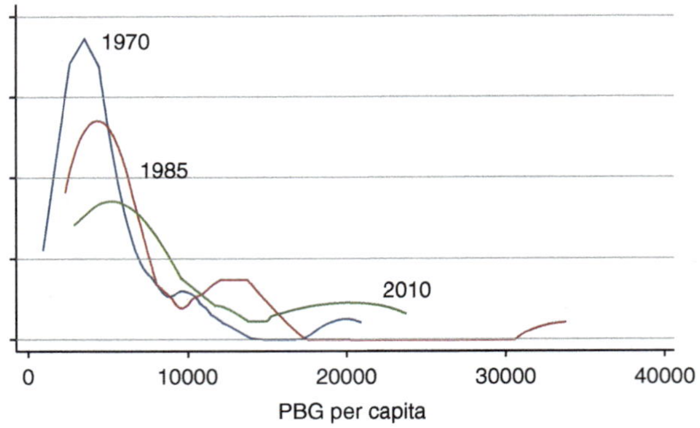

Fig. 11.1 Distribution of GDP in Argentina (Source: Own calculations and Elías 1996)

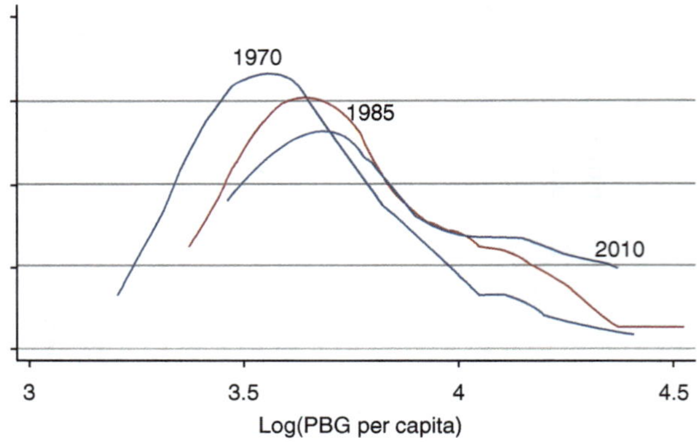

Fig. 11.2 Distribution of the logarithm of GDP in Argentina (Source: Own calculations and Elias 1996)

To account for this growth in income, in Fig. 11.2 we look at the distribution of log income per capita. When looking at the variable in logs, the spreading out of the distribution of income is less pronounced. This shows that even though there was an increase in the absolute gap between the rich and the poor provinces, the proportional gap has increased much less. Both figures show that there has been an increase in the density of relatively rich provinces, while some provinces still remain quite poor.

The variance in income across provinces can be due to wages and capital income variance. It looks that the variance in capital income is more important than wages variance In the case of wages, the variance is much larger among higher wages. The covariance between wages and capital income looks to be important too. This implies that migration across provinces is not enough to produce convergence.

Rates of growth of real per capita income are also diverse across provinces. For 1970–2010 we observe (see first row of Table 11.1), for example: Tierra del Fuego −0.4 % per year; La Rioja, −0.3 %; Tucuman, 0.1 %; Neuquen, 3 %; Catamarca, 5.4 %; the average for the provinces was 1.1 %. For 1985–2010, there are some

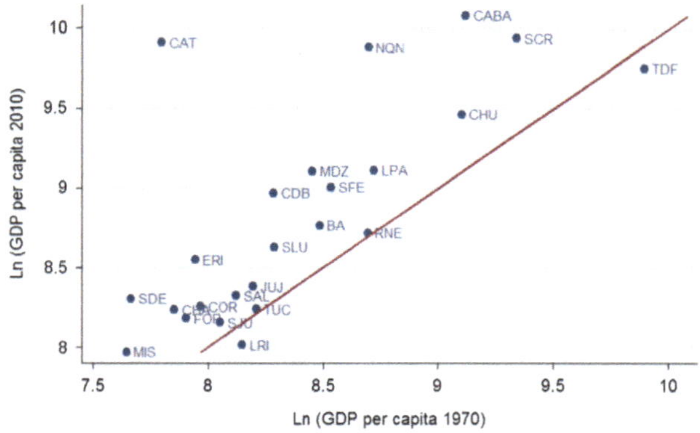

Fig. 11.3 Convergence – GDP in 1970 versus GDP in 2010 (Source: Own calculations and Elias 1996)

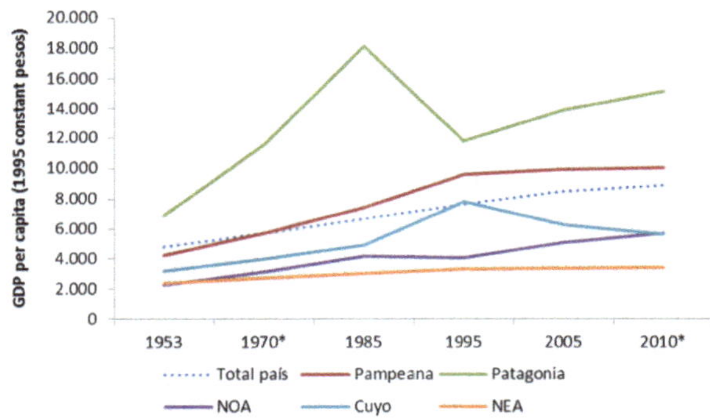

Fig. 11.4 Evolution of GDP per capita by region (1953–2010) (Source: Own calculations and Elias (1996). Note: * stand for estimated values)

miracles, Catamarca, 11.56 % per year, and some disasters, Salta, −0.38 %, and Tierra del Fuego, −2.54 %, with an average for the provinces of 1.3 %.

To evaluate whether this remarkable difference in growth rates explains today's income inequality across provinces, in Fig. 11.3 we plot log GDP per capita in 2010 versus the log GDP per capita in 1970, together with the 45° line. With the exception of Catamarca, most observations lie around the 45º line, what indicates little change in the ranking of provinces during the period and suggest that income distribution has been relatively stable. Moreover, the figure shows that the provinces of the NOA and NEA regions lie behind in relation to those in Pampeana and Patagonia region.

To summarize the long term trend over the period Fig. 11.4 shows the evolution of income per capita by region. Argentina's GDP per capita grew at an average annual rate of 1.3 % between 1970 and 2010, which means that the country was not able to double its GDP per capita in the last 40 years. However, NOA could do so by growing at an average annual rate of 2.9 %; NEA, Cuyo, Pampa and Patagonia regions failed to do so.

In general, GDP per capita increased for every region between 1953 and 1985. Over the following period (1985–1995) there was a slight fall in the GDP per capita for NOA and Patagonia, but it quickly recovered in the next period (1995–2005).

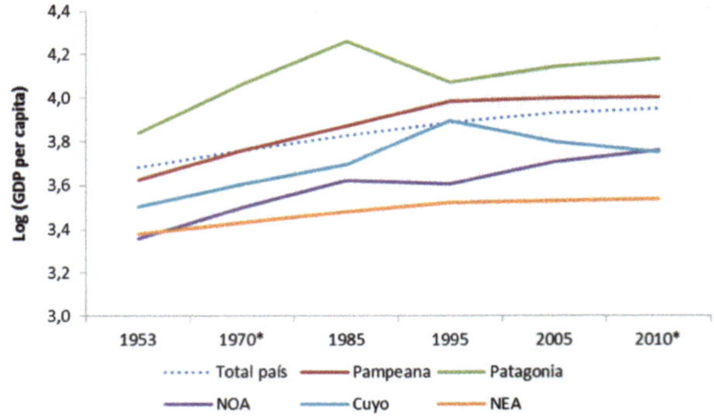

Fig. 11.5 Evolution of the logarithm of GDP per capita by region (1953–2010) (Source: Own calculations and Elias (1996). Note: * stand for estimated values)

Another useful comparison is to normalize the data to the GDP per capita of Buenos Aires in 1884. As compared to the existing GDP per capita in the province of Buenos Aires in 1884, we observe that in 2007 Patagonia shows a GDP per capita 3.8 times higher than Buenos Aires in 1884 whereas NEA's GDP per capita is just 1.45 times greater than it.

At this point, it is important to point out the extraordinary growth in income of Catamarca. Catamarca was at the bottom of the income distribution in 1970 (22th out of 24), by 2010 the province was in third place after Buenos Aires City and Santa Cruz. The force behind this miracle was mining, that went from 0.3 % of Catamarca's GDP in 1985, when Catamarca ranked 20th, to 60.7 % in 2006. This fact makes Catamarca an outlier when looking at simple correlations of growth and income with other variables and, what seems more important, it is unclear whether this prosperity was translated in other economic outcomes, such as health and investment in education. Because of this, we exclude Catamarca in some parts of the correlation analysis.

In this section we have documented the differences in income per capita across provinces and regions and its evolution. In particular, Figs. 11.5 and 11.6 suggests that during the 1970–2010 period there has been little, if any, unconditional convergence in per capita income at the province level. This is not confirmed when we look at the relationship between the average growth rate between 1970 and 2010 and the log of GDP in 1970 for the entire sample. As Fig. 11.7 shows, the association between initial income per capita and rates of growth over the period is negative, the coefficient of a simple regression of growth rates on initial income is −0.71. However, when we exclude Catamarca the association becomes slightly positive ().

Regarding the situation within the Province of Buenos Aires, the most important province of Argentina, the income per capita shows large differences across the cities in this province. For instance, in 2003 the GDP per capita of the city of Ensenada was almost four times the average for the province of Buenos Aires, while the GDP per capita of the city of Coronel Rosales was less than half the average for the province. In 1993 the situation was similar, though the gap was smaller. Rates of growth of real per capita income are also diverse across cities in

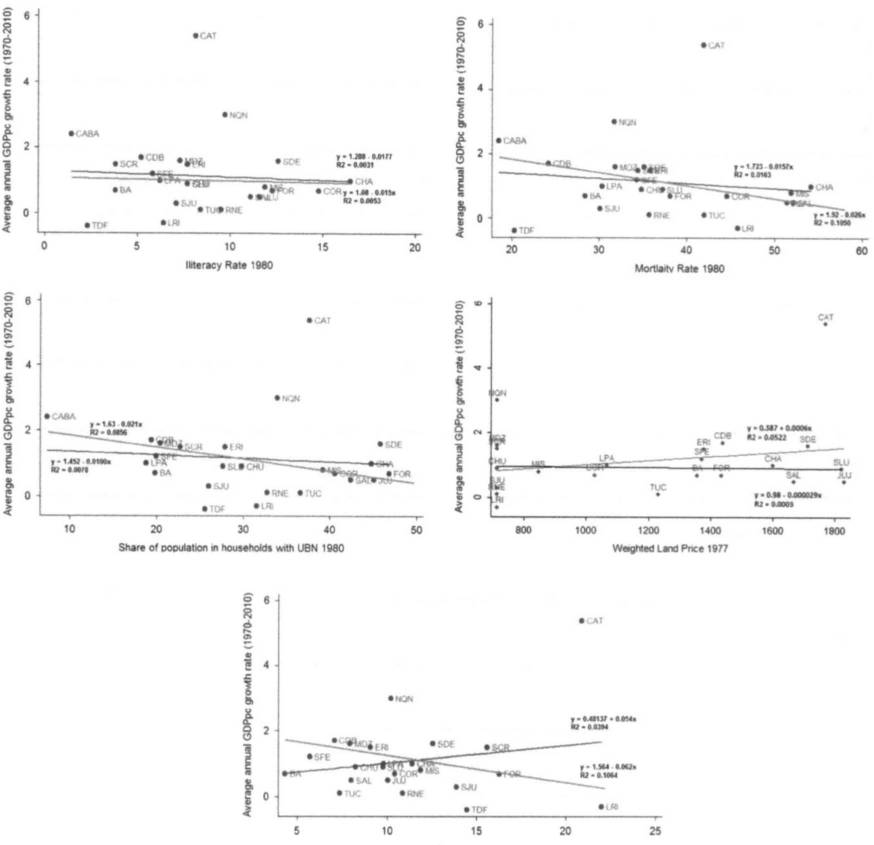

Fig. 11.6 (**a**) Average annual GDP per capita growth rate versus illiteracy rate at initial stage (1970–2010) (Source: Own calculations. CIAP Database and Elias (1996). Note: the *red line* shows the regression equation including all provinces while the *grey line* shows the regression equation excluding the province of Catamarca (CAT)). (**b**) Average annual GDP per capita growth rate versus infant mortality at initial stage (1970–2010) (Source: Own calculations. CIAP Database and Elias (1996). Note: the *red line* shows the regression equation including all provinces while the *grey line* shows the regression equation excluding the province of Catamarca (CAT)). (**c**) Average annual GDP per capita growth rate versus population with Unsatisfied Basic Needs at initial stage (1970–2010) (Source: Own calculations. CIAP Database and Elias (1996). Note: the *red line* shows the regression equation including all provinces while the *grey line* shows the regression equation excluding the province of Catamarca (CAT)). (**d**) Average annual GDP per capita growth rate versus Land Price at initial stage (1970–2010) (Source: Own calculations. CIAP Database and Elias (1996). Note: the *red line* shows the regression equation including all provinces while the *grey line* shows the regression equation excluding the province of Catamarca (CAT)). (**e**) Average annual GDP per capita growth rate versus Provincial Public Expenditures at initial stage (1970–2010) (Source: Own calculations. CIAP Database and Elias (1996). Note: the *red line* shows the regression equation including all provinces while the *grey line* shows the regression equation excluding the province of Catamarca (CAT))

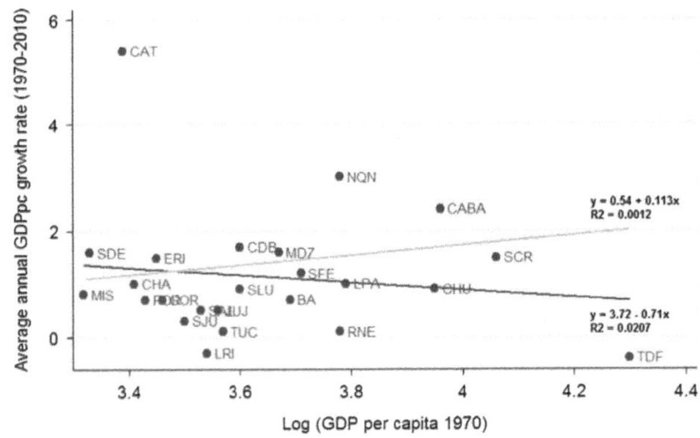

Fig. 11.7 Average annual GDP per capita growth rate versus GDP per capita at initial stage (1970–2010) (Source: Own calculations and Elias (1996). Note: the *red line* shows the regression equation including all provinces while the *grey line* shows the regression equation excluding the province of Catamarca (CAT))

the Province of Buenos Aires. There has been little change in the ranking of cities during the period, suggesting that income distribution has been relatively stable between 1993 and 2003. The income distribution across cities in Buenos Aires looks to be explained more by human capital differences than by the differences we observed across provinces.

This lack of convergence may be due to several factors such as differences in human capital per capita, differences in the composition of GDP among provinces, differences in the role of the national and provincial public sector with respect to each province. In what follows, we look at the patterns of factor accumulation, productivity growth, technological change and other correlates of economic growth and income level in the provinces and regions of Argentina.

11.5 Correlates of Economic Growth: 1970–2010

The discussion of the previous section raises the question on the determinants or characteristics of the provinces that might be related to economic growth. In this section we look at certain factors that correlate with economic growth. We start by looking at the factors suggested by the extended Solow model discussed briefly in Sect. 11.3, such as human capital and technology. Then we look at other factors that may affects or interact with the process of economic growth, such as the development of a particular economic sector, urbanization and public policies.

11.5.1 Population

The population of most provinces has considerably increased in the analyzed period (see Table 11.2, first panel). In the 1970 National Census, Argentina had 23 million people and in the recent 2010 Census, the population rose to more than 40 million people. The Pampeana Region has always been the leading region in terms of population, especially due to the presence of the city of Buenos Aires and its surroundings, while Patagonia is still the region with less population. However, the later region has experienced the largest growth in population.

The composition of the population has also varied during 1970 and 2010: the urban population has grown and the share of non-native population has considerably declined in every region.

11.5.2 Labor, Wages and Education

Labor and its quality are among the main inputs in production. The employment rate has been very similar across provinces along the last 40 years. Moreover there have been no significant changes in each province. However, its composition has varied over the period. The industrial employment declined in every region between 1996 and 2010 and Cuyo currently shows the highest share of industrial employment (24 % vs. 36 % in 1996) (Tables 11.1 and 11.3).

Regarding wages, it can be seen that there are large wage differentials among regions. In 1970, Patagonia was the region with the highest real unit wage, while the NOA had the lowest one. Wages along all regions fell drastically in the sub periods 1985–1995 and 1995–2005, but they start a process of recovering in the period after the 2001 economic crisis. In 2011 Patagonia still has the highest salary but wage inequality, as measured by the standard deviation, between provinces is even larger than in 1970. These differentials are related in part to investment in education and on-the-job training.

Figure 11.8 shows the well known positive relation between economic growth and education. This relationship is much stronger, when Catamarca is excluded. The percentage of people who attended secondary school aged between 13 and 17 increased impressively between 1980 and 2011 in every region. The existing gap between provinces in 1980 was much larger than today's. By 1980, NEA and NOA lagged behind the rest of the regions while Pampa clearly led with more than 50 % of the population attending Secondary School. In 2011 these differences have almost disappeared and now at least 84 % of the population in that age range attends Secondary School, though the northern regions are still located at the bottom in this aspect. This evidence suggests that we cannot confirm that convergence would have been greater if differences in human capital had not existed at the beginning of the analyzed period (Tables 11.2 and 11.4).

Table 11.3 Correlations between average annual growth rate of GDP per capita, wages and land prices

	Average annual wage (EPH) growth rate (1985–1995)	Average annual wage (EPH) growth rate (1995–2010)	Average annual GDP growth rate (1970–2010) %	Average annual GDP per capita growth rate (1970–2010) %	Average annual wage growth rate (1985–2010) %	Average annual land price growth rate (1977–2007) %	Average annual land price growth rate (1977–1997) %
Average annual EPH wage growth rate (1995–2010)	−0.33						
Average annual GDP growth rate (1970–2010) %	0.04	0.40					
Average annual GDP per capita growth rate (1970–2010) %	0.10	0.05	0.69				
Average annual wage growth rate (1985–2010) %	0.42	0.30	0.11	0.07			
Average annual land price growth rate (1977–2007) %	−0.43	0.14	−0.22	−0.32	−0.17		
Average annual land price growth rate (1977–1997) %	−0.44	−0.41	−0.32	−0.22	−0.32	0.32	
Average annual land price growth rate (1997–2007) %	−0.18	0.40	−0.02	−0.18	0.02	0.80	−0.30

Source: Own calculations

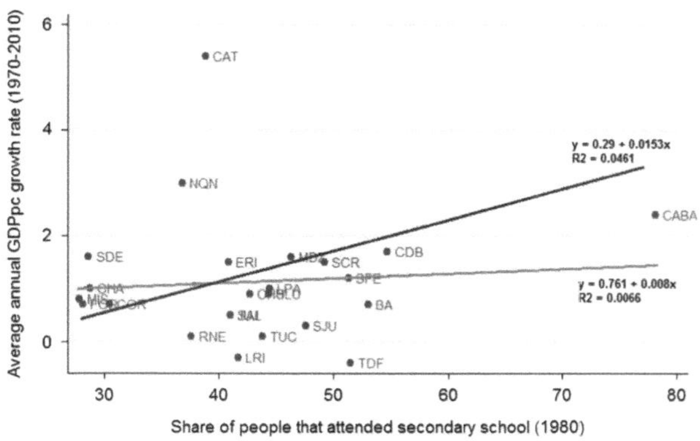

Fig. 11.8 Average annual GDP per capita growth rate versus share of people that attended secondary school at initial stage (1970–2010) (Source: Own calculations. EPH. INDEC and Elias (1996). Note: the *red line* shows the regression equation including all provinces while the *grey line* shows the regression equation excluding the province of Catamarca (CAT))

Table 11.4 Correlations with share of students attending private schools

Correlation with share of student attending private schools	In 1996	In 2010
Average annual GDP growth rate (1970–2010)	−0.274	−0.199
Average annual GDP per capita growth rate (1990–2010) %	−0.050	−0.050
Average annual GDP per capita growth rate (1970–2010) %	0.120	0.156
CONICET researchers per 1,000 inhabitants (2010)	0.710	0.727
Provincial exports as % of GDP (2007)	0.003	0.035
Companies per capita (2009)	0.707	0.746
ATM per 100,000 inhabitants (1998)	0.745	0.776
Population in household with unsatisfied basic needs (1980)	−0.698	−0.729
Provincial public expenditure per km^2 (2005)	0.748	0.679
Average wages according to EPH (1985)	0.429	0.415
Average wages according to EPH (1995)	0.396	0.434

Source: Own calculations

11.5.3 *Total Factor Productivity (TFP)*

In economics, we normally refer to TFP, or "technology", to capture factors other than physical capital and labor affecting economic growth. Differences in TFP across provinces may be reflecting differences in other factors, such as economic organization, other than technology. During the sub-period 1980–1990, TPF grew more than 50 % for Pampa and Cuyo Regions, the leading regions of Argentina, while it was more modest for Patagonia, a region with a growth driven by the oil industry, NEA and NOA, the regions with the poorer performance in terms of economic growth. The latter just experienced an increase of 10 % in the TPF in the 10-year period (see Table 11.2).

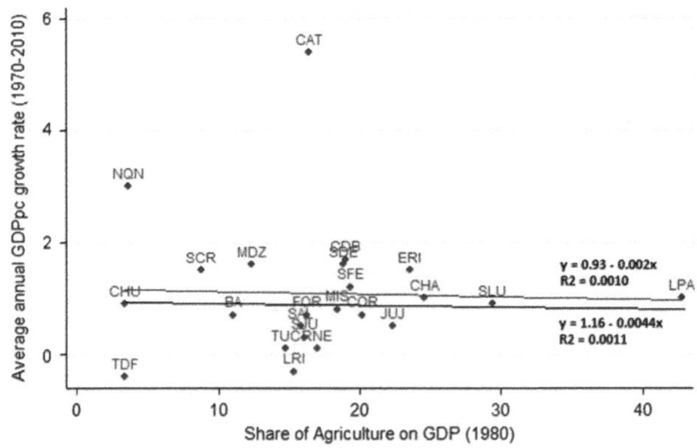

Fig. 11.9 Average annual GDP per capita growth rate versus share of agriculture on GDP at initial stage (1970–2010) (Source: Own calculations. CIAP Database and Elias (1996). Note: the *red line* shows the regression equation including all provinces while the *grey line* shows the regression equation excluding the province of Catamarca (CAT))

11.5.4 Agriculture

In relation to GDP composition, the share of Agriculture on GDP went down or at least stayed the same between 1980 and 2001 for every region. On the one hand, Pampa region have always had a high percentage of its GDP coming from Agriculture. Even though it has declined, it still takes 20.4 % of its GDP. On the other hand, Cuyo stays as the region with the lowest share of agriculture on its GDP. It declined from 17 % in 1980 to 11.5 % in 2001. In Patagonia, the share didn't change in a relevant way and stayed around 7 % along the whole period (Fig. 11.9).

11.5.5 Urbanization

As suggested by our discussion in Sect. 11.2, Fig. 11.10 shows a positive relationship between urbanization and economic growth. This figure therefore suggests that provinces that have grown faster are typically those with a higher level of urbanization. However, it is important to notice that these figures do not imply causation. Taking into account the importance of agriculture for the Argentinean economy this drives the question on whether agriculture promotes economic development and urbanization, or the reverse is true. The increase in land prices in rural areas over the period for all provinces, at an annual rate of 4.8 % on average, suggests that its use in agriculture has become more productive, but it is silent with respect to the role of cities. However, taking into account the endogeneity of most of the variables involved in the process of economic growth, our data suggest that there has been a process of development with increase in human capital and productivity growth accompanied by urbanization.

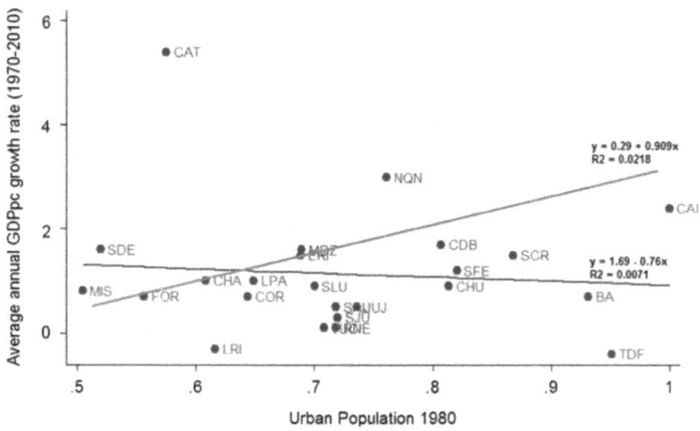

Fig. 11.10 Average annual GDP per capita growth rate versus share of urban population at initial stage (1970–2010) (Source: Own calculations. INDEC (1980) and Elias (1996). Note: the *red line* shows the regression equation including all provinces while the *grey line* shows the regression equation excluding the province of Catamarca (CAT))

11.5.6 Public Sector

The Public sector has an important role in provinces. Its importance can be measured through several indicators. On the one hand, public expenditure as percentage of GDP has largely increased from 1970 to 2005 in every region. While public expenditure was under 13.5 % for every region in 1970, that bound rose to 20 % in 2005 – except for Pampa region. In this regard, the Northern regions have always been the leading regions (37.9 % and 31.8 % for NEA and NOA in 2005). When measuring its importance as the public expenditure per squared kilometer, Pampa – excluding the City of Buenos Aires – shows the higher numbers along the whole analyzed period.

Figure 11.11 shows a negative relation between public employment per capita and growth. When looking at regional level, Patagonia appears as the leading region with 0.12 public employees per capita in 2000, followed by the northern regions. Regarding its evolution over time, the number of public employees per capita has not changed significantly since 1983 for Pampa. For the other regions – Patagonia, NOA, Cuyo and NEA-, total public employment declined to 0.12, 0.08, 0.07, and 0.08 in 2000 from 0.21, 0.16, 0.14, and 0.16 public employees per capita in 1983 respectively (Table 11.5) Porto and Sanguinetti (1996).

11.5.7 Taxes

Taxes are supposed to have an adverse effect on several indicators with direct impact on growth and development. For instance, Djankov et al. (2009) found that corporate tax rate have a large adverse impact on aggregate investment, Foreign

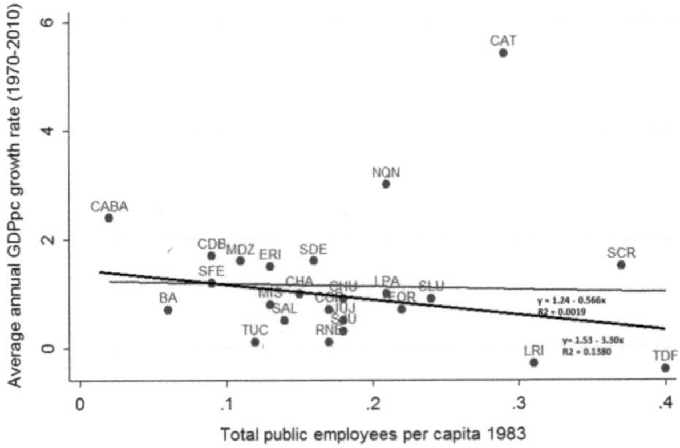

Fig. 11.11 Average annual GDP per capita growth rate versus total public employees per capita at initial stage (1970–2010) (Source: Own calculations, Interior Ministry Database and Elias (1996). Note: the *red line* shows the regression equation including all provinces while the *grey line* shows the regression equation excluding the province of Catamarca (CAT))

Direct Investment (FDI), and entrepreneurial activity. In Argentina there are both national and provincial taxes directly impacting provincial economies. Although Tax Pressure has remained relatively stable between the 1990s and 2000s, it is still very high. Pampa region has the highest rate at 4.6 % of provincial GDP.

Following Djankov interpretation, we should see what has happened with FDI during the last years. While taxing pressure did not changed significantly, FDI per capita augmented dramatically from 1990 to 2000. Patagonia is the region which had more FDI per habitant in 2000 while NEA was the opposite extreme (Djankov et al. 2002; Goerlich and Mas 2008).

Regarding the evolution of enterprises during this period, the number of companies per capita grew in every region from 1996 to 2009, but Cuyo and the Northern Regions are still far from Pampa and Patagonia. The size of enterprises, as measured by the average number of workers per firm, has also increased and while the largest companies used to be finds in Cuyo and NOA, in 2009 the largest ones are located in Patagonia and NEA. Still, the average size goes from 8 to 10.5 in 2009.

11.5.8 Government Debt

Since their existence, and particularly during the XX, provinces have indebted themselves as to face various charges or obligations. Provincial debt as percentage of GDP has largely increased during the last 10 years – at least ten percentage points in every region. Again the northern regions show the highest debts with respect to their GDP 67.2 % and 33.5 % for NEA and NOA respectively.

Table 11.5 Distribution of GDP and Employment through Provinces

	%	% GDP		% Profits	% Public employment		% Private employment			% Total employment
Province	km^2	1970	2010	2009	1983	2000	1996	2000	2010	2000
Buenos Aires	11.06	36.57	31.48	32.00	24.85	28.37	31.18	31.67	31.50	30.49
CABA	0.01	23.37	21.65	15.82	2.63	5.04	28.09	27.37	25.83	19.39
Córdoba	5.95	7.02	8.19	9.00	7.96	6.36	7.48	7.52	8.17	7.10
Entre Ríos	2.83	1.97	2.00	2.22	4.31	4.21	2.26	2.03	2.29	2.81
La Pampa	5.16	0.91	0.91	1.19	1.68	1.53	0.73	0.63	0.59	0.95
Santa Fé	4.78	9.35	8.19	8.70	8.64	7.91	8.10	8.28	8.13	8.15
Chubut	8.08	1.47	2.06	1.68	1.78	1.81	1.14	1.34	1.60	1.51
Neuquén	3.38	0.80	3.40	4.12	1.91	2.44	1.25	1.30	1.50	1.70
Río Negro	7.30	1.35	1.23	1.01	2.44	2.31	1.60	1.51	1.59	1.80
Santa Cruz	8.77	0.83	1.79	1.83	1.58	1.55	0.70	0.65	0.93	0.97
Tierra del Fuego	0.78	0.23	0.69	0.57	0.41	0.90	0.35	0.43	0.55	0.60
Catamarca	3.69	0.36	2.32	3.60	2.25	2.04	0.56	0.55	0.50	1.08
Jujuy	1.91	0.94	0.92	1.07	2.73	2.44	0.92	0.96	0.93	1.49
La Rioja	3.23	0.41	0.32	0.28	1.89	2.19	0.45	0.52	0.47	1.12
Salta	5.59	1.48	1.57	1.68	3.59	3.13	1.55	1.76	1.85	2.25
Santiago del Estero	4.90	0.91	1.11	1.50	3.52	3.04	0.75	0.80	0.79	1.60
Tucumán	0.81	2.42	1.72	1.65	4.49	3.81	2.25	2.29	2.57	2.83
Mendoza	5.35	3.93	4.93	6.06	4.93	4.39	4.18	4.01	3.91	4.15
San Juan	3.22	1.04	0.74	0.56	3.07	2.51	1.12	1.26	1.31	1.71
San Luis	2.76	0.63	0.76	0.69	1.91	1.60	1.00	1.03	0.93	1.24
Chaco	3.58	1.26	1.25	1.58	3.90	3.61	1.31	1.19	1.04	2.05
Corrientes	3.17	1.40	1.20	1.45	4.18	3.06	1.23	1.12	1.16	1.81
Formosa	2.59	0.55	0.59	0.80	2.48	2.81	0.38	0.36	0.40	1.23
Misiones	1.07	0.80	1.00	0.96	2.90	2.93	1.43	1.41	1.47	1.96

Source: Own calculations Zeller and Rivkin (2005)

11.5.9 Financial Sector

Financial development has been reported as a relevant factor to promote economic growth by many authors. For instance, Rajan and Zingales (1998) found that financial development actually facilitates economic growth by proving that financial development reduces the costs of external finance to firms.

In Argentina the level of financial development is still quite modest. However, the share of people with coverage of banking services has lately increased in every region compared with the 1990s. In this regard, the Northern regions continue to be the most backward with more than 26 % of the population without access to banking services.

Both banking branches and ATMs grew consistently from 1995 to 2005. Patagonia is the leading region in term of ATM per 100,000 people followed by Pampa Region, whereas NEA stays at the opposite end. The highest delinquency

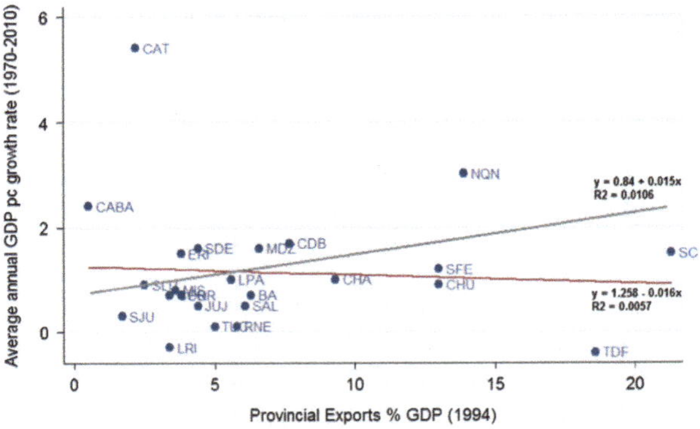

Fig. 11.12 Average annual GDP per capita growth rate versus provincial exports at initial stage (1970–2010) (Source: Own calculations. CIAP Database and Elias (1996). Note: the *red line* shows the regression equation including all provinces while the *grey line* shows the regression equation excluding the province of Catamarca (CAT))

rates are found in NEA and Cuyo Region, although they have drastically declined from 2001 to 2010.

11.5.10 Exports

For provinces, exports consist of sales to foreign countries and to other provinces. Regarding the evolution of external sales as share of the GDP, they increased up to 20 % of GDP for every region except for NEA, in which exports take 8 % of its GDP – and it stayed almost that same as in 1994. However, logistic costs are lower in this region than in NOA (16 % vs. 11.6 %) (Fig. 11.12).

11.5.11 Migration

Human migration continues to have an important role in the demographic composition and economic configuration of most countries of the world. In Argentina, the mass immigration of foreigners in the mid-nineteenth century and the internal migration between provinces and urban centers in recent decades, are the most important phenomena explaining population patterns in our country, as well as some of the economic disparities in development between regions.

The observation of rates of international and internal migration in Argentina in time allows to explain the relevance of these events placing the country among the one with most mobile population. While migration rates have varied in response to various phenomena according to historical times, the country is characterized by migration and experiencing high rates of spatial redistribution of population.

Internal migration in Argentina has in general been affected by the universal trend of migration from the countryside to the city; and the concentration of population in the City of Buenos Aires and Greater Buenos Aires.

However in the last decade, it has been also recorded a significant migration flow to Patagonia. Lagging behind Patagonia, Cuyo and NOA have also experienced an important migration flow whilst Pampa and NEA regions have experienced an emigration flow.

11.5.12 R&D

The literature suggests that roughly half of cross-country differences in per capita income and growth are driven by differences in Total Factor Productivity, generally associated with technological progress. However, adopting existing technology is not without cost. Firms and countries need to develop an absorptive capacity which, in turn are hypothesized to be functions of spending on research and development (R&D).

R&D is then crucial to meet development in a country. In Argentina the number of people devoted to research has remarkably increased in the last decades for every region. In 2008 Pampa Region appears as the leading region in terms of people devoted to research, in fact there are approximately seven researchers per 1,000 habitants (2008). NEA stays just at the opposite end with 0.48 researchers each 1,000 inhabitants.

According to the Ministry of Science, Technology and Innovation, expenditures on R&D per researcher has almost doubled between 2001 and 2008. Cuyo Region is the leader when looking at this variable, followed by Pampa and NOA regions.

11.5.13 FDI

Foreign direct investment (FDI) is an integral part of an open and effective international economic system and a major determinant to development. In Argentina FDI has increased for every region between 1990 and 2000. In this last year Patagonia appears as the principal region in terms of Foreign Direct Investment, principally because of energy investments. NEA and Pampa regions are the regions receiving less foreign investments.

11.5.13.1 Outcomes of Economic Growth: Health Improvements

Economic growth usually brings development in most dimensions of human welfare. In particular, it has a positive effect on health through the increase in income and education; on the one hand more education increases the net expected wealth of spending on education; producing a wealth effect that leads to an increase in health spending and therefore increasing the survival rate in subsequent years. On the other hand, education may directly affect the survival rate by making the person more productive in health investments.

The northern regions of Argentina are, as predicted by theory, the most backward ones regarding health. In 2008, the mortality rate was 17.1 per 1,000 newborn in NEA versus 9.4 in Patagonia. However, this ratio has considerably dropped over the period, since it was above 30 for every region by 1970 – Patagonia and NEA were also located at the opposite ends. Infant mortality has dropped by more than a half for all regions during the period.

11.5.14 Multiple Regression Analysis

Some of the multiple regressions performed, give some support to the effects of public employment and urbanization. We can think that public employment is higher in bigger cities. We also get that the speed of convergence were not much different between subperiods 1970–1990 and 1990–2010.

11.6 Regional Economic Policies (REP)

The evaluation of the economic policies at the regional and national level implemented during the period is an important and demanding issue that goes beyond the objective of this chapter.[5] However a review of the main policies implemented during the period is useful to contribute to the understanding of regional economic development.

Many REP were applied in the period 1970–2010. Some were general with regional effects, others were direct designed. In terms of tax revenue and expenditures, the federal government took many policies, like: (a) changes in the distribution of federal tax revenues between provinces and federal government and between provinces, some of them favoring provinces with less GDP per capita;

[5] This section is mainly based on a qualitative survey on regional public policies that we did among experts, Baruj et al. (2009), IERAL and Fundacion Mediterranea (2010), Porto and Cont (1998), Porto and Elizagaray (2011), Porto and Sanguinetti (1996), Krugman (1991), schultz (1968) and also on our own search.

some of them came by changing previous criteria, and others pushed by the inflationary finance (deficit distribution); (b) the federal government transferred to the provinces the budget corresponding to the primary and high schools, and health sector; (c) royalties coming from the mining and petroleum and gas exploitation corresponding to the provinces were going to be received directly by them; (d) the Federal Taxes Co-Participation Regime keeps the criteria of distribution inverse to the development level, favoring the poorest and delayed provinces; (e) many public works were jointly financed by the federal government and provinces; (f) expenditures planning were made, even though some of them without a complete project evaluation and financing sources; (g) many international loans (World Bank, Inter-American Development Bank) were used to finance provincial projects, in many cases paid by the provinces; (h) creation of Funds to promote Regional Growth (FIT then FDR).

Industrial policies were pursued by the federal government to support the industrial development in some specific provinces like: Tierra del Fuego, La Rioja, San Juan, San Luis, Catamarca, ant the Patagonic provinces. Some of them were tax exemptions, credit subsidies, regulations and administrative facilities. The provinces extended local tax exemptions too. In some cases they supported non-traditional manufacturing, like automotives, house appliances, paper, petrochemicals, and aluminum. Credit policies to favor small and medium size firms were implemented. However, these policies did not seem to be effective in inducing convergence and closing internal gaps.

Agricultural policies in favor of the so called regional products (wine, tobacco, sugar, forest, yerba mate, olives) were also in place during the period. The national government created the PROSAP to promote agricultural projects. Some of the trade integration had also regional effects, like ALADI and MERCOSUR.

Many federal Universities were created in less developed provinces and also in Gran Buenos Aires. Social programs were more general and part of it could have been more emphasized for less developed provinces (PAN, Jefes, ANH). The R&D expenditures in general had a high concentration on the Pampean Region, but some increases occurred in less developed regions.

Although there were some infrastructure projects across the federal and provincial governments, these were not adequate or too much concentrated in the City and Province of Buenos Aires, (i.e. the turnpikes financed with federal funds). There was also little regional energy policy. With regard to tariffs: (a) the natural gas tariffs have similar structure across provinces and are all subsidized relative to its opportunity cost; (b) The price of electricity was uniform in the 1990s with some distributional margins in the City of Buenos Aires and Great Buenos Airess below those observed in some provinces; (c) In railroad and bus transportation there is a federal subsidy mainly focused in the City and Great BsAs; (d) In air transportation there is a subsidy possibly favoring the less crowded routes; (e) Water and sanity is similar to electricity, although the wholesale cost of water varies across provinces.

Today there are in place many different programs and policies oriented in general to promote exports, industrial development and innovation. However, there is no systematic evaluation and follow up of the impact of these policies.

There were also some projects regarding the creation of regions to substitute the provincial organization, intending to reduce the number of public officials at the different government levels. Nevertheless, these projects did not advance and instead some regions covering many provinces each were implemented but without altering the provincial organization Baruj et al. (2009); Porto and Elizagaray (2011).

11.7 Summary and Conclusions

In this chapter we have characterized the evolution of provincial GDP per capita in Argentina in the period 1970–2010 across provinces and regions. According to the data, one the main feature of regional development in Argentina is the remarkable diversity across regions and provinces in measured per capita income levels and in growth rates. The convergence in living standards between provinces was very low. During the period, the income distribution has been relatively stable and there was little change in the income per capita ranking of provinces.

With the exception of Catamarca that had an unprecedented growth performance due to mining, provinces in the Northern region of Argentina lag behind by any economic measure. However, over the period there was important progress in these provinces in terms of education and investment in research and development.

When looking at correlates of economic growth, we find a positive relation between provinces economic growth and education, urbanization and provincial exports; and a negative relationship with the relative size of the public sector, as measured by public employees per capita. Even though our analysis cannot say anything about causality, these relationships point on the right direction in terms of economic theory.

There were many regional economic policies during the period. Most of them were targeted to increasing exports, industrial production and, some, to innovation and education. It is difficult to isolate the effect of these policies. Even though, we do not have elements to evaluate the impact of the regional economic policies over the period, theory combined with some of our finding suggests that policies directed toward promoting investment in human capital are the more promising for regional development.

References

Acemoglu D (2008) Introduction to modern economic growth. Princeton University Press, Princeton

Anastasi A, Blanco E, Elosegui P, Sangiácomo M (2006) La bancarización y los determinantes de la disponibilidad de servicios bancarios en Argentina BCRA. Documento de Trabajo N° 16

Banco Mundial (2006) Argentina: El desafío de reducir los costos logísticos ante el crecimiento del comercio exterior, Informe No. 36606-AR

Banco Central de la República Argentina (www.bcra.com.ar)

Barro R, Lee JW (2010) A new data set of educational attainment in the world, 1950–2010 NBER working paper, No. 15902
Baruj G, Kosacoff B, Ramos A (2009) Las políticas de promoción de la competitividad en la Argentina. Principales instituciones e instrumentos de apoyo y mecanismos de articulación público-privada, documentos de proyectos, N$^{\underline{o}}$ 257 (LC/W.257), CEPAL, CEPAL Office in Buenos Aires
Cerro A, Meloni O (2000) Distribución del Ingreso, Desempleo y Delincuencia: El caso de Argentina en los años 90. Universidad Nacional de Tucumán, Tucumán, Argentina
Compañía Argentina de Tierras (www.cadetierras.com.ar)
Consejo Nacional de Investigaciones Científicas y Técnicas (CONICET) (www.conicet.gov.ar)
Djankov S, La Porta R, Lopez-De-Silanes F, Shleifer A (2002) The regulation of entry. Q J Econ 117(1):1–37
Djankov S, Ganser T, McLiesh C, Ramalho R, Shleifer A (2009) The effect of corporate taxes on investment and entrepreneurship. Am Econ J Macroecon 2:31–64
Elias VJ (1992) Sources of growth: a study of seven Latin American economies. ICS Press, San Francisco
Elías V (ed) (1996) Informe sobre la Economía de Tucumán. Fundación del Tucumán
Glaeser E (2011) Triumph of the City, Penguin Books, New York
Goerlich FJ, Mas M (2008) Algunas pautas de localización de la población a lolargo del siglo XX. Investigaciones Regionales 12(primavera):5–33
Hoselitz BF (1953) The role of cities in the economic growth of underdeveloped countries. J Polit Econ 61:195–208
IERAL and Fundación Mediterránea (2010) Una Argentina competitiva, productiva y federal. Documento de Trabajo, Buenos Aires
INDEC, National Household Survey (1970–2011) Instituto Nacional de Estadísticas y Censos
INDEC, National Census of Population and Housing 1970, 1980, 1990, 2001, 2010. Instituto Nacional de Estadıstica y Censos
Krugman P (1991) Increasing returns and economic geography. J Polit Econ 99:483–499
Lucas R Jr (1988) On the mechanics of economic development. J Monet Econ Elsevier 22(1):3–42, July
Marshall A (1961) Principles of economics, 8th edn. Macmillan, New York
Ministry of Science, Technology and Innovation. Anuario FONTAR
Interior Ministry Database for provinces
Ministry of Labour, Employment and Social Security. Observatorio de Empleo y Dinámica Empresarial
Paz JA (2003) Transiciones en el mercado de trabajo y protección laboral en la Argentina (Estudio basado en datos de la Encuesta Permanente deHogares, 1997–2002), Seminario- Taller: Historias laborales y frecuencias deaportes al sistema de seguridad social
Porto A (2004) Disparidades regionales y federalismo fiscal. Editorial de la Universidad de La Plata, La Plata
Porto A (2005) Pujas y tensiones entre niveles de gobierno por los recursos fiscales. Documento de trabajo. Departamento de Economía -UNLP, La Plata
Porto A, Cont W (1998) Presupuestos provinciales, transferencias intergubernamentales y equidad. In: Desarrollo Económico, vol 38, Buenos Aires
Porto A, Elizagaray A (2011) Regional development, regional disparities and public polices in Argentina: a long-run view. In: Baer W, Fleischer D (eds) The economics of Argentina and Brazil. A comparative perspective, E. Elgart, Cheltenham/Northampton
Porto A, Sanguinetti P (1996) Las Transferencias Intergubernamentales y la Equidad Distributiva: El Caso Argentino, vol 88, Serie Política Fiscal. CEPAL, Santiago de Chile
Rajan RG, Zingales L (1998) Financial dependence and growth. Am Econ Rev Am Econ Assoc 88(3):559–586, June
Sarmiento DF (1845) "Facundo" Buenos Aires Ediciones Culturales, Buenos Aires
Schultz TW (1968) Economic growth and agriculture. McGraw-Hill, New York

Solow Robert M. (1956). A Contribution to the Theory of Economic Growth, Quarterly Journal of Economics, 70(1):65–94, February
Universidad de Buenos Aires, Faulted de Ciencias Económicas. Base de datos provinciales del Centro de Investigaciones en Administración Pública (CIAP Database)
Zeller N, Rivkin A (2005) El empleo público nacional: estudio de sus principales transformaciones. In: Thwaites Rey M, López A (eds) Entre tecnócratas globalizados y políticos clientelistas. Derrotero del ajuste neoliberal en el Estado argentino. Prometeo, Buenos Aires

Chapter 12
Territorial Inequality and Regional Policy in Chile

Patricio Aroca

12.1 Introduction

In their book on regional inequalities in small nations, Felsenstein and Portnov (2005) state that during a seminar held at Hebrew University of Jerusalem in 1957, Simon Kuznets argued that small nations had had more success than larger ones with distributing the fruits of growth among their inhabitants. In order to make this claim, he compared Scandinavian countries and Switzerland as examples of more equal distribution to nations like France, Germany and even the United States. Along these same lines, the literature on economic development posits that it is logical that larger countries present greater regional inequalities than small ones.

On the other hand, those who defend the idea of the market as an efficient mechanism for assigning an economy's resources to the production of goods and services argue that it provides adequate signals for reducing the inequalities that emerge in space. For example, migration will be the mechanism for reducing regional inequalities in unemployment and salary, while interregional commerce will be the instrument for arbitrating prices among regions. However, Aroca and Hewings (2002) show that in the case of Chile, even when migration follows the market's signals, inertial concentrating forces around large cities, particularly around the Metropolitan Region, are stronger, which leads to greater concentration rather than a reduction in inequality.

For its part, the new approach to economic geography posits that inequalities among regions can be maintained over time or even increase along with the growth of the economy due to the existence of a center that makes use of the benefits of growth while the regions on the periphery let the opportunities that this growth generates pass them by (Martin and Ottaviano 1999; Fujita and Thisse 2002; Baldwin and Martin 2004).

P. Aroca (✉)
University Adolfo Ibañez, Viña del Mar, Chile
e-mail: patricio.aroca@uai.cl

J.R. Cuadrado-Roura and P. Aroca (eds.), *Regional Problems and Policies in Latin America*, Advances in Spatial Science, DOI 10.1007/978-3-642-39674-8_12,

This chapter analyzes territorial inequalities in Chile, a small country, starting from the basis that it is one of most inequitable nations in the world and that this situation has a strong territorial component. We argue that between 1990 and 2010, regional differences have grown, presenting a center-periphery type pattern.

The second section of this chapter presents results regarding the evolution of regional inequalities in Chile. We argue that these inequalities have increased over time and that their origins lie in government actions and the expansion of the market as a mechanism for assigning resources to the production of goods and services. Next, we describe government actions that promote these inequalities, particularly through the centralization of decision-making and concentration of spending around the capital, the Metropolitan Region of Santiago. The following section describes the market mechanisms that promote concentration and inequality in the territory, and the final part contains conclusions and projections based on the current situation.

12.2 Regional Inequalities and Concentration

Geographically, Chile is a long, thin country. It consists of 12 regions, each of which has a name and a Roman numeral assigned in an order that runs north to south from I to XII. It also contains the Metropolitan Region ("RM" for its initials in Spanish), which is located in the central area of the country between Regions V and VI.[1]

The country's territorial inequalities vary. This chapter highlights those associated with the economic and political system over the course of two decades. Figures 12.1 and 12.2 present the regional per capita gross domestic product (GDP) and average income derived from the workers' main activity measured as an index compared to the Metropolitan Region (RM) for the two periods presented, 1992 and 2009. The value of the RM has been set at 100.

These figures suggest that the country is facing growing income inequality. The results for 1992 show that only two regions (II and XII) have higher GDPs than the RM: the northern copper producing region of Antofagasta and the southern oil and methanol producing region of Magallanes. No region presents higher average income than the capital, and the majority of the regions have less than 90 % of the average income reported for Santiago. If we compare the results for 1992–2003 or 2006, the years for which the information utilized from the CASEN study is available, the results are similar.

Regional per capita GDP presented positive evolution for all of the regions compared to the RM through 2009. During the period under study, the majority of the regions saw an increase in this area, which led the cluster of points to move

[1] Regions I and X were split in 2010 in order to create regions XIV and XV. However, the map of 13 regions will be used for this chapter.

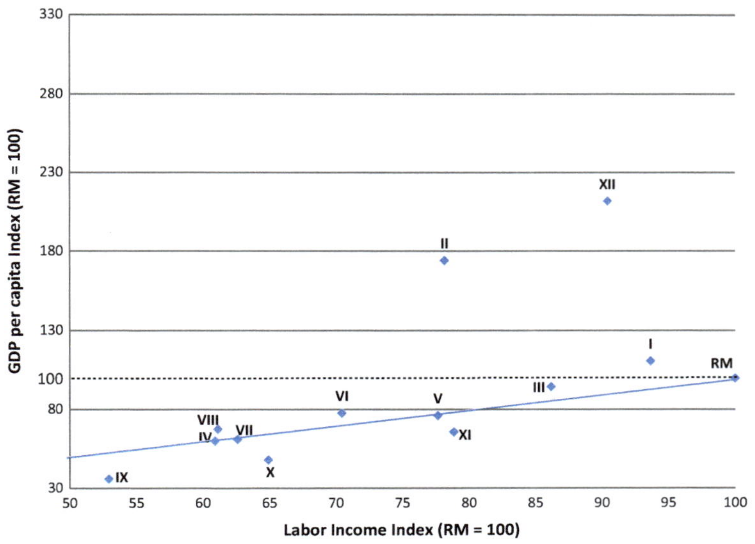

Fig. 12.1 Labor income versus GDP per capita – year 1992 (Source: Author with data from Central Bank and CASEN 1992)

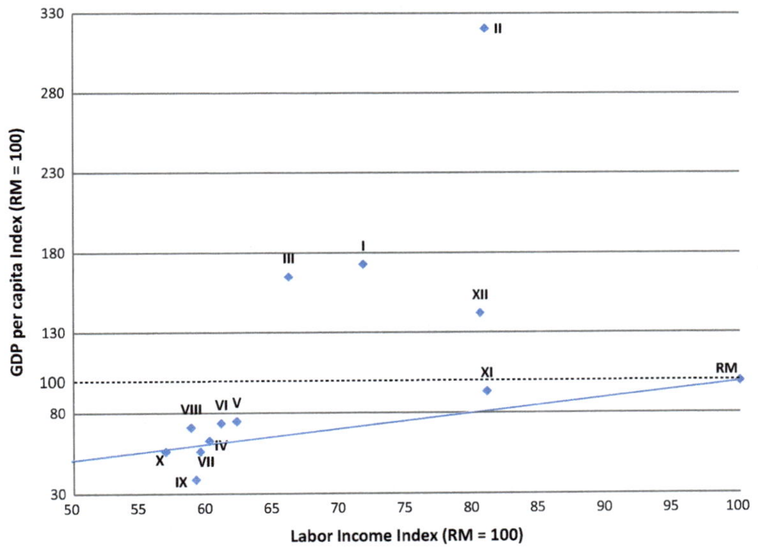

Fig. 12.2 Labor income versus GDP per capita – year 2009 (Source: Author with data from Central Bank and CASEN: National Socio-Economic Characterization Survey 2009)

upwards on the figure. However, the data on the average income of workers living outside of the capital is moving in unwanted direction. Although the regions' per capita GDP generally increased compared to that of the capital, their workers' income compared to that of Santiago workers decreased. This is particularly notable in the data on the country's central regions, which presented a mean of slightly less than 60 % of the average for Santiago. Meanwhile, the two northern- and southernmost regions of the country reported significant increases in production and small increases in workers' income.

In the 2009 figure, three groups emerge clearly: the low average income regions of the central part of the country, the medium income regions located at the extreme north and south, and the Metropolitan Region, which has the highest average income. A comparison of the two figures shows that the differences in average income increased among the regions over these two decades, bringing about differences in access to public goods and opportunities for development for their inhabitants and increasing concentrating forces around the Metropolitan Region.

12.3 The Concentrating Actions of the State

Foxley[2] (1987) wrote that Chile had a set of Gordian knots that had to be untied in order to be able to think about the developed country that we wanted to create when the dictatorship ended in 1990. He dedicated an excellent chapter on decentralization named "From Rhetoric to Action," where he argues that the country's growing concentration is due to the "gigantic voraciousness of Santiago" (*gigantismo insaciable de Santiago*).

Foxley argued that the situation of crisis of 1982 'reduced the scope of financial effort that has to be made to truly regionalize' and that at its best, the National Regional Development Fund (*FondoNacional de Desarrollo Regional*, FNDR) failed to exceed 2 % of public spending. He added that the 'phenomenon was exacerbated by the absence of a compensating and regulatory policy on the part of the State regarding the surpluses that were generated through single crop or mining exports by some regions.

While Foxley's book presents a summary of the proposal set forth by the Coalition of Parties for Democracy, a group led by the current Minister of Finance[3] presented the alternative proposal of the Alliance for Chile block, a continuation of the dictatorial government. Larrain (1987) argued in favor of the idea of making adjustments to the development model and the regional policy presented in a chapter by Arriagada (1987) in which he offers an assessment similar to that of

[2] Alejandro Foxley was the first Ministry of Finance in the new Chilean democracy from 1990 to 1994.

[3] Felipe Larrain is the current Ministry of Finance. He was appointed in 2010 and is to serve until 2014.

Foxley (1987). At one point, he argues that 'given the level of centralization that exists in Chile, "the solution cannot be left in the hands of the free forces of the market. State action and guidance is necessary, particularly during the period required to revert the centralizing inertia."

In 2006, Waissbluth wrote that 'Decentralization in Chile is a pending task.' He shows that effective public investment in municipal decision-making decreased from 17.2 % in 1990 until it stabilized around 10 % between 2000 and 2004. At the same time, effective regional investment increased from 10 % in 1990 to nearly 30 % by the end of the decade. However, this begins to systematically decrease beginning in 2000 until it reached 20.8 % in 2004. This implies that one third of effective regional public investment became effective sectoral public investment, which increased from 58 % to 68 % during the same period. This represents a huge step backwards in terms of the capacity for making decisions regarding the allocation of effective public investment in the decentralization process. At the same time, it is a step backwards towards the concentration of power through sectoral management that has ignored the heterogeneity of the country's regions.

Many hypotheses can be presented as potential explanations for this situation. For example, Waissbluth compares effective regional per capita public investment and shows that the Aysén Region has a value that is several times higher than that of the Metropolitan Region. This leads him to the erroneous conclusion that this fact invalidates 'a frequent regionalist complaint that those living in Santiago are taking the money'.

This is an erroneous conclusion because it ignores at least the following: economies of scale, economies of agglomeration and urbanization, mechanisms of concentration such as interregional spillover, and the benefits of interregional commerce that are concentrated in the Metropolitan Region. Rather than comparing effective investment levels in regions at the per capita level, one should look at the results of the process. The evidence from Figs. 12.1 and 12.2 regarding the growth process that took place between 1992 and 2009 is eloquent.

Some of these mechanisms are studied below. State actions are understood as those deployed by institutions such as government ministries and the Central Bank that impact the entities involved with the production and distribution of economic benefits in the territory. Four actions or policies are analyzed in terms of their impact on territorial inequalities: the National Regional Development Fund, the percentage of public spending on investment that is subject to regional or local decisions, the regional allocation of scholarships for graduate study abroad, and the Central Bank's efforts to control inflation.

12.4 The National Regional Development Fund (FNDR)

The law that created the FNDR stated that 'the National Regional Development Fund is a public investment program designed to provide territorial compensation and to fund actions in the various areas of social and economic infrastructure of the region in order to obtain harmonious and equitable territorial development' and that it is to come under the purview of the Office of the Secretary of Regional Development (*Subsecretaria de Desarrollo Regional*, SUBDERE), which is in turn part of the Ministry of the Interior.

Following two decades in which regional inequalities in income clearly increased -as seen in Figs. 12.1 and 12.2-, SUBDERE distributed the FNDR between 2003 and 2006 such that the region with the greatest increase (160 %) during the 3-year period was the Metropolitan Region while allocations to the remainder of the regions increased an average of 44 %. In other words, the fund that had been created to reduce regional inequalities increased allocations to the region with the greatest income in the economy by over 100 % more than the rest of the regions. The remaining regions, which required increased public spending to promote greater territorial equity, received a considerably lower percentage.

It is important to note that though FNDR is not the government's largest public find, it is the only one that was created with the objective of reducing regional differences. As such, there is no reason to expect other government investment funds to present different treatment when they were not designed to promote territorial equity.

Given that the FNDR's initial regulations from 1992 were consistent with the original definition of the fund, two approaches were used to increase the amount of funds allocated for investment in the Metropolitan Region. The first was the change introduced through Law 20.035 of June 23, 2005, which defined FNDR not only as a compensatory instrument but stated that it also had regional development purposes. This was interpreted as an alternative use of the resources, and made investing them in the capital of the country under the concept of regional development a valid option. The most significant change was a result of the creation of provisions that were incorporated into regional budgets which consisted of funds that had their own allocation regulations. Though they formed part of the FNDR, they completely ignored its allocation approach. As a result, the regulation of the provisions had a clear bias towards Santiago as shown in the aforementioned data from 2003 to 2006.

12.5 The Centralization of Public Spending

Waissbluth (2006) offers an analysis of the evolution of public investment based on data from MIDEPLAN (see Fig. 12.3).

In this context, the municipal and regional public investment amounts are decided in the municipality and the region respectively, while the sectoral amounts are determined by the country's government ministries. Figure 12.3 shows a trend with sustained growth through 2000, when the sum of municipal and regional public investment reached 41.2 % of total public investment. This is significantly higher than the level of 26 % reported in 1992. However, beginning in 2000, the percentage of local and regional investment begins to fall. By 2007, it represented

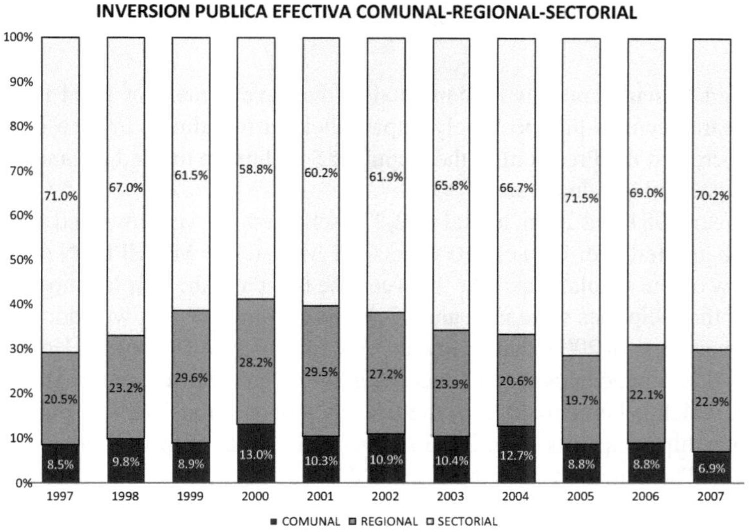

Fig. 12.3 Public investment by municipality, region and sector

just 29.8 % of all investment. In other words, there is a slide back towards levels that are only slightly higher than those of 1992. This evidence goes against the idea that efficiency in the allocation of resources was being improved by giving the power to make decisions about which projects are more socially profitable to regions and municipalities. At the same time, given that the central power is located in Santiago, the allocation for the RM will be more efficient because the individuals who make decisions about public spending have more precise knowledge of their own city.

In a study contracted by the IADB, Mancha et al. (2006) conclude that 'the distribution of powers in Chile is marked by a clear centralized dominance of normative and planning functions, the issuing of policies and instructions, and institutional handling of resources and supervision. As such, from a normative perspective, it is found that the regional/territorial economic development policies are national and sectoralized policies despite the description of functions related to this development offered in regional and municipal statutory laws that do not go beyond a mere statement of good intentions'.

In general, both the literature and political discourses evidence awareness of an over-centralization of decision-making with a clear bias towards investing in and spending on the RM and an excessive concentration of economic activity and population in it. However, as Foxley (1987) said, the country continues to wait to move from "rhetoric to action" in the decentralization process.

12.6 Advanced Human Capital and Scholarships

Advanced human capital is fundamental to the development of good universities and research centers that positively impact their surroundings. In view of this, the country created the President of the Republic Scholarship to fund advanced studies abroad, particularly doctorates.

Between 1981 and 2006, a total of 2,274 scholarships were awarded and 25,000 are to be granted over the next 10 years. The Minister of MIDEPLAN stated in an interview on the scholarships that 'between the launch of the scholarships and 2006, 73 % of the recipients were men and 27 % were women. When we adopted a blind selection process in 2006, that shifted to 53 % men and 47 % women'. However, her analysis does not address the fact that the granting has focused on the Metropolitan Region, which is home to 40 % of the country's population. The first published list of scholarship recipients from 2006 showed that 76 % of the grantees were from Santiago. The situation improved the following year, when the percentage of recipients from the RM dropped to 62 %.

Another matter of regional inequality is shown in the next figure. It is more attractive for new doctors or graduate students to join research teams in Santiago because they have more experience, obtain more funding, attend more conferences, etc. than peers elsewhere in the country. As a result, a significant portion of those who obtain the President of the Republic Scholarship who are from outside of the RM end up working in Santiago, which creates a brain drain for the regions.

It has recently been proposed that recipients be required to pay back the scholarship by working outside of the RM for a period of time similar to the period spent studying. However, this proposal has not gained momentum and it is thus expected that advanced human capital will continue to be concentrated in the RM.

12.7 The Central Bank's Monetary Policy

Chile's Central Bank is an independent state-run institution that is responsible for maintaining a low level of inflation. Three percent annual inflation has been set as the target of the policy. The main instrument used to achieve this has been the interest rate, which is increased when inflation is above that target point in order to increase the cost of debt and reduce family consumption with the resulting pressure to decrease prices.

This would not have territorial biases in an economy a priori. However, in Chile, inflation is only measured using data from the Gran Santiago area. In other words, information on the good whole prices are used to measure inflation is based exclusively on data from families and businesses located in the RM.

Given the heterogeneity of the Chilean economy, which has northern regions dominated by the mining industry, an industrial central region and the agricultural and aquacultural south, while it is quite likely that the shocks that produce changes in prices in Santiago also do so throughout the territory, these changes do not have to be equal in magnitude and direction.

As a result, the interest rate that acts as an efficient break or accelerator for Santiago is not necessarily adequate for the rest of the territory. The breaking mechanism may be applied before it is necessary in some regions, and acceleration may come too late because their inflation does not follow the dynamic of the RM. The National Institute of Statistics (*InstitutoNacional de Estadísticas*, INE) recently built a new basket with families and purchase points from throughout the country. However, it only distinguishes between the RM and the rest of the regions, which obscures Chile's regional heterogeneity.

Lopez and Aroca (2012) show that the inflation of housing prices reported between 2000 and 2009 demonstrates a high level of heterogeneity in the country. They describe a 'W' pattern with highs in the northern- and southernmost regions and lower rates in the central region with the exception of the RM, where the inflation rate is higher than the rest of the central regions but lower than those of the extremes. This pattern is accentuated during times of higher inflation. As a result, the regions that present inflation processes that differ from that of the RM will receive a monetary policy that is not optimal, generating increased costs of living or a loss of opportunities for growth depending on whether or not its inflation is higher or lower than that of Santiago, respectively.

In another study, Sarrias and Aroca (2011) analyze the synchronization of regional cycles in Chile and show that the further the region is from the RM, the less synchronicity is observed in their economic cycles, which supports the idea of the earlier article. In other words, monetary policy is more efficient for the RM than for any other region, and the further flung the region, the less adequate the monetary policy for promoting growth or limiting families' consumption.

12.8 The Concentrating Mechanisms of the Market

In their book on regional economics and policy, Armstrong and Taylor (2003) argue that the market contains a set of concentrating mechanisms, particularly when there is a dominant city or region like the RM. In these cases, there is a growing congestion of infrastructure and public services, and experience shows that the market and the public sector tend to resolve this problem through increased investment and provision of these goods rather than by reducing the demand for them through more balanced development of the territory.

The section below presents a description of some of the mechanisms of the market that contribute to promoting territorial inequality in Chile and concentration around the RM.

12.8.1 Labor Mobility: Migration and Interregional Commuting

Traditional economic theory teaches that labor migration is an important mechanism for reducing regional or territorial inequalities in salary and unemployment. It is thought that workers will leave regions with high unemployment and go to those that offer more employment opportunities. Reducing the unemployment rate in the region of origin, increasing it in the region of destination and arbitrating the salaries paid in the economy can lead to decreased territorial inequality.

However, Chile's 2002 Population and Housing Census showed that labor mobility in that nation is nearly twice as high as migration. This suggests that a significant percentage of workers have separated the decision about which region to live in from the decision regarding where they should work.

The labor code that regulates relationships between workers and employers has allowed for a shift system in all activities, which has been very attractive to commuters. These shifts range from four consecutive 12-h days with 3 days of rest to 22 consecutive work days with 8 days of rest. According to the 2002 Consensus, the Antofagasta Region had 16,500 workers from other regions. That number represents over 10 % of the local labor force.

In addition, labor commuters report higher average incomes than local workers because those who commute have higher levels of education. This means that the total amount represented by the salaries that are taken to other regions can be very significant. Aroca and Atienza (2008) estimate that the resources that commuters bring to the region of Antofagasta through salaries could be four times as high as the amount that the region receives through the National Regional Development Fund. They also show that only the southern- and northernmost regions of Chile present positive net commuting while the country's central regions report negative net commuting. In other words, the percentage of workers who go from the central region of the country to the north and south (Tarapacá and Antofagasta in the north and Aysén and Magallanes to the south) is higher than the percentage that travels from outlying areas to central regions. This labor mobility significantly concentrates income around the center of the country and is another source of territorial inequality.

12.8.2 Interregional and International Commerce

Hulu and Hewings (1993) developed a methodology that allowed them to show how the impacts of publicly funded projects or policies were distributed among the five sets of islands that comprise Indonesia: Sumatra, Java, Kalimantan, Sulawesi and the Eastern Islands.

They demonstrated that the impact of a project developed in one of the five groups of islands was also distributed to the four remaining groups. However, this distribution was not homogeneous and depended on the level of commerce among the regions. Those that exported more received a greater impact from the projects that were carried out in other regions while those that imported more retained less impact from the projects for themselves.

The results are surprising. For example, it was found that 94.2 % of the total impact of a project developed in the Banking and Financial Sector in Java remained in that region while a project developed in the Electricity, Gas and Water Sector in the Eastern Islands captured less than 10 % of the total impact generated by the project.

This figure shows some estimates for interregional commerce and commerce between Chile and the rest of the world for 1996. It shows that the RM presents a significant commercial surplus with the rest of the regions of the country while maintaining a proportionally greater commercial deficit with the rest of the world. In other words, Santiago imports goods from the rest of the world and exports them to other regions of the country.

The regions outside of the capital present the opposite: significant commercial surpluses with the rest of the world and a deficit with the rest of the country.

Based on the above, we reach a conclusion similar to that of the study on Indonesia in the sense that when a project is executed in a region, a significant portion of its expenditures will end up in the RM while a project carried out in the RM will have very little importance for the rest of the regions. Furthermore, it is likely that the impact on imports from the rest of the world will probably be much more significant. Another result of this is the greater concentration of the demand for goods and services in the RM given that projects developed throughout the country significantly increase demand in the Metropolitan Region but not in the remaining regions.

12.9 The Concentration of Private Sector Decision-Making

The concentration around the RM is not solely a matter of population, government, and a significant portion of the country's economic activity. It also involves the business sector's decision-making centers. For example, when a business needs to obtain a credit from the financial system of a region, it is evaluated in Santiago. This results in delays and reduces the likelihood that the applicant will receive the funds as compared to a situation in which the applicant appeals directly to the decision-maker.

Another example of this concentration can be found in the contributions that are made to the community and universities. Given that the decision-making centers are located in Santiago, its institutions receive greater contributions including those made by companies whose productive apparatus is located in outlying regions because their management entities are located in the RM. For example, mining companies make larger contributions to universities in the capital than to those in mining regions such as Antofagasta, Atacama or Tarapacá. This was reported in a local newspaper on May 20, 2008. The headline indicated that three Santiago universities –Universidad de Chile, Universidad Católica and Universidad de los Andes- received over 74 % of all of the private donations that were made to the Chilean university system.

12.10 Conclusions

Income inequality has been a serious problem in Chile for several decades. Following various governments' failure to significantly change this situation, the nation has been ranked as one of the most unequal countries on the planet. This phenomenon is distributed with some differences throughout the territory. However, studying the country from a spatial perspective shows an additional inequality, namely, a high concentration of income and the benefits of growth around the Metropolitan Region despite the fact that the growth of production in other regions has been higher. In other words, the Metropolitan Region has a very strong capacity to appropriate the income generated by growth in the country.

This article shows that this process of concentration is increasing over time. Over the past decade, three groups have emerged that present notable differences in average income levels, a variable that is posited as the closest thing to an indicator of the wellbeing of inhabitants of Chilean regions. The Metropolitan Region presents the highest income, and the difference between it and the rest of the regions of the country has grown over the course of a decade. A second group is formed by the southern- and northernmost regions, which produce primary goods such as copper, oil, and salmon. The rest of the regions, which are low-income, are located in the central part of the country to the north and south of the Metropolitan Region.

The reasons for the increase in inequality include government actions and the mechanism of the market. The former include the evolution of the fund designed to reduce regional inequalities, the increase in the centralism of public spending, the allocation of government grants for advanced human capital, and the monetary policy of Chile's Central Bank for controlling inflation.

The market mechanisms that increase regional inequality and concentration around the Metropolitan Region include labor mobility, particularly interregional commuting, interregional commerce, and the high concentration of private sector management or decision-making entities in the capital.

Finally, the results suggest that there is an urgent need for a strong regional policy that can revert the current trend, promote more balanced development throughout the country, and decrease concentration around Santiago, the country's capital.

Acknowledgments The author acknowledge the funding received through FONDECYT Project #1111061. Some of the ideas presented in this article were developed through the Regional Science and Public Policy Millennium Scientific Initiative Nucleus.

References

Armstrong H, Taylor J (2003) Regional economics and policy, 3rd edn. Blackwell, London
Aroca P, Atienza M (2008) La conmutación regional en Chile y su impacto en la región de Antofagasta. Rev EURE XXXIV(102):97–120
Aroca P, Hewings GJD (2002) Migration and regional labor market adjustment: Chile 1977–1982 and 1987–1992. Ann Reg Sci 36(2):197–218
Arriagada P(1987) Para un Efectivo Desarrollo Regional. Editado por F. Larraín. Cap. 9 de Desarrollo Económico en Democracia. Publicado por Ediciones Universidad Católica de Chile, Santiago
Baldwin RE, Martin P (2004) Agglomeration and regional growth. In: Henderson VJ, Thisse J-F (eds) Handbook of regional and urban economics, vol 4: cities and geography. Elsevier, North-Holland
Felsenstein D, Portnov BA (2005) Regional disparities in small countries. Springer, New York
Foxley A (1987) Chile y su futuro. Un país posible. CIEPLAN, Santiago
Fujita M, Thisse J-F (2002) Economics of agglomeration: cities, industrial location, and regional growth. Cambridge University Press, Cambridge, UK
Hulu E, Hewings GJD (1993) The development and use of interregional input-output models for Indonesia under conditions of limited information. Rev Urban Reg Dev Stud 5:135–153
Larraín F (1987) Desarrollo Económico en Democracia. (ed). Publicado por Ediciones Universidad Católica de Chile, Santiago
Lopez E, Aroca P (2011) Estimación de la Inflación Regional de los Precios de la Vivienda en Chile (2012). El Trimestre Económico LXXIX(3), # 315, 601–630
Mancha T, Cuadrado-Roura JR, Tripodi D, Rufian D, y Aroca P, Figueroa V (2006) Evolución, lecciones y desafíos de las políticas de desarrollo regional/territorial en Chile. Instituto Universitario de Análisis Económico y Social, Universidad de Alcalá, Madrid, Report for the Inter-American Development Bank and the Government of Chile
Martin P, Ottaviano G (1999) Growing locations: industry location in a model of endogenous growth. Eur Econ Rev 43(2):281–302
Sarrias M, Aroca P (2011) Regional business cycles synchronization in Chile. IDEAR Working Papers, UCN, Chile
Waissbluth M (2006) La reforma del Estado de Chile 1990–2005. De la Confrontación al Consenso. Publicado en el Boletín Electrónico de la ESADE, Barcelona, PUBLIC (www.esade.edu/public)

Chapter 13
The Paradox of Peruvian Growth: The Evolution of Territorial Disparities and Regional Policy

María Teresa Gallo-Rivera, Rubén Garrido-Yserte, Efraín Gonzales de Olarte, and Juan Manuel del Pozo-Segura

13.1 Introduction

The extraordinarily good performance of the Peruvian economy in the last 10 years, in the midst of a worldwide crisis, has been termed by many "the Peruvian miracle", given the spectacular outcomes shown by diverse economic variables, such as the rate of growth of GDP, the low rate of inflation and of unemployment, the increase in exports and the solidity of the financial system.

The rate of growth of Peruvian GDP in the last decade has been double that of Latin America and has increased since 2004 at a rate exceeding 5 % (in 2010 it increased by 8.8 %, compared to 5.9 % for the region). Furthermore, Peruvian GDP in 2010 was triple that registered in 2000 (while Latin American GDP overall in 2010 was double that recorded in 2000). In turn, GDP per capita in Peru has also displayed good performance in the last 10 years (in 2010 it was 2.5 times that of 2000), although it is still far from the average level in the region (which is 1.5 times greater), and far further if compared with Uruguay, Chile and Brazil, which more than double it, or with Mexico and Argentina, whose GDP per capita is 1.7 times that recorded in Peru.

In terms of exports the Peruvian economy has reached figures not previously seen (double those of 2000), increasing in the last 10 years at an average annual rate of 7 %, above the 5 % of the total exports of the region. In terms of imports, progress has been even greater (2.4 times imports in 2000), growing at an annual rate of 10 %, compared to 7 % in the region. This means the degree of openness to

M.T. Gallo-Rivera (✉) • R. Garrido-Yserte
Department of Economics and Business Management Department, University of Alcala, Madrid, Spain
e-mail: maria.gallo@uah.es; ruben.garrido@uah.es

E. Gonzales de Olarte • J.M. del Pozo-Segura
Catholic University of Peru, Lima, Peru
e-mail: egonzal@pucp.edu.pe; jmdelpozo@pucp.pe

J.R. Cuadrado-Roura and P. Aroca (eds.), *Regional Problems and Policies in Latin America*, Advances in Spatial Science, DOI 10.1007/978-3-642-39674-8_13,

the exterior has been greater than the average of the region, exceeding Brazil, Argentina and Colombia in 2010.

All this has been achieved while maintaining a rate of inflation of around 2.5 %, the lowest in the region, with adequate rates of activity of approximately 70 % (greater than the average of the set of Latin American countries) and with unemployment rates similar to those prevailing in the region, of approximately 9 % during the last decade.

Furthermore, poverty fell by 23 percentage points between 2001 and 2010, compared to the average 12 percentage points in the region. Extreme poverty has also fallen by 14 points (above all due to the sharp descent in rural zones, of approximately 28 percentage points), compared to the reduction of 6 percentage points in the region on average.[1]

According to Economic Commission for Latin America and the Caribbean (ECLAC), the Gini index moved from 0.525 to 0.458 between 2001 and 2010, while the ratio between the income of the richest quintile and the poorest quintile dropped from 17.1 to 11.5 in the same period (although the contraction has been lower depending on the geographical region, dropping from 11.6 to 8.0 in urban zones and from 9.9 to 7.6 in rural areas). However, despite the relative improvement, both indicators reveal that there still exist profound inequalities in Peru.[2]

Thus, macroeconomic dynamism conceals a much more complex reality affecting the Peruvian economy. Economic growth exists side by side with inequality which, despite the improvements registered, still displays certain disappointing features, namely its persistence and, especially, its territorial distribution. Growth with inclusion continues to be a pending task in Peru.

The persistence of inequality is reflected in the evolution of the distribution of GDP. According to data from the National Institute of Statistics and Informatics of Peru (INEI), while per capita GDP increased by 55 points between 2001 and 2010, real public and private salaries fell by 0.3 and one percentage points respectively, in the same period. Furthermore, between 2001 and 2010 the ratio between GDP per inhabitant between the richest region (Moquegua) and the poorest (Apurímac) was scarcely reduced, from 8.5 to 7.5 times.

In turn, the breach which separates Lima from the remaining regions persists. Today, Lima by itself concentrates 45 % of national production, accounts for 31 % of the economically active population, obtains 57 % of industrial production and 57 % of trade; it also concentrates 81 % and 88 % of financial loans and deposits, respectively.

---

[1] According to data from ECLAC, the 2011 Statistical Yearbook for Latin America and the Caribbean (ECLAC 2011).

[2] Various studies demonstrate the limitations of the national Household Surveys (ENAHO) for the calculation of the Gini index, as they do not capture a significant part of the incomes of the richest households. See, for the Peruvian economy the studies by Yamada and Castro (2006), Figueroa (2010) and Escobal and Ponce (2008), which obtain Gini coefficient values notably higher than those officially published, approximately 0.5 in 2009).

Thus, it can be stated that both the absence of quality in growth and the "tyranny of averages" are two characteristic features of the Peruvian economy and also of Latin America as a whole (UNPD 2010). The significant advances in terms of GDP per capita, in the reduction of poverty, and the advance in the HDI, conceal deep-seated inequalities, especially among territories, but which also include inequalities among groups (by gender or by ethnic or racial groups), and in different aspects related to development.

Such inequalities explain the origin of the paradox of why today the objective conditions of the Peruvian economy have improved (aggregate macro indicators regarding the progress of the economy are better than a decade ago) yet microeconomic malaise persists or has increased.

The thesis that the malaise of persons is an increasing function of the breach between the expectations of and the achievements in fact reached by persons is still in force (Schuldt 2004). Despite strong economic growth, the limited upturn in real salaries and earnings, and in employment levels (especially marked in sectors which make large investments that require little labor, such as mining, the financial sector and telecommunications), the deterioration in the quality of employment (with high levels of sub-employment and informality), and the unequal distribution of income and assets, are some of the reasons why this microeconomic malaise coexists with the notable macroeconomic performance in Peru.

Consequently, although sustained growth is a necessary condition for the reduction of poverty and an increase in welfare, growth in itself is not sufficient (Brady et al. 2007). This is especially true when such indicators are analyzed at territorial level. Thus, although the higher rate of growth of GDP may be responsible for a considerable part of the reduction of poverty, there exist other factors which are important and which may be, in some cases, determining. Examples are the change in the level of inequality or in income elasticities and the Gini coefficient of poverty, which may compromise the achievements of growth in terms of the reduction of poverty and the increase in welfare (Kalwij and Verschoor 2007).

Such factors, therefore, in the case of the Peruvian economy, may be responsible for the persistence of poverty in certain territories, and explain the persistence or widening of territorial gaps. High rates of inequality may make the effects on the reduction of poverty, given growth in GDP, less profound, and may even produce a reduction in the rate of growth of GDP itself.

Thus, the scenario is that economic growth in Peru is reducing poverty, but not in such a way that it produces a greater inclusion, since the dynamism of sectors which generate little employment, such as mining, forms the basis of this growth. Such sectors are generating more employment but not necessarily employment of greater quality, and thus high levels of informality and subemployment persist, without affecting positively and significantly affecting real salaries, which do not rise or in fact fall; this productivity is exported.

These results, therefore, reveal the limitations of the model of Peruvian economic growth, a model which represents benefits in the short term and not necessarily in the long term, as it is not based on solid foundations, thereby compromising future growth.

There exist viewpoints that Peruvian economic growth in recent decades has not been pro-poor, in the sense that the incomes of the poor have not increased by more than the average, to be able to reduce inequality (Francke and Iguíñiz 2006). However, perhaps the recent tendency regarding the contraction of poverty rates and inequality levels in recent years may indicate that advances are being made in the correct direction. Nevertheless, in the light of the economic indicators, it is not necessarily true the pro-poor growth may be the mechanism to reduce territorial differences.

Exploring other dimensions of pro-poor growth, on the basis of the evolution of non-income differences such as education, mortality, problems of nutrition and the delay in child growth, vaccination, or some multidimensional indicator of welfare would permit a deeper analysis of the true scope of the incidence of Peruvian economic growth on these other dimensions of welfare, key to the achievement of economic performance sustainable over time, insofar as they are to be found at the root of the process of the capitalization of society and of its territories (Groose et al. 2008; Klasen 2008).

In summary, the challenge is to unfurl the conditions necessary for the territories to generate an inclusive growth, understood as that capable of increasing the function of social opportunity (Ifzal and Hyun Hwa 2007). That is to say, that which ensures that a set of economic opportunities derived from growth is available to all, especially for the poor or those excluded from the benefits of growth. In referring to economic opportunities, defense is not being made of an equitable distribution of the fruits of growth, but instead of a guarantee that wider sectors of the population and more diverse territories participate in such growth. If the inequality of opportunities explains a significant part of inequality in consumer expenditure and of the capitalization of households and of the territories, the differences in the individual efforts made by their inhabitants would play, consequently, a secondary role (Ferreira and Gignoux 2008).

The objective of the present study is to demonstrate the recent evolution of Peruvian economic growth, which despite having reduced poverty significantly, coexists with and is partly tarnished by inequality. The territorial expression of inequality can be clearly seen in Peru in various social and economic aspects which are necessary to tackle in the task of promoting quality growth, so that the least fortunate sectors also benefit more and better from the fruits of growth and make it a process not only fairer but also more sustainable over time.

To this end, the contents of the study are organized into four sections, in addition to this introduction. The second section is intended to show some indicators which illustrate the perverse dynamic of Peruvian economic growth, in that it coexists with inequality and reinforces territorial disparities. It also shows the evolution of territorial disparities by analyzing certain household assets which reveal the unequal access of opportunities of households and of subnational territories, and offers some reflections regarding the complementarity of macro- and micro-perspectives in analyses of territorial convergence. The third section analyzes the origins of divergence and regional policies in Peru, with special emphasis on the process of decentralization and on the challenges of regional policy. The study ends with a series of final considerations and recommendations regarding regional disparities and their implications for regional policy.

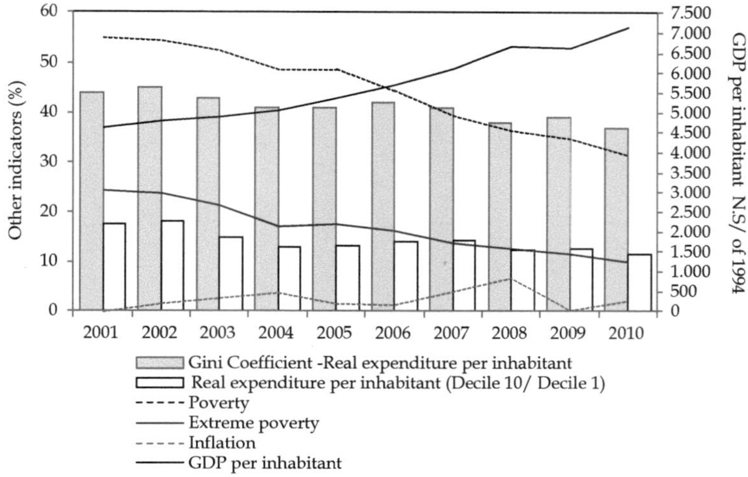

Fig. 13.1 Peru: evolution of socio-economic indicators, 2001–2010 (Source: INEI- statistical yearbooks. Own drafting)

13.2 Economic Performance and the Recent Evolution of Territorial Disparities in Peru

13.2.1 The Dynamic of "Imbalanced Growth" or "Non-inclusive Growth"

As stated in the introduction, the thesis of "imbalanced growth" appears to be still in force concerning the Peruvian economy. This is apparent from the analysis of the evolution of certain socioeconomic indicators for the period 2001–2010 (Fig. 13.1). GDP per capita in the last decade has shown good performance, increasing by almost 55 % compared to 2001. This performance has also been compatible with progressive reductions in poverty rates (in 2001 five of each ten inhabitants were poor, while in 2010 three of each ten were poor) and in extreme poverty rates (which fell from 24.4 % to 9.8 %), and with progressive advances in the Human Development Index (HDI) (moving from 69.1 in 2005 to 72.5 in 2011).[3]

Furthermore, this has been achieved while maintaining low rates of inflation, with high rates of exports and a healthy financial system (the rate of aggregated default of the banking system diminished significantly during the last decade, as a consequence of the growth in economic activity, reaching levels below 2 %, among the lowest in the region).

[3] See UNDP (2011).

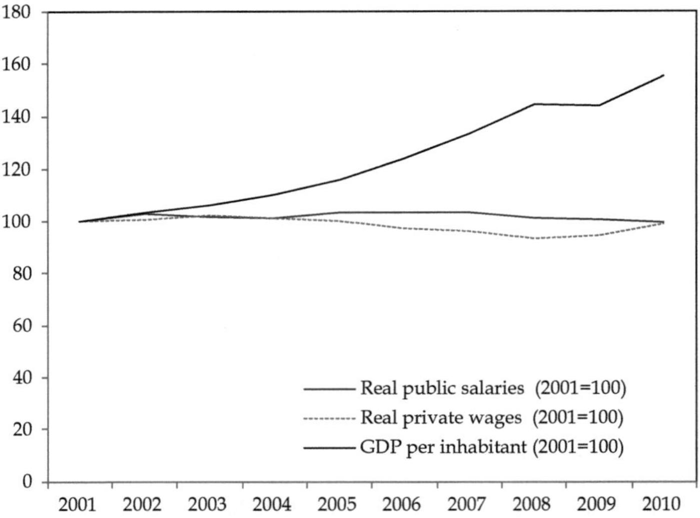

Fig. 13.2 Peru: GDP per inhabitant, public salaries and private wages, 2001–2010 (Source: INEI – statistical yearbooks. Own drafting)

Thus, in the current international context of economic crisis, all the elements which permit us to truly speak of the "Peruvian miracle[4]" are present, if it were not the case that economic growth continues to coexist with high levels of revenue inequality and with deep-seated regional disparities. In other words, the efforts made to reduce inequality in the distribution of income have not been sufficient; this continues to be high (between 2001 and 2010 the Gini coefficient of real expenditure per inhabitant fell from 44 to 37, and the ratio between the richest decile and the poorest decile dropped from 17.6 to 11.5[5]). Moreover, the gap separating the richest region, in terms of GDP per inhabitant, from the poorest scarcely fell (from 8.5 to 7.5). Thus, there appear to be no weighty reasons to affirm that the old tendency to regional divergence is being reverted.

The coexistence of economic growth and the persistence of income inequality is clear when observing the evolution of the real public and private salaries received by Peruvian workers in the last decade (Fig. 13.2). According to data from the INEI,

[4] This is understood to be a dramatic improvement in the economic conditions of a country. Chirinos (2008) offers a definition of economic miracle on the basis of the analysis of the upper quintile of the maximum rates of GDP growth in 1961–2002. It is assumed that the initial conditions constitute an accurate predictor of future growth and it is foreseen that there exists a strong probability that the Peruvian economy will constitute an economic miracle in the next 10 years.

[5] However, the limitations of household surveys must not be forgotten; such surveys are the basis of the estimations of the Gini coefficient and of income per quintile/decile, which according to diverse studies underestimate the true value of inequality as they do not adequately register the income of the richest segments of the population.

and taking 2001 as reference year, while GDP per inhabitant increased by 55 %, private and public salaries not only did not increase, but instead fell in this period.

The low productivity of labor (despite GDP per worker in Peru between 1995 and 2009 increasing at an annual rate of 1.4 %, above the 1 % in the region, this was below that of Argentina, Mexico, Chile, Venezuela, Uruguay and Colombia, above all due to the considerable occupation in low-productivity sectors), a high degree of informality (in 2008 participation in informal employment was 73 %, scarcely lower than the 76 % observed in 1997), and the slow growth of real salaries (due to a shifting of the supply of labor, which restrained real salaries but facilitated greater employment), constitute some of the important structural challenges to the Peruvian economy which cannot be tackled solely by economic growth (UNDP 2010).

The evidences found in the period 2001–2004 purporting to show that Peruvian economic growth would be beginning to take shape in improvements in the welfare of the population, especially the poorest sections (Casas and Yamada 2005), must be intensively reviewed, since the gap of a decade offers a wider perspective of the true accomplishments of the model of growth in Peru. The implications of this model of "imbalanced growth", are of great importance, not only because it does not allow advancing towards objectives of justice and equity, but also in terms of economic efficiency, since the underutilization of resources in specific backward territories acts against the welfare itself of the country, compromising future growth as well as the stability of such growth.

13.2.2 Territorial Disparities and Convergence in Peru from Macro and Micro Perspectives

The concurrence in Peru of macroeconomic dynamism with the maintenance or worsening of territorial disparities is influenced by the heterogeneity of its subnational territories, a feature which on the other hand is common to other Latin American countries. This heterogeneity is determined by the high level of demographic and economic spatial concentration, there coexisting a large quantity of small territories together with a very few extremely large regions. In distinction to the developed countries, Latin America displays a marked correlation between the geographical concentration of economic activity and the levels of territorial equity (measured by the territorial Gini coefficient); that is to say, the territorial concentration of GDP is accompanied in turn by greater levels of inequity (ECLAC 2010b).

In this way, economic territorial disparities constitute an expression of such heterogeneity and, consequently, of the unequal distribution of opportunities for development of the subnational territories. Frequently, use is made of the ratio of GDP per inhabitant between the richest and poorest regions of a country to evaluate the degree of existing territorial disparity. In the case of the Peruvian economy this ratio is 7.5, being one of the highest in the region, together with Argentina and

Brazil; by contrast, this ratio does not exceed the figure of 2 in the advanced countries.

On the other hand, the position occupied by each region in the national rankings, considering alternatively GDP per inhabitant and other socioeconomic variables, such as real average expenditure per household inhabitant and poverty rates (Table 13.1), do not reflect only the heterogeneity of the Peruvian territory, but also evidence the paradox of economic growth which mean that the most backward regions practically do not benefit from greater economic growth.

The departments of Pasco and Junín, located in the Sierra Central of Peru, and Ancash, on the coast, form part of the group of ten regions with the highest GDP per inhabitant in 2010, despite having levels of per capita expenditure which place them below the group of ten departments with the greatest levels of real per capita expenditure. Additionally, it can be observed that poverty rates are high, especially in Pasco where four of each ten persons are poor, despite the notable reduction of poverty (22 points) during the last decade. The opposite occurs with the coastal departments of Tumbes, Lambayeque and La Libertad; these are located among the ten departments with the highest real per capita expenditure, but their levels of GDP per inhabitant do not permit them to be situated among the top ten positions of the ranking.

From the comparison between GDP per inhabitant and poverty rates, it can be observed that the regions which occupy the final ten positions in relation to the first indicator are, with the exception of Tumbes and San Martín, those which display the highest rates of poverty (in Huancavelica and Apurímac, six of each ten persons were poor in 2010).

Other indicators to measure territorial disparities are those used in the traditional analyses of convergence (sigma (σ) and beta (β)). In the Latin American ambit, the studies by ECLAC constitute a reference point for this methodology (Silva 2003; Cuervo 2003, 2004; ECLAC 2009, 2010a). In general terms, such studies show that the diverse models of convergence estimated indicate not only that the advances in terms of sigma and beta convergence have been very modest in the last 40 years, but also that even in certain periods they appear to indicate the presence of divergence, or clear processes of stratification.

That is to say, there is no robust evidence of a process of regional convergence in absolute terms in recent decades, or that if this were the case it would have occurred only among the departments of greatest income. Neither is there evidence of conditional convergence, with paths of stable growth for the set of Peruvian regions in the long term, which could be explained by the presence of two stationary states (regimes) related to the initial levels of income (with a greater speed of convergence among rich regions), or because there existed the presence of stratification (various stationary states), each region converging to its own stationary state (Serra et al. 2006; Odar 2002; Gallo and Garrido 2006; Gallo 2009; Gonzales de Olarte and Trelles 2004; Gonzales de Olarte 2010).

Table 13.1 Peru: GDP per capita, real average expenditure per inhabitant monthly, and population in poverty by regions, 2001–2010

Regions	GDP per capita 2010 (NS 94)[a] (1)	Order	Real average expenditure per capita monthly 2010 (NS 2001)[b] (2)	Order	Poverty rate 2010[b] (3)	Order	Variation 2001–2010 (%) (1)	Variation 2001–2010 (%) (2)	Absolute variation 2001–2010 (3)
Moquegua	14,503.0	1	445.8	4	15.7	20	39.4	25.8	−13.9
Lima y Callao	9,990.0	2	534.4	1	13.5	22	54.8	20.7	−19.9
Arequipa	8,917.0	3	486.8	3	19.6	19	65.5	50.1	−24.5
Tacna	8,067.0	4	498.3	2	14.0	21	34.4	42.1	−18.8
Ica	7,973.0	5	390.4	5	11.6	23	96.6	53.9	−30.1
Pasco	6,187.0	6	269.9	16	43.6	10	20.4	25.7	−22.5
Ancash	5,979.0	7	338.0	11	29.0	16	48.1	48.6	−32.1
Madre de Dios	5,862.0	8	389.3	6	8.7	24	32.0	77.8	−28.0
La Libertad	5,269.0	9	374.8	7	32.6	13	66.6	43.2	−19.5
Junín	4,520.0	10	328.6	12	32.5	14	39.3	43.6	−25.0
Piura	4,241.0	11	296.8	14	42.5	11	55.2	32.3	−20.8
Lambayeque	4,240.0	12	351.4	9	35.3	12	44.2	54.7	−27.7
Cusco	4,202.0	13	246.2	18	49.5	7	91.5	30.7	−25.8
Ucayali	4,190.0	14	340.5	10	20.3	17	36.8	86.1	−50.2
Tumbes	3,957.0	15	367.1	8	20.1	18	44.2	42.5	−26.7
Loreto	3,621.0	16	279.3	15	49.1	9	28.1	53.8	−20.9
Cajamarca	3,235.0	17	240.1	21	49.1	8	29.8	50.8	−28.3
Huancavelica	3,090.0	18	193.5	24	66.1	1	14.4	67.1	−21.9
San Martín	3,075.0	19	323.1	13	31.1	15	51.8	66.5	−35.8
Ayacucho	3,020.0	20	240.7	20	55.9	5	68.9	37.3	−16.6
Puno	2,992.0	21	248.1	17	56.0	4	42.1	41.0	−22.0
Amazonas	2,959.0	22	222.8	22	50.1	6	61.3	30.4	−24.4
Huánuco	2,170.0	23	243.6	19	58.1	3	29.4	62.4	−20.8
Apurímac	1,946.0	24	216.7	23	63.1	2	60.0	37.5	−14.9

Note: Regions in descending order according to per capita GDP registered in 2010
[a]National Institute of Statistics and Informatics (INEI), GDP by Departments, 2001–2010
[b]National Institute of Statistics and Informatics (INEI), 2009–2010 Departmental Statistical Yearbook. Own drafting

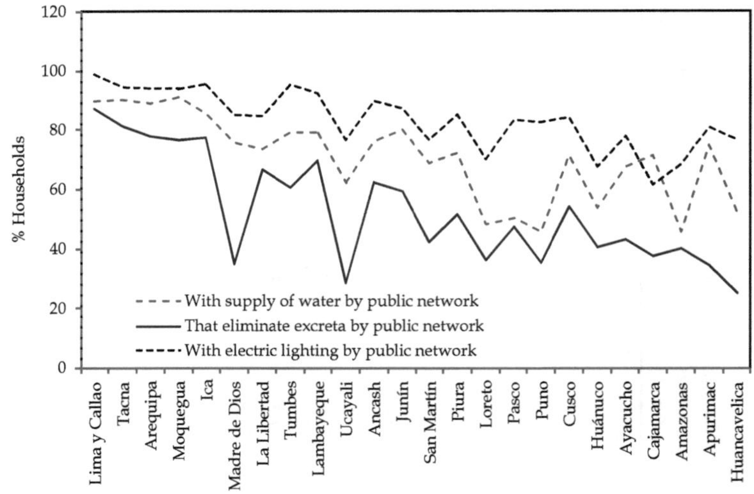

Fig. 13.3 Peru: households with availability of public capital by regions, 2010 (percentages) (Source: INEI – statistical yearbook. Own drafting)

Such results may be conditioned by the type of indicator utilized, since as a general norm use is made of aggregate indicators such as GDP per inhabitant or GDP per occupied person, which present problems of aggregation bias,[6] and which are only shown when an analysis is made of conditional convergence at regional level, combining information from censuses and household surveys or smaller territorial units (Escobal and Torero 2003; Gallo and Garrido 2006).[7]

Given that the majority of economic decisions are taken at family level, and end up by affecting the aggregate behavior of economic variables, it is pertinent to explore the fashion and the context in which such decisions are adopted, to explore more deeply in this way the dynamic of the territories (Attanasio and Székely 1999; Carter and Barret 2006). Figures 13.3 and 13.4, in which the regions have been ranked in descending order according to the levels of expenditure per capita of households (and not by GDP per capita), show that there exists a positive correlation for each of the three variables of access to basic services (public capital) and the level of expenditure, while there exists a negative correlation between the indicator of unsatisfied basic needs and the level of household expenditure.

Figure 13.5, in which the regions have also been ranked in descending order according to expenditure levels, shows territorial disparities in terms of the

[6] Such indicators are of limited use because they do not consider the multidimensional nature of regional growth and the true dynamics and structural problems of subnational realities, above all in countries with high rates of inequality in the distribution of income (Gallo and Garrido 2006: Gallo 2009).

[7] As examples in other countries, see the works of Azzoni et al. (2001); Figueroa and Herrero (2003); Herrero et al. (2010).

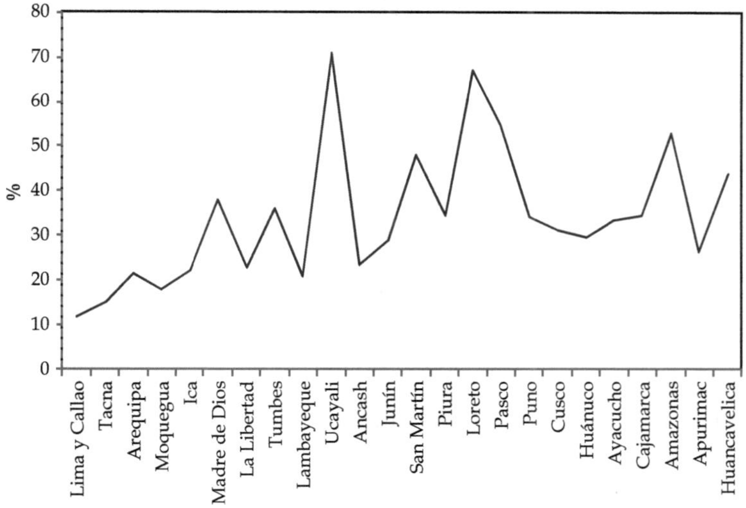

Fig. 13.4 Peru: population with at least one unsatisfied basic need by regions, 2010 (percentages) (Source: INEI – statistical yearbook. Own drafting)

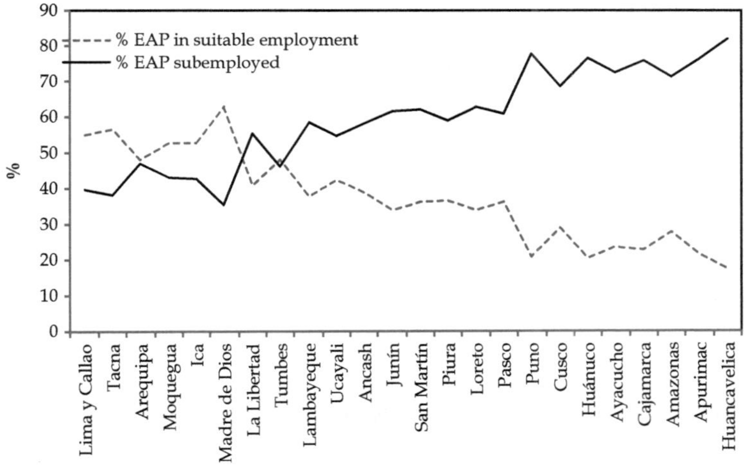

Fig. 13.5 Peru: economically active population (EAP), according to employment levels by regions, 2010 (percentages) (Source: INEI – statistical yearbook. Own drafting)

conditions of the labor market. There exists a positive correlation between the expenditure per capita of households and the percentage of the population which is adequately employed, while there is a negative correlation between the per capita expenditure of the household and the percentage of the population which is subemployed; in other words, a greater proportion of the workers who live in the poorest departments are subemployed (by hours or by income), in relation to those who live in the departments with higher levels of per capita consumption or expenditure.

Consequently, it can be stated that there exist notable differences in the assets possessed by Peruvian households (public, human and private), which are conditioned by the level of consumption (expenditure) per capita of them. In other words, there exist better life conditions and opportunities for development in those places in which the per capita expenditure of the household is relatively greater. These initial or starting conditions of the diverse Peruvian regional realities condition the path of growth and of regional development. It is therefore necessary to formulate political interventions in a differentiated fashion, since the necessities to be met or the assets to be promoted will be different in each region, as will the rhythms and sequences of such interventions (Attanasio and Székely 1999; Carter and Barret 2006).

To reduce the gap in territorial disparities, through policies of concentration on households, will require measures aimed at increasing the stock of their assets (productive, human, social, etc.); the modification of the rate at which these assets are used to generate greater revenue; and, also, the elimination of the limitations (income restrictions, access to credit and uncertainty) faced by households in accumulating assets which generate income.

Although these considerations may seem obvious, they are of extreme importance, since as has been shown, the extraordinary growth of the last decade has not permitted improvement in the capitalization of households, especially those located in the poorest territories. Thus, only a few agents have benefited from macroeconomic dynamism, leaving exposed the fragility of such growth, which places in question the stability and future growth of the regional territories. It is important to deep into the problematic experimented by the people excluding of the economic welfare, especially by the poor people and in the own perception they have of the well being. The arguments about the existence of conflicts between global and local discourses of development are useful to manage social change and public policy that are sensitive to the cultural and political biases (Copestake 2009; Muñoz et al. 2007).

13.3 The Origins of Divergence and Policies in Peru

13.3.1 The Origins of Regional Divergence

The territorial socioeconomic disparities in Peru form part of an economic model which permits macroeconomic growth based on productive sectors,[8] located in distinct regions, which are weakly articulated or, simply, not articulated among

[8] The most dynamic sectors, such as mining and services, are scarcely exchanged within the country and among regions. Mining exports practically all its production and services are not tradable.

each other (Gonzales de Olarte 2000, 2003a, b). This lack of articulation is one of the principal causes of the divergence in long-term growth among regions (Del Pozo and Espinoza 2011; Delgado and Del Pozo 2011), whose consequence is inequality of income among regions and its persistence.

The current Peruvian economic model is characterized by being an exporter of primary products and supplier of urban services (PESER) (Gonzales de Olarte 1993, 1998a, b), generated by the structural adjustment inspired in the Washington Consensus (Williamson 1990), which Peru complied with scrupulously. This model has three characteristics which generate conditions for divergence among regions: (1) the principal exporting sector is primary and predominantly that of mining (representing over 40 % of total exports since the year 1990), which functions on the basis of capital-intensive technologies. Consequently, this generates little employment, directly and indirectly, causing the mining regions to be characterized, in general, by low per capita incomes, low effective regional demand and a high level of rural poverty. (2) Given the world demand for raw materials and for gold,[9] Peru has resolved an old problem, that of "external restriction"; the flow of currency is such – due both to the accelerated growth of exports and to the increasing entry of capital- that the rate of exchange has shown a tendency to the revaluation of the nuevo sol during the last 11 years.

This means that imports have become relatively cheap and, consequently, there are no incentives for productive investment in sectors and regions which cannot compete with abroad, which has produced a situation very similar to the "Dutch illness". This scenario has inhibited the generation of greater employment and domestic revenue in the regions, since it is easier and cheaper to import than to produce. (3) The redistributive capacity of the Peruvian state is quite limited, for various reasons. Firstly, because total tax pressure, including the three levels of government, does not reach 18 % of GDP, which is insufficient to tackle the problem of redistribution via public expenditure. In second place, budget allocated to regions has been insufficient to promote a "big push" in regional growth, and also there was a political trade off for Central Government between to transfer more financial resources to regional governments and lose political power (Caravedo 1992). In third place the Fujimori's administration was anti decentralization, because its political regime close to a centralized dictatorship, which has not been exclusive of this when comparing to past administrations (Slater 1991), In fourth place a lack of bureaucratic and technical capacities to improve the efficiency of public expenditure arose, as an outcome of the reduction of the Peruvian State size. This meant the inability of the State to correct the tendencies towards regional disparity.

[9] The principal export product of Peru is gold, which has represented almost 20 % of total exports in at least the last 5 years (according to customs data). This is due above all to the enormous rise in its price, which in the context of the international crisis has become the safest refuge as a reserve value.

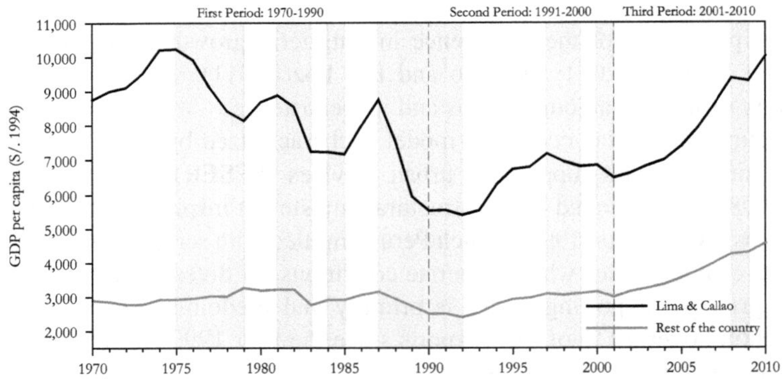

Fig. 13.6 Peru: GDP per capita in Lima and other regions, 1970–2010 (Note: shade intervals correspond to recessions of national GDP per capita. Source: INEI – statistical yearbooks. Own drafting)

These factors have been present during the last 40 years, with some variations, due above all to the "exogenous shocks" which Peru has suffered (Dancourt et al. 1997). This means that divergence has had a cyclical character, that is to say it has been strongly influenced by the international situation and by the economic model. The international situation has contributed to accentuating divergence in times of upswing, while in periods of recession the tendency reverts and moves towards convergence. However, it has been the economic model which has marked the long-term trend.

13.3.1.1 Long-Term Cycle 1970–2010

The long-term economic cycle of a regionalized Peru has had three characteristics (Fig. 13.6): (1) From 1970 to 2010 it had three phases: a recessionary one from 1970 to 1990, a transitionary one from 1991 to 2000 and one of sustained growth from 2001 to 2010. (2) The Lima cycle has been the most pronounced; both in the phase of upturn and in that of recession the rate of growth has been more pronounced than that of the remaining regions of Peru. (3) The tendency to convergence between Lima (the center) and the rest of the regions (the periphery) has occurred in periods of crisis, while in the phases of upturn the trend has been towards divergence (Del Pozo and Espinoza 2011).

Yet perhaps the most important characteristic of these 40 years is that the breach between GDP per capita in Lima and the rest of the country has fallen from 4 to 1 to 2 to 1 (in the periods of recession). This demonstrates a considerable productive disparity, which suggests the non-existence of mechanisms which permit the distribution of the fruits of growth in an endogenous fashion and which require the redistributive intervention of the state. This productive disparity is reflected in the distribution of income, which has not been corrected in recent years despite the striking growth of the Peruvian economy. As stated by Mendoza et al. (2011): "The distribution of income, approximated from national accounts with the real average income of independent and self-employed workers, of the country and the city, shows that Peru in 2010 is a more unequal country than at the beginning of the 1980s (...) The Gini coefficient in 2010 is exactly the same as that of 1980: 0.6" (pp. 101).

These fluctuations do not necessarily lead to regional convergence in the growth phase and, consequently, to the possibilities of a reduction in regional disparities; they have certain current causes which tend to deepen them. As growth is dependent on imports, this means that the growth of one region or another is relatively independent from the others, because they do not have the capacity to substitute the products imported. As a result, a parallel growth is occurring among them. The same is occurring between each city and its respective rural surrounding, whose economic relations depend on imported inputs and capital, largely due to the relative cheapening of the dollar. Consequently, as will be seen below, rural poverty decreases more slowly than urban poverty, since urban growth is not connected to rural growth. The process of investment has been concentrated in the sectors exporting primary products, above all in mining and gas, and in the cities in service sectors which, being exported and non-tradable, respectively, produce few linkages between city and country, in each region.

13.3.1.2 Scarcity of Spatial Integration

To a large extent, divergence is due to the fact that regional policies applied has not led to the physical, economic and state integration of the distinct regions (departments) is highly unequal. It has been shown that greater integration leads to greater human development and less poverty (Gonzales de Olarte et al. 2011; Gonzales de Olarte 2012).

A measurement to approximate the effect of regional policies is the global integration index (Table 13.2), which is a sum of economic integration via the labor and credit markets, of physical integration through roads, electricity and telephones, and of state integration through taxation and public expenditure by departments. As observed, a greater integration index means a greater human development index (HDI). The least developed departments are Huancavelica, Cajamarca and Huánuco, with an important mining sector. The relatively developed departments are Arequipa, Lambayeque and Lima-Callao. The distance of development between Lima-Callao and Huancavelica/Cajamarca is so great that convergence between the two, in terms of development, may take many years.

The main problem detected in each department is the quasi-divorce between the urban and rural dynamic. Using Granger causality analysis (Table 13.3) it can be observed that urban growth does not cause rural growth for selected departments

Table 13.2 Peru: indicators of integration, 2007

	Economic integration			Physical integration				State integration				
	% EAP employed	Loans/ GDP (%) 1/	Index	Paved roads (%)	Dwellings with electricity (%)	Household with landlines (%)	Index	Contribution tax system %	Gasto de gob/PIB (%)	Index	Human development index (HDI)	Global integration index
Total	43.0	51.8	47.4	15.9	74.1	27.7	39.2	14.2	6.6	10.4	0.62	32.3
Huancavelica	25.0	2.14	13.6	5.3	55.9	2.9	21.4	3.6	11.6	7.6	0.54	14.2
Cajamarca	30.3	10.1	20.2	9.5	40.2	7.1	18.9	5.2	8.9	7.1	0.56	15.4
Amazonas	28.8	7.1	18.0	15.1	48.5	5.0	22.9	5.1	12.4	8.7	0.57	16.5
Huánuco	28.3	13.3	20.8	9.0	43.1	7.3	19.8	6.1	12.8	9.4	0.57	16.7
Ayacucho	30.4	10.1	20.2	9.2	51.2	7.3	22.5	6.3	16.5	11.4	0.56	18.1
Pasco	38.5	4.2	21.3	7.1	69.0	6.6	27.6	6.6	5.3	6.0	0.59	18.3
Cusco	29.2	12.1	20.7	11.3	64.4	2.9	26.2	14.0	8.3	11.1	0.58	19.3
Puno	21.3	29.6	25.4	19.4	57.5	4.6	27.2	6.0	11.0	8.5	0.56	20.4
Loreto	31.3	10.9	21.1	18.9	61.3	19.9	33.3	7.4	10.9	9.2	0.59	21.2
San Martín	29.0	20.7	24.8	20.0	59.0	11.6	30.2	6.7	11.5	9.1	0.59	21.4
Apurímac	34.1	11.3	22.7	9.4	56.6	20.1	28.7	6.4	22.7	14.6	0.56	22.0
Junín	36.1	15.0	25.6	11.6	73.4	16.9	33.9	9.3	6.8	8.0	0.60	22.5
Ucayali	36.7	16.6	26.7	10.8	64.6	18.4	31.3	11.7	9.2	10.5	0.60	22.8
Piura	39.2	15.7	27.4	20.3	66.4	20.5	35.7	8.0	6.1	7.0	0.60	23.4
Ancash	41.8	9.0	25.4	19.2	73.2	20.1	37.5	8.6	6.1	7.3	0.60	23.4
La Libertad	45.7	20.0	32.8	13.8	71.9	16.9	34.2	8.8	4.9	6.9	0.62	24.6
Madre de Dios	47.1	16.9	32.0	18.3	68.3	10.3	32.3	13.7	8.6	11.1	0.63	25.1
Moquegua	42.9	5.9	24.4	22.7	80.3	17.7	40.2	19.4	4.8	12.1	0.65	25.6
Tacna	37.3	14.0	25.7	26.1	81.6	19.1	42.2	23.4	6.8	15.1	0.65	27.7
Tumbes	39.6	21.7	30.6	20.5	81.1	17.9	39.9	11.3	13.8	12.6	0.65	27.7
Ica	55.9	14.5	35.2	25.9	76.2	23.6	41.9	11.8	5.5	8.6	0.65	28.6
Arequipa	47.6	16.1	31.8	23.2	84.2	28.6	45.3	17.8	3.9	10.9	0.65	29.3
Lambayeque	46.7	24.2	35.5	33.7	76.1	28.2	46.0	10.1	6.4	8.2	0.62	29.9
Lima y Calla	52.7	79.6	66.2	24.9	93.0	49.7	55.9	24.0	5.8	14.9	0.68	45.6

Note: 1/ Corresponds to the variable Loans as % of GDP for the 2009. Departments sorted in ascending order according to Global Integration Index

Sources: UNDP/ Human Development Team. Peru, Human Development Report 2007 and various sectoral statistics. Own drafting

Table 13.3 Granger causality test between GDO urban and rural GDP in selected regions, 1970–2010

	Arequipa		Cusco		La Libertad	
	Var. urban GDP (t)	Var. rural GDP (t)	Var. urban GDP (t)	Var. rural GDP (t)	Var. urban GDP (t)	Var. rural GDP (t)
Var. urban GDP (t-1)	0.297	0.100	0.261	0.247[a]	0.358[a]	0.035
	(0.196)	(0.081)	(0.185)	(0.128)	(0.187)	(0.094)
Var. rural GDP (t-1)	0.174	0.118	0.323	0.335[a]	0.364	0.213
	(0.450)	(0.186)	(0.248)	(0.172)	(0.361)	(0.182)
Constant	107.728[b]	33.447[a]	42.303[a]	11.445	59.564	41.514[a]
	(47.650)	(19.647)	(22.746)	(15.762)	(40.592)	(20.483)
R-squared	0.102	0.093	0.146	0.259	0.190	0.065
Sigma (estimated)	251.2	103.6	127.5	88.34	222.1	112.1
F test GDP Urb/Rur (t-1)	0.150	1.522	1.699	3.728[a]	1.018	0.137

	Lima y Callao		Loreto		Synthetic region	
	Var. urban GDP (t)	Var. rural GDP (t)	Var. urban GDP (t)	Var. rural GDP (t)	Var. urban GDP (t)	Var. rural GDP (t)
Var. urban GDP (t-1)	0.534[c]	0.010	0.447[b]	0.096	0.392[b]	0.142
	(0.165)	(0.007)	(0.187)	(0.146)	(0.168)	(0.148)
Var. rural GDP (t-1)	−4.199	−0.113	−0.052	0.303	−0.134	−0.046
	(3.862)	(0.175)	(0.237)	(0.186)	(0.195)	(0.172)
Constant	1.116.542[a]	55.957[a]	32.750	5.932	106.233[b]	36.986
	(608.769)	(27.607)	(21.202)	(16.612)	(43.547)	(38.457)
R-squared	0.226	0.050	0.174	0.148	0.135	0.025
Sigma (estimated)	3.401	154.2	122.7	96.16	222.8	196.8
F test GDP Urb/Rur (t-1)	1.182	1.853	0.0488	0.431	0.471	0.915

Note: The number of observations is 39. Standard errors in parentheses. First differences of series to correct non-stationarity. GDP measured in millions of S/. 1994. GDP urban (rural) causes GDP rural (urban) in the sense of Granger if the F test of significance is significant at less than 10 %
[a]Significant at 10 %
[b]Significant at 5 %
[c]Significant at 1 %. Own drafting

(only in the case of Cusco, although weakly). We have included an economic region comprised of adjoining departments: Lambayeque, Cajamarca and Amazonas, but neither have we have found that causality exists. It is obvious that there exists a problem of integration among cities and their rural surroundings, and thus urban growth, which in general is high, is not transmitted to its rural periphery, which largely explains rural poverty. Thus, the Peruvian state must design policies for the alleviation of poverty, concentrated in rural zones.

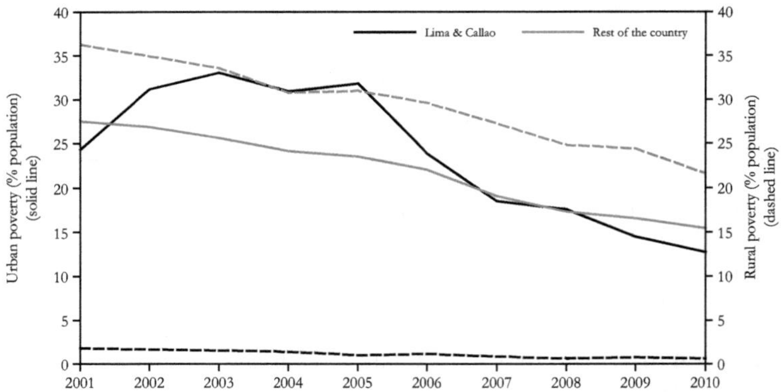

Fig. 13.7 Peru: evolution of urban and rural poverty in Lima and Callao and the rest of the country, 2001–2010 (Note: poor population includes those extreme and non-extreme poor. Extreme poor: those with an income lower than the basic food basket. Non-extreme poor: those with an income under an essential basket including basic food basket. Source: INEI – Household National Surveys. Own drafting)

13.3.2 Poverty, "Pro-poor" Growth Policies and Regional Policy

This lack of productive chains between the urban and rural zone of the country is reflected in the relative backwardness of the latter in terms of GDP per capita[10] and, principally, in the differences in the rate of poverty between the two zones, which contrasts with its progressive reduction achieved between 2001 and 2010, indicated in Sect. 13.2.1. This disparity is clearly apparent when poverty in both zones is disaggregated into that corresponding to Lima and Callao and to the rest of the country (Fig. 13.7).

On the one hand, in the case of poverty in Lima and Callao, that corresponding to the urban zone increased at the beginning of the decade and reached its most critical point in 2005 (32 %), when it even outstripped that of the rural zone in the rest of the country. From then onwards, the urban poverty of Lima and Callao displayed an accelerated reduction, to the point at which in the following 5 years it fell by 20 percentage points (12 % in 2010). In turn, rural poverty in the capital of the country has remained stable and at a considerably low level (under 2 %). The notable decline in the urban poverty of Lima and Callao suggests that this initiated a process of long-term convergence towards the level of poverty of the rural zone.

Moreover, although rural poverty in the rest of the country has displayed a greater level than urban poverty, both have shown a sustained decline (greater than 12 percentage points in both cases between the beginning and the end of the

[10] For 1970, the relation between urban and rural GDP per capita was 3–1. Although the quotient between the two fell by almost half for 2010 (1.8), rural GDP per capita continues to be low (around 4,000 soles at constant 1994 prices).

period). However, rural poverty has been, on average, eight percentage points higher than urban poverty. Thus, in contrast to what has occurred in Lima and Callao, the urban and rural poverty rates of the rest of the country do not show a process of convergence for the period studied, but instead have followed two differentiated paths.

Nevertheless, it is clear there was an important governmental effort to reduce the poverty rates. An important part of these pro-poor policies adopted the form of subsidies to reduce poverty with a focalized strategy, mainly in rural areas. The most important of these is "Juntos" (together), a comprehensive social program started in 2005, aiming to reduce child malnutrition and increase human capital in populations under social exclusion and poverty conditions. Its guidelines, inspired by other successful social programs in Latin America such as 'Bolsa-Familia' (Brasil) and 'Oportunidades' (Mexico), who reached its expected results in several dimensions of welfare (Perova and Vakis 2009).

In general, government expenditure per capita in the rest of the country displayed a sustained increase between 2001 and 2010, increasing at an average annual rate of 5.5 %, in distinction to what occurred in Lima and Callao, where it only increased by 2.5 % per year (Fig. 13.8). Nevertheless, there exists a persistent centralization of per capita expenditure in Lima and Callao, which is reflected in the greater levels of government expenditure in this region. Although the gap narrowed between 2001 and 2010, per capita expenditure in Lima and Callao is still 180 % of that of the rest of the country.

It is therefore fitting to ask what has been the role of government expenditure in the reduction of poverty rates in Lima and Callao and the rest of the country. In the case of the population in extreme poverty, the rate for the rest of the country fell dramatically, from 36 % at the beginning of the decade to 12 % at the end, in accordance with the notable increase in government expenditure per capita (panel A of Fig. 13.8). In the case of Lima and Callao, the reduction of the population in extreme poverty was not as drastic, as occurred with rural poverty in this region. Thus, the population in extreme poverty has been maintained at a low level and only fell by one percentage point.

The evolution of non-extreme poverty in the rest of the country displays a different trajectory to that of extreme poverty. Thus, in contrast to the notable reduction of the latter, the former was only reduced by five percentage points between 2001 and 2010, despite the sustained increase in government expenditure per capita (panel B of Fig. 13.8). By contrast, non-extreme poverty in Lima and Callao has displayed a rapid decline since 2005, causing the rate of non-extreme poverty to fall by half between 2001 and 2010 (24 % and 12.5 %, respectively). Similarly, note should be made in this last region of the similarity of the rates of extreme and rural poverty and the resemblance between non-extreme and urban poverty for all years. This provides indices that extreme poverty in Lima and Callao is concentrated principally in the rural zone and non-extreme poverty in the urban zone.

One way of quantifying by how much, on average, the increase in government expenditure per capita contributed to the change in poverty rates in the departments

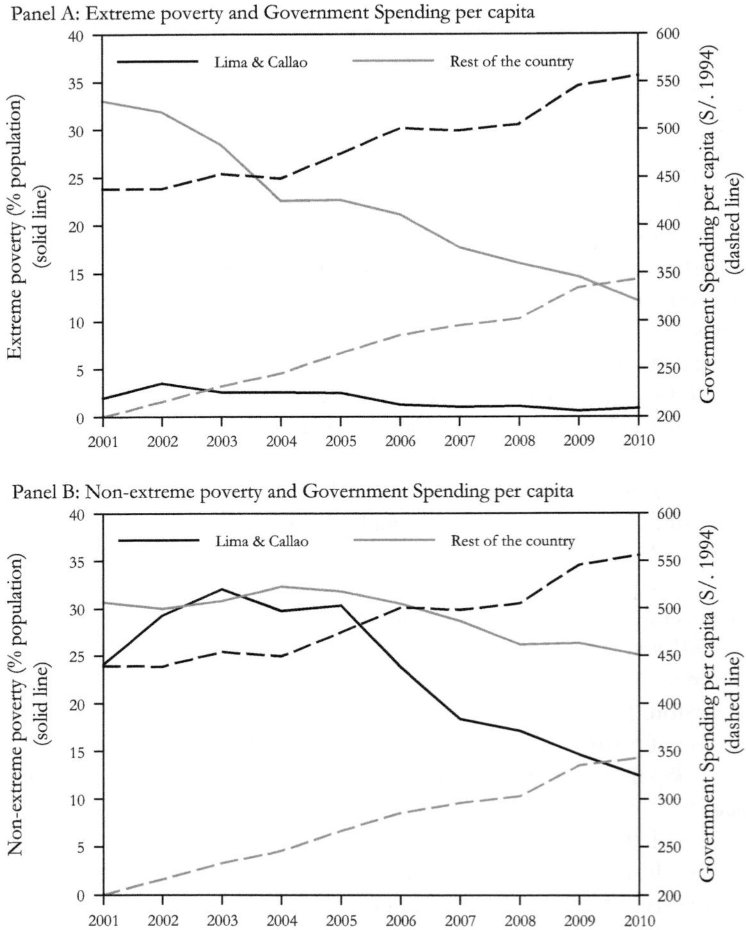

Fig. 13.8 Peru: poverty and per capita government spending of Lima and the rest of the country, 2001–2010 (Note: extreme poor: those with an income lower than the basic food basket. Non-extreme poor: those with an income under an essential basket including basic food basket. Source: INEI – Household National Surveys. Own drafting)

comprising the rest of the country consists of determining the elasticities of poverty with respect to government expenditure per capita for the last decade. If this were the case, government expenditure in the different departments would have been "pro-poor". The results (the dark bars in Fig. 13.9) indicate that in all departments the poverty-government expenditure per capita elasticity is negative, and thus the increase in government expenditure was accompanied by a reduction in poverty rates between 2001 and 2010. Nevertheless, there exists a strong variation between the values of the elasticity (the variation coefficient is 60 %).

The greatest elasticity corresponds to Ica (2.41 %), where an increase in government expenditure of 1 % produced a reduction of poverty of 2.4 % for the period.

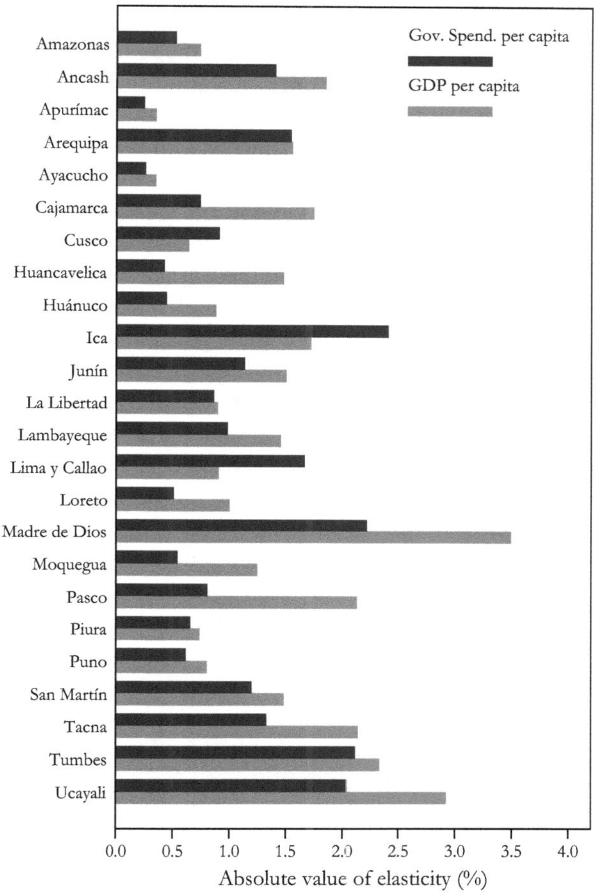

Fig. 13.9 Peru: poverty elasticity to GDP per capita and per capita government expenditure (%), 2001–2010 (Note: poor population includes those extreme and non-extreme poor. Extreme poor: those with an income lower than the basic food basket. Non-extreme poor: those with an income under an essential basket including basic food basket. Elasticities computed using the midpoint method (change over average value 2001–2010 of variables). Source: INEI – Household National Surveys and Statistical Yearbooks. Own drafting)

This is followed by Madre de Dios (2.22) and Tumbes (2.12). In only ten departments is this greater than 1 %, indicating that poverty is reduced more than proportionally by an increase in government expenditure. In turn, Ayacucho and Apurímac present the lowest elasticities: in both, an increase in government expenditure per capita of 1 % reduced poverty by 0.25 %. In general, in 14 departments poverty was reduced less than proportionally by the increase in expenditure. It having been established that per capita government expenditure has been, on average, "pro-poor", it is fitting to ask whether per capita GDP growth has also been "pro-poor". The answer to this question is to be found in the same previous graph and corresponds to the poverty-per capita GDP growth elasticity (the light-colored bars of Fig. 13.9).

The results confirm the "pro-poor" character of growth, since the departmental elasticities are negative, although the values continue to present a notable heterogeneity (the variation coefficient is 54 %). The maximum elasticity corresponds to that of the department of Madre de Dios (3.49), indicating that, on average, an increase of 1 % in GDP per capita produced a reduction of poverty of 3.5 %. This is followed by Ucayali (2.92) and Tumbes (2.33). In total, in 15 departments the elasticity is greater than one, indicating that GDP growth generates a more than proportional reduction of poverty.

Thus, the same two departments with the lowest elasticity regarding per capita government expenditure present the lowest elasticities in respect of growth. In these, an increase of 1 % in GDP per capita led to a reduction of poverty of only 0.35 %. In total, nine departments display an elasticity lower than 1. It is fitting to mention that Lima and Callao present the elasticity closest to 1 within this group, since an increase in GDP per capita of 1 % reduced poverty by 0.9 %.

Is growth more pro-poor than government expenditure? On the basis of the information in the graph, the poverty-government expenditure per capita elasticities are lower than the poverty-growth elasticity. In other words, poverty was reduced more by the growth of GDP per capita than by government expenditure per capita. In only three departments was the effect of the latter greater: Lima and Callao, Ica, and Cusco. A plausible explanation for this is that the centralization of the state has caused these to be characterized by the concentration of the majority of expenditure and government poverty reduction programs (especially in Lima and Callao) and by a greater concentration of such programs in these departments. As a result, the reduction of poverty was more a result of state activity than of the mechanisms of automatic reversion generated by growth, in contrast to what occurred in the rest of the country.

These elasticities can be linked to the impact of regional policies reflected in the Global Integration Index presented in Table 13.2. In general, a greater index is associated with a greater reduction of poverty, given the increase in government expenditure, since the correlation between the global index and the poverty-government expenditure per capita elasticity is positive (56 %) and statistically significant at 1 %. In fact, if Lima and Callao are left aside (due to their high index of global integration in relation to the other departments), the level of significance and correlation between the two variables increase (62 %). By contrast, an improved global integration does not have a statistically relevant relation to the poverty-growth elasticity, which is reflected in a low correlation whether Lima and Callao are included or not (12 % and 33 %).

13.3.3 The Decentralization Process, Advances and Limitations

Decentralization has been an old aspiration of the regions, from the end of the nineteenth century onwards, to achieve certain degrees of autonomy with regard to central government; its origin is obviously provincial, in opposition to the capital of Lima (Contreras 2002). At heart, decentralization is a process of power sharing, through the transfer of expenditure capacities and of tax collection to the subnational governments. The central idea has been that state decentralization, in addition to resolving the problem of governmental centralism, should promote local and regional development, understood as the increase of production, productivity and revenue, in addition to improving the efficiency of the state. That is to say, it has been thought that decentralization could correct the inequalities generated by the economic model and, consequently, should be a factor of convergence (Lessmann 2009). In general, more has been requested than can be given, above all taking into account the distributive situation in Peru and the size and efficiency of the state.

Consequently, Peru has experienced various attempts at decentralization (Contreras 2002; Planas 1998), all frustrated for one reason or another, the last being that which originated in the 1979 Constitution, corrected by the 1993 Constitution, which reduced the scope of the former due to the auto-coup of the government of Alberto Fujimori. When Peru returned to a democratic regime in the year 2000, decentralization was reinitiated, in compliance with an electoral promise of the government of Alejandro Toledo in the year 2001. To this end, the 1993 Constitution was modified and the decentralization law was promulgated, followed by various other measures.

The first important measure was the creation of as many regional governments as departments, probably to avoid the complex problem of establishing regions on the basis of integrating adjoining departments. This decision has generated more than a few obstacles to decentralization being a means of resolving various problems originating in political centralism and in territorial economic concentration.

Decentralization is a means of redistributing political power and changing the assignation of the public budget, which would contribute to the development and deepening of democracy. But it is also an end, insofar as it generates a new political and economic culture (Gonzales de Olarte 2004). This reform has already completed its first decade, and three consecutive regional governments have been elected, in addition to the election, dating from over 30 years ago, of local governments. However, what has decentralization changed?

Firstly, decentralization does not appear to be contributing to a greater growth of the regions and of local authorities, insofar as the principal factors behind regional growth have been private investment, central government public investment and trade opening. Due to rather rigid rules and regulations and the lack of management capacities, the majority of regional governments have not succeeded in investing all the resources available to them. For example, the resources of the fees on mining, oil or gas, which go directly to the regional governments, have been accumulated without being able to be spent. Secondly, decentralization has not yet produced local and regional governments with sufficient capacities to manage their finances and, consequently, their contribution to regional growth is due to the amounts invested more than to those investing them.

Nevertheless, decentralization has contributed to reducing poverty, insofar as local governments have had greater resources, although in general it is central government programs of poverty alleviation which have been more important in reducing poverty, above all due to the scale of expenditure. However, although in the majority of departments inequality, measured by the Gini coefficient, has fallen

Table 13.4 Regional Gini Indices (%), 2001–2010

	2001	2002	2003	2004	2005	2006	2007	2008	2009	2010	Var. (%)
Amazonas	59.6	59.5	60.1	55.8	56.2	54.4	57.8	55.8	57.5	58.6	−1.7
Ancash	56.2	57.8	55.3	53.7	55.4	51.3	53.0	51.5	47.6	50.3	−10.5
Apurímac	60.4	60.8	55.3	59.2	58.1	62.1	61.5	57.5	53.2	53.1	−12.1
Arequipa	51.9	46.2	49.1	47.7	45.3	42.8	46.2	45.9	45.9	44.9	−13.6
Ayacucho	56.8	58.2	55.1	55.1	59.5	56.6	57.2	53.5	52.0	51.0	−10.2
Cajamarca	56.3	57.0	56.3	55.4	55.3	56.7	58.5	60.0	55.4	59.1	5.0
Cusco	64.0	58.4	55.1	55.7	56.8	58.9	57.3	54.9	54.8	53.3	−16.7
Huancavelica	71.6	61.0	59.3	63.3	65.9	65.3	61.6	60.0	60.5	60.0	−16.3
Huánuco	65.1	66.0	68.7	64.4	64.3	68.0	60.5	58.6	54.7	57.2	−12.1
Ica	34.1	44.2	35.9	45.6	42.6	43.4	36.1	35.6	35.9	33.9	−0.5
Junín	47.0	52.2	45.3	46.5	49.1	48.8	49.3	52.9	45.3	43.0	−8.4
La Libertad	48.2	52.0	50.9	50.2	49.8	50.6	58.6	48.4	49.6	46.3	−4.0
Lambayeque	47.1	41.8	40.8	45.7	45.9	43.7	46.9	44.1	41.4	41.1	−12.8
Lima y Callao	50.0	53.3	55.5	46.2	50.9	47.7	47.7	45.2	46.4	44.8	−10.4
Loreto	62.2	60.1	56.4	54.5	53.3	56.6	59.0	55.6	61.2	59.0	−5.3
Madre de Dios	48.4	44.2	43.0	40.8	48.9	47.0	42.7	45.4	43.8	41.2	−14.9
Moquegua	44.1	48.1	48.8	52.3	51.6	51.3	56.3	55.7	52.7	51.9	17.8
Pasco	52.3	53.5	48.1	53.4	52.5	48.9	52.9	56.0	52.9	47.0	−10.2
Piura	54.8	54.7	57.5	49.6	48.3	47.7	49.5	47.1	45.5	46.1	−15.8
Puno	62.3	57.8	57.3	56.2	55.4	55.2	53.5	51.2	51.2	49.6	−20.4
San Martín	52.3	50.7	49.9	51.2	51.5	51.7	55.5	53.9	55.1	52.8	1.0
Tacna	46.2	43.1	48.8	45.1	50.2	49.5	44.2	45.4	43.8	38.7	−16.4
Tumbes	41.8	43.3	34.6	40.7	38.9	39.4	40.7	37.9	38.6	38.5	−7.9
Ucayali	52.5	51.1	52.2	52.7	53.8	50.2	51.4	47.9	44.6	41.7	−20.6

Note: Gini income per capita. Variation (%) refers to the period 2010–2001
Source: INEI-Household Survey. Own drafting

in the last decade, it still remains high (Table 13.4). For example, for 2010, the average difference in per capita income between two individuals in Apurímac and Cusco is, respectively, S/.2,570 and S/.3,900; for Lima and Callao the difference is S/.7,300.[11] A plausible reason for this is that the most important private investments have not been labor-intensive and have had limited multiplying effects upon regional employment.

The supply of state goods and services, at its three levels, has improved above all in coverage, because fiscal resources are greater than previously. What is not easy to determine is whether this is due to the greater availability of resources or to decentralization.

Has the quality of the Peruvian state improved with three levels of government? Yes, insofar as each level of government is fulfilling its functions and exercising its

[11] This occurs because the average difference in income between two individuals corresponds to the double of the Gini index as a percentage of average income (e.g.: a Gini coefficient of 0.4 signifies that the average difference in income between two individuals is 80 % of the average income) (Atkinson 1983).

budget. Thus, there are regions where decentralization is bearing greater fruit, as in the San Martín region, various provincial and district municipalities, where the central government itself has improved its performance, in areas such as the construction of infrastructure. Nevertheless, it is necessary to determine whether all these results are due to the greater availability of resources or to a decentralized public administration.

As a whole, decentralization is giving shape to another state, sustained on democratic forms, but it is not contributing to changing either territorial economic concentration or divergence among regions, which originate the inequality of opportunities in the distinct regions.

13.3.4 The Challenges of Regional Policy and of the Process of Decentralization

As shown, the process of decentralization is still insufficient, as it requires a combination of macroeconomic and sectorial policies and coordination among the levels of government, to promote economic de-concentration.

The lack of coordination among the levels of government, for example, make it possible that in practically all the departments the poverty-government expenditure per capita elasticity is lower than the poverty-growth elasticity, given the low incidence and effectiveness of social policies and of state-promoted welfare which originate such lack of coordination.

However, the articulation of the different levels of government may be beneficial for the regions, which could continue to reduce their levels of extreme poverty (as has been occurring), but in addition could reduce their levels of non-extreme poverty, whose incidence, although diminishing in recent years, continues to be above 25 %.

A good starting point for this is constituted by stimulation of the integration of the regions, understood not only from the economic viewpoint but also from the physical viewpoint (infrastructure) and that of the state. In fact, there exists a tendency for the regions where government policies reduce a greater percentage of poverty to be those characterized by greater overall integration.

Such departmental integration does not have merely an instrumental character. That is to say, the generation of conditions more favorable for a greater reduction of poverty compared with government aid would also permit the opening of markets for the populations within them. This latter factor is particularly important when it is considered that it could lead to a reduction in the Gini indexes and, consequently, to an increase in internal demand and the sustainability of the long-term growth of the regions.

For now, one of the greatest challenges to achieve this articulation lies in achieving an important connection between the urban and rural sectors of the different departments, given that, currently, there exist no indications that one stimulates the other. Thus, the reduction of the rates of rural poverty (above all extreme poverty) is faced with an immediate difficulty as its economy is left on one side, while urban poverty recurs to imports from abroad to support its productive apparatus.

A way for reducing regional and rural–urban inequalities would be carrying out social transfers to rural poor households. In addition that will generate simultaneously positive growth linkages among rural economies. However, a disadvantage of this measure is that such transfers would have little effect on economic growth at the national level. An alternative policy is to invest for improving agricultural and manufacturing productivities in rural regions, for instance: agricultural extension, credit provision and rural roads. Nevertheless, those policies can exacerbate rural–urban inequality, given that agricultural producers are price takers, who are affected by the fall of agricultural prices when output increases and price-elasticity of commodities are low. Thus, the inability of individual policy options to address both growth and inequality highlights the importance of packaging and sequencing interventions (Thurlow et al. 2009).

13.4 Final Remarks

The analysis performed helps the understanding of the nature of the extraordinary economic growth in Peru in the last decade, and its implications in terms of whether it is reversing the old tendency to divergence among the regions. Overcoming the limitations of the model of "imbalanced economic growth", or non-inclusive growth, constitutes one of the principal challenges of the Peruvian economy. This growth continues to coexist with high levels of inequality and socioeconomic territorial disparities, and thus has not resulted in generalized welfare for broad sections of society and for more diverse territories.

The Peruvian economic model possesses certain characteristics which generate the conditions for divergence:(1) the primary material export model, based largely on mining, does not generate the productive links necessary for the regions to be capable of endogenously activating greater effective regional demand and reducing their rates of rural poverty; (2) the dynamism of imports, favored by the revaluation of the *Nuevo Sol*, does not generate the incentives necessary for investment in productive sectors and in regions so that they can compete with the exterior; and, (3) the limited distributive capacity of the state, together with restrictions on undertaking an effective decentralization and improving the efficiency of public expenditure.

Together, this means that advances in terms of closing the gap among the regions are limited. Furthermore, the unequal physical, economic and state integration of the regional economies contributes to perpetuating such disparities. In addition, the problem of the integration of the cities with their rural environments deepens inequalities, as urban growth does not lead to lower rates of rural poverty.

As a result, the strong spatial concentration of economic activity, accompanied by greater levels of inequity, configures a type of perverse dynamic of growth, with a strong divergent center (Lima) which scarcely integrates the remaining regions. Reversing this tendency requires laying the bases to achieve solid growth with an integrating center, in which the state, given its limited capacity to correct regional disparities, uses public resources to promote the economic integration of the regions, which permits them to sustain the increase in internal demand and the sustainability of their growth in the long term.

The fruits of decentralization are still scarce, as it is not contributing to changing territorial economic concentration or divergence among regions. Greater efforts are required, involving the combination of macroeconomic policies and sectorial policies and coordination among the different levels of government, together with the private sector. Advances in the reduction of territorial inequity and the tendency to regional convergence will be the principal indicators that the Peruvian economic model, together with decentralization and public policies, is generating growth which is integrating and equitable for the regions.

References

Atkinson A (1983) The economics of inequality, 2nd edn. Clarendon, Oxford

Attanasio O, Székely M (1999) An asset-based approach to the analysis of poverty in Latin America, vol 3075, RES working papers. Inter-American Development Bank, Research Department, Washington, DC

Azzoni C, Menezes N, Menezes T, Silveira R (2001) Geografía y convergencia en renta entre los estados brasileños, 163–193. In: Mancha T, Sotelsek D (eds) Convergencia económica e integración; la experiencia en Europa y América Latina. Ediciones Pirámide, Madrid

Brady D, Kaya Y, Beckfield J (2007) Reassessing the effect of economic growth on wellbeing in less-developed countries, 1980–2003. Stud Complement Int Dev 42:1–35

Caravedo B (1992) Las regiones ¿descentralizarán al Perú? Balance del proceso regional. Eure XVIII(55):27–45

Carter M, Barret C (2006) The economics of poverty traps and persistent poverty: an asset-based approach. J Dev Stud 42(2):178–199

Casas C, Yamada G (2005) Medición del impacto en el nivel de vida de la población del desempeño macroeconómico para el período 2001–2004. Mimeo, Universidad del Pacífico, Lima

Chirinos R (2008) Puede el Perú ser un nuevo milagro económico, vol 2008–003, Serie Documentos de Trabajo. Banco Central de Reserva del Perú, Lima

Contreras C (2002) El centralismo peruano en su perspectiva Histórica, vol 127, Documento de Trabajo. Instituto de Estudios Peruanos, Lima

Copestake J (2009) Development and wellbeing in Peru: comparing global and local views, vol 09/48, WeD working paper. Wellbeing in Development Countries Research Group, University of Bath, Bath

Cuervo M (2003) Evolución reciente de las disparidades económicas territoriales en América Latina: estado del arte, recomendaciones de política y perspectivas de investigación, vol 41, Serie Gestión Pública. Instituto Latinoamericano y del Caribe de Planificación Económica y Social (ILPES) – CEPAL, Chile

Cuervo M (2004) Estudios de convergencia y divergencia regional en América Latina: balance y perspectivas. Investigaciones Regionales vol. Otoño, 5:29–65 Asociación Española de Ciencia Regional

Dancourt O, Mendoza W, Vilcapoma L (1997) Fluctuaciones económicas y shocks externos, Perú 1950–1996, vol 135, Documento de Trabajo. Departamento de Economía, Pontificia Universidad Católica del Perú, Lima

Del Pozo J, Espinoza L (2011) Un análisis exploratorio de convergencia en el PIB per cápita entre departamentos en el Perú 1979–2008. In: León J, Iguíñiz J (eds) Desigualdad distributiva en el Perú: Dimensiones. Fondo Editorial de la Pontificia Universidad Católica del Perú, Lima

Delgado A, Del Pozo J (2011) Convergencia y ciclos económicos departamentales en el Perú, Documento de Trabajo. Consorcio de Investigación Económica, Lima

Economic Commission for Latin America and the Caribbean (ECLAC) (2009) Economía y Territorio en América Latina y el Caribe. Desigualdades y Políticas, vol 99, Libros de la CEPAL. CEPAL, Santiago de Chile

Economic Commission for Latin America and the Caribbean (ECLAC) (2010a) Descentralización, divergencia y desarrollo regional en el Perú del 2010 In: Rodríguez J, Tello M (eds), Opciones de Política Económica en el Perú: 2011–2015. Fondo Editorial de la Pontificia Universidad Católica del Perú, pp 175–204

Economic Commission for Latin America and the Caribbean (ECLAC) (2010b) Time for equality: closing gaps, opening trails. Thirty third session of ECLAC, Brasilia, May 30th to 1st June. United Nations, ECLAC, Santiago de Chile

Economic Commission for Latin America and the Caribbean (ECLAC) (2011) Statistical yearbook for Latin America and the Caribbean. United Nations Publications, Santiago de Chile

Escobal J, Torero M (2003) Adverse geography and differences in welfare in Peru. United Nations University, World Institute for Development Economics Research, WIDER Discussion paper Nº. 2003/73

Escobal J, Ponce C (2008) Spatial disparities in living conditions in Peru: the role of geographic differences in returns vs. differences in mobile household assets endowment, a cross section analysis. Mimeo. World Bank-LAC, Lima, June 2008

Ferreira F, Gignoux J (2008) The measurement of inequality of opportunity: theory and an application to Latin America, Policy research working paper series, Nº. WPS 4659, The World Bank, Washington, DC

Figueroa A (2010) Crecimiento versus calidad de vida, in: Alarco (coordinador), Rutas hacia un Perú mejor. Qué hacer y cómo lograrlo. Centrum, Centro de Negocios, Aguilar, Lima

Figueroa V, Herrero L (2003) Análisis de la convergencia económica a través de indicadores sintéticos de desarrollo: aplicación al caso de Chile, Investigaciones Regionales vol. Otoño:41–63 Asociación Española de Ciencia Regional

Francke P, Iguíñiz J (2006) Crecimiento pro-pobre en el Perú. Mimeo. Pontificia Universidad Católica del Perú, Lima

Gallo M (2009) Crecimiento económico y desequilibrios territoriales en el Perú ¿Algo está cambiando. Foreign Aff Latinoam 9(1):33–44, Instituto Tecnológico Autónomo de México

Gallo M, Garrido R (2006) Disparidades económicas territoriales en el Perú: Una aproximación empírica a partir de microdatos. Investigaciones Regionales vol. Otoño:47–72 Asociación Española de Ciencia Regional

Gonzales de Olarte E (1993) Economic stabilization and structural adjustment under Fujimori. J Int Stud World Aff 35(2):51–80

Gonzales de Olarte E (1998a) La descentralización en el Perú: entre la fortaleza del centro y la debilidad de la periferia. In: Revesz B (ed) Descentralización y globalización en el Perú. Instituto de Estudios Peruanos – Centro de Investigación y Promoción del Campesinado, Lima

Gonzales de Olarte E (1998b) El neoliberalismo a la peruana: Economía Política del ajuste estructural 1990–1997. Consorcio de Investigaciones Económicas e Instituto de Estudios Peruanos, Lima

Gonzales de Olarte E (2000) Neocentralismo y neoliberalismo en el Perú. Instituto de Estudios Peruanos – Consorcio de Investigación Económica, Lima
Gonzales de Olarte E (2003a) Descentralización para el Desarrollo Humano en el Perú. Programa de las Naciones Unidas para el Desarrollo, Lima
Gonzales de Olarte E (2003b) Lineamientos Políticos y Económicos y Proyecto de Ley de Incentivos para la Integración y Conformación de Regiones. In: Alejos W (ed) Lineamientos Políticos y Económicos y Proyecto de Ley de Incentivos para la Integración y Conformación de Regiones. Fondo Editorial del Congreso del Perú, Lima
Gonzales de Olarte E (2004) La difícil descentralización fiscal en el Perú. Teoría y práctica. Instituto de Estudios Peruanos, Lima
Gonzales de Olarte E (2010) La matriz de capacidades y desempeños (MCD) y el algoritmo del desarrollo humano (ADH). Revista Economía, Departamento de Economía, Pontificia Universidad Católica del Perú 33(66):65–88
Gonzales de Olarte E (2012) Integración para la inclusión social en el Perú. Paper presentado en la III Conferencia Latinoamericana de Desarrollo Humano y Capacidades (ALCADECA), Buenos Aires
Gonzales de Olarte E, Trelles J (2004) Divergencia y convergencia regional en el Perú: 1978–1992, vol 31, Documento de Trabajo. Pontificia Universidad Católica de Lima, Departamento de Economía, Lima
Gonzales de Olarte E, Del Solar V, Del Pozo J (2011) Lima Metropolitana después de las reformas neoliberales: Transformaciones económicas y urbanas. In: De Mattos C, Ludeña W (eds) Lima – Santiago. Reestructuración y cambio metropolitano. Pontificia Universidad Católica del Perú-CIAC/Pontificia Universidad Católica de Chile-IEUT, Lima/Santiago de Chile
Groose M, Harttgen K, Klasen S (2008) Measuring pro-poor growth in non-income dimensions. World Dev 36(6):1021–1047
Herrero L, Figueroa V, Sanz J (2010) Disparidades económicas sobre unidades territoriales menores: análisis de convergencia. Investigaciones Regionales vol. Primavera, 17, pp 93–122, Asociación Española de Ciencia Regional
Ifzal A, Hyun Hwa S (2007) Measuring inclusive growth. Asian Dev Rev 24(1):11–31
Kalwij A, Verschoor A (2007) Not by grow alone: the role of the distribution of income in regional diversity in poverty reduction. Eur Econ Rev 51:805–829
Klasen S (2008) Economic growth and poverty reduction: measurement issues using income and non-income indicators. World Dev 36(3):420–445
Lessmann C (2009) Fiscal decentralization and regional disparity: evidence from cross-section and panel data. Environ Plan A 41:2455–2473
Mendoza W, Leyva J, Flor JL (2011) La distribución del ingreso en el Perú: 1980–2010. In: León J, Iguíñiz J (eds) Desigualdad distributiva en el Perú: dimensiones. Fondo Editorial de la Pontificia Universidad Católica del Perú, Lima
Muñoz I, Paredes M, Thorp R (2007) Group inequalities and the nature and power of collective action: case studies from Peru. World Dev 35(11):1929–1946
Odar J (2002) Convergencia y polarización. El caso peruano: 1961–1996. Estud Econ 29(1):47–70
Perova E, Vakis R (2009) El impacto y potencial del Programa Juntos en Perú: evidencia de una evaluación no experimental. Banco Mundial y Programa Juntos, Lima
Planas P (1998) La descentralización en el Perú republicano (1821–1998). Municipalidad de Lima Metropolitana, Lima
Schuldt J (2004) Bonanza macroeconómica, malestar microeconómico: apuntes para el estudio del caso peruano 1988–2004. CIUP, Lima
Serra M, Pazmin M, Lindow G, Sutton B, Ramirez G (2006) Regional convergence in Latin America, Working paper. IMF, Washington DC
Silva I (2003) Disparidades, competitividad territorial y desarrollo local y regional en América Latina. Serie Gestión Pública, 33. Instituto Latinoamericano y del Caribe de Planificación Económica y Social (ILPES)-CEPAL, Dirección de Gestión del Desarrollo Local y Regional, Santiago de Chile

Slater D (1991) Regionalización en una época de crisis social: Perú, 1985–1990. Eure XVII (51):33–41
Thurlow J, Morley S, Nin Pratt A (2009) Lagging regions and development strategies: the case of Peru, IFPRI discussion paper. International Food Policy Research Institute, Washington, DC
United Nations Development Programme (UNDP) (2010) Regional human development report for Latin America and the Caribbean 2010: acting on the future: breaking the intergenerational transmission of inequality. United Nations Development Programme 1st edn. San José
United Nations Development Programme (UNDP) (2011) Human development report 2011. Sustainability and equity: a better future for all. Palgrave Macmillan, New York
Williamson J (1990) What Washington means by policy reform. In: Williamson J (ed) Latin American adjustment: how much has happened? Institute for International Economics, Washington, DC
Yamada G, Castro JF (2006) Poverty, inequality, and social policies in Peru: as poor as it gets, vol 7, Documento de Discusión. Centro de Investigaciones Universidad del Pacífico, USA

Chapter 14
Growth, Clusters, and Convergence in Ecuador: 1993–2011

Marlon G. Ramón-Mendieta, Wilman S. Ochoa-Moreno, and Diego A. Ochoa-Jiménez

14.1 Introduction

Empirical research undertaken in Ecuador to study the country's regional dynamics uses the region as a unit of observation. Prior to 2007, Ecuador had 22 provinces (which would later be called regions). This study seeks to ascertain whether the regional growth and economic concentration that are evident in Ecuador are determining factors in the development of regional convergence.

The results obtained show sufficient empirical evidence of the economic growth process in Ecuador and the consequences that it has for the economic integration of the country's regions. The available literature suggests that spatial economic concentration is a basic characteristic of regional development processes. In view of this, the purpose of this study is to examine the interaction among the country's regions.

Solow and Swan (1956) developed -separately but with many similarities- an economic growth model in which they identified a specific type of convergence. This approach was crucial for the development of a number research projects on economic convergence. These models are known as neoclassical exogenous growth models. Later, Arrow (1962) discussed the role played by externalities in capital accumulation. Baumol (1986) analyzed the viability of the economic convergence model, concluding that such convergence only was observed in developed countries and that the underdeveloped nations would follow a pattern of divergence. Experts sought out a theory that would back his findings. A technological parameter was incorporated as an endogenous variable, and endogenous growth models were born. When convergence among developing countries was not found using the Solow and Swan model, an alternative model was developed to explain the possibility of a divergence in economic growth. Several studies (Romer 1986, 1990, and Lucas

M.G. Ramón-Mendieta (✉) • W.S. Ochoa-Moreno (✉) • D.A. Ochoa-Jiménez
Department of Economics, Universidad Técnica Particular de Loja, Loja, Ecuador
e-mail: mgramon@utpl.edu.ec; wsochoa@utpl.edu.ec; daochoa@utpl.edu.ec

J.R. Cuadrado-Roura and P. Aroca (eds.), *Regional Problems and Policies in Latin America*, Advances in Spatial Science, DOI 10.1007/978-3-642-39674-8_14,

1988) that facilitated the emergence of these latter models appeared in the late 1980s and early 1990s.

Quah (1996, 1997) incorporated the idea of the influence of space into the study of regional transaction dynamics. The author compared the influence of national and spatial determinants on the well-being of European regions and reached the conclusion that spatial factors are more important than national ones. It was found that regional growth is due to the fact that the economic trajectory of a country or region is not solely and exclusively explained by its key aggregate variables but also by the regions that comprise it.

This study consists of an introduction and four other sections. The second section offers an overview of Ecuador and its regions. In Sect. 14.3, we estimate the sigma and beta convergence equations. In the fourth section, we present general results on regional clusters and growth. Finally, the fifth section contains some final remarks.

14.2 The Physical Features of Ecuador

In 1830, Ecuador joined the movement for Latin American Independence, emerging from Spanish Colonial rule with a government structure based on three areas called *departamentos*. At the end of the nineteenth century, the country was administratively and politically structured into 16 territorial units known as provinces. In the mid-twentieth century, that number increased to 20. The twenty-first century began with 22 provinces, and as of 2007 Ecuador had 24 such units (which is currently the case).

The key feature of the young nation was the economic division that existed between the regions. This can be attributed mainly to the coastal areas' early focus on agricultural exports, the emphasis on grain and bean production for domestic consumption in the mountain regions, and the eastern areas' emphasis on crops for local consumption (Ramón 2011).

Given that export activities experienced a major boom, the agricultural sector posted strong growth. Rapid entry into foreign markets triggered by exports of agricultural products was the hallmark of the era. As a result, Ecuador based its economic growth model on exports of agricultural products (cocoa, rice, coffee, etc.). By the end of World War II, Ecuador was exporting large quantities of bananas mainly to Europe, where the country was gradually increasing its presence and expanding overseas sales to other markets. In the early 1970s, the country changed its growth model to one of import substitution. At the time, it was argued that this transition was a result of the nationalist surge being experienced in Ecuador and other Latin American countries. With the advent of the oil boom of the 1980s, Ecuador again shifted its economic model, this time focusing its efforts on that activity. In short, the growth model that has prevailed in the country since the beginning of the Republican Era has been agricultural export.

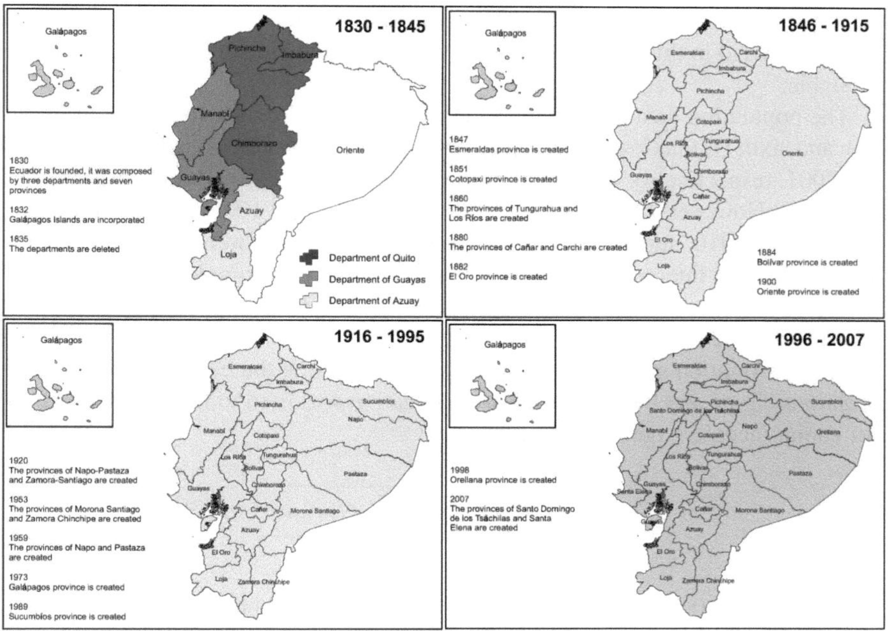

Map 14.1 Evolution of the territorial division of Ecuador

Ecuador has experienced strong territorial dynamism since from its birth (1830), and the number of provinces in the nation has steadily increased. In Ecuador's 181-year history as a republic, it has seen the creation of 24 provinces. On average, a new province has been formed every 7.5 years. One could thus argue that the country has undergone spatial subdivisions that have characterized it as having strong territorial dynamics since its inception.

A key aspect of the country's territorial configuration has been ongoing disputes, quarrels, and armed conflicts. While the country initially occupied a triangle-shaped area that included parts of modern-day Colombia, Peru, and Brazil, its current territory is smaller than what it once was (Ramón 2011) (Map 14.1).

14.3 Convergence Processes in Ecuador

The results of this research study are based on information provided by the National Statistics and Census Institute (INEC) and the Central Bank of Ecuador (BCE). INEC data[1] focus on the Ecuadorian population while BCE numbers[2] refer to Gross Value Added (GVA).

[1] Ecuador had 21 provinces until 1997. Orellana was founded in 1998. The INEC conducted the first Population and Housing Census in 2001, which yielded the first population data set. The BCE did the same with the GVA that year.

[2] This led to the first GVA data; therefore, this province will be subject to study as of 2001.

Note that the provinces of Santa Elena and Santo Domingo de los Tsáchil as will not be included in this study because they were founded in 2007 and data were not available.

The population data used in this study was prepared by the INEC based on the fifth and sixth Population Censuses and the fourth and fifth Housing Censuses (1990 and 2001, respectively). The projections for the other years also were developed by the INEC. However, GVA data are incomplete for 1994, 1995, 1997, 1998, 2000, 2008, 2009, 2010, and 2011. The numbers for those years were determined using the exponential interpolation method. Once the set was complete, the data were arranged in a linear function (using logarithms) to generate per capita provincial accounts for the country.

The information generated will be used to determine the classical convergence equations sigma and beta. The following equation was used to identify disparity in per capita income (sigma convergence):

$$\sqrt{\frac{\sum_{i=1}^{n} (lnGVApc_{it} - lnGVApc_t)^2}{n}} \tag{14.1}$$

in which $\ln GVApc_{it}$ is the logarithm of per capital value added in region i in year t, $\ln GVApc_t$ is the logarithm of per capita GVA of Ecuador as a whole (equivalent to a weighted average of the per capita regional GVA), and n corresponds to the number of regions studied. Two estimates were used to determine sigma convergence:

1. An estimate for 21 regions(Orellana is excluded);
2. An estimate for 20 provinces (excluding the Galápagos and Orellana).

Orellana is excluded in the second estimate because it is home to large-scale oil extraction operations. The Galápagos is excluded because it is a major tourist attraction, particularly for foreign visitors. Oil and tourism could affect the dispersion of national income. The sigma convergence is shown in Fig. 14.1.

In this first estimate, one can observe that the dispersion of income declines in the long term, which means that there is less regional inequality. In other words, national income tends to converge between regions. The figure establishes four stages:

1. Greater inequality is indicated from 1993 to 1996.
2. Less inequality in indicated from 1996 to 2004.
3. A slight increase in inequality is registered between 2004 and 2007.
4. There is a reduction in inequality between 2007 and 2011.

The first stage (1993–1996), which corresponds to a small incremental change of the slope, indicates an increase in inequality. Possible reasons for this include the presence of a neoliberal type government during that period which based part of its management plan on an aggressive policy of privatizations with the argument of modernizing the state. This sparked social upheavals that led to strikes and national

Fig. 14.1 Sigma convergence of per capita GVA in Ecuador (excluding Orellana)

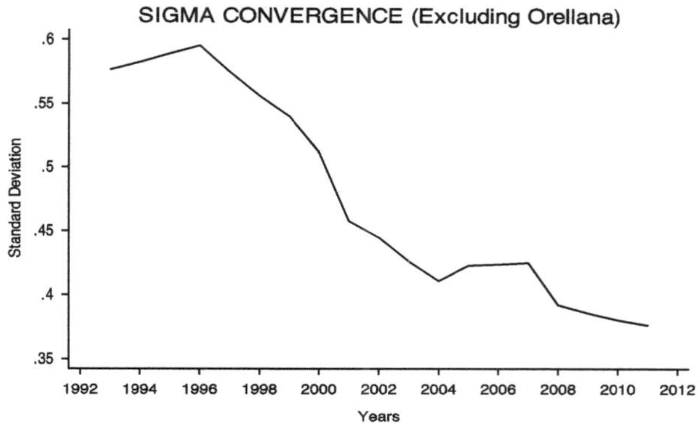

work stoppages as well as the first national uprising of indigenous peoples. In 1995, Ecuador was immersed in the "Alto Cenepa" conflict with Peru, and as a result a considerable amount of financial resources were earmarked for that situation at the expense of strategic sectors for national development. The effects of this situation included social unrest, price hikes, capital flight, and higher interest rates for loans.

The second moment (1996–2004), which corresponds to a decline in the slope, indicates less inequality. The factors that may have contributed to this situation include increased revenue from remittances entering the country as a result of the beginning of large-scale emigration and its subsequent boom (1999). In addition, the GVA growth rate was higher during this period. This was mainly due to the increase in oil prices beginning in 2000 following the application of a structural change in the local monetary economy that allowed the free circulation of the U.S. dollar. While this initially this made Ecuadorian exports less competitive, it was an important element in reducing inflation to single-digit figures in the domestic economy. This strategy was accompanied by decisions regarding how to manage public policies with the establishment of subsidies for the most vulnerable sectors along with public spending aimed at creating assets for industrial and trade competitiveness and social services.

National tax collection levels increased and though almost half of the private banks went under in 1998 and 1999, the national government assumed the debt, which led to a decline in income disparities. Finally, the political sphere was the big loser, as no constitutional period between 1996 and 2006 ended without vice presidential successions or military interventions.

The third stage (2004–2007), in which the slope increased slightly, was marked by an upturn in income inequality. One of the main causes was the weather. Ecuador faced a natural disaster known as El Niño, which swept away several large sections of the coast and the Ecuadorian seaboard. This led to a drop in exports of some of the main products of the country's trade balance (mainly bananas and shrimp). Meanwhile, as a result of tougher laws in the countries in which they work, Ecuadorians living abroad began to send fewer remittances home. As their work and legal statuses stabilized, they began to take steps toward family reunification, which also reduced remittances sent to Ecuador.

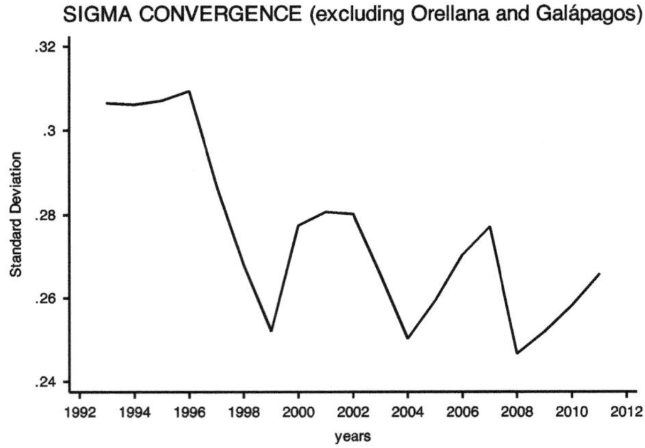

Fig. 14.2 Sigma convergence of per capita GVA in Ecuador (excluding Orellana and Galápagos)

The fourth stage (2007–2011) was characterized by a decline of the slope, suggesting that inequality had decreased. The reasons for this are varied; however, one important explanation is that Rafael Correa assumed the presidency and introduced a new approach to social policy. The main feature of this period is that considerable quantities of financial resources were earmarked for the poorest sectors of society through increasing the Human Development Dividend (which increased from USD 15 to USD 35). The government began to provide free medicine, built new health care clinics and improved existing ones, offered services and financial bonuses to people with disabilities, and introduced other programs. The evidence suggests that the income disparity between the provinces has decreased as a result of these efforts to increase income and improve the quality of life of the poorest sectors of society (Fig. 14.2).

The second estimate shows a decrease in long term income dispersion with less regional inequality. This shows that the trend in Ecuadorian national income levels is toward a convergence. Based on the figure, seven stages can be identified:

1. There is greater inequality between 1993 and 1996,
2. There is less inequality between 1996 and 1999,
3. Inequality increases between 1999 and 2000,
4. Inequality decreases between 2000 and 2004,
5. There is greater inequality between 2004 and 2007,
6. Inequality decreases from 2007 to 2008,
7. Inequality increases between 2008 and 2011.

The factors discussed in the previous projection will recur in this estimate. In general, it can be noted that the level of dispersion in per capita income has declined. However, it has not been constant over time as documented by the increases and decreases in inequality. Having excluded Galápagos from the analysis, it is believed that this region strongly affected income inequality since it receives a considerable volume of resources from tourism, especially, foreign visitors.

Table 14.1 Ecuadorian beta convergence, 1993–2011 (excluding Orellana)

β (value t)	−0.82 (−24.73)
Constant (value t)	−0.036 (−0.56)
R^2(adjusted)	0.97
Convergence velocity	0.091

The following formulas were used to determine the beta convergence and its velocity:

$$\Delta ln Y_{it} - \overline{\Delta lnY}_t = (\alpha_i - \overline{\alpha}) - \beta\left(ln\ Y_{i,t-1} - \overline{lnY_{t-1}}\right) + \varepsilon^*_{it} \qquad (14.2)$$

in which ($\alpha_1 - \alpha$) measures the autonomous growth differential on a regional scale and $\varepsilon^*_{it} = (\varepsilon_{it} - \varepsilon_t)$ represents the new element of random perturbation. A $\beta < 0$ coefficient indicates economic convergence, while the R^2 coefficient of the regression and the statistical significance of the coefficient (through statistic t) are indicators of the credibility of this measure.

The convergence velocity (β), also known as the measure of the speed at which the regions approach their steady-state, is obtained by comparing this equation to the prediction yielded by the neoclassical model via linear approximation around the steady-state(Sala-i-Martin 2004), which is expressed as follows (Table 14.1):

$$\beta = -\frac{1}{T}\left[1 - e^{-\beta^* T}\right] \qquad (14.3)$$

The beta convergence uses the two estimates presented above. In the first, the beta convergence (excluding Orellana) indicates that the beta coefficient has a negative slope. Therefore, per capita growth in the long term presents an inverse correlation with the level of real per capita income in the base year (1993), which demonstrates the existence of absolute convergence among Ecuador's regions. In this sense, it is argued that poor regions tended to grow faster than the wealthy regions in the long run, which suggests a trend towards a reduction in per capita income disparities.

The value of statistic t and its probability reveal the statistical significance of the beta coefficient. The result of the assessment is the presence of an absolute convergence in income in the long term, as the analysis of the beta coefficient is negative and statistically significant, and the association with initial income is high. These results corroborate the data obtained from the sigma convergence, which also indicated that income disparities declined in the long term. For the purpose of a reading of such data, the same analyses undertaken with the sigma convergence will be applied, which explain factors that could have produced the absolute convergence.

The regions have a convergence velocity of 9.1 % per year which is a high figure. Note that this value is a measure of the speed with which the regions approach their steady state (Table 14.2).

In the second estimate (excluding Galápagos and Orellana),the beta convergence indicates a negative slope (negative beta coefficient), with which long term per

Table 14.2 Ecuadorian beta convergence, 1993 – 2011 (excluding Orellana and Galápagos)

β (value t)	−0.46 (−1.9)
Constant (value t)	0.7 (3.26)
R^2(adjusted)	0.12
Convergence velocity	0.032

capita growth shows an inverse correlation to the level of real per capita income in the base year (1993). At the same time, it indicates the presence of an absolute convergence of income levels in Ecuador's regions. With these results, it can be assumed that the wealthy regions posted slower growth than the poor regions, and therefore it can be presumed that there is a shift towards a reduction in per capita income disparities between Ecuador's regions.

The fact that the value of t is greater than the expected value of t +/- 1.96 (95 % of the interval coefficient) also indicates the existence of an absolute convergence. A failure probability that is lower than the permitted value (5 %) proves this, as does the fairly moderate association with initial income. Finally, the resulting evaluation suggests the presence of absolute convergence in long-term income, given that the analysis of the beta coefficient is negative and statistically significant, and the association with initial income is fairly moderate. These results confirm those obtained from the sigma convergence, which show that the income disparities decreased in the long term.

The results of this convergence, in reaching trends similar to those observed for the sigma convergence, will assume the same analyses since they provide possible explanations for the absolute convergence.

In terms of convergence velocity, the regions grew at a considerable pace (3.2 %). It is important to note that the exclusion of the special cases of the tourist region (Galápagos) and the oil region (Orellana) yields a lower convergence velocity than the one obtained in the previous case (in which only Orellana was excluded), which demonstrates the influence of tourism on Ecuadorians' income.

14.4 Growth and Clusters in Ecuador

In previous estimates, the evaluation of the convergence process in Ecuador has shown that this process has slowed and been reversed in the past few years. In view of this, Exploratory Spatial Data Analysis (ESDA)will be used to determine whether the long term convergence process and its recent reversal is associated with the formation of wealthy and delayed regions that present specific steady states (convergence clubs).

The decision to exclude Galápagos was made based on the fact that this region is comprised of several islands, islets, and keys with no geographic contiguity with mainland Ecuador (located at a distance of about 1,000 km). Below, we will identify the convergence clubs in Ecuador. In order to do so, we must identify any regions whose behavior (per capita income) has been different than that of their

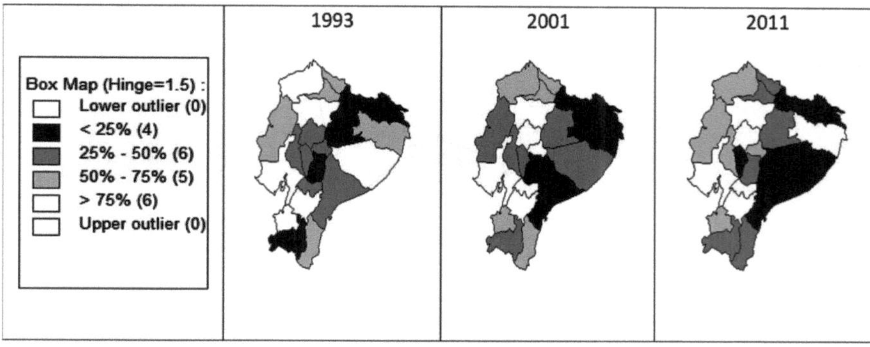

Fig. 14.3 Maps of per capita Ecuadorian GVA, 1993, 2001 and 2011

peers, that is, if there are regions whose income levels are above the others. In order to determine the atypical values, Box Plots were prepared and analyzed for 1993, 2001, and 2011.

Four conclusions stand out: (1) Azuay, Guayas, and Pichincha have experienced sustained long-term growth at rates higher than those of the other regions; (2) the regions of Cotopaxi and Orellana began to grow at higher rates in 2011 due to the recent emergence of industrial activities in Cotopaxi and oil extraction in Orellana; (3) the regions of Cañar, El Oro, Pastaza, and Tungurahua have entered and left the category of the fastest growing regions, which suggests that they have not been growing steadily; and (4) some regions have never been among the regions with the fastest growing economies (the rest of the regions).

In general, there are regions with higher growth rates (Azuay, Guayas, and Pichincha), as well as regions that sporadically post more rapid growth but that have not been able to consolidate their position within the group of the fastest growing regions, which would demonstrate a concentration in national income. Some regions have continued to lag behind the fastest growing economic provinces (the rest of the country).

In order to pin point the regions with faster or slower economic growth, clusters of regions that share similar characteristics are plotted on a map. The regions are represented in shades of gray that range from those with higher per capita income to those with lower per capita income. The results are presented below.

Figure 14.3 illustrates the behavior pattern indicated in the previous case. The regions of Azuay, Guayas, and Pichincha represent the group of provinces with higher incomes. Generally speaking, the regions of Napo and Sucumbios are characterized by low income levels. The higher income regions have better roads, industries and companies, airports (with the exception of the Azuay airport, the others are international airports), a larger number of schools and better overall infrastructure.

The poor regions present serious infrastructure deficiencies and fewer industries and companies. The placements of these two categories are also related to their population size, since there are fewer inhabitants in the poor regions. This confirms

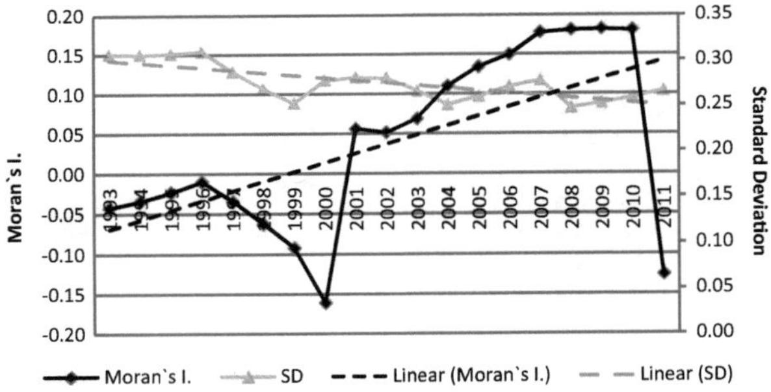

Fig. 14.4 Disparity and spatial dependence in Ecuador

the theory that spatial economic concentration of both economic activity and population is associated with higher income. Finally, it can be said that per capita income tends to concentrate in specific areas and does not occur in isolation, with groups of regions that present higher or lower income over periods of years.

A spatial autocorrelation analysis was applied using the Moran's Index (1950) in order to ascertain whether the categories of regions or convergence clubs display patterns of spatial dependence. According to Anselin (1995), the Moran's scatter plot is a tool for understanding spatial autocorrelation and provides a more disaggregated view of the nature of spatial dependence. Our study of the Moran's scatter plot for 1993, 2001, 2007, and 2011 and the estimation of the Moran's Index follow.

According to the results for 1993, 2001, and 2011, the slope of the Moran's index (MI) is not significant, which implies that there is no correlation between the per capita GVA and the average of the neighboring regions (the spatial lag). Alarger regional disparity can be noted, as each region is geographically distant the others and they tend to not occupy similar spaces.

For 2007, the MI reached 0.1774 and is significant and the Moran's scatter plot slope is positive. This suggests that there is a correlation and larger distance between their slopes.

Moreover, throughout the period under study, the regions analyzed tend to cluster in similar spaces (with certain exceptions). The results confirm the conclusions reached in the two previous cases, namely, that there is no spatial dependence of the convergence processes during the 1990s, that spatial dependence emerges at the beginning of this century, that it became more pronounced by the end of the period, and that as of last year (2011) there is once again no spatial dependence.

Figure 14.4 shows the evolution of Moran's Index over time as well as the standard deviation of provincial GVA. It should be noted that the MI is negative from 1993 to 2000 and positive in 2001 and that this trend is maintained until 2010 (in 2011 the MI was negative). The varied behavior of the Moran's Index reflects the absence of a random spatial distribution, if not the existence of possible clusters. Such clusters were comprised, above all, by the provinces of Azuay, Guayas and Pichincha, which house a significant portion of domestic production. This concentration leads to economic growth depending on the variables present locally.

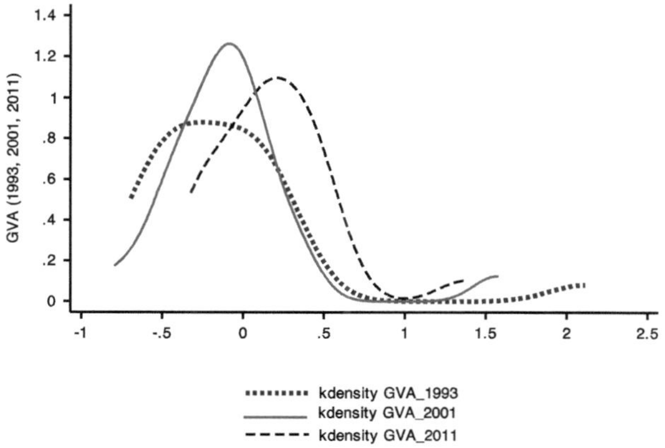

Fig. 14.5 Kernel density of Ecuadorian gross value added (GVA)., 1993, 2001, and 2011

The data thus suggest that income inequality decreased among the poorest regions beginning 2001, albeit not steadily. Ecuadorian economic growth has been accompanied by a moderate decrease in regional differences, with regional dependency continuing to be tied to the agro-export centers of the coast and the slightly industrialized areas of the central and northern highlands.

The increase in the Moran's index between 2001 and 2010 occurred because "when the economy became dollarized in 2000, GDP began to grow again. In 2004, Ecuadorian GDP growth was the highest in the region, reaching 5.4 %." (Correa and Ochoa 2007) (Fig. 14.5).

Kernel density helps us to understand how income distribution has shifted in Ecuador's provinces. The figure above illustrates the shift in income distribution over time, which suggests that Ecuadorian's income levels have improved. However, this shift suggests the presence of nodal regions of income concentration (Azuay, Guayas, and Pichincha), which, in turn, indicates the presence of disparities.

An easing in income distribution can be observed in 2001, which suggests improved distribution of national income. This is different from the situation observed for other years, in which there is greater asymmetry in income distribution.

14.5 Regional Policies in Ecuador

One of the recurring themes in Ecuador in terms of regional policy is centralization, a matter that has been widely discussed but poorly addressed. Many of the country's structural problems can be attributed to centralism given that it has resulted in the concentration of government functions, powers, and resources.

In terms of planning, Ecuador tends to be divided into geographical areas (the coast, the mountains, the Amazon, and the islands) rather than regions. As a result, regional policy measures have not been defined and actions have focused instead on social matters and territorial planning.

Early planning attempts in Ecuador were developed during the administration of Dr. Velasco Ibarra, which created the National Economic Planning and Coordination Board (JUNAPLA) in 1954. The Board was created to advise the government on the formulation of plans for the country's economic development and the coordination of its economic policy. JUNAPLA focused on issues related to foreign trade, the terms of trade, and industrialization as well as key pragmatic concerns such as the issuing of specific policies in relation to tariffs, taxes, credit, fiscal affairs, and the creation and training of the labor force. There was a focus on using industrial development to achieve economic growth (Santos 2007).

The National Development Plan was established in 1980under President Roldós-Hurtado (1979–1984). It included measures related to territorial integration and regional development as one of five general policy development areas. Policy objectives included the integration of the country's highways in nationwide system, support for economically disadvantaged areas, industrial decentralization, urban development, and environmental regulation. Issues related to regional policy were considered in mid-1980s in the National Economic and Social Development Plan for 1985–1992. However, regional issues were not viewed as a priority and instead were listed as one of the 13 "major national problems" posed by the country's development. The implementation of these policies was behind the call for the creation of a regional planning system, although a centralized policy schema remained in effect, which would change its name depending on the government in office (BCE 1995).

According to Moncayo (2006), during the following decade, neoliberal ideas would be introduced in the Americas and the last Andean country to adopt such neoliberal structural reform policies would be Ecuador in 1992. Under the administration of President Sixto Durán Ballén, Ecuadorian public policies followed the principles of the Washington Consensus, that is, financial and trade liberalization, reduction of social subsidies, an opening to foreign investment, flexibilization of the labor markets, and the privatization of state-run companies (telecommunications, oil, and electricity).

Over the years, some planning agencies were created and others were merged, but regional policies have not had a clear and applicable focus. In 2004, the National Secretariat for Planning and Development (SENPLADES) was created as a technical agency responsible for national planning. Its mandate included the creation of regions using the following criteria: two or more provinces that are territorially adjacent, a surface area of at least 20,000 km^2, and a number of inhabitants equivalent to 5 % of the national population (up to 20 % of the territory). The criteria focused on interregional balance, ecological complementarity, integrated water basin management, and historical and cultural affinity (Zamora and Carrión 2011)

Since 2007, mirroring the socialist trend in Latin American, SENPLADES participation was crucial in the creation of planning zones. President Rafael Correa proposed that the country be divided into seven planning zones in order to allow for the consolidation of regional equality in terms of power. The goal was to keep the potential of the regions and benefits of development from being centered exclusively

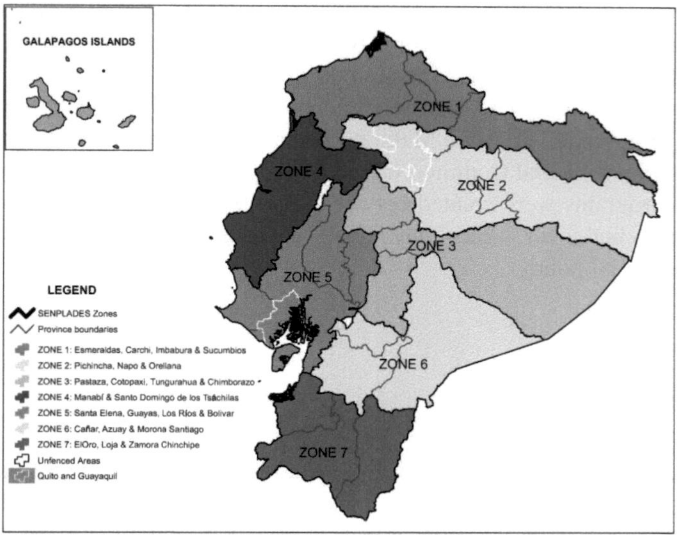

Map 14.2 Planning zones (Source: SENPLADES 2012)

on the country's two economic poles, Guayaquil and Quito. Correa further argued that the synergy or strengthening of the factors involved in the territorial components would make the sum of factors that would facilitate the full development of the individual become a reality in Ecuador (SENPLADES 2009).

The planning zones proposed by SENPLADES are as follows (Map 14.2):

Despite the progress made in recent years, the regional question in Ecuador is not assigned corresponding regional policies. As a result, public policies play a vital role in controlling regional imbalances. Social policies have received a boost from the government, with the corresponding policies and programs responsible for providing and producing services (education, health, housing, and social security), finance functions, procuring services (allocation of social spending and hiring and monitoring private services) and for the regulatory supervision and monitoring of their institutional aspects (regulatory framework for social policies). However, the focus of these functions has varied over time.

Currently, increased social spending and income redistribution are leading to an improvement and sophistication of policies aimed at reducing poverty and inequality, establishing equal opportunities and increasing capacity development and quality of life for individuals and thus the regions in which they live.

Social policy in Ecuador has focused on two intervention strategies:

1. Providing permanent universal social benefits such as education, healthcare, social assistance, sanitation, and housing, among other services (with higher percentages).
2. Specific social assistance programs aimed at the poorest sectors of society which use mechanisms involving cash, in kind, and/or service transfers.

These more recent programs involve the following intervention mechanisms: the Human Development Bond, Housing Bond, Operation Rescue the Children, Our Children Program, Child Development Program, Food and Nutrition Program, School Food Program, Feed Yourself Ecuador Program, Free Maternity, Popular Insurance Program, HIV/AIDS, Malaria Prevention, Tuberculosis, Water and Sanitation Program for Rural Communities and Small Municipalities, Basic Sanitation, etc. These programs were created between the 1980s and 1990s as compensatory mechanisms, but over time they have become permanent components of Ecuadorian social policy.

14.6 Final Remarks

Ecuador's economic growth has been accompanied by a moderate decrease in regional income disparities, which had tended to increase over time in the regions but have declined since 2005. Regional dependency continued to be tied to the agro-export centers of the coast and the slightly developed industrial areas of the central and southern highlands.

The sigma convergence suggests a reduction in per capita income and therefore, in regional disparities; however, that trend has not been constant. This has led to an exhaustion of growth factors and the beginning of a process of regional divergence. There is evidence of beta convergence given that the poor regions grew faster than the wealthier ones. However, this is not sufficient to reduce regional disparities, so it is assumed that the economic polarization has been maintained and regional clusters strengthened.

The convergence velocity is greater when Galápagos and Orellana are excluded. These regions present better economic performance than their peers. However, there is no spill-over effect in the rest of the country.

The exploratory analysis of spatial data demonstrates that the per capita income of Azuay, Guayas, and Pichincha has grown steadily and more than that of other regions. The opposite trend has been observed in Napo and Sucumbios. Therefore, the dynamic of economic convergence and divergence could be influenced by spatial factors that occur within the regions. The Moran's Index for 1993 does not suggest a correlation, but it does in2001. This would indicate that the productivity of a region is auto-correlated with the productivity of neighboring regions.

There is no significant spatial reconfiguration since most of the traditional economic clusters have not shifted or contracted. As a result, the emergence of new regions with considerable economic dynamism has been limited.

Until now, Ecuadorian public policy has been designed to control the territorial imbalances that have emerged as a result of the absence of regional policies.

References

Anselin L (1995) Local indicators spatial association – Lisa. Geogr Anal 27:93–113

Arrow K (1962) The economic implications of learning by doing. Rev Econ Stud 29:155–173

Baumol W (1986) Productivity growth, convergence, and welfare: what the long-run data show. Am Econ Review 76(5):1072–1085

Central Bank of Ecuador (1993) Cuentas provinciales del Ecuador, Quito-Ecuador

Central Bank of Ecuador (1995) Cuentas provinciales del Ecuador, Quito-Ecuador

Central Bank of Ecuador (1996) Cuentas provinciales del Ecuador, Quito-Ecuador

Central Bank of Ecuador (1999) Cuentas provinciales del Ecuador, Quito-Ecuador

Central Bank of Ecuador (2007) Cuentas provinciales del Ecuador, Quito-Ecuador

Correa R, Ochoa W (2007) Reconfiguración de Flujos Migratorios Internacionales. Gestión, 17

Lucas RE Jr (1988) On the mechanics of economic development. J Monet Econ 22:3–42

Moncayo E (2006) Las políticas regionales en América Latina y los países andinos: un análisis comparativo. Cuadernos del Cendes 23:99–125

Moran PAP (1950) Notes on continuous stochastic phenomena. Biometrika 37(½):17–23

National Secretariat for Planning and Development (2009) Sistema Nacional de Planificación y reinvención del Estado para el bienestar colectivo, Quito-Ecuador

National Statistics and Census Institute (1990a) V Censo de Población and IV de Vivienda, Quito-Ecuador

National Statistics and Census Institute (1990b) Proyecciones del V Censo de Población y IV de Vivienda, Quito-Ecuador

National Statistics and Census Institute (2001a) V Censo de Población and IV de Vivienda, Quito-Ecuador

National Statistics and Census Institute (2001b) Proyecciones del V Censo de Población y IV de Vivienda, Quito-Ecuador

Quah D (1996) Regional convergence clusters across Europe. European Econ Rev 40 (3–5):1951–1958

Quah D (1997) Empirics for growth and distribution: stratification, polarization and convergence clubs. J Econ Growth 2(1):27–59

Ramón M (2011) Dinámica poblacional en Ecuador. 1–16. Retrieved from Informe de coyuntura económica, Instituto de Investigaciones Económicas - UTPL website: http://www.utpl.edu.ec/comunicacion/wp-content/uploads/2012/12/utpl-Informe-de-coyuntura-economica-N-8-ano-2011.pdf

Romer P (1986) Increasing returns and long-run growth. J Polit Econ 94:1002–1037

Romer P (1990) Endogenous technological change. J Polit Econ 98(5, part 2):71–102

Sala-i-Martin X (2004) Apuntes de crecimiento económico. Antoni Bosch, Barcelona

Santos E (2007) Institucionalidad y Economía. Caso ecuatoriano. 1–10. Retrieved from Colegio de Economístas de Pichincha website: http://www.colegiodeeconomistas.org.ec/documentos/InstitucionalidadyEconomia.doc

Solow R (1956) A contribution to the theory of economic growth. Q J Econ LXX(1):65–94

Swan T (1956) Economic growth and capital accumulation. Econ Rec 82(4):755–782

Zamora G, Carrión A (2011) Planificación del desarrollo y ordenamiento territorial, Colección Nuevo Estado. I.a. Ed: Instituto de Altos Estudios Nacionales (IAEN), Quito, 199 pp

Part III
Horizontal and Comparative Analysis

Chapter 15
Population Distribution and Internal Migration Issues in LAC

Patricio Aroca and Jorge Rodríguez

15.1 Introduction

The evolution of the spatial distribution of the population of Latin America, in the last decades, is showing a heterogeneous path, while some countries have growing concentration around the main city or cities; others display an inverse pattern. Several factors are described in the first part of this chapter, affecting people and labor mobility across the territory.

There is not only one clear pattern of mobility in Latin America, but also a high heterogeneity of processes due to different policies, endowments, background, among others.

While three or four decades ago the main concern about moving across the territory was the migration from rural to urban areas, in the last decades Latin America has reach an urbanization rate comparable to developed countries, so the interested has moved to internal migration among the cities or regions within the country.

Internal migration has being one of the traditional concentration movements to the big cities. In this context, one of the aims of this chapter is to assess the impact of internal migration on population concentration around main cities for Argentina, Bolivia, Brazil, Chile, Costa Rica, Guatemala and Mexico.

In the period of analysis, most of the countries have implemented market policies in order to promote growth. In a competitive theoretical economy, the market arbitrages the wage and unemployment differential by moving people

P. Aroca (✉)
University Adolfo Ibañez, Viña del Mar, Chile
e-mail: patricio.aroca@uai.cl

J. Rodríguez
CELADE, CEPAL, Santiago de Chile, Chile
e-mail: jorge.rodriguez@cepal.org

J.R. Cuadrado-Roura and P. Aroca (eds.), *Regional Problems and Policies in Latin America*, Advances in Spatial Science, DOI 10.1007/978-3-642-39674-8_15,

across the territory. Other of the questions addressed in this chapter is whether migrants follow the market signal or there are others forces moving people around the country.

After a long descriptive analysis about population distribution and migration in several countries of Latin America, a model to explain migration for Argentina, Bolivia, Brazil, Chile and Mexico is estimated and the results reported showing how different are the process but the concentration still is a strong force attracting people to the main cities.

15.2 The Evolution of Population Distribution in Latin America

While the pattern of distribution of a territory's population depends on a complex range of economic, social, political, cultural, and environmental factors, from the demographic point of view, the spatial distribution of the population is mainly determined by three elements. The first is internal and international migration. Each time there are migratory displacements that generate migratory balances other than zero, there is a redistribution of the population. Said redistribution implies, *ceteris paribus*, an increase in the demographic weight of areas with net immigration and a reduction of the weight of areas with net emigration. The second is the natural growth differential which, *ceteris paribus*, elevates the representation of areas with above average growth and reduces that of areas with lower than average growth. Finally, there are processes of annexation, reclassification, redefinition and modification of borders that, without the two prior forces operating, modify the relative demographic weight of the various territories within a country.

The magnitude of the redistributive effect in the territory does not depend on migratory intensity (the likelihood of migrating) but on the size of the migratory balances. All in all, the intensity of internal migration is not irrelevant for the redistributive effect of the migration. A low intensity keeps the redistributive effect at low levels; even in a more redistributive theoretical scenario, which is one in which there are no countercurrents, if the population that migrates is limited, it is impossible for it to produce a massive redistributive effect. For its part, high intensity offers space for massive redistribution, though it is worth reiterating that its final effect would depend on the size of the balance and not the number of people who migrate.

In Latin America, internal migration has tended to come about in response to regional differentials in economic and social areas. Given that these inequalities are marked, the flows have been sizeable and have had significant redistributive effects because they have taken place between migrant-sending areas – typically those with lower relative development – and attractive areas, which tend to be those with greater relative development. By virtue of this relationship, migration has been many things. First, it has been the motor of urbanization – the gap that exists between country and city in the region is old, deep and systematically unfavorable for rural areas-, which supposes a massive and substantive redistribution of the population in demographic, economic, sociocultural, political and environmental terms. It also is the factor that explains the increase, which was sustained over the past 60 years in various countries of the region, in demographic concentration (and other types as well) in the main city and in the major administrative division in which it is located given that the city tends to provide better standards of living and greater labor and educational opportunities. Third, it is the mechanism that explains the rapid growth of the populations of certain subnational spaces that present accelerated economic dynamism in view of specific territorial development policies, market forces or the combination of the two. In some countries in the region such as Mexico with its northern border and the state of Quintana Roo, where Cancun is located, the emergence of these dynamic subnational spaces led to the consolidation of alternatives to the historic space of concentration (the metropolitan region). This in turn led to processes of demographic de-concentration. Fourth, migration is the force that has eroded demographic growth – leading to other demographic changes, such as premature aging- of regions that present chronic poverty, some of which are well-known. These include northeastern Brazil, the Peruvian *sierra*, the Bolivian *altiplano*, northwestern Argentina and Chile's Araucanía region, which systematically lose portions of their population due to migration.

However, internal migration in Latin American countries also has been influenced by other factors. These include development strategies and territorial public policies, several of them directly migratory, particularly in the past. In some cases, these factors have increased the effect of territorial inequalities on the size and direction of the flows, as occurred with the internally focused development strategy and country-to-city migration. But in others, they have had an effect that is different from the one that is derived from regional inequalities. This is the case of migration towards demographic border areas which in Latin America and particularly in South America tend to be large, sparsely populated areas that are rich in natural resources. Though these areas are not known for having greater income levels or better living conditions, they still receive large numbers of immigrants as a result of a combination of policy actions – including colonization, increased connectivity, productive, social and territorial investment and strengthening of the government and its agencies – and the arrival of private capital (which is frequently attracted by government incentives).

Finally, in a vein that diverges from the focus of this document but that should at least be mentioned, internal migration, including intra-metropolitan migration, is the variable that defines the redistribution of the population in the region's large cities. Until recently, this redistribution was marked by the massive exodus from central areas and the arrival of sizeable flows to the peripheries, which come from other parts of the country and within the same cities (precisely the flows that have come out of central and pericentral areas).

In addition to this very short and general description of the spatial redistribution patterns of the regional population and the role of migration in them, this study presents four empirical sections based on the latest available census information on the location of the population and migration. One of them offers specific calculations of internal migration intensity trends (considering migration among Major Administrative Divisions, which are called DAMs in Spanish, and Minor Administrative Divisions, which are called DAMEs in Spanish) and their redistributive effect on the population (in this case only among DAMs). The second addresses the process of urbanization and specifically the role played by rural–urban migration in it. The third, which is based on national cases, examines population concentration in the metropolitan DAM (which houses the main city) and a trend in which migration redistributes the population to alternative DAMs with the subsequent demographic de-concentration. The fourth section presents an overview of migration in regions that present chronic poverty. These analyses are based on recent publications by ECLAC (2012), Cunha and Rodríguez (2009), Rodríguez and Busso (2009) and Rodríguez (2011).

15.2.1 On Migratory Intensity and the Redistributive Impact of Internal Migration

Table 15.1 presents a generalized reduction of migratory intensity in the region. It is important to note that the data from the censuses of the decade of 2010 support this trend (Table 15.1), though they also show that there are exceptions. For example, Panama registered a higher Crude Migration Intensity in 2010 than it did in 1990 (though it was lower than that of 2000). Using micro data from three censuses from the decade of 2010 (Ecuador, Mexico and Panama), we present the results of a typification exercise using age for this rate in Table 15.2 in order to evaluate how much of this downward trend could be attributed to a change in the age group structure (Rodríguez and Busso 2009). The results are eloquent, as the typified rates maintain the trend of the observed rates.

There are several potential causes of this decrease, including the gradual reduction of the relative importance of rural–urban migration (a matter that will be examined in section C), the replacement of migration with commuting, and new forms of virtual interaction (Aroca and Atienza 2011). All in all, this trend and its determinants are the object of debate among the various theoretical frameworks that exist for understanding internal migration (Rodríguez 2011). Interestingly, a recent global study (Bell and Muhidin 2009) not only corroborates this trend in the case of Latin America but also verifies that it exists in other regions of the world as well. As a result, they configure a finding of global reach whose causes are probably also global in reach, which is effectively applied to the three determinants mentioned above.

In Latin America, there are two additional determinants that must be underscored. One of them is the sustained increase in international emigration, which can act as a substitute for internal migration in some countries or specific

Table 15.1 Latin America and the Caribbean: internal mobility rate, 1990 and 2000

	Absolute or life time migration		Recent migration (within last 5 years)	
Census round	Major administrative division (%)	Minor administrative division (%)	Major administrative division (%)	Minor administrative division (%)
1990	17.5	34.2	5.1	12.6
2000	17.7	35.2	4	8.7

Source: Rodríguez 2008, p. 139

Table 15.2 Evolution of the gross rate of observed mobility typified by age (per 1,000), three countries with censuses in the decade of 2010

Year	Country	Ecuador	Panama	Mexico
1980	Population	6,710,228		
	DAM migrants	568,556		
	Observed rate	**84.7**		
	Typical rate	**84.7**		
1990	Population	8,312,119	2,021,564	66,501,519
	DAM migrants	482,335	88,529	3,468,508
	Observed rate	**58.0**	**43.8**	**49.6**
	Typical rate	**57.7**	**43.8**	**49.6**
2000	Population	10,743,574	2,421,143	85,275,006
	DAM migrants	562,717	153,658	3,784,323
	Observed rate	**52.4**	**63.5**	**44.4**
	Typical rate	**53.1**	**64.1**	**44.8**
2010	Population	12,853,717	2,937,455	99,794,866
	DAM migrants	608,582	1,65,047	3,502,007
	Observed rate	**47.3**	**56.2**	**35.1**
	Typical rate	**48.9**	**55.1**	**36.3**

Calculations made by the authors based on MIALC and special processes from the 2010 censuses

areas within them. The second speaks to the end or interruption of major public programs for spatial redistribution of the population that was very important in the region between the 1950s and 1980s. In several countries in the region, these programs encouraged – sometimes in an imposing and/or not very transparent manner – the massive displacement of the population towards sparsely populated areas. The disappearance of these programs during the 1990s brought about the extinction of one of the motors of internal migration in the region (Rodríguez and Busso 2009).

This reduction of the intensity of internal migration can lead to a certain devaluation of the same by governments, researchers and public opinion. However, in this section, we will note that the size of internal migration is still very significant, that its profile is changing, presenting new challenges, and that its qualitative effects, which will be measured using innovative procedures, are relevant for places of origin and destination.

Linked to the above, the results show the attenuation of the redistributive effect of internal migration in a territory. This effect, on an aggregate scale (that is,

Table 15.3 Latin America: evolution of the global migratory effectiveness index and aggregate net migration rate between DAMs by country

	Migration effectiveness index, among DAMs				Aggregate net migration rate, among DAMs			
Country	1980	1990	2000	2010	1980	1990	2000	2010
Argentina			11.0				0.7	
Bolivia		23.8	28.8			2.7	3.4	
Brazil		25.4	17.6			2.0	1.2	
Chile	27.0	10.5	5.8		3.2	1.3	0.7	
Colombia		19.5	17.1			3.1	1.5	
Costa Rica	15.0		13.2		2.0		1.5	
Cuba			39.3				1.7	
Ecuador	51.6	28.1	30.9	14.2	8.7	3.3	3.2	1.41
El Salvador		48.1	15.7			4.6	1.0	
Guatemala		35.3	27.9			1.8	1.6	
Honduras	34.6		31.9		3.4		2.7	
Mexico		33.5	27.5	19.2		3.3	2.4	1.3
Nicaragua		33.6	21.1			2.4	1.0	
Panama		20.2	51.3	46.0		1.8	6.5	4.9
Paraguay	33.4	36.5	25.0		7.2	6.7	3.8	
Peru		28.7	29.7			4.9	3.2	
Dominican Republic			25.2				2.1	
Uruguay	21.2	22.9			3.2	3.0		
Venezuela			25.9				2.6	

Source: Calculated by the authors based on the MIALC and in special processing of databases of the 2010 censuses of Ecuador, Mexico and Panama

national) can be measured using two indices. One is the global migration effectiveness index, which relates the sum of the migratory balances of all entities (in absolute values so that they do not cancel each other out) to the sum of the gross migration of each entity. This ratio provides an estimate of the efficiency of the migration as a force that redistributes the population in the territory which is maximized when there are only currents and no countercurrents, that is, some entities only receive immigrants and others only report emigrants.

But this efficiency is measured in terms of migration undertaken and thus does not consider the size of the migration, which is key for its redistributive effect. In other words, there could be a country in which migration is very efficient as a mechanism for redistributing the population, but its final redistributive effect may be very low because the fraction of the total population that migrants represent is very small. In order to capture this total redistributive effect, one uses the second index, which is called the aggregate net migration rate. Here, the sum of gross migrations of each entity (DAM or DAME) is divided by the total population that is exposed to the risk of migrating (Bell and Muhidin 2009).

The calculation of the two indexes (Table 15.3) reveals the absence of a clear pattern in the case of migratory efficiency but suggests a clear reduction of the redistributive effect of the migration of the population among DAMs. This is linked

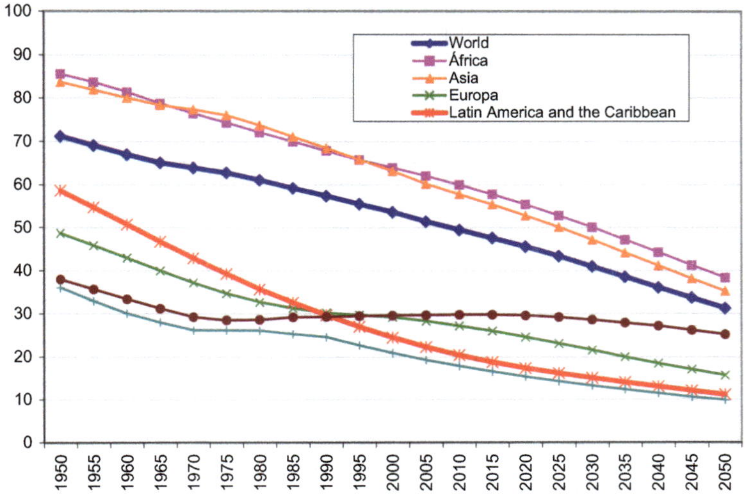

Fig. 15.1 World and regions: percentage of the population in RURAL areas, 1950–2050 (Source: Population Division of the Department of Economic and Social Affairs of the United Nations Secretariat, World Population Prospects: The 2010 Revision, http://esa.un.org/unpd/wpp/index.htm. Note: The term Latin America and the Caribbean refers to the 42 countries and territories identified by LACDC as comprising the region. The term Latin America refers to the 20 countries identified by LACDC as making up the sub-region (17 on the mainland and three Caribbean island territories: Cuba, Dominican Republic and Haiti). For further information, Guzmán et al. (2006))

to the decrease in migratory intensity. In fact, the results of the three countries with census micro data from the decade of 2010 suggest a continuation of this trend towards the decrease of the redistributive effect of migration.

This reduction in size notwithstanding, internal migration still involves large contingents of the population, has powerful implications for regional development, impacts regional balances in the area of employment and has a variety of qualitative impacts that we have only recently been able to estimate with relative precision (ECLAC 2012; Rodríguez and Busso 2009).

15.2.2 *Urbanization and Rural to Urban Migration*

Latin America and the Caribbean is the world's most urbanized developing region. Currently, only 20 % of the region's population is rural, as can be seen in Fig. 15.1. Only Northern America (USA and Canada) has a lower percentage. UN official population projections forecast a continuous decreasing of this percentage, reaching around 10 % in 2050 (Fig. 15.1).

This very rapid urbanization has been caused by an impressive rural exodus since 1930s, which had a peak between 1940 and 1980. In fact, 1950s levels of

Table 15.4 Latin America: net rural–urban migration and percentage of urban growth due to net rural–urban migration, by sex 1980–2010

	Net rural–urban migration rate (by thousand)					
	1980–1990		1990–2000		2000–2010	
Countries	Male	Female	Male	Female	Male	Female
Argentina	5.1	5.3	3.0	2.9		
Bolivia	21.2	23.9	8.0	8.4		
Brazil	10.6	11.4	7.6	8.6		
Chile	1.5	1.7	3.5	3.2		
Colombia	7.3	8.5	7.6	6.8		
Costa Rica	15.5	15.8	18.9	18.5		
Cuba	13.2	13.6	4.9	5.2		
Ecuador	15.1	16.0	10.5	10.2	5.3	5.4
El Salvador	15.4	15.1	16.6	16.5		
Guatemala	10.6	11.9	25.8	26.3		
Haití	29.0	12.1	32.6	12.8		
Honduras	17.5	20.7	14.2	15.6		
México	8.6	8.4	7.0	7.1	3.1	5.1
Nicaragua	8.4	9.5	4.7	6.2		
Panamá	10.5	11.6	16.7	15.9	6.4	6.8
Paraguay	18.6	21.0	13.0	14.4		
Perú	8.1	9.0	7.1	7.7		
Rep. Dominicana	6.9	6.7	13.1	13.7		
Uruguay	3.7	3.2	1.2	1.5		
Venezuela	5.4	6.3	4.9	4.9		

Source: ECLAC, 2012, Population, Territory and Sustainable Development, Santiago, Chile, ECLAC, LC/L.3474(CEP.2/3)

urbanization in Latin America and the Caribbean were lower than those registered in developed regions (North America, Europe and Oceania). In less than 40 years, the region reached urban levels of Europe and Oceania, thanks to rural exodus which generated an explosive urban growth. Subsequently, in the past 20 years, urban growth slowed down due to demographic transition and the reduction of emigration from de countryside. Nevertheless, rural exodus has continued, and so has urbanization. In fact, results from indirect techniques[1] applied to most recent censuses data show that rural to urban net migration rates are still positive indicating a persistent net out-migration from rural areas (Table 15.4).

The urbanization process in Latin America between 1950 and 1980 was driven by an industrialization strategy promoted by the governments from most LA countries. This strategy was named "internal development" or "import substitution", although most recently a newer – in our opinion a more acute term has been developed "State led industrialization" (Ocampo 2006). This strategy promoted

[1] Census Survival Ratio (CSR) method, http://www.un.org/esa/population/techcoop/IntMig/manual6/chapter2.pdf.

urban activities (industry and services) and favored "modernization" of countryside economy. Both changes involved a dynamic economic growth in cities and the creation of a large workforce surplus in rural areas of countries. During 1980s, most of the governments change this strategy by another called "neoliberal", based on free market, private sector and open economy. In spite of its anti-metropolitan or even anti-urban bias – due to the fact that commodities are the lion's share of Latin American exportations and the locus of commodity production are rural areas. However, urbanization process and rural exodus continued almost unaffected; the main reason was the persistent social gap between rural and urban areas. Nowadays the region has many development strategies (from socialist to neoliberal approaches), but any of them has closed this gap, and this is the explanation for the continuous urbanization and "rural exodus".

Latin American urbanization process has different characteristics from those achieved in the current developed countries, in which urbanization, industrialization and economic development were concomitant and synergistic. Although, industrialization has contributed to Latin America's modernization and has facilitated social achievements that positioned the region in compliance with most of the MDG's requirements, its progress was detached, at least partially, from an economic, social and institutional progress such as the one experimented by the current developed countries. On the other hand, this minor development involved a cumulative deficit in infrastructure, resources and regulations. This cumulative deficit is the main reason why Latin American cities' are marked by poverty, precariousness, informality and crime.

Expressions such as over-urbanization and hyper-urbanization have been used to describe the region's high levels of urbanization without accompanying the level of economic and social development typical of industrialized countries (Rodriguez and Martine 2008). Although it cannot be questioned that the region is quite below the developed regions in terms of per capita income, productivity and poverty, the over-urbanization hypothesis can lead to an erroneously negative evaluation of the Latin American urbanization. In fact, Latin America follows the classical pattern of positive association between urbanization and development because, in average, the higher urbanization the higher level of human development at country level (Fig. 15.2).

15.3 Concentration of and Migration to Metropolitan Regions

The urbanization process in Latin America has been historically linked to the concentration of the population in the major administrative division (MAD) containing the main city, usually the capital, of the country. In countries like Argentina, Chile, Panama and Uruguay, over 40 % of the population live in metropolitan MADs, (where the main city and/or capital is located). However, in

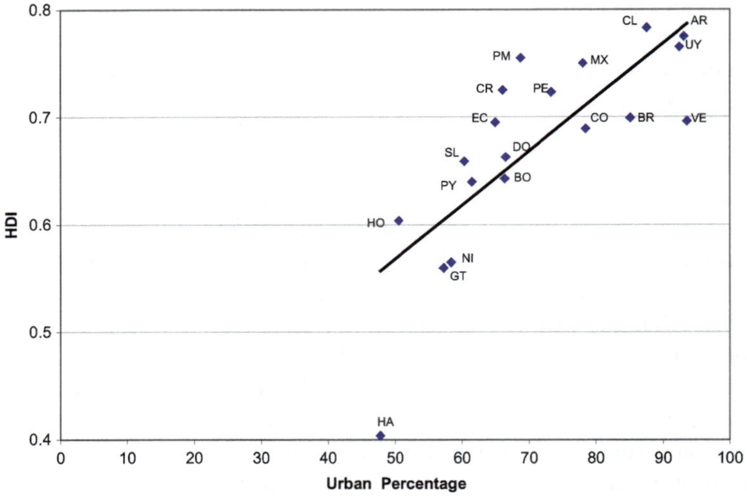

Fig. 15.2 Latin America, 2010: percentage of urban population and human development index by countries (Source: Based on Human Development Report 2010 and data base DEPUALC, 2009, CELADE, UN.)

other countries of the region (like Brazil, Colombia, Ecuador, Mexico and Venezuela (Bol. Rep.)) this highly concentrated pattern does not exist.

Since 1980 some signs of de-concentration became apparent. However, according to the systematized information taken from DEPUALC database (Spatial Distribution of Population and Urbanization in Latin America and the Caribbean) created and maintained by CELADE (www.cepal.org/celade/depualc/) there is no clear evidence of a sustained process of demographic de-concentration in Latin American countries, except for a few. Between 1980 and 2000, in Chile, Costa Rica, Ecuador, Panama, Paraguay and the Dominican Republic an increase of the relative participation of corresponding MAD in national population was registered. In the rest of countries included on Table 15.1, there is stability in the concentration process or a slight reduction of metropolitan concentration.

As Cunha (2002) stated, it is in fact "premature to claim that the demographic concentration that has taken place in the region, in the past 40 years is suffering a conclusive reversion of significant proportions". This same research underlined that "in the majority of Latin American countries, the metropolitan region (or the region's capital when MADs were not constituted yet) still presented an equal or even larger increase than the country's, at least up to the 80s". Indeed, this trend can be observed in Cunha and Rodriguez (2009).

It is also important to consider that even in countries where the main metropolitan region has grown slower than the national population, which is the case of Argentina, Bolivia, Brazil, Mexico, Nicaragua and Venezuela (Bol. Rep.), it does not mean that the metropolitan agglomeration phenomenon has stopped or simply disappeared. Data from DEPUALC reveals that in many countries in spite of the

Table 15.5 Latin America (three selected countries): metropolitan cities by total net migration, proximity and distance, absolute balances, census from the decade of 2010

	Net migration		
	Total	Closer	Farther
Panama City	70,789	2,553	68,236
Mexico City	−200201	−24386	−175815
Quito	23,284	−6992	30,276
Guayaquil	−7487	−11388	3,901

Source: Developed by the authors using processing of census microdata from Ecuador, Mexico and Panama 2010 with REDATAM

Note: Total migration: exchange of population between the city and the rest of the lesser administrative divisions of the country; Close migration: exchange of population between the city and lesser administrative divisions that form part of the DAM in which the city is located; Distant migration: exchange of population between the city and lesser administrative divisions outside of the metropolitan DAM

reduction of total increase, there are large agglomerations expanding faster than national average. Consequently, empirical evidence suggests that the decreasing importance of main cities or metropolitan regions of countries cannot only be substantiated on de-metropolitanization, demographic de-concentration; or the so called counter-urbanization as defined by developed countries. Gradual loss of importance of the greatest metropolises within the national population is not such a relevant phenomenon; however, the most interesting fact has happened in other agglomerations of smaller size, which have undergone a considerable population increase.

Leaving aside administrative regions to directly examine the metropolises, the data available from the 2010 censuses show a mixed situation in the area of migration from large cities, which may not be representative due to the exiguous number of countries available. Table 15.5 shows that Panama City is attractive to those living in its surrounding regions and those elsewhere in the country, while Mexico City presents a loss of population in the exchange with the rest of the country, a situation that has been present since 1990. Quito presents negative net migration with its surrounding areas (likely due to suburbanization), but a positive and larger net migration with the rest of the country that yields a positive balance. Guayaquil presents negative net migration in the exchange of population with its surrounding areas, and positive net migration with the rest of the country that is smaller in size and thus yields negative total net migration.

15.3.1 Interregional Migration, Development and Emigration from Areas Presenting Chronic Poverty

A stylized characteristic of internal migratory flows – adjusted, of course, to theoretical predictions – has been their direction from less developed regions to more developed ones. This is verified in a very elemental way through the

Table 15.6 Latin America and the Caribbean (select countries): simple linear correlation between the human development index and the net internal migration rate at the level of larger administrative divisions censuses from the decade of 2000

Country and year, indicator and reference year, number of large administrative divisions (DAM) with data			Index of simple correlation between the indicator and net migration rate (value p in parenthesis)	
Argentina, 2001	IDH 1996	24 DAM	0.407	(0.0242)
Bolivia, 2002	IDH 1994	9 DAM	0.619	(0.0378)
Brazil, 2000	IDH 1996	27 DAM	0.451	(0.0091)
Chile, 2002	IDH 1998	13 DAM	−0.01136	(0.5147)
Colombia, 2005	IDH 2000	24 DAM	0.414	(0.0222)
Cuba, 2002	IDH 1996	14 DAM	0.77	(0.0006)
Ecuador, 2001	IDH 1999	15 DAM	0.65	(0.0044)
Guatemala, 2002	IDH 1995–1996	22 DAM	0.442	(0.01972)
Honduras, 2001	IDH 1996	18 DAM	0.697	(0.0006)
Mexico, 2000	IDH 1995	32 DAM	0.408	(0.0102)
Nicaragua, 2005	IDH 2000	17 DAM	0.055	(0.4170)
Panama	IDH 2000	12 DAM	0.484	(0.0554)
Paraguay, 2002	IDH 2000	18 DAM	0.133	(0.29936)
Uruguay, 1996	IDH 1991	19 DAM	0.063	(0.60097)
Venezuela, 2001	IDH 1996	23 DAM	0.0686	(0.3780)

Source: Rodríguez 2008, p. 140, IDH stand by Human Development Index

correlation between the net migration rate presents, which reveals the attractive or emigrant-sending condition of a given DAM, and the human development index. It was determined that, almost without exception, higher human development levels are concomitant with higher average net migration rates, that is, with greater attraction or less sending (Table 15.6).

As we noted previously, the most important regularity is that between emigrant-sending areas, there are DAMs that present the areas of greatest relative poverty, those that are most affected by marginalization and those in which indigenous communities are found. These include nearly all of northwestern Argentina (with the exception of Catamarca), the four *altiplano* provinces of Bolivia (Chuquisaca, La Paz, Oruro and Potosí), seven of the nine states in northeastern Brazil, central-southern Chile (particularly Region IX, Araucanía), practically all of Guatemala and southern Mexico, the Peruvian sierra, a good part of Ecuador's Andean provinces (with the exception of Pichincha, which is a metropolitan DAM), and the indigenous areas of Panama. Examples that correspond to historically delayed areas of Chile in economic and social terms (Regions VII, VIII and IX, the central-southern part of the country where the Mapuche population is located), Bolivia (the *altiplano*, where there is a high concentration of Quechua and Aymara people), and Brazil (the northeastern region). These three areas are noteworthy because they generate emigration. The data from the 2010 censuses show continuity in this trend in Panama's Kuna Yala province, which presents a net emigration rate of around 4 % per year. In Bolivar and Carchi, two poor provinces in the Ecuadorean sierra, one finds the greatest amount of emigration. Mexico's states of Chiapas, Guerrero and Oaxaca (the three poorest in the nation located in the southern region of the country) maintain net emigration. The erosion of the base of qualified human resources that this tenacious emigration implies for regions presenting chronic poverty is as important as or perhaps more important than the above, though its analysis goes beyond the reach of this text (ECLAC 2012; Rodríguez and Busso 2009).

15.3.2 A Model for Migrants

The model to be developed should possess the capability to evaluate the effect of different variables on the workers' migration decisions. In a free market, it is usually proposed that prices are the main sources of information upon which decisions are made. Thus, labor, under a free market, should focus mainly on salaries in each of the regions in the process of making the migration decision.

In addition, there will be other variables that affect migration and these are well documented in the literature. For example, attention is often directed to the role of amenities, development of the regions, the age of the migrant and his/her family status and so forth.

In order to set the model, we follow Kanaroglou and Ferguson (1996, p. 272), who stated that "because choice models are firmly rooted in behavioral theory, aggregation must result in models consistent with theory", and Borjas (2001), who used a similar model to study the worker's internal migration decision in USA.

This model is drawing on classical consumer theory. It is assumed that a worker's migration decision can be represented by the following index function determined by the utility maximization problem over possible locations $j \in \{1, 2 \ldots n\}$, (Aroca and Maloney 2005).

Therefore, $I^* = V_j - V_i - C$, where I^* is the index, V the indirect utility function in the context of random utility theory and C is the migration cost. In addition, V is a linear function of location characteristics X, such that $V_j = X_j \beta + \varepsilon_j$. Thus, if region j is preferred to the residential region i, the worker will move to region j if $I^* > 0$. Extending for the whole population, we might state the probability of migration as:

$$P(I^* > 0) = P(V_j - V_i - C > 0) = P(\varepsilon_i - \varepsilon_j \leq X_j\beta - X_i\beta - C)$$

Following Gourieroux (2000), for aggregate data we will estimate:

$$F^{-1}[p(I^* > 0)] = X_j\beta - X_i\beta - C$$

Where the probability function F is determined by the structure of the errors. Therefore, the estimation of this model will be done by a weight least square, given that $F^{-1}[.]$ will be heteroskedastic.

15.3.3 The Results

In order to estimate the model, data for Argentina, Bolivia, Brazil, Chile and Mexico was collected. The dependent variable is the rate of migration from region *i* to region *j*. This was calculated as the ratio between the number of people that have move from region *i* to region *j* over the number of people living at region *i* at the initial period.

Explanatory variables were included in the model to capture three different dimensions:

1. Public good availability and agglomeration benefits for people,
2. Market signals to reallocate labor force,
3. Level of regional development and
4. Moving costs.

The population size at the origin and destination region were included in the model to capture the pull effect associated to the public good and agglomeration benefits that people might get from larger populated regions, or the push effect or lack of attractiveness of regions with small size of population. Therefore, we expect that people tend to move to those regions with larger population size, leaving those regions less populated, promoting a population concentration process.

In order to capture the market signal, we include the wages paid at the regions. The literature has reported that in developing countries the wages or income at the origin region can have to effect, when it is increasing some people might deter movement to other region because local conditions have improve relatively to other regions. However, other people that had decided migration but could not afford the moving cost, after the increasing in income they can pay the moving cost and migrate to other region. In Aroca and Maloney (2005) is used the origin income or wage as a level variable to capture the later effect (Ln w_i), and they use the relative income or wage between the regions to capture the former effect (w_j/w_i), we follow them.

In addition, the GDP per capita at the origin and destination region was introduced to capture the level of development of each region (yppp) as well as an Human Development Index (idh), expecting that people tend to move to those more developed areas. Finally, logarithm of the distance (ldist) was introduce to capture moving or migration costs, which are higher the farter is the destination region from the origin one.

The results are showed in Table 15.7 for the five countries under study: Argentina, Bolivia, Brazil, Chile and Mexico.

15.3.4 Moving Costs

The variable logarithm of distance is introduced in the model for capturing the moving cost. The coefficients estimated for the five countries have the expected

Table 15.7 Probit estimation for dependent variable: (Migrant from *i* to *j*/population in *i*)

	(1)	(2)	(3)	(4)	(5)
	Argentina	Bolivia	Brazil	Chile	Mexico
Population_i	0.012**	−0.112	−0.007***	−0.057***	−0.013**
	(0.005)	(0.071)	(0.003)	(0.020)	(0.006)
Population_j	0.069***	0.215***	0.019***	0.161***	0.055***
	(0.005)	(0.049)	(0.003)	(0.017)	(0.004)
Ln w_i	−0.078	0.625*	0.242***	0.394	0.126
	(0.108)	(0.362)	(0.080)	(0.246)	(0.155)
W_j/w_i	0.063*	0.346**	−0.016	−0.304**	−0.290***
	(0.035)	(0.170)	(0.054)	(0.119)	(0.087)
yppp20	0.036***	0.084	−0.005	−0.002	-0.015**
	(0.005)	(0.059)	(0.011)	(0.009)	(0.008)
yppp2D	0.014***	−0.132***	0.004	0.014*	0.029***
	(0.004)	(0.047)	(0.009)	(0.007)	(0.006)
Idh0	−5.877***	1.220	−0.051	−0.568	1.342
	(2.257)	(0.860)	(0.313)	(0.885)	(0.970)
idist	−0.432***	−0.517***	−0.384***	−0.124***	−0.306***
	(0.050)	(0.075)	(0.032)	(0.038)	(0.025)
Constantt	7.029***	−1.891	0.070	−4.166**	−1.287
	(1.383)	(2.851)	(0.702)	(1.739)	(1.213)
N	552	72	702	156	987
R^2	0.847	0.741	D.621	0.824	0.754

Standard errors in parenthesis
$^{*}p < 0.1$, $^{**}p < 0.05$, $^{***}p < 0.01$

sign and all of the very significant, indicating that people tend to move closer to their origin region. The impact of the moving cost on the migration decision is larger for Bolivia and smaller for Chile, while the other countries are in the average of those two. This is showing that moving costs is less important in the decision for Chilean than for Bolivian workers.

15.3.4.1 Public Good Availability and Agglomeration Benefits

The size of the population in the spatial unit, like region, state or province, at destination and origin is used to proxy the public good availability and agglomeration economies for the people. In this context, the larger the population it is supposed the more the availability of public good that makes a region more attractive.

The results show very consistent results, in the five countries, for the variable population size at the destination region. The estimates coefficients are strong significant, positive and systematically larger than the estimates for the population size at the origin region, which has the expected sign and are significant for Brazil, Chile and Mexico. However, it is not significant for Bolivia and for Argentina has a positive size. This result might be explained because people is migrating more from more populated region to Buenos Aires that dominated the whole migration process.

This result is an indication that the countries have a strong inertial force to keep concentrating around the main city or cities, because they attract more people than the ones migrating to less populated areas, as is reported in Atienza and Aroca (2013) in this volume.

15.3.4.2 Market Signals to Reallocate Labor Force

Logarithm of the wage at the origin region and relative wage between the destination and origin region were the two variables used to evaluate migration as the market mechanism to reallocate people across the territory.

The results in Table 15.7 show different patterns. For Chile and Mexico there is a negative relation between relative wage and migration, which is contrary to what we expected. For these two countries there is an explanation that might be plausible. These two countries, especially Chile, have an important production of raw materials that are exported. That production is done in the periphery regions, so a significant number of people do not go to live there, but work there through a long distance commuting scheme. People are leaving those regions even though there are an increasing number of workers commuting to those areas. This fact might be behind what it is captured by these coefficients for Chile and Mexico, given that those areas show high wages however they are not attracting people to live there.

For Argentina, Bolivia and Brazil, the significant coefficients have the expected sign, however there are some differences. For Argentina only the relative wage are significant, which means that there is not income effect at origin region promoting migration, while in Brazil is the other way around, the only significant effect is the log of wage at origin region, which means that for those low income Brazilian states, the increase in income promotes significantly migration to other states. In the Bolivian case, both effects are strong and higher than any of the other four countries.

15.3.4.3 Level of Regional Development

In addition to public good availability, market signal we include some variables that intent to capture the effect of regional development on migration, under the assumption that more developed areas attract people, while less developed ones push people to other regions.

The results in Table 15.7 show that Brazilian migration is not motivated by regional development, while it is for Chile and Mexico; people tend to move to those more developed areas.

Argentina is the most interesting result in this dimension, because it shows a negative effect associated to the Human Development Index (idhO) at origin region. A similar process was reported by Molho (1995) for some Britain remote areas. He called this "cumulative inertia" and described as a process where fewer out-migration opportunities jointly with a low development generate longer residence durations which become self-perpetuating, this results is complementary with the positive sign in the size of the population of the origin region. It means, people from less developed and populated areas are not the ones that are migrating, and it is reinforced with the positive sign associated to the gross domestic product per capita at the origin region.

15.4 Conclusions

Migration in Latin America is not a homogeneous process across the countries analyzed in this chapter. In the last decades, we find for some countries, people following the market signals, while in others movement of people across regions is dominated for some inertia that is there for other factors, like culture, institutions, and sociological characteristics.

In addition, it seems that there is not policy to promote movement of the people to those areas where they might have a better quality of life. In general, countries shows a reduction of the migration, so it is likely to find strong persistence in those processes that it is supposed are affected migration in the equilibrium direction.

According to the results of the estimated model, the most robust result is associated to the size of population at the destination region. It is an indication that people is moving to larger city than where they were living. This result explains in part, what other chapters in this volume have reported, which is a large concentration around the largest city of the country.

It also allows concluding that the migration as a market mechanism to reduce spatial inequality in the territory, like unemployment or wage differentials, is not working properly, so again, regional policy is required to promote a more balanced development in the countries territories.

References

Aroca P, Atienza M (2011) Economic implications of long distance commuting in the Chilean mining industry. Resources Policy 36:196–203

Aroca P, Maloney WF (2005) Migration, trade, and foreign direct investment in Mexico. World Bank Econ Rev 19(3):449–472, Oxford University Press

Atienza MP, Aroca (2013) Concentration and growth in LA countries. Chapter 5 of this volume

Bell M, Muhidin S (2009) Cross-National Comparisons of Internal Migration. Human development research paper, No 2009/30, (PNUD)

Borjas G (2001) Does immigration grease the wheels of the labor market? Brook Pap Econ Act 32 (1):69–134

Cunha, M da (2002) Urbanizacion, redistribucion espacial de la poblacion y transformaciones socioeconomicas en America Latina, Serie Poblacion y desarrollo, 30 (LC/L.1782-P), ECLAC, Naciones Unidas, Santiago de Chile

Cunha M, Rodríguez J (2009) Urban growth and mobility in Latin America, en SuzanaCavenaghi (organizer), demographic transformations and inequalities in Latin America historical trends and recent patterns. ALAP, Rio de Janeiro, pp 25–63, Serie Investigaciones No. 8, www.alapop.org/docs/publicaciones/investigaciones/DemogTransformations.pdf

ECLAC (2012) Population, territory and sustainable development, Santiago, Chile, ECLAC, LC/L.3474(CEP.2/3)

Gourieroux C (2000) Econometrics of qualitative dependent variables. Cambridge University Press, Cambridge

Guzmán JM et al (2006) La démographie de l'Amériquelatine et de la Caraïbedepuis 1950. Popul-F 61(5–6):623–733, InstitutoNacional de EstudiosDemográficos (INED), París

Kanaroglou PS, Ferguson M (1996) Discrete spatial choice models for aggregate destinations. J Reg Sci 36:271–290

Molho I (1995) Migrant inertia, accessibility and local unemployment. Economica 62(245): 123–132

Ocampo JA (Ed.) (2006) La cooperación financiera regional: Experiencias y desafíos. Libros de CEPAL, No 91 (LC/G.2319-P/E), Comisión Económica para América Latina yel Caribe (CEPAL). Publicación de las Naciones Unidas, Santiago de Chile, No de venta: S.06.II.G.103

Rodríguez J (2008) Distribución espacial, migración interna y desarrollo en América latina y el Caribe, vol 96 (LC/G.2396-P), Revista de la CEPAL. Comisión Económica para América Latina y el Caribe (CEPAL), Santiago de Chile

Rodríguez J (2011) The spatial distribution of the population, internal migration and development in Latin America and the Caribbean, en population distribution, urbanization, internal migration and development: an international perspective. United Nations, Department of Economic and Social Affairs, Population Division, Nueva York, ESA/P/WP/223, pp 54–80

Rodríguez J, Busso G (2009) Migración interna y desarrollo en América Latina entre 1980 y 2005, Un estudio comparativo con perspectiva regional basado en siete países. Libros de la CEPAL No. 102, LC/G.2397–P. CEPAL, Naciones Unidas, Santiago de Chile, N° de venta: S.09.II.G.14

Rodríguez J, Martine G (2008) Urbanization in Latin America: experiences and lessons learned. In: Martine G, McGranahan G, Montgomery M, Castilla-Fernandez R (eds) The new global frontier: cities, poverty and environment in the 21st century. IIED/UNFPA and Earthscan, London, pp 353–367

Chapter 16
Education, Innovation and Economic Growth in Latin America

Miguel Ángel Mendoza-González, Marcos Valdivia-López, and Jorge Isaac-Egurrola

16.1 Introduction

The population of Latin America has doubled three times in the past 60 years; today around 550 million people live in the region, representing 7 % of the world's entire population. The region's workforce (those aged 15 or over) has increased continuously and reached 75 % of the total population in 2010, up from 60 % in 1950. Young people with primary or secondary schooling now face additional restrictions to get higher wages: they are unemployed for long periods in some countries of the region, uneducated working force remain without a job up to 9 months (CEDLAS and the World Bank 2012) and in the past two decades this process has accelerated even more with trade liberalization and the internationalization of tertiary education in the region (Hans de Wit et al. 2005). At the same time, firms are now demanding skilled workers with more than formal and elementary education because of the technological innovation which is taking place in many production processes (Schwartsman 2001). For this reason, the role of unskilled and skilled workforce against innovation and the use of new technologies are important to explain the poor average growth of GDP per capita (1.8 %) in Latin America during the period 1950–2010 (Astorga 2010).

This paper analyzes how economic growth in Latin America is affected by the linkages between population in school (net enrollment rate) and population with different educational skills enrolled in the job market; and in particular, this study

M.Á. Mendoza-González (✉)
FE-UNAM, México
e-mail: mendozag@unam.mx

M. Valdivia-López
CRIM, UNAM
e-mail: marcosv@correo.crim.unam.mx

J. Isaac-Egurrola
FES-Acatlán, UNAM
e-mail: jeiemx@yahoo.com.mx

J.R. Cuadrado-Roura and P. Aroca (eds.), *Regional Problems and Policies in Latin America*, Advances in Spatial Science, DOI 10.1007/978-3-642-39674-8_16,

focuses in whether skilled workers are engaged in production processes through practices of imitation or innovation of technologies and, how this affects economic growth performance. To analyze the challenges that education in Latin American faces to promote economic growth, we take the approach of United Nations's Millennium Development Goals (United Nations 2006) using coverage indicators designed by CEDLAS and World Bank (2012) and also considering the methodology of Barro and Lee (2010) to adjust workforce schooling at the primary, secondary and tertiary levels.

It is generally accepted that education has a strong effect on the training of human capital and economic growth (Deutsch and Silber 2009) and it is recognized that formal education is one component of human capital, the others being people's education, training, experience and/or IQ (Castelló-Climent and Hidalgo 2010; Breton 2011; Ram 2007). On the other hand, it has been pointed out that it is important to define the role of the levels of human capital and the use and generation of technological innovation in production processes, as the basis to promote long-term economic growth (Aghion et al. 2009; Galor 2011). Workers need secondary or higher education for the imitation and/or generation of technology, but it is not enough to develop scientific capabilities or creative skills (Florida 2002). It is also established by others authors that the necessary capabilities or skills for the imitation or generation of technological innovation are complementary and only match the concepts of human capital and creativity in specific analytical situations (Marrocu and Paci 2010).

Relying on the mentioned analytical framework, this chapter focuses on assessing the ability of countries in Latin America to innovate or imitate technological processes, and how it could trigger long-term and sustained economic growth from 1950 to 2010. We elaborate empirically this approach using five panel models of economic growth that involve the identification of the technological frontier through the choice of a leading regional economy with three options (Mexico, Argentina and Chile) and, a leading continental economy (United States). The main result of implementing these models is that tertiary or qualified education had long-term effects on the region's economic growth performance, but only through processes of technological imitation instead of innovation.

This chapter is structured with six sections including this introduction: the second one assesses an evaluation of Latin America's education performance against those established by United Nation's Millenniums goals; the third analyzes the characteristics and trends of education of the workforce in Latin America, based on schooling years; the fourth section presents the theoretical framework used in this research to understand the relationships among education, innovation and economic growth; the fifth section provides the econometric specification, estimation and results of the models proposed to evaluate the effects of education under a framework of innovation and long-term economic growth in Latin America (1950–2010); and the last section includes some final remarks.

16.2 Challenges for Education in Latin America

For several decades the discussion on Latin America's economic performance has focused on issues of macroeconomic stability, especially hyperinflation, restrictions in the accumulation of reserves and, more recently, the effect of trade liberalization on economic growth (Astorga 2010; Bengoa and Sánchez-Robles 2003; Díaz-Bonilla and Robinson 2010). Yet there has been little discussion on the relevance of education or human capital as a decisive factor on the region's long-term economic growth (Chumacero and Fuentes 2006; Díaz-Bonilla and Robinson 2010; De Gregorio 1992). Therefore most governments in the region have targeted their public policies on reducing poverty and improving their populations' quality of life. As a result, the creation and implementation of education policies that could have a direct impact on the living conditions of people remains an unresolved issue in most Latin American countries (Blanco and Cusato 2009; Tarabini 2010; Tarabini and Jacovkis 2012).

In the past decade, the most important public policy on education in Latin America has been focused on addressing the huge lack of coverage of basic education. Most countries, therefore, have worked toward meeting the second objective of the Millennium Development Goals, namely ensuring that everyone received a primary education and that children finished a complete cycle of primary schooling. The millennium goal implies that specific policies are established to reach terminal efficient to primary schooling, such as the increase in literacy rates for the population in general and for women aged 15–24 in particular (United Nations 2006).

According to the net enrollment rate indicator for primary-level education for 18 countries in Latin America, one can observe that good progress has been made toward achieving the second objective of the millennium goals (see Fig. 16.1). A group of countries has achieved net enrollment rates equal to or higher than 97 %, practically the same as those in high-income countries(Bassi et al 2012); Argentina and Chile lead this group, followed by Costa Rica, Paraguay, Peru, Panama, Mexico, the Dominican Republic, Brazil, Ecuador and Venezuela. Another group of countries lags slightly further behind with net enrollment rates lower than 97 % but higher than 93 % and which may take some years to reach the millennium goal; in order of importance, these countries are: Colombia, Bolivia and Honduras. Finally, there is a group of countries with enrollment rates lower than 93 % which will probably have difficulties reaching the millennium goal by 2015: El Salvador, Nicaragua and Guatemala. According to the regional report on Regional Human Development Report for Latin America and the Caribbean (UNDP 2010), a variety of structural conditions for each country have affected the speed of progress toward the millennium goals in the area of universal primary schooling by 2015. The most important of these factors include the schools' infrastructure, monetary and/or financial aspects, and cultural and social conditions in the home.

The information shown in Fig. 16.1 shows us that there is a large diversity in the net enrollment rates in secondary education reached by each country. This tells us

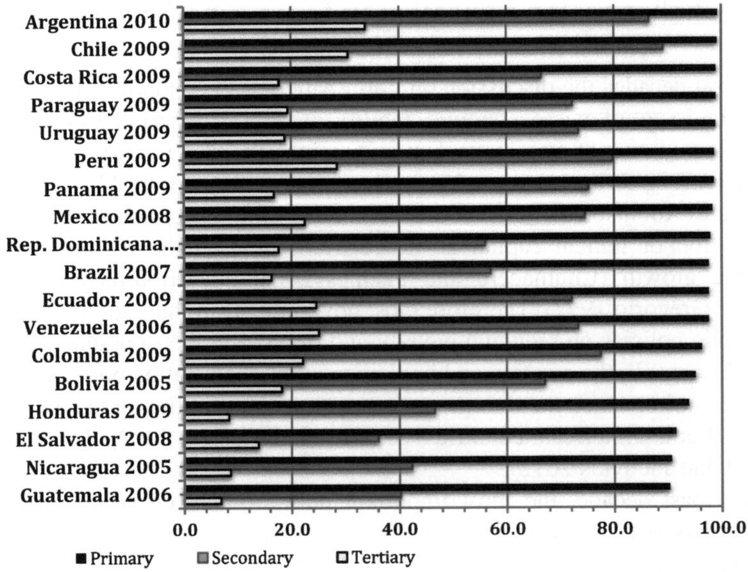

Fig. 16.1 Net enrollment rate for primary, secondary and tertiary education in Latin America: 2005–2010 (Source: Data from Socio-Economic Database for Latin America and the Caribbean CEDLAS and the World Bank 2012. Note: In the figure there is specified the year of reference for the net enrollment rate, which is measured as the proportion between the number of children officially of school age who are enrolled in primary, secondary or tertiary education and the total population of children officially of school age (United Nations 2006))

that the variety in enrollment rates in the region can be explained partly by the region's lack of a concept of public policy on education, which might coordinate efforts between countries to make progress similar to the millennium goals for primary education less unevenly. For example, countries such as Chile and Argentina that are leaders in meeting the millennium goal for primary education have a successful education policy that can be seen in the results of the secondary education enrollment rates that are very close to those specified in the millennium goals (rates higher than 90 %), in contrast to the results achieved by the other countries. A second group consists of ten countries which have a highly varied net enrollment rate for secondary level education between 60 % and 80 % coverage; this shows not only a major shortfall in terms of coverage at that level compared to the two leaders in the region, and also that the gap within the same group appears hard to close in the short term. This group consists of Peru, Colombia, Panama, Mexico, Uruguay, Venezuela, Paraguay, Ecuador, Bolivia and Costa Rica. And finally, there is a group of six countries who have fallen far behind with enrolment rates between 30 % and 60 %: Brazil (57 %), the Dominican Republic (56 %), Honduras (46 %), Nicaragua (42 %), Guatemala (40 %) and El Salvador (36 %). The disparity in secondary enrollment levels is clearly evident when we consider the differential in net enrollment rates between the leading country (Chile) and the poorest performer in secondary level education (El Salvador), which has a rate of

53 %. This shows that any education policy that seeks to improve the secondary education enrolment rates must look for very long-term political strategies and policy among countries in the region.

Public policy on tertiary education followed by some countries in Latin America seems to respond to a combination of internal needs and international conditions (Teichler 1999), which have arisen when the region began down the path toward trade liberalization and internationalization of services. The region's leading economies that have focused on a strategy of market liberalization have also sought a policy of educational internationalization, such as the academic mobility of students and teachers, the building of international networks, agreements and projects, and new international research programs (Hans de Wit et al 2005). Nevertheless, national public policy on higher education in this group of leading countries seems to be prioritizing the incorporation of younger students in higher education, so that countries like Argentina, Chile, Peru, Venezuela, Ecuador, Mexico and Colombia continue maintaining low enrollment rates between 25 % and 30 %. Most countries in Latin America have a coverage of between 16 % and 25 % in higher education, and countries that have fallen far behind such as Nicaragua, Honduras and Guatemala have levels lower than 10 %. The disparities in the rate of tertiary enrollment in the region are even more pronounced when comparing the enrollment rate of Argentina (34 %) with that of Guatemala (7 %) – see Fig. 16.1.

16.3 Educational Characteristics and Trends for Latin American Workforce

In the past 60 years, the time it has taken young people to join the workforce has changed dramatically. For example, in countries such as Argentina, Bolivia, Brazil and Venezuela, a young person between 15 and 24 years old can spend between 7 and 9 months without finding work; the young in Colombia, Costa Rica, the Dominican Republic, Ecuador, El Salvador, Honduras, Panama and Paraguay, take an average of between 3 and 6 months to join the workforce; meanwhile, the young take less time to find work in Chile, Peru, Uruguay, Guatemala and Nicaragua (CEDLAS and the World Bank 2012). In addition to the unemployment and its duration that affects the young, secondary education is no longer enough to find well-paid employment; now their salaries are lower on average and they tend to be concentrated on low added-value economic activities. This problem is exacerbated by the lack of tools and educational quality offered by the education system which is inadequate to compete in a job market that requires greater adaptation and/or technological innovation to be prepared for the trade liberalization and internationalization facing Latin American economies on the whole (Bassi et al 2012).

In order to analyze the characteristics and trends of the level of education for people at the moment of joining the workforce in the Latin American region, below we present various indicators of education estimated by Barro and Lee (2010).

Their proposed methodology has the virtue of building indicators of average years of education for the population of working age, based on completed studies that depend, among other factors, on the enrollment rates according to educational level (primary, secondary and tertiary). Barro and Lee's work has undergone a series of changes since the first version of their paper was published in 1993, in which they built indicators for a group of 129 countries, divided into 5-yearly periods from 1960 to 1985, considering the adult population over 25 years' old who were classified as having no formal education, primary, secondary and higher. In the second version of the study in 2000, the number of countries increased to 142 and the population of a working age was changed so that the threshold was 15 rather than 25 years' old, which was more relevant to the situation of the workforce of many developing countries such as those in Latin America. The study was improved by incorporating the estimates of the average years of education, the adjusted enrollment rates in the case of students who repeat the school year at a primary and secondary level, the existing changes in the length of schooling, etc.

In Barro and Lee's revised 2010 study, the set of data on completed education was built for 146 countries from 1950 to 2010. On this occasion they break down the figures by gender and by age cohorts of 5 years and four categories of education: no formal education (*lu*), primary (*lp*) secondary (*ls*) and tertiary education (*lh*). Primary includes complete and incomplete primary studies; secondary includes lower and upper secondary, and tertiary education includes both junior-level and higher-level tertiary.

The number of years of education for the age group a, $s^a{}_t$, is estimated as:

$$s_t^a = \Sigma_j h_{j,t}^a Dur_{j,t}^a \tag{16.1}$$

Where $h^a{}_{j,t}$ is the fraction of age group a at the level of completed education $j = 0$ for no education, $j = 1$ for primary, $j = 2$ for secondary and 3 for the highest level during time t. For the populations aged 15 and above, 13 age groups of 5 years were constructed, $a = 1$ (15–19 age group) to $a = 13$ (75 and above). And the variable *Dur* indicates the corresponding duration of the education cycle.

The years of schooling for the population aged 15 and above, s_t, was constructed as an aggregation of the years of schooling of age group, considered as the participation of the population of group g in the population aged 15 and above, $l^g{}_t$,

$$s_t = \Sigma_{a=1}^A l_t^a s_t^a \tag{16.2}$$

The interesting aspect of this proposal by Barro and Lee (2010) is that the years of schooling can be aggregated or disaggregated by primary, secondary and tertiary level of schooling to analyze the characteristics and tendencies of the levels of education of the population of working age (15 and above) in Latin American countries for the 1950–2010 period.

16.3.1 Characteristics and Trends of the Population with Years of Schooling at Primary Level

To analyze the effect of primary education on the workforce, firstly a box plot is used for the average years of schooling at primary level among the Latin American countries, for the 1950–2010 period. According to the average years of schooling at primary level, represented by white lines within the box plot in Fig. 16.2, the countries are ordered from higher to lower averages and the results show that Argentina, Chile and Uruguay are those with the largest population with years of schooling at primary level throughout the entire period. The indicator of standard deviation or sigma convergence for the average years of primary education between Latin American countries from 1950 to 2010 (see charts in the second column of Fig. 16.2) complements the results shown with the box plots. The trend of the indicator shows that there was a process of divergence from 1950 to 1975, when countries with higher per capital income made progress toward achieving better enrollment rates and thus increased the proportion of the population with primary education. After this process, most Latin American countries followed an educational policy that led the poorest countries to close the gap between them and the larger ones; this process lasted almost 25 years. It is interesting to note the trend after the millennium development goals were set in 2000, when the countries committed to attaining them by 2015 (United Nations 2006). Countries increased resources to raise the level of enrollment at primary level, and therefore the working age population with primary school education grew quickly. As a result, for a short period, the disparities in the populations' average years of schooling at primary level increased (in the 2000–2004 period). Following this initial process of divergence, the less-developed countries could channel more resources and this led to a process of convergence between Latin American countries. In Fig. 16.2, the sigma convergence chart shows the years of schooling at primary level that clearly demonstrates the divergence and convergence for the 2000–2004 and 2005–2010 periods respectively.

Similarly, with the analysis of the functions of the normal kernel density estimations for the years of schooling at primary level among countries during the 1950–2010 period (see charts on the right side of Fig. 16.2), we can find behaviors that confirm the aforementioned trends. For an improved reading of the kernel functions, the 1950 distribution is highlighted in black and light gray for subsequent years. The results clearly show a typical behavior for 1950, where the average years of schooling at primary level was 2.2 years, with two groups of countries distributed evenly underneath and over this average, and with limit values close to zero and to 5 years of primary education. The second notable aspect is the movement of distributions toward the right over time, implying that Latin American countries were systematically increasing years of schooling over time. Another important result of the estimated distributions is the reduction in the dispersion of years of schooling during the 1950–2010 period, as this indicates a steady closing of the gap between countries in terms of years of schooling at primary level.

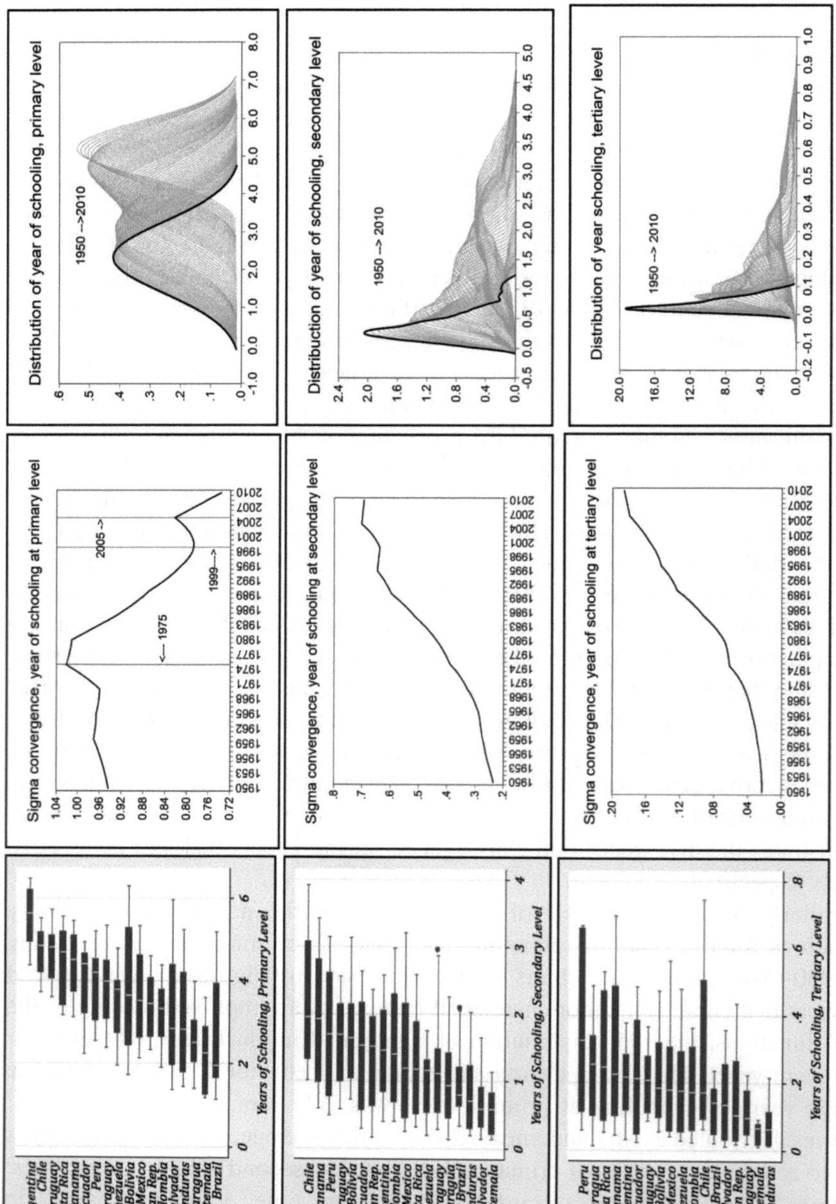

Fig. 16.2 Structure and trends for average years of schooling at primary, secondary and tertiary level of the workforce in Latin America, 1950–2010 (Source: Compiled by authors based on Barro and Lee (2010))

16.3.2 Characteristics and Trends of the Population with Years of Schooling at Secondary Level

The panorama for the population with years of schooling at secondary level among Latin American countries is very different to that observed in primary education. Firstly, the averages shown in the box plots show that Chile, Panama and Peru have made the most progress in terms of the size of population with secondary education; but if we look at the limit values of the box plots, Chile, Panama and Mexico have the highest schooling levels. At the other extreme, Guatemala, El Salvador and Honduras have the region's lowest levels of years of schooling at secondary level, as shown in the averages of the box plots.

Secondly, the sigma convergence chart showing the years of schooling at secondary level in Latin American countries shows a process of divergence that began in 1950 and which accelerated in the 1970s prior to the setting of the millennium development goals, and halted in the mid-1990s before increasing again in the early 2000s and stopping again in the middle of the decade. The 1950 kernel density shows a very compact distribution, indicating that the initial disparities were very small since the majority of countries in the region had very low levels of schooling at secondary level.

Nevertheless, the distributions begin to move rapidly toward the right over time, but now they are more stretched out and less spiky. This means an increase in the disparities in the levels of schooling years at secondary level, with countries with 0.5 years of secondary schooling at one extreme, and those with less than 3 years of secondary schooling at the other.

16.3.3 Characteristics and Trends of the Population with Years of Schooling at Tertiary Level

The disparities between Latin American countries in terms of the population with years of schooling at tertiary level is more serious still, because none of the countries have a population of 15 years or above with an average of more than 1 year of tertiary education. Secondly, the box plots clearly show the peculiarity of the disparities in tertiary education: on the one hand, countries such as Peru, Nicaragua and Costa Rica have high averages but they are not necessarily the countries with the highest populations with years of schooling at tertiary level at the end of the period in question; in this group we find, in order of importance, Chile, Panama and Peru. The sigma convergence chart (Fig. 16.2) reveals that the disparities in years of schooling at tertiary level have tended to increase constantly over the period, highlighting the accelerating disparities since the 1980s up until their apparent deceleration after 2005. According to the estimated distributions, most countries had a population with an average of less than 0.1 years of tertiary education in 1950; and therefore the distribution shape for that year is compact and very high (see the last chart in Fig. 16.2). The distributions since 1950 move right but not symmetrically around the average; unlike primary and secondary schooling, the distributions are slanted toward the left, indicating that a high concentration of countries have few years of tertiary schooling and a small group of countries have years of schooling at tertiary level far above the average.

16.4 The Relationship Between Education, Innovation and Economic Growth

Differences between Latin American countries in terms of net enrollment rates have been reduced as a result of public policies implemented in order to attain the millennium development goals for primary education. Most countries have a coverage of primary level education above 90 % in the 2007–2010 period, and everything indicates that the millennium goals can be reached by most Latin American countries by 2015. This policy of increased primary level coverage has in turn had an impact on the population entering the workforce. The proportion of the population aged 15 or over with primary education has grown sharply in the countries lagging furthest behind, such that it generated a process of convergence between Latin American countries in the average years of schooling at primary level. This regional convergence process contrasts with the particular and specific policy of a set of countries which, as a result of trade liberalization and globalization of tertiary services and in particular education services, has aimed to improve coverage of secondary level education and to transform the tertiary educational system (Bassi et al. 2012), without this necessarily resulting in a greater coverage of higher education.

There is a clear link between coverage and education of the workforce. However, this is not so evident when analyzing the skilled workforce's role and function in adapting to or creating innovation, and therefore its influence in generating long-term economic growth in Latin America. The trends of convergence in primary education and the divergence in the secondary and tertiary education of the workforce in Latin America suggests that the participation of the workforce in technological processes is noted less for generation and more for the imitation of innovation.

As Deutsch and Silber (2009) mention, various studies have found that education is an important source human capital formation and economic growth. However, as it is known, this focus on considering education as the sole source of human capital has been fiercely criticized (Florida 2002; Marrocu and Paci 2010; Ram 2007), and has led to the development of two important trends in the definition of the concept of human capital and its corresponding empirical measurement in economic development and growth studies.

The first trend establishes that the education obtained from the school system is the most important part of human capital, but that it must also consider the quality of people's education, training, experience and/or IQ (Castelló-Climent and Hidalgo 2010; Breton 2011; Ram 2007). In the case of educational quality, a proposal exists to include different aspects of knowledge such as the measuring of cognitive aspects which consider IQ levels and which have been identified through two pillars to construct the skill sets required by the job market; math and language. The OECD's PISA (Program for International Student Assessment) survey is an international assessment system focused on measuring the abilities of the population with 15 or more years of schooling in writing, math and science. The PISA survey has the virtue of focusing on measuring abilities and skills that are developed in the education system and which can be used to resolve problems encountered in daily life and in the job market.

The second trend focuses on differentiating human capital for production purposes in regard to the use and creation of technological innovation, thus creating an indicator for the impact on long-term economic growth. For Aghion et al. (2009), the possibility of generating companies' research and development activities is derived from linking the highly educated workforce to economic growth and innovation. Under these conditions, one expects that skilled workers generate a process of technological innovation that in turn leads to a greater production of goods and services, and companies' long-term growth. However, there also exists the possibility that skilled workers are hired but only to imitate and adapt technology in production processes, with a greater effect on companies' sustained growth in the long term.

Using the aforementioned analytical schemes, we can suppose that less-skilled workers neither adapt nor generate technology in production processes (Papageorgiou 2000, 2003; Simões 2011). In this sense, it is recognized that workers with primary and secondary-level education can only meet some of companies' production needs. Furthermore, workers need to have medium or higher level education in order to carry out technological imitation and/or generation activities, but it is not enough to develop scientific knowledge or creative skills (Florida 2002). It is also recognized that many of the skills or abilities needed to imitate or generate technological innovation complement come before or even match the concepts of human capital and the creative class in specific analytical situations (Marrocu and Paci 2010).

16.5 The Effects of Education in a Framework of Innovation and Long-Term Economic Growth in Latin America: 1950–2010

The theoretical model underpinning this part is the study carried out by Papageorgiou (2000, 2003) consists of a proposal to establish economic growth through the combination of human capital, innovation and technological adoption. The most important concept that uses the notion of contiguous knowledge – the idea that knowledge can be disseminated over a short distance, meaning that only economies existing near to the technological frontier can grow rapidly and ensure an advantage or benefit by adopting a specific technology. The proposal also includes the relationship between technological innovation-adoption and growth that forms the basis of an empirical proposal. Papageorgiou's theoretical and empirical proposals are used to analyze the role of the workforce in technological processes, to note whether it is due to the imitation or generation of innovation and to measure the effects of long-term economic growth for Latin American countries. But unlike Papageorgiou who only studies the levels of primary and post-primary education, this paper follows a strategy similar to that of Simões (2011), Ang et al. (2011) and Palacios (2009), which analyze the importance of primary, secondary and tertiary education in the explanation of long-term growth. For this purpose, a set of econometric specifications are estimated with panel model with the aim of assessing the impact of the workforce's three levels of education in the economic growth of 18 Latin American countries for the 1950–2010 period.

16.5.1 *Specification of the Panel Model*

Three types of workforce were considered for the analytical model, according to the criteria proposed by Barro and Lee (2010): with primary, secondary and tertiary education respectively, and the capital-work ratio is included as an indicator of the technology used.

The analytical model has the following panel econometric specification

$$\begin{aligned} \ln\left(y_{i,t}/y_{i,0}\right) &= c_0 + c_{0,I} + c_1 HA, ter_{i,t} + c_2 HA, ter_{i,t}\left(y^{*}{}_0/y_{i,0}\right) + c_3 \ln\left(K_{i,t}/L_{i,t}\right) \\ &+ c_4 \ln\left(HY, pri_{i,t}/HY, pri_{i,0}\right) + c_5 \ln\left(HY, sec_{i,t}/HY, sec_{i,0}\right) + u_{i,t} \end{aligned} \tag{16.3}$$

Where the Latin American countries are identified by $i = 1, 2,.., 18$ and the years by $t = 1950, 1951,..,2010$.

The model establishes that the long-term economic growth $[\ln(y_{i,t}/y_{i,0})]$, measured according to Gross Domestic Product, is explained by the highly-skilled workforce with tertiary education ($HA,ter_{i,t}$), where it is supposed that they are involved in the processes of technological change through innovation and imitation of new technologies. Therefore it is established that the measurement of the process of imitation (μ) is obtained directly with the parameter c_2 and the innovation process (δ) indirectly from the imitation parametersandc$_1$; $\delta = c_1 + \mu$ (Papageorgiou 2003). It is important to note that the process of technological imitation is measured by the educated workforce involved in research and development multiplied by the $y^{*}{}_0/y_{i,0}$ ratio, which represents the proximity of an economy's technology ($A_{i,0}$) to the technological frontier ($A^{*}{}_0$). From the empirical point of view and following Benhabib and Spiegel (1994), ($y^{*}{}_0/y_{i,0}$) is used in the specification as a good predictor of the $(A^*_0/A_{i,0})$ relationship. The proportion of capital accumulation to the workfare is measured by capital/work ratio. And finally, the growth of the workforce with primary education $(\ln(HY,pri_{i,t}/HY,pri_{i,0}))$ and secondary education $(\ln(HY,sec_{i,t}/HY,sec_{i,0}))$ is included, implying a short-term influence on long-term economic growth. In the panel specification, it is very important to record the heterogeneity of economic growth through the individual constants and that measure the regional differences between countries, which are a combination of the average effect (c_0) and an individual effect $(c_{0,I})$.

16.5.2 Identifying Latin America's Leading Economy

In order to define the technological frontier(y^*_0), different indicators were analyzed to help identify the region's leading economy, while keeping the possibility open of finding more than one leading country. In principle, by analyzing the net enrollment rates for primary, secondary and tertiary levels of education, Argentina and Chile stood out as the leaders. Argentina and Chile also led the way in terms of years of primary schooling, while Argentina and Panama ranked highest for years of secondary schooling; and, finally, Peru, Panama and Chile came top in tertiary and higher education. From the economic perspective, it was important to consider countries with the highest levels of income per capita and/or per worker, under the following characteristics: (1) The countries that stood out a being leaders at the beginning of the period; (2) Those that maintained their leadership throughout the period, for which an average income indicator was used; and, (3) Countries that maintained the highest incomes throughout the period. According to these characteristics, Argentina, Venezuela and Mexico had the highest income for the period per capita and/or per worker, while Mexico and Chile maintained a leading position throughout the period, and Mexico had the highest GDP per capita and per worker. With this combination of education indicators and GDP per capita, for the purposes of this analysis the following countries were identified as the regional leaders: Argentina, Chile, and Mexico. And for making comparisons with other studies, the United States was identified as the continental technological leader. For example, in the study by Papageorgiou (2003), Switzerland was identified as the technological leader, since it had the highest per capita income for the first year of the period in question.

16.5.3 Analytical Design, Econometric Estimates and Results

To analyze the context in which the primary, secondary and tertiary education levels create long-term economic growth in Latin American countries, five models were designed with different specifications in terms of educational level and possible technological leaders in the region.

Table 16.1 Panel models for education, innovation and economic growth in Latin America Panel Data Set: 18 countries, 1950–2010

	Aggregated schooling and regional leader: Mexico	Schooling level (Pri, Sec and Ter) and regional leader: Mexico	Schooling level (Pri, Sec and Ter) and regional leader: Argentina	Schooling level (Pri, Sec and Ter) and regional leader: Chile	Schooling level (Pri, Sec and Ter) and regional leader: United States
Const.	0.005	0.002	−0.002	−0.002	0.000
prob.	(0.55)	(0.73)	(0.00)	(0.00)	(0.00)
Δ(K/L)	0.549	0.566	0.639	0.626	0.631
prob.	(0.00)	(0.00)	(0.00)	(0.00)	(0.00)
ΔH	0.052				
prob.	(0.56)				
ΔHy, pri		−0.186	−0.275	−0.213	−0.259
prob.		(0.09)	(0.00)	(0.00)	(0.00)
ΔHy, sec		0.115	0.137	0.120	0.121
prob.		(0.05)	(0.00)	(0.00)	(0.00)
H	−0.009				
prob.	(0.10)				
HA,ter		0.004	0.001	−0.003	−0.001
prob.		(0.16)	(0.00)	(0.00)	(0.00)
$H^*(A^*/A)$	−0.020				
prob.	(0.00)				
HA,ter*(A^*/A)		0.012	0.004	−0.002	0.001
prob.		(0.00)	(0.00)	(0.00)	(0.00)
Innovation (δ)	−0.009	0.004	0.001	−0.003	−0.001
Imitation (μ)	−0.020	0.012	0.004	−0.002	0.001
Adjusted R-squared	0.15	0.16	0.16	0.15	0.15
Obs	982	982	982	983	1,041

Method Estimation: Fixed-Effects, EGLS (Cross-section weights); Cross-section SUR (PCSE) standard errors & covariance

16.5.3.1 Model 1: Aggregated Schooling and Mexico as Regional Leader

The first model uses the years of average aggregate years of schooling to analyze the short-term effect and to record the effects of innovation and imitation on long-term growth. In regards to the regional leaders in Latin America, Mexico had the highest GDP per capita in the indicator showing the average and maximum levels for the entire period, and therefore the technological border (y^*_0) is measured as the GDP per worker in Mexico.

This is a model with a panel data set that is estimated according to fixed effects, least squares generalized with considerations of a cross-section and efficient errors with SUR restrictions on the variance-covariance matrix (see Column 2a in Table 16.1). The increase of the (Δ(K/L)) ratio was significant, with a positive and the highest parameter value, making it the main source with which to explain the region's economic growth. The increase in the years of average schooling in the region (ΔH) has the expected parameter but is not significant, the long-term impact (H) has negative and insignificant parameter, and its interaction with the differential in regard to the technological frontier ($H^{*}(A^{*}/A)$) was negative and significant. This implies that in this model, education does not affect economic growth in the short term, and nor does it affect it in the long-term and instead of leading to a closer proximity it has the effect of furthering the distance from the technological frontier of the regional leader, which is Mexico in this case. Therefore there is a negative innovation coefficient, and a negative and insignificant imitation coefficient, indicating a different process than the one suggested in the theoretical model.

16.5.3.2 Model 2: Levels of Primary, Secondary and Tertiary Education, and Mexico as Regional Leader

For the second model (see Column 3a of Table 16.1), three levels of education are included in terms of the average years of schooling at primary (Hy,pri), secondary (Hy,sec) and tertiary (HA,ter) level. As was proposed in the specification of the model in Eq. 16.3, the hypothesis is that the workforce with primary and secondary training participates solely in direct production processes, while the skilled workforce influences the innovation or technological imitation processes. The model of average years of primary and secondary schooling incorporates the growth rate and years of tertiary schooling and multiplied by the differential regarding the technological frontier ($HA,ter^{*}(A^{*}/A)$) that, for the model, remains the GDP per worker for Mexico.

This model uses a panel data set and applied the same type of estimate and correction to obtain the efficient parameters such as in the case of Model 1. The growth of the (Δ(K/L)) ratio keeps maintaining the status of the principal source for explaining the region's economic growth. After incorporating the three levels of education in this model, it is found that the growth in the average number of years of primary schooling in the region (ΔHy,pri) has a negative and significant parameter, which implies that it is restricting rather than boosting economic growth in Latin America. The result for the growth of secondary level schooling years (ΔHy,sec) shows that it tends to increase economic growth, but it has a lower parameter than that of the years of primary schooling. The combination of the effects of the years of primary and secondary schooling implies that instead of complementing one another, one replaces the other to limit or boost growth in Latin America; for example, economic growth is restricted if the proportion of the workforce is more biased toward primary education, while the opposite state of affairs can reduce this restriction and boost economic growth.

The long-term effect of education on economic growth is measured by the years of tertiary or skilled education, and is identified by the parameters of the innovation processes (HA,ter) or imitation processes ($HA,ter^{*}(A^{*}/A)$) or δ and μ, respectively. The results of the estimates show that the parameter for the innovation process has a positive but insignificant parameter, and therefore it is not a relevant factor in explaining economic growth; the parameter of the process of technological imitation, meanwhile, is positive and significant. The results imply that in a model of Latin American economic growth with a technological frontier anchored in Mexico, countries with a greater proportion of their workforce with primary schooling are limiting their economic growth, while an increase in the population with years of secondary schooling would foster economic growth. Tertiary or skilled education has long-term effects on economic growth, but through a process of imitation rather than technological innovation.

16.5.3.3 Model 3: Primary, Secondary and Tertiary Education Levels, and Argentina as Regional Leader

The only difference between this model and Model 2 is that Argentina is being considered as the technological frontier in this case. In this framework, the constant is significant and the growth parameter of the ratio (Δ(K/L)) increased, therefore it continues maintaining the status as the principal source in the explanation of economic growth in the region. Similarly, there was a slight growth in the positive and negative effects of the growth in the average years of schooling at primary and secondary levels. A difference from Model 2 is the effect of tertiary or skilled education has on the long-term economic growth, here the mechanism operates through the processes of innovation and technological imitation.

16.5.3.4 Model 4: Primary, Secondary and Tertiary Education Levels, and Chile as Regional Leader

With Chile as the regional leader in this technological frontier models (see Column 5a of Table 16.1), the conclusions are similar to those in the case of Argentina in terms of the K/L Ratio and effects of primary and secondary education on economic growth. The difference is the effect of tertiary or skilled education on the long-term economic growth, since here the mechanism resembles Model 1, with aggregated education, innovation processes and technological imitation indicating the contrary.

16.5.3.5 Model 5: Primary, Secondary and Tertiary Education Levels, and the United States as Regional Leader

As in the previous three models, the K/L ratio and the effects of primary and secondary education on economic growth do not change. In this case, the effect of tertiary or skilled education on long-term economic growth is based on a (negative) move backward in terms of the innovation process and technological innovation toward the United States' economy.

In brief, the results of the models analyzed in this section indicate that a higher rate of enrollment has an impact on the long-term growth of various Latin American economies. However, the results also suggest the long-term growth in the region may not be sustained (or desirable) even when countries increase the rates of enrollment in higher education; and this is because the skilled workforce is mainly working in processes of technological imitation rather than innovation; these are very similar results to those found by Papageorgiou (2003)in his models for low-income countries. This risk of only working on imitation processes is in turn also linked to a marked heterogeneity in the enrollment at secondary and tertiary level, a situation that has prevailed and even become more entrenched in countries in the region (see Sect. 16.4). As a final remark, this raises the possibility that the region as a whole might start out on a path of a far-reaching dynamic of growth – depending on a global policy among Latin American countries that seeks to close the gaps in the higher education enrolment rates and to encourage educational practices that go beyond technological imitation.

16.6 Conclusions

This chapter analyzed the links between the population attending school (net enrollment rate), the population joining the job market with different skills provided by education system (population with completed education), and their impact both on the production processes and on the imitation or generation of innovation (population with years of schooling at primary, secondary and tertiary level) as well as on the short and long-term growth of Latin American countries.

The second and third part of the chapter examined the challenges facing education in Latin America on the basis of the UN's Millennium Development Goals. We concluded that the levels and trends of the net enrollment rate, as well as the workforce's years of primary level schooling (the population calculated from those aged 15 and above), show: (1) that most countries in Latin America can achieve the goal of universal primary level education by 2015 (Objective 2 of the Millennium Goals); and (2) that the workforce with primary level schooling years is relatively homologous among Latin American countries.

The situation is very different when analyzing the enrollment rates and the years of schooling for secondary and tertiary education. Currently a great disparity exists between different countries in the region in terms of the coverage, with a sizeable distance between the leading countries and those lagging furthest behind. The differences in the proportions of the population with completed secondary and tertiary education, accumulated over the past 60 years, do not seem easy to reduce in the short term.

With this outlook, the discussion sought to assess the ability of Latin American countries to innovate or imitate technological processes, and thus contributes to short and long-term economic growth. Five economic growth models were defined for this purpose, notably identifying the technological frontier by choosing the three possible leading regional economies (Mexico, Argentina and Chile) and another continental and world leader (United States of America). We conclude that the workforce with primary education is restricting short-term economic growth, regardless of which is the leading economy. The population with secondary education helps boost short-term growth, and the skilled workforce or those with tertiary education do not generate innovation but instead participate in technological adaptation processes that favor long-term economic growth for countries in the region.

Databases and Indicators

The variables for GDP, investment, completed education and average years of schooling used in all the estimates are sourced from two general databases: New Data Set of Educational Attainment in the World, 1950–2010 by Barro and Lee (2010), and the Penn World Table Version 7.0 by Heston, Summers and Aten (2011).

Barro and Lee (2010). This database was used for the indicators of completed education and the years of average schooling at the three education levels (primary, secondary and tertiary). All the indicators are constructed on a 5-yearly basis, and therefore the non-linear interpolation methods was used to cover the intermediary years from 1950 to 2010. CEDLAS and the World Bank (2012) Socio-Economic595 Database for Latin America and the Caribbean (http://cedlas.econo.unlp.edu.ar/eng/index.php).

References

Aghion P, Boustan L, Hoxby C, Vandenbussche (2009) The causal impact of education on economic growth: evidence from the United States. Brook Pap Econ Act conference draft, spring 2009

Ang J, Madsen J, Islam M (2011) The effects of human capital composition on technological convergence. J Macroecon 33:465–476

Astorga P (2010) A century of economic growth in Latin America. J Dev Econ 92:232–243

Barro RJ, Lee J-W (2010) New data set of educational attainment in the world, 1950–2010, working paper 15902 http://www.nber.org/papers/w15902, National Bureau of Economic Research 1050

Bassi M, Busso M, Urzúa S, Vargas J (2012) Disconnected, skills, education and employment in Latin America, Inter-American Development Bank, IADB

Bengoa M, Sánchez-Robles B (2003) Foreign direct investment, economic freedom and growth: new evidence from Latin America. Eur J Polit Econ 19:529–545

Benhabib J, Spiegel M (1994) The role of human capital in economic development: evidence from cross country data. J Monet Econ 34(14):173

Blanco R, Cusato S (2009) Desigualdades educativas en América Latina: todos somos responsables, working paper, UNESCO

Breton T (2011) The quality vs the quantity of schooling: what drives economic growth? Econ Educ Rev 30:765–773
Castelló-Climent A, Hidalgo A (2010) Quality and quantity of education in the process of development, working paper, Institute of International Economics and University Carlos III, Madrid
Chumacero R, Fuentes R (2006) Economic growth in Latin America: structural breaks or fundamentals? Estudios de Economía 33(2):141–154
De Gregorio J (1992) Economic growth in Latin America. J Dev Econ 39:59–84
Deutsch J, Silber J (2009) Estimating an educational production function for five countries of Latin America on the basis of the PISA data. A report on a research project funded by RBLAC-UNDP 2009 Regional Report on Inequality in Human Development, Department of Economics, Bar-Han University
Diaz-Bonilla E, Robison S (2010) Macroeconomics, macrosectoral policies, and agriculture in developing countries. Handbook of Agricultural Economics, Elsevier B.V. 4:3035–3213
Florida R (2002) The rise of the creative class. Basic Books, New York
Galor O (2011) Inequality, human capital formation, and the process of development. Handbook of the Economics of Education, Elsevier B.V. 4:441–493
Hans de Wit Jaramillo I, Gacel-Avila J, Knight J (eds) (2005) Higher education in Latin America: the international dimension. The World Bank, Washington, DC
Heston Summers, Aten (2011) Penn world table version 7.0. Center for International Comparisons of Production, Income and Prices at the University of Pennsylvania, Philadelphia
Marrocu E, Paci R (2010) Education or creativity: what matters most for economic performance? Working Paper, Centro Ricerche Economiche Nord Sud
Palacios N (2009) Los efectos de la educación en el crecimiento de América Latina. Facultad de Economía de la Universidad del Rosario, Thesis Research
Papageorgiou C (2000) Technology adoption, human capital, and growth theory, Working Paper, Louisiana State University
Papageorgiou C (2003) Distinguishing between the effects of primary and post-primary education on economic growth. Rev Dev Econ, November 7(4):622–635
Ram R (2007) IQ and economic growth: further augmentation of Mankiw–Romer–Weil Model. Econ Lett 94:7–11
Schwartsman S (2001) The future of education in Latin America and the Caribbean, Working Paper for the seventh meeting of the regional inter-governmental committee of the major project of education in Latin America and the Caribbean
Simões M (2011) Education composition and growth: a pooled mean group analysis of OECD countries. Panoeconomicus 4:455–471
Tarabini A (2010) Education and poverty in the global development agenda: emergence, evolution and consolidation. Int J Educ Dev 30:204–212
Tarabini A, Jacovkis J (2012) The poverty reduction strategy papers: analysis of a hegemonic link between education and poverty. Int J Educ Dev 32:507–516
Teichler U (1999) Higher education policy and the world of work: changing conditions and challenges. High Educ Policy 12:285–312
United Nations (2006) Indicators for monitoring the millennium development goals: definitions, rationale, concepts and sources. United Nations Development Group, New York
UNDP (2010) Regional human development report for Latin America and the Caribbean. United Nations Development Programme – UNDP, New York

Chapter 17
The Geography and Determinants of Regional Human Capital in Eight Latin American and Caribbean Countries

Francisco Rowe

17.1 Introduction

There is broad consensus concerning the importance of human capital in economic development (Lucas 1988; Barro 1992). Human capital accumulation stimulates economic growth and development through direct and indirect transmission channels (Lucas 1988; Mathur 1999). Large endowments of highly educated individuals in a region plays a key role in local economic performance, accelerating the rate of technological change, innovations, diffusion inventions and emergence of entrepreneurs (Mathur 1999; Desrochers and Leppäla 2011). Spatial concentration of human capital also promotes knowledge spill overs, enhancing the linkages between new ideas, technology and economic development (Jacobs 1969).

Recognising the importance of human capital in economic development has driven the need to derive a better understanding of the various economic and non-economic factors shaping its spatial distribution. Most prior analyses have been focused on Western European and North American countries (e.g. Florida 2002b; Boschma and Fritsch 2009; Mellander and Florida 2011). In Latin America and the Caribbean (LAC), however, the economic geography of human capital has remained an unexplored issue, probably due to the lack of temporally consistent spatial data. In Western European and North American countries, along with other factors, previous studies have paid special attention to the role of high-technology industries and diversity (in terms of immigrants) in determining the spatial concentration of highly educated individuals (Florida 2002b, c; Clifton 2008; Boschma and Fritsch 2009). In contrast, in LAC countries, these factors appear to be less important in explaining the spatial distribution of human capital since these countries have a lower level of development of high-technology industries and more homogenous populations (smaller proportions of immigrants) (Hill 2002;

F. Rowe (✉)
Queensland Centre for Population Research, School of Geography, Planning and Environmental Management
e-mail: f.rowegonzalez@uq.edu.au

J.R. Cuadrado-Roura and P. Aroca (eds.), *Regional Problems and Policies in Latin America*, Advances in Spatial Science, DOI 10.1007/978-3-642-39674-8_17,

World Bank 2011). Thus, while there are grounds for arguing that a different set of factors have shaped the geography of human capital in LAC, there is not empirical evidence demonstrating these arguments.

This paper aims to redress this gap in the existing literature by analysing the spatial concentration of human capital and the factors that shape its configuration in LAC countries. In particular, it seeks to answer four questions: (1) How has the stock of human capital changed in LAC countries over the last five decades? (2) What is the degree of spatial concentration of human capital in these countries? (3) Does it concentrate in particular regions? (4) What are the factors that explain regional differences in human capital accumulation across LAC countries? In addressing these research questions, the analysis focuses on eight LAC countries: Argentina, Brazil, Bolivia, Chile, Colombia, Ecuador, Mexico and Peru. These are the LAC countries for which a dataset of temporally consistent spatial data could be assembled from two consecutive census rounds (i.e. the 1990 and 2000 census rounds).

The paper is structured as follows. The next section reviews previous work on human capital, and identifies the importance and influence of four sets of factors in shaping its spatial distribution. Section 17.3 discusses the obstacles to cross-national comparative analysis, followed by a description of the approaches adopted to address these obstacles, and the data, methods and variables used in the analyses in Sect. 17.4. Section 17.5 begins the analyses by examining the national stock and temporal variations of human capital in the eight LAC countries in the sample. Section 17.6 explores the spatial distribution of human capital before investigating the role of four sets of factors in explaining the regional differentials in human capital accumulation using fractional regression models. Finally, Sect. 17.7 summaries the main findings of the analyses.

17.2 Literature on Regional Human Capital

This section first considers the importance of human capital in regional economic development, and then reviews the literature with a focus on two current issues which are relevant to this study: (1) the measurement of human capital and (2) the factors influencing its spatial distribution.

In economic geography, theoretical work has stressed the associations between human capital and economic growth. In the 1950s, Ullman (1958) pointed out the importance of human capital in the concentration of regional economic development, before Jacobs (1969, 2000) articulated this link by stressing the role that cities play in economic development through accumulation of knowledge and skills embodied in individuals. She argued that larger and more diverse cities increase human creativity and knowledge spill overs, leading to an acceleration in the generation of new ideas and innovations. In the same vein, Andersson (1985) emphasised the role of communications, culture environment, knowledge and creativity on regional performance. He argued that human capital accumulation is an essential component in reinforcing regional creativity and economic development. According to endogenous growth theory (Romer 1986; Lucas 1988) human capital accumulation can impact economic growth through two channels: schooling and learning-by-doing (Romer 1986; Lucas 1988). In sum, all this work recognise that spatial concentration of human capital creates and accelerates knowledge spillovers and creativity, foresting regional economic growth.

Confirming these theoretical linkages, empirical evidence in various geographical contexts has substantiated the positive influence of human capital accumulation on economic growth. Barro (2001) and Benhabib and Spiegel (1994), for instance, provided evidence on this association from a national-scale perspective. Boschma and Fritsch (2009) and Fischer et al. (2009) verified this association at the regional level for a group of European countries; while other analyses have corroborated this connection for regions within single countries, such as the United States (Rauch 1993; Simon 1998), the United Kingdom (Simon and Nardinelli 1996), Sweden (Mellander and Florida 2011) and the Netherlands (Marlet and Van Woerkens 2004).

While there is consensus on the importance of human capital in regional economic development, there has been lively debate on two key issues (Florida et al. 2008; Mellander and Florida 2011). The first is concerned with the measurement of human capital. Generally, educational attainment indicators are used to measure human capital. Individuals with bachelor's degree or above are commonly considered as measure of human capital. With the emergence of Florida's (2002c) creative class, more recent studies have suggested occupational-based indicators. These indicators attempt to measure what people do, rather than what they study. These measures have led to a controversy over whether or not members of the creative class differ from highly skilled and educated individuals (Marrocu and Paci 2012). Glaeser (2005) persuasively claimed that there is not benefit from including indicators of the creative class in economic growth models that already account for the influence of human capital in terms of educational attainment. This is because most members of the creative class are skilled and highly educated. Running regressions with Florida's data, Glaeser (2005) demonstrated that creative class variables become statistically insignificant and negative (opposite to the expected effect) when an educational attainment variable (i.e. the percentage of adults with bachelor's degree) is considered.

In contrast, other studies have shown that creative class measures outperform educational indicators in accounting for regional development (Marlet and Van Woerkens 2004; Mellander and Florida 2011). Considering both classes of measures, others have found contrasting evidence. Boschma and Fritsch (2009), for example, demonstrated that educational measures outperform creative class indicators in the Netherlands, whereas the opposite occurred in Germany. Despite these contrasting findings, most studies have found that the spatial distributions of both indicators are highly correlated (e.g. Glaeser 2005; Marrocu and Paci 2012).

Based on this evidence, given that the focus of this paper is on the spatial distribution of human capital, rather than on the impact of different categories of human capital or creative class on economic growth, the conventional definition of human capital is adopted here i.e. the regional share of individuals with bachelor's degree or above. It is important to note that although measures for the various categories of creative class are not considered here, the concepts and hypotheses developed by Florida are of great utility in explaining the geography of human capital. This study considers his concepts and the findings of associated empirical work testing his hypotheses.

The second issue relates to the factors that determine the spatial distribution of human capital. Three consistent findings have been pointed to underpin the relevance of this issue: (1) the growing spatial concentration of human capital in major cities; (2) the positive impact of human capital on economic development; and (3) the high mobility rates among highly educated individuals(Berry and Glaeser 2005; Florida et al. 2008; Mellander and Florida 2011). These findings have given rise to, the key question on: What are the main driving forces shaping the uneven distribution of the human capital across regions? We now consider the evidence accumulated by studies addressing this question based on North American and Western European contexts in order to formulate hypotheses that can be tested in the LAC context.

Various factors have been found to shape the spatial distribution of human capital. Four broad categories can be distinguished: (1) regional culture and climate, (2) regional amenities, (3) high-technology industries, and (4) controlling factors. The discussion next focuses on, the way in which each of these sets of factors influences the geography of human capital.

Studies have argued that differences in regional culture and climate influence the spatial distribution of human capital. Specifically, the climate of tolerance and diversity plays a key role in the attraction and retention of human capital (Florida 2002c). Talented individuals are attracted to regional societies that are tolerant and open-minded to diversity (Florida 2002b). Individuals view a tolerant and open environment as having low barriers to entry for human capital and as being positive to creativity since diversity inspires innovation (Jacobs 1969; Florida 2002c). Ottaviano and Peri (2005) demonstrated how diversity in terms of immigrants boosts productivity. Mellander and Florida (2011) noted that immigrants have complementary skills to the native population; they can perform different tasks, and also, bring different skills to the same tasks. Together with immigration, empirical analyses have shown that regions with high shares of bohemian population are associated with high shares of human capital (Florida 2002a; Boschma and Fritsch 2009). Bohemians add a sense of liveliness and tolerance to regions, making them attractive to talented individuals (Florida 2002a). In addition, Mellander and Florida (2011) argued that the geographical concentration of gay and lesbian households can also be a good indicator of tolerance and openness to diversity as high representation of these groups of population symbolise a society free from prejudices.

Studies have also emphasised the influence of regional amenities on the geography of human capital. Clark (2003) argued that amenities attract and retain talented and innovative individuals because these amenities redefine the local context and lifestyle. Amenities like operas, health facilities, news media, theatres, museums, restaurants, sports stadiums and local universities contribute to a city being cool, driving location decisions of individuals (Clark 2003). From these factors, local universities are likely to be one of the most significant factors as they play a key role in the local production of human capital, and therefore in its spatial distribution, increasing the local stock of highly skilled people (Comunian and Faggian 2011). In fact, it has been reported that despite of their high mobility rates, the vast majority of highly skilled individuals tends to stay in the same location where they graduate (Corcoran, Faggian and McCann 2010). Mellander and Florida (2011) demonstrated that the presence of local universities, relative to other factors, plays the most important role influencing the geographic distribution of talent in Sweden.

Boschma and Fritsch (2009) measured the influence of regional amenities on a segment of highly skilled individuals (creative core class) including two indicators in a regression-based analysis. They separated the effect of public provision amenities (e.g. universities, health facilities and parks) from that of cultural amenities (e.g. cinemas, restaurants and operas). In their regressions, whereas coefficients for public amenities were statistically significant for five of the six countries in their sample, those for cultural amenities were insignificant. These results thus point to the importance of differentiating between these two types of regional amenities.

The spatial concentration of human capital has also been associated with the geographical concentration of high-technology activity. Using data on US metropolitan areas, Florida (2002b) found a statistically significant association between the spatial distribution of talent and high-technology activity, indicating that, in the context of a knowledge-based economy innovative, high-technology activities are highly dependent on educated individuals. This thus appears to be the reason for which US knowledge-based industries firms have tended to cluster spatially to exploit the advantages of agglomeration that stem from common labour pools (Audretsch and Feldman 1996), and to have implemented strategies to retain and attract highly educated people (Florida 2002b). In addition, Berry and Glaeser (2005) demonstrated that places with higher initial endowments of human capital experienced faster growth of their stock of highly skilled individuals. They suggested that start-ups of new based-knowledge firms increase the local labour demand for highly educated individuals, and hence the local stock of human capital. Although Florida (2002b) also recognises the positive association between the geographical distribution of talent and high-technology activity, he focuses on the reverse causality of this association. He noted that the availability of talent may drive the location of firms in this industry. In the same vein, Simon and Nardinelli (2002) argued that highly skilled individuals are better able to implement existing knowledge and create new knowledge, enlarging the number and scope of local innovative and high-technology industries.

To isolate the influences of the three categories of factors discussed above, two controlling variables are commonly considered: population size and employment growth. As a result of their market size, larger regions attract company head offices, have important historical legacy, provide more consumer amenities and offer a more diverse ethnic and cultural environment. McGranahan and Wojan (2007) argued that these are all elements that may contribute to shape the geography of human capital. The economic literature also recognises that individuals are sensitive to local economic conditions. Economically more vibrant economies have been associated with high concentrations of human capital. Boschma and Fritsch (2009) found that employment growth is the most consistent factor in explaining the geographical distribution of particular creative groups (i.e. creative core and professional classes) in Western European countries.

Thus, this review identified four sets of factors which have been found to influence the regional distribution of human capital in North American and Western European countries (i.e. regional climate and culture, regional amenities, high-technology industries and controlling factors). Before we determine the importance of these factors in explaining regional differentials in human capital in the LAC countries, the next section considers the main obstacles involved in cross-national comparative analysis of the spatial distribution of human capital.

17.3 Impediments to Comparative Analysis

There are a number of challenges that prevent readable comparisons across countries. Various sources can introduce noise into the analysis, giving rise to 'artificial' differences across countries i.e. differences that are not related to the underlying pattern under analysis. Hence, it is important to identify the main sources of noise and seek approaches to minimise these differences.

In the current analysis, three major sets of obstacles to cross-national comparisons are identified. These obstacles derive from differences in (a) how human capital is measured, (b) the division of space and (c) temporal comparability.[1] Each of these issues is considered in the context of LAC countries.

(a) *How human capital is measured.* Since national educational systems and occupational structures differ across LAC countries, some countries employ different numeric classification systems to code data on education and occupation of employment. Hence, regardless of whether indicators of educational attainment or occupation are adopted to measure human capital, reconciliation of codes is essential to minimise errors in cross-national comparisons. The University of Minnesota holds a large compilation of census data from various countries, labelled Integrated Public Use Microdata Series, International (IPUMS). To make data from different countries comparable, the University of Minnesota uses international standard classification systems (the

[1] It is also recognise that differences in cross-national comparisons can also arise from differences in population coverage and data quality. However, in practice, there is little that can be done to minimise such differences after data collection and processing. Hence, this issue is not discussed in this section.

International Standard Classification of Education (ISCED) and International Standard Classification of Occupations (ISCO)) to homogenise education and occupation variables for various LAC countries, facilitating comparative analysis (Minnesota Population Center 2011). As will be discussed in the next section, these classification systems were adopted for the analyses in this study.

(b) *The division of space*. Differences in the size and shape of countries, and in the number and shape of regions within countries also prejudice cross-national comparisons. The degree of spatial concentration of human capital or the influence of factors driving its spatial distribution may vary with the level of geography. LAC countries usually code data to some zonal system based on administrative boundaries. Although these zonal systems are far from ideal, the UN-regional Office for LAC has developed two sets of spatial frameworks the DAM (División Administrativa Mayor) spatial framework which comprises major administrative divisions of LAC countries and the DAME (División Administrativa Menor) spatial framework which includes minor administrative divisions. These spatial framework seek to enable national comparisons across LAC countries by minimising differences in division of space. For the current analysis, since the theory and concepts reviewed in the previous section were developed in a city-level spatial framework, data were organised on the DAME level of regions which is equivalent to city-level regions.

(c) *Issues of temporal comparability*. Various changes in zonal boundaries occurred within individual LAC countries. From one census to another, zones were amalgamated or new zones were created. These changes cause discrepancies in zonal boundaries over time, compromising the temporal comparability of spatial indicators. In the context of single regression-based analyses, to avoid endogeneity problems, indicators for the drivers of the spatial distribution of human capital are normally measured in a period earlier than that for human capital. Thus, a temporally consistent spatial framework is crucial to explore the factors shaping the geographic distribution of human capital.

The next section describes the approach adopted to address these three issues in combination with a description of the data, methods and variables used in the analysis.

17.4 Data, Methods and Variable Definitions

The analysis is divided in two stages. In the first stage, the analysis explores the extent and temporal variations of human capital from a national scale using descriptive statistics. In the second stage, it examines the spatial distribution of human capital in each of the LAC country in the sample. To this end, the analysis first investigates the degree of spatial concentration of human capital, and then, seeks to determine the factors that explain the spatial differentials in human capital in a regression framework.

For the national-scale analysis, data from the 1960, 1970, 1980, 1990 and 2000 census rounds were extracted from the IPUMS database (Minnesota Population Center 2011). This database holds census microdata samples for 68 countries. It also offers consistently coded data in an effort to facilitate comparability across countries and over time, all crucial issues for cross-national comparability relevant to the current study as discussed in the pervious section. For the spatial analyses, a dataset of 5,978 city-level regions was assembled from the two latest, available rounds of censuses i.e. the 1990 and 2000 rounds.[2] In the process of this assembly exercise, actions were taken to address each of three issues described in the previous section.

A temporally consistent spatial framework was created to minimise temporal discrepancies in zonal boundaries (issue c, Sect. 17.3). A freeze history approach was implemented (Blake et al. 2000). This approach involves to freeze the geographical system at a certain point in time and track systematically subsequent alterations in geographical boundaries. In doing so, later observations can be adjusted back to an earlier geography. In the context of this study, it involves the reorganisation of the 2000 census data according to the spatial framework at the 1990 census round (see Appendix 1). To this end, data for Chile and Colombia were drawn directly from the censuses, while data for the six remaining countries were extracted from IPUMS. As mentioned earlier, the result of the harmonisation process was a dataset that covers a total of temporally consistent 5,978 city-level regions.[3] For the countries in the sample, these regions represent the smallest administrative level to which data were available (i.e. municipalities, departments, cantons and provinces). As mentioned in the previous section (issue b), this spatial framework corresponds to the DAME level of regions used by the UN-LAC Office to set comparative analysis for LAC countries.

For the regression analysis, the dependent variable was measured using 2000 census round data, while all independent variables were measured using 1990 census round data to avoid endogeneity problems.[4] Below details of the definitions of these variables are provided (Appendix 2).

---

[2] Data from the 2010 census round were not yet accessible for most countries in the sample (excluding Mexico); or they were only available in predetermined tables (e.g. Argentina, Brazil, Ecuador and Mexico). However, the analysis required customisable data to harmonise education- and occupation-based variables.

[3] It is important to note that, in addition to the procedures employed to create a temporally consistent spatial framework, the final number of regions in the dataset was also conditioned by the data available from IPUMS. Since IPUMS data are publicly available, its data holdings are restricted in spatial detail. Within larger regions, spatial units with populations smaller than 20,000 are amalgamated. Hence, for small geographic scales, this procedure reduces the number of spatial units for which data were originally collected.

[4] It is important to point out that the data used in this paper for Colombia (from the 2005 census) and for Peru (from the 2007 census) lie in 'the 2010 round of censuses' of UN classification scheme. This differs from what appears in Appendix 1.

17.4.1 Dependent Variable

The conventional educational attainment indicator was used to measure human capital. Human capital was measured as the share of the regional workforce with a bachelor's degree or above. The workforce was defined as those employed or unemployed individuals aged 15–64. To minimise differences across countries due to discrepancies in data classification systems (issue a, Sect. 17.3), the harmonised IPUMS variable of education attainment based on the ISCED-1997 developed by UNESCO (1997) was utilised.[5]

17.4.2 Independent Variables

From Sect. 17.2, the spatial distribution of human capital was found to have been associated with four categories of factors: regional culture and climate, regional amenities, high-technology industry and controlling factors. Most of these variables are based on data on occupation and industry of employment. Hence, the approach taken to minimise cross-national differences due to differing classification systems (issue a) is explained before describing each variable. For occupational-based variables we used the ISCO-88 developed by the International Labour Organisation (1988), while for industry-based variables we used the International Standard Industrial Classification, Rev.3 designed by the United Nations Statistics Division (1989). Occupational-based variables were measured at the three-digit level, while industry-based variables were gauged at the four-digit level. In the cases in which data at three or four-digit level of disaggregation was not available, the following upper level of the respective classification system was used.

Regional culture and climate. As noted in Sect. 17.2, more diverse, opened-minded and tolerant regions are expected to have over-representations of talented individuals. Following Boschma and Fritsch (2009), two indicators were considered to capture this influence. The first indicator was the share of regional workforce in bohemian occupations. Based on ISCO codes, various occupations were combined to define bohemian occupations. Appendix 2 lists the selected ISCO categories. High proportions of bohemians in a region represent a different local culture, lifestyle and values from those of mainstream, all elements which are expected to attract talented individuals.

The second indicator was the so-called openness index, which corresponds to the share of foreign-born population. This indicator was used to account for the degree of local tolerance, diversity and open-mindedness. As mentioned earlier, it is important to emphasise that immigration to the eight LAC countries in the sample is small. In 2000, the foreign-born comprised less than 4 % in all eight countries, whereas in European countries it made up over 9 % and over 13 % in North

[5] Data on Chile and Colombia were also harmonised using the ISCED-1997.

American countries (The World Bank 2011). Hence, the effect of the openness index on human capital in LAC countries is expected to be positive but less important than in European and North American countries.

Regional amenities. Boschma and Fritsch (2009) considered two indicators to account for the expected positive influence of greater diversity in the provision of local amenities on the spatial concentration of human capital. The authors included one indicator for measuring the effect of public amenities, and one for assessing the influence of cultural amenities. Following Boschma and Fritsch (2009), two measures were considered here. The first is an indicator of public provision which was measured as the share of regional labour in education and health care. The second is an indicator of cultural amenities which was measured as the share of regional workforce in cultural and recreational activities. Appendix 2 lists the ISIC codes used for the definitions of these indicators. Since great diversity of local public and cultural amenities is thought to be important for educated individuals, high scores of these two indicators are expected to be associated with large shares of talented people.

High-technology industry. In the context of a knowledge-base economy, innovative and high-technology industries have been linked to a high incidence of highly educated individuals (see Sect. 17.2). Firms in these industries are expected to raise the local demand for knowledge, and hence for talent. To account for this effect, the share of regional workforce in high-technology industries was considered. To define high-technology industries, the definition of the Milken Institute (DeVol et al. 2004) was adopted. Following Boschma and Fritsch (2009), knowledge-intensive service industries were also incorporated to this definition. Appendix 2 catalogues the ISIC codes corresponding to these industries. As for the openness index, it is important to emphasise that the share of workers in high-technology industries was considered despite the fact that high-technology manufacturing activities appear to play a less important role in LAC economies relative to European, Central Asian and North American countries (Hill 2002). Brazil and Mexico could be considered as exceptions. High-technology manufacturing exports have become increasingly important in these countries, accounting for over 80 % of all LAC high-technology manufacturing production in 2000 (Alcorta and Peres 1998; Hill 2002).

Controlling variables. To isolate the effect of the three aforementioned factors, two controlling variables were used: regional job opportunities and population size. Population size was considered to account for a scale effect in the provision of local amenities and cultural climate. Larger and more urbanised regions tend to offer a more diverse environment and more consumer amenities. To measure regional regional economic conditions, the rate of employment growth between 1990 and 2000 was calculated, using data from the corresponding census round. This variable is expected to reflect the positive influence of regional economic conditions on the local accumulation of human capital.

Having described the data and methods, the next section starts the analyses by examining the extent and temporal variations of the stock of human capital in the

Table 17.1 National stock of human capital, census rounds

Census round					
Country	1960	1970	1980	1990	2000
Percentage					
Argentina	–	1.0	1.4	1.9	2.6
Bolivia	–	0.4	–	1.2	1.9
Brazil	0.3	0.5	1.2	2.3	2.8
Chile	0.4	0.7	1.0	1.7	2.7
Colombia	0.3	0.5	1.7	0.5	4.4
Ecuador	0.2	0.4	0.9	2.1	2.9
Mexico[a]	0.3	0.5	2.1	3.6	3.7
Peru	–			2.8	5.0
Number					
Argentina	–	229,150	387,772	624,186	945,840
Bolivia	–	19,350	–	78,040	156,570
Brazil	171,540	476,420	1,482,040	3,333,548	4,740,030
Chile	30,627	59,230	116,440	227,830	404,510
Colombia	47,650	105,370	465,933	159,120	1,766,395
Ecuador	10,230	26,767	74,870	201,290	356,040
Mexico[a]	84,219	244,400	1,739,530	3,240,232	3,626,965
Peru	–	–	–	624,130	1,374,550

Source: IPUMS
[a]The data on Mexico for 1980 and 1990 correspond to the 1990 and 1995 censuses, respectively

eight LAC countries, before Sect. 17.6 turns to examine the spatial distribution of human capital.

17.5 The Extent and Trends of Human Capital in Latin America

From the 1960s to the 2000s the national stock of human capital increased sharply in all eight LAC countries.[6] The data suggest that countries like Colombia, Ecuador and Mexico expanded their numbers of individuals with higher education qualifications by more than 30 times, while Brazil and Chile did by more than 13 times. Despite this substantial rise, the stock of human capital in the eight LAC countries remained smaller than in advanced countries. In 2000, it accounted for less than 3 % of the national population in five of the eight countries (Argentina, Bolivia, Brazil, Chile and Ecuador) and less than 6 % in the remaining three

[6] Note that cross-country differences in the number of individuals with university attainment are not directly comparable since they reflect differences in national population size and other demographic processes.

(Colombia, Mexico and Peru). In contrast, it made up more than 10 % of national population in advanced economies, such as Australia (15 %), New Zeeland (14 %), Japan (12 %) and the US (25 %) (Barro and Lee 2001).

Despite the efforts to harmonise the data and enable cross-national comparisons, national differences in the stock of human capital for the eight countries under analysis should be interpreted with care. For instance, the data suggest that Colombia reduced its stock of human capital by 1 % between 1980 and 1990, and then expanded it by more than 4 % between 1990 and 2000. This is the largest variation observed in the sample. The data also suggest that Colombia, along with Peru, had the largest percentage of people with higher education attainments of the eight countries. However, UNESCO data indicate that these two countries have consistently had a lower gross enrolment rate in tertiary education than Argentina from the 1970s and than Chile from the mid-1990s, suggesting that Colombia and Peru could not have achieved such large shares of highly skilled population (The UNESCO Institute for Statistics 1999). These data inconsistencies could be attributed to the existing difference in time interval between census dates. The time difference between censuses is larger (12 and 15 years) for Peru and Colombia than for the remaining countries (only 9 or 11 years). Given this discrepancy, we could only conclude that differences in the stock of human capital across the six remaining countries have been small (of less than 3 %), with Bolivia reporting the smallest accumulation of human capital.

While this section has shed light on the extent and temporal variations in the national stock of human capital in the eight LAC countries, it has not illuminated the spatial distribution of human capital within their borders. The next section explores this geographical arrangement.

17.6 Spatial Distribution of Human Capital in Latin America

This section is divided into two parts. The first analyses the spatial distribution of human capital in the eight LAC countries. Specifically, it seeks to measure the degree of geographical concentration of human capital and to identify regions with large human capital accumulation.[7] The second seeks to determine the factors shaping the uneven distribution of human capital using fractional response regression models.

[7] Efforts were made to map the data. However, discrepancies in geographic boundaries between data files prevented this action. Digital boundaries for the administrative units of each country, at hand, differ from those on which IPUMS data are geographically organised. To create consistent boundaries, an automatised procedure was not possible. Instead, a manual procedure was needed. However, harmonising zonal boundaries manually resulted impractical due to the large number of geographic units involved in the analysis.

Table 17.2 Gini coefficients of human capital, employment and population (2000 census round data)

Country	Human capital	Employment	Population
Argentina	0.73	0.56	0.56
Bolivia	0 88	0.61	0.55
Brazil	0.86	0.68	0.66
Chile	0.82	0.68	0.64
Colombia	0.62	0.45	0.43
Ecuador	0.83	0.61	0.58
Mexico	0.91	0.79	0.74
Peru	0.84	0.68	0.60

Note: For the calculations, 0 values were included using the algorithm developed by Stephen (1999)

17.6.1 Spatial Concentration of Human Capital

Table 17.2 shows the Gini coefficients for human capital, population and employment of the eight LAC countries. The Gini coefficient measures the degree of spatial concentration. It fluctuates from 0 (indicating an even distribution across regions) to 1 (indicating complete concentration in one region). The Gini scores suggest that human capital is highly concentrated at the city-level region. In all countries, human capital is more spatially concentrated than employment and population. These scores also suggest that the geographical concentration of human capital, employment and population is consistently higher in Mexico than in the seven remaining countries. By contrast, we could say that the spatial clustering of these variables seems to be lowest for Colombian regions. However, such comparison is avoided due to the data inconsistencies discussed in the previous section.

Analysing this spatial concentration from a different perspective, the share of regional workforce with bachelor's degree or above is considered. The box plots in Fig.17.1 reveal the spread of these shares within each of the eight LAC countries in the sample. The white middle band in the box represents the 50th percentile i.e. the median. The bottom and top of the box are the 25th and 75th percentile of the distribution i.e. the second and third quartile. The ends of the whiskers (lines extending from the box) represent the adjacent values. To calculate these values, the interquartile range (IQR) was used i.e. the difference between the first and third quartiles (Q3–Q1). In Fig. 17.1, the lower adjacent value is the smallest data score that is equal or greater than the first quartile minus 1.5*IQR, while the upper adjacent value is the largest data score that is equal or less than the third quartile plus 1.5*IQR. Data values beyond the lower and upper adjacent values are labelled outside values and are represented by dots in Fig. 17.1. From this Fig. 17.1, we can observe that differences in human capital endowment are the smallest across Bolivian regions, whereas they are the greatest across Mexican regions, with the region of San Andres Huayapam in the outskirts of the main city of Oaxaca having the largest share.

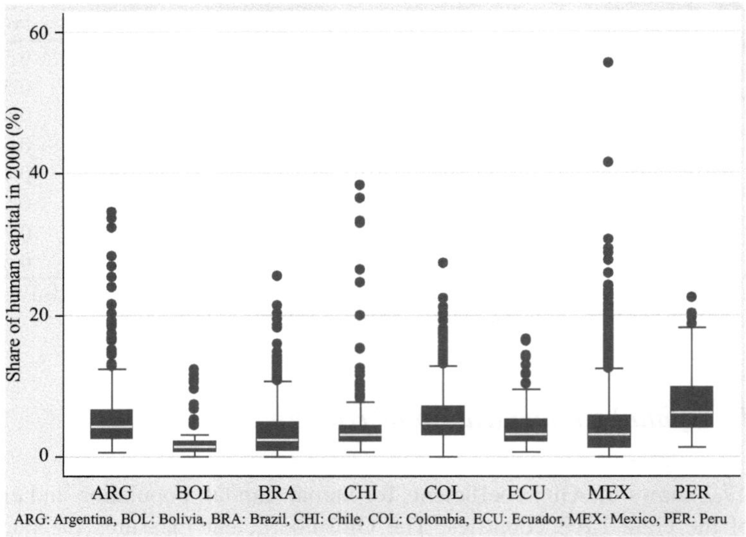

Fig. 17.1 Spatial distribution of human capital across regions in LAC countries in 2000 (%)

The most striking feature from Fig. 17.1, however, is the large number of outlier regions with high shares of human capital. These outliers regions include areas of capital cities of countries, major cities, capital cities of larger geographic administrative divisions (such as states, regions, provinces or departments) and their immediate surrounding areas (Table 17.3). In Argentina, for example, the outlier regions include the Federal districts of the Great Buenos Aires, Vicente Lopéz and the capital city of Mendoza. In Brazil, some of these outlier regions comprise areas of Sao Paulo, Rio de Janeiro and Santa Catarina. In Chile, the highest shares of human capital are in regions of the Great Santiago, Viña del Mar and Concepción. In Peru, outlier regions encompass the capital city of Lima and major cities, such as Arequipa and Cuzco.

The data for Colombia contrasts with these findings. These data suggest that most outlier regions include rural areas and small size city-towns (population $< 20{,}000$), with the exceptions of the capital city of Bogota and the main urban agglomerations of Barranquilla and Envigado. Together with the considerable temporal variations in the national stock of human capital noted in the previous section, this issue raises concerns about the quality of the data at hand for Colombia.[8] The problem may be associated with the use of individual data weights to create customised tables. It is unclear why individual data weights are used since the data are supposedly retrieved directly from the national census, which is

[8] The data used for Colombia were extracted from the RedatamWebServer of the UN population division for LAC (CELADE).

Table 17.3 Top/bottom ten human capital regions (%)

Top 10 regions		Bottom 10 regions	
Region name	Share of HC	Region name	Share of HC
Argentina			
District I	34.5	Rivadavia	0.6
District IX	33.6	25 de Mayo	0.6
District X	32.3	Lavalle	0.7
District II	28.3	Copo	0.7
Capital (Mendoza)	26.9	Department in Santiago del Estero province*	0.8
District VIII	25.4	General Manuel Belgrano	0.9
District VII	24.0	Federal	0.9
District XV	21.5	Guarani	0.9
District XVII	21.4	Independencia	0.9
Vicente López	20.2	Burruyacu	1.0
Bolivia			
Oropeza	12.3	Muñecas	0.0
Cercado (Cochabamba)	11.6	Provinces in Panda department	0.0
Cercado (Oruro)	10.9	Tapacari	0.1
Cercado (Tarija)	10.5	Loayza	0.1
Tomás Frías	9.5	Cornelio Saavedra	0.2
Murillo	9.5	Ayopaya	0.3
Andrés Ibáñez	7.3	Camacho	0.3
Cercado (Beni)	6.7	Bolívar Arque	0.3
Quillacollo	5.2	Charcas	0.3
Chapare	4.8	Tiraque	0.3
Brazil			
Niteroi	25.4	Conde	0.0
São Caetano do Sul	21.3	Pocao de Pedras	0.0
Florianópolis	20.4	Primeira Cruz merged	0.0
Vitória	19.4	Rio Real	0.0
Santos merged	18.6	Curralinhe	0.0
Porto Alegre	18.2	Jeremoabo merged	0.0
Rio de Janeiro	15 9	Itambe	0.0
Campinas	I4.8	Riachao das Neves	0.0
Curitiba	14.8	Jitauna	0.0
João Pessoa	14.1	Ribeira do Amparo merged	0.0
Chile			
Providencia	38.3	Rio Claro	0.6
Lai Condes	33.2	Ñinhue	0.7
Vitacura	32.9	Ñiquen	0.7
La Reina	26.4	San Clemente	0.8
Ñuñoa	24.6	La Pintana	0.9
La Barnechea	19.9	Longavi	1
San Miguel	15.3	Yerbas Buenas	1.1
Santiago	15.2	Juan de la Costa	1.1
Concepción	12.5	Retiro	1.1
Viña del Mar	12.0	Teno	1.1

(continued)

Table 17.3 (continued)

Top 10 regions		Bottom 10 regions	
Region name	Share of HC	Region name	Share of HC
Colombia			
Envigado	27.3	Papunaua	0.0
Bogota	22.3	Jurado	0.0
Barranquilla	21.2	Barranco Minas	0.0
Tabio	21.1	Puerto Colombia (GUA)	0.0
Arroyohondo	21.0	Yavarate	0.0
Chia	20.3	Mapiripan	0.0
Puerto Colombia	20.2	Miriti Parana	0.0
La Calera	19.2	Argelia	0.0
Pueblo Nuevo	18.1	La Guadalupe	0.0
Guamal	18.0	Rio Iro	0.0
Ecuador			
Loja	16.6	Guamote	0 66
Samborondon	16.3	Colta	0.67
Rumiñahui	14.3	Cantons in Cotopaxi province*	0.78
Quito	14.0	Pichincha	0.82
Portoviejo	12.9	Rio Verde	0.86
Cuenca	11.8	Urbina Jado	1.03
Guayaquil	11.7	Colimes	1.14
Riobamba	11.5	Alausi	1.19
Machala	10.4	Flavio Alfaro	1.29
Cantons in Galapagos province	10.3	Muisne	1.3
Mexico			
San Andres Huayapam	55.5	San Sebastian Río Hondo	0.0
Benito Juárez	41.3	San Martin Huamelulpam	0.0
San Pedro Garza Garcia	30.6	San Miguel Mixtepec	0.0
Coyoacan	29.3	Santiago Nacaltepec	0.0
Emiliano Zapata	28.6	San Martin Peras	0.0
Tlaxcala	27.7	San Pedro Quiatoni	0.0
Ciudad Madero	25.5	Santos Reyes Yucuna	0.0
San Sebastián Tutla	24.2	Santa Catarina Quioquitani	0.0
San Pedro Comitancillo	24.0	Tekom	0.0
Miguel Hidalgo	23.6	San Mateo Tlapiltepec	0.0
Peru			
Arequipa	22.4	El Dorado	1.3
Cuzco	20.2	Mono	1.7
Ica	20.2	Hualgayoc	1.8
Huaraz	19.6	Paucartambo	1.8
Huancayo	18.7	Cajabamba	2.1
Trujillo	18.3	Lamas	2.1
Lima	18.2	Bellavista	2.3
Puno	18.1	Paruro	2.3
Huaura	17.7	Canas	2.3
Huamanga	17.6	Pachitea	2.4

theoretically carried out to cover the entire population. Given the lack of clarity of the use of weights, no further analysis was conducted on these data.

For the seven remaining countries, the ten regions with the smallest endowments of human capital were also identified (Table 17.3). These regions tend to include poor areas, rural localities and small-medium size city/towns with a population between 20,000 and 50,000. In Bolivia, for instance, these regions include provinces, such Muñecas, Tapacarí, Loayza, Conelio Saavedra and Ayopaya. In Ecuador, among the bottom ten regions are the cantons of Guamote, Colta, Pichinga, Colimes along with small cantons (population $< 20{,}000$) in the Cotopaxi province. In Mexico, these regions include municipalities, such as San Sebastian Río Hondo, San Martin Huamelulpam, San Miguel Mixtepec and Santiago Nacaltepec, all which display a share of human capital of zero.

Thus far, the analysis of this section has demonstrated that particular regions (areas of capital cities of the respective countries, major cities, capital cities of larger geographic administrative divisions and their immediate surrounding areas) in LAC countries possess considerably higher endowments of human capital than other regions (poor areas, rural localities and small-medium size city/towns). In the next subsection, the analysis attempts to determine the factors underlying these regional differentials in human capital accumulation.

17.6.2 Explaining Differentials in Human Capital Accumulation Across Regions

To determine the factors underlying the uneven regional distribution of human capital, regression models were separately estimated for each of the seven remaining countries in the analysis: Argentina, Bolivia, Brazil, Chile, Ecuador, Mexico and Peru. In these regressions, the dependent variable was the share (proportion) of regional workforce with bachelor's degree or above. To define this variable, data from the 2000 census round were used. As described in Sect. 17.4, seven explanatory variables were included in the regressions to account for four broad groups of influences: regional climate and culture, regional amenities, high-technology industry and controlling factors. Specifically, the explanatory variables included were: the share of bohemian workers and the share of foreign-born employees (i.e. the openness index) to account for the influences of regional climate and culture; an indicator of the public provision and an index of cultural amenities to account for the effects of regional amenities; the share of employment in high-technology industries to account for their influence on the local demand of highly skilled individuals; and population size in logarithmic form and the rate of employment growth to control for scale and economic condition effects (for details, see Sect. 17.4).

Since the dependent variable is a proportion (share), there are certain properties of its distribution that prevent the valid application of linear regression models. A proportion tends to have a right-skewed distribution (see Fig. 17.1) and is bounded between 0 and 1 (Kieschnick and McCullough 2003). These properties imply that the influence of explanatory variables tends to be non-linear, and that the variance tends to decrease when the mean approaches to one of the boundaries (Kieschnick and McCullough 2003). To handle these type data, Baum (2008) advises the use of the fractional response model proposed by Papke and Wooldridge (1996). In a Generalised Linear Model (GLM) framework, this approach utilises the logit link function and binomial distribution to handle proportion data with zero and one values through the maximisation of the Bernoulli log likelihood. Consequently, this approach was adopted here to run the regressions. To account for spatial autocorrelation, the estimation strategy followed Cameron and Miller (2011) and Partridge et al. (2012). Using the Stata cluster command, city region residuals were assumed to be spatially correlated with neighbouring city regions within the same larger geographic area (such as provinces for Argentina) but independent from city region residuals in a different area. In doing so, the variance-covariance matrix of the estimators and standard errors were affected but not the estimated coefficients. Since estimates were derived from a non-linear model, marginal effects at mean values of the explanatory variables were also estimated.

In assessing the regressions, the squared-correlation between the observed and predicted values of the dependent variable (R^2) was used as a goodness-of-fit indicator. This measure ranges from 0 (indicating a poor fit) to 1 (indicating a perfect fit). To evaluate the significance of individual coefficients and multicollinearity, hypothesis tests and Variance Inflation Factors (VIFs) were used. The presence of multicolinearity is generally considered to be of concern when a VIF value exceeds ten (Chartterjee and Hadi 2006). For the variables in the analysis, these values were in most cases below three and never over six, suggesting that multicollinearity was not a problem of concern.

Table 17.4 presents the estimated model coefficients, marginal effects and diagnostic statistics. For six of the seven countries, high values of R^2 (>55 %) indicate that the fitted model explains a large proportion of the regional differences in human capital accumulation. The only exception was Brazil where other factors (not included in the model) seem to have also played an important role in shaping the geographic distribution of human capital at the city-region level.

The results provide little support about the importance of regional culture and climate factors in explaining regional differences in human capital endowment in LAC. For the share of regional workforce in bohemian occupations, although coefficients were positive for six of the eight countries, they were statistically insignificant in four countries (Bolivia, Ecuador, Peru and Mexico). For the openness index, coefficients were statistically significant only for Argentina and Brazil. For the former, contrary to our expectations, this coefficient was negative, suggesting that regions with high shares of foreign-born population (high diversity) tend to have low human capital endowments. For the remaining countries, coefficients associated with the openness index (the share of regional foreign-born population) were insignificant. This is likely to reflect the fact that the foreign-born population in these countries is too small (less than 2 % of national

Table 17.4 Regression models for the share of human capital in the workforce (Fractional response model)

Variables		Argentina Coefficients	Argentina Marginal effects	Bolivia Coefficients	Bolivia Marginal effects	Brazil Coefficients	Brazil Marginal effects	Chile Coefficients	Chile Marginal effects
Regional culture and climate	Share of bohemians	1.007***	0.052***	0.051	0.001	0.374***	0.012***	0.776***	0.03***
		(0.169)	(0.009)	(0.300)	(0.006)	(0.080)	(0.002)	(0.151)	(0.006)
	Openness index	−0.032*	−0.002*	−0.033	−0.001	0.235**	0.007**	0.016	0.001
		(0.014)	(0.001)	(0.042)	(0.001)	(0.090)	(0.003)	(0.011)	(0.000)
	Public provision	0.081***	0.004***	0.204***	0.004***	0.071***	0.002***	0.108***	0.004***
		(0.021)	(0.001)	(0.033)	(0.001)	(0.015)	(0.000)	(0.020)	(0.001)
Regional amenities	Cultural opportunity index	−0.031	−0.002	0.184	0.004	0.06	0.002	0.068*	0.003*
		(0.059)	(0.003)	(0.146)	(0.003)	(0.034)	(0.001)	(0.031)	(0.001)
High-technology industry	High-technology industry employees	−0.002	0.000	0.249	0.005	0.148***	0.005***	0.038	0.001
		(0.031)	(0.002)	(0.326)	(0.007)	(0.029)	(0.001)	(0.059)	(0.002)
	Rate of employment growth (1990–2000)	0.003**	0.000**	0.010*	0.000*	−0.003	0.000	0.001	0.000
		(0.001)	(0.000)	(0.004)	(0.000)	(0.002)	(0.000)	(0.003)	(0.000)
Controlling factors	Population(In)	0.18	0.009	0.307***	0.006***	0.140**	0.004**	−0.092	−0.004
		(0.092)	(0.005)	(0.078)	(0.002)	(0.049)	(0.001)	(0.083)	(0.003)
	Constant	−5.362***		−8.488***		−5.981***		−3.425***	
		(1.056)		(0.695)		(0.688)		(0.838)	
	Number of observations	307		84		1447		335	
	Log pseudolikelihood	−47.83		−6.46		−156.18		−42.17	
	Akaike (AIC)	111.65		28.92		328.37		100.34	
	R^2	0.71		0.81		0.44		0.69	

(continued)

Table 17.4 (continued)

		Ecuador		Mexico		Peru	
	Variables	Coefficients	Marginal effects	Coefficients	Marginal effects	Coefficients	Marginal effects
Regional culture and climate	Share of bohemians	1.194	0.05	−0.042	−0.002	0.109	0.007
		(0.623)	(0.025)	(0.031)	(0.001)	(0.205)	(0.014)
	Openness index	−0.057	−0.002	0.015	0.001	−0.09	−0.006
		(0.035)	(0.001)	(0.033)	(0.001)	(0.085)	(0.006)
	Public provision	0.308***	0.013***	0.082***	0.003***	0.119***	0.008***
		(0.034)	(0.001)	(0.007)	(0.000)	(0.021)	(0.001)
Regional amenities	Cultural opportunity index	0.389*	0.016*	0.116***	0.005***	0.257***	0.018***
		(0.187)	(0.008)	(0.024)	(0.001)	(0.047)	(0.003)
High-technology industry	High-technology industry employees	1.202***	0.05***	0.060***	0.002***	0.242	0.017
		(0.216)	(0.008)	(0.015)	(0.001)	(0.139)	(0.01)
	Rate of employment growth (1990–2000)	0.001*	0.000*	0.000	0.000	0.000	0.000
		0.000	(0.000)	0.000	(0.000)	(0.001)	0.000
Controlling factors	Population(In)	−0.022	−0.001	0.209***	0.008***	0.036	0.002
		(0.075)	(0.003)	(0.021)	(0.001)	(0.052)	(0.003)
	Constant	−4.056***		−5.841***		−4.059***	
		(0.774)		(0.233)		(0.604)	
	Number of observations	119		2403		169	
	Log pseudolikelihood	−15.58		−303.1		−32.47	
	Akaike (AIC)	47.79		622.19		80.94	
	R^2	0.65		0.58		0.72	

Note: Robust estimates (standard errors in parentheses). ***, **, and * indicate significant at 0.1 %, 1 %, and 5 % respectively. R^2 corresponds to the squared correlation between observed and predicted values of the regional share of human capital population) to exert any significant influence on promoting human capital accumulation. In contrast to the North American and Western European countries (e.g. Florida 2002c; Mellander and Florida 2011), the results suggest that regional differences in cultural climate, tolerance and diversity contribute little to explain regional differentials in the stock of human capital in LAC countries.

In contrast, the analysis suggests that regional disparities in public and cultural amenities are key in influencing regional differentials in the share of human capital. Coefficients for public provision were positive and statistically significant for all seven countries, indicating that highly educated individuals are especially sensitive to the local supply of educational and health services in LAC. Coefficients for the cultural opportunity index were positive for six of the seven countries (excluding Argentina) and statistically significant for Chile, Ecuador, Mexico and Peru. For these four countries, this finding could be interpreted as an indication that high level of local cultural amenities influences positively the local presence of highly skilled individuals. The results thus suggest that regional amenities play an important role in explaining the regional share of human capital in LAC. In particular, educational and health amenities seem to have been the most consistently influential factor across LAC countries.

The analysis also suggests that high-technology industries contribute to explain differences in human capital accumulation across regions in only three of the seven countries. Coefficients for the share of regional workforce in high-technology industries were positive and statistically significant only for Brazil, Ecuador and Mexico. For these countries, this result may indicate that firms in high-technology, knowledge-intensive industries have contributed to boost the local demand for highly educated individuals, and therefore increased the local stock of human capital. Whereas this result was expected for Brazil and Mexico, it was not anticipated for Ecuador. In the former countries, the share of regional workforce in high-technology industries was expected to influence the local accumulation of human capital because high-technology manufacturing activities in these economies have become increasingly important, accounting for more than 80 % of all high-technology manufacturing production of LAC economy as a single unit, in 2000 (Hill 2002). In Ecuador, however, the importance of high-technology industries influencing local human capital accumulation is more difficult to explain since these industries accounted for less than 0.01 % of employment in Ecuador.

Regarding population size and employment growth, the results indicate that these factors were important in explaining the regional share of human capital in only certain countries. For the rate of employment growth, coefficients were positive and statistically significant for Argentina, Bolivia and Ecuador, suggesting a strong impact of local labour demand on their regional stocks of human capital. By contrast, insignificant coefficients for Brazil, Chile, Mexico and Peru appear to indicate that employment grew faster in regions with both small and large shares of human capital, concealing the positive influence of local prosperous economic conditions on human capital accumulation. For population size, coefficients were positive and statistically significant for Bolivia, Brazil and Mexico, indicating that larger and more urbanised regions in these countries tend to have larger shares of highly educated individuals. For Argentina, Chile, Ecuador and Peru, insignificant coefficients for population, instead, reflect the presence of some small-medium size regions (10,000 < population < 50,000), with large endowments of human capital in the immediate surroundings of main cities. Regions in this group include the departments of Yerba Buena in Tucumanin Argentina; the municipalities of Lo Barnechea, Calera de Tango and Pirque in the Metropolitan region in Chile; and the province of Ilo in the department of Moqueguain Peru.

Overall, the results suggest that the provision of public amenities is the most prevalent factor in explaining regional differentials in human capital accumulation across the seven LAC countries. This is the only factor that was positive and statistically significant for all seven countries. In part, this finding may point to the key role of higher educational institutions (HEIs) in the local production, attraction and retention of human capital in LAC. This finding resembles those of Mellander and Florida (2011) for Sweden. In addition to the provision of public amenities, the regressions suggest that a unique combination of other factors contributes to shape the regional differences in the stock of human capital in each country. In Argentina, for example, the share of bohemians and employment growth also play significant roles in the regional distribution of human capital. In Mexico, instead, high-technology industry and population factors appear as the other two important drivers of the regional concentration of human capital. On the other hand, of all the factors, the results suggest that the openness index is the least prevalent factor in explaining regional differences in human capital accumulation in LAC countries. It is only significant in Brazil. This may point to the low degree of diversity or cultural openness in LAC countries as reflected by their small shares of foreign-born population.

17.7 Conclusion

In the economic geography literature, there has been a growing attention concerning the geography of human capital due to its key role in regional economic development. Most research has, however, been restricted to North American and Western European countries. In LAC, the spatial distribution of human capital has remained an unexplored topic, probably as a result of the lack of temporally consistent spatial data. Addressing this research gap, this paper examined the geography of human capital in eight LAC countries.

The evidence assembled here revealed that the national stock of human capital has risen in all eight countries. However, it has, remained considerably smaller compared to advanced economies. It accounted for less than 6 % in the eight LAC countries in the sample, while it made up more than 10°% in the United States, Australia, New Zeeland and Japan. The evidence also revealed that human capital is unevenly distributed across LAC regions. Human capital tends to be more spatially concentrated than employment and population. It tends to cluster in regions which include areas of capital cities of countries, major cities, capital cities of larger administrative units and their immediate surroundings areas. The analysis also revealed that the provision of public amenities is the most prevalent factor in explaining these regional differentials in human capital accumulation in LAC countries. In part, this may be due to the importance of HEIs in the local production, attraction and retention of highly educated individuals. In addition to public amenities, the results suggested that a distinctive combination of other factors plays a key role in shaping the geography of human capital in each country.

These results provide interesting insights for public policy. They suggest that governments in LAC should pay special attention to the provision of public amenities in their decentralisation policies. Specifically, they suggest that governments should promote policies oriented to increase the provision of local health and educational amenities in order to increase the local stock of human capital. At the same time, it is important, to note that increasing the provision of public amenities does not necessarily imply a rise in the local accumulation of human capital since it is also likely to depend upon a wide range of inherent factors of public amenities, such their quality and availability in relation to their demand. This is, in addition to other regional factors associated with economic conditions, regional climate and culture and presence of high-technology activities as these factors may act simultaneously, with the provision of public amenities, to shape the spatial distribution of human capital.

The evidence assembled here for LAC countries appears to contrast with that from North American and Western European countries in two regards (Florida 2002b, c; Boschma and Fritsch 2009). First, unlike North American and Western European countries, the analysis revealed that regional differences in tolerance and diversity contribute little to explain the uneven spatial distribution of human capital in LAC countries. This result is likely to be a reflection of the relatively low degree of population diversity in LAC in terms of immigration. Second, the analysis revealed that high-technology industries have been less important in shaping the geography of human capital in LAC. Whereas high-technology industries have contributed to the spatial concentration of human capital in Brazil, Ecuador and Mexico, they have played a less important role in Argentina, Bolivia, Chile and Peru. For the latter, the low influence of high-technology industries in human capital accumulation appears to reflect their low level of development in innovative and knowledge-intensive services and products. This evidence contrasts with North America and Europe where the spatial distribution of human capital appear to be associated with the geographical spread of high-technology activity (Florida 2002b, c; Clifton 2008).

This study thus delivers a first comprehensive analysis on the spatial concentration of human capital in LAC countries. However, compared with other branches of regional science, progress in understanding the spatial dynamics of human capital in LAC countries remains at an early stage of development. As data and digitalized maps become readily available in these countries, it is expected that more researchers embark on the challenging agenda of understanding where highly educated individuals move, and how spatial concentration of human capital affects regional economic performance in LAC regions.

Appendix 1: Spatial Resolution, Number of Regions and Census Rounds

				Census round	
Code	Country	Spatial resolution	Number of regions	1990	2000
ARG	Argentina	Department	307	1991	2001
BQL	Bolivia	Province	84	1992	2001
BRA	Brazil	Municipality	1,447	1990	2000
CHI	Chile	Municipality	335	1992	2002
COL	Colombia	Municipality	1,114	1993	2005
ECU	Ecuador	Canton	119	1990	2001
MEX	Mexico	Municipality	2,403	1990	2000
PER	Peru	Province	169	1993	2007

Note: The census round column indicates the data that were used in the regression analysis
Data on Colombia were extracted from http://www.eclac.cl/redatam/. For this country, the 2005 geographic structure was adopted, since analyses were only conducted the 2005 census data – see text

Appendix 2: Definition of Variables

Variable	Description[a]
Human capital	People in the workforce with, bachelor degree or above
Bohemians	People employed in
	245 writers and creative or performing artists
	3131 photographers and image and sound recording equipment operators
	347 Artistic. entertainment, and sports associate professionals
	521 fashion and other models
Openess index	Foreign-overseas population (1990 census round)
Public provision	Persons employed in
	80 education
	85 health
Cultural index	Persons employed in
	5,520 restaurants bars, and canteens
	9,211 motion picture and video production and distribution
	9,212 motion picture projection
	9,213 radio and television activities
	9,214 dramatic arts, music, and other arts activities
	9,219 other entertainment activities n.e.c
	9,231 library arid archives activities
	9,232 museums activities and preservation of historical. sites and buildings
	9,233 botanical and zoological gardens and nature reserves activities

(continued)

Variable	Description[a]
	9,241 sporting activities
High-technology industries	2,423 manufacture of pharmaceuticals, medicinal chemicals, and botanical products
	3,000 manufacture of office, accounting, and computing machinery
	3,210 manufacture of electronic valves and tubes and other electronic components
	3,230 manufacture of television and radio receivers, sound or video recording or reproducing apparatus, and associated goods
	3,311 manufacture of medical and surgical equipment and orthopedic appliances
	3,312 manufacture of instruments and appliances for measuring, checking, testing, navigating, and other purposes, except industrial process control equipment
	3,320 manufacture of optical instruments and photographic equipment
	3,330 manufacture of watches and clocks
	6,420 telecommunications
	7,210 hardware consultancy
	7,220 software consultancy and supply
	7,230 data processing
	7,240 data base activities
	7,250 maintenance and repair of office, accounting and computing machinery
	7,290 other computer related activities
	7,310 research and experimental development on natural sciences and engineering (MsE)
	7,320 research arid experimental development on social sciences and human it les (SSH)
	7,421 architectural and engineering activities and related technical consultancy
	7,422 technical testing and analysis
Employment growth	Employment (2000 census round) – employment (1990 census round)
population	Population (1990 census round)

[a]Note that the International Standard Classification of Education (ISCED) was used to define human capital. The International Standard Classification of Occupations (ISCO-88) was used to define bohemians. The International Standard Industrial Classification of All Economic Activities (ISIC Rev. 3) was used to define public provision, cultural index and high-technology industries

References

Alcorta L, Peres W (1998) Innovation systems and technological specialization in Latin America and the Caribbean. Res Policy 26(7–8):857–881

Andersson Å (1985) Creativity and regional development. Pap Reg Sci Assoc 56(1):5–20

Audretsch D, Feldman M (1996) R&D spillovers and the geography of innovation and production. Am Econ Assoc 86(3):630–640

Barro R (1992) Human capital and economic growth. In: Policies for long-run economic growth, a symposium. Federal Reserve Bank of Kansas City, Kansas

Barro R (2001) Human capital and growth. Am Econ Rev 91(2):12–17, Papers and Proceedings of the Hundred Thirteenth Annual Meeting of the American Economic Association
Barro R, Lee J (2001) International data on educational attainment. Oxf Econ Pap 53(3):541–563
Baum C (2008) Stata tip 63: modeling proportions. Stata J 8(2):299–303
Benhabib J, Spiegel M (1994) The role of human capital in economic development. Evidence from aggregate cross-country data. J Monet Econ 34(2):143–173
Berry C, Glaeser E (2005) The divergence of human capital levels across cities. Pap Reg Sci 84 (3):407–444
Blake M, Bell M, Rees P (2000) Creating a temporally consistent spatial framework for the analysis of inter-regional migration in Australia. Int J Popul Geogr 6(2):155–174
Boschma R, Fritsch M (2009) Creative class and regional growth: empirical evidence from seven European countries. Econ Geogr 85(4):391–423
Cameron C, Miller D (2011) Robust inference with clustered data. In: Ullah A, Giles D (eds) Handbook of empirical economics and finance. Chapman and Hall/CRC Press/Taylor and Francis Group, Boca Raton, pp 2–28.
Chartterjee S, Hadi A (2006) Analysis of collinear data. In: Regression analysis by example. Wiley, New Jersey, pp 221–258
Clark T (2003) Urban amenities: lakes, opera, and juice bars: do they drive development? In: Clark T (ed) The city as entertainment machine (Research in urban policy, vol 9). Emerald Group Publishing, Bingley, pp 103–140
Clifton N (2008) The creative class in the UK: an initial analysis. Geogr Ann B Hum Geogr 90 (1):63–82
Comunian R, Faggian A (2011) Higher education and the creative city. In: Andersson D, Andersson S, Mellander C (eds) Handbook of creative cities. Edward Elgar, Cheltenham, p 574
Corcoran J, Faggian A, McCann P (2010) Human capital in remote and rural Australia: the role of graduate migration. Growth Change 41(2):192–220
Desrochers P, Leppäla S (2011) Opening up the 'Jacobs Spillovers' black box: local diversity, creativity and the processes underlying new combinations. J Econ Geogr 11(5):843–863
DeVol R, Koepp R, Ki J (2004) State technology and science index: enduring lessons for the intangible economy. Milken Institute, Santa Monica
Fischer M, Bartkowska M, Riedl A, Sardadvar S, Kunnert A (2009) The impact of human capital on regional labor productivity in Europe. Lett Spat Resour Sci 2(2):97–108
Florida R (2002a) Bohemia and economic geography. J Econ Geogr 2(1):55–71
Florida R (2002b) The economic geography of talent. Ann Assoc Am Geogr 92(4):743–755
Florida R (2002c) The rise of the creative class. Basic Books, New York
Florida R, Mellander C, Stolarick K (2008) Inside the black box of regional development: human capital, the creative class and tolerance. J Econ Geogr 8(5):615–649
Glaeser E (2005) Review of Richard Florida's the rise of the creative class. Reg Sci Urban Econ 35:593–596
Hill D (2002) Latin America: high-tech manufacturing on the rise, but outpaced by East Asia. National Science Foundation (NSF), Washington, DC
International Labour Organisation (1988) ISCO: International Standard Classification of Occupation, ILO, http://www.ilo.org/public/english/bureau/stat/isco/isco88/index.htm
Jacobs J (1969) The economies of cities. Random House, New York
Jacobs J (2000) The nature of economies. Random House, The Modern Library, New York
Kieschnick R, McCullough B (2003) Regression analysis of variates observes on (0,1): percentages, proportions and fractions. Stat Model 3:193–213
Lucas R (1988) On the mechanics of economic development. J Monet Econ 22(1):3–42
Marlet G, Van Woerkens C (2004) Skills and creativity in a cross-section of Dutch cities. Discussion Paper Series 04–29. Tjalling C. Koopmans Research Institute, Ultrecht School of Economics, Ultrecht University
Marrocu E, Paci R (2012) Education or creativity?: What matters most for economic performance? Econ Geogr 88(4):369–401.

Mathur V (1999) Human capital-based strategy for regional economic development. Econ Dev Q 13(3):203–216
McGranahan D, Wojan T (2007) Recasting the creative class to examine growth: processes in rural and urban counties. Reg Stud 41(2):197–216
Mellander C, Florida R (2011) Creativity, talent, and regional wages in Sweden. Ann Reg Sci 46 (3):637–660
Minnesota Population Center (2011) Integrated public use microdata series, International: Version 6.1 [Machine-readable database], University of Minnesota, Minneapoli
Ottaviano G, Peri G (2005) Cities and culture. J Urban Econ 58(2):304–337
Papke L, Wooldridge J (1996) Econometric methods for fractional response variables with an application to 401 (k) plan participation rates. J Appl Econ 11(6):619–632
Partridge M, Rickman D, Olfert MR, Ali K (2012) Dwindling U.S. internal migration: evidence of spatial equilibrium or structural shifts in local labor markets? Reg Sci Urban Econ 42 (1–2):375–388
Rauch J (1993) Productivity gains from geographic concentration of human capital: evidence from the cities. J Urban Econ 34(3):380–400
Romer P (1986) Increasing returns and long-run growth. J Polit Econ 94(5):1002–1037
Simon C (1998) Human capital and metropolitan employment growth. J Urban Econ 43 (2):223–243
Simon C, Nardinelli C (1996) The talk of the town: human capital, information and the growth in English cities. Explor Econ Hist 33(3):384–413
Simon C, Nardinelli C (2002) Human capital and the rise of American cities, 1900–1990. Reg Sci Urban Econ 32(1):59–96
Stephen PJ (1999) INEQDECO: Stata module to calculate inequality indices with decomposition by subgroup, S366002 edn. Boston College Department of Economics, http://ideas.repec.org/c/boc/bocode/s366002.html
The UNESCO Institute for Statistics (1999) Gross enrolment rate, tertiary education (%), The UNESCO Institute for Statistics (UIS), July, 1st http://www.uis.unesco.org
The United Nations Educational Scientific and Cultural Organization (1997) International Standard Classification of Education. ISCED 1997, UNESCO. http://www.unesco.org/education/information/nfsunesco/doc/isced_1997.htm
The United Nations Statistics Division (1989) ISIC Rev.3: international standard industrial classification of all economic activities, Rev.3, UNSTATS, http://unstats.un.org/unsd/cr/registry/regcst.asp?Cl=2&Lg=1
The World Bank (2011) World development indicators: international migrant stock (% of population), The World Bank (WB), July, 1st http://data.worldbank.org/
Ullman E (1958) Regional development and the geography of concentration. Pap Proc Reg Sci Assoc 4(1):179–198

Chapter 18
Labor Income and Poverty in Brazil and Mexico: A State Level Analysis, 2000–2009

Carlos Salas and Anselmo Santos

18.1 Introduction

During the twentieth century, Latin America had a continuing history of income distribution inequality, accompanied by high poverty levels (Engerman and Sokollof 1997; Williamson 2009). For the first decade of the twenty-first century, (López-Calva and Lustig 2010) writing on the results of a large research project, present evidences of a common process of diminishing inequality and poverty in many Latin American countries. Nevertheless (Helwege and Birch 2007) give a cautionary tale, showing that ample differences exist among inequality measures among the Latin American economies. Two countries stand out in that process because of their relative economic size and because of the contrasting economic policy paths observed in recent years: Brazil and Mexico. As the following table shows, both countries exhibited a common fall of their Gini indexes as well as of their poverty headcount ratios. However, after 2007, those paths started to show divergences: While Brazilian data shows a continuing improvement towards more income equality and lower poverty levels, Mexican data shows a rising level of income inequality and growing poverty levels. It should be noticed that, in the case of Mexico, improvement in the 2010 Gini index is a consequence of income falls both for the richest and poorest families.

C. Salas (✉) • A. Santos
CESIT, Institute of Economics, University of Campinas, Campinas, Brazil
e-mail: csalasp51@gmail.com

J.R. Cuadrado-Roura and P. Aroca (eds.), *Regional Problems and Policies in Latin America*, Advances in Spatial Science, DOI 10.1007/978-3-642-39674-8_18,

	1998	1999	2000	2001	2002	2003	2004	2005	2006	2007	2008	2009	2010
Brazil Gini Index	60.4	59.8		60.1	59.4	58.8	57.7	57.4	56.8	55.9	55.1	54.7	
Brazil Poverty headcount ratio							33.7	30.8	26.8	24.2	22.6	21.4	
Mexico Gini Index	49.0		51.9		49.7		46.1		48.1		48.3		46.0
Mexico Poverty headcount ratio	63.7		53.6		50.0		47.2	47	42.7		47.7		51.3

Source: World Bank, World development indicators

Writing on the evolution of Brazilian an Mexican economies up to the mid-1980s, Agnus Maddison and associates (Maddison et al. 1992) conclude that both countries had development paths that were quite parallel, up to the point where the slowdown of the 1980s could be traced back "major errors in macroeconomic policy" and not to the exhaustion of the past growth regimes of each country. Nevertheless, both countries went through a major economic transformation, and the parallel paths continued through the trade opening period of the 1990s, to depart at the beginning of the 2000s.

Some of the reasons behind those economic and social results were discussed in (Salas and Santos 2011). Our goal here is to analyze the evolution of income and income distribution inside Brazil and Mexico, i.e. at the state level. These objectives arise for two reasons, first it could be that a convergence process might be going between the Brazilian states that includes labor income convergence, thus explaining the lower levels of inequality and poverty, while the opposite process could be acting in the Mexican case. Second, convergence analysis done using gross national product data tend to obscure the impact those processes (or absence of them) have on the working population. Both countries have a story of entrenched state disparities at the economic and social levels, and the analysis of the recent evolution of income distribution and poverty, might show evidences of the regional impact of national economic policies.

We will use descriptive non parametric techniques to examine the evolution, at state level, of labor income – from wages and self-employment incomes, between 2001 and 2009. The data used comes from the national occupation and employment household surveys of both countries, and after examining the behavior of both variables, we turn to the issue of poverty. Instead of fixing a common poverty line for both countries, we examine the evolution of the first two deciles of the labor income distribution, as a proxy for poverty – e.g., Chap. 10 in (Martin and Morrison 2003). This is the first time occupation surveys are used to examine labor income convergence and conditional convergence, at state level in Mexico and Brazil. Also this is the first time labor income evolution is analyzed separating wage and self-employed workers. So this work must be seen as first step towards an explanation of the forces behind the regional convergence/divergence processes seen in Brazil and Mexico. A common theme in most explanations, both for Brazil and for Mexico, is that convergence processes can be explained, in part, by education levels (references needed here). Thus overall rises in education, seen throughout Latin America in general, would explain a fall in inequality (Lopez-Calva and Lustig). But since 2000, the Mexican case shows that other forces are working, that have greater impact on inequality and poverty. Some of those forces have to do with a segmented labor market, both in terms of the existence of precarious and non-precarious occupations and with a regional segmentation, mainly in terms of the economic structure of regions. Thus, the examined processes could be explained in terms of these two segmentation processes. It has been shown by (Ortiz et al. 2008) that such segmentation exists in the case of Colombia, but they do it just for a point on time. For the cases of Brazil and Mexico, we examine how the distribution of average labor income (derived from wage labor and self-employment) has evolved at the state level. Afterwards, we will examine the evolution of poverty, using the conditional distribution (Hyndman 1996) for poverty at the state level. The combination of both results shows the existence of a segmentation of labor income and a differential process of convergence of poverty levels (in the case of Brazil) and of divergence (in the case of Mexico). In fact, our results show the existence of a sort of convergence clubs of poverty in Mexico, and of a convergence of income and of lesser poverty levels in Brazil.

The chapter is organized as follows. First we will discuss the evolution of poverty in Brazil and Mexico, with particular stress on the 1992–2009 period, highlighting different patterns of evolution of poverty and extreme poverty. In the case of both countries, economic policy changes can explain those transformations. In particular, the shift from inward based development to an outward, export oriented economy, can explain major changes in income distribution and poverty trends. The second section exams the evolution of average labor income, separating wage income from self-employed income in Brazil and Mexico, using state level data. Next we look at the evolution of poverty, using the income levels of the first two deciles of the labor income distribution as reference. In the third and final section, we discuss the results and point out to future research topics that arise from this paper.

18.2 Poverty Trends in Brazil and Mexico 1990–2009

18.2.1 The Brazilian Case

The Brazilian economy had one of the highest economic growth rates in the world during its industrialization period, that is, between 1930 and 1980. Especially in the post-World War II and during the period of heavy industrialization – from the second half of the 1950s – Brazil's economy diversified, modernized and integrated a highly productive structure under the leadership of the manufacturing activities along with a process of fast growth both in per capita income and in urbanization rates.

This development process, albeit concentrated and exclusionary, did not prevent the social betterment of important segments of the population (Barbosa de Oliveira and Henriques 2010). That period was one of a huge gap between the capacity for producing material wealth and the capacity for raising the living standards of the majority of the population, a gap expressed in the high rates of inequality and in massive poverty levels. Using a criteria of insufficient income, Sonia Rocha (2004) showed that the proportion of the population in poverty, went through significant reduction from 68.4 % in 1970 to 34.6 % in 1981, a period marked by military dictatorship, but also by high rates of economic growth and a deepening of the industrialization process.

The steady advance in wealth generation capacity of the Brazilian economy, however, could have been accompanied by widespread improvements in the living standards and in the poverty eradication programs that could have lowered poverty to minimum levels. The reasons why this didn't happened can be found in the arguments developed in Barbosa de Oliveira and Henriques (2010), where they point out to three major determinants of poverty in Brazil: "the way in which the agrarian problems were handled, the particular structure of the labor market and the nature of social policies with regards to their historical-structural characteristics."

The legacy of colonial slavery, the lack of democracy and the prevalence of large state in the agrarian structure, not only contributed to the very low living standards in rural areas, but also prevent the majority of the population from access to land ownership, they also contributed to hinder the organization and unionization of farm workers. These traits were responsible for a rapid and violent rural–urban migration, which contributed decisively to the creation of unfavorable conditions for workers in the urban labor market, as well as to the explosion of poor settlements surrounding big cities.

Thus, despite the high dynamism of industrial, construction and modern service industries employment, the huge surplus labor force, "dumped" in large Brazilian cities, contributed to the creation of an occupational structure marked by low wages and urban informality, even in the context of the creation of an institutional framework that regulated union organization and guaranteed an expressive set of labor rights in the urban areas.

Finally, with regard to social policies, it is observed that under the military rule (1964–1985) the Brazilian government did not developed extensive compensatory social policies, and mainly concentrated spending in support of the industrialization project. During the military regime, the structure of the financing of social spending was mainly based on the contributions of the workers themselves, many social programs mainly benefited the middle class – and were defined and guided by bureaucratic interests, corporate patronage and a huge set of private interests entrenched in power, in the context of a closing public space – trends that ultimately reaffirmed the concentration profile of income, without ever reaching the low-income segments.

Even with the significant upward social mobility, expansion of small businesses, of typical middle-class occupations in large companies and in the public sector, resulting from the vigorous and sustained process of economic growth and industrialization, it is no surprise that poverty, misery and hunger, reached outrageous heights in the early 1980s, as an expression of "a conservative society and a conservative state too, dominated by private interests and by a coalition of classes from which the subaltern classes were excluded"(Barbosa de Oliveira and Henriques 2010).

In the 1980s, despite the slow process of "democratization" of the country, the situation becomes even more complicated, as economic dynamism was lost, a dynamism that was the main mechanism responsible for upward social mobility and the maintenance of a minimum social cohesion in a society strongly marked by inequality and poverty. With the debt crisis, the sharp rise in inflation and the break with the previous path of accelerated growth, social conditions became even more severe, with negative impacts on the already difficult process of poverty reduction. Clear evidences show that as early as the late 1970s, there was an increase in the proportion of the population in extreme poverty, a trend that would continue until 1993 (Paes de Barros 2009).

Especially during the period 1981–1993, and associated with the Brazilian foreign debt crisis, the evolution of the Brazilian economy was marked by low economic growth rates, rising unemployment and informality, accelerating inflation and even hyperinflation, reduction of the average wage and the real value of the minimum wage. Besides the increase in extreme poverty, and in spite of the democratization process of the country, effective in 1985, a high level of inequality was maintained in equity and property, in relation to access to land, in relation to functional income distribution, in labor income, from a regional point of view, in relation to access to public policies (urban, social, social security, etc.).

The evolution of extreme poverty in this period reinforces the idea that during the "lost decade" the picture of poverty changed little: using the criteria of per capita household income, the proportion of people in extreme poverty increased from 20.2 % in 1981 to 21.4 % in 1989, staying for most of that period above 20 %, and reaching higher levels (23–26 %) in the worst recession periods (1983 and 1988) and/or high inflation rates (1984, 1988–89).

In the early 1990s, before the process of monetary stabilization in the Franco government in 1994, extreme poverty remained high, reaching in 1993 (23 %) the same level as in 1976 (see Table 18.1). With the positive impacts of the Real Plan and the reduction of inflation on the income of the poorest, along with a higher rate of economic growth, falling unemployment and the recovery of the purchasing power of wages and of the minimum wage, in 1994, the proportions the population in poverty and extreme poverty declined significantly (see Table 18.1).

The neoliberal social policies of Cardoso Government (Community Solidarity Program) were not even able to significantly reduce extreme poverty, in view of the negative impacts of liberalizing economic policies that strongly increased external vulnerability of the Brazilian economy (see Table 18.2). Even in the period (1995–1996), with increased economic growth and wage recovery, the proportion

Table 18.1 Poverty and extreme poverty headcount ratio (Brazil, 1990–1995)

Years	President	Poverty headcount ratio[a]	Extreme poverty headcount ratio[b]
1990	Collor's	44.2	22.1
1992	government	44.0	22.6
1993	Itamar Franco's	44.1	22.9
1994	government	–	–
1995	Beginning of Cardoso's government	33.2	17.3

Sources:
[a]PNAD/IBGE. Special crosstabs calculated by Sonia Rocha. Site IETS. North rural áreas are excluded
[b]PNAD/IBGE. Taken from PAES de BARROS, Ricardo. Sobre a evolução recente da pobreza e da desigualdade. IPEA, Brasília, DF. September 2009

Table 18.2 Poverty and extreme poverty headcount ratio under Fernando Henrique Cardoso's Government (Brasil, 1995–2002)

Years	Poverty headcount ratio[a]	Poverty headcount ratio[b]	Extreme poverty headcount ratio[b]
1995	33.2	38.6	17.3
1996	34.1	38.2	17.7
1997	34.1	38.7	17.8
1998	33.4	37.4	16.8
1999	35.0	39.0	17.4
2001	35.1	38.7	17.4
2002	34.0	38.3	16.5

Sources:
[a] PNAD/IBGE. Special crosstabs calculated by Sonia Rocha. Site IETS. North rural áreas are excluded
[b] PNAD/IBGE. Taken from AFONSO et al 2011

of people in extreme poverty showed a slight upward trend, and poverty declined slightly, revealing the ineffectiveness of anti-poverty targeted policies (see Table 18.2).

No more than 3 years after the beginning of his administration, were needed to show that the huge mistakes of Cardoso's economic policy, strongly increased external vulnerability of the Brazilian economy, through the negative effects of the Asian and Russian crisis, which resulted in a new external sector crisis, with Brazil pleading anew plea for help to the IMF in 1998, and a submission to their liberal-conservative policies of recessive macroeconomic adjustment.

Thus, after 1997, while inflation was relatively controlled, a minimum wage with a slightly higher purchasing power, a number of targeted policies to combat poverty helped to avoid an increasing proportion of poor or extremely poor population. On the other hand, the reduced pace of economic growth, a strong and progressive reduction in real average wages (until 2003), the explosion of

Table 18.3 Poverty and extreme poverty headcount ratio according to different estimates (Brazil, 2002–2009 (%))

Anos	Poverty headcount ratio[a]	Poverty headcount ratio[b]	Poverty headcount ratio[c]	Extreme poverty headcount ratio[b]	Extreme poverty headcount ratio[c]
2002	34.0	38.3	–	16.5	–
2003	35.6	39.4	–	17.5	–
2004	33.2	37.0	28.0	15.1	15.0
2005	30.5	34.2	–	13.3	–
2006	26.9	29.7	–	10.8	–
2007	25.1	28.1	–	10.3	–
2008	22.9	25.3 (a)	–	8.8 (a)	–
2009	21.9	–	18.0	–	9.0
Var 2009/2002	−35.6	–	–		–
Var 2008/2002	−32.7	−33.9	–	−46.7	–
Var 2009/2004	−34.0	–	−35.7		−40.0

Fonte:

[a]PNAD/IBGE. Special crosstabs calculated by Sonia Rocha. Site IETS. North rural areas are excluded

[b]PNAD/IBGE. Taken from AFONSO et al 2011 (a) PNAD/IBGE. Taken from PAES de BARROS, Ricardo. Sobre a evolução recente da pobreza e da desigualdade. IPEA, Brasília, DF. Setembro de 2009

[c]PNAD/IBGE – Taken from: IPEA (2011). Mudanças recentes na pobreza brasileira. Comunicados do IPEA n.111. Brasília/DF, September 2011

unemployment and informality were factors that contributed to the incidence of poverty at the end of the Cardoso government, when it reached almost the same level as the beginning of his first term, while extreme poverty had small decrease – 4.6 % – (see Table 18.2).

Among all the aspects that made up what was known as the "cursed legacy" of Cardoso's Government – high debt, submission to IMF programs, high domestic public debt, record unemployment and informality, rising inflation etc. – one should highlight the proportion of extreme poverty (16.5 %) and, especially, the headcount ratio in 2002 (38.3 %) that remained virtually the same as in 1995 (38.6 %).

Under Lula's Government a more intense process of reducing poverty and extreme poverty was started. Several studies have examined poverty levels using the criterion of household income. Their common result is that the proportion of poor fell by more than one-third, between 2002 and 2009. Depending on the sources used, the range goes from 34 % to 38 % in 2002, to a range of 18–25 % in 2009 (see Table 18.3). By the criteria of insufficient income, the number of poor people was reduced by about 17 million between 2002 and 2009.

With regard to extreme poverty, also measured by the criteria of household income/family, some researchers indicate that the reduction was even higher, 40–47 %. Just over 16 % in 2002, the proportion of the population living in extreme poverty felt to about 9 % in 2009 (see Table 18.3). This movement means taking about 9.0 million people out of extreme poverty (IPEA 2011).

Table 18.4 Poverty gap, poverty severity, extreme poverty gap and extreme poverty severity under Lula's Government (Brazil, 2003–2008 (in %))

Years	Poverty gap	Poverty severity	Extreme poverty gap	Extreme poverty severity
2002	17.2	10.3	6.6	3.9
2003	18.2	11.1	7.3	4.4
2004	16.2	9.6	6.1	3.6
2005	14.7	8.5	5.3	3.1
2006	12.4	7.2	4.4	2.6
2007	11.9	7.1	4.5	3.0
2008 (a)	10.4	6.0	3.7	2.4
Var 2008/2002	−39.5	−41.8	−43.9	−38.5

Sources: PNAD/IBGE. Taken from AFONSO et al 2011 (a) PNAD/IBGE. (a) Taken from PAES de BARROS, Ricardo. Sobre a evolução recente da pobreza e da desigualdade. IPEA, Brasília, DF. September 2009

Also the depth of poverty and extreme poverty, measured by the poverty gap, was reduced substantially between 2002 and 2008. In the case of poverty, the reduction was about 40 %, with slightly higher proportions in case of extreme poverty, of about 42 %. Also the severity of poverty and extreme poverty has been reduced significantly, in the 2002–2008 period (see Table 18.4).

Workers' conditions in Brazil went through systematic improvement, notably since 2004. This is reflected in the increase in protected work, mainly on permanent contracts, the raising of the minimum wage, the recovery of the average wage, a drop in open unemployment and curbs on unprotected subcontracting. Families have seen a rise in average income, and a considerable reduction of poverty. All of this comes as a result of the minimum wage revaluation policy, social security, income transfers and improved wage bargaining. In spite of these improvements, a number of structural problems remain, such as high labor turnover, unprotected employment, structural unemployment and the strongly heterogeneous nature of the Brazilian occupational structures (Baltar et al 2010).

18.2.2 The Mexican Case

At the end of the 1930s the then president Lázaro Cardenas, was able to stabilize the post-revolutionary Mexican economy, and took the initial steps to launch a new development path (Moreni-Brid and Ros 2009). This development policy was based on a closed market model that imposed elevated tariffs on imports and prohibited or restricted the import of many kinds of goods. Nevertheless, there was a lack of an efficient program to substitute the imported inputs that domestic industry depended upon. Ultimately the external restrictions led to a major crisis in 1982, as domestic production was dependent on foreign currency to buy needed inputs abroad. But, from 1941 to 1970, Mexican GDP growth rate hovered around the 6.0–6.7 % range, making it one of the fastest growing economies in Latin America. This growth was fueled by a combination of industrialization and agricultural development; the latter concentrated in the northern states. Manufacturing flourished in the period from 1956 to 1970, but was never able to reach high technological levels, in part due to the fact that the more advanced industrial processes were owned by foreign based firms, with local branches in the country. In fact, the share of capital goods in total manufacture production was smaller than in Brazil (Moreni-Brid and Ros 2009).

Foreign currency was obtained through international trade of agricultural and agro-industrial products, and from extractive industries. By mid-1970s, the agricultural sector entered into a crisis (Solís 1981). The discovery of large petroleum-rich zones and their exploitation beginning in the mid-1970s postponed an imminent crisis by facilitating accelerated foreign indebtedness, which occurred effectively in 1982.

This growth cycle came to a stop in the mid-1970s, along with the first major devaluation since 1954. The discovery and exploitation of huge oil reserves rescued the economy from a long period of slow growth after 1976. External debt and oil revenues helped to bring growth back, a necessary condition for better income distribution and lower poverty levels. When the price of petroleum fell in the beginning of the 1980s, it was impossible to avoid a larger crisis. As the debt crisis erupted in 1982 and a new President took office, another development path, more outward oriented, started gaining control of the national economic policies.

The domestic market oriented model(or import substitution model) was able to maintain high per capita GDP growth rates which were accompanied by a reduction in the inequality of income distribution and an increase in labor income (Altimir 1983; Hernández Laos 2003). Different estimates of poverty show a sharp decline from 1955 to 1970 (Székely 2005; Van Ginneken 1980), along with a mild growth of inequality, as measured by the Gini index (Székely 2005).

Beginning with the government of Miguel de la Madrid (1982), the turn to an export led growth strategy, was carried out by means of privatizations and re-privatizations (of nationalized banks), changes to the laws, abandonment of income re-distribution mechanisms, liberalization of foreign trade and greater labor flexibility (Salas y Gallahan 2004; Zapata 1997). In 1986, the economic opening process was consolidated with Mexico's entrance into GATT. By diminishing direct State participation in the economy and reducing per capita social spending, the market opening had the effect of accelerating a polarized economic structure, by reinforcing low income levels and poverty at the state level.

The government of Carlos Salinas (1988–1994) presented access to foreign markets as a means for the country to ascend into the First World (Aspe 1993). As an instrument to achieve this goal and in order to assure foreign markets of the reliability of the open economy model, NAFTA was signed in 1993.

Mexican capitalism was restructured in a stage during which the global economy was characterized by a great increase in productive capacity, along with a decline in the ability of national economies to generate large numbers of stable, decent-paying jobs. Economic restructuring meant an accelerated process of installing production sites outside the areas that traditionally had been the geographical centers of the old model of accumulation. This movement has its most palpable expression in the

Table 18.5 Headcount poverty and extreme poverty rates

Year	Extreme poverty	Asset poverty
1992	21.4	53.1
1994	21.2	52.4
1996	37.4	69.0
1998	33.3	63.7
2000	24.1	53.6
2002	20.0	50.0
2004	17.4	47.2
2005	18.2	47.0
2006	13.8	42.7
2008	18.4	47.7
2010	18.8	51.3

Source: Consejo Nacional de Evaluación, Mexico, 2012

maquiladora[1] activities along the country's northern border. However, the geographical relocation process cannot be reduced to the maquiladoras. It has also involved the growth of several mid-size cities located away from the central area of the country, that traditionally concentrated most of the economic activities.

Despite these regional expansions, the working population has experienced a long crisis at the national level, expressed in a growing and asymmetrical concentration of income and a systematic deterioration of living standards. This deterioration can be explained, basically, by the decline in labor income. In fact, there are two parallel processes at work here, creating a clear expression of the polarization of the present-day Mexican economy. On the one hand there is an insufficient creation of stable, well-paying jobs in large and mid-size establishments; on the other hand, there is a growing generation of jobs in micro-enterprises, with very low payment levels.

We are now in a position to present and analyze the evolution of poverty and extreme poverty in Mexico since 1992, measured in terms of income. The needed figures can be found in Table 18.5, where extreme poverty (*pobrezaalimentaria*) means lack of access to the minimum food intake levels, and asset poverty (poverty or "pobreza patrimonial") means lack of access to shelter, transport, health care or minimum food intake levels. A fact that should be kept in mind is the existence of targeted programs to lower poverty rates. Initially named *Progresa* and later named *Oportunidades*, these programs are conditional cash transfers programs, whose objectives are twofold, to help families to overcome poverty and to induce them to "invest in the human capital" of their children.

The results shown in Table 18.5 go almost parallel to the evolution of the Mexican economy, as the sharp rise of poverty and extreme poverty in 1996, are a consequence of the 1995 crisis and its aftermath. Although there is a trend towards

[1] These are firms that operate in Mexico, using U.S. tariff code provisions (HTS 9802), which allows U.S. firms to send U.S-made inputs abroad for assembly and then return those semi-finished or finished products to the U.S., paying a tariff only on value added abroad. Most of these 'Maquiladoras' are owned by U.S. firms.

Table 18.6 Household count poverty and extreme poverty

Year	Extreme poverty	Asset poverty
1992	16.4	44.5
1994	16.1	43.6
1996	29.1	60.2
1998	26.3	55.7
2000	18.5	45.7
2002	15.6	42.4
2004	13.8	39.7
2005	14.1	39.6
2006	10.7	35.5
2008	14.5	40.5
2010	14.8	43.7

Source: Consejo Nacional de Evaluación, Mexico, 2012

lower poverty levels, that trend suddenly stops in 2006, even before the onset of the 2008 financial crisis. In 2000, after 70 years of a one party political rule in Mexico, the new President came from an opposition party. No wonder there was an expectation of great social changes, that were never materialized. The economy grew at sluggish rates, and job creation was leaded by self-employment and very small economic units.

In 2010 the levels of asset poverty are higher than the 2002 levels and at the same time income inequality, as measured by the Gini index, is lower than in 2008. This is a result of the fact that income felt both for the upper and lower deciles of income distribution.

Tables 18.5 and 18.6 show that poverty levels can change in spite of the efforts of conditional cash transfers programs. What is relevant here is the fact that the conditional cash transfer programs work well to keep people over poverty lines (extreme or standard) but they definitely do not take people permanently out of poverty. This is a consequence of the fact that poverty levels tend to grow during slowdowns or crisis, and then recede slowly (Cortez et al. 2003). In this vein, (Zepeda et al 2007) show that an important factor of per capita household labor income evolution is the change in earnings, followed by changes in employment levels. Thus, for people in extreme poverty conditions, access to a job and steady labor income levels are a way to definitely come out from poverty (Cecchini and Madariaga 2011).

18.3 Regional Evolution of Incomes and Poverty

18.3.1 Regional Differences in Brazil

Brazil is be divided along the lines of economic growth and income in major regions: North and Northeast, Center South, Southeast and South(Cano 2007; Diniz 1993), where the North and Northeast have relative low income levels and

Table 18.7 Gini coefficient for labor income, 2001 and 2009

	Wages	Self-employed labor income
2001	0.21908	0.27727
2009	0.19759	0.25127

Source: Calculations done with DASP Stata routines, using PNAD data

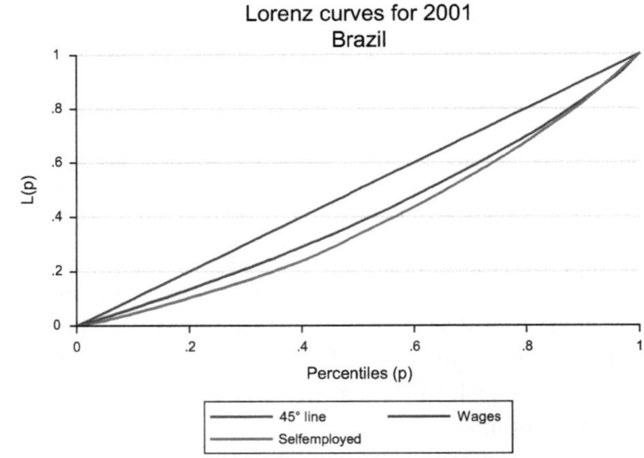

Fig. 18.1 Lorenz curves for 2001, Brazil

big shares of poor working people, while the Southeast and South have higher income levels and lesser shares of poor people. As (Gondim et al. 2007) point out, this differentiation – or convergence clubs – is hidden when the analysis of income convergence is done under the traditional beta or sigma convergence techniques.

The Gini coefficient for the average wages and self-employed labor income, we see a convergence process between 2001 and 2009 (Table 18.7). The relatively low values are the result of a more or less uniform distribution of labor income among the Brazilian states and regions.

The respective Lorenz curves for 2001 and 2009 show that aside from converging, wages continue to be less concentrated than non-wage income (Figs. 18.1 and 18.2).

The maps showing the income percentile profiles of the Brazilian states, between 2001 and 2009, show clearly a divide between the northern and southern regions, albeit a diminishing one. By means of this graphical technique, in the case of wages, clearly three convergence groups stand up, the northern states, the southern states and Sao Paulo and Rio de Janeiro (Figs. 18.2 and 18.3). The case of the geographical distribution of self-employed income is different, as can be seen in Figs. 18.4 and 18.5. These differences arise from the fact that that variable has a more unequal distribution (Fig. 18.6).

Now we turn to analysis of the evolution of poverty along the period 2004–2009. In this case, survey data includes the whole country, and it's the period where poverty levels dropped quickly. This is a combination of greater and deeper

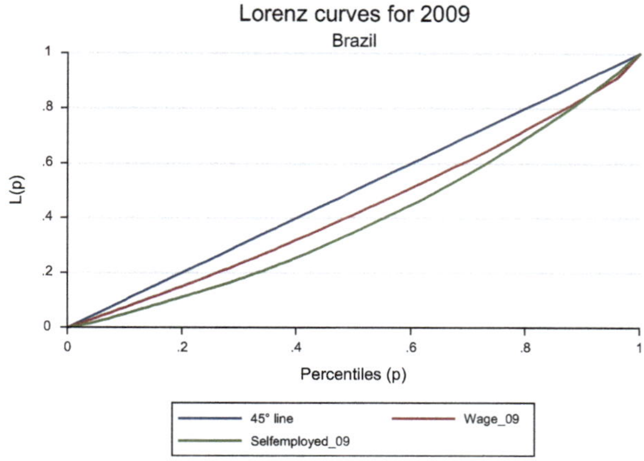

Fig. 18.2 Lorenz curves for 2009, Brazil

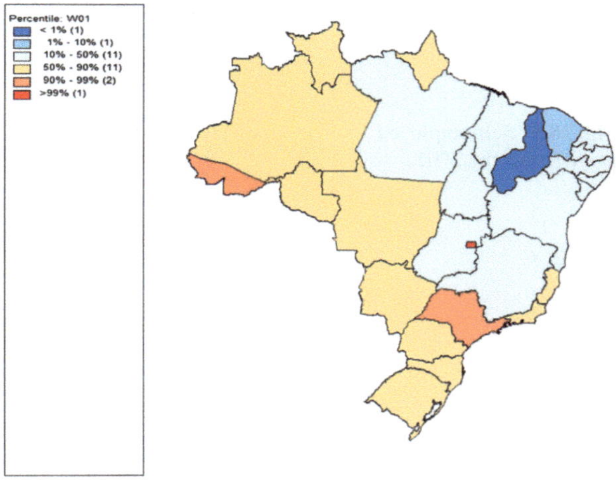

Fig. 18.3 Average wages 2001

convergence that can be seen when we look at the entire distribution of the data (Quah 1993, 1997). Figure 18.4 shows the conditional distribution function (Hyndman 1996a; Hyndman and Grunwald 1996) for the poverty rates of the Brazilian states in 2004 and 2009. The picture shows two different groups, one moving to lesser poverty levels at slow rates and the other maintaining its relative position at higher poverty rates (Fig. 18.7).

The above mentioned trends are confirmed when we look at the movement of the probability mass in the highest density regions (HDR) of 2009 poverty levels, conditioned on 2004 levels (Fig. 18.8). There is a group where the modes show a growing trend, that is the final position is a higher share of poverty, while there is another one where this mode shows a falling trend. This is the result of the regional

Fig. 18.4 Average wages 2009

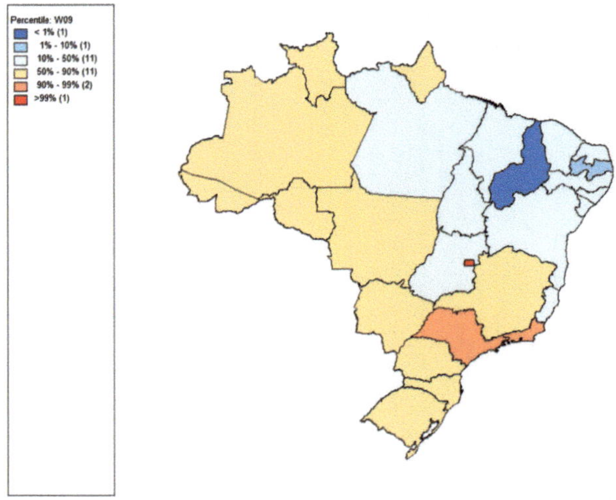

Fig. 18.5 Self-employed average income 2001

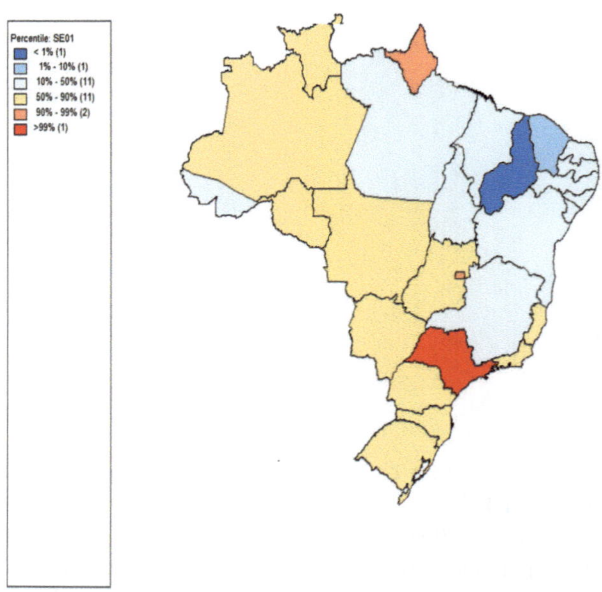

polarization of self-employed incomes, incomes associated with greater poverty levels, along with a group of states that have become relatively richer during this period.

We now turn to analyze the case of Mexico.

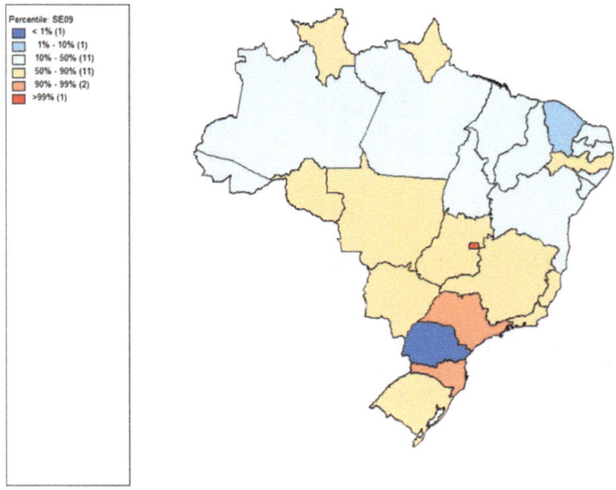

Fig. 18.6 Self-employed average income 2009

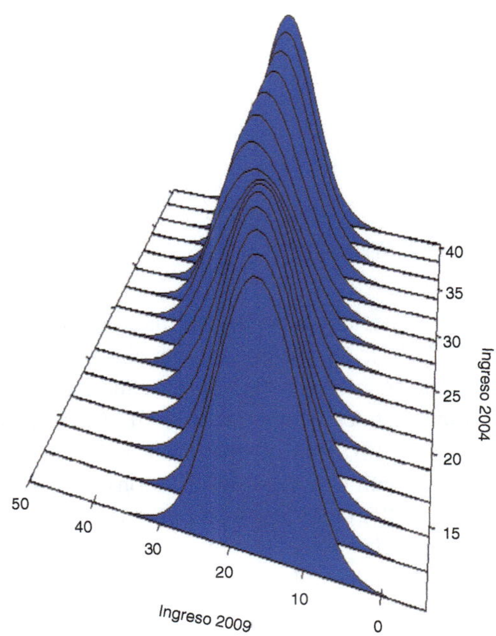

Fig. 18.7 Conditional Densities of State Poverty in Brazil 2004–2009

18.3.2 Regional Differences in Mexico

As in the case of Brazil, Mexico has a regional division, in terms of economic structure and incomes that separates, in gross terms, the northern, central and southern states. This divide runs along the lines from high to low income and

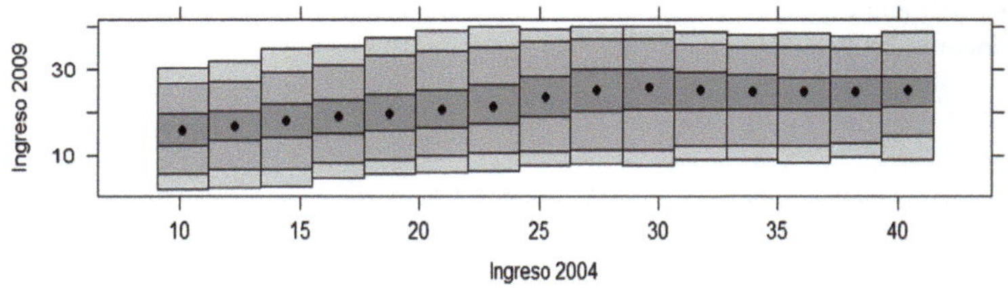

Fig. 18.8 Highest Density Regions Plots for State Poverty in Brazil 2004–2009

Table 18.8 Gini coefficients for wage na self-employed income, 2000 and 2009

GINI_wages_00	GINI_selfemployed_00
0.151462	0.293698
GINI_wages_09	GINI_selfemployed_09
0.108989	0.178466

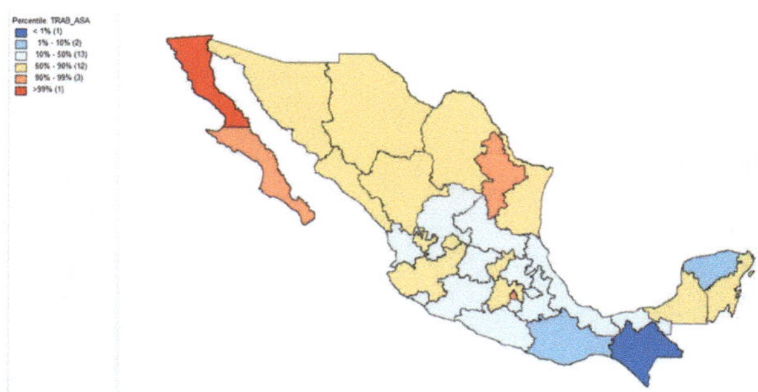

Fig. 18.9 Wages 2000

from a specialization in manufactures to one in primary sector activities (Asuad et al. 2007), As was pointed out above, the signing of NAFTA resulted in a greater integration between the Mexican and the US economies, with initial benefits for the northern states, where most of the Maquila activities were initially concentrated, but after 18 years of operation, NAFTA impacts are fading and what is left is country with new regional divisions, as was pointed out by (Aroca et al. 2005).

From the table below, it could be inferred a convergence process from 2000 to 2009 (Table 18.8).

Nevertheless, the following percentile graphs for wages and self-employment income, show a very different picture for 2000 and 2009. Although the relative position of most of the northern states remained constant, in the case of wages, the gap between them and the rest of the country, in particular, the south, remained. In the southern states, the traditionally poor states in the Pacific coast, didn't see much relative advance, as Oaxaca fell behind (Figs. 18.9 and 18.10).

But the distribution of income levels for the self-employed shows that the central and southern states remained in general with lesser relative income (Figs. 18.11 and 18.12).

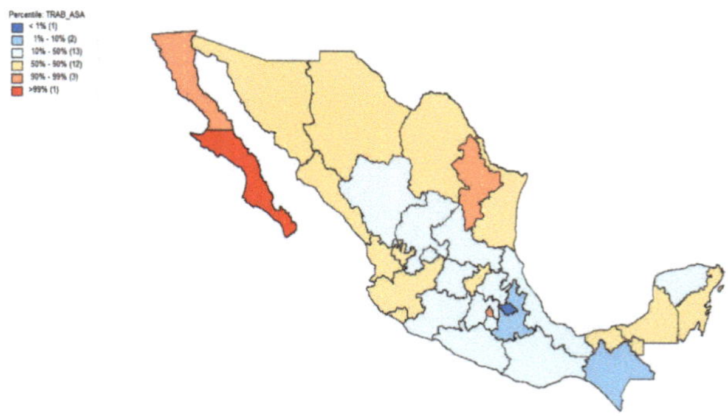

Fig. 18.10 Wages 2009

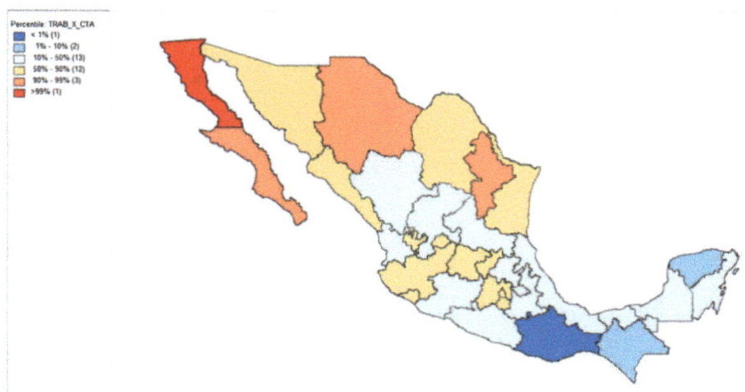

Fig. 18.11 Self-employed income 2000

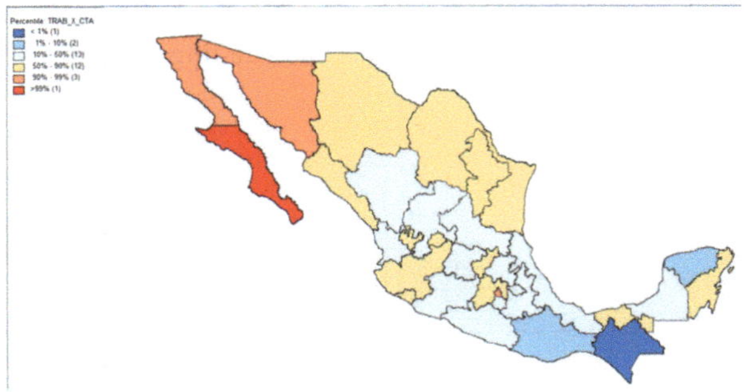

Fig. 18.12 Self-employed income 2009

When we turn to the evolution of poverty, what emerges is a bleak picture of growing poverty levels that comes out in the conditional distribution graphics.

There is a group where their relatively good position does not change, and two more groups where is poverty rates were already high in 2000 and stay high in 2009 (Fig. 18.13). And this regional divide is visible only when we look at the entire distribution of the data. Figure 18.13 that shows the conditional distribution function (Hyndman 1996a; Hyndman and Grunwald 1996) for the poverty rates of the

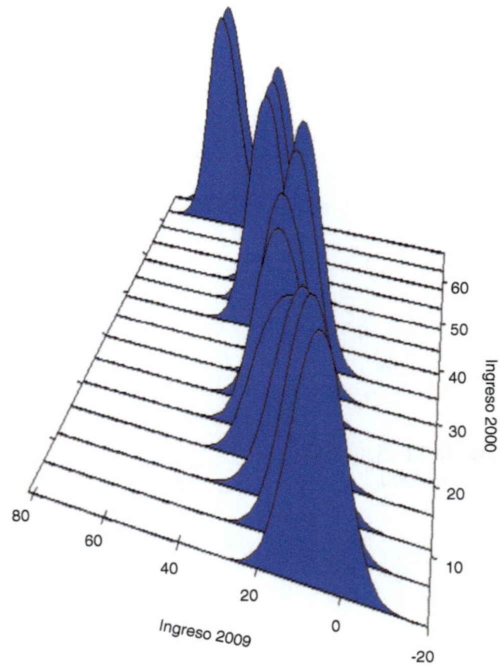

Fig. 18.13 Conditional Densities of State Poverty in Mexico 2000–2009

Mexican states at 2009 conditioned on 2000 data really shows three groups, one maintaining their relatively low levels of poverty and two others, at higher rising levels.

And the HDR plot confirms those results, with three different set of mode movements, here shown under the heading of Ingreso 2000 against Ingreso 2009.

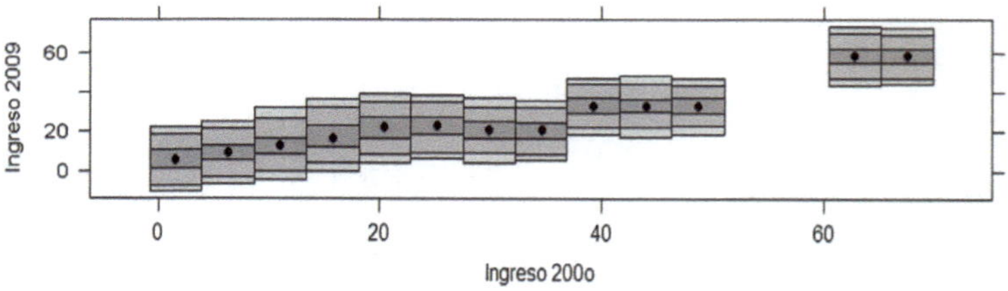

18.4 Conclusions

The comparisons of both countries, during a crucial period in their history, show clearly diverging outcomes in poverty levels. In Brazil, due to a major policy change (Salas and Santos, 2011), incomes were raised, jobs were created and poverty felt throughout the whole country. Along with job creation, the numbers of wage workers protected by the labor, also rose significantly. This is a true convergence process towards a more egalitarian society. Nonetheless, there is a group of hardcore poverty areas, where the standard policies are not enough to rise the living standards of millions of people, due to their isolation, low levels of education and the impact of poverty ridden generations. So, specific policies have already been implemented for this group.

In the case of Mexico, greater integration into the North American economic area didn't translate in a convergence process, whereby the less developed areas started growing faster, to catch up with the rest of the country, thereby diminishing poverty levels in a more definite and permanent way. The impact of the 2008 crisis and the slow rate of creation of quality jobs, had an impact on the general well-being of Mexican workers. Since 2007, micro economic units (i.e. those with less than 6 workers, including self-employed workers) were creating more jobs than the rest of the economy. The working and payment conditions of these units are bad (Salas 2013), which might explain the surge in poverty levels. And the call for more education as means for better jobs is meaningless when the quality of jobs created is so bad. That is why we don't use educational levels as conditionals on the evolution of poverty, as the causality runs always the other way around: poverty always implies low educational levels. As Magrini (2009) expresses this idea:

> Thus, if a conditioning explanatory variable is not actually determining an economy's economic position as in the standard neoclassical approach but, rather, is evolving endogenously as a response to initial factors determining club membership, a traditional researcher would incorrectly attribute growth and convergence to the conditioning variable and never discover the true growth determinants. (Magrini 2009)

The country analysis also shows that the cumulative causation processes, can be changed in direction by the forces of policy intervention. It is not always true that when government retires from the economy, what is left is a pure competitive market. As Joan Robinson remarked, sometimes the Invisible Hand of the Market acts by strangling.

References

Afonso LE et al (2011) O salário mínimo como instrumento de combate à pobreza extrema: estariam esgotados seus efeitos? Economia Aplicada, 15(4), Oct–Dec 2011. Ribeirão Prêto, São Paulo

Altimir O (1983) La distribución del ingreso en México, 1950–1977. Distribución del ingreso en México. Ensayos, Serie de Análisis Estructural. Banco de México, Cuaderno 2, tomo 1, México

Aroca P, Bosch M, Maloney WF (2005) Spatial dimensions of trade liberalization and economic convergence: Mexico 1985–2002. The World Bank Econ Rev 19(3):345–378

Aspe Armella P (1993) El camino mexicano de la transformación económica. Fondo de Cultura Económica, México

Asuad Sanén NL, Romero Q, Hernández R (2007) Convergencia espacial y concentración regional agrícola en México 1970–2003. Problemas del Desarrollo. Revista Latinoamericana de Economía 38(149):79–111

Baltar P et al (2010) Moving towards decent work. Labour in the Lula government: reflections on recent Brazilian experience, Global Labour University working papers num 9

Barbosa De Oliveira CA, Henriques W (2010) Determinantes da Pobreza no Brasil. Carta Social e do Trabalho. Cesit/Instituto de Economia, Unicamp

Cano W (2007) Desequilíbrios regionais e concentração industrial no Brasil, 1930–1970, 3ªth edn. Editora UNESP, São Paulo

Carlos S, Santos A (2011) Diverging paths in development: Brazil and Mexico. Int J Labour Res 3(1):115–132

Cecchini S, Madariaga A (2011) Programas de Transferencias Condicionadas. Balance de la Experiencia Reciente en América Latina y el Caribe, CEPAL, Santiago

Cortés F, Hernández D, Hernández Laos E, Székely M, Vera Llamas H (2003) Evolución y características de lapobreza en México en la últimadécada del siglo XX. Economía Mexicana XII(2):295–325, NUEVA ÉPOCA, segundo semestre de

Diniz CC (1993) Desenvolvimento poligonal no Brasil: nemdesconcentração, nemcontínuapolarização. Nova Economia, EconomicsDepartment, Universidade Federal de Minas Gerais (Brazil), vol 3(1):35–64

Engerman SL, Sokoloff K (1997) Factor endowments, institutions and differential paths among new world economies. In: Haber S (ed) How Latin America fell behind, essays in the economic histories of Brazil and Mexico 1800–1914. Stanford University Press, Stanford, pp 260–304

Gondim JLB, Barreto FA, Carvalho JR (2007) Condicionantes de clubes de convergência no Brasil. Estudos Económicos 37(1):71–100 [online]

Helwege A, Birch MBL (2007) Declining poverty in Latin America? A critical analysis of new estimates by international institutions. September, Tufts University, http://ase.tufts.edu/gdae

Hernández Laos E, Velásquez Roa J (2003) Globalización, desigualdad y pobreza. Lecciones de la experiencia mexicana, UAM-Plaza y Valdez, México

Hyndman RJ (1996) Computing and graphing highest density regions. Am Stat 50:120–126

Hyndman RJ, Grunwald GK (1996) Estimating and visualizing conditional densities. J Comput Graph Stat 5(4):315–336

IPEA (2011) Mudanças recentes na pobreza brasileira. Comunicados do IPEA n.111. Brasília, September 2011

López-Calva LF, Lustig N (eds) (2010) Declining inequality in Latin America: a decade of progress? Brookings Institution Press and UNDP, Washington, DC

Maddison A et al (1992) The political economy of poverty, equity and growth. Brazil and Mexico. Oxford University Press-World Bank, London

Magrini S (2009) Why should we analyse convergence using the distribution dynamics approach? Scienze Regionali – Italian. J Reg Sci 8:34

Martin R, Morrison PS (eds) (2003) Geographies of labour market inequality. Routledge, London

Moreni-Brid JC, Ros J (2009) Development and growth in the Mexican economy: a historical perspective. Oxford University Press, London

Ortiz CH, Uribe JI, Badillo ER (2008) Segmentación inter e intrarregional en el mercado laboral urbano de Colombia, 2001–2006. Ensayos Sobre Política Económica 27(58):194–231, Edición Especial, Economía Regional Y Urbana

Paes De Barros R (2009) Sobre a evolução recente da pobreza e da desigualdade. IPEA, Brasília, September 2009

Quah D (1993) Empirical cross-section dynamics in economic growth. Eur Econ Rev 37 (2–3):426–434

Quah DT (1997) Empirics for growth and distribution: stratification, polarization and convergence clubs. J Econ Growth 2:27–59

Rocha S (2004) Pobreza no Brasil: o que mudou nos últimos 30 anos? vol 83, Estudos e Pesquisa. INAE, Rio de Janeiro

Salas C, Callaghan G (2004) Labour and free trade: Mexico within Nafta. In: Bromley S, Mackintosh M, Brown W, Wuyts M (eds) A world of whose making? Making the international: economic interdependence and political order. Pluto Press/Open University, London, pp 251–272

Salas C (2013) Labour, income and social programmes in contemporary Mexico. In: United Nations development programme, social protection, growth and employment: evidence from India, Kenya, Malawi, Mexico, Peru and Tajikistan, UNDP, New York, pp 201–230

Solís L (1981) La realidad económica de México. Retrovisión y perspectivas, Siglo XXI, México
Székely M (2005) Pobreza y desigualdad en México entre 1950 y el 2004. El Trimestre Económico LXXII(288):913–951
Van Ginneken W (1980) Socio-economic groups and income distribution in Mexico. Palgrave MacMillan, London
Williamson JG (2009) Five centuries of Latin American inequality, NBER working paper No. 15305, August
Zapata F (1997) The paradox of flexibility and rigidity: the Mexican labour market in the 1990s. In: Amadeo EJ, Horton S (eds) Labour productivity and flexibility. Macmillan, London
Zepeda E, Alarcón D, Soares F, Guerreiro R (2007) Growth, poverty and employment in Brazil, Chile and Mexico, International Poverty Center working paper number 42, December

Chapter 19
Decentralization and Democracy in Latin America: Reshaping the Development Paradigm

Clemente Ruiz-Duran

Regional development and decentralization has been at the core of political and economic development in large countries of Latin America (Argentina, Brazil and Mexico). All of them were born as Federal states, and assumed distribution of power among the three levels of government, but di facto central government held the decision making process until late twentieth century, when a governance crisis emerged as a result of the debt crisis, forcing governments to rebuilt their social contracts: Argentina reformed its Constitution in 1994, Brazil enacted a new Constitution in 1988 and reformed it in 1996; and Mexico reformed the Constitution in 1983 and 1999. Reforms have strengthened municipal finance and have delivered a larger political autonomy to local governments.

Administrative and fiscal decentralization brought in a larger political competition, that has increased as democracy has opened the doors to new political forces at subnational level which has emerged in response to *renewed citizen participation*. All this has helped to promote a reallocation of central budget into subnational levels contributing to reduce inequality among regions and improving living standards in the poorest areas of Latin America. This chapter explores how *decentralization has been an interactive process*, with a mix of politics, fiscal and administrative and financial innovation that has built up a framework for local participation helping to improve living standards and reducing the gap among regions.

Theoretical framework for this discussion is rooted in different approaches for regional development. On the productive side, Perloff's et al. (1960) seminal paper on "Regions, Resources and Economic Growth" states that decentralist trends have

"Response change is evolution; change of question is revolution".

Development of this paper was enriched with comments from Juan R. Cuadrado-Roura, Rolando Cordera Campos and Victor Manuel Durand Ponte, and support for data base elaboration and revisions came from Eduardo Cendón, Moises Portillo, Christopher Sánchez and Jorge Martinez.

C. Ruiz-Duran (✉)
National Autonomous University of Mexico, Mexico, DF, Mexico
e-mail: ruizdc@servidor.unam.mx

J.R. Cuadrado-Roura and P. Aroca (eds.), *Regional Problems and Policies in Latin America*, Advances in Spatial Science, DOI 10.1007/978-3-642-39674-8_19,

been reinforced by technological change and the differentiation of regional labor markets, which have been modified by historical conditions in particular localities and the structural dynamics of the market economy, that has delivered new patterns of regional growth and development. This was reinforced by Oates (1972) who proposed his ***decentralization theorem***, which argues that fiscal (and regulatory) decentralization has potential welfare gains from diversifying local public outputs in accordance with local circumstances (encompassing both differences in preferences and costs), and he has argued that since he wrote his theorem, empirical literature has shown that these gains has been quite large (Oates 2007). This discussion was enriched late in the twentieth century with the claim for a more effective regional development policy that has to be conceived as a multilevel process characterized by the ***principle of subsidiarity*** (Breton et al. 1998; Gorun 2009), this means that, contrary to past dominant practice, those processes and decisions that can best be performed at local or regional levels should be executed there (Stöhr 2001). All this has been combined with a political approach that argues that ***the basic structure of governance is being transformed in countries around the world as authority and resources migrate from central to subnational governments*** (Rodden 2004; Atsushi Limi 2005) and that ***it has happened in a sequential form*** (Falleti 2010).

Evolution of decentralization in Latin America has been captured by socio-economic disruptions and is far from being a linear process (Palma 1985; Willis et al. 1999), instead it has evolved within passions of politics – that has been quite unstable in the last 40 years, old regimes has disappeared but new ones have not been able to heal wounds that were open in socio-political transformation of the region, everything, every stone is still on the move, so this essay is a reflection on the move, trying to find some paradigms that will allow societies to reach the coast of a more egalitarian socio-political agreement within the vast geography of a subcontinent that has common roots within the diversity of cultures.

19.1 Latin America Debt Crisis: Space Consequences of Its Resolution

Debt crisis of the early 1980s was a breakdown in Latin American development; its resolution was complex and delayed, pushing Latin America into a long-term crisis, which lasted for a decade (Bértola and Ocampo 2012). Literature has focused on the reforms carried out at macro level, but little has been discussed on what might be called its space consequences.

Latin America's state-led-industrialization financing was linked to external debt, as export earnings were dim to support the import substituting process, Brazil, Argentina, and Mexico, borrowed huge sums of money from international creditors especially to built up the required infrastructure for the new productive capacities. Through the debt mechanism the region was able to solve the twin deficit (fiscal and external) inherent in the model. After its collapse in 1982, twin deficits got a different resolution, fiscal deficit was solved by a dramatic collapse of expenditures in search of equilibrium and external deficit was pushed toward foreign direct investment for its financing. What were the space consequences of this process?

By one side *central government* austerity programs reduced its capacity to face unequal social structures, due to its low revenue level, pushing central governments to adopt decentralization as a road to reduce unrest among the population. From this point of view decentralization took place not as a bureaucratic decision (top-down) but was supported by political, administrative and fiscal reforms in most Latin American countries (Falleti 2005), first steps of this evolutionary process could be summarized, as follows:

- Argentina sequential process begun with the transfer of all primary public schools, which were under federal jurisdiction to the provinces. The transfer of responsibilities was unilaterally imposed from above and was not accompanied by revenues (Eaton 2001). It was followed by fiscal decentralization. In 1983, popular elections were reinstalled; in 1988, the territorial interests of the governors coincided, surpassing their partisan interests and leading to the formation of a subnational coalition that pushed for a co-participation formula for incomes; and in 1994 the mayor of the City of Buenos Aires became an elected official. This measure was designed to explicitly target a subnational polity.
- Brazil's in 1988 introduced a new concept of Federalism in the Constitution, giving municipalities the quality of federal agencies (Art. 1 and 18). By 2010, the Constitution had been amended 67 times, with most of the constitutional amendments relating to changes in economic policy and government structure. Constitution states that Federative Republic of Brazil is the "indissoluble union" of States, Federal District and Municipalities. There is no hierarchy among the three federal branches; they are autonomous, and they should act in an auxiliary form.
- Mexico brought in Federalism in the 1917 Constitution (Article 115), but effective Federalism came in with the reforms of 1983, that introduced political, economic and administrative decentralization, and the definition of specific sources of revenue for local governments (municipalities) as was the case with property taxation. In 1999 a new reform reinforced political governance schemes, defined municipal services to be provided by municipal authorities (drinking water, drainage, sewage, treatment and disposal of waste), redefined procedures for allowing citizens lawsuits against authorities, established municipal planning and it defines mechanisms for joint actions by a group of municipalities.

Beside political, administrative and budgetary decentralization, debt crisis brought also a *development financing switch* from *foreign debt(FDt)* to *foreign direct investment* (*FDI*), unwrapping a process of decentralization, in the old model central government allocated budget decision in the territory – especially through infrastructure programs – while in the FDI model flows are located in the territory by foreign investors, within a bargaining procedure in which state and local authorities offer a bundle of conditions to attract projects. This unwrapped a competition among communities and developed the concept of regional competitiveness indexes to show strengths and weaknesses of each region. For this purpose states and local authorities developed a new economic bureaucracy at subnational level, coexisting with Federal government. Competition among regions became very successful, attracting large flows of FDI to develop clusters, giving life to Perl off writings of the 1960s.

- Argentina got 36.2 billion dollars of FDI flows in the period 2000–2010 (CEPAL 2011) the sectorial distribution of the inward FDI stock has been relatively stable: manufacturing, natural resources and services (including financial services) each accounted for approximately one third of the stock (Nofal Beatriz et al. 2010). Traditional location of FDI flows has been the Buenos Aires region, but with the emergence of natural resources investments and the emergence of Mercosur, northern provinces have become central to the new project, restructuring the investment geography of the country (Chudnovsky et al. 1997; Castro et al. 2007).
- Brazil has become the number one destination of FDI in the region, for the period 2000–2010, flows reached 192 billion dollars, the main location have been industrial south and southeast regions, but the northeast rich in mineral resources, with most of petroleum and natural gas production, as well as mines of granite and precious and semi-precious stone, combined with hydroelectricity, for irrigated fruit culture and tourism, has been attracting FDI helping the boost of the region's development (Ögütçü 2002). In this case it has been an *incentive-based competition* among state governments for the location of investment that has led to regional development.
- México's flows of FDI reached in the period 153 billion dollars, half of it are located in Mexico City, but since the enactment of NAFTA in 1994, there has been a larger competition for attracting foreign and domestic investors, the area that has been able to get one fifth of all flows are Border States, where foreign investors have located export plants, incentive-based competition has developed among states allowing central states to compete as they have become a connection between US-border states and the surrounding area of Mexico City.

From the above discussion it becomes clear that decentralization has evolved in a multidimensional scheme, strengthening local governance, decentralizing institutions and fiscal resources and creating an incentive-based competition to attract domestic and foreign investment.

19.2 Strengthening Local Governance: Emergence of a New Political Class

Return to democracy, brought in more open pluralistic forms of government, one of the aspects that accompanied this change in style of governance was the devolution of political power to the state and municipal level. Faced with fiscal crisis and

Table 19.1 Latin America: political structure for governance

	Argentina	Brazil	Mexico	Latin America
Area (thousands of km^2)	2,780	8,516	1,985	19,347
Population (millions)[a]	40.4	194.9	113.4	589.0
Percentage of population aged 15 years and over[a]	75.1	74.5	70.8	72.1
Local/provincial governments	24	27	32	246
Municipal governments	512	5,564	2,457	10,875

Source: CEPAL, World Bank, INEGI and INDEC
[a]Last data available 2010

increased political demands for urban public services, many Latin American states began to adopt administrative decentralization policies in an attempt to reduce financial pressures on the federal government and to increase the efficiency of public service provision. The logic behind this type of reform was straightforward: returning administrative responsibilities to states and municipalities would not only result in greater locative efficiency, given that local governments were better suited to assess their priorities and design cost-effective solutions, it would also improve the overall quality of governance because local constituents were thought to be in a better position to monitor public expenditure and policy outcomes in their communities (Edmond Elias 1997). Reforms have led to a change in the governance structure in Latin America that respond to a framework built on political agreements, cultural traditions and partnerships at city level, which shows the existence of a complex system with more than 246 intermediate governments, and 10,875 local governments, where Argentina, Brazil and Mexico share is above 75 % (Table 19.1).

The new structure has helped to develop what can be called a *new political class in the region*; nowadays Argentina has around 202 local parties, Brazil 12 and Mexico 30, which are not directly linked with National Parties. This has led to more citizenship participation, in Argentina in the 2012 elections around 78.7 % of voters attended the polls for Federal and Local elections, in Brazil around 77.3 % at Federal level, and 81 % at local level, the weakest case is Mexico where only 57.7 % of voters attended last Federal election, and 54 % at local level. The new structure of power has provided local majors and state governors the capacity to form coalitions, which changed the way national politics are developed. Emergence of the political decentralization can be summarized for each country as follows:

- Argentina political decentralization occurred in the constitutional reform of 1994, it established the direct election of the mayor of the City of Buenos Aires, previously appointed by the president. Other constitutional reforms also aimed at strengthening federalism and provincial capacities, such as giving the system of revenue sharing constitutional status, and granting the provinces the capacity to create economic regions and to enter international treaties. This constitutional reform resulted from a negotiation between the national leaders of the two major political parties; it was a national level type of coalition that brought about political decentralization (Falleti 2009 and 2010).

- Brazil is the one with the largest participatory process since the Constitutional change municipal power has been linked to grassroots associations that have allowed that 140 Brazilian cities use participatory budgeting since the 1990s (Goldfrank 2007). The key in the Brazilian context has been the formation of a social movement party – Partido dos Trabalhadores (PT) – that was able to serve as the focal point and to channel social movement demands. It emerged as the most distinct and consequential new political force of the time. With its deep ties to movements, the PT self-consciously projected itself as a vehicle for translating civil society demands into party platforms, with a specific commitment to the democratizing of state institutions. While state-level contests favored the political machines and established powerful families, the first fully free municipal elections of 1985 opened space to many outsiders. The PT, representing the paradigmatic case of the "social turn" of the Left in Latin America increasingly took advantage of these spaces. After winning a prefeitura in the limited 1982 elections, then two in 1985, and then 36 in the 1988 contests, it won 50 in 1992 and 104 in 1996. It has continued to win municipal contests, some state elections and finally the presidency in 2002 (Baiocchi et al. 2011).
- In Mexico the Constitutional reform of 1983 opened a space for strengthening local governance; the reform was linked to a struggle that began with the 1968 movement claims for democratization, which opened spaces for opposition parties in the Congress. The process allowed mayors and governors of political opposition to win key elections that strengthened the political system. Opposition parties rarely won municipalities until 1981 and never won state elections until 1989 in Baja California (Tulchin and Selee 2004) it was followed in 1991 by Guanajuato, 1995 Jalisco, followed then by the capital city in 1997. From there on, the 'Partido Revolucionario Institucional' (PRI) lost 14 states. Municipal elections followed the same pattern, the process increased citizenship participation (Torres 2005), but Mexican governors and mayors have only recently asserted their political autonomy as the regime changed with the weakening of the PRI's monopoly (Montero and Samuels 2004). Political trends changed in 2009, in that year election PRI recovered two states (Queretaro and San Luis Potosi) and lost Sonora. In 2012 elections, with a larger citizen participation in both levels, PRI recovered the Presidency and Chiapas and Jalisco, but lost Tabasco to the left coalition of parties (PRD, PT and Movimiento ciudadano) today it holds 21 states and 11 are in the opposition.

19.3 A Departing Point for Decentralization: Tax Distribution Among Different Levels of Government

Remaking public finances after debt crisis was very heterogeneous in Latin America. Readjustment was agreed with debtors, but the path and final decision were on central government in each country, the outcome was the emergence of different size of governments. Strongest outcome was Brazil, whose public expenditure share of GDP set around 39 %, Argentina 30 % and México 27 % at the beginning

Table 19.2 Tax distribution among levels of government

Tax/Country	Argentina	Brazil	Mexico
Enterprises profit tax	(F)	(F)	(F)
Wage tax	–	(S)	(S)
Enterprises or people assets tax	(F)	(F)	(F)
Value added tax	(F)	(F)	(F)
Other indirect taxes	Energy and fuels (F)	Industrial production tax (F)	Fuels (F)
Natural resources tax	Royalties (S)	–	–
Vehicles tax	Property (S)	Property (S)	Use and property (S)
Real property tax	Property (E)	Land:(F) Heritage tax: (S) Transference: (M)	Transference: (S) Property: (M)
Enterprises tax	–	Services (M)	Industry and trade (M)

Note: (F) Central government; (S) State or province government; (M) Municipal government
Source: Own elaboration based on Banco Interamericano de Desarrollo (2010), "La Alternativa Local: Descentralización y desarrollo económico"

of the 1990s. Within this differential floor, is that discussion of decentralization took place, seeking to determine which level of government was more effective to perform the tasks of providing basic public services or to build the infrastructure required for a stronger local development.

Governance structure of the three countries does not correspond to an income structure that would allow sub-national governments to meet expectations derived from political decentralization. This problem has been outlined in the OECD report "Latin American Economic Outlook" (2009), which shows that the level of subnational government spending in the region is smaller than the equivalent of the OECD measured as a percentage of GDP, a problem caused by several factors: in come from sub-national governments are low, as well as central government transfers, providing a limited capacity to these entities to modify their environment.

The debate on decentralization of public finances took on a renewed importance with the emergence of the debt crisis in the 1980s, together with the effort to establish macrofiscal balances, which imposed a restriction on state intervention in economy. However, in this environment, there were higher degrees of freedom to subnational governments so they could implement financing schemes for local development. This resulted in an extensive debate on what should be the sources of income for different levels of government, with severe restrictions by the central government, but it made some basic agreements that changed tax collection structure, opening a new income structure that included subnational governments. Table 19.2 summarizes tax allocation of the different levels of government, noting that much of the collection is concentrated on central government, which show the weakness of state/provincial and municipal governments to carry out revenue policies to foster development projects.

Income structure within this distribution relies in Central government, in Argentina federal government collects around 60% of public resources, in Brazil

Table 19.3 Total income and expenditure by government level by country (percent of GDP)

		Argentina[a]			Brazil			Mexico		
		Federal (%)	Provincial (%)	Municipal (%)	Federal (%)	State (%)	Municipal (%)	Federal (%)	State (%)	Municipal (%)
1995	Income	14.0	7.4	2.3	22.4	11.1	5.5	13.2	7.0	1.1
	Expenditure	17.1	12.7	2.6	21.9	12.1	5.9	13.7	5.2	0.9
	Balance	−3.1	−5.4	−0.3	0.5	−1.0	−0.4	−0.5	1.8	0.2
2000	Income	15.0	8.5	2.4	20.1	12.1	6.2	13.7	7.1	1.3
	Expenditure	15.7	13.5	2.8	21.7	12.8	5.9	15.0	6.2	1.3
	Balance	−0.7	−5.0	−0.4	−1.6	−0.7	0.3	−1.3	0.9	0.0
2005	Income	16.4	9.4	2.4	22.7	12.9	7.4	15.3	8.4	1.8
	Expenditure	15.0	13.3	2.7	26.3	12.7	7.1	16.4	7.5	1.8
	Balance	1.4	−3.9	−0.3	−3.6	0.2	0.3	−1.1	0.9	0.0
2010	Income	20.8	12.4	N.A.	26.2	12.0	7.7	15.9	10.4	2.0
	Expenditure	23.4	16.5	3.2	26.0	13.5	N.A.	18.6	9.4	2.0
	Balance	−2.7	−4.1	N.A.	0.2	−1.5	N.A.	−2.7	1.0	0.0

Source: Argentina (MECON, Secretaria de Politica Económics y Planificación del Desarrollo); Brazil (Tesouro Nacional, Banco Central de Brasil); Mexico (INEGI, Finanzas públicas estatales y municipales)

N.A. no data available

[a] Last data available 2009

around 57 %, and in Mexico 69%. In the three countries, municipal revenue is below 20 %. Argentina and Mexico, does not show an effort to develop municipal income, Brazil seems to be an exceptional case as it has raised state and municipal taxes systematically, strengthening local governance. This could be considered first stage bargaining, second stage is related to co-participation formulas to define transfers amounts, which derives from a bargaining process to structure what has been called co-participation criteria (Table 19.3).

19.4 Transfers as a Bargaining Political Process

Transfers from national government represent in most cases the main source of income for subnational governments. These may be conditional or not, depending on the objectives of national public policies. They are conditioned if the transferred funds must be spent with a limited purpose (usually sectoral), whereas the unconditioned have no restrictions to be used according to the priorities of local governments. Generally subnational governments tend to prefer unconditional transfers, enabling them to make use of resources according to their own priorities, but this reduce incentives for subnational governments to generate their own resources. Moreover, due to large regional heterogeneity of production in each country, the ability to generate income through taxes is greatly affected. As there is no correspondence between expenditure and income tax themselves, a dependency on the system of intergovernmental transfers is generated (Rodden 2003).

Transfers can have different purposes: vertical if they cover imbalances between central and subnational government, as expenses are usually greater than income in sub-national governments; and horizontal if they improve redistribution among subnational governments, ensuring a minimum of public goods to compensate regional disparities, as the financing of public goods such as health, education or correction of negative externalities, compensating those who may be affected. However, the greater the horizontal imbalance, the greater the vertical imbalance, and the higher the level of tax funding centralization, the greater the dependence on transfers to cover the funding gap of subnational governments.

In an optimal distribution of functions with the impossibility of full fiscal correspondence, intergovernmental transfers are essential, but there are two main dilemmas: the degree of autonomy of subnational governments versus the search for sectoral policy objectives (Bardhan 2002). Discussion has been tied to the process of democratization in Latin America where electoral reforms have allowed democratic election of local authorities that has led for the search of greater resources for local and regional authorities so they could concentrate on those preferences of their constituencies generating new demands for empowerment basis for taxation. The result has been a gradual but clear trend towards decentralization of public spending in Latin America since 1985. Linked to this view has been the discussion that decentralization would allow a more efficient allocation of public goods to a sub-territorially diverse citizenship, allowing, in turn, improved channels of citizen participation and political accountability (Finot 2002). In most cases in Latin America, central government transfers have been very important, in Brazil accounted for 36.9 % of the revenues of the states, in Argentina, 54.7 % of provincial revenues, Bolivia 62.7 %, Colombia 60 %, Chile and Mexico 36 %, Peru 80 % and Ecuador 89 %. This heterogeneity of results derived from the construction of tax practices where two views are mixed, the former has been the capacity building of the resources of the towns – as in Brazil, with the idea of a decentralization based on the transfer of activities previously undertaken by the central public sector, and in the second case it was decided to decentralize without increasing the capacity of collection as in the case of Mexico. Table 19.4 describes main co-participation funds and the income source they will be sharing and how it will be distributed, Brazil is the one with a more complex system as it takes into account general taxes, but also some specific taxes related to exports and creates a fund for regional development.

- *Argentina Transfer System.* Spatial organization of public expenditure in Argentina is based on federal government decentralized social spending that is over 10 % of GDP. Social spending (education, culture, housing, urban planning, social security and welfare) has been transferred to sub-national governments, but the provinces are also responsible for the provision of basic public services, administration and public safety (provincial and local). Active role of provinces in the management of social spending looks to solve huge social deficits as result of recurrent episodes of economic crises (the most recent of these was the 2000–2001). Intergovernmental transfers are based on the Federal Tax Sharing agreement (FTC), which is based in law 23,548. Legislation sets primary distribution to the provinces of 54.66 % of total proceeds of national taxes such as Value Added Tax (VAT), income taxes and a part of the fuel taxes collection. These funds are not tied to a specific purpose, so its assignment can be determined freely. Other transfers are *conditional* on a sector or activity with a specific purpose. These funds finance decentralized services to the provinces, such as: education, health and other activities associated with housing (National Housing Fund, FONAVI), basic infrastructure (ConurbanoFund), electrical work (National Fund for Development Electrical Interior FEDEI), social security and roads.

  The distribution of the transfer system depends on a number of variable parameters for the FTC. The funds are distributed according to the percentages directly established by law 23,548 and are not labeled; suburban and basic social infrastructure transfers are financed by a levy of 14 % on income tax, the same happen to FONAVI, electrical works and roads that are funded through withholding taxes on fuel, gas and electricity. There are also transfers that support national public service decentralization to provinces whose distribution is a function of the transferred services. Finally, the Fund to Compensate Provincial Imbalances are equally distributed, while the National Treasury Contributions (NTC) are distributed in a discretionary form. The process of

Table 19.4 Coparticipation criteria

Country	Funds	Bag for sharing	Distribution criteria	Conditioned
Argentina	Provinces coparticipation fund	54.66 % of total fiscal resources	Individual sharing coefficients	✗
	Specific provinces and emergency fund	3 % for the total of fiscal income	1 % for financial emergencies of a province or natural disaster and the other 2 % is for Buenos Aires, Chubut, Neuquén y Santa Cruz	✓
Brazil	States participation fund	21.5 % of the net proceeds of the IR (income tax) and IPI (sale tax)	Individual fixed share coefficients; Contribution 25 % to the national fund for development of basic education	⊙
	Municipalities participation fund	22.5 % of the net proceeds of the IR and IPI	10 % for the municipal seats and 90 % in other municipalities	⊙
	Fund for compensating for the exports of industrial goods	10 % of the net proceeds of the IPI	75 % of the value added generated by each municipality with criteria set by state law	✗
	Regional funds	3 % of the net proceeds of the IR and IPI	Distribution to the north, midwest and northeast of the country	✗
Mexico	General fund for participation	20 % of total revenue sharing	General formula and 20 % for the municipalities	✗
	Contribution fund	Resources of the federal budget (Ramo 33)	Specific formulas for each fund	✓

Note: (✗) Not conditioned; (✓) Conditioned; (⊙) Partial condition
Source: Argentina (Ley de Cooparticipación, 1988); Brazil (Lei Complementar N.101); Mexico (Ley de Coordinatión Fiscal, 1978)

evolution of provincial revenues has been on the rise from 10.5 % of GDP in 2003, to 13.6 % in 2009, this results from increased provincial own revenue sources that have grown faster than income transfers themselves. In this case the increase in transfers appears to have stimulated provincial and local fiscal effort made by the provinces, developing a virtuous circle for provincial public finances.

- *Brazil transfer system* Brazilian legal framework sets guidelines for preparing national budget, but not for state and municipal governments, in other words, public spending in Brazil has a degree of ambiguity and discretion. Amendments to Brazilian Constitution in 1988, left pending the demarcation of responsibilities, especially in the social field. The characteristics of the Brazilian fiscal federalism are explained by the existence of strong regional and municipalities disparities, which promotes pressures, in two different direction, one from the most backward regions to the federal government to get a larger amount of financial resources, and the other from the more advanced regions governments that demand greater autonomy. Thus, transferred social spending from federal sources coexist with actual expenditure by local governments. Entitiesto which Federal Government has transferred a greater amount of resources are Bahia, Minas Gerais and Sao Paulo, with very un even conditions of development. Intergovernmental transfers for the case of states in Brazil are composed of several funds, of which the most important are the *Participation Fund States (FPE) and the Participation Fund for Local Governments (FPM)*, which sets up that of total national government revenue from Income Tax (IR) and on Industrialized Products (IPI), 21.5 % were participating States and 22.5 % to municipalities, and States must allocate to municipalities 25 % of the Receipts on Circulation of Goods and Services Tax (ICMS). Other intergovernmental transfers associated with other taxes are: States are entitled to receive 20 % of any tax created by the federation; and States allocate to municipalities 50 % of the Rural Land Tax and various concepts related transferred public services as listed in the federal budget. Finally transfers of the Unified Health System (USU) allows states and municipalities access to federal funds according to criteria of population (50 %) and with respect to development projects to the attention of public health (50 %)
- *Mexico transfer system.* Currently, decentralized spending is transferred through what is called federalized budget with four sources: income share – expenditure for free exercise under the Federal Revenue Sharing Agreement (Ramo 28), federal contributions to subnational government for specific activities, and previsions(Ramos 25 and33), expenditure for social and productive development in poor regions(Ramo 26) and previsions for wage and salaries and security in subnational governments (Ramo 23 y 24). Share of all federalized funds account for 28.6 % of Federal Budget for 2012 (around 6.9 % of GDP).

Federal Revenue Sharing Agreement (Ramo 28) linked to the evolution of federal tax revenues in a year, plus oil and mining excise duties. Due to the funding sources, it varies year by year; by this reason, it is consider a non-programmable expenditure. Distribution to the states are set based on equity (45.17 %), collection efficiency (45.17 %) and balance (9.66 %) and it is distributed in inverse proportion to the share of the per capita income of each state. It includes different funds: General fund for participations, Fund for municipal promotion, Control Fund, Compensation Fund, Oil extraction fund,

Special duties over production and services, Special duties over oil extraction, and 0.136 % of over Federal Collection.

Federal contributions to subnational government for specific objectives (Ramo 33 and 25) are more stable, around 13.2 % of Federal Budget and includes different funds: basic education (FAEB), health (FASSA), social infrastructure (FAIS), fund for strengthening municipal governments including Federal District (FORTAMUNDF), public security (FASP), state strengthening fund (FAFEF), technological and adult education (FAETA).

Bargaining with states and local governments is also used for distribution of Federal investment projects in different regions, summing up to 11.9 % of total budget, nevertheless, most populated states are the ones that get the largest share of it. Beside there are at least three large programs to support regional development: the first is the Municipal Development Fund (FFM) comply with the 1 % of the RFP and distributed as follows: (a) 16.8 % Municipal Development Fund, (b) and 83.2 % are entities that are coordinated in rights as set out in Article 10-A of LCF; (b) Contingency Reserve equivalent to 0.25 % of the RFP for each year. It is used to support all those entities whose full participation in the FGP and the FFM does not reach the growth experienced by the RFP for the current year compared to the year 1990. The distribution of this fund starts with the smaller entity participation rate and continues on until exhausted the resources of this fund. This ratio is obtained by dividing the shares actually received by each entity by the total number of shares paid in the exercise of the question; the third one is the Compensation Reserve is intended to compensate those states that are affected by the change in formula units. This reserve is formed by the remaining 1 % of the RFP, as well as that derived from the part of the FFM. The amount of the impairment is determined by subtracting the shares that would have accrued in accordance with the provisions in force at December 31, 1990, effective participation of the relevant year. Regarding distribution, this is from the institution least affected to most affected until exhausted the resources of this fund.

19.4.1 Overview of the Transfer Systems

Using the methodology applied by Finot (2005), which classifies the different transfer systems in Latin America, it could be argued that transfer system could be classified according to its contribution to local development and to their use (Table 19.5).

Co-participation schemes varies from country to country, but although schemes are different, all of them have reached an agreement with subnational governments to link contributions to the delivery of *basic public services*, in order to enhance contribution of transfers to local development. This sort of decentralization is assumed that increases the "sensibility" of the local public servants to the demands of the collectivity, giving larger attention to local diversity, and regarding political,

Table 19.5 Transfers conditions and type decentralization

Conditions		Contribution to local development: No	Contribution to local development: Yes
According to their use	No	Political decentralización of expenditure	Political decentralization
	Yes	Decentralization of operative policy	Operative decentralization > political dencentralization

Source: Based on Finot (2005)

ethnical, religious and cultural aspects. Thus, good practices and a sense of cooperation has been developed (Nobrega 2011). Good practices on the delivery of services has become more efficient as control of expenditure at local level has been linked to more citizen participation, that has promoted the development of evaluation methodologies for a better delivery of municipal services.

One problem – in the transfer mechanism – has been that given the political context in which transfer processes were developed, the required distinction between territorial and social distribution was never established, so its was easier to ensure the entire population certain levels of access, instead of creating a mixed mechanism that could satisfy both goals. This can be seen in the case of Brazil where decentralization processes have focused mainly on the implementation of social policies.

This trend has been extremely varied and the effects have been unequal, it could be argued that the emergence of new forms of government, has helped to a more efficient public service provision, and has widened citizen control over public affairs (Scott 2009). Although it has to be recognized that in some cases, where social, political and economic structures are fragmented, social cohesion and citizen involvement have been limited; such is the case of Indonesia, where interests of *local gangsters* have hijacked democracy, as pointed out by Hadiz (2004) and by Barron and Clark (2006).

19.5 Expenditures and the Trap of Megacities

Decentralized expenditure in education and health (first, second, and third level) has been translated from central government to states or provinces, and basic infrastructure services (sewage and provision of drinking water) to local governments in Argentina, Brazil and Mexico. The main approach to this sort of decentralization has been that their delivery could be more effective, and that citizenship surveillance could improve the quality. This sort of decentralization helped also to develop administrative skills at subnational level. One problem with decentralization have been the emergence of megacities in all Latin America, that has led to an ambiguous process of decentralization as all formulas benefit large urban areas.

Table 19.6 Megaconcentrations and public expenditure absorption

Country	States/provinces		Population share	Public expenditure absorption
			Share (%)	
Brazil	First three	São Paulo, Minas Gerais and Río de Janeiro	40.3	45.0
	First five	Previous three, Bahía and Rio Grande do Sul	53.2	51.0
Argentina	First three	Buenos Aires, Córdoba and Santa Fe	55.2	40.0
	First five	Previous three, Cd. Autónoma de Bs. As. and Mendoza	66.7	53.0
Mexico	First three	Estado de México, México D.F. and Veracruz	28.2	36.0
	First five	Previous three, Jalisco and Puebla	39.9	46.0

Source: INEGI, INDEC, IBGE

- In Argentina, the provinces of Buenos Aires, Cordoba, Santa Fe, Cd. Autonoma de Buenos Aires and Mendoza absorb 53 % of total spending;
- In Brazil, Sao Paulo, Minas Gerais, Rio de Janeiro, Bahía, Rio Grande do Sul absorb 51 % of the budget.
- Mexico would be the less concentrated, as spending in the Federal District, Estado de México, Veracruz, Jalisco and take 46 % of total provincial spending.

The three cases shows that the level of decentralized spending in states and local governments is limited, which hardly could generate substantial changes. The only mechanism for this level of expenditure to have a greater effect would be through a supra-regional planning framework that could define territorial change (Ochs 1974), otherwise subnational expenditures may be lost in bureaucratic procedures reducing the impact of decentralization (Table 19.6).

19.6 New Political Class and Indebtedness of Subnational Governments

As the new political class at subnational level developed management skills, they began a search for different revenue sources of financing to allow them some autonomy over the budget; borrowing from US experience, they decided to open the door of subnational government indebtness, i.e. bond market. Reasons to open this disequilibrium door, has been discussed by Dillinger and Webb (1999): “giving SNGs autonomy over spending is, of course, the way in which decentralization can improve efficiency in matching the needs and desires of a diverse population” Two aspects are usually important regarding the effects on macro fiscal management. One is whether the central government can dictate which functions the subnational governments must take on, at least in exchange for receiving transfers from the center. If the central government can do this, central spending and deficits are contained.

Central governments were unable to set up such rules, under the pressure of the new political class federal government allowed indebtness of subnational governments. Unfortunately local governments were not ready for such a challenge, there was a weak accounting practices at this level, in most cases, local accounting is on cash basis only and does not distinguish between recurrent and capital expenditures. In such a situation it is difficult to ensure that long term borrowing is for capital investments only, and prudential rules limiting the financing of recurrent deficits to short term borrowing are not enforceable. At subnational level, few local governments apply multi-year budgeting processes, as a result is very difficult for them to assess the impact of alternative investment financing scenarios (Noel 2000). The learning process led Argentina, Brazil and Mexico to face a debt crisis at subnational level in the late 1990s and early in the twenty-first century. The whole process led to the setting of indebtness rules to avoid recurrence to crisis; each country set up a different framework:

- Argentina set up in May 2010, the Federal Debt Relief Program of the Argentine Provinces (PFD) which aims to reduce the debt of the Argentine Provinces. As such, there is no regulation for the debt ceiling, however, Federal Government monitors the stock of debt to avoid an excessive growth of debt. Restructuring includes programs for financial assistance, infrastructure, monetary unification, and the Provincial Public Debt Conversion. Debt reduction was carried out by contributions of the Federal Government through the Treasury, distributed in each Province according to its debt stock, rescheduling repayment, extending them to 2030, with a fixed interest rate of 6 %. The program was joined by 18 Provinces (Buenos Aires, Catamarca, Cordoba, Corrientes, Chaco, Chubut, Entre Ríos, Formosa, Jujuy, La Rioja, Mendoza, Misiones, Neuquen, Rio Negro, Salta, San Juan, Tucuman, Tierra del Fuego) and reduction led to a reduction of 18 % of the debt, that stands today at 6.6 % of GDP (Decreto 660/2010)
- Brazil subnational indebtness at the turn of the century reached 20 % of GDP, pushing for a reform that led to a new legislation named Fiscal Responsibility Law (RTF) to set management rules for all levels of governments (Federal, State and Municipal governments), it states borrowing limits as percentage of NCI (net current income), that for Federal government is 3.5 % of NCI, at State level is 2.0 % and at Municipal level is 1.2 % (Ministerio de Economía y Finanzas 2005). Brazil subnational debt is around 7 % of GDP.
- Mexico is the most complex system, as debt emission is regulated by subnational legislation, based on Article 115 and 117 of the Constitution. Nineteen of the 32 states have set up a guideline, eight of them has linked it to a limit of budget expenditure which varies between 2.5 % and 25 % and ten has set up a limit based on incomes which varies between 0.5 % and 15 %. Overall subnational debt is of 3 % of GDP (Table 19.7).

Ten years later public debt of subnational governments is around 2 % of GDP, but with a great heterogeneity among states, provinces, and municipal

Table 19.7 Deficit and indebtness rules by level of government

Country	Brazil	Argentina	Mexico
Current legislation	Ley de Responsabilidad Fiscal (2000)	Régimen Federal de Responsabilidad Fiscal (2004)	Ley Federal de Presupuesto y Responsabilidad Hacendaria (2006)
Government level (Federal, state/provincial, municipal)	Federal and subnational	Federal	Federal
Level or indebtness	Federal 3.5 (% of NCI)[a] State 2 (% of NCI) Municipal 1.2 (% of NCI)	Federal Debt Relief Program of the Argentine Provinces (2010)	Purchase of obligations by states, is regulated by a state law itself which sets the guidelines for this purpose

Source: based on government documents

[a]NCI (Net current income). NCI is the sum of tax revenues, contributions, heritage, industrial, agricultural, services, current transfers and other revenue flows less: (a) at Federal Government, legal contributions to social security system; (b) in the states quotas given to municipalities by constitutional rules, and (c) in the three levels or government, the contribution of public servants for the costing of its social security system, plus social assistance and income from financial equalization among the various social security schemes

governments. In Mexico subnational debt range is between 8.6 of GDP in the state of Coahuila and 0.1 % from Tlaxcala; and in Brazil the largest indebtness is 3 % of GDP in Sao Paulo and the lowest is in Amapa with 0 %. Indebtness has brought in a more complex system to finance different levels of government, supporting a new framework for development that still is under construction. It has opened a door for leveraging subnational governments for strengthening their capacity to undertake a major role in their own development.

19.7 Measuring the Impact of Decentralization

As mentioned above, the decentralization of states pending has been focused on maintaining and enhancing a more efficient cover age of basic services and some aspects related to the welfare of the population in the regions. In this regard, we explored the correlation between state spending in Mexico, Brazil and Argentina through a model affixed effects panel in which the individuals analyzed were the states and the period 2000 and 2010.

The fixed effects model assumes the individual effect is correlated with the state spending, for this purpose a simple model is proposed; dependent variables are Human Development Index (HDI), education and public services coverages, and the state public spending as an independent variable, the proposed model can be specified as:

Table 19.8 Fixed effects model

Variable	Model 1. HDI	Model 2. Literacy	Model 3. Drinking water	Model 4. Sewage	Model 5. Electricity	Model 6. Health
State public expenditure	0.1241***	7.9436***	6.2211	11.1924**	8.5438***	56.6514***
ci	0.7343***	87.8979***	86.0241***	56.4489***	92.3914***	17.7855**
N	166	166	166	166	166	166
r2	0.2216	0.1359	0.0116	0.0888	0.1268	0.2104
r2_o	0.0336	0.0455	0.0002	0.0022	0.0304	0.0048
r2_b	0.0311	0.0443	0.0001	0.0019	0.0324	0.0026
r2_w	0.2216	0.1359	0.0116	0.0888	0.1268	0.2104
sigma_u	0.0891	7.7178	9.8067	33.1635	5.9426	42.051
sigma_e	0.0264	2.2701	6.5049	4.0618	2.5408	12.4354
rho	0.9195	0.9204	0.6945	0.9852	0.8454	0.9196

Source: Own elaboration
Statistically significant coefficients: $^{*}p < 0.05$; $^{**}p < 0.01$; $^{***}p < 0.001$

$$Y_{it} = c_i + x_{it}GPE + ci + u_{it}$$

Where:
i = state
t = 2000 and 2010
GPE = State public expenditure
Y = HDI, schooling coverage, drinking water, sewage, electricity and health
ci = non observable individual effect (Table 19.8)

Based on the above, the results allowed to find that:

- State public expenditure is positive and significant related to HDI and also with the increase in literacy coverage, sewage, health, and electricity,
- Drinking water coverage does not show a significant correlation;
- Regarding HDI, increased of spending by one percentage, gets a positive impact of 12 %.
- Noteworthy is the effect of states pending on health coverage, in which government spending in this period, get the largest multiplier effect.

Decentralization in Latin America has lived up to its promise, even when the constitutional and legal frameworks have not been clearly defined and enforced. Local governments had been given access to additional resources, but still the institutional framework has not been developed to monitor and control the pace and allocation of spending, and there has not been the training for local bureaucrats to keep the pace, so in many cases results has tend to be disappointing. More planning is required, in order to pair spending responsibilities with revenue sources. Despite the difficulties in implementation, the arguments for decentralization are sound and powerful. The process can and does live up to its promises.

19.8 How Much Decentralization Has Fostered Development?

Latin America decentralization has been interactive, fostered by the financial crisis of the 1980s, led to politicians to look for alternative ways to carry on development process. Emergence of a new political class at local level led to a new governance scheme; Argentina has multiplied political parties increasing citizen participation with a very high share of effective voting; Brazil, with its participative budget processing, has been able to have the highest share of effective voting; and Mexico, where political parties development has been the weakest, with the lowest share of effective voting (Table 19.9). In all cases new governance schemes has prevailed pushing the creation of local institutions that have helped to a more efficient delivery of public goods.

Decentralization has helped to ensure a better provision of basic infrastructure and has been through this way in which local governments have contributed to local economic development. It has not been an easy task, resources has not been adequate and in some cases there has been also a lack of political commitment. Local governance has helped to strengthened State and Provincial governance and is at that level that institutional change has happened, decentralized promotion of economic activity has taken place, as they have bid for foreign investment flows and have successfully developed clusters in their regions, diversifying their economic activity; for that purpose incentive packages have been developed by Ministries of subnational governments, bargained with Federal authorities, in a menu that has included local taxes, tax breaks, provision of advisory and support services for businesses and infrastructure development, i.e. Jalisco electronic industrial parks, that has been named the Mexican Silicon Valley, Rafaela in Argentina with its successful industrial park focus on metal mechanic industry and Brazil with Santa Rita do Sapucaí, known as the Brazilian Silicon Valley. In all cases local promotion has been structured and has developed a competence for attracting foreign investors into their communities.

State and Provincial governments has also get into what can be called second stage policies, that is linked to the development of higher education centers in business related subjects that has helped to strengthened human capital within the regions to help business development. In some regions research and development centers has been fostered and has helped regional development to take place.

Decentralization has helped also to reduce inequalities among regions, in Graph 19.1 appears estimates of sigma convergence, with Brazil and Mexico in a clear-cut trend toward convergence, while Argentina lacks behind in this process.

Decentralization agenda has helped to strengthened territorial development In Latin America, but it has to be recognized that lack of planning has diminished positive effects. Brazil experience seems to be the most successful as it has been able to set a larger mechanism of participation through a participative budget that has allowed a more solid model of development. Mexican experience has been rooted more in a decentralization combined with foreign investment promotion, but

Table 19.9 Democracy and citizen participation

Country	Type of election	Share of effective voting	Political parties
Argentina[a]	Federal	78.69	32
	Local	78.69	202
Brazil[b]	Federal	77.34	17
	Local	81.46	12
Mexico[c]	Federal	63.34	7
	Local	56.74	30

Source: Electoral institutes of each country
[a]Local elections were held in 2012 with the exception of Corrientes (2009) and Santiago
[b]2010 Election data
[c]Local elections were held between 2007 and 2012, some data are preliminary

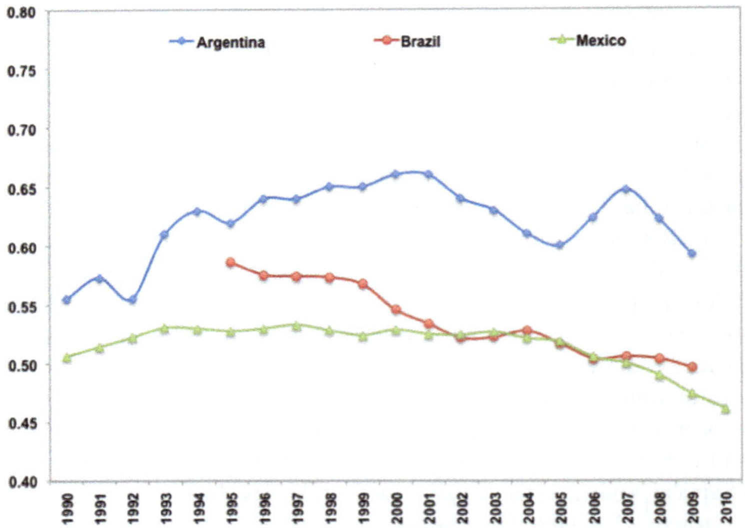

Graph 19.1 Sigma convergence, 1990–2010 (Source: INDEC, INEGI, IBGE)

with credibility problems that has affected citizen participation as shown in the voting system. In the Argentinian case, decentralization could be considered that has come from above and that still is the need for further citizen involvement in public sector development, it has to combined politics with delivery of public goods. The three case study shows that there is no linear processing of decentralization, that it is a case by case study, to find how political organization can really improve delivery of public goods at local level and induce a change at political level. But it has to be recognized that this process has been a very dynamic one, where new rules are being built and new forms of participation are being found.

References

Baiocchi G, Heller P, Silva M (2011) Bootstrapping democracy transforming local governance and civil society in Brazil. Stanford University Press, Brazil

Bardhan P (2002) Decentralization of governance and development. J Econ Perspect 16 (4 (Autumn, 2002)):185–205

Barron P, Clark S (2006) Decentralizing inequality? Center – periphery relations, local governance and conflict in ACEH social development papers, Conflict prevention and reconstruction paper No. 30. Conflict Prevention & Reconstruction, Washington, DC

Bértola L, Ocampo José A (2012) Latin, America's debt crisis and "lost decade". Institute for the Study of the Americas. University of London & Development Bank of Latin America, London

Blanco Valdes RL (2012) Los Rostros del Federalismo. Alianza Editorial, Espan˜a

Breton A, Cassone A, Frschini A (1998) Decentralization and subsidiarity: toward a theoretical reconciliation. Int J Law Econ 19:1

Castro L, Regis, Saslavsky D (2007) Infrastructure and the location of direct investment MPRA paper No. 6736, posted 14. January 2008/15:04

CEPAL (2011) Foreign direct investment in Latin America and the Caribbean, 2010

Chudnovsky D, López A, Porta F (1997) Market or policy driven? The foreign direct investment boom in Argentina. Oxf Dev Stud 25(2):173

Decreto 660/2010 (2010) Programa Federal de Desendeudamiento de las Provincias Argentinas. http://www.infoleg.gov.ar/infolegInternet/anexos/165000–169999/167212/norma.htm

Dillinger W, Webb S (1999) Fiscal management in federal democracies: Argentina and Brazil. World Bank, Washington, DC

Eaton K (2001) Decentralization, democratization and liberalization: the history of revenue sharing in Argentina, 1934–1999. J Lat Am Stud 33:1–28, Cambridge University Press

Elias EE (1997) Fiscal decentralization and municipal governance in Mexico, the case of Chihuahua. Paper prepared for Latin American studies association Guadalajara April 2997

Falleti T (2005) Sequential theory of decentralization. Am Polit Sci Rev 99(3):327–348

Falleti TG (2009) El federalismo y los gobiernos locales en Argentina y Brasil en Espacios Políticos. Revista de la Sociedad Argentina de Análisis Político, Buenos Aires, August 2009, pp 22–24

Falleti TG (2010) Decentralization and subnational politics in Latin America. Cambridge University Press, New York

Finot I (2002) Decentralización y participación en América Latina: una mirada desde la economía. Rev de la CEPAL 78:139–149

Finot I (2005) Descentralización, transferencias territoriales y desarrollo local. Rev de la CEPAL 86:29–46

Goldfrank B (2007) The politics of deepening local democracy: decentralization, party institutionalization, and participation. Comp Polit 39(2 (Jan 2007)):147–168

Gorun A (2009) Regional politics, decentralization and subsidiarity. In: Paper presented to the international conference on economics and administration, faculty of administration and business, University of Bucharest, Romania. ICEA-FAA Bucharest 14th–15th Nov 2009

HadizVedi R (2004) Decentralization and democracy in Indonesia: a critique of neo-institutionalist perspectives. Dev Chang 35(4):697–718, Blackwell Publishing

Iimi A (2005) Decentralization and economic growth revisited: an empirical note. J Urban Econ 57:449–461

Jack O (1974) Public finance. Harper and Row, New York

Ministerio de Economía y Finanzas (2005) Implementación de reglas, informe especial de la Dirección General de Asuntos económicos y sociales

Montero Alfred P, Samuels David J (2004) Decentralization and democracy in Latin America. J Lat Am Stud 37:173–231, The University of Notre Dame Press

Nobrega M (2011) Fiscal decentralization and the control of public expenditure: improvement in the performance of governmental programs by principal-agent model: the BolsaFamilia case. Harvard Law School, Cambridge
Noel (2000) Building subnational debt markets in developing and transition countries: A framework for analysis, policy reform and assistance strategy. Policy Research Working Paper 2339. World Bank, Private and Financial Sectors ,Development Unit, Europe and Central Asia Region, Washington, DC
Nofal B, Nahon C, Fernandez C (2010) Inward FDI in Argentina and its policy context VALE Columbia center on sustainable international investment May 17, 2010
Oates WE (1972) Fiscal federalism. Harcourt, Brace and Jovanovich, New York
Oates WE (2007) On the theory and practice of fiscal decentralization, in Centro di Ricerca Interdipartimentale di Economia delle Istituzioni ROMA TRE Università degli Studi. Working paper no. I/2007
Ögütçü M (2002) Foreign direct investment and regional development: sharing experiences from Brazil, China, Russia and Turkey. OECD DAFFE/INV/RD(2002)38
Palma E (1985) El tema de la descentralización en la transición hacia la democracia. Rev EURES 1:34–35
Perloff HS (1960) Lagging sectors and regions of the American economy. In: American Economic Review, vol 50(2), Papers and proceedings of the seventy-second annual meeting of the American Economic Association (May, 1960), pp 223–230
Real Instituto ElCano (2012) Anuario Iberoamericano 2012
Rodden J (2003) Reviving leviathan: fiscal federalism and the growth of government. Int Organ 57 (4 (Autumn, 2003)):695–729
Rodden J (2004) Comparative federalism and decentralization: on meaning and measurement. Comp Polit 36(4):481–500
Carlos S, and Mariano T (2012) Institucionalización de las instituciones políticas y su impacto sobre las políticas públicas Banco Interamericano de Desarrollo
Scott Z (2009) Decentralization, local development and social cohesion: an analytical review. Governance and Social Development Resource Centre
Stöhr BW (2001) In: Stöhr WB, Edralin JS, Devyani Mani (eds) Subsidiarity: a key concept for regional development in New regional development paradigms, vol 3, decentralization, governance and the new planning for local-level development. Greenwood Publishing Group, Inc, Westport
Torres Estrada, P (2005) La distribución del poder hacia el municipio en el sistema federal mexicano. In: La autonomía municipal y su garantía constitucional directa de protección. Cap. 2. Instituto de Investigaciones Jurídicas, UNAM, pp 45–101
Tulchin J, Selee A (2004) Decentralization and democratic governance in Latin America. Woodrow Wilson Center for Scholar, Washington, DC
Willis E, Da Garman CBC, Haggard S (1999) The politics of decentralization in Latin America. Lat Am Res Rev 34(1):7–56

Chapter 20
Political and Fiscal Decentralization in South America: A Comparative Analysis of Bolivia, Chile, Colombia, Ecuador, and Peru

M. Camilo Vial-Cossani

20.1 Introduction

Since the 1980s, government decentralization has been one of the most important areas of reform in Latin America. Over the years, decentralizing processes have been developed at varying rates of speed and with different areas of emphasis and motivations. All of this has led to a regional variety that provides an interesting opportunity for comparative analysis.

Despite this highly heterogeneous reality, many of the major decentralizing reforms have not met the expectations that were generated. Though there have been substantive advances such as democratic elections through direct voting for a large number of sub-national officials, following three decades of decentralization, centralism continues to be a common denominator in Latin America.

The purpose of this study is to compare the current state of political and fiscal decentralization at the intermediate and local levels of government in five countries: Bolivia, Chile, Colombia, Ecuador and Peru. These cases have been chosen based on two main criteria: they are constitutionally unitary governments that are administered in a decentralized fashion in contrast to Argentina, Brazil and Venezuela, which have federal models, and they belong to the same continental sub-region that, while highly diverse, shares a recent history with authoritarian governments (with the exception of Colombia) followed by democratic restorations that came about in a relatively parallel manner.

Decentralization is understood as a public policy process that transfers responsibilities, resources or authority from the central government to sub-national ones, endowing the latter with autonomy (Falleti 2005). There are three types of decentralization: political, fiscal and administrative. This analysis is focused on the first

M.C. Vial-Cossani (✉)
Complutense University, Madrid, Spain
e-mail: camilovial@gmail.com

J.R. Cuadrado-Roura and P. Aroca (eds.), *Regional Problems and Policies in Latin America*, Advances in Spatial Science, DOI 10.1007/978-3-642-39674-8_20,

two and provides a brief explanation of the contexts in which the decentralizing processes and political-administrative divisions began in each country.

20.2 General Description of Decentralization Processes

One of the common characteristics of decentralization processes in Latin America is that they began to develop in the 1980s as democratic systems were recovered following dictatorial periods.

The designs of new governments following years of authoritarianism had to be modern, democratic and pluralist given that they would necessarily have to have a decentralized face (Mascareño 2008). As a result, the decentralization process began with a strong political motivation and included expectations such as improved allocation of public goods and services, the promotion of accountability mechanisms and the encouragement of citizen participation (Daughters and Harper 2006) in addition to opening up a wider range of options for plurality and territorial representativeness (Restrepo 2006).

All of this encouraged the proliferation of a wide range of mechanisms that converted several countries into unique cases for interesting analysis. The countries' varying political contexts, institutional characteristics and demographic, geographic, ethnic, productive and other features meant that each country would follow its own path. This explains the differences that can be observed today in their administrative divisions, the mechanisms that have been introduced for electing sub-national officials, the design of local and intermediate government and the models that have been used to endow them with resources. Despite this broad diversity, in each of the cases studied, a significant portion of those objectives have not been met, leaving "la sensación que la descentralización no ha logrado generar los procesos de inclusión política, social y económica que se esperaban"[1] (Montecinos 2005, p. 84).

On occasion, large decentralization reforms have resulted in formal changes that failed to substantially modify the design in practice or to satisfy the high expectations generated among the populace. Central governments continued to make important decisions, transferred limited powers to the sub-national level and allocated resources to local and intermediate governments whose expenditures are highly conditioned by the center.

In addition, the generalized crisis of the second half of the 1990s forced a change in focus in what Gómez Sabaini and Jiménez call the second wave of decentralizing policies. "No se priorizaron los regímenes de coparticipación de impuestos (habitualmente de libre disponibilidad), como en los años anteriores, sino que se dio preferencia a canalizar los recursos federales a los gobiernos subnacionales para

[1] Translation: "(...) the feeling that decentralization has failed to generate political, social, and economic inclusion processes".

educación y salud, fortaleciendo los mecanismos de transferencia con asignación específica"[2] (2011, p. 15). As we will see, this type of transfer tends to reduce receiving governments' power to manage resources at their own discretion, which ends up strengthening the position of the central government. There is no doubt that three decades after these policies were first implemented, Latin America is more decentralized than before. However, public affairs are still centralist in nature, and it seems that this situation will not change in the short term.

20.2.1 Bolivia

Following the 1982 return to democracy, Bolivia was again ruled in accordance with the Political Constitution of 1967, which allowed for the democratic election of mayors in the provincial capitals and the constitutional recognition of the governments of each *departamento* (department; region level). In the mid-1990s, decentralization was expanded at the municipal level, which meant that mayors throughout the country could be elected. However, the intermediate level of government faced a significant setback when the constitutional recognition of regional governments was eliminated in order to increase efficiency.

In 2005, the country was in the midst of a strong political and social crisis. Under the administration of Carlos Mesa, the regional governments were strengthened once again and the democratic election of their officials was allowed. These entities also were granted a series of attributes that allowed them to work with greater levels of autonomy. Following the rise to power of Evo Morales in 2006, the country experienced increasing political tension dominated by ethnic and territorial variables in which the opposition argued strongly for the autonomy of the departments and for Sucre to be considered the capital. In May 2008, Santa Cruz declared its autonomy and manifested its intention to charge special taxes, which the government declared unconstitutional (La Nación May 18 2008).

In this context, a new constitution was passed in 2009 that defined Bolivia as a unitary, plurinational, decentralized state with autonomies. The text states that due to the "existencia precolonial de las naciones y pueblo indígena originario campesinos y su dominio ancestral sobre sus territorios, se garantiza su libre determinación en el marco de la unidad del Estado, que consiste en su derecho a la autonomía, al autogobierno"[3] (Asamblea Constituyente de Bolivia 2009, p. 3). While the Constitution addresses issues of decentralization, the administrative model has not managed to resolve substantive matters such as poverty and

---

[2] Translation: "The tax-sharing arrangements were not prioritized (usually freely available), as in previous years. Preference was given to lead federal resources to sub-national governments for education and health, strengthening specific transfers".

[3] Translation: "(...) existence of pre-colonial nations and indigenous people and their ancestral dominion over their territories, is guaranteed self-determination within the framework of the unity of the State, which consists in their right to self-government".

inequality. "Las críticas se concentran propiamente sobre este punto, el de la fragilidad endémica del Estado boliviano que no ha logrado consolidar su institucionalidad en casi dos siglos de existencia"[4] (Herman 2010, p. 39). In addition to this new imbalance between expectations and results, there are ethnic and territorial tensions in the country which undoubtedly will generate more than one internal conflict in the future.

20.2.2 Chile

Following the return to democracy in 1990, Chile quickly began to develop a decentralizing process based on the territorial structure inherited from the dictatorship. Early on in Aylwin's administration, the statutory laws of Municipalities (1991) and Regional Government and Administration (1992) were passed. These pieces of legislation set the stage for the institutional structure that continues to be in place to this day at the territorial level. The former restored the democratic election of local officials and eliminated authoritarian enclaves within municipalities. It also restored autonomous administrative capacities and partially modified sources of income. The latter created regional governments for each of the regions as an intermediate-level agency, though one that was not completely autonomous from the central government.

While the creation of regional governments has led to unprecedented innovation, its effects on decentralization have been very limited. This is due to the fact that officials are not elected through direct democratic voting processes. In addition, the regional governments have limited budgets that come almost entirely from central transfers (they are not authorized to introduce their own taxes). There is also a lack of autonomy from the central level as well as technical and human limitations that keep these governments from successfully completing the tasks assigned to them.

20.2.3 Colombia

This country has been characterized by marked territorial differences that have created regional and local leaderships throughout its republican history.

The Constitution of 1991 expanded a decentralizing process begun in 1986 by allowing for the democratic election of governors, granting greater political and administrative autonomy to *departamentos* and municipalities, modifying the distribution of responsibilities among the three levels of government and elevating the transfer of resources to sub-national governments to a level of constitutional import.

---

[4] Translation: "The criticism focuses on this point, the endemic weakness of the Bolivian State has failed to consolidate its institutions in nearly two centuries of existence".

Under the administration of Luis Uribe (2002–2010), Colombia stopped the progress that it was making on its road to decentralization. The period saw, among other things, cuts in municipal budgets and an increase in the resources of the central government that were invested in municipalities. Matters of decentralization returned to the fore beginning in 2010, when José Manuel Santos was elected. In 2011, the Territorial Organization Law which promotes planning and competitivity in the regions was passed.

Colombia is considered one of the most decentralized countries in the region and is regularly compared to the federal states of Argentina and Brazil (Subsecretaría de Desarrollo Regional y Administrativo 2009). However, it would seem that the desired results are far from being achieved. The current model generated the conditions necessary for the sub-national governments to satisfy an adequate provision of services, decrease territorial inequities and promote citizen participation. However, a significant number of them have not managed to meet the basic needs of their population and present deficient performance, "lo cual está asociado a prácticas de captura de los aparatos públicos, de corrupción y de clientelismo"[5] (Maldonado 2011, p. 1).

20.2.4 Ecuador

When democracy was restored in 1979, Ecuador returned to the practice of holding democratic elections for local and regional officials. The country also passed a new Political Constitution (1978) which stated that "Ecuador es un Estado constitucional de derechos y justicia, social, democrático, soberano, independiente, unitario (...). Se organiza en forma de República y se gobierna de manera descentralizada"[6] (Asamblea Constituyente 1978, p. 16). In 1992 a set of fiscal reforms was approved that created important sub-national transfer funds. One year later, the National Council on Modernization was established in order to generate a national decentralization and de-concentration plan. In 1998 a new transfer tool known as the '15 % Law' was created and the Special Law on Government Decentralization and Social Participation was passed.

However, this entire process was characterized by its voluntary nature, as sub-national governments were allowed to request greater jurisdiction; the meager organization of the methodology for doing so; the ambiguity with which the government would transfer – or not – the resources requested; and the lack of clarity with which it planned interaction with territorial stakeholders (Verdesoto 2006).

[5] Translation: "Which is associated with harvesting practices of public agencies, corruption and clientelism".

[6] Translation: "Ecuador is a constitutional State of rights and justice, social, democratic, sovereign, independent, unitary (...). It is organized as a Republic and is governed in a decentralized way".

Recent institutional changes have reenergized the decentralizing process. These include the constitutional reform of 2008 and the Statutory Code of Territorial Organization, Autonomy and Decentralization (COOTAD, acronym in Spanish) of 2010. These two pieces of legislation set out the general structure of the current and incipient decentralizing process. One year later, the National Jurisdiction Commission was created to transfer responsibilities from the central government to sub-national ones. Finally, the 2012–2015 National Decentralization Plan was created. This instrument was based on massive citizen participation and is designed to develop strategic medium-range plans that promote greater inter-territorial equity.

While it is still too early to evaluate this entire new institutional framework, the current model already presents some weaknesses. For example, there are Decentralized Autonomous Governments with uneven institutional capacities. As a result, some of them cannot meet some of their mandatory responsibilities while others have already moved voluntarily towards a larger transfer of responsibilities in the earlier process. The latter must now slow down their pace in order to reach uniformity among the entities that share a level. The definition of the system of responsibilities is not yet complete. There are still loose ends, mainly in the area of fiscal decentralization (Serrano and Acosta 2011a).

20.2.5 Peru

In 1979, Peru passed a new Political Constitution that eliminated the authoritarian government, recognized a series of powers of local governments and restored the democratic election of their officials. Ten years later – and strongly influenced by electoral calculations that forecast a loss at the polls in the presidential election of 1990-, the government of Alan García strengthened the intermediate level of government, creating 12 regions. However, none of the changes that he proposed were ever implemented.

Peru's democracy was halted during the Fujimori administration. His authoritarian government even closed the regional governments in 1993 along with Congress and the courts through a self-coup. One year later, following strong internal and international pressure, a new Constitution was passed that restored recognition of sub-national governments and established that Peru is a Republic that is "democrática, social, independiente y soberana. El Estado es uno e indivisible. Su gobierno es unitario, representativo y descentralizado"[7] (Tribunal Constitucional del Perú 1993).

However, most of the initiatives that changed the territorial institutional structure and strongly promoted sub-national governments came in the twenty-first

---

[7] Translation: "(. . .) democratic, social, independent and sovereign. The State is one and indivisible. Its government is unitary, representative and decentralized".

century. The Law on Regionalization was passed in 2002. It allowed for the direct election of regional officials. The Statutory Law on Regional Governments, which set out resources and jurisdictions for those entities, was passed the same year. The Statutory Law on Municipalities was put in place in 2003, strengthening their powers and resources, and the following year brought the introduction of the natural resources canon, the most important budgetary transfer system implemented for sub-national governments by Lima.

The election of Ollanta Humala brought a new focus on the regional level and the promotion of greater levels of autonomy. However, the agents and stakeholders involved in the process have proved critical of this approach, claiming that the practice is far from what is established in the law and that it leads to "dependencia de decisiones del nivel central, duplicidad de competencias, falta de visión estratégica regional y de capacidades de gestión en los equipos técnicos y profesionales, pérdida de vitalidad del componente participativo, entre otros"[8] (Serrano and Acosta 2011b, p. 7).

20.3 Political-Administrative Divisions

It is interesting to observe the variety that exists in the region with regard to the countries' political-administrative divisions. Some nations have a large number of territorial units, and some even allow for the creation of indigenous territories with distinctive administration models, such as Bolivia, Colombia and Ecuador.

Bolivia is organized into *departamentos*, provinces, municipalities, autonomous regions and rural indigenous territories.[9] Colombia has *departamentos*, municipalities, districts, *corregimientos departamentales*, *corregimientos municipales*, and indigenous territories. In Ecuador, the new institutional structure introduced through the constitutional reform of 2008 and the COOTAD added six types of Decentralized Autonomous Governments, one for each territorial level: regional governments,[10] provincial governments, metropolitan governments, municipal governments, *juntas parroquiales* and governments for areas with a high presence of indigenous and Afro-Ecuadorian peoples.

---

[8] Translation: "(...) dependency on central level decisions, overlap of responsibilities, lack of regional strategic vision and management skills in technical and professional teams, loss of vitality of participatory component, among others".

[9] The autonomous regions and rural indigenous territories are territorial units that were created once a series of requirements set out in the law were met. Bolivia currently has the autonomous region of Chaco Tarijeño, while there are 11 municipalities that have opted to become rural indigenous territories.

[10] The Ecuadorean regions do not yet exist, but according to COOTAD they must be created by 2018, grouping two or more geographically contiguous provinces together and meeting surface area and population criteria.

Table 20.1 Intermediate Governments (IG) and Local Governments (LG)

	Intermediate unit	IG name	IG #	Local unit	LG name	LG#
Bolivia	*Departamento*	*Gobierno departmental*	9	*Municipio*	*Gobierno municipal*	327
Chile	*Regiόn*	*Gobierno regional*	15	*Comuna*	*Municipalidad*	345
Colombia	*Departamento*	*Gobierno departmental*[a]	33	*Municipio*	*Municipalidad*	1,114
Ecuador	*Provincia*	*Consejo provincial*	22	*Cantόn*	*Municipalidad*	219
Peru	*Departamento*	*Gobierno regional*[b]	25	*Distrito*	*Municipalidad*	1,838

Source: Generated by the author
[a]Includes capital district (Bogotá)
[b]Includes constitutional province of Callao and 'Lima Provincias'. Excludes the province of Lima

However, in all of the cases studied, there are two territorial units with their own governments that stand out because of their responsibilities, resources and territorial authority: the local ones (with their respective local governments, LG) and the intermediate ones (intermediate governments, IG), which can be viewed in Table 20.1.

An analysis of territorial units and their respective population densities reveals a notorious atomization at the municipal level. As the data in Table 20.2 show, 70 % of the districts in Peru and nearly half of the municipalities in Bolivia and Colombia have fewer than 10,000 inhabitants. While Chile and Ecuador have a lower percentage of LG under that standard, the number of units with over 50,000 inhabitants is relatively low. As one can imagine, the average population of the IG is much higher. However, in all of the countries studied, significant numbers of IGs rule areas with fewer than 500,000 inhabitants.

The creation of sub-national administrations that govern small populations decreases their strategic positions regarding the central government, facilitating the possibility that the latter may domesticate them. This is even more likely when peripheral governments depend on a high percentage of transfers from the center. As we will see in Sect. 20.5, these are usually highly conditioned on financial ministries.

20.4 Political Decentralization

Political decentralization is directly related to the mechanisms that allow the people elect sub-national officials without being dependent on the central government. This allows, among other things, for elected representatives to answer to their territorial citizenry and not the edicts issued from the center. Since the 1980s, all of the countries studies meet this criterion with the exception of Chile, which recovered its democracy in 1990 but does not yet democratically elect its highest-ranking regional officials (see Table 20.3).

Table 20.2 Sub-national governments and populations

	LG			GI		
	Inhabitants/LG	LG < 10,000	LG > 50,000	Inhabitants/IG	IG < 200,000	IG > 500,000
Bolivia	25,304	49.8	5.2	919,369	10	60
Chile	49,069	28.4	25.5	1,128,585	20	73.3
Colombia	37,225	44.3	9.7	1,256,618	21.2	66.7
Ecuador	6,531	27.4	19	650,131	45.8	25
Peru	13,484	73.8	6.2	1,096,486	8	64

Source: Generated by the author based on national census data (The years and Websites of the censuses consulted to make the calculations are as follows: Bolivia, 2001, Instituto Nacional de Estadística: http://www.ine.gob.bo; Chile, 2002, Instituto Nacional de Estadística: http://www.ine.cl; Colombia, 2005, Departamento Administrativo Nacional de Estadísticas: http://www.dane.gov.co; Ecuador, 2010, Instituto Nacional de Estadística y Censos: http://www.inec.gob.ec; and Peru, 2007, Instituto Nacional de Estadística e Informática: http://www.inei.gob.pe)

Table 20.3 Democratic election of sub-national officials

	LG				IG			
	Mayor election	Terms	Re-eligibility	Popular revocation	President election	Terms	Re-eligibility	Popular revocation
Bolivia	1985	5	Yes, but only for two terms	Yes	2005	5	Yes, but only for two terms	Yes
Chile	1992	4	Yes	No	–	–	–	–
Colombia	1986	4	Not consecutively	Yes	1991	4	No	Yes
Ecuador	1983	4	Yes	No	1983	4	Not consecutively	No
Peru	1980	5	Yes	Yes	2002	4	Yes	Yes

Source: Generated by the author

Both LG and IG are composed of an executive branch (which is responsible for the highest level of administration of the sub-national government) and another branch that tends to be called legislative, but that in practice is more nominative and oversight-related.

At the LG level, mayors are democratically elected for periods of 4 years in Chile, Colombia and Ecuador and for 5 years in Bolivia and Peru. With the exception of Colombia (and the limitation of immediacy in Bolivia), they may be reelected. The situation of municipal council members (which are called *regidores* in Peru) is similar. They vary in number within each country depending on the population that the LG governs. However, there are differences. Some council members are not democratically elected in Bolivia but are selected by indigenous communities through their own electoral processes. In Colombia, council members can be reelected immediately and in Ecuador the mayor presides over the municipal council with a right to cast a vote in order to break a tie.

The democratic election of IG officials has come later with the exception of Ecuador, which introduced this process for both levels of government simultaneously. As a result, the governors in Bolivia and Colombia, prefects in Ecuador and regional presidents in Peru are elected directly,[11] with greater restrictions on their reelection compared to the local sphere. Chile is the only exception, as the *intendente* is appointed by the President of the Republic as a de-concentrated agent of the central government. He or she is also the highest ranking official in the regional government, thus playing a double role. This open paradox has meant that in practice the *intendente* prioritizes his or her role of representative of the Executive over that of the regional government. These officials remain in office at the sole discretion of the President.

In regard to legislative bodies, the members of the assemblies of *departamentos* in Bolivia and Colombia, provincial councils in Ecuador and regional councils in Peru also are elected democratically and have similar characteristics to those presented by their counterparts in the LG: some of these officials in Bolivia are selected by their indigenous groups through their own processes and prefects preside over provincial councils in Ecuador with the right to a tie-breaking vote.

The exception continues to be Chile, where regional council members are still selected by the municipal council members. A change was made to the Constitution in 2009 that establishes democratic elections in this case, but the law which regulates the election is still under discussion (it entered Congress in September 2011).

Finally, in Bolivia, Colombia and Ecuador, the highest-ranking sub-national officials may be removed from their positions by citizen initiatives via referendums.

However, the democratization of sub-national governments has not led the central government to cede significant amounts of responsibility. The LGs, which are frequently stronger than the IGs, tend to have nearly exclusive responsibilities

---

[11] In both Peru and Ecuador, the Executive Branch has a Vice President and Vice Prefect, respectively. In the latter case, he or she is elected at the same time as the Prefect.

with high levels of discretion over basic services (sanitation, potable water, drainage, public lighting and waste management, among other) as well as planning. However, in regard to social services such as health, education and housing, they share responsibilities with other levels of government, mainly at the central level, from which they receive the transfer of responsibilities and highly conditioned transfers.

20.5 Fiscal Decentralization

This type of decentralization is understood as a group of public policies designed to increase the income or fiscal autonomy of sub-national governments. Decentralization can be studied based on income source and in terms of expenditures. While "la asignación de responsabilidades del gasto a los gobiernos subnacionales es importante, la forma en cómo los gobiernos subnacionales financien tales servicios es una preocupación clave"[12] (Gómez and Jiménez 2011, p. 11). The focus of this study is decentralization based on income, specifically in regard to three main areas: self-generated resources (creation of sub-national taxes, delegation of tax authority to officials at this level and non-tax income), transfers (usually from the central government) and debt capacity (Falleti 2005).

Table 20.4 presents an investigatory summary of the fiscal reality of the intermediate governments of the five countries. The first matter to be considered is the capacity that the IGs have to generate their own resources. Only Colombia and Ecuador give these bodies the power to collect taxes; they may not do so in Chile, Peru and Bolivia. Not however that in Bolivia, while autonomous governments in the *departamentos* do not directly collect taxes, the central government is required by law to transfer the monies earned through the exploitation of natural resources in their areas. In other words, though the *departamentos* cannot collect taxes, they are assigned to them. Chile is the only country whose IG do not collect money through the payment of fees and licenses, though as we will see in the pages that follow, those sources of income are not truly significant in the other cases. Also Chile is the only country whose IG do not have debt capacity. It is important to note, however, that while this measure restricts their budgetary autonomy, it is also a barrier to a lack of balance in public finances. South America has presented critical cases in which central governments have had to severely restrict borrowing, such as Argentina and Colombia in 2001 and 1997, respectively (Subsecretaría de Desarrollo Regional y Administrativo 2009).

Table 20.5 presents information on the distribution of income and public spending by level of government. The fiscal centrality in both income and expenditures is notorious, as is the budgetary strength of LGs compared to IGs (with the exception

[12] Translation: "(...) the allocation of expenditure responsibilities to sub-national governments is important, the way how sub-national finance such services is a key concern".

Table 20.4 Fiscal responsibilities of IG in South America

	Do IG collect taxes?	Do IG collect fees or licenses?	Have IG debt capacity?	Do IG receive transfers related to industries or exploitation of natural resources in their areas?	Have they freedom to spend at least the 50 % of their transfers?
Bolivia	No	Yes	Yes	Yes	No
Chile	No	No	No	Yes	No
Colombia	Yes	Yes	Yes	Yes	No
Ecuador	Yes	Yes	Yes	Yes	No
Peru	No	Yes	Yes	Yes	No

Source: Generated by the author

Table 20.5 Share of income and public expenditures by level of government

	Incomes			Expenditures		
	Central	Intermediate	Local	Central	Intermediate	Local
Bolivia 2011	81.0	9.6	9.2	81.0	9.6	9.2
Chile 2011	85.1	3.0	11.7	82.7	3.9	13.2
Colombia 2010	65.1	12.1	22.6	61.0	13.4	25.5
Ecuador 2010	96.0	0.4	3.5	81.9	4.7	13.4[a]
Peru 2011	75.3	8.4	16.1	63.4	18.4	18.0

Source: Generated by the author based on the execution of national budgets
[a]This line item combines the expenditures of municipal governments (12.8 %) and those of parish boards (0.6 %)

of Bolivia) and the apparent fiscal responsibility of sub-national governments, which have balanced income and expenditures. However, these data do not reflect an important vertical fiscal imbalance. In other words, the income collected directly by peripheral governments is considerably lower than the amount that they must spend based on their obligations. This is only balanced through transfers (mainly from the central government) and royalties (also central transfers, but based on the exploitation of non-renewable natural resources).

Figure 20.1 shows transfers and royalties as percentages of the income of IGs and LGs. The latter far outweigh the former particularly in Chile due to the greater strengths of municipalities when it comes to generating their own income, particularly taxes. Finally, the Chilean case is notable in that it has the third-lowest income at the municipal level but is less dependent on transfers and presents greater capacities to generate own income.

All of the countries have vertical transfers (from the central government to peripheral ones) related to the exploitation of natural resources. These programs generally benefit the areas in which the natural resources are obtained more than others. The exception is Chile. It almost does not have allocations of this type and there are no vertical transfers at the municipal level. There is a mechanism for horizontal transfers at the local level in Chile.

The resources produced by transfers and royalties represent a very high percentage of the total sub-national income and are also very much conditioned on their

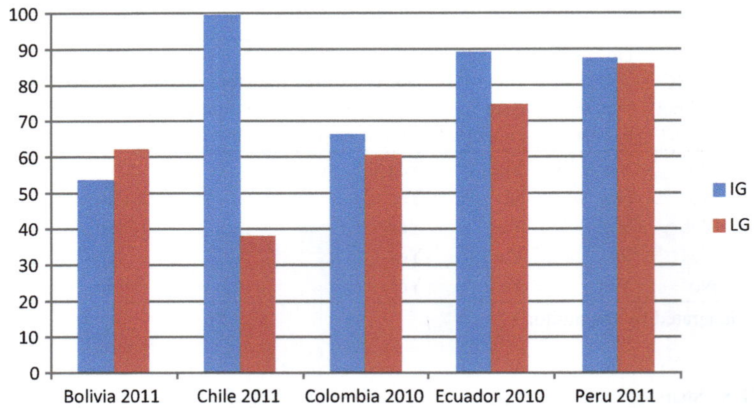

Fig. 20.1 Transfers and royalties as percentages of total income of sub-national governments (Source: Generated by the author based on national budgets)

expenditure either due to their nature (regular or capital expenditures) or the specific sectors to which they must be allocated. As a result, autonomy in public spending at the sub-national level is highly conditioned by the basis for the transfer.

In order to analyze the situation of sub-national taxes by country, the self-generated income (tax and other) and transfers (including royalties, where applicable) are considered due to the fact that these are the most important line items in their budgets. There are, however, other sources of income including balances from previous periods, social contributions and debt capacity. Finally, all of the numbers presented here reflect the executions of the income of sub-national governments and not their budgets. This is done in order to allow the reader to appreciate how many of the resources effectively enter at the sub-national level with more certainty.

20.5.1 Bolivia

20.5.1.1 Self-generated Income

At the level of *departamento,* while autonomous governments are to receive taxes and fees on natural resources, they do not have the authority to collect them.[13] The income that is generated through this route is received through transfers related to the hydrocarbon industry. The greatest sources of self-generated income at this level are collected through the sale of assets. However, in 2011, this source was

[13] The following data were consulted in the documents of the Budgetary Execution Office of the Ministry of Economics and Public Finance of the Plurinational State of Bolivia (2012).

responsible for just 1.25 % of the income of the *departamentos*, while fees and licenses represented only 0.26 %.

The Autonomous Municipal Governments receive shared tax transfers and collect taxes. The most significant taxes are those related to real estate, sales, vehicles and assets, among others. In 2011, this item represented 12.43 % of all income at this level.

20.5.1.2 Transfers

Bolivia's sub-national governments receive a wide range of transfers from the central government. The most important is the Direct Hydrocarbon Tax (IDH, acronym in Spanish), which applies to all *departamentos* and municipalities. It represents 32 % of total hydrocarbon production, and the resources must be spent on education, health, infrastructure and economic development. Ten percent goes to the *departamentos* and 31 % goes to the municipalities, with priority placed on areas that produce hydrocarbons. The remainder is distributed to universities, the National General Treasury, the program *Renta Digna* and the Indigenous Fund. In 2011, resources collected through the IDH represented nearly 68 % of all transfers received by autonomous regional governments.

At this level there is also the Special Tax on Hydrocarbons and Their Derivatives (IEHD, acronym in Spanish), which corresponds to 25 % of the monies collected on internal sale of hydrocarbons and the importation of their derivatives. Half of these resources are distributed in equal parts while the other half is disbursed in relation to the number of inhabitants of each *departamento*. In 2011, the IEHD covered nearly 30 % of transfers at the *departamento* level. Finally, there is the *Departamento* Compensatory Fund, which applies to all of the areas that are under the national average for royalties per inhabitant. Funds are transferred from the National General Treasury until that average is met as long as it does not exceed 10 % of the monies collected through the IEHD. The expenditures related to this transfer also operate based on conditions: 85 % must be used on capital spending and 15 % is to be used on regular spending.

Income from royalties, by contrast, is obtained through the Hydrocarbon Law of 2005, which establishes that 18 % of monies generated through hydrocarbon exploitation is to be distributed as follows: 11 % to the *departamentos* where hydrocarbons are produced, 1 % to the *departamentos* of Beni and Pando, and 6 % to the National General Treasury.

In 2011, transfers to the autonomous governments of the *departamentos* represented 53.86 % of their income. Royalties totaled 26.55 %. These two sources represented 80.41 % of the budget. The *departamento* that was least dependent on transfers and royalties that year was Beni (67.27 %) and the rest showed high levels of dependency (over 96 %).

At the municipal level, in addition to the IDH (which represented 42.86 % of the income received through transfers in 2011), there are three other instruments that make transfers from the central government. The main one and the principal source of all municipal income is the Popular Tax Co-Participation Fund. Twenty percent of the monies that are collected through a total of eight taxes (included the value added tax, the corporate tax and tax on transactions) go directly to the municipalities and are distributed proportionally based on the number of inhabitants. Eighty-five percent of this fund must be spent on public investments. In 2011, tax co-participation represented nearly 50 % of the income received through transfers.

There are also resources that come from the National Dialogue Law of 2000. These funds are generated through external debt remission. They are resources that are allocated to remedy deficits in municipalities with the highest poverty and risk levels in the areas of health and education. Twenty percent of the monies collected is allocated to education, 10 % goes to health and 70 % is placed in the National Economic and Social Investment Fund. In 2011, these resources represented a little over 7 % of all municipal transfers. Finally, the Autonomous Municipal Governments receive transfers from the Hydrocarbon Licenses, which are charged to the Bolivian Government Oil Facilities. The central government transfers 50 % of the monies collected to the municipalities that produce this material to be spent on public investment and environmental management projects.

Transfers to the Autonomous Municipal Governments in 2011 represented 62.33 % of their income. That same year, over 80 % of the total budget of 233 municipalities was dependent on transfers.

20.5.2 Chile

20.5.2.1 Self-generated Income

Regional governments do not generate income through taxes or fees or licenses.[14] In 2011, only 0.05 % of their budgets came from self-generated income. A small exception was introduced in 2005 with the budgetary category of "Self-generated Income Allocated by Law." However, these are not necessarily new resources because a significant portion of them were already in place through transfers from the central government. Though the name suggests otherwise, the term self-generated income only refers to a very small portion of this category (mining and geo-thermal licenses, resources generated through the laws on gaming casinos and national goods, and others) and these monies are not collected at the regional level. As a result, the central government transfers them.

Municipalities do have self-generated tax income. In 2011, this source represented 41.28 % of all municipal income. The most important category is municipal licenses (mainly related to commerce, exploitation and cleaning

[14] The following data were gathered from the general and municipal governments' Operating Reports and the Budgetary Execution Reports (Dirección de Presupuestos 2012a, b).

contracts), which represent 26.93 % of the self-generated tax income, followed by territorial taxes (25.61 %) and taxes collected through vehicle registration permits and drivers licenses (11.04 %).

20.5.2.2 Transfers

In 2011, transfers were the source of 99.91 % of the income of regional governments. The most important of these was the National Fund for Regional Development (FNDR, acronym in Spanish), whose resources correspond to a portion of total public investment established in the National Budget each year.

There are two major types of FNDR: traditional or distributed and provisional. The former is composed of resources from the national budget that are mainly allocated to social infrastructure projects. This type of fund is the oldest and allows for the greatest amount of decision-making power at the regional level. It is distributed as follows: 90 % of the fund is set out in the Budgets Law in function of two criteria. They are that (a) 50 % of this amount is distributed in accordance with regional poverty and indigence indicators and (b) the remaining amount is allocated in accordance to indicators that express the region's territorial characteristics (likelihood that the population will access public services and cost differentials of paving and construction projects, for example). The remaining 10 % is distributed equally based on two criteria: standards of efficiency (measured in the health and education sectors and based on the investments made by the FNDR) and emergency spending. In 2011, this represented 37.57 % of all regional government income.

The FNDR for provisions is composed of funds that are to be invested regionally in sectors that are identified in advance. In this case, the Ministry of Finance makes the investment decisions while the regional governments play a secondary role. This fund represented 35.39 % of the total income of regional governments in 2011.

Other less important mechanisms include the aforementioned Self-Generated Income Allocated by Law and other transfers that are not part of the regional governments' budget but do require their approval so that the investments related to them can be made.

At the local level, there is the Common Municipal Fund (FCM, acronym in Spanish). In contrast to the rest of the inter-governmental transfer programs described in this study, the FCM is a horizontal municipal transfer tool meant to redistribute resources at this level. It has historically been composed solely of municipal contributions, though beginning in 2005 it has included resources from the government. It is distributed as follows: 25 % is allocated in equal parts to all of the municipalities in the country; 10 % is allocated based on the number of individuals living in poverty in the municipality; 30 % is granted based on the number of tax exempt properties; and 35 % is allocated proportionally to the municipalities with the lowest permanent self-generated income the preceding year.

In 2011, the FCM represented 28.77 % of all municipal income. However, according to data from the Municipal Information System (*Sistema de Información*

Municipal, www.sinim.cl), the importance of this transfer system is more notorious when one considers that it represents over 50 % of the income of half of the country's municipalities.

In addition, the municipalities receive a series of transfers linked to their responsibilities in the areas of health and education by law, as well as other programs (housing, urban improvement and others). In 2011, these sources represented 9.37 % of their income.

20.5.3 Colombia

20.5.3.1 Self-generated Income

The governments of the *departamentos* are authorized to collected taxes.[15] The most important ones are beer and liquor consumption taxes (which represent nearly 50 % of all taxes collected at this level) followed by registration and licensing (11.38 %), cigarettes and tobacco (7.86 %), motor vehicles (7.52 %) and the tax on gasoline (5.65 %) as well as other smaller taxes. In 2010, that income represented 26.1 % of the total for the *departamentos*. There are significant differences among these units. For example, nearly 45 % of the income of the valley or Atlantic *departamentos* comes from self-generated income, while less than 10 % of the income of Vichada, Guainia, Arauca, Vaupes, Putumayo and Amazonas comes from this source. Non-tax self-generated income represented 5.7 % of the total income.

The municipal tax system is composed of 19 taxes, including those applied to commerce and industry (41.52 % of the total municipal taxes in 2010), property (30.66 %) and the tax on gasoline (10.1 %). In 2010, 30.76 % of all municipal taxes corresponded to the collection of taxes at this level. That same year, non-tax self-generated income totaled 5.49 %.

As a result, the total self-generated income of the *departamentos* represented 33.42 % of all of their income while that of the municipalities was 39.31 %.

20.5.3.2 Transfers

For 10 years following the passage of the Constitution of 1991, Colombia had a system for transfers based on two mechanisms. The first was the *Situado Fiscal,* which was directed at the *departamentos,* and the second was the municipalities' share. The increase in fiscal imbalance and diverse deficiencies in the allocation of

[15] The following data were consulted in the Budgetary Execution Reports of the *Departamentos* and Municipalities (Departamento Nacional de Planeación 2012), and the Execution Reports (Ministerio de Hacienda y Crédito Público 2012).

these resources led the government to replace the two mechanisms with a single General Participation System (SGP, acronym in Spanish). The SGP is responsible for a significant portion of the budgets of sub-national entities. In 2010, it represented 46.88 % of the municipal budget and 47.18 % of the budget of the *departamento*.

Meanwhile, royalties are distributed in two groups. Some go to the territories that produce them and others go through the National Royalty Fund. In 2010, royalties represented 14.95 % of the total income of the *departamentos* and 5.22 % of that of the municipalities. Royalties and SGP transfers combined represented 66.58 % and 60.69 % of their budgets, respectively.

Budgetary dependence on these sources of income is considerable in sub-national governments. According to data from the National Planning Department, transfers and royalties represented nearly 90 % of the income of four *departamentos* while 90 % or more of the income of nearly 200 municipalities came from these income sources (Departamento Nacional de Planeación 2010).

20.5.4 Ecuador

20.5.4.1 Self-generated Income

Prior to the passage of COOTAD, provincial councils had very limited tax income generation capacities, receiving only 1 % of the *alcabala* sales taxes and 0.1 % of registrations.[16] In 2010, self-generated income (taxes and other sources) in the provinces represented only 10.4 % the entities' total income.

By contrast, the municipalities have a broad fixed tax base that is applied to local residents under the principle of fiscal co-responsibility. These include taxes on urban and rural property, vehicles, registrations and licenses, assets, public performances, gaming, sales tax and gains through the purchase and sale of real estate. COOTAD modified the fiscal decentralization model, assigning tax authority on these same taxes to provincial councils.

Self-generated income for municipalities other than taxes mainly consists of fees, investment income, rent and fines. Municipal self-generated income represented 24.8 % of total income for these units in 2010 (40.5 % of self-generated income came from taxes).

[16] The following data were taken from the National Decentralization Plan for 2012–2015 (Consejo Nacional de Competencias and Secretaría Nacional de Planificación y Desarrollo 2012).

20.5.4.2 Transfers

Ecuador has 18 transfer funds that shift resources from the central government to sub-national ones, contributing most of the income of the latter. In 1998, the Political Constitution was modified and it was established that fiscal transfers would only be made with the corresponding transfer of responsibilities. This meant that transfers would be highly conditioned. The most important of these mechanisms are the Special Transfer Law of 15 % of the National Government to Local Governments (better known as the '15 % Law'), the Provincial Development Fund and the Local Development Fund.

The 15 % Law transfers that percentage of the net income to provincial councils (30 %) and municipalities (70 %) based on criteria such as surface area, population and need. It is mainly meant to finance investment plans for economic, social and cultural development.

Transfers represented 89.5 % of the provinces' total income in 2010. The main mechanisms were the 15 % Law (48.8 %) and the Provincial Development Fund (16.3 %). Municipal transfers represented 75.1 % of all income for those entities and the 15 % Law represented over half of these resources.

20.5.5 Peru

20.5.5.1 Self-generated Income

While regional governments are given a share of import taxes by law, they cannot collect them and receive them only through transfers.[17] (Note that in 2011, such income represented only 0.005 % of the total for the *departamentos*.) As a result, at the level of the *departamento,* all income is non-tax in origin (fees, fines, administrative interests and the sale of foods, mainly). These sources represented 9.27 % of all income for these entities in 2011.

By contrast, the municipalities can collect taxes. Self-generated income from local taxes represented 8.82 % of these entities' total income in 2011. The main tax collected is the property tax, which represented 61.94 % of self-generated income at this level in 2011. The tax on production and consumption took a distant second place, representing 5.54 % of self-generated income. If non-tax self-generated income is included, the total self-generated income for municipalities in 2011 represented 12.83 % of total income for this level.

[17] The data for this section are from the Public Sector Budget Closure documents for the 2011 Fiscal Year (Ministerio de Economía y Finanzas 2012).

20.5.5.2 Transfers

At the *departamento* level, the main transfer mechanism is the Regional Compensation Mechanism, which constitutes nearly all of the budgets of the Regional Governments (Subsecretaría de Desarrollo Regional y Administrativo 2009). It is distributed based on factors of poverty, unmet needs, location on a border, population, tax contribution to the government and performance indicators related to the execution of investments. The resources from this fund go directly to regional investment projects mainly in the areas of agriculture, fishing, mining, energy, tourism, roadways, communications, health, education and the environment.

Thirty percent of the Camisea Socio-economic Development Fund, which is focused on areas through which the main hydrocarbon channels pass, is distributed among the *departamentos* affected by that infrastructure and Ucayali. With the exception of the last one,[18] the resources are distributed based on indicators linked to population, social need and longitude of the channels and are to be spent mostly on regional investment projects and economic infrastructure maintenance.

Regional governments receive significant income in the form of royalties, which come in two forms: the canon and the mining royalties. The former is a share that sub-national governments receive as a result of compensations generated by the economic exploitation of non-renewable natural resources based on the income obtained by the central government as a result of that activity. There are several types of canons: mining, hydro-energy, gas, fishing, forestry and oil. In addition to mining royalties, each of these is highly conditioned on being spent on regional investment projects. As a whole, transfers and royalties represented 87.73 % of the total income of the regional governments in 2010.

At the municipal level, there is a Municipal Compensation Fund. It is distributed based on criteria such as population, mortality rate, unmet basic needs and rate of rural population and benefits the country's most outlying and depressed municipalities. In addition, municipalities have significant resources made available to them through the canon concept. While 25 % go to regional governments, 75 % go directly to local ones according to the following format: 10 % goes to local governments in which the resource is exploited; 25 % goes to the local governments that belong to the same province as place in which the exploitation takes place; and 40 % goes to the local governments that belong to the same *departamento* where the exploitation takes place. In 2011, municipal transfers and grants represented 86.13 % of all income.

[18] By law, it is distributed in different percentages to all of the local governments in the *departamento*.

20.6 Conclusions

Three decades after the process began there is no doubt that Latin America now presents a more decentralized face. Proof of this is, for example, the democratic election of key sub-national officials; the political and administrative recognition of ethnic groups in some cases; and the greater – though incomplete – levels of autonomy and budgetary and jurisdictional responsibilities that have been assigned to peripheral governments, at least compared to the early 1980s. In the preceding pages, we have seen how some major decentralizing reforms are limited to formal aspects that do not manage to generate practice or fail to meet the high expectations created, which once again generates incentives for the center to take on greater leadership. Proof of this is the generalized tendency to promote sub-national financing through conditioned transfers from the capitals, the limited transfer of significant responsibilities to the periphery and the institutional weaknesses that persist in sub-national governments. While important efforts to make progress in this area have been observed in all of the cases studied, it is clear that there is a need for more than a set of reforms to untangle a sort of centralist culture that poses more obstacles from those inherent to a decentralizing process.

Regarding the specific analysis of the five countries selected, significant differences and common patterns are observed. One overarching characteristic is the presence of two sub-national levels of government: local and intermediate. The first has greater levels of political, administrative and financial authority while the second reflects somewhat weak strategic positions, constituting their political autonomies later and reflecting practically no opportunity to generate their own tax income (with the exception of Colombia and, recently, Ecuador).

It also was found that the countries studied present significant vertical fiscal imbalances that stem from a diversity of transfers and benefits that come from the center almost without exception. In addition these limit the fiscal and administrative autonomy of peripheral governments by highly conditioning the expenditure of the resources allocated to them and representing a significant portion of their budgets. It also was determined that there was a generalized horizontal fiscal imbalance in that there are substantial differences in the level of budgetary dependence shown by sub-national governments from the same level regarding transfers from the central government.

In regard to the differences observed, the diversity of the administrative units is noteworthy. Colombia and Bolivia present strong territorial traditions as well as high levels of decentralization and have integrated ethnic diversities into territorial policies. In Bolivia, this is very much in line with its policy towards its nations of origin, as indigenous peoples are given the opportunity to govern themselves using autonomous statutes in their territories. Colombia and Ecuador also recognize their ethnic and cultural diversity by providing an opportunity to establish special territories in which representatives of these groups have greater participation in local politics. Chile is on the opposite side of the spectrum, as is Peru, though to a lesser extent, as these are both traditionally centralized nations. The latter has presented a recent openness towards greater levels of political decentralization at the regional level, while the former is still on its way to achieving that and is the only country whose highest-ranking regional officials continue to be appointed by the central government.

From a fiscal perspective, the case of Colombia stands out in that it is the only country that has a wide range of taxes collected by its intermediate-level governments. (Ecuador is following in its footsteps.) This is true to a lesser degree in Bolivia and to a much lesser extent in Peru, where intermediate governments do not have the authority to collect takes but benefit from the tax monies transferred to them by the central government.

References

Asamblea Constituyente (1978) Constitución de la República del Ecuador. http://www.asambleanacional.gov.ec/documentos/contitucion_de_bolsillo.pdf. Accessed 22 Jun 2011

Asamblea Constituyente de Bolivia (2009) Nueva constitución política del estado. http://www.presidencia.gob.bo/download/constitucion.pdf. Accessed 22 Jun 2011

Consejo Nacional de Competencias, & Secretaría Nacional de Planificación y Desarrollo (2012) Plan nacional de descentralización 2012–2015. http://www.senplades.gob.ec/c/document_library/get_file?uuid=19efd899-1543-4eb6-8d80-b6e8c2fc2046&groupId=18607. Accessed 28 Sept 2012

Daughters R, Harper L (2006) Fiscal and political decentralization reforms. In: Lora E (ed) The state of State reform in Latin America. Washington: Banco Interamericano de Desarrollo. Stanford University Press, Stanford

Departamento Nacional de Planeación (2010) Desempeño fiscal de los departamentos y municipios 2009. Departamento Nacional de Planeación, Bogotá

Departamento Nacional de Planeación (2012) Ejecuciones presupuestales. http://www.dnp.gov.co/Programas/DesarrolloTerritorial/FinanzasP%C3%BAblicasTerritoriales/EjecucionesPresupuestales.aspx. Accessed 26 Sept 2012

Dirección de Presupuestos (2012a) Estado de operaciones del Gobierno General. http://www.dipres.gob.cl/572/propertyvalue-15495.html. Accessed 26 Sept 2012

Dirección de Presupuestos (2012b) Informes de ejecución presupuestaria. http://www.dipres.gob.cl/572/multipropertyvalues-15490-20971.html. Accessed 26 Sept 2012

Falleti TG (2005) A sequential theory of decentralization: Latin American cases in a comparative perspective. Am Polit Sci Rev 99(3):327–346

Gómez Sabaini JC, Jiménez JP (2011) El financiamiento de los gobiernos subnacionales en América Latina: un análisis de casos. CEPAL, Santiago (Serie Macroeconomía del desarrollo), 111

Herman C (2010) Estado y descentralización en Bolivia. La difícil configuración de un orden territorial para una sociedad plural. Estudios en Gobierno y Derecho, Vol 3, No 1

La Nación (2008) Santa Cruz se declaró autónoma en Bolivia. http://www.lanacion.com.ar/1012749-santa-cruz-se-declaro-autonoma-en-bolivia. Accessed 26 Jun 2011

Maldonado CA (2011) Descentralización territorial en Colombia: situación y perspectivas de política. Friedrich Ebert Stiftung Colombia (Policy paper 1). http://library.fes.de/pdf-files/bueros/kolumbien/08286.pdf. Accessed 2 Sept 2012

Mascareño C (2008) Descentralización y democracia en América Latina: ¿Una relación directa? Elementos conceptuales para su estudio. Latin American Studies Center. University of Maryland, College Park, working paper No 23

Ministerio de Economía y Finanzas (2012) Cierre del presupuesto del sector público: año fiscal 2011. http://www.mef.gob.pe/index.php?option=com_content&view=article&id=2896%3Aestadistica-anual-cierre-del-presupuesto-del-sector-publico-ano-fiscal-2011&catid=216&Itemid=100292&lang=es. Accessed 26 Sept 2012

Ministerio de Hacienda y Crédito Público (2012) Informe de ejecución acumulado a Diciembre. http://www.minhacienda.gov.co/HomeMinhacienda/presupuestogeneraldelanacion/EjecucionEPGN/2011. Accessed 26 Sept 2012

Montecinos E (2005) Los estudios de descentralización en América Latina: una revisión sobre el estado actual de la temática. EURE 31(093):73–88

Restrepo D (2006) Historias comparadas. Las fracturas del estado en América Latina. In: Restrepo D (ed) Historias de la descentralización. Transformaciones del régimen político y cambio en el modelo económico. América Latina, Europa y EUA. Universidad Nacional de Colombia, Facultad de Ciencias Económicas, Bogotá

Serrano C, Acosta P (2011a) El proceso de descentralización en el Ecuador. http://www.rimisp.org/FCKeditor/UserFiles/File/documentos/docs/gobernanzaterritorial/documentos/proceso-descentralizacion-ecuador.pdf. Accessed 29 Sept 2012

Serrano C, Acosta P (2011b) El proceso de descentralización en Perú. http://www.rimisp.org/FCKeditor/UserFiles/File/documentos/docs/gobernanzaterritorial/documentos/proceso-descentralizacion-peru.pdf. Accessed 29 Sept 2012

Subsecretaría de Desarrollo Regional y Administrativo (2009) Descentralización en América Latina: un análisis comparado de los casos de Colombia, Bolivia, Perú, Brasil y Argentina. Ministerio del Interior, Santiago de Chile

Tribunal Constitucional del Perú (1993) Constitución política del Perú. http://www.tc.gob.pe/legconperu/constitucion.html. Accessed 11 Jun 2011

Verdesoto L (2006) ¿Quién hace qué en el territorio? Quito: Proyecto PRO-ODM, AECI, CONCOPE

Chapter 21
Impact Assessment of Interregional Government Transfers: Lessons from the Brazil Experience

Eduardo A. Haddad, Carlos A. Luque, Gilberto T. Lima, Sergio N. Sakurai, and Silvio M. Costa

21.1 Introduction

The aim of regional policy is the attainment of a more efficient and/or equitable interregional distribution of economic activity (Temple 1994). Haddad (1999) has demonstrated that in the last 20 years or so Brazil has undergone deep structural changes that have been responsible for the setback in the process of polarization reversal in the economy. After 1988, with the new Constitution, the central government was hampered in advancing its regional policy agenda by a profound loss in its revenues to the state and municipal governments. Nevertheless, the fiscal crisis reached all levels of government, decreasing their financial capability for carrying out new investment ventures. One of the major consequences has been the paucity of investment in economic infrastructure that has contributed to increasing the average cost of production. Therefore, producers' costs increased since they faced inefficient mechanisms for trade and transportation, many of which lagged technologically.

The regional de-concentration trend that has been verified for the period from the 1960s to the early 1980s was heavily influenced by an active government intervention, manifested in actions such as direct investments in regional development projects and tax incentives in the less developed regions of the country. However, with the fiscal crisis generalized to all levels of government, there were fewer

E.A. Haddad (✉)
Department of Economics, University of Sao Paulo, Sao Paulo, Brazil; CNPq and Fapesp scholar
e-mail: ehaddad@usp.br

C.A. Luque • G.T. Lima • S.N. Sakurai
University of Sao Paulo, Sao Paulo, Brazil
e-mail: cluque@usp.br; giltadeu@usp.br; sakurai@usp.br

S.M. Costa
Brazilian Central Bank, Brasilia, Brazil
e-mail: silvio@usp.br

J.R. Cuadrado-Roura and P. Aroca (eds.), *Regional Problems and Policies in Latin America*, Advances in Spatial Science, DOI 10.1007/978-3-642-39674-8_21,

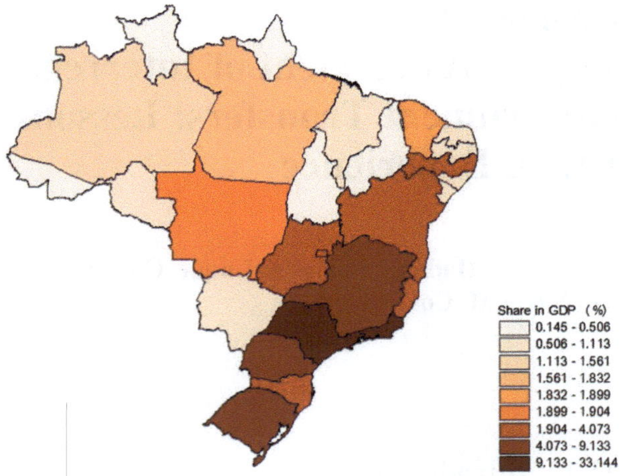

Fig. 21.1 Regional shares in national GDP, Brazil, 2006

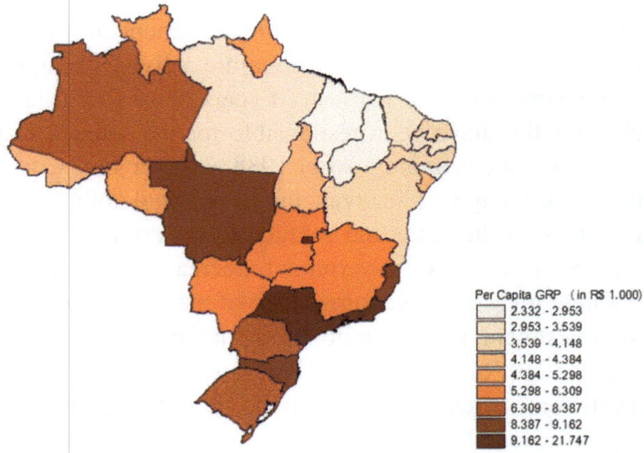

Fig. 21.2 Per capita gross regional product, Brazil, 2006

options for new public ventures. Even though the country witnessed a process of regional de-concentration and an improvement in regional inequality at that time, the situation is still striking in Brazil. In terms of the distribution of economic activity, Brazilian GDP is heavily concentrated in the Center-South of the country (Fig. 21.1). Regarding regional inequality related to per capita GDP, the picture is not different, with many states in the poorest region of the country (Northeast) achieving per capita GDP levels more than half-way below the national average (Fig. 21.2).

The agreed agenda for Brazil includes the competitive integration of the country in the global trade network, with additional domestic concerns focused on of sustainable stabilization and social cohesion. This implies the attraction of foreign investments and a responsible (balanced) budget policy for all levels of government, reinforced by the promulgation of the "Lei de Responsabilidade Fiscal"

(Fiscal Responsibility Law) in 2000. The latter precludes regional policies that are based primarily on redistributional expenditures, as was the case in the 1970s. For foreign investors, the search is dominated by attention to maximal financial returns with little concern for regional equity; location is defined on a purely economic basis.

The results presented in Haddad (1999) suggest that the interplay of market forces in the Brazilian economy favors the more developed region of the country. *In other words, the trickling-down effects generated by market forces are still very unlikely to overtake the polarization effects from the Center-South.* If regional equity is part of the country's development agenda, an active regional policy by the central government is still needed, in order to reduce regional economic disparities, and specifically to address the problems of the North and Northeast, traditionally backward areas reliant on low technology activities. The improvement of the economic infrastructure in those regions, as well as the establishment of enduring competitive advantages, through a consistent human capital policy, are necessary to attenuate the adverse regional effects of the development strategy to be pursued by the public authorities.

Nowadays, the regional policy carried out by the central government consists of isolated subsidies and industrial incentives to growth centers, in addition to constitutional transfers to less developed regions and rural areas. In the context of the fiscal adjustment process of the 1990s, the role of the central government in stimulating directly productive activities and enhancing the social overhead capital in the lagging regions is being neglected. In the conception of the Real Plan, in 1994, there was no explicit concern about the formulation of a regional development policy for the country. The Real Plan was conceived as a global stabilization plan, that would include economic reforms (privatization, concessions and deregulation) and institutional reforms (tax system, social security and administrative), without proposing any strategy for medium and long-run development. However, with the benefits from the stabilization and the reforms, a new cycle of private investments emerged. These investments tended to concentrate in the South and Southeast regions, which provided a full range of non-traditional (e.g. technical skills and urban agglomeration) and traditional (e.g. friction of distance – Mercosul) locational factors to attract the incoming capital. The lack of investments by the central government, allied to the spurt in private investments, has led regional governments to engage in strong competition for private capital through fiscal mechanisms (see Baer and Hewings 2007).

In this context, we can argue that nothing much has been done since the 1988 Constitution. In terms of what might be termed a "clearly-defined" regional policy, the central government has relied only on constitutional intergovernmental transfers through regional funds. As can be seen from Fig. 21.3, such mechanism provides an explicit strategy of geographic targeting to reduce spatial disparities in Brazil. Whether they achieve the goal of classical regional policies – namely, the

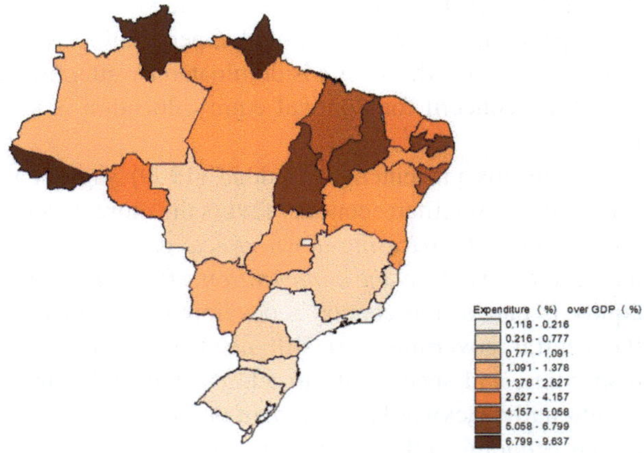

Fig. 21.3 Ratio of the shares in interregional government transfers to shares in national GDP, Brazil, 2006

reduction of regional disparities – through direct income transfers to poorer states remains to be tested.

While it is commonly accepted that Brazil's interregional government transfers system provides initial distributional effects, there have been few attempts to formally assess the implications this has had for the domestic pattern of industrial location. Moreover, it is still to be measured the broader impacts on regional growth, considering not only its direct effects, but also the indirect and induced effects closely associated with the role played by the existing economic structure. Over the next few pages, this paper aims to address this somewhat overlooked issue by adopting the following approach. After a brief review of the main institutional aspects of interregional government transfers in Brazil, an attempt is made to characterize its recent structure. Having established the nature of these transfers, the paper then goes on to evaluate their implications for the pattern of regional development within Brazil. In order to achieve this objective, an interregional input-output model is prepared and then tested to assess the recent impact of interregional government transfers on such variables as regional output and income levels. Finally, the tractability of these results is discussed before the possible policy implications are drawn.

21.2 Interregional Government Transfers in Brazil

21.2.1 Some Analytics and Empirics of Government Transfers

Considerable shares of public revenue and public expenditure consist of transfers, which are payments with no direct counterpart. On the revenue side, that applies to taxes and social contributions. Even though the government uses these revenues to finance, for instance, public facilities and social benefits, those come to be indirect counterparts. On the expenditure side, meanwhile, it applies to social benefits – such as pensions, unemployment benefits, and public health care expenditure – and other transfers of income and capital as subsidies granted to enterprises or households.

Three kinds of economic reasons are usually invoked to justify the role of transfers. First, central governments have advantages over subnational governments in raising revenues from many types of particularly productive sources, while subnational governments have advantages in providing many types of public services. Quite often, there is an imbalance between expenditure responsibilities of subnational governments and their revenue raising powers, which ends up resulting in an inability of local governments to provide adequate levels of public service. Another rationale for intergovernmental transfers is provided by the need of equalization, as there is often a great deal of disparities in revenue-raising capacity across decentralized levels of government. Third, when local governments are left to make their own decisions, they may end up under spending on certain services where there are substantial external benefits to third parties, such as surrounding local governments. Moreover, resources from the central level can be used to ensure that basic national priorities will be met in all subnational jurisdictions. In case of existence of externalities on other jurisdictions, the central government financially supports sub-national authorities in order to guarantee the provision of some public services on the local level. As summed up in Nam and Parsche (2001), intergovernmental transfers are aimed at rectifying not only the vertical imbalance caused by the unequal own tax revenues and expenditures of different tiers of governments but also the horizontal imbalance which is led by the different fiscal capacities among jurisdictions at the same level. The compensation for the presence of spillovers or externalities between jurisdictions in the provision of regional and local public services is likewise a usually accepted rationale for introducing fiscal transfers from central government. We may define vertical fiscal imbalance, following Bird and Tarasov (2002), as the resulting difference between expenditure and own-source revenues at different levels of government. Following the same source, the notion of horizontal fiscal imbalance may be defined as the difference in the resources available to governments at the same (subnational) level, where this difference stems from the heterogeneity in wealth of subnational jurisdictions.

Meanwhile, transfers from or to the central government can be broken down by region. Transfers between the government and households are based on the place of residence, while transfers between the government and businesses are based on the place where the business is conducted or value is created. As it turns out, it is possible to conduct a regional comparison of the relative scale of the public transfers thus broken down. A region is seen as a contributor of interregional transfers in terms of public revenues if the per capita transfers by that region's residents to the federal government or social security are higher than the per capita national average. Conversely, a region is regarded as a recipient of such transfers if its contribution is proportionately lower than would be expected on the basis of its percentage of the population. Therefore, evaluation of the interregional transfers on the basis of both public revenue and public expenditure reveals the net position of each region in terms of interregional transfers.

The empirical literature on the determinants and impacts of the government transfers on regional performance is huge, and a small sample includes the following. Groenewold et al. (2003) analyze the regional effects of intergovernmental transfers by a federal government, having done so in a two-region model in which regional governments determine their tax and expenditure policies so as to maximize the utility of the representative household in their region subject to a budget constraint consisting of a CGE model describing the regional economy. The model is then calibrated using Australian data, with the authors conducting a series of six simulations of an increase in the federal government's transfer to one region matched by a decrease in the transfer payment to the other. In each simulation one of the six Australian states was taken as region 1 and the remainder of the country as region 2. The authors find that substantial changes in the amount transferred by the federal government from one region to the other had little effect on welfare, per capita consumption and wages.

Garcia-Milà and McGuire (2004) evaluate the effectiveness of the transfers received by the regional governments of Spain from both the central government and the European Union. They do so by comparing the economic performance of the regions before and after the implementation of the transfers programs, and find that these policies have not been effective at stimulating private investment or improving the overall economies of the poorer regions. Dias and Silva (2004), meanwhile, evaluate the effectiveness of the transfers received by the regional governments of Portugal from the central government, and do not find strong and robust evidence that these transfers have been stimulating convergence among Portuguese regions and improving the overall economies of the poorer regions.

As the simulation exercise to be conducted in the next section is based on the Brazilian experience, it should be pointed out that the redistributive role the government played through the federal fiscal system was a common practice in the 1970s and 1980s. As reported in Haddad (1999), the regional shares of the central government revenues in the poorer regions were recurrently smaller than the shares of central government expenditures in those regions over the period. In particular, the specific figures suggest the existence of an effective redistribution of public funds to the North and Northeast over the period.

The pioneering efforts by Rolim et al. (1996) provide a more complete interpretative scheme on interregional flows in Brazil, based on available statistics on trade balance, government accounts, public investment, and savings. Indeed, their preliminary results for 1985 reinforce the character of interregional government transfers just suggested. Even though the analysis covers only 1 year, it can give a rough idea on how interregional flows were oriented in the years preceding 1985. As shown in Haddad (1999), the repeated pattern of government fiscal transfers observed in the previous decade, together with the estimates of interregional and international trade balances for the Northeast and North in the same period, support the following generalization of the results. The North and Northeast presented trade deficits recurrently over the period. In the case of the Northeast, the perennial interregional trade deficits were partially compensated by international trade surpluses, indicating a transfer of foreign exchange earnings to other regions of the country. The continual overall interregional trade deficits of these two regions had to be financed by public and/or private savings, so that the conditions for macroeconomic balance were met. The conjecture, taking 1985 as a typical year, is that the transfers of federal resources to the Northeast, for instance, had to be greater than the trade gaps in order to compensate the interregional flows of private capital oriented towards other regions. Even though the figures show a net outflow of private capital from the Center-South, less aggregated figures, for 1985, show a tendency of net private capital gains to the states of São Paulo and Rio de Janeiro, as well as the Center-West. The orientation of public capital to the less developed regions has often been offset by the flight of private capitals. Rolim et al. (1996) argue that this represents the synthesis of bad allocation of government funds from the point of view of an efficient regional policy. However, it might be argued, based on the previous discussion, that government transfers to the North and Northeast, during the 1970s and early 1980s were necessary to build the social overhead capital in those regions in order to strengthen the potential spread effects from the Center-South and create self-reinforcing mechanisms in the regions to generate their own sustainable growth.

In other words, government transfers might have achieved a greater relevance in the less developed regions by creating the necessary infrastructure to foster development and attract, in a second moment, private investments to directly productive activities. This hypothesis would be better tested by looking at estimates of investments in the region; if it is somehow relevant, the relation between the share of public investments in the target region to the share of public investments in the country should show an increasing trend during the 1970s with an inflection point after the necessary time for the economic infrastructure to have matured. From the estimates for the Northeast, however, an increasing path in the share of public investment in the region, compared to the national average, is apparent from 1973 to 1989. Even though there seems to be a declining tendency towards the national average in the first years of the1990s, empirical evidence to support the conjecture on the existence of a change in gears is very weak.

Meanwhile, redistributive policies carried out by the central government in Brazil through interregional government transfers is still a relevant feature of the Brazilian federal fiscal system. Regional shares of the central government revenues in the poorer regions have been recurrently smaller than the shares of central government expenditures in those regions, a feature on which we elaborate down the road. Indeed, appeal to core-periphery arguments could be made, as São Paulo, the wealthiest state in the country, concentrated, in 2006, over 40 % of total Federal tax revenue, receiving less than 10 % of Federal expenditures. These figures suggest the existence of an effective redistribution of public funds from the spatial economic core of the economy to the peripheral areas.

Monteiro Neto (2006) evaluates the federal government transfers to Brazilian regions and states over the 1970–2000 period, and analyze the actual direction taken by the flows of those government transfers in comparison with the income flows occurring among states through their interregional and international trade. Drawing on Celso Furtado's hypothesis that underdeveloped regions have to spend a huge amount of income to buy sophisticated wage goods and capital goods produced in the developed regions to maintain a certain level of economic growth, the author shows that in 2000, the resources directed by the federal government to the poor regions (North, Northeast and Center-West) were able to offset their current trade deficits.

21.2.2 An Overview of the Constitutional Transfer System in Brazil

One of the main characteristics of the Brazilian economy is the excessive concentration of the income in the states of South and Southeast (Fig. 21.1). This feature, as stressed earlier, lessens the power of the states and municipalities located mainly in the North and Northeast regions in providing public services to the population. The constitutional transfer system in Brazil was built in order to overcome or at least to reduce this disparities of economic power between the states and municipalities.

With this objective, the mechanisms of transfer from the Union to the States and Municipalities can be divided in three kinds: constitutional transfers, legal transfers and voluntary transfers. The main constitutional transfers from the Union to States and Municipalities are the State Participation Fund (FPE); the Municipalities Participation Fund (FPM), the Constitutional Fund of the Center-West; Constitution Fund of the North; Constitution Fund of Northeast and the Constitution Fund of Compensation of Industrialized Products. The legal transfers are regulated by specific laws like the automatic transfers to education and transfers to the health care system. The volunteer transfers are connected to specific projects made by states and municipalities and submitted to federal institutions.

Our focus in this article is concentrated in the federal constitutional transfers specifically in the State Participation Fund (FPE) and Municipalities Participation Fund (FPM), established by the article 159 of the Federal Constitution. The FPE is constituted by 21.5 % of the Income Tax (IR) and 21.5 % of the Excise Tax on Industrialized Products (IPI). On the other hand, the FPM is constituted by 22.5 % of the Income Tax (IR) and 22.5 % of the Excise Tax on Industrialized Products (IPI).

The FPE is distributed according to the following rule: 85 % of the resources go to the States of the North, Northeast and Center-West and 15 % are transferred to the States of the South and Southeast. The regional distribution is: 25.37 % to the North Region; 52.46 % to the Northeast; 7.17 % to the Center-West; 6.52 % to the South and 8.48 % to the Southeast.

The FPM is distributed according to the population of the municipality and inversely distributed according the average income of the municipality. We have also a division between the State capitals and other municipalities (hinterland). Of the total of resources, 10.0 % are distributed to the State capitals; 86.4 % for the rest of municipalities and 3.6 % to municipalities with population above 142.633 inhabitants excluded the capitals.

21.2.3 Some Descriptive Figures on the Brazilian Transfers System

In this study, we basically have two sets of information. The first concerns the tax revenues collected by the Central government along the Brazilian states and the second, in turn, provides information regarding the amount of resources transferred to the Brazilian States via the Federal constitutional funds, both during the year of 2006. In this section of the paper, we will present a broad description of these two datasets.

Table 21.1 presents the regional distribution of the joint FPE and FPM expenditures in 2006 compared to the regional distribution of the originating resources that composed the funds in the same year. A very important point to be clarified is that the regional origin of these resources is very heterogeneous: column A of Table 21.1 shows that over 40 % of Federal tax revenues come from just one state, namely, São Paulo, the richest one. Once considered that other 20 % come from Rio de Janeiro state, it is possible to verify that about two-thirds of the total tax revenue are collected in only two states. Distrito Federal, Minas Gerais, Rio Grande do Suland Paraná are other important unities, given that their total contribution is approximately 25 %. The remaining share are divided among 21 states, most of them located in the North (six states with a total share of 1.70 %), and Northeast (nine states with a share of 5.34 %) regions.

The previous discussion presented an overview concerning of how each Brazilian state contributes to the Federal taxation system. Altogether, such constitutional transfers represent around 3.1 % of Brazilian GDP. In order to analyze our second set of information, Table 21.1, column B provides information regarding the regional distribution of constitutional resources transferred by the Federal government to each Brazilian state. Noteworthy is that São Paulo state receives only 7.15 % of the total amount of transfers against a contribution of 43.59 % to the revenues – a similar effect is observed to other rich states like Rio de Janeiro and Distrito Federal, i.e., their (proportional) contributions to the Federal revenues are higher than the (proportional) amount received via the constitutional funds. On the other hand, we observe exactly the opposite for poorer states like Maranhão, for instance, which generated only 0.25 % of the Federal tax revenues but received 5.63 % of the total constitutional transfers. This example helps one to understand how the allocation of resources by the Central government works in Brazil, in the

Table 21.1 Regional shares in federal government tax revenue[a] and expenditures[b], Brazil – 2006

	Regional revenues (A)	Regional expenditures (B)	(A) – (B)
North	***1.7***	***16.88***	***–15.18***
RO	0.13	1.84	–1.71
AC	0.04	1.96	–1.91
AM	0.86	2.15	–1.29
RR	0.04	1.38	–1.34
PA	0.48	4.81	–4.33
AP	0.05	1.88	–1.82
TO	0.09	2.86	–2.77
Northeast	***5.34***	***43.88***	***–38.54***
MA	0.25	5.63	–5.38
PI	0.14	3.44	–3.3
CE	0.82	6.25	–5.43
RN	0.24	3.34	–3.10
PB	0.26	4.03	–3.77
PE	1.27	5.88	–4.62
AL	0.2	3.27	–3.07
SE	0.2	2.8	–2.61
BA	1.98	9.24	–7.26
Southeast	***70.9***	***19.85***	***51.05***
MG	6.24	8.94	–2.7
ES	1.43	1.61	–0.18
RJ	19.64	2.16	17.48
SP	43.59	7.15	36.45
South	***10.64***	***12.18***	***–1.54***
PR	A.\2	4.92	–0.81
SC	2.14	2.62	–0.48
RS	4.38	4.63	–0.25
Center-west	***11.42***	***7.21***	***4.21***
MS	0.27	1.45	–1.18
MT	0.32	2.08	–1.75
GO	0.83	3.26	–2.43
DF	10	0.43	9.57

Source: Secretaria da Receita Federal
[a]Manufacturing tax (44.0 %) and income tax (44.0 %)
[b]Constitutional transfers (FPE and FPM)

sense that the poorest regions are relatively more benefited than the richest ones. The last column of Table 21.1 summarizes such allocation presenting those regions that directly benefit from such constitutional transfers (negative values) and those that are net transferors (positive values).

In the next section, we use an interregional input-output model for the Brazilian economy for purposes of regional impact assessment. The model is to be used to capture the role of inter industrial and interregional relations in the economic development process through the evaluation of the regional impact of the existing interregional government transfers mechanisms in Brazil. The use of this modeling approach is very relevant to the Brazilian case. Its ability to handle detail at a disaggregated level is useful for analyzing the role played Brazil's spatial productive structure from a systemic perspective.

21.3 Assessing the Regional Impacts of Interregional Government Transfers in Brazil

We start by describing the model used to analyze the regional effects of interregional government transfers in Brazil. The general equilibrium nature of economic interdependence and the fact that the policy impacts in various regional markets differ are considered in the results of the model. Attention is directed to one main issue, namely the differential regional impacts of the current interregional transfers structure on regional value added, a proxy for the tax base effects. As the simulations try to mimic a "typical year", we have selected as our case study the transfers' estimates for 2006. In this paper, we intend to use the fiscal parameters to simulate different arbitrary allocations of the interregional government transfers.

21.3.1 Theoretical Background

The intersectoral flows in a given economy can be represented by the following system:

$$X = AX + Y \tag{21.1}$$

where X is a $(nx1)$ vector with the value of the total production in each sector, Y is a $(nx1)$ vector with values for the final demand, and A is a (nxn) matrix with the technical coefficients of production. In this model, the final demand vector can be treated as exogenous to the system, such that the level of total production can be determined by the final demand, i.e.,

$$X = BY \tag{21.2}$$

$$B = (I - A)^{-1} \tag{21.3}$$

where B is a (nxn) matrix of the Leontief inverse.

According to Miller and Blair (1985), an interregional model for two regions L and M can have its coefficients matrix represented in matricial terms as:

$$A = \begin{bmatrix} A^{LL} & A^{LM} \\ A^{ML} & A^{MM} \end{bmatrix} \tag{21.4}$$

Vectors X^L and X^M will constitute the total production vector, X

$$X = \begin{bmatrix} X^L \\ X^M \end{bmatrix} \tag{21.5}$$

The final demand vector, Y, will be composed of vectors Y^L and Y^M

$$Y = \begin{bmatrix} Y^L \\ Y^M \end{bmatrix} \tag{21.6}$$

As such, the system presented by Eq. 21.2 can then be used to represent an interregional system; in this way, it is possible to evaluate the impact of the final demand on total production, and from there, on value added, employment, etc., for each one of the regions considered in the model.

21.3.1.1 Multipliers

From the multiplier results it is possible to measure the direct and indirect effects of a change in the final demand on production, value added, employment, etc. (see Miller and Blair 1985).

From the Leontief inverse matrix (B) defined above, one sees that the production multiplier of type I for each economic sector is given by:

$$P_j = \sum_{i=1}^{n} b_{ij} \qquad j = 1, \ldots, n \tag{21.7}$$

where P_j is the production multiplier for sector j, and b_{ij} is an element of matrix B.

Using the structure of derivation elaborated below for the value added multipliers, all the other multipliers in the economy can be derived.

The first step is to estimate the coefficients of value added, given by

$$w_j = \frac{va_j}{x_j} \tag{21.8}$$

where w_j is the coefficient of value added in sector j, va_j is the total value added in sector j, and x_j is the level of production in sector j.

The total value added multiplier of type I (VA_j), generated in sector j, is given by

$$VA_j = \sum_{i=1}^{n} w_i b_{ij} \tag{21.9}$$

where b_{ij} is an element of matrix B described above.

21.3.2 Hypotheses for Simulations

In order to grasp the differential effects associated to interregional government transfers, the interregional input-output model briefly described in the previous sub-section was estimated for 2004 considering the 26 Brazilian States and the Federal District. The interstate input-output model also considers 110 products and 55 sectors in each region. A major effort in data compilation was undertaken in order to estimate the model.[1] The simulation strategy is to introduce a shock related to the existing structure of interregional government transfers – as indicated in Table 21.1 – and to evaluate its distributional impacts (benchmark simulation). The main research question is to check whether the production structure acts in favor of more developed regions countervailing the redistributional effects of government transfers through the operation of indirect and induced multiplier effects. A counterfactual simulation is also carried out in which we consider that the structure of interregional government transfers would follow exactly the regional structure of Federal government's tax revenue. To reach this goal we use a closed input-output model in which the regional household sectors are endogeneized.

21.3.3 Results

As for the benchmark simulation, Table 21.2 presents the first set of results whose focus is on the regional distribution of value added effects. For reference, column A shows the regional shares in GDP; column B replicates the regional distribution of the shocks while column C shows the regional distribution of the effects of transfers expenditures on the generation of value added in the Brazilian economy. Comparing such distributions in the last column of Table 21.2, one can have an idea on the presence of relevant leakages from lagging regions to more developed regions. For instance, while the States in the Southeast receive about 20 % of total interregional transfers, they achieve one third of total value added associated with such expenditures. On the other hand, the Northeast region also achieve about the same share in the impact on value added (34.63 %) but receiving almost 44 % of total interregional transfers. States highlighted in the last column – Espírito Santo, Rio de Janeiro, São Paulo, Paraná, Santa Catarina, Rio Grande do Sul and Distrito

[1] For details on the methodology, see Haddad et al. (2002) and FIPE (2008).

Table 21.2 Regional value added effects of interregional transfers in Brazil: benchmark simulation

	Regional share in GRP (A)	Regional share in expenditures (B)	Regional share in total VA impact (C)	(C) – (B)
North	***4.95***	***16.88***	***12.86***	***−4.02***
RO	0.58	1.84	1.44	−0.41
AC	0.2	1.96	1.38	−0.58
AM	1.56	2.15	2.04	−0.11
RR	0.14	1.38	0.96	−0.42
PA	1.83	4.81	3.8	−1.01
AP	0.2	1.88	1.32	−0.56
TO	0.43	2.86	1.92	−0.94
Northeast	***12.72***	***43.88***	***34.63***	***−9.25***
MA	1.11	5.63	3.73	−1.90
PI	0.51	3.44	2.31	−1.13
CE	1.9	6.25	5.35	−0.91
RN	0.8	3.34	2.49	−0.85
PB	0.77	4.03	2.91	−1.12
PE	2.27	5.88	5.22	−0.66
AL	0.66	3.27	2.46	−0.82
SE	0.63	2.8	2.26	−0.55
BA	4.07	9.24	7.91	−1.33
Southeast	***55.83***	***19.85***	***32.21***	***12.36***
MG	9.13	8.94	8.78	−0.15
ES	2.07	1.61	1.65	0.04
RJ	11.48	2.16	4.85	2.69
SP	33.14	7.15	16.92	9.78
South	***17.39***	***12.18***	***13.48***	***1.30***
PR	6.31	4.92	5.15	0.23
SC	3.99	2.62	3.17	0.55
RS	7.1	4.63	5.15	0.52
Center-west	***9.11***	***7.21***	***6.82***	***−0.39***
MS	1.09	1.45	1.17	−0.27
MT	1.9	2.08	2.05	−0.03
GO	2.47	3.26	2.74	−0.52
DF	3.64	0.43	0.86	0.43

Federal – are those that have shown to receive benefits "beyond their contribution", i.e. their share in total benefits is higher than their share in total expenditures.

Another way of looking at these results is through the computation of the truncated regional value added multipliers, which shows the value added creation in the region per money unit of regional transfers received *by the State*. Such multipliers compare the region-specific value added effect based on the overall transfers (Column C) – thus capturing all interregional effects –, with the total amount of transfers accruing to the State (column B). The results are presented in Table 21.3. In the case of São Paulo, for instance, for each BRL 1.00 received from

Table 21.3 Regional value added multipliers of interregional transfers in Brazil: benchmark simulation

	Regional transfers in BRL millions (A)	Regional VA in BRL millions (B)	(B)/(A)
North	***12,296.66***	***13,703.88***	***1.11***
RO	1,343.92	1,532.68	1.14
AC	1,425.02	1,469.5	1.03
AM	1,567.57	2,177.22	1.39
RR	1,004.46	1,023.34	1.02
PA	3,505.69	4,052.11	1.16
AP	1,367.28	1,405.5	1.03
TO	2,082.72	2,043.53	0.98
Northeast	***31,968.35***	***36,889.68***	***1.15***
MA	4,099.9	3,969.83	0.97
PI	2,504.3	2,463.41	0.98
CE	4,554.73	5,694.64	1.25
RN	2,430.27	2,652.47	1.09
PB	2,934.73	3,103.27	1.06
PE	4,285.98	5,562.4	1.30
AL	2,384.13	2,616.6	1.10
SE	2,043.17	2,402.52	1.18
BA	6,731.13	8,424.54	1.25
Southeast	***14,460.25***	***34,307.6***	***2.37***
MG	6,509.35	9,353.89	1.44
ES	1,173.14	1,759.28	1.50
RJ	1,572.03	5,167.66	3.29
SP	5,205.73	18,026.76	3.46
South	***8,869.58***	***14,357.08***	***1.62***
PR	3,587.49	5,490.96	1.53
SC	1,907.48	3,376.25	1.77
RS	3,374.61	5,489.87	1.63
Center-west	***5,252.89***	***7,263.82***	***1.38***
MS	1,053.64	*\2A%A1*	1.18
MT	1,512.47	2,183.32	1.44
GO	2,374.61	2,919.15	1.23
DF	312.17	912.87	2.92
Brazil	***72,847.73***	***106,522.06***	***1.46***

the Federal Government – and considering the transfers to other States as well – the State generates BRL 3.46 in value added, a proxy to the tax base. In the other extreme, Maranhão, one of the poorest states, generate only BRL 0.97 of value added per BRL 1.00 received as transfers.

One can also look at output effects. In this case, Table 21.4 presents the results for the benchmark simulation. The last column highlights those states with above-the-average multipliers. Again, states in the Center-South of the country perform better, including also the Sate of Amazonas, in the North region. It is clear from

Table 21.4 Regional output multipliers of interregional transfers in Brazil: benchmark simulation

	Regional transfers in BRL millions (A)	Regional gross output in BRL millions (B)	(B)/(A)
North	***12,296.66***	***21,139.75***	***1.72***
RO	1,343.92	2,242.44	1.67
AC	1,425.02	2,008.04	1.41
AM	1,567.57	4,459.04	2.84
RR	1,004.46	1,432.22	1.43
PA	3,505.69	6,081.84	1.73
AP	1,367.28	1,885.61	1.38
TO	2,082.72	3,030.57	1.46
Northeast	***31,968.35***	***60,583.94***	***1.90***
MA	4,099.9	6,401.13	1.56
PI	2,504.3	3,790.98	1.51
CE	4,554.73	9,368.72	2.06
RN	2,430.27	4,205.55	1.73
PB	2,934.73	4,533.62	1.54
PE	4,285.98	9,363.88	2.18
AL	2,384.13	4,065.56	1.71
SE	2,043.17	3,571.92	1.75
BA	6,731.13	15,282.58	2.27
Southeast	***14,460.25***	***66,430.91***	***4.59***
MG	6,509.35	16,039.84	2.46
ES	1,173.14	2,887.3	2.46
RJ	1,572.03	9,859.47	6.27
SP	5,205.73	37,644.3	7.23
South	***8,869.58***	***28,506.28***	***3.21***
PR	3,587.49	10,712.93	2.99
SC	1,907.48	6,482.69	3.40
RS	3,374.61	11,310.66	3.35
Center-west	***5,252.89***	***13,048.16***	***2.48***
MS	1,053.64	2,261.7	2.15
MT	1,512.47	3,932.77	2.60
GO	2,374.61	5,177.63	2.18
DF	312.17	1,676.05	5.37
Brazil	***72,847.73***	***189,709.05***	***2.60***

these results that interregional feedback effects operate in favor of the more developed regions of the country.

So far, we have looked at the gross effects of constitutional interregional transfers. Given the known methodological limitations of our approach to deal with general equilibrium issues that involve price changes through the tax system,[2] we still can have a rough idea about the net effects of such transfer mechanism. To

[2] See, for instance, Shoven and Whalley (1992).

Table 21.5 Net regional value added effects of interregional transfers in Brazil: comparison of the benchmark and the counterfactual simulations

	Benchmark simulation (A)	Counterfactual simulation (B)	(C) = (A) − (B)	(C)/(B)
North	***13,703.88***	***1,979.12***	***11,724.76***	***5.92***
RO	1,532.68	209.13	1,323.55	6.33
AC	1,469.5	61.15	1,408.35	23.03
AM	2,177.22	870.92	1,306.3	1.50
RR	1,023.34	40.97	982.37	23.98
PA	4,052.11	597.96	3,454.15	5.78
AP	1,405.5	48.73	1,356.77	27.85
TO	2,043.53	150.27	1,893.26	12.60
Northeast	***36,889.68***	***5,653.73***	***31,235.95***	***5.52***
MA	3,969.83	308.64	3,661.19	11.86
PI	2,463.41	144.8	2,318.61	16.01
CE	5,694.64	839.84	4,854.8	5.78
RN	2,652.47	263.19	2,389.28	9.08
PB	3,103.27	275.44	2,827.82	10.27
PE	5,562.4	1,148.79	4,413.61	3.84
AL	2,616.6	251.27	2,365.32	9.41
SE	2,402.52	253.49	2,149.04	8.48
BA	8,424.54	2,168.27	6,256.27	2.89
Southeast	***34,307.6***	***72,029.43***	***−37,721.83***	***−0.52***
MG	9,353.89	7,357.64	1,996.25	0.27
ES	1,759.28	1,553.57	205.71	0.13
RJ	5,167.66	17,636.73	−12,469.07	−0.71
SP	18,026.76	45,481.49	−27,454.72	−0.60
South	***14,357.08***	***12,832.3***	***1,524.79***	***0.12***
PR	5,490.96	4,894.74	596.22	0.12
SC	3,376.25	2,912.26	463.99	0.16
RS	5,489.87	5,025.29	464.58	0.09
Center-west	***7,263.82***	***9,432.45***	***−2,168.64***	***−0.23***
MS	1,248.47	476.28	772.19	1.62
MT	2,183.32	842.71	1,340.61	1.59
GO	2,919.15	1,630.09	1,289.07	0.79
DF	912.87	6,483.38	−5,570.5	−0.86
Brazil	***106,522.06***	***101,927.04***	***4,595.03***	***0.05***

reach this goal, we have designed a counterfactual simulation in which we have used the regional structure of Federal government's tax revenue to hypothetically distribute the interregional government transfers expenditures. The difference between the impacts of the benchmark simulation and the counterfactual simulation may be seen as a first approximation of the net results of the constitutional interregional transfer mechanism in Brazil. The results are presented in Table 21.5.

Column A presents the value added effects in the case interregional transfers are spent according to constitutional rules (*status quo*); column B shows the value added effects based on an hypothetical distribution of interregional transfers in which regional shares are the same as those verified in the revenue side. A first approximation of the net effects of interregional transfers is given by the difference between A and B. Two points deserve to be mentioned. First, it is clear that the constitutional transfer mechanisms favor the less developed regions of the country. Even though the existing economic structure lessens such redistributive effects, they help to achieve a more equitable interregional distribution of economic activity. Second, given this static picture, there does not appear a trade-off between equity and efficiency. As a matter of fact, total value added effects are a little bit (5 %) higher in the benchmark simulation. This basically happens because of the stronger foreign import dependence of the states in the Center-South of the country. With higher import coefficients from the rest of the world, a higher share of expenditures in this region produces smaller multipliers. It is important to highlight that such static results should be viewed, as emphasized above, as a first approximation of the impacts.

21.4 Final Remarks

The main goal of this paper was to evaluate the implications of interregional government transfers in Brazil for the pattern of regional development within the country. The main research question was to check whether the production structure acts in favor of more developed regions countervailing the redistributional effects of government transfers through the operation of indirect and induced multiplier effects. As for regional concentration, which is therefore the main object of this paper, the effects are clearly favorable. The Northeast and North regions increase their share in national GDP, as their shares in total value added effect exceed their respective shares in GDP. Thus, interregional government transfers present a clear, favorable regional impact. Since it is targeted to poor regions, with a clear spatial focus, it ends-up producing a de-concentration effect. This effect is, of course, larger if government expenditures follow the proposed transfer mechanisms, since the regional pattern of central government tax revenue, if followed, would be more pro-concentration.

One last point that should be further emphasized is the role played by the existing economic structure in terms of reducing the initial redistributive effects of interregional government transfers. Our analysis has shown that interregional linkages within the Brazilian economy operate favoring the more developed regions of the country, as there are relevant leakages from lagging regions to more developed regions. Actually, while the States in the Southeast receive about 20 % of total interregional transfers, they achieve one third of total value added associated with such expenditures. Meanwhile, the Northeast region also achieve about the same share in the impact on value added (34.63 %) but receiving almost 44 % of total interregional transfers. As it turned out, Espírito Santo, Rio de Janeiro, São Paulo, Paraná, Santa Catarina, Rio Grande do Sul and Distrito Federal are the States that have shown to receive benefits "beyond their contribution", i.e. their share in total benefits is higher than their share in total expenditures. While the design of constitutional interregional transfer funds in Brazil do present a strong spatial focus – "poorer regions get more" –, the persistence of regional dualism in Brazil is nonetheless reinforced by the structure of productive interdependence of the economy, as our results have demonstrated.

References

Baer W, Hewings GJD (eds) (2007) Equity distortion in regional resource allocation in Brazil. Haworth Press, New York

Bird R, Tarasov A (2002) Closing the gap: fiscal imbalances and intergovernmental transfers in developed federations. International studies program, working paper 02–02. Andrew Young School of Policy Studies

Dias MF, Silva R (2004) Central government transfers and regional convergence in Portugal. Paper presented at the 2004 European Regional Science Association Conference, Mimeo

Garcia-Milà T, McGuire TJ (2004) Do interregional transfers improve the economic performance of poor regions? The case of Spain. Int Tax Public Finance 8(3):281–296

Groenewold N, Hagger A, Madden JR (2003) Interregional transfers: a political economy CGE approach. Pap Reg Sci 82:535–554

Haddad EA (1999) Regional inequality and structural changes: lesson from the Brazilian economy. Ashgate, Aldershot

Nam CW, Parsche R (2001) Municipal finance in Poland, the Slovak Republic, the Czech Republic and Hungary: institutional framework and recent development. MOCT-MOST Econ Policy Transit Econ 11(2):113–134

Miller RE, Blair PD (1985) Input-output analysis: foundations and extensions. Prentice-Hall, Englewood Cliffs

Monteiro Neto A (2006) Fluxos de Renda fiscal versus Fluxos de Renda via Comércio: O Que Há de Novo na Direção e Magnitude da Ação Redistributiva do Governo Federal nas Regiões Brasileiras. Texto para Discussão 1230, IPEA, Brasilia

Rolim CFC, Machado CC, Lavinas L, Lemos MB, Magina M, Rios-Neto E (1996) Saldo Comercial, Transferências Governamentais e Movimento de Capitais Inter-regional. Estudos Econômicos 26(1):5–19

Shoven JB, Whalley J (1992) Applying general equilibrium Cambridge surveys of economic literature. Cambridge University Press, Cambridge

Temple M (1994) Regional economics. St. Martin's Press, New York

Chapter 22
Regional Policies in the Andean Nations: A Comparative View

Edgard Moncayo-Jiménez

Andean countries
Basic facts
(2011)

	Population	Square kilometers	GDP	Income PPP pc (current US$)	Income PPP pc/income PPP pc of USA
Bolivia	10,088,108	1,098,581	24,426,829,466	4,920	10.06 %
Colombia	46,927,125	1,138,914	331,654,672,814	9,640	19.72 %
Ecuador	14,666,055	283,561	67,002,768,302	8,310	17.00 %
Perú	29,399,817	1,285,216	176,662,074,713	10,610	20.78 %
Venezuela	29,278,000	916,445[a]	316,482,190,800	12,620	25.81 %
Total	**130,359,105**	**4,722,717**	**916,228,536,095**		

Source: World Bank (databank)
[a]Disputed areas are not included

E. Moncayo-Jiménez (✉)
Research Associate Fellow (Non resident), United Nations University-Institute of Comparative Regional Studies (UNU-CRIS), Brugge, Belgium
e-mail: edgardmoncayo@yahoo.com

J.R. Cuadrado-Roura and P. Aroca (eds.), *Regional Problems and Policies in Latin America*, Advances in Spatial Science, DOI 10.1007/978-3-642-39674-8_22,

22.1 Introduction

The Andean countries (Bolivia, Chile, Colombia, Ecuador, Peru, and Venezuela) constitute a special geographic and geopolitical environment in South America because of their distinctive location along the Andes mountain range.[1] The Andean nations share a long, ethnical and cultural tradition that, dates back to pre-Columbian Inca and Aymara civilizations. Politically, that tradition can be traced back to military alliances during the wars of independence against the Spanish colonial regime led by Bolívar and San Martin in the early nineteenth century.

Since the second half of the last century these countries have established close economic relationships by means of various agreements, of which the most comprehensive and ambitious was the one currently named the Andean Community (CAN for its acronym in Spanish). This supra-national community was, created in 1997, was the result of the transformation of the Cartagena Agreement (Andean Group),[2] signed in 1969 to create a 'common market' integrated by Bolivia, Chile, Colombia, Ecuador, Peru, and Venezuela.

[1] The Andes are the longest mountain range in the world, the second highest (after the Himalayas), and extend along 7,250 km from Patagonia in southern Chile to the Caribbean coast in Venezuela.

[2] The Andean Group was formed within the framework of The Latin American Free Trade Association – LAFTA – created in 1960, in which, besides the Andean nations, other Latin American countries like Argentina, Brazil, México, Paraguay, and Uruguay took part.

In practice, after a long and difficult process of nearly 45 years, the Andean integration is far from having achieved its original objective. Among a variety of contributing factors there are two that deserve to be highlighted!: (a) the growth model based on Ricardian international trade (comparative advantage) adopted by some member countries in the early 1990s, and (b) the political tensions arising from the sharp turn to the left of the political spectrum by the governments of Venezuela, Bolivia, and Ecuador in the first decade of this century. The former left the idea of integration based on productive complementarities by means of import substitution broadened to an Andean scale without foundations. The latter led, for example, to the withdrawal of Venezuela in protest of the signing by Colombia and Peru of bilateral free trade agreements with the United States.[3]

Currently, as a consequence of the distancing of most Latin American nations from the principles of the Washington Consensus, the cartography of integration has become more complex with the emergence of several initiatives that might be labeled "post-neoliberal", such as the case of the Union of South American Nations or 'Unasur' (2008) and the Bolivarian Alternative for Latin America and the Caribbean ('Alba', for its Spanishacronym) (2004).[4] Some common aspects of new integration models are: (a) the search for productive complementarities, (b) the return to active participation of the State in that search, and the inclusion of social development among its objectives.

However, the Andean Community continues to promote integration among its four current members (Bolivia, Colombia, Ecuador, and Peru), particularly on trade and the social and political areas, including some early steps toward defining a common territorial development strategy.[5]

This paper presents an analysis of the evolution of regional policies in the Andean countries, including Venezuela, from the 1960s until the present. Despite Venezuela's aforementioned withdrawal from Andean Community, this country continues to maintain strong commercial and political ties with the four current members. There is even a possibility that Venezuela may again become part of the community.

The rationale of forming a subgroup within LAFTA was to associate economies with greater homogeneity than the broader set of countries in order to advance more quickly toward the formation of a common market.

[3] Chile had left the association in 1976, during the Pinochet regime.

[4] For a comprehensive account of these developments in Latin American integration, see: Sanahuja (2009).

[5] The author of this article took part, as a consultant to the General Secretary's office of the CAN, in preparing some foundational documents for this initiative. See Moncayo (2003, 2011).

22.2 The Latin American Context

From the perspective of major structural trends, Andean regional policies have evolved in a pattern quite similar to most Latin-American countries. These, in turn, have followed the path of the dominant international trends.

Such synchronicity is explained by the fact that regional policies — just like all other public policies- evolve *paripassu* with the role assigned to the State in the process of development, which has undergone very similar transformations in all Western capitalist economies.

In the developed countries, during the post-World War II period until themid-1970s, the Keynesian Welfare State —KWS— gave rise to interventionist public policies that from the territorial perspective were designed, with a top-down approach.

The simultaneous crises of the world economy and the KWSled to a transformed role for the State, characterized by a scaling back to certain basic functions and by the decentralization of responsibilities to sub national levels. This new stage arrived in the context of deep structural changes in Western capitalism (post-Fordism, technological revolution, and globalization).

The combined effects of these processes have resulted in a profound re-scaling of the role of the State in three directions: (a) upward, because of globalization, (b) horizontally, because of the recurring crisis of the KWS, and (c) downward, because of decentralization toward the subnational territorial governments (Brenner 2003).

In this context, the "active" and "redistributive" regional policies characteristic of the KWS have given way to approaches based on the competitiveness of individual regions, based on the mobilization of endogenous capabilities (Helmsing 1999).

The change of direction of public policies, including regional ones, in Latin America resulted from the dismantling (in the late 1980s) of the "developmental" State. Though at a smaller scale and intensity, this State model shared many features of KWS and had its zenith during the 1960s and 1970s.

As a consequence, two clearly distinct periods regarding public policies can be highlighted in the Latin American context: (a) the post-War period until the late 1980s, and (b) the period dating from that time until the present.[6]

In the case of three Andean countries -Bolivia, Ecuador and Venezuela it is relevant to distinguish yet another stage, characterized by "post-" or "anti-neoliberal" policies of governments that aim at establishing a new kind of socialism in their respective States.

[6] See Boisier's article in this same volume.

22.3 Evolution of Regional Policies of the Andean Countries: A Comparative View

Political geography, regional balance and the territorial organization of the State have been permanent topics in the history of the Andean countries. From the inception of these nations as republics the allocation of power among the territories and its impact on the centralism–federalism tension as constitutional models of political organization of the State, are matters that have permeated the historical evolution of these nations over the past two centuries.

In the first half of the nineteenth century, the Andean countries oscillated between centralist systems suited to the imperatives of the independence wars and the federalist systems that better reflected the reality of nations fragmented into economically autarkical regions under the military power of local *caudillos*.

It was not until the second half of the nineteenth century that the unfolding of forces favorable to the integration of national markets led to the advent of political regimes that favored centralist constitutions. In several cases, this was made possible by cruel civil wars in which the victors would impose a new constitution according to their own preferences.

The process of consolidation of the nation-state – inspired by progress in the integration of national markets – began to be promoted in Venezuela by the autocratic governments of Antonio Guzmán Blanco (1870–1887) and Juan Vicente Gómez (1908–1935); in Ecuador during the "Garcian" period (after president Gabriel García Moreno 1861–1865, non-continuously); in Bolivia by president Narciso Campero in 1880; in Colombia by the so-called Regeneration led by Rafael Núñez during the last two decades of the nineteenth century; and in Peru by the government of Nicolás de Piérola in 1895.

Centralist constitutions resulting from such economic and political developments remained in force until the end of the twentieth century, when re-invigorated decentralizing forces revived the centralism – federalism antagonism that had been considered to be overcome.

Synchronic developments in the configuration of state policies in the Andean countries are not limited to major constitutional parameters, but can also be found in the evolution of public policies related to territory. In this regard, these five countries show remarkable parallels, which, in turn, follow the pattern, as mentioned above, of the general trends of Latin America and the developed countries.

22.3.1 The Period from the Postwar Until the 1970s: The Rise of Regional Policies

Just like in the developed countries and the whole of Latin America, the postwar years marks the beginning of a stage in which the State assumes the leadership of development, adopting features of the Keynesian Welfare State. Basically, the aims of development were defined as the achievement of accelerating growth rates through industrialization and economic planning.

Active policies for promoting industrialization via import substitution were applied in the Andean countries since the late 1950s and gained strength in the subsequent decades in the context of the consolidation and strengthening of innovative forms of State intervention. Accordingly analysts such as Ocampo (2008) and Thorp (1998), among others, label name this stage as "State-led industrialization", in order to emphasize the role that government policies played in leading the process.

Thus in Venezuela, the *Junta Cívico–militar* that took power in 1945, initiated a State capitalism model which, under the slogan "sowing oil", aimed at industrializing the country as well as the construction of large-scale infrastructure. To this effect, the State, through the Development Corporation of Venezuela – DCV – , fostered huge projects during the 1960s that had a big impact on the economic geography of Venezuela and allowed for the takeoff of Zulia and Bolívar states (in the Guayana region).[7] Among these, it is worth mentioning the ones regarding, iron and steel (Cerro Bolívar, in the Guayana region),[8] hydro-electricity (Caroní and Orinoco rivers, in the Guayana region) and oil and chemicals (Zulia).

Similarly, Ecuador's Industrial Development Law of 1957 was an attempt on the part of the State towards redirecting the surpluses of the banana boom (of the late 1950s) to the industrial sector. Ever since the boom of banana prices and the establishment of industrial firms in Guayaquil have made the Province of Guayas one of the most dynamic in the country (along with the traditional pole of Quito in the Pichincha Province).

During this same period, Mariano Ospina Pérez and Laureano Gómez also took protective measures in Colombia to stimulate a process of industrialization that had been spontaneously taking place in a highly decentralized way. The role of the Development Corporation of Venezuela was played in Colombia by the Industrial Development Institute, created in the 1940s.

Although the focus on industrialization would only appear many years later in Bolivia, the early 1950s also represents a historic milestone, in the country's path to modernity. Overdue social reforms were made especially regarding labor rights and land reform. As Venezuela, Bolivia developed a model of state capitalism to turn the surplus of the mining sector, at that time completely in private hands, into resources for national development.

National Revolution governments (Víctor Paz Estensoro and Hernán Siles Suazo) undertook three projects of great regional significance: oil industry expansion, the Cochabamba–Santa Cruz highway, and the opening up of the eastern

[7] Regarding this experience, see: Rodwin et al. (1969).

[8] During the period of 1960–1971, Venezuela created six large corporations to foster development in six specific regions (Guayana, Andean Region, Northern-western Region, Zulia, Northern-Easter Region, and Central-western Region). By the late 1970s and especially along "the lost decade" (1980s), these corporations faded away, and eventually disappeared in the 1990s (Sanabria 2010).

region. These three activities brought development benefits for the department of Santa Cruz, initiating a take-off process that would make it the most prosperous department in the country.

Finally, in Peru (as in Bolivia), the import substitution strategy was implemented relatively late. In fact, in November 1959 (the last year of Manuel Odría's government) the Industrial Development Law No. 13270 was passed establishing various incentives for industry, causing high growth rates in the sector in the 1960s.

In the framework of these structural transformations, along the gradual consolidation of a developmental and interventionist State, planning policies and institutions emerged: the Planning Office in Colombia (1951); the National Council of Coordination and Planning in Bolivia (1953); the National Planning Committee in Ecuador (1954); the Central Planning Office and Coordination of the Presidency of the Republic in Venezuela; and the National System for Planning and Economic and Social Development in Peru (1962).

It is important to highlight that in the emergence of planning in the Andean countries, several international organizations had a strong influence. This is the case of the ECLAC[9] missions to Bolivia (1953), Ecuador (1953), Colombia (1955), and Peru (1962 and 1963); and those of the World Bank to Colombia (1947)[10]; the United Nations to Bolivia (1953); David Lilienthal, director and founder of Tennessee Valley Authority (1954), as an advisor for the creation of the Valle del Cauca Regional Corporation in Colombia; and Arthur D. Little (1960), who designed a Regional Industrial Development Program in Peru.

The first official plans were put into practice in Colombia and Venezuela around the same period and under similar political circumstances. In fact, the General Plan of Economic and Social Development 1960–1970 (*Plan Decenal*) was devised during Lleras Camargo's Administration (1958–1962), the first in an arrangement called the *National Front* that represented the return to democracy after the dictatorship of General Gustavo Rojas Pinilla (1953–1957),as a result of a governance agreement between the two traditional political parties (Liberal and Conservative). Under this plan – greatly influenced by ECLAC's proposals – a model of import substitution was formalized and the notion of mandatory state investment planning was introduced.

Equivalent to Colombia's *Plan Decenal*, Venezuela's First Plan of the Nation 1960–1964 was devised by Rómulo Betancourt's government (1959–1964), the first democratic administration after the dictatorship of General Marcos Pérez Jiménez (1952–1958) and the result of a governance agreement called the *Pacto de PuntoFijo*, similar to *National Front* in Colombia.

The Punta del Este Conference in 1961, and the subsequent implementation of the *Alliance for Progress*, validated the developmental policies applied in several

---

[9] Economic Commission for Latin America and the Caribbean (ECLAC – CEPAL)

[10] According to Alacevich (2010, p. 64), this mission was "a paradigm for future missions of the Bank, and its report was used for many years as a model for studying the economic conditions of a country".

countries in Latin America, including economic planning that was associated by some with the suppression of the free market characteristic of socialist systems. Thus, the use of planning techniques was spread over the Andean countries, including Peru in1962, Ecuador in 1963, and Bolivia in 1966.

Using Müller's (2002) terminology, the first development plans in Andean countries had exclusively *vertical–sectorial* logics, in which there was no room for the *horizontal territorial* dimension. That is, spatial issues were not present in the contents of those plans. In this regard, however, it is important not to forget that outside central planning, States carried out megaprojects and policies that boosted regional development in Santa Cruz, Bolivia, Guayas province in Ecuador, and the (subnational) state of Bolívar in Venezuela; and also created institutions for the promotion of regional development.

The first Andean program that appears to explicitly consider spatial provisions is the *Second Plan of the Nation* 1963–1966 enacted in Venezuela. This document discussed the issue of "backward" regions in contrast with those it called "of high productivity" and remarked upon the usefulness of designing regional development programs for several states in the country.

The concept of "Regionalization" also appeared strongly during the Lleras Restrepo administration (1960–1970) in Colombia. This president proposed a "Regionalization Model" with the objective of articulating urban and regional policies with the national ones, so as to achieve physical, economic, and sociopolitical integration at a regional level. In this model, influence from the French *Amènagement du Territoire* becomes evident. Lleras Restrepo's administration promoted the Constitutional Reform of 1968 that for the first time introduced the concept of (administrative) decentralization in Colombian public management.

During the late 1960s and early 1970s, the incorporation of spatial variables in planning is generalized, as can be seen by the analysis of the *Third Plan of the Nation* 1965–1968 and the *Fourth Plan of the Nation* 1970–1974 in Venezuela, the *Socio–Economic Plan of Development* 1971–1991 in Bolivia (that introduces the concept of *development poles*); and the *Integral Plan of Transformation and Development* 1973–1977 in Ecuador. In this last case, General Rodríguez´s administration (1972–1976) launched a wide variety of activities at the regional level after passing the Regional Industry Development Law (1973), Regional Industry Development Law of Small and Medium-sized Industry (1973) and Industrial Parks Development Law (1975). All three aimed at fostering the establishment of industrial enterprise outside Pichincha and Guayas provinces.

Along these lines, General Rodríguez's administration started an integral development initiative in the basin of the Guayas River, and introduced rural development programs, following the guidelines regarding this subject promoted by the World Bank at that time in other Latin American countries such as Colombia.

In Peru, during the first phase of the military government (Velasco Alvarado, 1968–1975) and within the framework of a state capitalism model, the National Development Plan for the period 1971–1975 foresaw large investment by the State in mining and oil, which in spite of its considerable regional impact did not manage to balance an investment pattern highly concentrated in the coastal area.

The consideration of territorial issues in the development plans of Andean countries continued to be on the rise until peaking in the late 1970s and first half of 1980s. Bolivia was the first country where this phenomenon became noticeable. In fact, the "National Program for Economic and Social Development 1976–1980", enacted during the first administration of Hugo Bánzer (1971–1978), is the first in the Andean context in placing regional development as a high-priority strategy. This has several characteristic elements of the first generation of regional policies applied in developed countries, such as reduction of regional disparities, territorial integration, and regionalized investment budgets.

In practical terms, however, the policies mentioned above mainly favored the region of Santa Cruz, which thus received a new stimulus. During Bánzer's first term of office regional development corporations, in existence since 1945, were regulated.

Programs dealing with regional issues as the centerpiece for development were designed subsequently in Colombia, Ecuador, and Venezuela. Thus, Turbay Ayala's administration (1978–1982) in Colombia enacted the National Integration Plan that, as its name suggests, made the physical integration of territory its *leitmotif* and began to speak the language of endogenous development, which was just beginning to be formulated in the developed countries. This plan also included decentralization, conceived not as an end, but as a means for regional development.

The *National Development Plan* 1980–1984 devised by the Roldós–Hurtado administration (1979–1984) in Ecuador considered policies related to spatial articulation and regional development as one of the five general policies in the program. Among the objectives of the policy were: (a) the integration of the roads within the territory; (b) support for economically depressed zones; (c) industrial deconcentration; (d) urban development, and (e) environmental regulation. The implementation of these policies called for setting up a *regional planning system*.

Similarly in Perú, no longer in a development plan but in the Constitution of 1979 itself (of interventionist orientation), steps toward decentralization were taken through three, provisions: regional representation in the Senate, granting regions the status of intermediate levels of government, and turning municipalities into bodies of local government.

Finally, the last Andean country to arrive at regional planning was Venezuela, with the *Sixth Plan of the Nation* 1981–1985 enacted during Luis Herrera Campins' term of office. This plan, as in Bolivia, Colombia, and Ecuador, considered the territorial dimension one of the key pillars of the development strategy.

In addition to the Sixth Plan, Herrera Campins' administration updated and complemented the institutional structure of regional policy in Venezuela (Executive Decree No. 478/80); promoted approval of the Spatial Regulation Law in Congress and strengthened the role of regional development corporations. For these reasons, it is appropriate to say that this government devised a complete model of *Regional Development Management*.

In Bolivia, the ascendant phase of regional policies continued until 1984, when Siles Suazo's second administration (1982–1985) enacted the "National Plan for

Rehabilitation and Development, 1984–1987", the first drawn up by a democratic government after almost 20 years of military dictatorship. Although the Rehabilitation Plan diverged from prior programs, it contained Regional Development Policies that represented a line of continuity as compared to Bánzer's program.

In that sense, the main concerns of Regional Development Policy were: (a) physical integration of national territory; (b) reduction of regional disparities through investment in less-developed areas; and (c) applying appropriate institutional structures to conduct participatory planning processes of Regional Development. To this end, Regional Development Corporations were used and assigned a budget. It is noteworthy that Siles Suazo's plan was the first to introduce the concepts of decentralization and economic de-concentration.

In Ecuador, the inertia of regional policy also lasted until the mid-1980s, since in the "National Economic and Social Development Plan 1985–1992" regional issues were still deemed a priority and considered to be one of the 13 "biggest national problems" obstructing national development.

22.3.2 *Regional Policies in Decline: Neoliberalism and Decentralization (The Period Dating from 1980 Until the Late 1990s)*

The Andean countries did not escape the crisis of the Welfare State of the 1980s in the developed countries and in the rest of Latin America. This group of countries, with the exception of Colombia, was not exempt from the severe contraction in growth rates that affected all Latin American countries.

Similarly, the therapy that was applied followed the Latin America formula: less State and more market.[11] As a logical consequence, public policies previously designed to guide the direction of the economy and of private agents were abandoned.

Bolivia was the first Andean country to firmly advance in this new direction. In 1985 under a new presidential term of Victor Paz Estensoro (the same president who led the National Revolution during the 1950s), Bolivia applied economic policies based on the principles of neoliberalism.[12] The so-called New Economic Policy -NEP-preceded the famous Washington Consensus formulated by John Williamson in 1990 (Williamson 1990), by nearly 5 years.

In this context, the government formulated the plan "Economic and Social Development Strategy 1989–2000" that, in accordance with the NEP, limited government intervention to provision of infrastructure and social services; and set

[11] An analytic review of how Andean countries took on neoliberal policies can be found in Moncayo (2006, Chap. 2).

[12] The American economist Jeffrey Sachs, hired by the Bolivian government, was the key advisor on this policy (see: Sachs 2005: Chap. 2).

out a strategy to boost the private sector and direct foreign investment. Interestingly, the program, of neoliberal orientation, resumed the decentralization process started by Siles Suazo's Rehabilitation Plan.

Bolivia's decentralization finally came into being during the administration of Sánchez de Lozada (1993–1997), which included the topic in the 1994 constitutional reform and encouraged the approval of the Popular Participation Law (1994) and Departmental Administrative Decentralization Law (1995) in Congress. Although these two laws refer to both departments and municipalities, the decentralization model in Bolivia had a notably municipal bias. Specifically while the former granted municipalities diverse (political, economic and administrative) responsibilities, the latter only decentralized administrative functions to the departments. During the Sánchez de Lozada administration, the National Planning System was organized, and the participation of civil society was included in the process of planning at three levels (nation, department and municipalities).

What emerged back then could be characterized as one of the *regularities* in the long-term evolution of public policies in the Andean countries: *substitution of regional policy by decentralization*. At the same time, decentralization began a difficult journey due to the antagonism of those who thought of it as a requirement for wider democratic participation and promotion of balanced territorial development; and others who understood it as a mere mechanism to alleviate the fiscal burden of the central state.

After Bolivia, the next country to adopt neoliberal policies was Venezuela. In a paradoxical twist of history – similar to Paz Estensoro's in Bolivia – Carlos Andrés Pérez, one of the main architects in the design of the State capitalism model in Venezuela, implemented a neoliberal model during his second presidential term (1989–1993). Consequently, in the plan of this government ("*Seventh Plan of the Nation* 1990–1994" –The Great Change–) regional policy was given a lower profile and fused with environmental conservation policy.

The Great Change accepted as a fact that in an environment of open competition, regional growth was bound to be heterogeneous; but at the same time, it proposed the transfer of fiscal resources to (subnational) states as a compensation mechanism. Consistent with these conceptions, political, administrative and fiscal decentralization began in earnest in Venezuela, during Pérez's second term of office (Mascareño 2006, p. 149–166).

At this point, neighboring Colombia was undergoing a very similar transition starting with the plan named "Change with Equity" enacted by the Betancur administration (1982–1986). Under this plan, regional policy was replaced by decentralization (popular election of mayors, among other measures). In the case of Colombia, where armed insurgency was escalating, decentralization was deemed to be part of a wider political project that involved incorporating local elites into the traditional leadership by opening new channels of democratic participation.

The momentum of decentralization in Colombia reached its highest expression with the Constitution of 1991, which eclectically blended the concepts of "unitary republic" and "territorial autonomy". This hybrid formula was a result of a compromise between members of the Constitutional Convention who favored more federal institutions and those who conversely favored less drastic reforms involving only the deepening and improvement of decentralization.

President Cesar Gaviria (1990–1994) put into practice a broad set of decentralizing measures, strongly biased toward transferring fiscal responsibilities and resources to the municipalities. These provisions were based upon the broad platform provided by the Constitution of 1991 (which Gaviria himself had promoted), and in the context of an economic model inspired by the Washington Consensus. Thus, the conception of decentralization as a means to fostering regional development and productive deconcentration was postponed until very recently. This will be discussed later.

As in Colombia, the Washington Consensus was the main point of reference for the economic policies applied during Fujimori's first term of office in Peru starting in1990. Nonetheless, in contrast to other Andean countries, Peru's neoliberal reforms were not accompanied by a new impetus to decentralization but, on the contrary, by a return to hyper-centralist schemes of territorial governance. Such reforms were included in the 1993 Constitution. While nominally committed to decentralizing schemes, this Constitution established an autocratic presidency and a single congressional house elected by a single national district. As a result regional and municipal governments were significantly weakened through cuts to their revenues and powers.[13]

Led by President Six to Durán Ballén (1992–1996), Ecuador became the last Andean country to adopt the neoliberal package of structural reforms was Ecuador in 1992. Parallel to what happened in Bolivia (1985), Venezuela (1989), Peru (2000) and Colombia (1991), Ecuadorian public policies followed the principles of the Washington Consensus. Namely, trade and financial liberalization, reduction of social subsidies, opening to foreign investment, flexibilization of labor markets, and the privatization of public enterprises (telecommunications, hydrocarbons and electricity).

In this context, the National Development Council prepared the "Government Action Plan 1993–1996" (Development Agenda), thereby replacing policies related to Regional Development, by decentralization. To this end, the State Modernization Law passed in 1993, appointed the National Modernization Council to coordinate administrative, political, and fiscal decentralization. (Carrión 2006, p. 441–483).

[13] In 1992, Fujimori performed a self-coup-d'état, with the support of the high military command. He closed Congress and constitutionally autonomous controlling bodies, and under pressure from the OAS member nations convoked a Constituent Assembly in 1993 that replaced the 1979 Constitution (Pease 2003, p. 105).

22.3.3 The Post-Washington Consensus or Post-Neoliberal Period

In 2003, Joseph Stiglitz argued that:

> A reform strategy [the Washington Consensus] which promised to bring unprecedented prosperity [. . .] The outcomes have been worse than many of its critics feared: it has not brought growth to much of the region [Latin America] but, at least in some parts of the region, it has brought increased inequality and poverty. . .
>
> The neoliberal reform agenda failed even in its more narrow objectives of promoting growth. . . we should not be trapped into the narrow vision that that agenda supported. . . As we reform the economic agenda, we must place that agenda within the broader context in which it must reside (Stiglitz 2003, p. 38).

Disappointment with the outcomes of structural reforms based on the postulates of the Washington Consensus, along with the decline of the political parties that had promoted them, led to an unprecedented wave of governments that can generically be called "left" or "center-left" in Latin America in the first decade of the twenty-first century.

Hugo Chávez in Venezuela, Néstor and Cristina Kirshner in Argentina, Tabaré Vázquez in Uruguay, Fernando Lugo in Paraguay, Ricardo Lagos and Michelle Bachelet in Chile, Evo Morales in Bolivia, Rafael Correa in Ecuador, and Ollanta Humalain Peru, rose to power via popular elections and marked a "left turn" in the political models of their respective countries (Saint-Upéry 2008: Introd.).

Supported by very diverse political bases such as popular and student movements, traditional center-left and left parties, unions, ethnic organizations, and other groups coming from different political backgrounds (ex-priests, soldiers, union leaders, professional politicians, independent intellectuals and indigenous leaders), and also with very dissimilar economic policies, these governments nevertheless shared several common features. Among these are inclusive social policies, rejection of the neoliberal tradition (and therefore the reassertion of the State in economic management), recognition of the rights of indigenous peoples, and a determination to act with independence from the demands emanating from Washington (Hershberg and Rosen 2006: Chap. 1).

In the case of the Andean countries, Bolivia and Ecuador, state political-economic transformation promoted by Evo Morales and Rafael Correa (elected in 2005 and 2006, respectively) have prioritized the rights of "the original indigenous nations and peoples". As a consequence, these two States (Ecuador in 2008 and Bolivia in 2009) have been defined in their constitutions as "plurinational and intercultural states".

From the human rights perspective these developments have represented a considerable advance compared to the treatment of native communities throughout the history of the republics of Bolivia and Ecuador. However, in fact the concepts of "self-government" and "territorial autonomy" for indigenous nationalities expressed in the Constitutions pose many problems of governability for governments like those of Morales and Correa that aspire to build active States capable of carrying out policies on a wide sectorial and territorial spectrum (Cordero 2012). In Bolivia, for example, the ethnic factor has sharpened the atavistic conflict between the preponderantly indigenous highlands and the low eastern lands inhabited by whites and mestizos.

Evo Morales introduced a series of reforms in Bolivia that for many analysts represent a true "new foundation of the Bolivian state" (De León 2011, p. 72). The nationalization of hydrocarbons, the agrarian reform law, and the constitutional self-definition of the country as a "plurinational state" are among the most outstanding features in this process of profound changes.

In this context and with regard to regional issues, the Development Plan "Dignified, Sovereign, Productive and Democratic Bolivia for Good Living" does not include any particular dimension of territorial development. Nonetheless, it does consider cross-dimensional strategies and policies for infrastructure, rural development, and transformation of the productive structure.

Moreover, the plan is very sensitive to approaches based on endogenous development theories, for which it defines an interesting instrument called Integral Productive Complexes (IPC)[14] IPCs are "an articulated set of social actors, activities, conditions and relations of production with regard to the productive matrix, on the sectorial and territorial levels where the state intervenes to generate equity in the redistribution of wealth and the distribution and redistribution of income, prioritizing the strengthening and empowering of small urban and rural producers for good living" (National Development Plan 2007, p. 149).

IPCs incorporate the European-school concepts of Local Endogenous Development, complemented by the strong redistributive action of the central State. It also explicitly contains elements of the *Ayllu*, which were collectively owned territories of Andean communities in pre-Columbian America.

After reelection in 2009, President Morales designed the Development Plan "Bolivia and its Citizens First" (2010–2015). Just as in the previous plan – regional policy as such is not one of the four *transformation axes* considered in the document. One thing that does constitute one of these four axes is "Autonomic Transformation", presented in the plan in the following manner:

> Our country has begun a process of state reconfiguration. This involves the transition from a centralist system inherited from the colonial era toward a de-concentrated system in the framework of regional and municipal autonomies that come to comprise a new vision about the management of the Republic. This must be configured on three levels, properly articulating their responsibilities: national, departmental, and municipal" (Government Program 2010–2015, "Bolivia and its citizens", Sect. 5.4).

As mentioned in the last section, the issue of decentralization has been on the public policy agenda in Bolivia at least since the second Siles Suazo administration (1982–1985) and has followed a troubled path ever since.

[14] A complete analysis of development policies and instruments applied in Bolivia can be found in Muñoz-Reyes (2009).

With the above mentioned decentralization and popular participation laws of the Sánchez de Lozada government (1993–1997) significant progress was made in the provision of public services to the municipalities (Faguet 2000). However this was postponed on the departmental (regional) level. This level would take on greater importance with the traumatic constitutional processes leading to the approval in 2009 by popular referendum of the new Constitution,[15] in which, besides the Plurinational State, departmental autonomies are recognized and confirmed.

According to the new constitution, such autonomies were to be exercised by means of directly elected governments and with departmental assemblies with deliberative, oversight, and legislative powers in the areas under their responsibility, along with representation by the aboriginal nations.

Ultimately, aside from the popular election of prefects in the departments, the constitutional mandates and the development plan with respect to autonomy have so far been scarcely developed. As a result large differences remain in the way the Morales government and the departments promoting the most radical forms of decentralization understand the concept of *autonomy*. The former has a project based on a strongly interventionist central State,[16] while the latter aspire to a level of autonomy that would allow them to manage their own economic model consistent with neoliberal principles.

In Ecuador, as in Bolivia, the new political constitution of 2008 promoted by President Correa also established a "plurinational State"[17] and a renewed role of the State in promoting development by means of planning and in leading strategic sectors of the economy. In order to develop the constitutional mandate on State intervention, President Correa reorganized the national planning system by creating the National Planning Council and the National Secretariat for Planning and Development (*Senplades*), there by strengthening the public development bank system.

This new regulatory and institutional framework entailed a radical distancing from neoliberal principles in force in Ecuador since early 1998; and gave regional policy a low profile. Aside from scarce and scattered mentions of "territorial integration" contained in the National Development Plan for 2007–2010, the

[15] The approval of the new Constitution by referendum on January 25, 2009 was the last episode of an intensely conflictive process during which blood was even shed, following two other referendums and a failed attempt to pass autonomy laws at the Constitutional Assembly of 2007. The forces in the conflict were the MAS, headed by President Morales, and on the other side the civic and business leaders from the eastern departments of *Media Luna* led by Santa Cruz (the other departments are Beni, Pando, and Tarija) (Burbano de Lara 2012, pp. 225–236).

[16] In May of 2006, the Morales government decreed the nationalization of hydrocarbons, located mainly in Tarija and Santa Cruz (which, along with Beni and Pando, comprise the region known as the *Media Luna* or Half Moon).

[17] As a result of an electoral process that marked the end of the traditional parties in Ecuador, the economist Rafael Correa assumed the Presidency of the Republic on January 15, 2007. Correa headed an alternative political movement known as "Alianza País" a heterogeneous alliance comprising diverse social, environmentalist and political organizations

economic strategies promoted by Correa do not consider active regional policies as a priority.

On the other hand, and in accordance with the previously mentioned Andean pattern (p.?), the processes of decentralization and territorial autonomy have acquired a new force and a new scope. As discussed earlier, decentralization policies were first proposed in Ecuador in the early 1990s and achieved constitutional status in the Constitution of 1998.

Since then, and until the new constitution approved in 2008, the Ecuadorian decentralizing model had a strong municipal bias. Additionally a discriminatory and asymmetric character emerged where by the central State had the discretionary power to transfer differential responsibilities at the request of the territorial entities. Naturally, under these rules, the greater the economic and political power of the region, the greater the transfer of responsibilities.[18]

During the government of Rafael Correa, decentralization has acquired connotations that markedly contrast with the prior model. Firstly and under the premise of are insertion of the State through planning on all territorial levels, decentralization stopped being voluntary and differential, taking on an obligatory and holistic character aimed at inter-territorial cohesion and equity. Secondly, the new model recognizes intermediate territorial levels besides the municipal level, such as regions and territorial districts, which can be comprised of indigenous peoples, Afro-Ecuadorians, and Montubios. Lastly, the new territorial organization foresees a broad scheme of popular participation to include communities, peoples, and nationalities.

The new Ecuadorian territorial order was codified in the Constitution of 2008, in the "Good Living" Development Plan of 2009–2013, and in Basic Code of Territorial Organization, Autonomy and Decentralization of 2010. In order to develop this regulation, the National Decentralization Plan was passed in 2012 (CNC and Senplades 2012).

With respect to the new model of decentralization, the autonomy granted to the decentralized governments is different from a federal scheme, because Ecuador is still by Constitution a "unitary" state.

In marked contrast to his counterparts in Bolivia and Ecuador, the left-wing government of Hugo Chávez[19] departed from the decentralizing pattern and revived (though without explicitly acknowledging it) some of the main elements of the phase we have called "regional policy in ascendance" (1960–1980s). On the basis of diagnoses that point to the polarization of economic activity and of the population, very similar to those of the Plan of the Nation 1981–1985, the political project led by Hugo Chavez known as "21st Century Socialism" has within its strategic

[18] An illustrative assessment of decentralization in Ecuador up to the early part of the last decade can be found in Carrión (2006).

[19] Hugo Chávez was elected President of Venezuela (currently "the Bolivarian Republic of Venezuela) in 1998 (Dec.) and since then has twice (2006 y 2012) been reelected to consecutive 6-year periods.

core the creation of conditions for diversified productive development *with balanced territorial development*.

In pursuit of this objective, a wide range of *active* regional policy instruments have been launched, such as the reactivation of regional development organizations, Endogenous Development Nuclei (*Nudes*), and Special Zones for Sustainable Development (*Zedes*). This package of instruments has its legal origin in a broad legislative and institutional frame work that includes the Constitution of 1999, the Central Planning Commission, the Regional Development Plan 2001–2007, and the Simón Bolívar National Planning Project -First Socialist Plan 2007–2007.

Problematically, in counterpoint to the search for territorial balance from a perspective of location of productive activity, the Chávez regime has been enacting another strong process that neutralizes and undermines that objective: the project of geopolitical control over the territory. Thus, in spite of the National Constitution of 1999 (art. 4) that defines the Venezuelan State as "federal and decentralized", and of progress in political decentralization (popular election of governors and mayors) achieved in the 1980s, the central executive level retains broad powers to: (a) designate regional planning authorities, (b) create Strategic Defense Regions, and (c) make decisions about the huge investments required for the development of the new territorial axes.[20] In conclusion, it is a process of productive delocation rigidly controlled by the central government (Rojas and Pulido 2009).

Reluctance of the Fifth Republic, as self-named by the Chávez regime since taking power, to advance the decentralization model of the 1990s became clear since the Constitution of 1999, promoted by Chávez himself. Nominally the new political Magna Carta preserves the federalist spirit of the previous constitution (1961) and the popular election of governors and mayors has been enforced. However, in practice most of the constitutional provisions on fiscal decentralization and territorial responsibilities have not been subject to any substantive development (Mascareño 2006, pp. 166–176).

Similarly to Bolivia and Ecuador, regional aspirations in Venezuela toward autonomic federalism, granted formally in the constitution, clash in terms of concrete political dynamics with markedly centralist and authoritarian presidential regimes.

Of all the Andean countries, only Peru and Colombia continued in the first decade of the twenty-first century to practice the neoliberal policies that were adopted in the early 1990s. However, there were substantial differences between them with regard to regional policies.

In Peru, the Fujimori regime represented a true "hyper-centralistregression" (Dammert 2003, Chap. 1), considering that, as mentioned earlier, the 1979 Constitution had come to define the Peruvian state as unitary, representative, and decentralized, and that important progress had been made in terms of municipal

---

[20] Toward this end, Chávez has had at his disposal the huge revenues generated by high oil prices over the last decade.

responsibilities (Municipality Basic Code of 1984) and in the regionalization of the country, including popular election of regional governments in 1989 and 1990.

The road to decentralization in Peru would only be retaken a decade later during the democratic government of Alejandro Toledo, with the passage in 2002 of reforms to Chap. 14 of Title IV of the 1993 Constitution on decentralization, to the Foundations of Decentralization Law, and to the Basic Law on Regional Governments. This legislation defined the rules that would regulate administrative, political, and fiscal decentralization and also introduced the novel concept of economic and productive decentralization.

In 2003, the National Council on Decentralization was created, headed by a president with ministerial status. The Council elaborated the National Decentralization Plan 2004–2006 as well as the National Plan for Territorial Development 2004–2013, conveniently linking the economic dimension to the decentralization process.

This package of reforms and regulations defined a model of territorial organization whereby Peru is a unitary State with regional and local governments that are politically, economically, and administratively autonomous with regard to the matters under their jurisdiction. In this framework, the formation of regions is guided by a *sui generis* procedure that is not based on a previously determined delimitation, but on the political initiative (referendum) of the territories interested in creating a region.

To the previous "a la carte" regionalization, the reforms added a transfer of differential responsibilities that depend on the management capabilities of the agencies that receive them.

In this way, Peru in the last decade chose a decentralization policy in which territory is a geometrically variable social construction and responsibilities are transferred in a random process of varying speeds that share some similarities to the Spanish autonomy model.

During the democratic post-Fujimori administrations (Alejandro Toledo and Alan García), which continued, the neoliberal economic policies in place since the early 1990s, economic growth in Peru was the highest in Latin America. Even so, the presidential elections of June, 2011 favored Ollanta Humala, the left-wing opposition candidate with an openly anti-neoliberal program.

Humala's campaign sharply criticized the macroeconomic policies of the previous two decades, as well as the regional and decentralization policies that were emphatically dismissed. In practice, however, Humala's administration has been very pragmatic and has continued the policies – including regional policies – inherited from his predecessors without significant changes.

In the case of Colombia, starting with the government of Cesar Gaviria (1990–1994) that introduced structural reforms based on the Washington Consensus to the economic model, public policies dealing with regional development changed course dramatically. In this sense, three dominant directions can be distinguished: (a) the leading role of decentralization (b) the absence of explicit regional policies, (c) the emergence of sectorial-territorial policies, and (d) territorial economic activism (Moncayo 2006, pp. 72–98).

With regard to the first of these, the above-mentioned Constitution of 1991 granted constitutional status to a decentralization process that had begun in the 1960s, and introduced the notion of "autonomy" of territorial units. Given that the 1991 Constitution itself defines Colombia as a "Unitary Republic", the concept of "territorial autonomy" in Colombia has the same eclectic and ambiguous connotation seen in the recent Constitutions of the other Andean countries.

This central-federal hybrid, codified at the constitutional level, explains the difficulties the Colombian legislature had in enacting its Basic Law of Territorial Structure called for by the Constitution. After numerous failed attempts, not until 2011 did the Colombian Congress manage to enact this law (*Ley 1454*). Furthermore, it did so in a way that did not significantly resolve the lack of definition about the level of autonomy the territorial units have (Estupiñan 2012, p. 291).

In general, in the neoliberal period decentralization has not had a clear and strategically defined direction, and there has been a notorious absence of an integral policy for territorial development (Maldonado 2011, p. 17). There has been, for example, important progress in poverty reduction and in the decentralized (at the municipal level) provision of public utilities and of social services (education and health) (Faguet y Sánchez 2009). However there are also clearly perceptible recentralizing tendencies in the administrative responsibilities for the management of decentralized fiscal resources and of public order[21] (Restrepo 2006, pp. 377–381).

Currently, in both the regulatory framework and the concrete dynamics of decentralization in Colombia, and in spite of the 2011 law, one of the "weakest links" remains the political and administrative articulation between the municipality and the nation. Another "loose wire" is the connection between the different territorial levels with respect to citizen security (Gutierrez et al. 2010, pp. 175–179).

Active regional policies have slowed down notoriously in the post-structural reform period, though they have not disappeared completely. Thus, in the official development plans of the Gaviria (1990–1994), Samper (1994–1998), Pastrana (1998–2002) and Uribe 2002–2010) administrations, regional policies are only tangentially mentioned and usually in regard to the territorial distribution of sectorial policies, as discussed see below.

During this period, however, some measures and actions were taken toward directly encouraging regional development, among which the following should be highlighted: the Territorial Development Law (1997) making the preparation of territorial organization plans mandatory for all municipalities; the Rural Modernization and Peasant Business Development Policy (1994); and specific programs for certain areas of the country.

[21] A perverse effect of fiscal decentralization has been the intensification of the military conflict between the State and illegal armed groups, which has been going on for more than 50 years in Colombia. Decentralized resources can become an incentive for these illegal organizations to try to take control of the territories that receive more transfers (Sánchez and Palau 2006).

Contrary to these tendencies, the development plan of the Santos administration (2010–2014) treats the regional dimension as one of its central themes (R. of C. 2011). To operationalize this concept, a new regionalization of the country is created. Further concepts like regional convergence in quality of life and the definition of prioritized territorial development zones, largely forgotten in Colombian planning since the 1980s, have been revived.

Although beyond the conceptual claims the plan comes up short on the formulation of a plan for regionalized investments, the Santos government recently promoted a constitutional reform to create a General System of Royalties[22] that established a fund for financing projects for social, economic, and environmental development projects at the level of the territorial units.

The third important tendency in Colombia during the last two decades is the emergence of regional policies that authors like Helmsing (1999) and Cuadrado-Roura (1995) call "second generation" and "third generation", and Müller (2002) label sectorial-territorial, in the sense that they combine the vertical logic of conventional sectorial policies with the horizontal logic of territory.

Typical instruments of this new generation of regional policies include industrial and technological parks, business incubators, technological development centers, and clusters, among others, as well as institutional arrangements such as regional systems for technological innovation, regional competiveness councils, *inter alia*.[23]

Parallel to the second generation or sectorial-territorial policies, there is a perceptible tendency in Colombia that might be referred to as "regional and local activism". Such activism is characterized by which regions and localities are adopting their own development initiatives without resorting to the national agencies. In the face of the retreat of the State in the neoliberal model, the territorial units are equipping themselves with their own institutions and instruments to generate development. Some of the most advanced metropolitan regions like Bogotá and Medellín have even established very dynamic relationships of decentralized cooperation with regions of other countries (Jiménez 2012).

The journey that some territorial governments are taking from delegated management of public services to activism and entrepreneurship is manifested in the numerous strategic and prospective planning exercises being carried out in the majority of regions of Colombia. These processes find support in the conceptual frameworks developed by the European school of "local endogenous development"[24] and by Michael Porter.

[22] Legislative Act 05 of 2011. Royalties are payments to the State derived from the exploitation of non-renewable natural resources.

[23] A complete description of these instruments can be found in World Bank (2007).

[24] Authors such as Juan Ramón Cuadrado Roura, Antonio Vásquez Barquero, and the Italian theorists of industrial districts are the most frequently referenced.

22.4 Conclusions

Based on the previous sections, the following conclusions can be drawn:

1. Issues related to spatial structuring and the territorial organization of the State have permeated Andean history since the early years of the republics in the five countries up until our times. The centralism-federalism division caused several civil wars in the nineteenth century, and during the twentieth century this dialectic motivated multiple constitutional changes and partisan conflicts. These contradictions remain without being fully resolved today in the twenty-first century.
2. During the second half of the twentieth century, Andean regional policies followed a path that is closely associated with the evolution of the role assigned to the State in development processes, which is very similar to the cycles of the welfare state and regional policy in the developed countries and in Latin America as a whole (see Table 22.1). Considering that territorial policies are highly path dependent and are necessarily influenced by the specific geographies of the countries where they are applied, such synchronicity in the evolution of policies is surprising. Leaving aside as prosaic the hypothesis of simple mimicry, a possible explanation can be found in the theoretical approach of Wallerstein, according to which:

   > World-system analysis questions the way we conceive of social change. This kind of change is usually described referring to societies as equivalent to countries: thus we speak about "British society", "American society", "Brazilian society", "Chinese society" etc. Since in today's world there are more than 200 States, those who study social change would have to do so for more than 200 different societies. Orthodox social science accepts this concept that can be named the multiple-society assumption; but world-system analysis does not accept this assumption as a valid starting point for understanding the modern world.
   >
   > Instead of arguing that social change happens country by country, Wallerstein (1979) postulates the existence of a "world-system" that currently has a global extension. If we accept this assumption of a "single society", the many "national societies" simply become part of a larger whole, and any given social change can only be understood in its entirety in the wider context of the modern world–system (Taylor and Flint 2000, p. 5 y 6).

3. The ascendant stage of regional policy in the Andean countries was produced in the context of the gradual configuration of a 'developmentalist' (*desarrollista*) and interventionist state that in Bolivia, Peru, and Venezuela even took on features of State capitalism, with the central aim of directing the surplus generated by the export of natural resources toward import substitution industrialization.

   In this stage, which runs from the postwar to the 1980s, national policy objectives were very similar and mainly focused on the reduction of interregional inequality, the physical integration of the territory, and the promotion of new centers of development.
4. The efficiency of active regional policies has been seriously questioned by different analysts. However it should be recognized, on the one hand, that they

Table 22.1 Transformation of the regional development paradigm (specially adapted to Colombia and Perú)

	Classic regional policy	Second generation or sectorial–territorial policy
Dominant problems and general policy orientation	Cross-regional inequalities	Efficiency and competitiveness
	Backward regions	International insertion
	Exploitation of local natural resources (e.g. hydrographic basins)	Innovation and technological change
	Physical articulation of the territory	Endogenous development as an objective of sectorial-territorial policy
	Equity and redistribution as an objective of regional policy	Bottom-up approach
	Top down approach	
National development model	State-led industrialization	Expansion of range of action of the market without sectorial emphasis
	Keynesian welfare state	Schumpeterian work state
State model of political organization	Unitary and centralist republic	Eclectic mixtures combining unitary models (except Venezuela) with different degrees and modes of regional autonomy
Interpretive theories and approaches	Growth stages (Fisher, Clark)	Lack of a formal theoretical framework
	Cumulative circular causality (Myrdal, Kaldor, Hirshman)	Identification of determinants of endogenous growth (Porter, industrial districts, New Economic Geography)
	Development poles (Perroux, Boudeville)	
Instruments	Direct state investment in target areas	Hardware
	Regional development corporations	Infrastructure for connection to international markets (ports, airports, waterways)
	Incentives (e.g. tax exemptions)	Connectivity: telecommunications and telematics
	Controls (e.g., restrictions on new investment in congested areas)	Software
	Territorial regionalization for development planning	Business development
		Support for small and medium enterprises
		Regional agendas for sectorial development (e.g. agriculture; c and t)
		Productivity centers
		Technological development centers
		Regional systems for technological innovation
		Regional competitiveness councils
		Regional export plans
		Clusters

(continued)

Table 22.1 (continued)

Classic regional policy	Second generation or sectorial–territorial policy
	Industrial and technological parks
	Human resource training
	Orgware
	Integration of the economic dimension into decentralization
	Territorial restructuring programs
	Cooperative alliances between government, the private sector, universities, and NGOs
	Strategic development projects on the regional and local scale (e.g. city-regions)

Source: Author's own elaboration

turned out to be pro-cyclical to real processes of decreasing regional inequalities driven by structural forces,[25] and on the other hand that during their period of application they successfully consolidated very important alternative poles of development such as the Santa Cruz region in Bolivia, Guayas in Ecuador, and to a lesser degree Guayana in Venezuela.

5. The crisis of the welfare state in the 1970s, the impact of imbalances in the world economy in the 1980s, and the adoption of the neoliberal model in the 1990s determined the dismantling of the 'developmentalist' state in the Andean countries – as in most of the other Latin American countries – and thus the decline of active public policies, including regional policies.

   In the particular case of regional policies, these were replaced by decentralization for the distribution of fiscal resources with a municipal emphasis, which has delayed decentralization for regional development.
6. During the 1990s, in addition to decentralization, three new approaches to regional development appeared: *regional-sectorial* policies for technological innovation, productive development, and competitiveness; (a) territorial restructuring; and (b) local economic development.
7. Disenchantment with the results of structural reforms of the economy inspired by the neoliberal paradigm and the demise of the political parties that promoted them led to a wave – unprecedented in Latin America – of governments on the left side of the political spectrum. This was the case in Venezuela, Bolivia, and Ecuador, where rejection of the neoliberal model was reinforced by the emergence of powerful ethnic and social movements.

   In these countries, specifically regional policies seem to have been left aside. As a result, today this field is dominated by the search of a model of political-

[25] A study on Colombia found that regional income inequality in this country decreased substantially between 1930 and 1990 (see: Bonet and Meisel 1999).

territorial organization. The distribution of powers between the national state and the territorial units, under a framework of profound transformations in their development model, is one of the most crucial issues on the agenda of governability faced by Venezuela, Bolivia, and Ecuador.

8. In Colombia and Peru, where neoliberal policies were implemented in the early 1980s and have continued since then without interruption, "second generation" regional policies have been adopted, characterized among other features by a withdrawal of the central state and greater participation by the territorial units and the private sector (see Table 22.1).

   Ultimately, this suggests that the great challenges the Andean countries will face in the future with regard to regional policy are: (a) developing systemic rationality needed to connect a variety of currently dispersed actions and instruments, (b) reorienting decentralization toward the competitive development of regions and localities, and (c) preserving the integrity of the nation-state in the face of the external demands of globalization and internal demands for greater powers and responsibilities on the part of subnational entities.

22.5 A Final Reflection

In a world in which globalization tends to widen the gap between the very rich and the very poor in all latitudes, Latin America "has the largest 'excess' inequality of any region in the world vis-à-vis its income per capita" (Palma 2006, p. 19). In this context, the interregional gaps within the Latin American countries, as measured by various indicators, remain one of the core problems on the development agenda (Ilpes 2009: Chap. 2).

While in the last three decades such disparities have not shown a definite rising trend, it is an undeniable fact that they are very pronounced and show a stubborn persistence.

Interregional levels of per capita income exhibited a slow but continuous propensity toward convergence through the 1990s. Since then, this trend has stagnated and in some cases turned to divergence[26] (Bolivia[27] and Colombia[28]).

This suggests that the cycle of convergence coincided with the cycle of active regional policy, and the cycle of stagnation in the reduction of inequalities with that of neoliberal policies and globalization. While it would be reckless to claim a simple causality between the economic model and the magnitude of interregional disparities, we can say that here we find a clearly probable stylized fact.

[26] A meta-analysis of international studies on regional convergence conducted between 1990 and 2003 found that these same tendencies were happening in Europe (Moncayo 2004a, b).

[27] On Bolivia, see: Schroeder (2007).

[28] On Colombia, see: Galvis and Meisel, in this same volume (Chap. 9)

Finally, it must be noted as a positive feature that, even though the territorial gaps in terms of income are not decreasing, policies in recent decades to decentralize public spending may have contributed significantly to convergence in terms of quality of life (access to public services and human development – health and education –). This has been shown in some studies of the Colombian case (Faguet and Sánchez 2009; Braniza and Cardozo 2009).

References

Alacevich M (2010) La economíapolítica del Banco Mundial – Los primerosaños. MayolEdiciones, Bogotá (Original Title: The political economy of the world bank: the early years. Banco Mundial, Washington, DC, 2009)

Bonet J, Adolfo M (1999) La convergencia regional en Colombia: Una visión de largo plazo, 1926–1995, vol 62, Documentos de Trabajo sobre Economía Regional. Banco de la República/ Centro de Estudios Económicos Regionales, Cartagena

Branisa B, Adriana C (2009) Revisiting the regional growth convergence debate in Colombia using non-income Indicators. University of Goettingen, Goettingen

Brenner N (2003) Metropolitan institutional reform and the rescaling of state in contemporary western Europe. Eur Urban Reg Stud 10(4):297–324

Burbano de Lara F (2012) Movimientos regionales y autonomías políticas de Bolivia y Ecuador. Ph.D. thesis final text, Universidad de Salamanca

Carrión F (2006) Ecuador es la suma de sus partes, en: Restrepo (2006)

Consejo Nacional de Competencias y Secretaría Nacional de Planificación del Desarrollo (2012) Plan Nacional de Descentralización 2012–2015. Senplades, Quito

Cordero S (2012) Estados plurinacionales en Bolivia y Ecuador, Nuevas ciudadanías ¿más democracia? Nueva Sociedad 240:134–148

Cuadrado JR (1995) Planteamientos y teorías dominantes sobre el crecimiento regional. Eure Mag 21(63):5–32

Dammert M (2003) La descentralización en el Perú a inicios del siglo XXI: de la Reforma Institucional al Desarrollo Territorial, vol II, vol 31, Serie Gestión Pública. Cepal, Santiago de Chile

Daude C, Stein E (2007) The quality of institutions and foreign direct investment. Econ Polit 19 (3):317–344 (Wiley Blackwell)

De León O (2011) Bolivia: la construcción participativa del desarrollo, en: Déniz J, De Leon J, and Palazuelos A (2011), Ecuador y Venezuela. Catarata/Madrid

Déniz J, De León O, Palazuelos A (2011) Nuevas estrategias económicas en América Latina. Los casos de Bolivia, Ecuador y Venezuela. Catarata/Madrid

Estupiñan L (2012) Desequilibrios territoriales. Estudio sobre la descentralización y el ordenamiento territorial colombiano. Una mirada desde el nivel intermedio de gobierno, Universidad del Rosario; Ediciones Doctrina y Ley Ltda, Bogotá

Faguet JP (2000) Does decentralization increase government responsiveness to local needs? Decentralization and public investment in Bolivia, London School of Economics, Center Economic Performance, Working Paper Nr.999

Faguet JP, Fabio S (2009) Decentralization and accesto social services in Colombia, vol 2009-6, Documents CEDE. CEDE, Universidad de los Andes, Bogotá

Gutierrez F (2010) 25 años de la descentralización en Colombia. Konrad Adenauer Stifjung, Bogotá

Helmsing AHJ (1999) Teorías del desarrollo industrial regional y políticas de segunda y tercera generación, vol XXV(75), Eure review. Pontificia Universidad Católica de Chile, Santiago de Chile

Hershberg E, Fred R (2006) Latin America after neoliberalism. Turning tide in the 21st century. The New Press, New Baskerville

Ilpes (2009) Economía y territorio en América Latina y el Caribe. Desigualdades y políticas. CEPAL, Santiago de Chile

Jiménez WG (2012) Gestión pública e internacionalización como estrategia para el desarrollo de los gobiernos subnacionales en Colombia. Instituto Nacional de Administración Pública A.C. et al., México

Maldonado A (2011) Descentralización territorial en Colombia: situación y perspectivas de política, vol 1, Policy paper. Friedrich Ebert Stiftung en Colombia -Fescol, Bogotá

Mascareño C (2006) Venezuela: no se hacen revoluciones sin unidad de mando, en Restrepo, ed. (2006)

Moncayo E (2003) Geografía económica de la Comunidad Andina: regiones, nuevos actores de la integración. Secretaría General de la Comunidad Andina, Lima

Moncayo E (2004a) El debate sobre la convergencia económica internacional e interregional: enfoques teóricos y evidencia empírica. EURE XXX(90):7–26

Moncayo E (2004b) Las políticas regionales en Colombia. Universidad Externado de Colombia, Bogotá

Moncayo E (2006) Neoliberalismo en los países andinos: balance de dos decenios. Editorial Oveja Negra y Universidad Católica de Santiago de Guayaquil, Bogotá

Moncayo E (2011) Elementos para una estrategia de desarrollo territorial en el marco de la integración andina. Universidad Pontificia Bolivariana, Medellín

Monroe J (2006) Condiciones históricas y sentidos de la cuestión territorial en el Perú. en Restrepo, ed. (2006)

Müller P (2002) Las políticas públicas. Universidad Externado de Colombia, Bogotá (Original Title in French: Les politiques publiques. PressesUniversitaires de France, Paris)

Muñoz-Reyes C (2009) Políticas e instituciones para el desarrollo económico territorial. El caso de Bolivia, vol 6, Serie Desarrollo Territorial. CEPAL, Santiago de Chile

Ocampo JA (2008) Etapas del pensamiento sobre desarrollo en América Latina., en Altimir O, Iglesias E, Machinea JL (2008) Hacia la revisión de los paradigmas del desarrollo en América Latina. Cepal; Secretaría General Iberoamericana, Santiago de Chile

Palma JG (2006) Globalizing inequality: 'Centrifugal' and 'Centripetal' forces at work. Desa Working paper No.35

Pease H (2003) La autocracia fujimorista. Del Estado intervencionista al Estado mafioso. Pontificia Universidad Católica del Perú; Fondo de Cultura Económica, Lima

República de Colombia (2011) Plan nacional de desarrollo 2010–2014. Prosperidad para todos. Departamento Nacional de Planeación, Bogotá

Restrepo DI (ed) (2006) Historias de la descentralización. Transformación del régimen político y cambio en el modelo de desarrollo en América Latina, Europa y EUA. Universidad Nacional de Colombia, Bogotá

Rodwin L et al (1969) Planning urban growth and regional development: the experience of the Guayana program of Venezuela. The MIT Press, Clinton

Rojas J, Pulido N (2009) Estrategias Territoriales recientes en Venezuela. ¿Reordenación viable de los sistemas territoriales o ensayos de laboratorio? Eure Review XXXV(104):77–100

Sachs J (2005) The end of poverty. How we can make it happen in our lifetime. Penguin Books, London

Saint-Upéry M (2008) El sueño de Bolívar. El desafío de las izquierdas sudamericanas. Ediciones Paidós Ibérica, S.A, Barcelona, Original title in French: Le rêve de Bolívar. Le dêfi des gauches sud-américaines, París: La Découverte 2007

Sanabria S (2010) La ordenación del territorio o política territorial en Venezuela. Terra Nueva Etapa 40:13–44, Universidad Central de Venezuela

Sanahuja JA (2009) Del 'regionalismo abierto' al 'regionalismo post-neoliberal'. Crisis y cambio en la integración regional en América Latina. Anuario de la Integración Regional de América Latina y el Gran Caribe, 7:11–54, Coordinadora Regional de Investigaciones Económicas y Regionales, Buenos Aires

Sánchez F, del Pilar Palau M (2006) Conflict, decentralization and local governance in Colombia, 1974–2004, vol 2006-20, Documento CEDE. Universidad de los Andes, Bogotá

Schroeder K (2007) Economic globalization and Bolivia's regional divide. J Lat Am Geogr 6 (2):98–120

Stiglitz J (2003) El rumbo de las reformas. Hacia una nueva agenda para América Latina. CEPAL Mag, Nr. 80:7–37

Taylor P, Flint C (2000) Geografía política, economía-mundo, Estado-nación y localidades, 4th edn. Trama Editorial, Madrid

Thorp R (1998) Progreso, pobreza y exclusión. Una historia de América Latina en el Siglo XX. IDB, Washington, DC

Union of South American Nations or "Unasur": Argentina, Bolivia, Brasil, Chile, Colombia Ecuador, Guayana, Paraguay, Suriname and Venezuela

Wallerstein I (1979) The capitalist world economy. Cambridge University Press, Cambridge

Williamson J (1990) What Washington means by policy reform, Latin American adjustment. In: John W (ed) How much has happened? Institute of International Economics, Washington, DC

World Bank (2007) Colombia: inputs for subregional competitiveness policies. Report, World Bank, Washington DC

No. [illegible]

Chapter 23
Export Specialization and Regional Growth: The Chilean and Colombian Cases

Miguel A. Márquez, M. Teresa Fernández, and Julián Ramajo

23.1 Introduction

Unequal regional development is a feature of most Latin American countries [LAC] (see Cuadrado-Roura and González-Catalán 2013). As the spatial agglomeration of economic activity has become an important determinant of a country's economic growth pattern (Puga and Venables 1999), much of the existing empirical research in Latin American has been focused primarily on the relationship between regional inequality and development (see, for example, Aroca and Hewings 2002). Nevertheless, although authors like Venables (2005) stress the theoretical root for the relationship between exports and spatial development, studies which examine regional exports as determinant of regional inequalities are less frequent. While different theoretical models make different predictions with respect to the impact of regional exports on regional growth differentials, the empirical evidence on the relationship between regional export diversity (that is, less specialization) and regional growth have only recently begun to be measured.

Traditionally, international trade and export specialization are closely interrelated. According to the more orthodox theories of international trade, one of the arguments that support the possibility of specialization in export patterns between countries is the mechanism of comparative advantages. These advantages stem from countries' different relative production factor endowments or technologies and the intensity with which these factors are used in the production of each good traded (Heckscher-Ohlin model and Ricardo's theory). Thus, trade between countries based on comparative advantages might lead to big differences in their export patterns. More recently, developments framed in the new economic

M.A. Márquez (✉)
Department of Economics, University of Extremadura, Badajoz, Spain
e-mail: mmarquez@unex.es

M.T. Fernández • J. Ramajo
University of Extremadura, Badajoz, Spain
e-mail: teresafn@unex.es; mmramajo@unex.es

J.R. Cuadrado-Roura and P. Aroca (eds.), *Regional Problems and Policies in Latin America*, Advances in Spatial Science, DOI 10.1007/978-3-642-39674-8_23,

geography or in endogenous growth theories emphasize the role of economies of scales, the product differentiation and dynamic spill-over effects as key determinants in the volume of trade between countries with similar factor endowments (Krugman 1980; Helpman and Krugman 1985). These investigations seem to contradict the traditional trade theory, highlighting the concept of new varieties of products and so, export diversification.[1] This way, export diversification has become a relevant issue in the recent economic research.

At national level, the main question is why it is important for a country to diversify exports. One reason to justify export diversification is export instability (Herzer and Nowak-Lehnmann 2006; Hesse 2008). A high dependency on a few sector exports may be dangerous for the growth if they are affected by both prices and volume shocks. Sachs and Warner (2001) argue that risk may be bigger when the specialization is based on primary products. In this case, countries may suffer from the Ducht Disease effects (among others Reinhardt 2003; Sinnot et al. 2010). Thus, widening the number of export sectors (horizontal export diversification) may contribute to maintain stable export earnings (Al-Marhubi 2000; Herzer and Nowak-Lehnmann 2006). Furthermore, and following Prebisch–Singer hypothesis (1950), increasing exports of manufactured products to the detriment of primary products (that is, vertical export diversification) may also help to stabilize export earnings (Athukorola 2000). This could be explained by the fact that prices of manufactured goods are less volatile than primary products.

Many endogenous growth models (Matsuyama 1992; Gutiérrez de Piñeres and Ferrantino 2000) also emphasize the importance of vertical export diversification for growth. Manufactured exports tend to offer more possibilities for learning by doing and more knowledge spillover effects to other activities than primary products. The sources of these spillovers might be related to improvements in productivity, more technological advances and managerial practices, and to the increase in labour force training (Herzer and Nowak-Lehnmann 2006; Capello 2009).

Recently, an emerging literature emphasizes the role played by the composition of a country's exports on growth. In this framework, productive specialization is connected to growth possibilities; and also, the economic growth is driven by countries' diversification instead of the concept of comparative advantage (Hesse 2008). Some researchers such as Hausmann et al. (2007) argue that countries that are able to export higher productivity goods relative to their income tend to offer greater potential for growth. However, authors like Hwang (2006) posit that countries with room for quality upgrading within the existing export package would grow faster. Thus, the key would be to diversify toward higher productivity goods or to an export basket with opportunities to create space to upgrade the quality within products. Finally, other authors such as Hidalgo et al. (2007) and Hausmann and Klinger (2007, 2008) instead of test the relationship between export

[1] We use this term as opposed to specialization. In line with Dennis and Shepherd (2007), export diversification involves expanding the variety of products that a country exports.

diversification and growth, they diagnose the export challenge facing a country. They stress that countries with room to move from existing export packages to another export basket specialized in "nearby" products tend to have more opportunities for structural transformations. Consequently, they have more possibilities for expanding export and growth.

Based on the expectation that export diversification promotes national economic growth, many empirical researchers have worked at a country level. In this context, the research has been focused mainly on the causality relationship between export diversification and economic growth (Awokuse 2007). However, neither theoretical models nor empirical evidence has managed to clarify it (Benedictis et al. 2009).[2] Some scholars have argued that export diversification affects economic growth positively (Matsuyama 1992; Lederman and Maloney 2007; Hesse 2008; Agosin 2009; Benedictis et al. 2009; Parteka and Tamberi 2013). Moreover, other authors have stated that diversification can derive from economic development (Imbs and Wacziarg 2003; Koren and Tenreyro 2007). In any case, the empirical evidence has showed that there is a positive link between economic growth and export diversification (Al-Marhubi 2000).

Based on the aforementioned expectations, the previous empirical evidence has focused mainly at a country level, being only a few studies which have researched the link between regional growth and regional export diversity. Due to the heterogeneity of the regional economies within a country in terms of their export baskets, results might differ from the one obtained for the national aggregate. Nevertheless, few previous empirical works have examined the extent to which regional specialization in exports is related to regional growth. For example, Mattee and Naudé (2007) analyzed this relationship within South-Africa over 1996–2004 period. They find that, in general, regions with more diversified exports (less specialization) experienced higher economic growth rates. By comparison, Guerrieri and Ianmarino (2003) studied the case of the regions of the Italian Mezzogiorno along 1985–2000. These authors find that there is no any one way relationship due to the coexistence of different specialization patterns at provincial and different growth paths. Digging deeper into the opportunities for growth according to the level of sophistication of export basket, Hausmann and Klinger (2008) diagnose the export challenge facing Colombia's growth at both, national and regional, level. They conclude that the low levels of long term growth in Colombia are not independent of the lack of export dynamism. But also, they show big differences in the level of sophistication of the export basket across regions.

Due to this lack of studies within the regional economic literature, this chapter aims to give empirical evidence on this relevant issue. Therefore, the main contribution of this study is mainly empirical. We use an empirical model where it is hypothesized that outward-oriented regions grow more rapidly, and alongside this hypothesis we test the relevance of the link between export specialization and the

---

[2] Some authors point out that the data and the measure of specialization may generate different results across countries (see e.g. Benedictis et al. 2009)

economic growth on a regional level. The empirical model is implemented focusing on the different regions of Chile (over 1992–2006) and the distinct departments in Colombia (over 2000–2010), using export data disaggregated by industries at ISIC 3 digit level. We also use various measures of export diversity at regional level. This study doesn't show conclusive evidence in favour of diversification of export-led growth. For the Chilean and Colombian cases, export diversification (export specialization) in regions seems to be negatively (positively) correlated with regional growth. This finding might be of great interest for policy purposes.

This Chapter is structured as follows. Firstly, it is necessary to make an exploratory analysis about both the country export pattern and the regional export patterns. Hence, Sect. 23.2 presents the export pattern for countries in Latin America. Section 23.3 analyzes the evolution and structure of regional exports for the different regions/departments within both the Chilean and the Colombian economies. Section 23.4 shows an empirical analysis about the relationship between export diversification and regional growth for Chile and Colombia. Finally, Sect. 23.5 concludes.

23.2 Export Pattern in Latin America

This section provides a descriptive overview of export composition in some countries in Latin America along the last two decades. Export data (in nominal US dollars) comes from the BADEDEL database (CEPAL). We use data of trade disaggregated by industries at 2 digit SITC (Rev. 3).

Unequal economic development is a traditional feature of countries in Latin America Furthermore, the evolution of LAC economies has been very different across countries during the last two decades. Cuadrado-Roura and González-Catalán (2013) stress that its behaviour is related not only to issues such as territorial dimension in each country, but also, to the cultural, political and economic issues in each of them.[3] Besides, these authors link the growth of these countries with the export growth in resource-natural based sectors. As we mentioned above, recent researchers point out the composition of a country's export basket as a key in the economic performance. Thus, it is very important to know how export composition has evolved and which are the basic stylized facts in this issue across countries and time.

Table 23.1 shows GDP performance and export growth from 1990 to 2010 in eight LAC countries. These economies account for more than 80 % of the total Latin American GDP and more than 65 % of the total export. We can find that their behaviours in terms of trade have been very different in the past two decades. For example, while export performance in Chile and Mexico has been the most

[3] Cuadradro-Roura and González-Catalán analyze these differences in the Chap. 5 of this book. From their analysis emerge five stylized facts in LAC countries.

Table 23.1 Degree of openness and export and GDP growth rates, 1990–2010

	Degree of openness (exports/GDP)(constant 2,000 US$)		Average growth exports (constant 2,000 US$)			Average growth GDP (constant 2,000 US$)		
	1990	2010	1990–2000	2000–2010	1990–2010	1990–2000	2000–2010	1990–2010
Chile	24.24	33.39	9.26	4.45	6.83	6.40	3.88	5.13
Colombia	12.86	16.65	5.17	4.25	4.48	2.66	4.08	3.37
Bolivia	16.94	23.39	4.56	6.44	5.49	3.77	3.84	3.80
Argentina	8.95	12.46	6.62	5.76	6.19	4.55	4.33	4.44
Brazil	6.56	13.08	6.94	6.46	6.70	2.54	3.61	3.07
Mexico	12.41	39.66	13.37	4.32	8.75	3.47	1.76	2.61
Peru	10.90	17.26	8.04	6.47	7.26	3.97	5.67	4.82
Ecuador	24.84	35.43	5.96	4.13	5.04	1.80	4.60	3.19
LAC	12.20	22.30	8.66	4.38	5.64	3.21	3.33	3.27
World	16.54	32.03	7.08	5.19	5.83	2.85	2.51	2.68

Source: Authors' calculation from World Bank, WDI

successful in Latin American countries, this performance has been quite poor in Colombia. The radical trade policy reforms implemented in Chile have made it a leader in the opening-up process in the Latin American regions since the mid-1980s (Gutiérrez de Piñeres and Ferrantino 1997; Alvarez and Fuentes 2003; Reinhardt 2003). In Mexico, after the country joined North American Free Trade Agreement export grew faster. However, after trade liberation in the early 1990s in Colombia, the relationship of Colombian economy with the world economy remained low (Ramirez et al. 2007). By way of comparison, between 1990 and 2010, the degree of openness of the Chilean economy rose from 24.24 % to 33.39 %; in Mexico from 12.41 % to 39.66 %, and, in the case of Colombia increased from 12.86 to 16.65.

In this framework, countries in Latin America present unequal economic growth. In general, the most dynamic economies in terms of export have been the most dynamic in term of economic performance. In fact, Chile's performance has been the most important in comparison to the rest (see Table 23.1). By contrast, Colombia's GDP growth rate has been lower. These results may suggest that the levels of long-term growth in these countries cannot be independent of the export dynamism.

Differences across countries are also showed up in the geographical patterns of exports (see Table 23.2). Trade policies might have been keys in this issue. In this sense trade agreements established between countries are very important.[4] In general, all LAC countries have increased their trade relationships each other in the last two decades. However, while some economies have diversified its exports by different regions in the world, others such Colombia or Mexico continue to focus a significant share of their exports in the USA markets, being more vulnerable to growth. China has become a main trading partner for Latin America. Thus, between 1990 and 2010, destination markets have experienced some changes. There have been shifts from advanced countries to emerging economies.

According to the most traditional trade theory, a country that opens to trade would tend to specialize in those goods in which has comparative advantage. Developments more recent, framed in the endogenous growth and the new trade theories, emphasize into the new varieties of goods. Thus, following these models, structural transformations in the economy might play a key role in the growth performance. Therefore, the trade composition might be relevant on growth. Some authors such as Hausmann et al. (2007) stress that the composition of a country's exports matters. In this sense, differences in export basket may be behind the different dynamism in the export of countries.

Observing the export basket in LAC countries in the last two decades, three stylized facts are worth noticing. First fact, most of LAC countries are highly dependent on primary product exports (commodity exports). Despite of great

[4] For example, Mexico joined North American Free Trade Agreement (NAFTA) in 1994. This fact explains that USA to be the main trading partner of Mexico. On the other hand, Argentina, Brazil, Paraguay (suspended today), Uruguay and Venezuela built MERCOSUR in 1991.As a result, the commercial relations are bigger each other.

Table 23.2 Destination markets of exports (%)

		Regions						
		LAC	China	Japan	EU 15	USA	Other member OECD	Rest of world
Chile	1990	12.67	0.40	16.25	38.76	16.76	4.63	10.53
	2010	17.14	24.41	10.55	17.17	9.68	10.56	10.48
Colombia	1990	19.57	0.03	3.83	28.32	41.29	2.89	4.07
	2010	27.28	4.50	1.29	12.46	41.96	5.46	7.05
Argentina	1990	27.65	1.95	3.20	30.96	13.48	4.42	18.34
	2010	41.99	8.51	1.25	15.27	5.18	6.51	21.28
Brazil	1990	19.62	1.22	7.48	32.54	24.17	6.77	8.21
	2010	27.05	15.20	3.53	18.68	9.60	5.66	20.28
Mexico	1990	6.98	0.03	5.47	12.77	70.03	3.07	1.65
	2010	7.10	1.41	0.65	4.61	79.99	4.63	1.60
Peru	1990	15.00	1.67	12.68	32.68	22.87	4.27	10.82
	2010	16.88	15.57	5.17	16.60	16.04	23.82	5.92
Ecuador	1990	22.15	0.00	1.87	10.20	48.55	1.15	16.09
	2010	39.91	1.88	2.30	12.47	34.57	1.32	7.56

Source: Authors' calculation from CEPAL, BADECEL database

heterogeneity among LAC countries,[5] they have a commodity share of more than 65 % of total exports. Mexico is a notable exception (25 % of total exports). Commodity exports lost importance in export basket in LAC in the 1990s, falling more dramatically for Mexico. However, in the last decade in all LAC countries they boomed and they remained very large (Table 23.3). Thus, these economies are lagging in manufactured goods. This feature makes LAC countries very vulnerable to terms of trade shocks This export basket is typical of poor countries, not rich countries (Hausmann et al. 2008). Moreover, it may not be well suited to drive future growth. Some empirical studies, especially two influenced papers by Sachs and Warner (1995a, b) have supported that a large share of natural-resource exports in total exports is related to slower growth. Deteriorating terms of trade, excess volatility and low productivity growth are the main arguments for this negative relation (Cadot et al. 2012). To the extent the abundant resources are exported, countries may suffer from the "Ducht Disease", that is, there may be a tendency for the real exchange rate to become excessively appreciated, which reduces the incentive to promote the production of other tradable goods (manufactured products). Thus, with terms of trade declining, the expectation would be that economies specializing in primary products would no benefit from positive spillovers involved in manufacturing – more technological progress and innovation due to the learning by doing – and consequently, it would hinder economic growth. Furthermore, primary product-exporting countries are more exposed to commodity price volatility. Commodity price shocks may have stronger effects on both

[5] Chile is highly dependent on copper, Colombia on oil, Bolivia on natural gas, Argentina on agricultural export commodities, Brazil on metals and petroleum, Mexico on hydrocarbons, Peru on mining and Ecuador on petroleum.

Table 23.3 Primary product exports as a share of total export (%), 1990–2010

	1990	2000	2010
Chile	89.1	84.0	89.6
Colombia	74.9	65.9	77.9
Bolivia	95.3	72.3	92.6
Argentina	70.9	67.6	67.8
Brazil	48.1	42.0	63.6
Mexico	56.7	16.5	25.3
Peru	81.6	83.1	89.1
Ecuador	97.7	89.9	90.2
LAC	66.8	42.1	54.1

Source: CEPAL, BADECEL database

economic performance and export earning stability (Athukorola 2000; Sinnot et al 2010). This may bring more difficulty to growth and to follow an accurate economic policy.

However, recently an emerging literature has questioned the importance of the resource curse and the means by natural-resource dependence may be damage growth. For example, Frankel (2010) has pointed that resource-abundant countries are not always destined to grow lower and he also stress that the countries must be careful to these advantages and to find the successful route. Otherwise, Sinnot et al. (2010) suggest that countries may suffer some risks and weaken economic growth if natural resources are badly managed. Nevertheless, it is widely accepted that Dutch disease effects are real (Sinnnot et al. 2010). Thus, commodity export countries might be risk to drive growth in the future.

Second fact, exports are mainly concentrated in a few sectors. This aspect may imply more volatile terms of trade, which may increase output volatility and reduce growth (Lederman and Maloney 2007; Sinnot et al. 2010). In most of the countries the leading export sectors are resource-natural based sectors. In addition, the central export sectors in 2010 continued to be the same as in 1990. Only there have been changes in their relative weight over time. As we can appreciate in Table 23.4, the top five export sectors account for more than half of the country's exports. Even its share has increased over time. This feature may also indicate that the type of export-led growth strategy is simply export more of the same and no new products.

Third fact, countries have maintained Revealed Comparative Advantages (RCA) in leading exports[6] along the period considered. This fact may suggest that

[6] RCA index (Balassa 1965) is defined as:

$$RCA^{j}_{i,t} = \left(\frac{X^{j}_{it}/X^{j}_{t}}{X^{LAC}_{it}/X^{LAC}_{t}}\right)$$

where X denotes the value of exports, i the sector, j the country, t the year considered, and LAC is the Latin American economy. The index measures the importance of sector i in the export bundle of country j with respect to the importance of the same sector in Latin American export flows. If the index is bigger (smaller) than 1, then country j is said to be specialized (de-specialized) in sector i.

Table 23.4 Leading export sectors (%) in Latin America, 1990–2010

Chile				**Colombia**			
1991		2010		1991		2010	
Sector	%	Sector	%	Sector	%	Sector	%
68. Non ferrous metal	33.16	68. Non ferrous metal	39.59	33. Petroleum	20.10	33. Petroleum	40.71
28. Metalliferous ore	13.27	28. Metalliferous ore	23.79	7. Coffee	19.54	32. Coal, coke	15.17
5. Vegetables and fruits	11.02	5. Vegetables and fruits	5.81	32. Coal and coke	8.67	7. Coffee	5.64
3. Fish	6.40	3. Fish	4.17	84. Articles of apparel	8.16	97. Gold, no monetary	5.35
8. Miscell. Edible	5.40	25. Pulp and waste paper	3.56	5. Vegetables and fruits	7.00	29. Crude animal materials	3.20
Leading exports	69.25	Leading exports	76.92	Leading exports	63.47	Leading exports	70.07
Bolivia				**Argentina**			
1992		2010		1991		2010	
Sector	%	Sector	%	Sector	%	Sector	%
97. Gold no monetary	50.00	97. Gold no monetary	50.00	8. Feeding stuff for anim.	10.61	8. Feeding stuff for anim.	12.89
28. Metalliferous ore	17.71	34. Gas	19.84	42. Fixed veget. Fats and	10.07	78. Road vehicles	11.68
34. Gas	8.14	28. Metalliferous ore	13.17	4. Cereals	9.63	33. Petroleum	7.93
68. Non ferrous metal	6.61	68. Non ferrous metal	2.95	22. Oil-seeds	8.98	4. Cereals	7.86
24. Cork and wood	3.03	8. Miscell. Manuf.	2.43	1. Meat	7.45	22. Oil-seeds	7.79
Leading exports	85.49	Leading exports	88.40	Leading exports	46.74	Leading exports	48.15
Brazil				**Mexico**			
1991		2010		1991		2010	
Sector	%	Sector	%	Sector	%	Sector	%
67. Iron and steel	13.01	28. Metalliferous ore	16.29	33. Petroleum	29.02	78. Road vehicles	17.28
28. Metalliferous ore	9.15	33. Petroleum	11.38	78. Road vehicles	16.56	76. Telecommunications	14.60
7. Coffee	6.03	1. Meat	6.57	71. Power generating	5.73	33. Petroleum	13.61

(continued)

Table 23.4 (continued)

78. Road vehicles	4.99	6. Sugars	6.42	5. Vegetables and fruits	5.65	77. Electrical machinery	9.64
68. Non ferrous metal	4.82	78. Road vehicles	5.76	75. Office machines	2.77	75. Office machines	4.92
Leading exports	38.00	Leading exports	46.44	Leading exports	59.73	Leading exports	60.05
Peru				**Ecuador**			
1991		2010		1991		2010	
Sector	%	Sector	%	Sector	%	Sector	%
68. Non ferrous metal	28.84	28. Metalliferous ore	29.60	33. Petroleum	40.40	33. Petroleum	55.30
28. Metalliferous ore	16.62	97, Gold, no monetary	22.11	5. Vegetables and fruits	25.70	5. Vegetables and fruits	14.01
8. Miscell. Edible	13.74	68. Non ferrous metal	10.58	3. Fish	20.08	3. Fish	9.71
65. Textile yarn	6.22	33. Petroleum	8.00	7. Coffee	7.87	29. Crude animal materials	3.53
33. Petroleum	6.10	8. Miscell. Edible	4.94			7. Coffee	3.41
Leading exports	71.52	Leading exports	75.23	Leading exports	94.05	Leading exports	85.96
		LAC					
		1991		2010			
		Sector	%	Sector	%		
		33. Petroleum	22.95	33. Petroleum	12.73		
		78. Road vehicles	5.89	78. Road vehicles	9.29		
		67. Iron and steel	5.80	28. Metalliferous ore	8.77		
		68. Non ferrous metal	5.63	76. Telecommunications	5.82		
		5. Vegetables and fruits	5.31	68. Non ferrous metal	5.10		
		Leading exports	45.59	Leading exports	41.71		

Source: Authors' calculation from CEPAL, BADECEL database

specialization according to comparative advantage is optimal; but also, it may indicate that behind this specialization is found the improvement of products with higher value-added or the upgrading quality within the resource based sectors (Reinkardt 2003). In other words, LAC countries seem to move toward more sophisticated products. In this sense, some authors such as Ferranti et al. (2002) have studied many cases in which mining, forestry and agriculture have evidenced a high degree of innovation.

Measuring a country's overall export pattern and its changes over time is not so easy. It is convenient to use indicators most appropriate to measure the degree of export concentration. But also, it is necessary to use measures that are able to assess changes in countries' export basket. In other words, it is necessary to tackle the issue of similarity with the aim of examining how the export composition of a country has shifted along the time or how it has changed respect to that of a reference area (mainly trade partners).

The most commonly used statistic for measuring concentration is the Herfindahl index. Following Cadot et al. (2012), for a given country and year the Herfindahl index of export concentration, normalized to range between zero and one, is defined by the following formula:

$$H_j = \frac{\sum_{i=1}^{n} \left(x_i^j\right)^2 - (1/n)}{1 - (1/n)}$$

where x_i^j denotes the share of each sector i in total exports of country j and n is the total number of sectors.[7] It is positively related to a country's concentration level: the bigger the value the larger the concentration level (or the lower the diversification level).

In order to assess structural transformation in exports, we use two similar indices. First, we calculate self-similar index (SS). This indicator allows to measure how countries' export composition has evolved over time. Starting from the Finger and Kreinin index, this indicator is given by the following formula:

$$SS_{x_t, x_{92}} = \left[1 - \frac{\sum_i \left|x_i^t - x_i^{92}\right|}{\sum_i \left(x_i^t + x_i^{92}\right)}\right] * 100$$

In this case, the benchmark year is 1992.[8] A value of 100 shows identity with the initial situation. In other words, a value of 100 implies that there are no changes in export basket; moreover, lower values represent the distance to the starting point. Thus, lower values shows structural changes in export pattern.

[7] In this study, we consider 67 sectors.

[8] 1992 is considered as a benchmark because of the availability of export data.

Second, we evaluate changes in country's export pattern relating to the export pattern of a reference area. In this case, Latin American as a whole is considered as a benchmark.[9] Thus, LAC-Similarity index (SI) is defined as:

$$SI_{j,LAC} = \left[1 - \frac{\sum_i \left| x_i^j - x_i^{LAC} \right|}{\sum_i \left(x_i^j + x_i^{LAC} \right)} \right] * 100$$

where x_i^{LAC} represents the share of each sector i in total exports of Latin American.[10] A value of 100 indicates similarity with the LAC, and a lower value represents the extent of the difference.

All indicators are calculated using sector exports at 2-digit SITC.[11] In Fig. 23.1 we show the Herfindahl index. The evidence reveals significant differences across countries. Furthermore, the distance between them tends to be similar over time.[12] Ecuador and Bolivia, which were the most specialized export basket in 1992, are still in the same position in the ranking after two decades. The same is true for the main diversified, Brazil and Argentina. Broadly, Herfindahl index shows that countries tend to be more specialised. Chilean and Colombian economies have experienced the higher increase in export concentration. This feature may indicate that export specialization is a persistent phenomenon in Latin American countries, widely dependent on country-specific characteristics that are difficult to move in the time (Parteka and Tamberi 2013).

Changes in countries' export pattern are displayed in Fig. 23.2. On the vertical axis is presented self-similarity index (SS) and on the horizontal axis the yearly LAC-Similarity index (SI). Each mark displayed on the graph plotted for each country corresponds to one year of the period analyzed. Vertical movements indicate the range of the changes over time in a country export composition, and rightward horizontal movements show convergence toward Latin American trade pattern (as a whole).

This figure highlights the unequal evolution of the countries' export structure. The country that changed the most initial trade structure seems to be Colombia, followed by Peru and Brazil. Bolivia has experienced lower changes. These structural transformations have not led toward a convergence process in Latin America. In this sense, Brazil and Argentina seem to have the most similar structure to the Latin America as a whole. Chile and Bolivia have the most divergence composition.

[9] Latin America is considered as a benchmark because all countries have increased their exports each other in the last two decades

[10] In order not to generate important distortions, the country considered is not included in Latin American a whole.

[11] It is worth indicating that the degree of concentration changes with the level of disaggregation of export data.

[12] The standard deviation of the Herfindahl index between countries tend to be constant along the period considered.

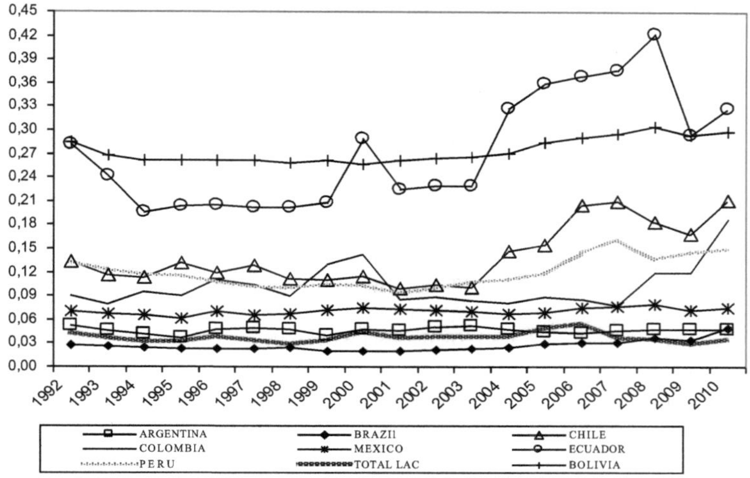

Fig. 23.1 Export concentration by country, 1990–2010 (Herfindahl index) (Source: Authors' calculation from CEPAL, BADECEL database)

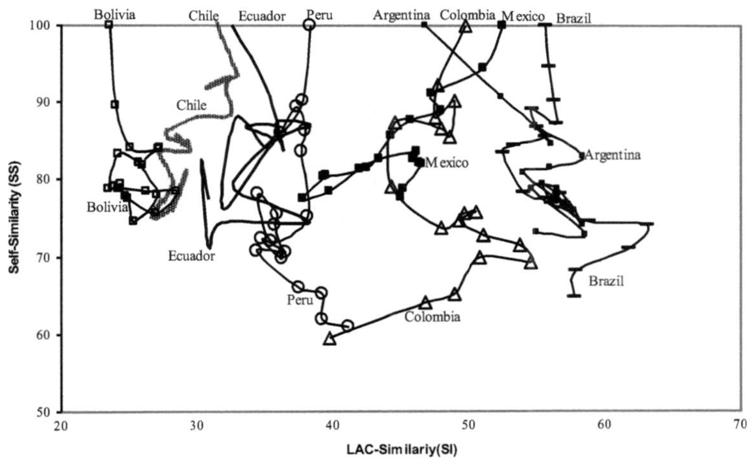

Fig. 23.2 Self and LAC similarities (1992–2010) (Source: Authors' calculation from CEPAL, BADECEL database)

This behaviour in export patterns in Latin America contrasts to the one in the European Union (see Fernández and Márquez 2009). While the differences among the European countries export baskets are decreasing over time, the pattern among the Latin American countries shows a rise on specialization.

In addition, comparing export basket between countries, we can also appreciate important disparities (see Table 23.5). Broadly, each country shows a different trade pattern. Chile and Bolivia are the most separate from Latin American export pattern. Peru seems to have the most similar structure. On the other side, Colombia

Table 23.5 Similarities in trade composition among countries (1992–2010)

		LAC	Bolivia	Peru	Ecuador	Mexico	Colombia	Chile	Brazil
Argentina	1992	46.82	13.40	35.43	24.46	35.54	34.92	29.56	45.09
	2010	55.03	21.22	35.91	26.39	43.44	32.75	24.58	52.38
Brazil	1992	55.62	25.03	35.64	16.33	45.10	33.58	37.64	
	2010	57.79	27.02	42.28	29.00	43.85	37.78	34.80	
Chile	1992	31.40	33.77	64.51	25.85	20.07	21.45		
	2010	28.14	24.44	50.13	19.38	16.86	14.60		
Colombia	1992	49.76	10.21	28.94	40.48	43.13			
	2010	39.77	14.70	30.85	59.35	36.43			
Mexico	1992	52.50	11.86	25.70	27.44				
	2010	45.04	12.08	24.99	27.22				
Ecuador	1992	32.61	5.61	20.02					
	2010	30.85	9.30	25.57					
Peru	1992	38.33	38.26						
	2010	41.17	49.47						
Bolivia	1992	11.51							
	9010	11.92							

Source: Authors calculation from CEPAL, BADECEL database

is approaching its pattern to other countries such as Ecuador. Consequently, although the main feature in Latin American export basket is the high degree of export specialization in resource-natural based sectors, each country differs from the others, showing their own characteristics.

In summary, we conclude that specialization according to comparative advantage has become optimal in Latin American. The type of export-led growth strategy has been simply export more of the same, that is, movements within existing products and no to new products (export diversification). However, this strategy has led to different dynamism in export and growth performance in countries. It might be expected that differences in export basket across countries may be behind the unequal dynamism. In general terms, export basket in Latin American may not be well suited to drive future growth. It is dominated by natural resource based sectors. Furthermore, according to the "Ducht disease hypothesis" a high dependency on primary product sectors may hamper the development of other tradable sectors by means of cost inflation and exchange rate appreciation. These negative effects may also be magnified by inadequate policies. In this sense, it will be necessary to stimulate the diversification of productive structure.

23.3 Export Pattern Within Regions in Colombian and Chilean Economies

Unequal regional economic development and high concentration of production in the territory are two important stylized facts in Latin American countries (Cuadrado-Roura and González-Catalán 2013). These features are particularly pronounced in Colombia (Galvis and Meisel 2013) and Chile (Aroca 2013). These disparities have persisted over time. It is recognised that these features play a key role in the country's economic development pattern (Matthee and Naudé 2007).

As we mentioned in Sect. 23.2, trade composition may also be relevant on growth. In this sense, differences in export basket between regions, might contribute to explain the different dynamism in regional growth. Thus, a matter of concern is the potential importance of export composition at regional level for spatial economic growth and development. Therefore, this Section examines the export structure and its evolution for the different regions/departments within Chilean and Colombian economies. Regional export statistics for Chile come from Division of Regional Planning, MIDEPLAN. They cover the period 1992–2006. In the case of Colombia, export data are sourced from DANE. They are referred to the period 2000–2010. All data set contain information of exports disaggregated by industries at ISIC 3 digit-level. All the variables are expressed in real terms in local currency. In addition, data for regional GDP from ODeplan (Central Bank of Chile) and from DANE are employed. Finally, the official exchange rates (LCU per US$, period average) is derived from the World Bank (WDI).

Geographically, Chile is divided into 13 regions (we also consider the Metropolitan Region). They present unequal degree of openness. As we can appreciate in the Fig. 23.3, the export and economic growth performance have varied across regions. Among other factors, differences in export composition might be behind these disparities. Traditionally, the broad-based export capacities identified at national level are concentrated in Antofagasta, Valparaíso, O'Higgins, Biobío and Metropolitan Region. Their exports represent more than 70 % of the Chilean total trade during all the period. In this context, between 1996 and 2006, Antofagasta is the only one that incremented its share (from 29 % to 34 %,), improving its leader position into export regions By contrast, Metropolitan Region[13] and Valparaiso showed higher decreases (from 15 % to 10.5 % and from 13.6 % to 8.3 %, respectively).

Observing the export basket at regional level, two stylized facts emerge. First, exports are mainly concentrated in a few sectors. In most regions the leading export sector are still natural resource based sectors, bringing an important risk to drive regional future growth. The export basket in the northern regions is mainly dominated by copper. Regions in the center of Chile, such as Maule, Biobío and Araucanía show a high export concentration in pulp and paper, and food industry. However, in Metropolitan Region is dominated by different groups of manufactured products. In part, this difference may be explained by the public policy implemented in Chile in the last decades (Aroca 2013). The most important sector in southern regions is food industry. Second, the regional leading export sectors in 2006 continue to be the same. Only there have been significant changes in Tarapaca, moving from a high export concentration in copper to another in food

[13] It is very surprising that this region reduced its share of export, because it has been one of the most benefited from the public policy (Aroca 2013)

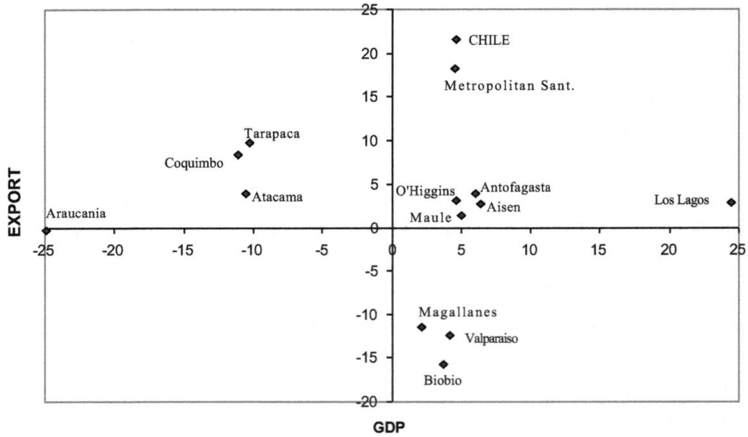

Fig. 23.3 Export and GDP growth rates by regions in Chile, 1992–2006 (in constant 2005 local currency) (Source: Authors' calculation from WDI (World Bank), ODEPLAN and MIDEPLAN)

industry. This evidence may indicate that the type of export-led growth strategy in most of Chilean regions is to export more of the same and no diversify export to new activities.

On the other hand, Colombia consists of 33 departments. There are many differences among them in terms of international opening. Figure 23.4 shows the unequal behaviour in terms of export and GDP across departments in the past decade. Colombian exports are concentrated in a few departments located in the Andina Region (Antioquia, Bogotá, Cundinamarca and Valle del Cauca) and in the Caribbean Region (Atlántico, Bolívar, Cesar and Guajira). Only these eight departments accounted for more than 81 % of total export in Colombia. This percentage has decreased in the last decade, achieving the 70 % of Colombian exports.[14] From 2000, Bogota has emerged as an important export area. This behaviour may be derived from the public policy that the Colombian government has implemented in the last decade (see Galvis and Meisel 2013). By contrast, Cundinamarca has become the worst exporter in the context of these eight departments. Really, this fact would show that the country's economic activity tends to be concentrated in the capital.

Observing the export basket at departmental level, two stylized facts become evident. First, exports are also mainly concentrated in a few sectors. Considering the most important export departments, Cesar and Guajira are mono-export sector (they only export coal). The rest of them mainly incorporate agricultural products, chemical products, precious and non-ferrous metals. The emergence of some manufacture products made trade pattern less dangerous for the economic growth. Second, from 2000 to 2010, basically the leading export sector has been the same.

[14] We only mention the departments which account for more than 5 % of Colombian export in the period analyzed.

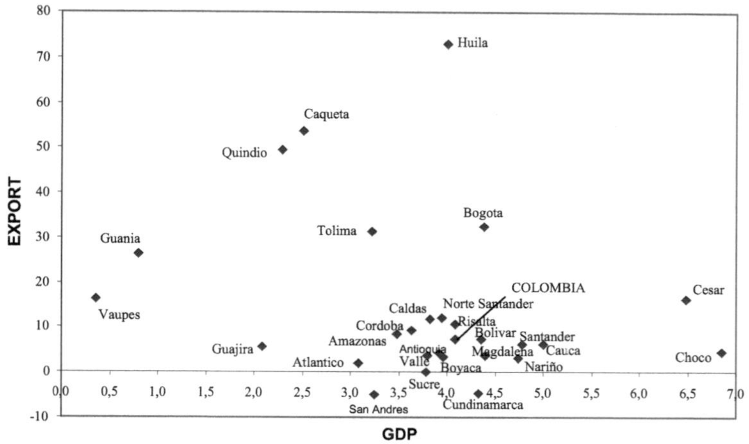

Fig. 23.4 Export and GDP growth rates by departments in Colombia, 2000–2010 (in constant 2005 local currency) (Source: Authors' calculation from WDI (World Bank) and DANE)

However, Antioquia and Bogota have experienced deep changes.[15] This feature may suggest that some departments in Colombia have shown higher odds for structural transformation than others.

In order to analyze properly the degree of concentration of regional exports and to assess structural transformation in export baskets, the methodology applied in Sect. 23.2 is used. Firstly, we measure the degree of specialization in terms of internationality exchanged good by every region/department. We use the Herfindahl index and examine its evolution over time. Secondly, we tackle the issue of similarity. We apply two similarity indexes. On the one hand, Self Similarity indicator with the aim of knowing how a region's (department) export composition has changed with respect to a starting point. On the other hand, Country-Similarity index in order to evaluate how the export composition of a region/department has changed in relation to the export structure of both Chile and Colombia.

For Chilean and Colombian economies the Herfindahl-index evidences significant differences across regions and departments. The regional export pattern tends to be more specialized than national export pattern. Consequently, this feature should have important implications to the growth performance in the country. It should be noted that shocks abroad that impact demand for export should have different impacts within de country according the specializations of the regions. While a negative shock might affects significantly to some regions, it might not affect at all the other ones.

[15] In 2000 the leading export sector was agricultural products in Antioquia and vehicles in Bogota. After 10 year, the leader sector has become precious and non-ferrous metals in the former and Chemical products in the later.

Herfindahl index also shows that regional inequalities have been persistent during the last decade, being greater in Colombia. Both countries show an increase in regional export concentration along the time. By comparison, between 2000 and 2010, the simple average of Helfindahl index in Colombia rose from 0.47 to 0.54, and the standard deviation fell slightly from 0.35 to 0.33. For Chile, the average Herfindahl index increased from 0.45 in 1992 to 0.50 in 2006, and the standard deviation remained next to 0.25. The four regions/departments with the highest and the lowest overall export specialization in the periods considered are presented in Table 23.6.

On the other hand, it would be also interesting to examine spatial and temporal variation in the regional specialization of exports across both Chilean and Colombian regions. To our knowledge, our work is the first exploratory study of this type.[16]

After the computations, different spatio-temporal patterns are shown for the two regional economic systems. Firstly, for all the analyzed years, there is no evidence of significant negative spatial autocorrelation in the distribution of regional specialization in regional economies of Chile and/or Colombia. Nevertheless, the evolution of the spatial dependence was not the same for both regional systems.

With respect to regional economies in Chile, they were increasing their spatial dependence (see Table 23.7 and Fig. 23.5). As can be seen, the Moran's I increases along the period, with no significant positive values during 1992–1997, and significant positive values during 1998–2006. In Fig. 23.6, the Moran scatterplots for years 1992 and 2006 are illustrated. While Moran's scatter plot for the initial year (1992) does not show evidence of spatial dependence, the final year (2006) of the sample shows the result of a clear positive spatial dependence. The Moran's scatter plot in year 2006 indicates that five regions in the center of Chile (Valparaiso, O'Higgins, Del Maule, Biobío and Santiago Metropolitan) presented low levels of specialization and they had low levels of specialization in its adjacent regions. The rest of regions had got higher levels of specialization while their adjacent regions presented high levels of specialization in their exports (from Fig. 23.7, regions in the North and South). The main indication is shown in Fig. 23.7: similar values of specialization on the map tend to cluster together.

On the other hand, the spatial dependence of regional specialization in Colombia varied along the period, although it follows a different evolution than the Chilean case.

---

[16] Moran's I statistic was used to assess the presence of significant spatial autocorrelation of regional specialization for the cases of both Chilean and Colombian regions. The global Moran's I test statistic was calculated in every year using GeoDa software (Anselin 2005). As it is well known, Moran's I ranges from -1 to 1: a value close to 0 indicates spatial randomness; a positive and significant value indicates positive spatial autocorrelation, and a negative and significant value indicates negative spatial autocorrelation. Statistical significance was tested using randomization based on 999 permutations. The weight matrix W, necessary for the computation of spatial autocorrelation statistics, was based on a row standardized binary queen contiguity matrix (it takes the value of 1 if the regions are geographically adjacent, and 0 in another case).

Table 23.6 Regions in Chile and departments in Colombia with the lowest and highest overall specialization in exports (Herfindahl index)

	Chile		Colombia	
	1992	2006	2000	2010
Four lowest specialization	Santiago Metropolitan (0.04)	Santiago Metropolitan (0.07)	Valle del Cauca (0.07)	Bogota (0.06)
	Biobio (0.23)	Del Maule (0.20)	Norte de Santander (0.09)	Valle del Cauca (0.08)
	Coquimbo (0.24)	Biobio (0.23)	Atlantico (0.09)	Atlantico (0.09)
	Del Maule (0.26)	O'Higgins (0.33)	Caldas (0.10)	Cundinamarca (0.12)
Four highest specialization	Araucania (0.72)	Los Lagos (0.85)	Vaupes (1.00)	Cesar (1.00)
	Los Lagos (0.72)	Antofagasta (0.85)	Caqueta(1.00)	Arauca (1.00)
	Atacama (0.71)	Atacama (0.73)	Choco (0.99)	Amazonas (1.00)
	Antofagasta (0.70)	Tarapaca (0.73)	Guajira (0.97)	Casanare (0.99)

Note: value of a Herfindahl index is in brackets. Values range from 1 to 0
Source: Authors calculation from MIDEPLAN (Chile) and DANE (Colombia)

Table 23.7 Spatial autocorrelation in specialization of exports in the Chilean regions

Years	Moran's I	p-value
1992	0.261	0.111
1993	0.250	0.119
1994	0.269	0.108
1995	0.254	0.109
1996	0.307	0.083
1997	0.274	0.102
1998	0.361	0.056
1999	0.565	0.012
2000	0.601	0.008
2001	0.654	0.003
2002	0.629	0.003
2003	0.605	0.004
2004	0.718	0.002
2005	0.627	0.002
2006	0.616	0.004

Source: Authors' calculation from MIDEPLAN

From the data in Table 23.8, there was a significant spatial positive autocorrelation of regional specialization for 3 years (during 2000–2002); later, there was a decrease in spatial autocorrelation over the period 2003–2010, reaching the lowest value during 2005–2007. Finally, the Moran's I in year 2011 indicates a significant and positive spatial autocorrelation.

These differences in the spatio-temporal patterns of regional specialization may be related to the allocation of natural resources in the Colombian regional economic system. But also, with the successful penetration of new products that point to new opportunities for future structural transformation (Figs. 23.8, 23.9, and 23.10).

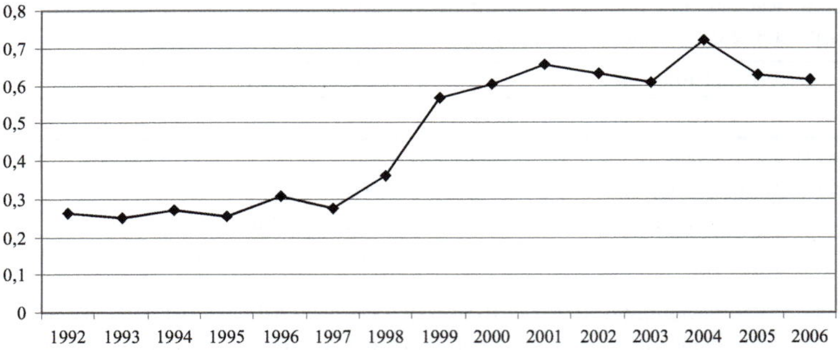

Fig. 23.5 Moran's I for the specialization in Chilean regional economies (1992–2006) (Source: Authors' calculation from MIDEPLAN)

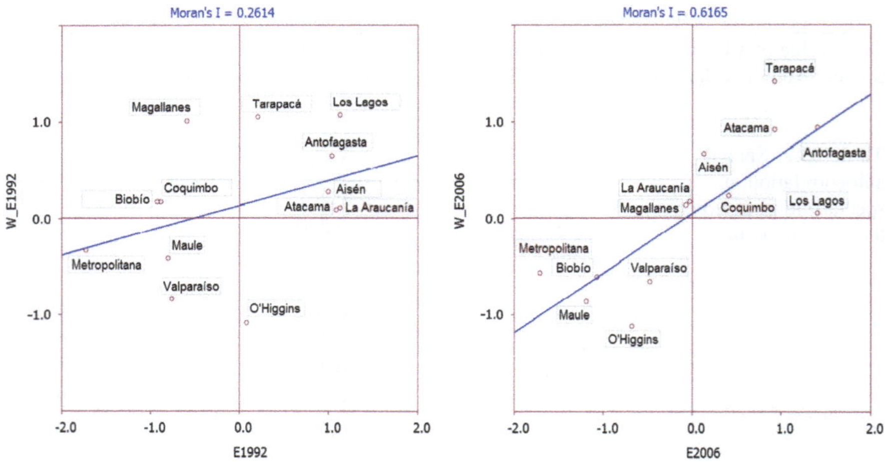

Fig. 23.6 Moran scatter plot for specialization in Chilean regional economies (years 1992 and 2006) (Note: The horizontal axis is based on the values of the regional export specializations – years 1992 ("E1992") and 2006 ("E2006"). The vertical axis is based on the weighted average (spatial lag using the matrix W) of the corresponding specializations on the horizontal axis – years 1992 ("W_E1992") and 2006 ("W_E2006"). Thus, the Moran scatter plot provides a representation of the geographic relationship between regional export specializations in the Chilean regional neighborhood. Source: Authors' calculation from MIDEPLAN)

As general conclusion, positive spatial autocorrelation seems to emerge in the last year in both, the Chilean and the Colombian regional economies. The trend would imply that similar values of specialization in exports are clustering in the space of the regional economic system.

Otherwise, Figs.[17] 23.11 and 23.12 show the dynamic of the regions' self-similarity and the process of convergence of each region's export structure toward

[17] We only plot the most relevant regions/departments in terms of exports.

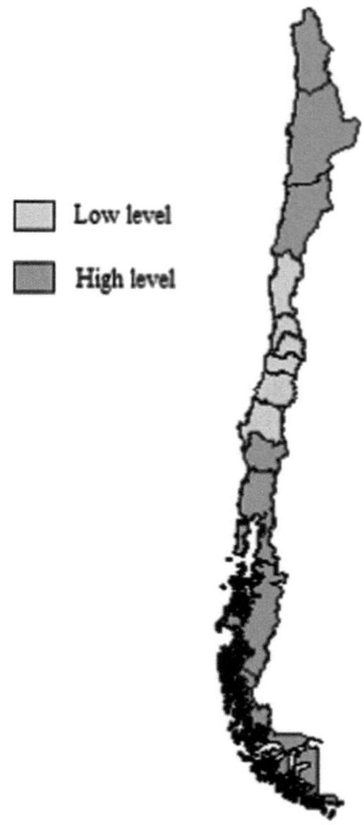

Fig. 23.7 Spatial patterns of regional specialization of exports in Chile (average for the period 2002–2006) (Note: Low level (High level) corresponds to a value of regional export specialization between 0.06 and 0.47 (0.48 and 0.81). Source: Authors' calculation from MIDEPLAN)

Table 23.8 Spatial autocorrelation in specialization of exports in the Colombian departments

Years	Moran's I	p-value
2000	0.139	0.07
2001	0.218	0.023
2002	0.297	0.005
2003	0.096	0.134
2004	0.048	0.221
2005	−0.083	0.334
2006	−0.004	0.618
2007	0.021	0.307
2008	−0.145	0.147
2009	0.105	0.118
2010	0.100	0.121
2011	0.247	0.016

Source: Authors' calculation from DANE

the national trade pattern. Broadly, regions/departments have changed their patterns along the time but not with the same intensity.[18] These changes have not led toward

[18] It is worth noticing that both countries have unchanged regions/departments.

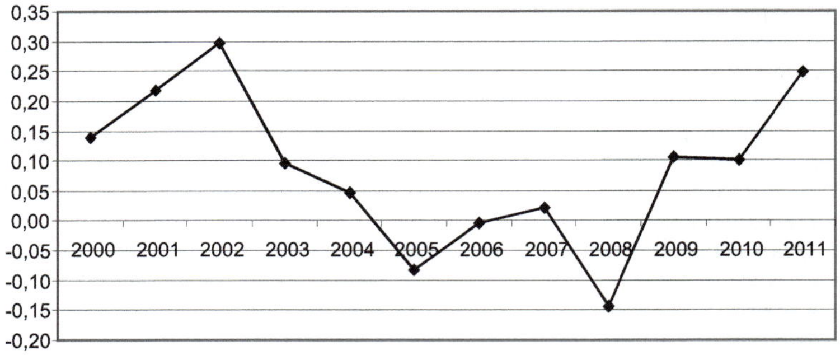

Fig. 23.8 Moran's I for specialization in Colombian departments (years 2000–2011) (Source: Authors' calculation from DANE)

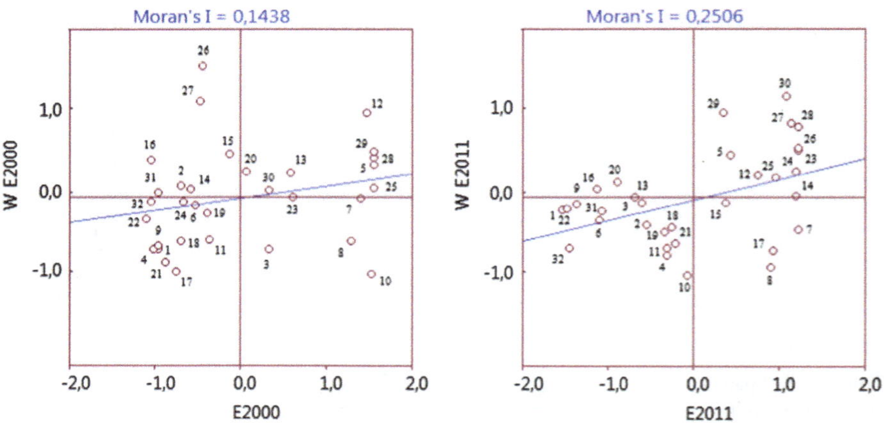

Fig. 23.9 Moran's I for specialization in Colombian department economies (years 2000 and 2011) (Notes: (1). The horizontal axis is based on the values of the regional export specializations – years 2000 ("E2000") and 2011 ("E2011"). The vertical axis is based on the weighted average (spatial lag using the matrix W) of the corresponding specializations on the horizontal axis – years 2000 ("W_E2000") and 2011 ("W_E2011"). The Moran scatter plot represents the geographic relationship between regional export specializations in the Colombian regional neighborhood. (2). Legend: The numbers into the figure represent the Colombian Departments (*1* Bogota, *2* Bolivar, *3* Boyaca, *4* Caldas, *5* Caqueta, *6* Cauca, *7* Cesar, *8* Cordoba, *9* Cundinamarca, *10* Choco, *11* Huila, *12* Guajira, *13* Magdalena, *14* Meta, *15* Nariño, *16* Norte de Santander, *17* Quindio, *18* Risaralda, *19* Santander, *20* Sucre, *21* Tolima, *22* Valle del Cauca, *23* Arauca, *24* Casanare, *25* Putumayo, *26* Amazonas, *27* Guania, *28* Guaviare, *29* Vaupes, *30* Vichada, *31* Antioquia, *32* Atlantico). Source: Authors' calculation from DANE)

a convergence process with the national export pattern. In fact, if we measure this process of convergence by the standard deviation of the regional similarity respect to the country, one can observe an increase on its value over the period considered in both countries. By comparison, while in Chile it rose from 18.19 to 25.43 over 1992–2006 period; in Colombia between 2000 and 2010 it increased from 10.28 to 13.39.

Fig. 23.10 Spatial patterns of regional specialization of exports in Colombia (Note: "Low level" corresponds to a value of regional export specialization between 0 and 0.38, "Middle level" between 0.4 and 0.84, and "High level" between 0.85 and 1. Source: Authors' calculation from DANE)

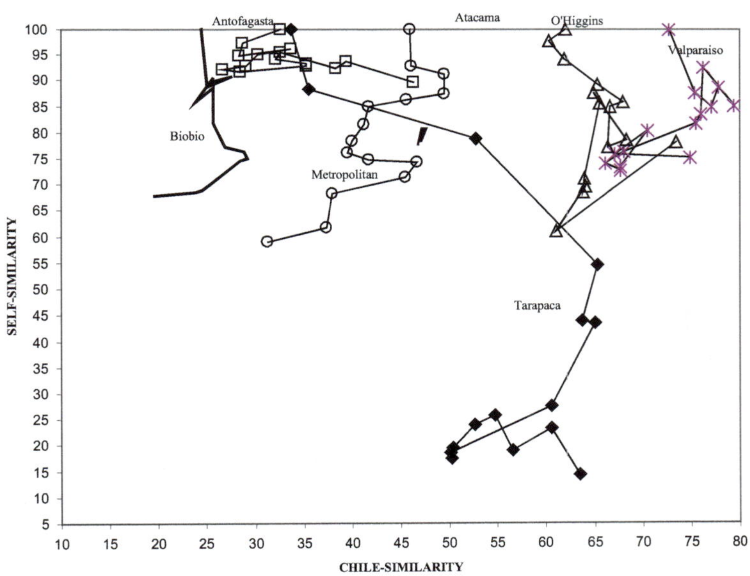

Fig. 23.11 Self and Chile similarities (1992–2006) (Source: Authors' calculations from MIDEPLAN)

In general terms, these results might suggest that specialization in regions/departments in both Chilean and Colombian economies according to comparative advantage is optimal. Regions/departments are mainly specialized in commodity

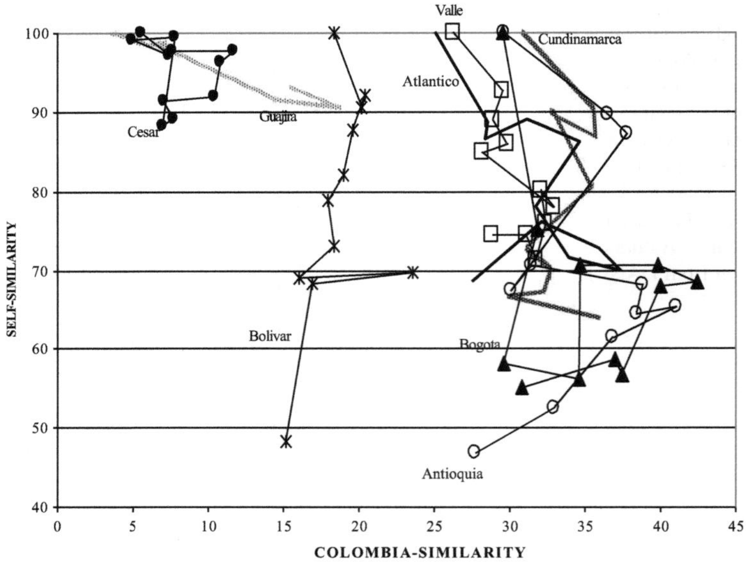

Fig. 23.12 Self and Colombia similarities (2000–2010) (Source: Authors' calculations from DANE)

exports, bringing important risks to drive regional growth in the future. Specialization is a persistent phenomenon in regions/departments, widely dependent on region-specific characteristics that are difficult to move in the time. This feature, should also suggest that the growth performance of these economies should not be independent of their trade patterns.

23.4 Exports, Export Specialization and Regional Growth: An Econometric Analysis

In this section we test the hypothesis that export specialization (or less diversification) is a significant component of development in regions of Chile and Colombia. For this purpose, we propose an empirical model where it is hypothesized that outward-oriented regions grow more rapidly, and alongside this hypothesis, we test the relevance of the link between export specialization and the economic growth process (using as measure of specialization the regional Herfindahl index constructed in Sect. 23.3).

Although there is a widely shared belief that regional exports induce regional economic growth (Armstrong and Taylor 2000), it is not clear the effect that export specialization can produce on regional growth. Research on the level of countries tend to concur that export specialization may be important for economic growth (Gutierrez de Piñeres and Ferrantino 1997), but so far very little research have focused on the regional level. Thus, in the case of the Colombian and Chilean regional economies, narrow specialization in primary and agricultural goods may make regions vulnerable to external shocks. Besides, the dominance of primary-product exports can imply deterioration in the trading terms of the less developed regions against their developed counterparts, being a factor of regional growth-inhibiting (Cadot et al. 2012). On the other hand, as it was mentioned in Sect. 23.1, export diversification (or less specialization) may lead growth. Consequently, the expected influence from regional export specialization on regional growth is ambiguous, and it is necessary to show empirical evidence about this influence.

The reduced form used to explain the Colombian and Chilean regional aggregate growth takes the following fixed-effects panel data form:

$$\Delta\log(RGDP_{it}) = \alpha_{0i} + \alpha_1 t + \alpha_2\Delta\log(NGDP_t) + \alpha_3\Delta\log(REXP_{it}) + \alpha_4\Delta(SPEC_{it}) + e_{it}$$

where $\Delta\log(RGDP)$ is the first difference of natural log of real regional gross domestic product (this variable measures approximately the real regional GDP growth), t is temporal trend, $\Delta\log(NGDP)$ is the first difference of the natural log of real national (Chilean or Colombian) gross domestic product (approximately the growth rate of aggregate real national GDP), $\Delta\log(REXP)$ is the first difference of natural log of real regional exports (growth rate of real regional exports), and finally $\Delta(SPEC)$ is the first difference of the specialization index of each region (Herfindahl index).

In this specification, regional growth is supposed to depend on national growth and regional export fluctuations, and are hypothesized potential additional marginal effects of regional export structure through the introduction of the *SPEC* variable analysed in Sect. 23.3.

The results of the estimation of the proposed empirical model are in Table 23.9. From this table, the GDP regional growths in Chile and Colombia are highly correlated (and significant) with the growth rate of the respective real aggregate national outputs. In the same way, the growth rate of regional exports influence positively the GDP regional growths; being more significant in the Chilean case than in the Colombian. However, both Chilean and Colombian regional GDP growth is positively correlated with export specialization although the respective coefficients are not statistically significant. This coefficient implies a negative correlation between export diversification and growth.[19]

As general conclusions, and for the analyzed period, regions with more exports generally experienced higher economic growth rates. Besides, regional specialization (less diversification) in exports seems to enhance regional growth. Although this result could be based on different underlying mechanism (economies of scale in markets of intermediaries, spillover effects resulting from intra-industry

[19] A positive coefficient and significant at 0.10 % was obtained by Gutierrez de Piñeres and Ferrantino (1997) for the Chilean case (at national level).

Table 23.9 Estimation results of GDP regional growth equations

Explanatory variables	Chile (1992–2006)	Colombia (2000–2010)
Trend	−0.002	0.003
	[−2.97]	[2.85]
Δlog(*NGDP*)	0.483	0.607
	[5.15]	[5.98]
Δlog(*REXP*)	0.020	0.026×10^{-3}
	[1.72]	[4.08]
Δ(*SPEC*)	0.018	0.007
	[0.27]	[0.29]
R^2	0.234	0.202
Time periods (after adjustments)	14	10
Cross-sections included	13	33
Total pool observations	182	330

Notes: (1) t-statistics are in brackets
(2) In the Colombian case, because regional exports were null in some periods, Δ(*REXP*) was used instead of Δlog(*REXP*)

knowledge, and/or productivity improvements resulting from higher international competition), in the cases of the Chilean and Colombian regional economies, the fundamental explanation is the dependence on natural resource sectors (high shares of primary and agricultural goods within their respective export basket). This type of specialization has important risks for these regions, since external shocks for regional export will have negative impact on them.

Consequently, the policy recommendation would be to promote regional growth by means the stimulation of the orientation of these regional economies towards activities related to exports. From a regional policy point of view, it is necessary to promote government actions that stimulate the diversification of the productive structure in these regions as a way to encourage regional development. Effectively, a region can attain export diversification using two ways that have different implications: changing its shares of commodities in its existing export portfolio or including new commodities in its export basket. The recommendation is clear, to include new commodities in their export mix.

23.5 Concluding Remarks

This paper attempts to examine whether the economies in Latin America have become more specialized or less specialized in their exports over the years. Additionally, we have presented an empirical analysis on the potential influence of export specialization on regional growth for the Chilean and Colombian economies. It is important to emphasize the lack of this type of analysis in the regional economic literature.

The main finding of the analysis at national level is that current export basket in Latin American countries (agricultural products and natural resource exports) is not suited to drive future growth. So, movements to new sectors will be necessary but, as it is well known, this is not an easy task.

For Chilean and Colombian economies the regional export pattern tends to be more specialized than national export pattern. Export specialization is a persistent phenomenon in regions/departments in both economies. Regional export pattern is widely dependent on region specific characteristics. Regional export basket is mainly dominated by natural resource based sectors. Only the regions/departments next to the capital of both countries are the less lagging in manufacture products, bringing more opportunities for structural transformations.

In addition, positive spatial autocorrelation seems to emerge recently in both, the Chilean and the Colombian regional economies. The trend would imply that similar values of specialization in exports are clustering in the space of the regional economic system.

We have estimated a positive (no significant) impact of regional specialization on the regional growth. That is, in the cases of Chile and Colombia, the export diversification in the regions does not induce regional growth.

Summarizing the findings of the above analysis, regional exports and export specialization better than export diversification seem to enhance regional growth. However, the current export basket does not offer an adequate path to lead future growth. There will be troubles on the horizon for the analyzed regional economies. The type of export-led growth strategy has been within existing sectors, that is, exporting more of the same, or upgrading quality within products. In this context, it may be easier to reduce the growth capability in the future. Following Hausmann et al. (2008), it will be necessary the emergence of new export activities. In this sense, it is worth noting that a type of export-led growth strategy based on moving from existing sector to new export sector have emerged slightly in some Colombian departments, bringing more opportunities for regional grow.

Consequently, our policy recommendation would be to promote regional growth by means the stimulation of the orientation of these regional economies towards activities related to exports. From a regional policy point of view, it is necessary to promote government actions that stimulate the diversification of the productive structure in these regions as a way to encourage regional development. In line with Hausmann et al. (2008) the structural transformation might be led towards goods with similar capabilities to those that already exist in the different regions. In this context, it will be necessary the cooperation between the government and the private sector: the aim will be to achieve better knowledge about the drawbacks and advantages they face, to be able to deal with them in an efficient way.

In addition, efforts should be made to create a framework to promote the location of new businesses or new multinationals to be able to explore and develop new productive activities.

In general the results suggest that regional economic growth in Chile and Colombia requires promoting regional export performance. For the regions with more specialized export, it will be necessary a regional policy framework that generate opportunities for structural transformation. Such changes would enhance the development on new activities and new export sectors.

References

Agosin M (2009) Export diversification and growth in emerging economies. CEPAL Rev 97:115–131

Al-Marhubi F (2000) Export diversification and growth: an empirical investigation. Appl Econ Lett 7(9):559–562

Alvarez R, Fuentes R (2003) Trade reforms and manufacturing industry in Chile. In: Aroca P, Hewings GJD (eds) Structure and structural change in the Chilean economy. Ashgate Publishing, England

Anselin L (2005) *GeoDa 0.95i* ed. Urbana

Armstrong H, Taylor J (2000) Regional economics and policy, 3rd edn. Blackwell, London

Aroca P (2013) Territorial inequality and regional policy in Chile. In: Cuadrado-Roura JR, Aroca P (eds) Regional problems and policies in Latin America. Springer-Verlag

Aroca P, Hewings GJD (2002) Migration and regional labor market adjustment: Chile 1977–1982 and 1987–1992. Ann Reg Sci 36(2):197–218

Athukorola PC (2000) Manufacturing exports and terms of trade of developing countries: evidence from Sri Lanka. J Dev Stud 36:89–104

Awokuse T (2007) Causality between exports, imports, and economic growth: evidence from transition economies. Econ Lett 94:389–395

Balassa B (1965) Trade liberalization and "revealed" comparative advantage. Manchester School 33:99–123

Benedictis L, Gallegati M, Tamberi M (2009) Overall trade specialization and economic development: countries diversity. Rev World Econ 145:37–45

Cadot O, Carrère C, Strauss-Kahn V (2012) Trade diversification, income, and growth: what do we know? J Econ Surv. Doi: 10.1111/j.1467-6419.2011.00719.x

Capello R (2009) Spatial spillovers and regional growth: a cognitive approach. Eur Plan Stud 17 (5):639–658

Cuadrado-Roura JR, González-Catalán S (2013) Growth and regional disparities in Latin America. Concentration and regional policy challenges. In: Cuadrado-Roura JR, Aroca P (eds) Regional problems and policies in Latin America. Springer-Verlag

De Ferranti D, Perry D, Lederman D, Maloney W (2002) From natural resources to the knowledge economy: trade and job quality, Latin American and Caribbean studies. World Bank, Washington, DC

Dennis A, Shepperd B (2007) Trade costs, barriers to entry and export diversification in developing countries, vol 4368, Policy research, working paper. World Bank, Washington, DC

Fernández MT, Márquez MA (2009) Análisis de la capacidad competitiva relativa de las exportaciones intracomunitarias de productos agroalimentarios: el caso de la Unión Europea (UE12). Información Comercial Española 851:135–146

Frankel J (2010) The natural resource curse: a survey. National Bureau of Economic Research, Working paper N 15836

Galvis LA, Meisel A (2013) Regional inequalities and regional policies in Colombia: the experience of the last two decades. In: Cuadrado-Roura JR, Aroca P (eds) Regional problems and policies in Latin America. Springer-Verlag

Guerrieri P, Iammarino S (2003) The dynamics of export specialisation in the regions of the Italian Mezzogiorno: persistence and change. SPRU electronic working paper series 105. University of Sussex, SPRU – Science and Technology Policy Research

Gutiérrez de Piñeres S, Ferrantino MJ (1997) Export diversification and structural dynamics in the growth process: the case of Chile. J Dev Econ 52:375–391

Gutiérrez de Piñeres S, Ferrantino MJ (2000) Export dynamics and economic growth in Latin America. Ashgate Publishing, Burlington

Haussman R, Hwang J, Rodrik D (2007) What you export matters. J Econ Growth 12(1):1–25

Hausman R, Klinder B (2007) The structure of the product space and the evolution of comparative advantage. Working Paper, N. 146, Center for International Development, Harvard University

Hausman R, Klinder B (2008) Achieving export-led growth in Colombia. Working Paper, N. 182, Center for International Development, Harvard University
Haussman R, Rodrik D, Sabel C (2008) Reconfiguring industrial policy: a framework with an application to South Africa. Center for International Development, Harvard University, Working Paper, N. 168
Helpman E, Krugman P (1985) Market structure and foreign trade. MIT Press, Cambridge
Herzer D, Nowak-Lehnmann D (2006) What does export diversification do for growth? An econometric analysis. Appl Econ 38(15):1825–1838
Hesse H (2008) Export diversification and economic growth, commission on growth and development, vol 21, Working paper. World Bank, Washington, DC
Hidalgo CA, Klinger B, Barabási AL, Hausmann R (2007) The product space conditions the development of nations. Science 317:482–487
Hwang J (2006) Introduction of new goods, convergence and growth. Job market paper. Harvard University, Cambridge, USA
Imbs J, Wacziarg R (2003) Stages of diversification. Am Econ Rev 95:704–723
Korem M, Tenreyro S (2007) Volatility and development. Q J Econ 122(1):243–287
Krugman P (1980) Scale economies, product differentiation and the pattern of trade. Am Econ Rev 70:950–959
Lederman D, Maloney W (2007) Trade structure and growth, In Lederman D and Maloney W (eds) Natural resources: neither curse nor destiny. The World Bank, Washington, DC
Matsuyama K (1992) Agricultural productivity, comparative advantage, and economic growth. J Econ Theory 58:317–334
Matthee M, Naudé W (2007) Export diversity and regional growth: empirical evidence from South Africa, research paper, UNU-WIDER, United Nations University (UNU), No. 2007/11
Parteka A, Tamberi M (2013) What determines export diversification in the development process empirical assessment. World Econ 36(6):807–826
Puga D, Venables A (1999) Agglomeration and economic development: import substitution vs. trade liberalization. Econ J 109:292–311
Ramírez JC, Osorio H, Parra-Peña R (2007) Escalafón de la competitividad de los departamentos en Colombia. Serie Estudios y Perspectivas, 16. CEPAL
Reinhardt N (2003) Chile's export structure, 1970–2006. In: Aroca P, Hewings GJD (eds) Structure and structural change in the Chilean economy. Ashgate Publishing, England
Sachs JD, Warner A (1995a) Economic reform and the process of global integration. Brook Pap Econ Act 1:1–118
Sachs JD, Warner A (1995b) Natural resource abundance and economic growth, vol 5398, Working paper. National Bureau of Economic Research, Cambridge
Sachs JD, Warner A (2001) The curse of natural resources. Eur Econ Rev 45(4–6):827–838
Sinnot E, Nash J, de la Torre A (2010) Natural resource in Latin America and the Caribbean. Beyond booms and busts? World Bank, Washington, DC
Venables A (2005) Spatial disparities in developing countries: cities, regions and international trade. J Econ Geogr 5:3–21

Chapter 24
Trends and Realities in Foreign Direct Investments in Latin America

Michael Penfold and José Luis Curbelo

24.1 Introduction

Latin America is currently in a favorable economic situation, given the very uncertain conditions of the global economy. In particular, the region shows relatively high growth rates, co-exists in an environment of democratic opening and, with certain exceptions, has achieved a reduction in its poverty rates. A central element behind this great economic dynamism has been the renewed interest recovered by foreign investment in continuing to increase its participation in Latin America.

Many of the developed countries, both from North America, Asia and Europe, have begun to see in Latin America a central ally in the construction of their strategies for stimulating the growth of their various economies, which has increased foreign direct investment (FDI) even in sectors which go beyond the exploitation of natural resources and in areas related to telecommunications and financial services. No doubt these are encouraging news, but it also constitutes an opportunity to promote a new cycle of changes and assume new challenges which must be tackled by the various countries with responsibility and without complacency.

Latin America has achieved economic growth, after more than a decade of reforms, mainly due to a responsible fiscal policy, a strengthening of the regulatory frameworks of the financial sector and obviously to the high world commodity prices which have enabled them to increase their traditional exports considerably.

M. Penfold (✉)
Public Policies and Competitiveness of the CAF Development Bank of Latin America and Associate Professor, Caracas, Venezuela
e-mail: mpenfold@caf.com

J.L. Curbelo
Strategies of Development and Public Policies of CAF Development Bank of Latin America, Caracas, Venezuela
e-mail: jcurbelo@caf.com

J.R. Cuadrado-Roura and P. Aroca (eds.), *Regional Problems and Policies in Latin America*, Advances in Spatial Science, DOI 10.1007/978-3-642-39674-8_24,

This external situation, so positive in the context of an adequate macroeconomic policy, has paid off making the region even more attractive.

But despite these macroeconomic triumphs, the microeconomic and social inadequacies remain evident: the region maintains high levels of inequality and poverty; the quality of employment is precarious given the high rates of informality; public institutions are still weak, which is evidenced by high crime rates and the low levels of public approval of the functioning of the rule of law; the industrial sector is highly dependent on the production of goods and services of low value added; investment in infrastructure is scarce; rates of innovation and entrepreneurship are low and financial access continues to be a limiting factor for entrepreneurial development. Besides, environmental concerns have been spreading out across the region and more attention should be paid to aspects such as environmental protection, biodiversity, water resources and soil fertility depletion and climate change. Furthermore, Latin America has lagged behind in the adoption of new technologies which is evidenced by the low penetration rates of information technology (IT), particularly among small and medium enterprises, as well as in those areas oriented towards promoting energy efficiency and the development of a green economy.

In this context, foreign investment looms large in contributing to offset -and even overcome- many of these weaknesses. The type of investment that is attracted, in the event that countries continue in their effort to strengthen their political and legal institutions, maintaining sustainable fiscal policies and reducing extreme poverty levels, can contribute perfectly to facing these challenges related to entrepreneurial development. Interestingly, foreign investment in the region shows some positive contrasts in regard to its behavior in the decade of the 1990s – a decade which was also characterized by high investment, although marked by the privatization processes of numerous state assets in a context of fiscal adjustments and trade liberalization.

With regard to the contrasts, the following transformations can be identified: (a) greater diversification in the origin of the FDI (which was initially highly concentrated in foreign investment originating from Europe and the USA) towards greater participation from Asia, especially China, and also foreign investment originating from Latin American companies which have expanded to other countries (known as "multilatinas"); (b) The region has started to see the entry, although very incipient, of foreign investment linked to the venture capital industry, oriented towards the identification of dynamic and innovative companies and sectors; (c) the growth in domestic markets, especially of the middle class, has been an important source of attraction for foreign investment in the area of services, for the purpose of taking advantage of the expansion in consumption, as well as physical infrastructure (airports, ports, telecommunications, highways, etc.) and social (health) needs, raising the standards both of educational demand as well as supply; and (d) the specific decision, albeit in incipient form, of some foreign companies to install Research and Development Centers in countries such as Mexico, Chile, Panama and Brazil, in which they have expanded their operations, which could result in the strengthening of the potential for innovation and increase the technological content of some non-traditional sectors within the Latin American economies.

However, the continuities in the behavior of foreign investment are equally outstanding: (a) the increased growth in FDI is concentrated in sectors linked to the export of *commodities* based on natural resources (energy, mining and agriculture) and also in services; (b) FDI oriented towards using Latin American countries as export platforms in non-traditional sectors remains scarce; and (c) the dynamism of FDI is closely linked to the opportunities generated by changes in government policies; in the 1990s by the privatization processes and currently by the processes of concessions or public-private investment projects in infrastructure and services and in the opening up of capital intensive sectors, such as oil, gas and mining.

To illustrate each of these points, the chapter has been divided into three parts. In the first section the behavior of foreign investment in Latin America is characterized based on various indicators. The second, contains an analysis of the relevance that Asian investments have been acquiring, with a special focus on China, as well as the investment of the "multilatinas" as a mechanism of intra-regional integration, respectively. In this same section some incipient elements relating to FDI are dealt with, such as the installation of Research and Development Centers by multinational companies and the emergence of a venture capital industry which has begun to channel investment resources towards local sectors and companies with innovative potential. The chapter concludes with the identification of new challenges which the Latin American countries are going to have to deal with in order to increase FDI and, above all, to positively impact in the different economies of the region.

24.2 Characterization of FDI in Latin America

Several works have been carried out to identify the determining factors of foreign investment in Latin America (Stein and Daude 2001; Fernández Arias and Haussman 2000; Levy Yeyati et al. 2004; Stein and Daude 2007). In these studies, several variables are analyzed that would appear to be statistically significant, such as the institutional quality of the countries, the size of the economy, the geographical proximity, linguistic similarities and time difference (Daude and Stein 2001). Other works with greater scope, both in the sample of countries as well as the evolution over time in the behavior of foreign investment, have identified commercial variables, among them, the number of free trade agreements as well as the degree of liberalization of the economies, as aspects which have a strong impact on the attraction of investments (Buthe and Milner 2008).

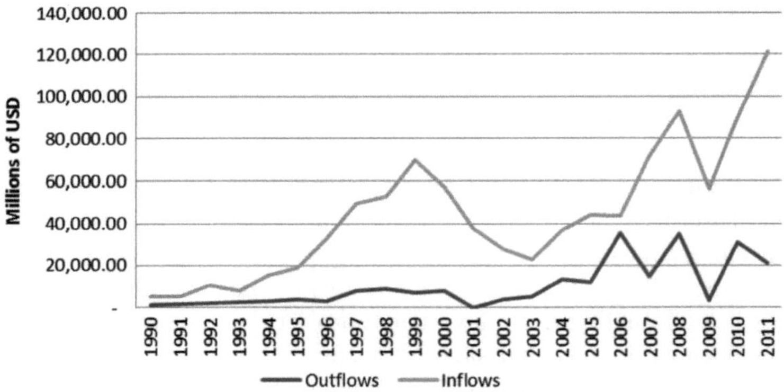

Fig. 24.1 Flow of foreign direct investment into Latin America (Source: UNCTAD (2011))

24.2.1 Investment Flows

In general terms, Latin America has shown relatively high foreign investment figures during the last decade (see Fig. 24.1). FDI has even been growing consecutively, with the exception of a single year (2008) which showed a decrease as a consequence of the global financial crisis. By the year 2011, foreign investment in Latin America had not only recovered, but it achieved its maximum historic levels, exceeding 120 billion dollars, with Brazil, Mexico and Colombia as the countries which attracted the greatest amount of flows in the last few years.

In terms of GDP, the story is less positive for Latin America. The weight of the stocks of foreign investment in terms of their size within the Latin American economies is lower than in some other regions of the world, such as those of Southeast Asia or Eastern Europe, in which stocks of FDI have reached levels of more than 50 % of GDP. In the case of Latin America, said stocks have represented almost 30 % of GDP. However, the figure is particularly high, above all, when compared with China, where the stock reaches almost 10 % of GDP (see Fig. 24.2). This behavior does not change significantly in relative terms, with regard to the annual flows of investment against GDP, in comparison with Eastern Europe, Southeast Asia and China.

During the last 5 years, a large part of the annual flows of FDI in Latin America have been concentrated in a small group of countries: Brazil, Mexico, Colombia, Chile, Peru and Panama. In terms of the importance of FDI within their economies, the performance of some of them clearly stand out, especially when these countries are compared over the last three 5-year periods (1996–2000; 2001–2005; 2006–2011). As a result, some countries such as Chile, Panama, Brazil and Mexico have shown high levels of attraction of foreign investment. This process has been continuous during these three periods. In the cases of Panama and Chile, FDI is close to or higher than 8 % of GDP; and close to 3.5 % and 2.5 % of GDP in the cases of Brazil and Mexico, respectively. In the cases of Colombia, Uruguay and

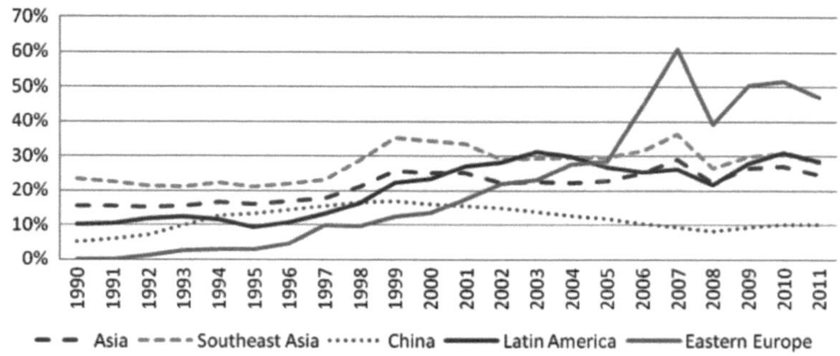

Fig. 24.2 Incoming stocks by region as a percentage of GDP (Source: UNCTAD (2012))

Peru there has been a significant increase in FDI upon comparing the importance of the amounts they attracted in the period 1996–2000 in relation to the high levels of attraction achieved for the period 2006–2011. In the cases of Uruguay and Colombia, FDI for 2006–2011 reached 5.5 % and 3.5 % of GDP respectively. Finally, countries like Venezuela, Bolivia and Argentina have shown a significant fall in the importance of FDI as a percentage of GDP throughout these three periods (see Fig. 24.3).

24.2.2 Origin of the Investment

The origin of the FDI in Latin America has changed significantly upon comparing the periods 2000–2005 and 2006–2011. In the first period, both the European Union as well as the United States had a very high percentage weight in terms of their participation as originators of FDI. In particular, the European Union had a clear leadership in the process, representing almost 45 % of the origin of the annual flows. In the second period, the European Union maintained its leadership, but despite that it declined in importance with 40 % of the total amounts. The investments from the United States fell from 37 % in 2000–2005 to almost 28 % in 2006–2011 (Fig. 24.4).

Curiously, the emergence of other alternative sources of origination marked the dynamism of foreign investment in Latin America during this second period. The participation of Asia in FDI passed from 11 % in 2000–2005 to almost 17 % in 2006–2011. Furthermore, Latin America began to observe in both periods the expansion of the companies known as "multilatinas", which have been dominated by processes of strong expansion of their markets within the region itself, through the extensive use of FDI mechanisms (Santiso 2008; Guillén and García-Canal 2011, 2012). In the period 2000–2005, the Latin American origination of FDI represented little more than 10 % of the annual flows; while for the second period, these flows reached almost 17 % of the total amounts received by the different

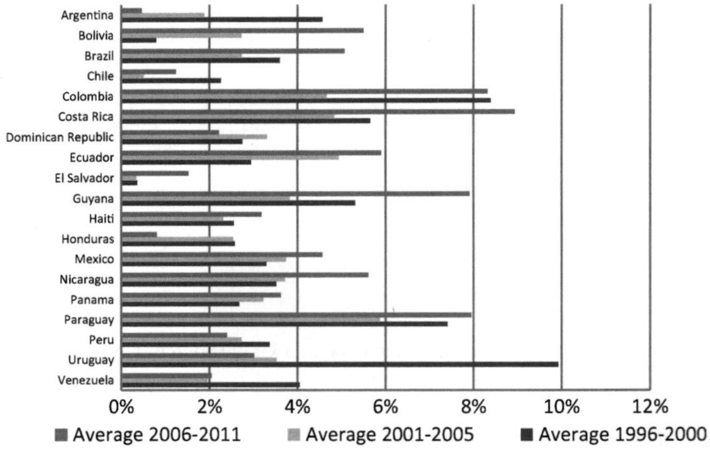

Fig. 24.3 Inflows of DFI as a percentage of GDP (Source: UNCTAD (2012))

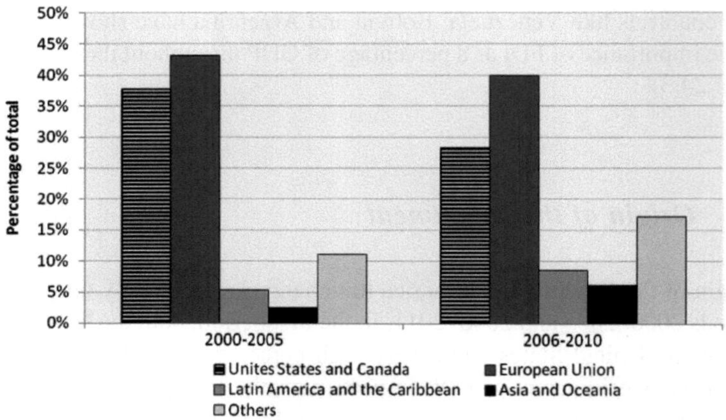

Fig. 24.4 Origin of the FDI in Latin America (Source: CEPAL (2011))

countries. In other words, in the period 2006–2011, both the Asian as well as the Latin American sources grew strongly in terms of importance, while the FDI from Europe and the United States – which continued to represent the greatest proportion of funds-, experienced a clear decrease in terms of their relative importance.

24.2.3 *Sectorial Behavior*

The sectorial behavior of the FDI has shown some interesting changes, particularly when it is compared with the 1990s. These changes are particularly striking given the growing external dependency of the region of the exports based on natural

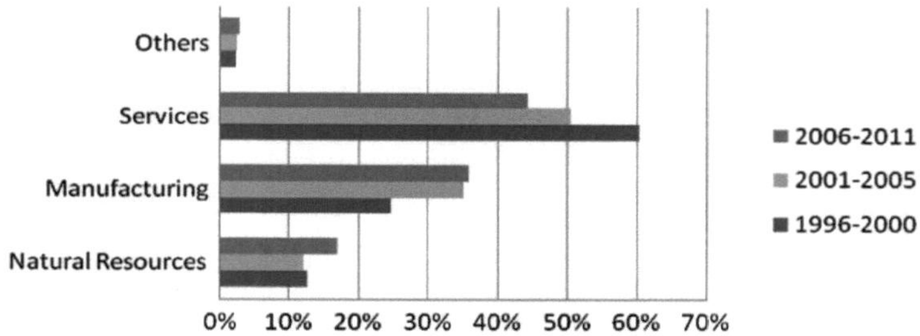

Fig. 24.5 Average sectorial distribution of FDI in Latin America (Source: UNCTAD (2012))

resources, among them, petroleum, gas, mining and food, as well as the high prices of these *commodities* in the international markets.

During the 1990s, the FDI in Latin America was highly concentrated in the attraction of investments in the service sector mainly due to the opportunities generated by the privatization processes and the opening applied to the financial sectors, telecommunication sectors and also public service sectors (electricity and water). In this same period, the FDI also took advantage of opportunities in the manufacturing sector, especially to capitalize the opportunities of the economic opening that certain markets such as Brazil, Argentina and Mexico represented. It should be stated that during the 1990s Mexico had a high performance in the attraction of investments in manufacturing oriented towards exports, taking advantage of its commercial integration with the United States and Canada. In this manner 60 % of the FDI in Latin America was concentrated in the service sector and 23 % in the manufacturing sector. The FDI in industries based on natural resources hardly represented 12 %; much of this regional investment was concentrated in Venezuela, given the opening process of the petroleum industry which characterized this country during the middle of that same decade and that was reversed soon afterwards.

By the end of the first decade of the millennium, some new sectorial trends began to be observed. The proportion of FDI in the service sector maintained its importance (although declining) attracting 43 % of total flows from 2006 to 2011. FDI in the manufacturing sector reached 33 % between 2006 and 2011, representing a significant increase compared to previous periods of time. On the other hand, the FDI in natural resources increased significantly, representing in this same period 17 % of the total flows of FDI in Latin America. Interestingly, in the last 2 years (2009–2011) FDI in natural resources increased to 28 % of total inflows towards Latin America (Fig. 24.5).

Various causes explain these trends. In the service sector, there has been a clear transition from the specific opportunities which were generated by the privatization processes, especially in the financial and telecommunications sector, towards a growing expansion of the internal markets marked by the growth of the middle classes and the reduction in the poverty gaps (Birdsall 2012; Lustig et al. 2011). This new social and economic reality has created *downscaling* opportunities which

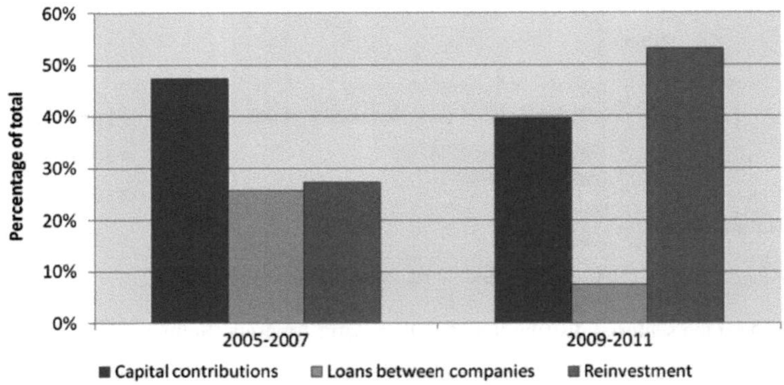

Fig. 24.6 Net FDI inflows by component. Average for Latin America (Source: CEPAL (2011))

have allowed many of these foreign companies to reinvest to increase the expansion of their services to the various sectors of the population, even the lowest income sectors.

The growth of the purchasing power of the new middle classes has increased the attraction of the internal Latin American markets becoming even more demanding. This has not only had an impact on the service sector but also on the manufacturing sector. The growth in purchasing power has forced the mass consumption industry to invest more in innovation; especially, in a greater knowledge of the new trends of these markets, as well as in the design of adequate processes and products which cannot always be imported from more developed countries. Likewise, these same industries, to be able to adapt themselves to the low cost requirements of these new middle classes, have had to develop new production and distribution schemes that require a greater investment on the part of the different multinational companies.

With regard to the industries related to natural resources, the emergence of public policies more favorable to the entry of foreign capital in sectors such as petroleum and mining, accompanied by the discoveries of new deposits in various Latin American countries, including Colombia, Brazil and Peru, have promoted a large inflow of FDI. This is particularly true for the countries that consolidated a regulatory framework that permits the participation of private investment in various large scale projects, such as for example, Chile, Peru, Colombia, Brazil and Peru. On the other hand, other countries such as Argentina, Bolivia and Venezuela, which modified their public policies to seek a more strategic control of these industries by the State, have experienced disinvestment processes. Despite this, the investments in the exploitation of natural resources which the first group of countries has been able to attract (those with more open investment frameworks) have been really large (Fig. 24.3).

Finally, in the period 2005–2007, the central component of FDI in Latin America was provided by capital contributions (Fig. 24.6). In effect, more than 48 % of the net income of foreign investment was of this nature. Between the years 2009–2011 this same percentage had reduced to 40 %, increasing instead the importance of the reinvestment of the profit (which came to represent more than 50 % of all the components of the net income of FDI). This quantitative change reflects the perception by the foreign companies in Latin America of a fall in the risk levels and a greater desire to finance their expansion in the region through reinvestment processes. This is undoubtedly an obvious change and a process that can have positive long term effects on the economic and productive performance of the region. However, as we will see later, the FDI in Latin America continues to respond more to the search for high returns derived from opportunities that arise from changes in the regulatory frameworks (privatizations or opening of sectors), than the attractiveness itself of the countries with regard to their competitive improvements.

24.2.4 Territorial Dynamism

There is very little information regarding the geographic location of the FDI and its agglomeration patterns in Latin America. However, the data presented until now permits some hypotheses to be derived. The first is that given the high percentage of foreign investment in the service sector, it is possible to assume that it follows market expansion criteria, thus it should be concentrated in high growth urban zones. The second hypothesis is that foreign investment in natural resources, especially petroleum, gas and mining, tends to be concentrated in geographically isolated zones with few spillover effects on the rest of the economy.

Both realities suggest that the FDI must be favoring two clearly differentiated territorial spectra: high urban concentration zones that demand services and geographically isolated zones with access to natural resources. This localization pattern of FDI – with little emphasis on manufacturing industries with export potential and with a bias that rather favors territorial centers with large internal markets or access to natural resources-, could be contributing to produce certain territorial inequalities.

In fact, some recent studies (CAF 2010; CEPAL 2009) have identified that the territorial dynamics in Latin America are marked by two problematic processes: (a) lack of economic convergence between the territories with lowest and highest incomes; and (b) inequity with regard to the opportunities of individuals depending on their geographical birthplace, mainly due to the difference in the quality of the public services and barriers to the mobility between jurisdictions. In this sense, the territorial dynamics suggested with regard to the agglomeration patterns of FDI observed in Latin America, may not in themselves necessarily be contributing directly to resolving or counteracting both problems.

This new reality leads us to believe that the subject of foreign investment and the territorial dynamics, and in particular the role that could be played by the intermediate cities, are an indisputable matter of public policy. The intermediate cities in Latin America can help to offset some of these imbalances to the extent that public policy favors greater investment in public services, an increase in the investment in physical and social infrastructure and an adequate insertion of these emerging urban spaces into the international markets. However, to validate this assertion or understand the channels through which FDI can aggravate or resolve these territorial imbalances is an issue that requires a rigorous empirical work that is beyond the scope of the present study.

24.3 Some Tendencies of FDI in Latin America

This chapter does not seek to identify the determinants of FDI in Latin America, but it does attempt to discern some dynamics that would seem to be regionally guiding this process. As we will see, some data suggests that not all the countries have been able to match their attraction potential with their performance in terms of FDI, while other countries appear to have had an exemplary performance. Equally, some of these trends are new and permit the establishment of some differentiated patterns compared with previous decades.

For this we would like to identify four processes that are very striking: the high relationship between economic liberalization and FDI; the low relationship between competitiveness indicators and FDI; the emergence of venture capital investments directed towards the search for innovative business ideas or companies with high growth potential; the decision of some multinational companies to expand their investment spectrum towards Research and Development Centers; the growing presence of Chinese investment throughout the region, especially in South America; and the emergence of the "multilatins" as a new source of investment.

24.3.1 Economic Liberalization

As shown in the following graph, there would seem to be a high correlation between the degree of economic liberalization of the countries (measured in terms of imports plus exports versus GDP) and their performance in the attraction of FDI. This is a new relationship, since in similar studies for the decade of the 1990s (Daude and Stein 2001) a high correlation between commercial integration processes and investment levels was not observed. Those Latin American countries with greater degrees of liberalization currently show higher attraction levels of foreign investment (Fig. 24.7).[1]

[1] Upon analyzing the graph Nicaragua stands out as a statistical outlier for this period. The fundamental reason for this performance is that Nicaragua has notably improved its commercial opening levels and also its indicators of ease of doing business. Likewise, with regard to investment levels, much of the foreign investment that it is receiving originates from state "multilatin" companies from Venezuela, which has become one of the main partners commercially as well as in investment aspects.

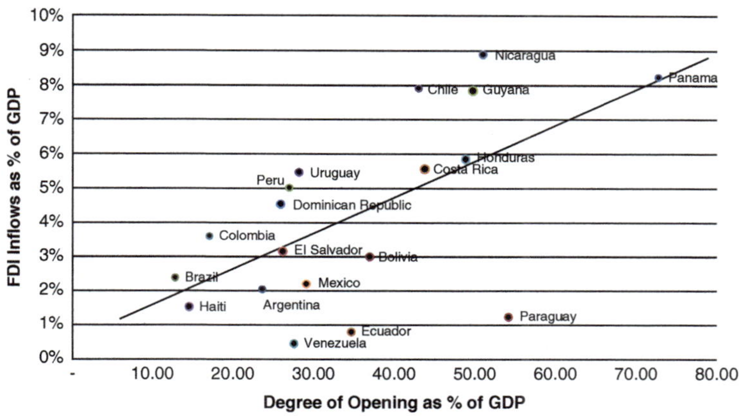

Fig. 24.7 Flows of foreign direct investment in relation to degree of opening (average 2006–2011) (Source: UNCTAD (2012))

Certainly, it is difficult to establish a causal relationship between both factors, since different variables, among them, institutional factors, may well cause relationship to be spurious (Daude and Stein 2001). However, it would seem evident that the greater integration of the countries with the global economy stimulates the participation of FDI within their economies (Buthe and Milner 2008). Perhaps a possible explanation of this phenomenon is that commercial opening – as well as financial- basically permits easier entry to FDI to capture the potential of that market, due to the elimination of customs barriers and controls on capital inflows. Opening permits the elimination of various institutional barriers that the FDI exploits to capture the market potential of the country involved.

24.3.1.1 Competitiveness

However, as shown in this other graph, the relationship in Latin America between competitiveness indicators (measured both through the WEF as well as by Doing Business) and FDI is relatively low. Better competitiveness levels would not seem to guarantee on their own greater attraction levels of FDI. This result is somewhat paradoxical, due to the enormous effort and the amount of resources assigned by the countries to improve their investment climates (Fig. 24.8).

A possible explanation is that FDI in Latin America is seeking higher returns – in the framework of acceptable risk levels- regardless of the competitive characteristics of the countries. Once FDI has possibilities to enter a developing country (thanks to its opening and the low probability of being confiscated), it does so based on opportunity and profitability criteria more than for reasons strictly related to competitiveness. It is also possible to think that the causal relationship is the reverse: to the extent to which countries have attracted a certain level of FDI, then pressures start generating to improve and even sophisticate the

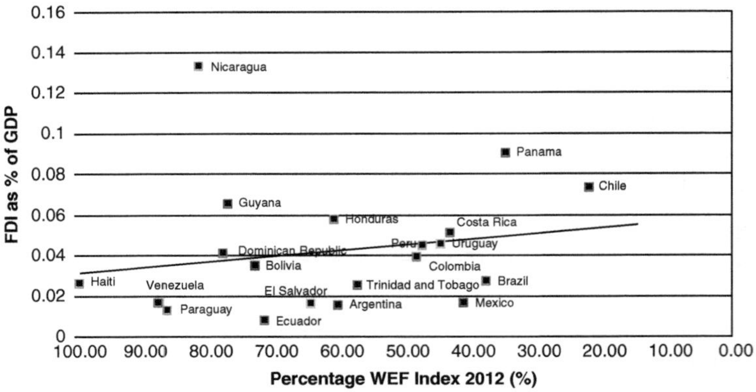

Fig. 24.8 Relationship of WEF and FDI as % of GDP in Latin America (Source: UNCTAD and WEF (2012))

competitiveness indicators. Besides this, the relationship may not be linear but it may present a relationship related to a certain development threshold based on which these competitive demands are activated by investors.

24.3.1.2 Venture Capital

Latin America, although to a lesser extent than Asia or Eastern Europe, has seen the appearance of new forms of foreign investment, especially under the method of venture capital funds. This phenomenon has been mainly concentrated in Brazil and Mexico and with an incipient presence in Chile, Peru and Colombia. For the year 2011, these funds had committed close to 6.5 billion dollars in investment for the region, which represents close to 5 % of the total funds invested globally (Ernst and Young 2011; McKinsey and Company 2012).

In terms of amounts, these are scarcely relevant on a global level. Additionally, many of these funds operate more as development capital – oriented towards equity investment in ongoing companies- than in the financing of risk investments per se. However, as a recent phenomenon this process is tremendously significant. For the first time, Latin America begins to receive investment oriented towards identifying dynamic growth companies, as well as the identification of new innovative projects. This is a fundamental boost for business development that permits the injection of dynamism to the growth of medium companies with high potential. However, the sustainability of this process will depend on the capacity of the countries not only to attract risk capital but also to strengthen their capital markets, as well as their national and regional innovation systems and the existence of a greater flow of business projects that are attractive for this type of investor.

24.3.1.3 Research and Development

One of the most outstanding characteristics of the recent behavior of FDI in Latin America is related to the fact that the most significant component in net income is being provided by the reinvestment of profit. As mentioned previously, this reality shows that the region has been earning the trust of foreign investors with regard to their future growth decisions, which has had an impact on the expansion of the range of activities carried out by multinational companies within the different industries in which they have established themselves.

Additional evidence of the increased confidence is the expansion of the spectrum of activities of some multinational companies which have chosen to install Research and Development Centers in certain Latin American countries. This process is still very incipient and requires an adequate public policy (in matters of sector policy as well as science and technology) to be able to stimulate and consolidate the economic and scientific impact of this type of investment.

Although the total investment in terms of R&D in Latin America is comparatively low (Navarro 2010), it is also true that the public component is the most important and the private component presents significantly low levels. However, certain countries, such as Brazil, Mexico and Chile have started to show some changes that deserve to be highlighted (Unesco 2011). The private sectors in Chile and Mexico are financing almost 50 % of the total investment in R&D. In Brazil this amount is little more than 40 %. Among these amounts, the increase in private financing reflects the decisions of various multinational companies – such as for example Siemens, GE, Cargill, P&G among others- of opening their research and development centers in some of these Latin American nations. This tendency undoubtedly reflects one of the most positive aspects of the recent dynamic of FDI in the region, since it permits the leverage of innovation processes based on technological transfers with a high productive impact in the economic development of these countries.

24.3.1.4 China as Investor

Although it is true that the growth of the investment of Chinese origin is a global process that began more than a decade ago, and that reflects the growing economic importance of this country on a global level, it is no less true that in Latin America this is a relatively new process (CEPAL 2011). The presence of Chinese FDI in Latin America, has basically concentrated on the sectors related to the exploitation of natural resources (petroleum and mining) and incipiently in the agricultural and telecommunication sectors.

It is evident that the main "driver" of the Chinese investment has been the need to ensure the provision of certain raw materials considered strategic to guarantee their future economic growth (fundamentally energy) and for which the region plays a privileged geopolitical role (Downs 2011). Besides this, in many of these investment processes, especially in the petroleum sector, the state companies of China have played a preponderant role, financed additionally through their development banking institutions (Downs 2011; Dussel Peters 2012). In this sense, the tendency of a greater presence of Chinese investors in Latin America is not only something new due to its "origin", but also due to the characteristics of the companies which have driven this process (state companies) and due to their high sectorial focus (raw materials).

In terms of relative importance, the region has become the second geographical destination for China. The countries which have received greatest investments in recent years are Venezuela, Brazil, Argentina, Ecuador and Peru. Of the total amounts, during the last decade, China has invested close to 26 billion dollars, which represents close to 11 % of its total flows (Dussel Peters 2012). This investment amount involves a total of 862 transactions with an average amount of 300 million dollars. From this number of transactions, only eight have been carried out by private companies while the rest involve companies with state participation (Dussel Peters 2012). In terms of the amounts of the transactions, the FDI promoted by the state companies represents close to 87 % of the total invested amounts (Dussel Peters 2012). Most of these transactions are concentrated in sectors related to raw materials, especially petroleum and mining and most recently some operations in the agriculture sector are observed.

24.3.1.5 The 'Multilatinas'

The emergence of the so-called multilatins reflects how globalization has a reverse side: the growing role of originators of FDI from developing countries towards countries also in the process of development (south-south) and even also of developing country to developed countries (south-north). In fact, of the 100 biggest companies of the emerging markets, nine of them have their headquarters in Latin America. Cemex, Telcel, Embraer, Votorantim, Vale Do Rio Doce, among others, represent some of the most emblematic multilatin companies.

On a global level, the multilatins went from originating 0.5 % of the global amounts of FDI in the period 1970–1990 to 3.7 % for the period 2000–2009 (Lopez and Ramos 2011). These amounts currently represent 27 % of the total FDI flows originated in the developing countries since more than 60 % are being made by companies based in Asia (Lopez and Ramos 2011). Although compared to Asian companies, the multilatins are far from wielding the global leadership of this new process, it is no less true that their growth is significant and has, among Mexican and Brazilian companies, its most distinguished examples (Santiso 2008).

In the same manner, and as mentioned previously, more than 17 % of the FDI received by the region originates within Latin America, which results in the so-called multilatins acquiring a leading role in the processes of market expansion and productive integration in the region. This tendency of the multilatins to invest within the region is due to the consolidation of internationalization strategies that usually begin through entry to neighboring countries. This type of expansion tends to take place through merger and acquisition processes and also greenfield investment which are the FDI schemes most commonly used by the multilatins to begin their operations. The investment decisions of the multilatins in a determined country have often been the logical stage following greater knowledge of the market thanks to previous export activity. However, on other occasions these decisions of the multilatins have been guided by strategic diversification decisions of geographical risk that lead large companies to venture to operate directly in neighboring countries with growth potential.

Contrary to the dynamic observed in the case of FDI of China in Latin America, the sectors in which the multilatin companies show greater activity are more diversified. In particular, investments in food and beverages, engineering and construction, steel and metallurgy, transport, petroleum and mining stand out. Furthermore, this is a process in which there is a growing participation of medium sized companies that attempt to emulate the internalization patterns of the large Latin American companies, through which they tend to be integrated as suppliers. This expansion in the size range of the investors (from large to medium and their greater diversification) is probably showing that the FDI originating from the multilatins is having a growing regional integration impact.

24.4 The New Agenda of FDI in Latin America

The trends that have been described throughout this chapter show some notable changes in the behavior of FDI in Latin America. These changes are accentuated when compared with the decade of the 1990s. In general terms, Latin America continues to increase its attraction for FDI as a result of the consolidation of its economic and commercial liberalization processes. Simultaneously, Latin America achieved greater diversification in the origin of FDI and the presence of new types of investment as well as activities more oriented towards innovation objectives are also evident. These processes have been the result of the appearance of venture capital funds as well as the decisions of multinational companies to install Research and Development Centers in some specific countries. However, foreign investment has shown growth in primary sectors and a high concentration in the service sectors. Therefore there are some challenges that deserve to be mentioned as part of a new development agenda.

The first is the need to understand in more detail the territorial dynamic of FDI in Latin America. This has most probably been marked by access to natural resources as well as the expansion of the internal markets – especially of its middle classes – which have stamped a dual dynamic on the behavior of FDI, that is, the search for natural resources irrespective of their geographic location and its concentration in urban zones of high economic growth. A central point to be able to develop adequate public policies is to have a clear diagnosis – maybe in some countries such as Brazil, Colombia, Mexico and Chile – through the construction of agglomeration maps that permit the verification from the territorial point of view of some observable patterns in terms of FDI. In any case, this perspective opens the need for Latin American cities, especially its intermediate cities (as is being done by various cities in Asia and Eastern Europe), to begin to plan on a territorial basis the process of attraction of investments as a mechanism to increase the productivity of these localities, but also as a policy to balance territorial development. This process requires the institutional strengthening of those cities with high potential of investment attraction and also the continued strengthening of the political, economic and administrative decentralization processes of these entities.

A second matter is the need to stimulate a greater link between competitiveness and the investment attraction agenda on a country level and also of the territorial localities. This link necessarily requires the attraction of a greater number of investments – especially in the manufacturing sector and with a greater export focus – that generates sufficient demand to sophisticate the competitive agenda of the countries and drive the territorial development of the localities. This process is irrevocably related to the productive consolidation of those business clusters (new and old) located throughout the entire territory, so that given increases in the levels of association between the various actors, the attraction of new investments and technological dissemination and adoption, demands that stimulate competitive solutions for the business challenges being faced are generated.

The emergence of the multilatins as a new investment channel is undoubtedly another matter that arises from this analysis, especially for its regional integration effect as well as its greater sectorial diversification. Some of the multilatin companies, especially the largest ones, have advanced to compete not only regionally but also globally. However, there is evidence that this investment tendency of Latin American origin is not only limited to major companies, but is also being expanded to the medium companies of the region. In this sense, a new agenda must include the most rigorous analysis of the profile of these medium companies and the characterization of their internationalization strategies. This is an area in which the development banking of the different countries – as well as on a multilateral level–, can play a decisive role in supporting the internationalization of this business segment through FDI and not only emphasizing support processes for export activity.

Finally, Latin America observes in an incipient manner the appearance of new forms of foreign investment (venture capital) as well as new related activities (research and development). This leads us to assume that innovation will be one of the central elements of a certain type of foreign investment in the region, especially in those countries that show competitive improvements in their institutional frameworks. Based on this it becomes imperative to document the characteristics and the experience of the venture capital funds and the type of investments that they are carrying out. Furthermore, it is also necessary to document the various business cases that led to the installation of some Research and Development Centers in order to understand the success factors and the public policy requirements that were demanded by the companies. These types of studies are fundamental to be able to promote adequate regulatory frameworks that make the region more competitive and to identify potential innovative sectors in which greater FDI levels could be attracted.

References

Birdsall N (2012) A note on the middle class in Latin America. Working Paper 303. Center for Global Development

Birdsall N, Lustig N, McLeod D (2011) Declining inequality in Latin America: some economics, some politics. Working Paper 251. Center for Global Development

Buthe T, Milner H (2008) The political determinants of foreign direct investment into developing countries: increasing FDI through international trade agreements. Am J Polit Sci 52 (4):741–762

CAF Banco de Desarrollo de América Latina (2010) Desarrollo Local: Hacia un Nuevo Protagonismo de Regiones y Ciudades. Reporte de Economía y Desarrollo

CEPAL (2009) Economía y Territorio en América Latina y el Caribe. Desigualdades y Políticas

CEPAL (2011) Inversión Extranjera Directa en América Latina y el Caribe 2010

CEPAL (2012) People's Republic of China and Latin America and the Caribbean: Ushering in a New Era in the economic and trade relationship

Daude C, Stein E (2001) Longitude matters: time zones, the location of FDI, and trade. Inter-American Development Bank. Working Paper

Daude C, Stein E (2007) The quality of institutions and foreign direct investment. Econ Polit 19(3):317–344 (Wiley Blackwell)

Downs E (2011) Inside China, Inc: China Development Bank's cross-border energy deals. John L. Thornton China center monograph No. 3. Brookings Institution

Dussel PE (2012) Chinese FDI in Latin America: does ownership matter? Discussion Paper # 3. Working Group on Development and Environment in the Americas

Ernst & Young (2011) Globalizing venture capital. Report

Guillén M, García-Canal E (2013) Emerging markets rule: growth strategies of the new global giants. McGraw Hill, New York

Guillén M, García-Canal E (2011) Multilatinas: causas y Efectos de su Expansión. Política Exterior 25(144):128–137

Hausmann R, Fernández-Arias E (2000) Inversión extranjera directa: ¿Buen colesterol? Research Department Publications 4204. Inter-American Development Bank. Research Department, Washington DC

Levy Yeyati E, Stein E, Daude C (2004) The FTAA and the location Of FDI. Working Papers Central Bank of Chile 281. Central Bank of Chile, Santiago

Lopez A, Ramos D (2011) Las Multilatinas de Expanden en Asia. Observatorio Económico Red Mercosur

McKinsey & Company (2012) Private equity Asia-Pacific: is the boom back? Report

Navarro, JC (2010) The importance of ideas: innovation and productivity in Latin America. Volume edited by Carmen Pages. The Age of Productivity. Palgrave Macmillan, New York

Porzecanski R, Gallaher K (2007) Economic reform and foreign direct investment in Latin America: a critical assessment. Prog Dev Stud 7:217–233

Santiso J (2008) La Emergencia de las Multilatinas. Rev de la Cepal 95:7–23

UNCTAD (2012) FDI outflows by region and economy 1990–2011

UNESCO (2011) Global investments in R&D. UIS fact sheet. No.15

Wu H (2009) Has Latin America become China's backyard? Contemp Int Relat 19(3):16–26

MIX
Papier aus verantwortungsvollen Quellen
Paper from responsible sources
FSC® C105338

If you have any concerns about our products,
you can contact us on
ProductSafety@springernature.com

In case Publisher is established outside the EU,
the EU authorized representative is:
Springer Nature Customer Service Center GmbH
Europaplatz 3, 69115 Heidelberg, Germany

Printed by Libri Plureos GmbH
in Hamburg, Germany